HUMAN RESOURCE MANAGEMENT IN IRELAND

SECOND EDITION

Patrick Gunnigle, Noreen Heraty
& Michael Morley

GILL & MACMILLAN

Gill & Macmillan
Hume Avenue
Park West
Dublin 12
with associated companies throughout the world
www.gillmacmillan.ie

© 1997, 2002 Patrick Gunnigle, Noreen Heraty and Michael Morley
0 7171 3362 1

Index compiled by Yann Kelly
Print origination in Ireland by
Carrigboy Typesetting Services, County Cork

This paper used in this book is made from the wood pulp of managed forests.
For every tree felled, at least one tree is planted, thereby renewing natural resources.

A catalogue record is available for this book from the British Library.

Contents

1

Human Resource Management: an Introduction

People are the lifeblood of organisations. An organisation's workforce represents one of its most potent and valuable resources. Consequently, the extent to which an organisation's workforce is managed effectively is a critical element in improving and sustaining organisational efficiency. It is widely argued that effective workforce management is one of the pivotal factors that characterises high-performing organisations (Buchanan and McCalman 1989; Tiernan *et al.* 1996). However, the challenge is also great. Managing people is one of the most difficult aspects of organisational management as it is concerned with people related problems and issues. This difficulty largely stems from the fact that people are inherently different. Managing an organisation's workforce means dealing with people who differ physically and psychologically. This is the essence of *human resource management* (HRM): that aspect of organisational management concerned with the management of an organisation's workforce.

This chapter provides an overview of the field of HRM. It explores the nature of HRM and identifies key human resource (HR) activities within organisations. The objective of this chapter is to place HRM in Ireland within a national and international context, and thus facilitate an analysis of Irish developments in the context of broader contemporary developments in the field. This chapter places particular focus on the issue of *HR policy choice* in an attempt to explain the considerable variations in approaches to HRM management across organisations. However, before engaging the debate on the nature and role of HRM, it is useful to consider the historical development of HRM in Ireland.

THE HISTORICAL DEVELOPMENT OF HRM
Early Days: The Emergence of the HR Role
The origins of contemporary HRM lie in the dramatic changes brought about by the industrial revolution in Britain (see Niven 1967). A central component of this was the growth of the 'factory system' whereby owners of capital employed large numbers of wage labourers to produce standardised goods in larger quantities for bigger markets. Such developments had dramatic effects on the organisation of work. From the owner's perspective, the new factory employees required direction, equipment had to be maintained, production controlled and goods distributed and sold. Here we have the origins of

modern management: the need to plan, organise, direct and control the use of equipment, capital, materials and employees within organisations. These early stages of industrial society were often characterised by extremely poor working conditions for the bulk of the new 'factory' labour. Workers themselves could do little to improve their position since they had little economic or political power. It was not until the growth of organised labour through the trade union movement that concerns of workers could command the attention and action of employers and, indeed, Governments.

However, two important developments emerged in the late nineteenth and early twentieth century which represent the first significant influences on the evolution of HRM and, particularly, the specialist HR function. These were (i) the welfare tradition and (ii) scientific management (see Niven 1967; Foley and Gunnigle 1994).

THE WELFARE TRADITION

The origins of modern HRM are generally traced back to what has become known as the welfare tradition, which developed in a few large companies in Britain during the late nineteenth and early twentieth century. In the early stages of industrialisation, many factory owners regarded their labour force in largely instrumental terms. Working conditions were poor and employees enjoyed few of the benefits we now associate with employment such as sick pay, pensions, and basic welfare provisions (Niven 1967). The welfare tradition refers to a series of voluntary initiatives undertaken in certain companies to improve the conditions of factory workers, particularly in relation to pay, working hours and health and safety provision.

This phase is particularly important in the development of HRM as it was characterised by the appointment of welfare officers who are seen as the forerunners of the modern HR practitioner. Welfare officers first emerged in the mainly Quaker-owned firms in the food and confectionery industries in Britain in the late 1890s. These progressive employers, often influenced by their religious beliefs, took various steps to improve working conditions including the appointment of a welfare officer. The early 1900s saw the appointment of welfare officers in some Irish Companies such as *Jacobs* and *Maguire and Paterson* in Dublin (Byrne 1988).

The First World War added some impetus to the welfare movement in Britain because of the need to accelerate factory production. However, large scale unemployment and depression in the post-war period meant that developments in the area of welfare and HR work were abandoned in many organisations. In 1919 the Welfare Workers' Institute, founded in Britain in 1913 as the Welfare Workers' Association, had a membership of 700. By 1927, when it had been renamed the Institute of Industrial Welfare Workers, its membership had fallen to 420 (Farnham 1984).

The impact of the welfare approach is still very apparent in contemporary HR practice. Welfare has been inextricably linked with a 'caring' approach to employees, dealing with issues such as health, working conditions and personal problems. This is very much in evidence in modern HRM practice in areas such as counselling and occupational health and safety provision. On a rather different level, the welfare tradition has been a source of some confusion about the position of the HR practitioner in the managerial hierarchy. The early welfare officer occupied a semi-independent position in the factory system, with employees the main beneficiaries of their work. This led to the so-called 'middle man' perception of the welfare role with employees seeing them as the representatives of worker interests. However, it is clearly apparent that modern HR practitioners operate as an integral part of the management team and primarily represent employers' as opposed to workers' interests.

SCIENTIFIC MANAGEMENT

Another important early influence on the emergence of HRM was the advent of scientific management and what became known as 'Taylorism'. As the welfare tradition succumbed in the face of economic depression, Taylorism and its associated notions of labour efficiency became an increasingly popular managerial approach. By the early years of the twentieth century improvements in technology coupled with increases in company size and complexity forced employers to investigate new ways of improving industrial performance. In the US, F. W. Taylor led the way by pointing to the efficiency and profitability benefits to be gained through greater standardisation of work systems and methods.

Based on his work at the Bethlehem Steel Company (1900–11), Taylor encouraged employers to adopt more systematic approaches to job design, employment and payment systems (Taylor 1947). Such scientific management approaches were widely adopted in both the US and Britain in the inter-war years. Particular emphasis was placed on job analysis, time and motion studies, and the creation of incentive bonus schemes, thereby extending the work of the emerging HR function. Scientific management led to a shift in the emphasis of HR away from the employee oriented 'caring/do gooding' agenda of the welfare tradition and towards the more managerial 'efficiency/profitability' agenda of the work study officer. From an HR perspective, the spread of scientific management placed greater weight on the careful selection and systematic training of employees. Associated with this trend was an increased attention to job design, working conditions and payment systems. HR also took responsibility for much of the research and administration required to underpin such initiatives.

Despite extensive criticism, the principles of Taylorism had, and continue to have, a profound impact on management practice. Probably its most significant legacy is the notion that work *planning* (seen as a management task) should be separated from work *doing* (seen as a worker task). This separation delineated the primary role of management as that of establishing work standards, procedures and methods. Such approaches to work organisation were dominated by a desire to maximise the productive efficiency of the company's technical resources. Management's role was to ensure other organisational resources, including employees, were organised in such a way as to facilitate the optimal utilisation of the technical system.

This efficiency approach, based on Taylorist principles, has been a characteristic of employers' approaches to job design since the early years of the twentieth century. Jobs were broken down into simple, repetitive, measurable tasks requiring skills, which could be easily acquired through systematic job training. Taylorism helped improve efficiency and promoted a systematic approach to selection, training, work measurement and payment. However, it is also seen as the source of many of the problems associated with industrial work, such as high levels of labour turnover and absenteeism, and low levels of employee motivation (see, for example, Mowday *et al.* 1982; Steers and Mowday 1987). Indeed, the growth of the behavioural science movement (discussed below) can be traced to criticisms of Taylorism and to suggestions that improvements in organisational effectiveness could be achieved through greater attention to workers' needs and, particularly, by providing workers with more challenging jobs and an improved work environment.

The Behavioural Science Movement

The emergence of the behavioural sciences gave a major impetus to HRM by establishing a body of knowledge to underpin many aspects of HR work such as selection, training, motivation, industrial relations and payment systems. It also served to focus attention on some of the problems created by work organisation in the large factories of the new industrial era, such as monotony and low morale.

The emergence of the behavioural science movement is most commonly associated with the work of Elton Mayo and of Roethlisberger and Dickson (see Roethlisberger and Dickson 1939). Based on their studies of workers' productivity, it was suggested that employees' behaviour and performance was influenced by motivation and needs as well as by working conditions and payment practices. This research highlighted the importance of issues such as social factors, group dynamics, and employees' motivation in affecting both individual performance and organisational effectiveness. Although the work of the human relations school has been the subject of methodological criticisms (see Carey 1967), it has had an important influence on management practice, particularly in the sphere of HRM. Possibly, their major contribution was in initiating interest in applying behavioural science principles to the study of organisational and worker behaviour. Subsequent work on the application of the behavioural sciences to the study of organisations helped inform our understanding of organisational functioning and particularly, workers' motivation. Indeed, much of the subsequent work in the field has focused on investigating employees' motivation and attempting to reconcile employers' and workers' needs through appropriate organisation structures, work systems and managerial styles. In chapter five, dealing with employee motivation and the design of work, we consider this literature.

Industrial Relations as a Key HR Activity

A particularly significant development affecting the nature of HRM and the role of the emerging HR function was the growing significance of industrial relations. The growth of an industrial relations emphasis in HR work was a direct result of the increasing influence of trade unions. In Ireland, the trade union movement had become well established in the early 1900s in industries in the major cities of Dublin, Belfast, and Cork (McNamara *et al.* 1988). A particularly important development was the emergence of the 'new unionism', involving the organisation of unskilled or 'general' workers.

In Britain economic depression after the First World War saw a re-emergence of autocratic management styles. A combination of factors, particularly low pay and poor working conditions, contributed to high levels of industrial conflict which culminated in the General Strike of 1926. During this period workers and their trade unions became increasingly suspicious of management motives in introducing welfare initiatives in the workplace. Trade unions became quite anti-welfare, viewing this as an employer strategy to prevent worker organisation.

In Ireland, the 'new unionism' also began to take hold, led by Jim Larkin's Irish Transport and General Workers' Union. A period of conflict between employer and worker interests came to a head in the 'Dublin lockout' of 1913. An important implication of this turbulent period was that it served to accelerate the organisation of employees into trade unions and employers into employers' associations and thus placed an ever increasing emphasis on industrial relations as a critical aspect of workforce management (Gunnigle and Flood 1990).

Employer opposition to trade unions slowly gave way to reluctant acceptance of their role and legitimacy. Trade union membership increased steadily from the early 1930s. Employers were forced to accommodate the reality of organised labour and responded through multi-employer bargaining via employers' associations, and in the employment of 'labour relations officers' to deal with HR and industrial relations matters at organisation level.

A related and important factor contributing to the growth in significance of industrial relations was the nature of pay bargaining. During the Second World War wages were controlled under the Emergency Powers Orders. The rescinding of these in 1946 marked the start of a new era for industrial relations with the establishment of the Labour Court. The removal of the Emergency Powers Orders and the negotiation of a general pay increase for unionised employees constituted what became known as the first *wage round* (see Nevin 1963; McCarthy *et al.* 1975; O'Brien 1989). A wage round was essentially a period of intensive collective bargaining between employers and trade unions occurring at regular intervals and resulting in a similar general wage increase for unionised employees (Gunnigle *et al.* 1995).

The nature of collective bargaining in the immediate postwar period had important implications for the development of HRM in Ireland. Growth in the size and complexity of organisations demanded greater specialisation and knowledge in workforce management, particularly in the area of industrial relations. In the public sector and among some larger private companies these needs were achieved through the establishment of specialist HR departments, whose key activity was industrial relations (O'Mahony 1958). By the 1960s levels of unionisation among manual workers had increased significantly and *shop stewards* began to emerge as a significant grouping in establishing plant level bargaining as a central component of workforce management (Roche and Larragy 1989; Marsh 1973). This situation was accentuated by the growth in white-collar trade unionisation from the 1960s (Bain 1970; Kelly 1975). The decade of the 1960s was also characterised by a marked increase in levels of industrial conflict.

A further development contributing to the increasing significance of industrial relations as a critical concern in HRM was the onset of the *national wage agreement* era (1970–82). The negotiation of the first national wage agreement marked a transformation from the rather unclear system of wage rounds, which had existed since the end of the war. An important effect of national wage agreements was to move major pay bargaining issues away from the level of the enterprise. This development was initially seen as freeing management from complex negotiations with trade unions and giving them more certainty in corporate planning. However, the reality was somewhat different. At a time of relative economic prosperity and substantial growth in union membership, the key workplace role for trade unions, namely pay bargaining, was removed. With the expectation that pay increases would be derived by means of national agreements, trade unions increasingly focused their attention on matters that could be negotiated at local (workplace) level such as employment conditions, pay anomalies and productivity deals. Indeed, far from eliminating enterprise level bargaining, national agreements merely changed their focus, and the period saw the negotiation of various types of productivity deals. These became an important means by which trade unions could gain pay increases above the stated maxima laid down in national wage agreements. The emphasis on industrial relations therefore continued to expand during the national wage agreement era.

For the HR function, industrial relations remained a priority with HR practitioners heavily involved in workplace bargaining with trade unions. Industrial harmony was the objective, and industrial relations specialists, through their negotiating, inter-personal, and procedural skills had responsibility for its achievement. Increased industrial unrest from the mid-1960s to the end of the 1970s served to confirm industrial relations as a key concern of employers. It gave the emerging HR function a central management role. HR departments whose major responsibility was industrial relations became established in most medium and larger organisations. The Donovan Report in Britain (1968) was also influential in encouraging collective bargaining, the adoption of comprehensive industrial relations procedures and greater specialisation in industrial relations management.

Increased Government intervention in the management sphere since the 1970s has also had a significant influence on the HR function. As discussed above, this was particularly evident in the area of centralised pay bargaining. The early seventies also witnessed the introduction of an unprecedented wave of *employment legislation*, which was to impinge on the industrial scene and significantly impacted upon the role of the HR practitioner. This legislation primarily focused on extending the individual employment rights of workers in areas such as dismissals and equality. Key legislation approved in this period included the Unfair Dismissals Act 1977, the Anti-Discrimination (Pay) Act 1974, the Employment Equality Act 1977, and a number of Redundancy Acts.

Organisations have had to come to grips with the application of such legislation. Much of this responsibility was assumed by the emerging HR function. HR practitioners were expected to provide expert advice and guidance on the new legislation and to oversee its implementation in the workplace.

Chapters ten, eleven and twelve of this text review employee relations issues in Ireland.

The Multinational Influence

Multinational companies (MNCs) exert a much greater influence on the Irish economy than in any other European Union (EU) member state. We now have some 1,200 overseas companies operating in Ireland, employing approximately 120,000 people directly and an additional 15,000 people on a temporary basis (Hannigan 1999, 2000; Gunnigle and McGuire 2001). Employment in MNCs now accounts for roughly one third of the industrial workforce, with the main sectors being electronics, pharmaceuticals and health-care, software and 'teleservices'. MNCs account for 55 per cent of manufactured output and some 70 per cent of industrial exports (Tansey 1998). US-owned firms represent by far the most significant grouping. Ireland has over 400 US MNCs employing over 50,000 people. The UK and Germany are also important sources of DFI (see table 1.1).

Table 1.1 MNCs in Ireland: country of ownership 2000

Ownership	% of Firms
US	41
UK	16
Germany	14
Netherlands	4
Japan	4
Canada	3
France	3
Sweden	2
Italy	2
Switzerland	2
Others	9

Given the significance of multinational companies in Ireland it is hardly surprising that they have had an important impact on the development of HRM. MNCs have been to the fore in developing comprehensive policies and procedures across various aspects of HRM, and in giving a greater impetus to the role of the specialist HR function (HR department).

A particularly important legacy of MNC investment has been the diffusion of new HR techniques. In areas such as selection testing, training methods, reward systems and communications, MNCs have been to the fore in introducing new developments and methods. We have evidence, for example, that MNCs have also been associated with innovation in areas of high performance work systems (Mooney 1988), performance related pay (Gunnigle, Turner and D'Art 1998) and with enhancing the status of the specialist HR function (Gunnigle 1998). At a general level, the effect of MNCs has been to contribute to establishing HRM as a more central component of the management process.

The impact of MNCs on HRM in Ireland is considered throughout this text with particular mention of their impact on employee relations in chapter eleven.

HRM EDUCATION
Another important factor, which has contributed to the growth and expansion of the HR role, has been a progressively increasing emphasis on the professional education of HR practitioners since the 1970s. Clearly increasing specialisation in the HR sphere required commensurate growth in the education and training of HR specialists. Many of the newer multinational and larger indigenous organisations emphasised the appointment of qualified and experienced HR practitioners. While the origins of formal courses in aspects of HRM can be traced back to the 1940s, the most significant developments have taken place since the 1960s.

The establishment of AnCO as the national training agency in 1967 added impetus to the development of the HR role through increased emphasis on training and development. In the 1970s the first courses leading to membership of the Chartered Institute of Personnel and Development (CIPD – then called the Institute of Personnel Management) were offered at centres in Dublin and Limerick. Since then full- and part-time undergraduate and postgraduate programmes have been established at most universities and a number of other colleges of higher education. In 2000, courses leading to various categories of membership of the CIPD were available at thirteen third level centres throughout the Republic of Ireland.

We also find that courses in HRM, organisation behaviour and/or employee relations form part of most undergraduate programmes in business and related disciplines, while personnel/HR modules are generally a core component in MBA programmes. Thus, we have had a progressive increase in formal education of HR practitioners which has served to enhance the status and competencies available across the broad field of HRM.

This growth in HR education has occurred in parallel with growth in membership of the CIPD in the UK and Ireland. The CIPD is the professional body for HR practitioners in Ireland and the UK. It began its life in the UK in 1913 as the Welfare Workers' Association, operated for many years at the Institute of Personnel Management (IPM) and became the Institute of Personnel and Development in 1994 – the name being a derivative, resulting from the merger between the Institute of Personnel Management and the Institute of Training and Development in the UK. It was granted a Royal Charter from July 2000 in acknowledgement of its role as the major management association in the HR field. The resulting change in title to CIPD reflects this change in status. Membership of the CIPD in the UK and Ireland is more than 100,000. In Ireland membership has increased dramatically; from a base of just fourteen registered members in 1937, membership passed the one thousand mark in 1987 and by 1999 there were over 3100 CIPD members in Ireland.

RETRENCHMENT AND RE-DEFINITION

In evaluating the development of the HRM in Ireland, it is clear that increased industrialisation, direct foreign investment and commercial activity since the 1960s have contributed to the establishment of HR as a discrete management function. By the late 1970s the HRM role was firmly established in most of the larger Irish organisations. HR or 'personnel' departments operated as a distinct management function with responsibility for a well-defined range of HR activities. Industrial relations was the key activity area with most emphasis on collective bargaining.

However, the 1980s heralded a period of considerable major change for HRM. A depressed economic climate together with increased competitive pressures, led to a slump in business activity for most of the decade. These developments helped to change both the focus of HRM and the nature of HR activities. Competitive pressures combined to set new priorities, forcing the HR function to act under tighter cost controls and to undertake a wider range of activities (Berridge 1992; Tyson 1987; Foley and Gunnigle 1994). The recessional climate reduced the need for many hitherto 'core' activities such as recruitment and, particularly, industrial relations. The harsh economic atmosphere of the 1980s dramatically changed the industrial relations environment. An economic climate characterised by widespread redundancies and high unemployment significantly altered the bargaining environment with adverse consequences for trade unions. Increasingly employers sought to address issues such as payment structures and levels of wage increases, the extent of demarcation and restrictive work practices and, ultimately, the erosion of managerial prerogative by trade unions.

Restrictive trade union legislation in Britain and hard-line management approaches in many firms indicated a more offensive approach to dealings with trade unions. This was reflected in the adverse outcomes for trade unions of strikes by miners in Britain and air traffic controllers in the US in the early 1980s. Trade unions were in retreat and membership began to fall in many Western countries. In Ireland trade union membership fell significantly throughout the 1980s and industrial unrest has also declined from the highs of the 1970s.

At the same time increased market competition forced many organisations to seek ways of establishing competitive advantage. One apparent source of such improvements lay in the better utilisation of human resources. Some organisations began to investigate different approaches to workforce management, particularly in areas such as work organisation and job design, reward systems, employee relations and training and development.

However, the most widely debated development over the period was the emergence of what became known as *human resource management*. In this text we use the term 'human resource management' (HRM) in a generic fashion to encompass all aspects of workforce management in organisations. HRM has indeed become the umbrella term for what was formerly known as 'personnel management'. From an academic perspective, HRM has also become the umbrella discipline encompassing research and education in the fields of industrial relations, personnel management, organisational behaviour, human resource development and management strategy.

This was not always the case. The use of the term 'human resource management' (HRM) only came into popular usage in the early 1980s. In its initial conception, HRM essentially referred to the development of a more integrated and strategic approach to workforce management. It had its roots in the US, which has been receptive to the application of organisational psychology and behavioural science principles in an attempt to improve organisational performance (Beaumont 1992). The central contention, this specific conception of HRM, was that organisations incorporate human resource considerations into strategic decision-making, establish a corporate human resource philosophy and develop a complementary and coherent set of HR strategies and policies to improve HR utilisation (Guest 1987; Beer *et al.* 1984). Although over two decades have now passed since this debate began, the implications for practice remain unclear. Some contributors argue that HRM merely involved a retitling exercise or 'old wine in new bottles' with little substantive change in HR practice (Armstrong 1987; Keenoy 1990). Others have argued, however, that the emergence of (strategic) HRM involves a complete reorientation of the HR role and function in organisations (Beer *et al.* 1984; Storey 1992). The emergence of HRM and its implications is considered in some detail in chapter two (which also addresses the linkages between business strategy and HR), and briefly below where we consider some contemporary developments in the field.

Contemporary Developments

When we consider the exceptionally high levels of economic growth and employment creation from the early 1990s, it is sometimes difficult to appreciate the pessimism that characterised the Irish economy for much of the 1980s. Economic growth during the first half of the decade was extremely low, unemployment and inflation rose steadily, and the country's fiscal debt was unsustainable. Substantial employment decline was recorded during this recessional period when unemployment rose from less than 8 per cent to almost 20 per cent of the labour force and resulted in the resumption of large-scale emigration. As public debt and unemployment reached record proportions, the economy became locked in deep recession. A quote from *The Economist* in 1988 captures the situation in which the Irish economy found itself:

> . . . the country was on the skids. In four years its national debt had doubled. As a proportion of Gross Domestic Product, Ireland's debt was the biggest in Europe. Servicing costs were gobbling one third of annual tax revenue and 90 per cent of the revenue from income tax. Real interest rates of 10 per cent were driving business to despair. A panicky flight of capital had begun. The International Monetary Fund expected a call for help.

As we now know, IMF intervention was not called for. Rather, towards the end of the decade, the Irish Government embarked on a programme of fiscal rectitude, encompassing severe cutbacks in public expenditure. A confluence of favourable developments, both in the domestic and Irish economy, has since contributed to a remarkable transformation in the Irish economy. Indeed, the Irish economy has now recovered to such an extent that by the late 1990s it was widely heralded as a model of effective economic management. Expansive growth in the Irish economy characterised this period. Real GDP growth rates since 1994 averaged over 9 per cent a year or almost four times the European Union (EU) average (Economist Intelligence Unit 1999). Ireland became the OECD's fastest growing economy with levels of economic performance at or above the levels of most of the world's high growth economies. In terms of international competitiveness, the 2000 World Competitiveness Report ranked Ireland as the fifth most competitive world economy (www.imd.ch) up from tenth in 1997, achieving particularly strong scores in areas such as education, Government, and technological capacity. However, more recently the poor economic performance of the US economy and the associated downturn in the high technology sector has become a source of considerable concern especially in relation to employment losses.

The transformation from a comparatively poor and under-developed economy in the late 1950s to one characterised by industrial expansion and strong economic growth involved major changes in the structure of employment and a substantial restructuring in the labour market. Trends in the sectoral distribution of employment indicate a progressive decline in agricultural and traditional industrial employment, and a dramatic rise in the service sector, particularly private services. Between 1980 and 1996, Irish non-agricultural employment growth of 26 per cent exceeded that of the EU (7 per cent) and the US (15 per cent). Of the current labour force of 1.6 million people, approximately 10 per cent are employed in agriculture, 29 per cent are employed in industry and the remaining 61 per cent are employed in services. Over recent years, the largest share of employment creation was accounted for by the growth in the services sector.

However, employment growth in manufacturing and construction sectors has also remained strong. Unemployment, a traditional problem in the Irish economy and the source of large scale emigration from the country over many decades, has also fallen significantly in recent years (from 18 per cent in 1986 to just under 4 per cent in 2001); skill shortages have now emerged in some sectors of the economy. Indeed, a number of commentators fear that decreased labour supply may arrest Ireland's economic growth and – particularly – its capacity to attract foreign direct investment.

From a HRM perspective, the arrival of the 'Celtic tiger' brought very different challenges. Probably the most pressing of these concerns the 'attraction and retention' of workers. Rapidly falling unemployment levels combined with increased demand for labour has made for a very tight labour market. Employers were increasingly forced to compete for new workers and sought to develop innovative means of retaining current employees. Related issues include pressures from workers and trade unions for better rewards and some increase in employee relations disputes, often related to pay and working conditions. We have also seen an increased emphasis on the training and development of workers, as organisations seek to both enhance its workforce competencies and give workers adequate opportunity for personal development.

This changed economic climate provides the context for our treatment of each major area of HR activity and is referred to throughout the text, while developments in the Irish labour market are specifically addressed in chapter three. However, we now move beyond our historical review to consider HRM practice in organisations.

THE NATURE OF HRM

During discussions some years ago with a class of mature students taking an introductory HRM course, a number of class members suggested that 'personnel' did not really operate in their organisations since they had 'no personnel department'. This interpretation of HRM as being the responsibility of HR specialists is a common, if flawed, conception. HRM is concerned with the management of an organisation's workforce. Thus conceived, it is a *generalist* responsibility, which constitutes an important aspect of the job of everyone with managerial responsibilities. It incorporates all policies and practices involving workforce management and is therefore an inherent aspect of the management process. All organisations have important HR responsibilities, with the deployment, development, motivation and reward of employees representing core HR activities.

However, HRM may also be seen as a *specialist* management function. In this context, certain HR activities are seen as the responsibility of HR specialists who have particular responsibility for developing and monitoring their organisation's HR strategies, policies and practices. Even where a specialist function exists however, line management will

10

continue to play a central role in operational day-to-day HR activities, such as recruitment or on-the-job training. The key role of the specialist HR function is to provide adequate assistance, advice and administrative support. However, it may play more of an executive role by taking direct responsibility for certain activities. Common examples here might include collective bargaining with trade unions or approving promotion decisions.

This conception of HRM in *generalist* and *specialist* terms is important. Firstly, it recognises that HRM is a key responsibility of all managers. It also recognises that in some particularly large organisations, HR specialists are employed to undertake particular aspects of the HR role. Thus, although HR involves managers at all levels in the organisation's hierarchy, it is useful to consider the respective roles of three critical layers, namely top or senior management, line management and the specialist HR function.

At the highest level of organisational decision-making, HRM involves *senior management* developing the organisation's HR philosophy and strategy. Senior management may comprise of the owner or manager of a small retail store or the corporate board of directors of a multinational corporation. At an operational level, HRM primarily involves *line management* undertaking the day-to-day operational activities of HR: communicating with employees, monitoring performance, handling employee grievances, etc. In most larger organisations one generally finds a *specialist HRM function*. This involves the employment of one or more HR specialists who together may constitute an HRM department. The primary role of the specialist function is to help devise and execute the organisation's HR strategies and policies (Cole 1988). It also undertakes specialist tasks and acts as a source of expert advice and guidance to line and top management.

HRM Activities

If we accept that HRM is concerned with the management of an organisation's workforce, it is clear that the range of HR activities, which may be undertaken by an organisation, is extensive. Many of these are basic activities common to all types of organisation, such as recruiting and rewarding workers. Certain HR activities may only be appropriate in particular organisational contexts and require more specialist skills. Examples here would include the administration of job evaluation schemes or negotiating collective agreements with trade unions. Other HR activities may be more optional in character and their incidence related to preferred managerial approaches or styles. Examples of the latter might include the operation of profit sharing schemes or the establishment of employee assistance programmes. Since there is a wide range of HR activities, which may be undertaken in an organisation, it is clear that the nature of HRM may differ considerably between organisations.

At a general level it is possible to identify critical HRM activities which are shared by all types of organisations. Possibly the most comprehensive attempt to chart these activities was that undertaken by the Personnel Standards Lead Body (1993) in the United Kingdom which identified the following core activities:

1. **Strategy and Organisation**
   This involves contributions to organisational strategy, organisation structure and processes; influencing culture and values and developing personnel/HR strategies and policies.
2. **Employee Resourcing**
   Incorporating human resource planning, recruitment and selection; deployment and termination of employment.

3. **Employee Development**

   Incorporating training and development, management development, career development and performance management.

4. **Reward Management**

   Incorporating the selection of reward strategies and administration of payment and benefit systems.

5. **Employee Relations**

   Incorporating industrial relations, employee involvement and participation, communication, health, safety and welfare and employee services.

6. **Employment and Personnel/HR Administration**

   Incorporating administration of employees' records, employment policies and practices, working conditions and personnel/HR information systems.

The Impact of Organisations' Size

A useful approach in considering the nature of HRM is to reflect on the extent and variation of HRM activities as organisations' size increases. In *smaller organisations* one finds that responsibility for all HR matters normally rests with line management (Gunnigle and Brady 1984). For obvious financial and structural reasons, such organisations would not normally employ a HR specialist. Nevertheless, effective HRM remains a vital consideration. Since payroll is often the largest ongoing cost in many small firms, performance and profitability can often be increased by better human resource utilisation (Gunnigle 1989; McMahon 1994). Indeed poor recruitment, inadequate training or conflicting employee relations can have a proportionately more serious effect in smaller organisations than in their larger counterparts. Of course, the nature of HRM is made potentially simpler in small firms due to the scale of operations, which eases the burden of communications and reduces the level of administrative support required.

In the majority of small companies, HRM will be concerned with basic activities essential to the effective running of the organisation. For such organisations key HR activities incorporate human resource planning; recruitment and selection; training and development; reward management; employee relations; health, safety and welfare and administrative support.

When we consider larger organisations we find that increases in the organisation's size will normally make the HRM process more complex. It expands the scale of HRM activities and increases the complexity of HR administration. Normally there is also greater formality and sophistication of HR policies and procedures. However, while such changes simply affect the nature of the HRM process, the basic objectives and activities remain the same.

A common response of many larger Irish organisations is to have a specialist HR department which co-ordinates HR activities and carries out much of the administrative work (Shivanath 1987; Foley and Gunnigle 1994; Monks 1992). Such specialist departments may comprise of one or two individuals with general responsibility for HR matters. Alternatively, very large organisations may employ an extensive HR department characterised by a high degree of task specialisation as outlined in figure 1.1.

It is apparent that increases in the size and complexity of organisations result in specialisation and formalisation in the conduct of HR activities. One also finds that the specialist HR function takes responsibility for a larger range of activities. However, the key role of top management in deciding upon the corporate HR approach, and of line management in undertaking a range of operational HR tasks, should remain intact.

The specialist HR function normally operates in a *staff* capacity. This means that its primary role is to provide assistance and advice to line management (at all levels) in undertaking their HR responsibilities.

12

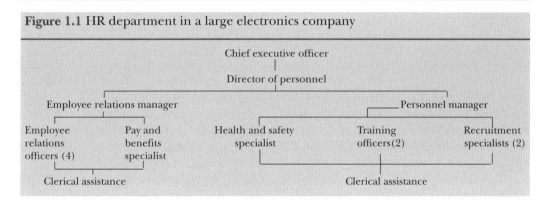

Figure 1.1 HR department in a large electronics company

STRATEGY, POLICY AND PRACTICE IN HRM

The study of *business strategy* has achieved increasing prominence as organisations seek to adapt to a changing business environment (see chapter two). Business strategy is concerned with policy decisions affecting the entire organisation, the main objective being to best position it to deal effectively with its environment. Strategic decisions are long-term in nature, affect the future of the organisation, and serve to guide subsequent decision-making at lower levels.

In recent years, the HRM literature has placed an ever increasing emphasis on the need to align HR strategies and policies with overall business strategy (Beer *et al.* 1984; Fombrun *et al.* 1984; Schuler 1987, 1998, 1992; Schuler and Jackson 1987a and b). It is suggested that HRM activities should be guided by the overall business strategy and related HR strategies. It has further been argued that a well-aligned business and HR strategy can contribute to improvements in organisational performance (Huselid 1995). Thus, it is argued that the role of HR strategy, policies and activities is to contribute to the organisation's primary business goals (Fombrun *et al.* 1984). This link between business strategy, HRM strategies and HR activities is illustrated in fig. 1.2.

Figure 1.2 Business strategy and HRM

Business strategy
(incorporating marketing and product development strategies)

Personnel management strategy
(incorporating the company's desired approach to personnel management and its key personnel management objectives)

Personnel management policies and procedures
(incorporating key polices in areas of employment, rewards, and employee relations)

Strategy & organisation	Employee resourcing	Employee development	Reward management	Employee relations
Organisation strategy and structure; personnel strategy	Human resource planning; recruitment; selection; socialisation; deployment	Training; development; performance management	Pay systems; benefits; employment conditions	Industrial relations; communications; employee involvement; health and safety; employee services

Personnel information systems and support

HRM STRATEGY

An HRM strategy incorporates an organisation's basic philosophy, overall approach and long-term objectives in managing human resources (Gunnigle and Flood 1990). It involves identifying the organisation's beliefs and values about how employees should be managed and forms the basis for the subsequent development of more explicit HR policies and procedures in critical areas of workforce management, such as employee selection and reward management. The responsibility for developing HR strategy rests primarily with top management aided, as appropriate, by the specialist HR function. HR strategies are normally designed to complement the overall business strategy and may often be expressed in the form of general statements outlining the important organisational philosophies and values concerning HRM. Table 1.2 outlines examples of such statements from two companies.

Table 1.2 Statements of corporate beliefs in HRM

Company 1: Key beliefs in managing people
- To treat each employee with dignity, as an individual.
- To maintain an open atmosphere where direct communications with employees affords the opportunity to contribute to the maximum of their potential and fosters unity of purpose.
- To provide personal opportunities for training and development to ensure the most capable and most efficient workforce.
- To respect senior service.
- To compensate fairly by salary, benefits and incentives.
- To promote on the basis of capability.

Company 2: Core values and beliefs about how employees should be managed (selection)
- *Employment:* Employees are recruited and promoted on merit and we believe in maximum openness in competition and appointments. We respect our employees and value each as an individual. All employees have equal opportunity for development and advancement according to their qualifications, abilities and the needs of the business. We seek to use individual talents and skills to the best advantage of the person and the company.
- *Pay and conditions:* We have pay and conditions of employment designed to attract the right people, motivate employees, stimulate quality work and reflect performance, while taking account of national economic circumstances and policy. We try always to be fair and equitable in the treatment of individuals and in responding to their needs.

The examples in table 1.2 are explicit indications of particular espoused organisational strategies in HRM. However, in practice one finds that a majority of companies do not have such explicit statements. Data generated from the Cranfield-University of Limerick (CUL) study of HR practice in Irish organisations found that approximately four in every ten firms had a written HR strategy (Gunnigle, Morley, Clifford and Turner 1997). The latter study focused on larger firms (i.e. those employing fifty or more employees). Clearly the incidence of formal HR strategies is likely to be much lower among smaller organisations. Does this imply that such organisations do not a have HR strategy? Generally not. Virtually all organisations have a philosophy and broad approach concerning how it views and manages its workforce. While this may not necessarily be written, it can be inferred from how employees are treated and rewarded within the organisation. In such situations the organisation's HR philosophy is implicit rather than explicit in nature (Gunnigle and Flood 1990). This approach may sometimes reflect a lack of strategic awareness of HRM considerations on the part of the organisation.

HRM Policies

Of course, broad HR strategies and related HR philosophy statements expressing corporate beliefs and values are likely to be ineffective unless they are implemented in the day-to-day practice of HRM. To effectively bridge the gap between espoused beliefs and workplace practice, organisations normally develop a set of HR policies in key activity areas of HRM such as recruitment, rewards and employee relations. The primary role of such policies is to guide managers in the execution of their HRM responsibilities. They also act as an important yardstick for workers in outlining the standards and approaches they should expect from the organisation, and the norms the organisation expects from its workforce. Examples of HR policy statements are outlined in table 1.3.

Table 1.3 HR policy statements (indicative)

Company 1: Policy statement on promotion and development
This company encourages everyone to prepare for career enhancement thorough its educational assistance and training programmes. It is our policy to promote from within whenever suitable and experienced candidates are available.

Company 2: Policy statement on employment equality
It is our policy to ensure that all employees are afforded equal treatment irrespective of their sex, marital or parental status, race or religion. This company ensures equal access to employment, training, development and promotion solely based on essential job requirements and the individual's ability and fitness for work.

Company 3: Policy statement rewards on pay and employment conditions
It is our policy to provide pay and terms of employment, which are competitive with the top quartile of comparable firms in our industrial segment.

Company 4: Policy statement on employee relations
We seek to develop good relations with employees and their trade unions. Where difficulties arise, the company will seek to resolve these quickly and as close to the workplace as possible. The company is committed to adherence to agreed procedures in the resolution of employee relations' difficulties.

HRM Procedures

Policy statements, therefore, establish the parameters within which managers, supervisors and team leaders execute their various operational HRM responsibilities. To further aid this process, organisations very often have a set of HRM procedures which are detailed statements to guide managers and workers in the detailed and effective implementation of policies. These procedures normally embrace detailed statements covering a range of operational HR activities such as recruitment, promotion, performance management and industrial relations. Examples of such HR procedures are outlined in table 1.4. The specialist HR function normally plays a key role in developing HR policies and procedures. They also provide support and direction to line managers in the implementation of procedures through advice, guidance and administrative assistance (Tyson and Fell 1986).

Table 1.4 HRM procedures (indicative)

Company 1: Procedure on educational assistance
To help personal development and maintain the company's competitive position, all relevant educational courses or parts thereof, which have been successfully completed and are appropriate to your career will be paid for by the company. All such courses must be approved, prior to the commencement of the course, by your department manager and the Human Resource Manager in order to be considered for reimbursement. Application forms are available from the Human Resource Department.

Company 2: Procedure on probationary period
The first six months of your employment will be considered a probationary period. During this time, your supervisor will assess your suitability for the job. He/she will sit down with you and discuss your performance after one month, after three months and, again, after six months service. You will be given every opportunity and assistance to make a success of your new position. Within this time the company shall have the sole and absolute right of deciding on your suitability for continued employment. Your employment may be terminated by the company at any time during this period without recourse to the disciplinary or grievance procedure.

HRM POLICY CHOICE: VARIATIONS IN STRATEGY, POLICY AND PRACTICE IN HRM

The preceding discussion has alluded to the fact that, in practice, one finds immense variation between organisations in their approach to workforce management. This is manifested in differing HRM strategies, policies and procedures and may be attributed to the differential impact of factors in the external or internal environment of organisations. Purcell (1987) notes the tendency to identify and contrast prominent organisations according to their 'employment policies and practices'. While many of these differences are due to external environmental factors such as product market performance, Purcell also identifies *strategic choice* (exercised by senior management) as a key factor explaining differences in organisational approaches to HRM (also see Beer *et al.* 1984; Kochan *et al.* 1986).

Strategic choice addresses the extent to which management (i) possess and (ii) exercise choice in developing their HRM strategies, policies and procedures. This implies that senior managements possess some room for manoeuvre, and while environmental factors may constrain the range of choice, they retain considerable power in making decisions on 'appropriate' styles and policies. Senior management can therefore use their resources and power to make strategic choices, which both influence environmental factors and affect particular management approaches or 'styles'. Organisational approaches to HRM should therefore be evaluated in terms of the interplay between environmental factors, managerial ideology and values and strategic choice. As Marchington and Parker (1990, 99) state:

> Choice should be viewed as both a cause and a consequence of environmental influences, that is, managements have some influence over the kind of markets in which they choose to operate, and in some cases over the structure of the market itself, as well as having some choice over the way in which they respond to environmental pressures.

The interplay of such factors will clearly lead to consequential variations in patterns of HRM. Such disparity will become manifest in a vast range of HR activities such as recruitment and selection, reward systems and employee development.

The Context for Choice: Variation in Organisational Approaches to HRM

In order to identify and explain variations in organisational approaches to HRM it is necessary to examine the interplay between a diverse range of external and internal factors that influence and constrain managerial choice and practice in the sphere of workforce management. A particular focus of such analysis is the external environment (such as product and labour markets), management values, business strategy and historical factors as key factors impacting on organisational approaches to HRM (Kochan *et al.* 1986).

It is argued that changes in environmental conditions affect decisions on business strategy and ultimately HRM. Such decisions will be conditioned by managerial values and constrained by historical factors and current organisational practice in HRM. Figure 1.3 presents a framework for evaluating variation in organisational approaches to HRM. This framework is further discussed below.

Figure 1.3 HRM policy choice: context and variation

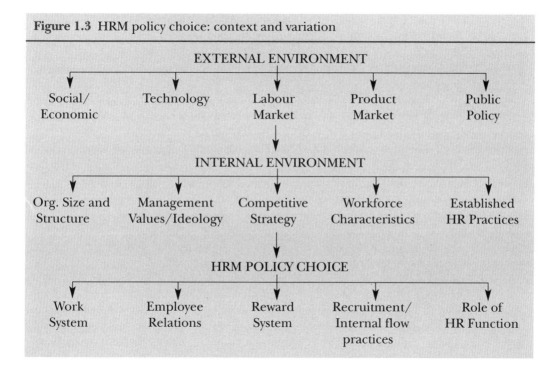

The External Environment

The external environment is a major influence on organisational decision-making. Trends in the socio-economic context, such as *levels of economic performance* and *trends in cultural and societal norms and values,* will impact upon business strategy and management practice. Economic performance and public policy, as manifested in areas such as levels of economic activity, state intervention and control, and approaches to organised labour, clearly exert a significant impact on management approaches to HRM (Gunnigle, McMahon and Fitzgerald 1999). We have already seen that while levels of economic activity in Ireland remained depressed for much of the 1980s, they have now recovered remarkably over the past decade. This created a boom in business activity across almost all sectors of the economy. Labour shortages and pressures for production are just some of the spin-offs with important implications for HRM. At the same time we have seen increased competition in certain sectors (such as telecommunications) and, most recently, a downturn in the high tech sector. This has exposed many organisations to increased levels of market pressure, which, in turn, may encourage organisations to focus on initiatives to reduce labour costs and improve labour productivity.

Broader social changes in areas such as education, living standards, and class mobility also exert significant influence on organisational approaches to workforce management. For example, higher education levels can contribute to increased worker expectations in relation to issues such as rewards, working conditions and opportunities for personal development.

Developments in *technology* are another key external environmental factor affecting organisational approaches to HRM. Technology, seen in generic terms as the equipment used to perform particular tasks, and the way in which it is organised, has a major influence on approaches to workforce management (Beer *et al.* 1984). Guest (1987) identifies techno-logical/production feasibility as a requisite condition for the successful implementation of more 'strategic' HRM approaches, and suggests that large-scale investment in short-cycle, repetitive, assembly-line technology mitigates against the job design principles and autonomous teamworking characteristic of 'strategic' HRM (see chapter two for more details).

Technology also affects cost structure, and consequently impacts upon important aspects of HRM, such as reward systems. Marchington (1982) suggests that in labour-intensive sectors, where wage costs are high, organisations may be more constrained in developing employee-oriented management styles. However, in capital-intensive sectors, where labour constitutes a small proportion of total costs, organisations may have greater scope to adopt 'softer' HRM approaches, incorporating, for example, attractive reward and employee development policies. Developments in technology also impact directly on job content and changes in technology may lead to changes in the competencies required to effectively carry out particular job tasks. These issues are addressed in greater detail in chapter five (specifically concerning the issues of work systems and job design).

The *labour market* has exerted possibly the most profound influence upon HRM in Ireland, especially in the areas of recruitment, training and reward systems. Looking at the Irish labour market, the most notable development has been the huge growth in employment levels since the early 1990s and the resultant decline in unemployment (from almost 20 per cent at one stage in the 1980s to current levels of approximately 4 per cent). An associated and significant development has been the change in the sectoral distribution of employment encompassing a progressive decline in agricultural employment and growth in industrial and – particularly – service sector employment. This means that the Irish labour market has been transformed from one of over-supply labour to that characterised by a significant reduction in labour availability, and indeed labour shortages in certain sectors of the economy. This has meant that 'dipping' into the external labour market is no longer a ready option for employers. Such conditions increase the onus on organisations to establish more elaborate training and development policies, and more generally to employ HR policies designed to attract and retain workers. Lower unemployment also tends to exert upward pressure on wages and fringe benefits, and can also impact on other aspects of HRM such as labour turnover and power relations in collective bargaining. Other notable developments in employment structure are the increased feminisation of the workforce and the growth of 'atypical' employment forms, that is any form of employment which deviates from the full-time, permanent format, includes self-employment, temporary and part-time work.

Product market performance is also a significant influence on strategic decision-making and organisational approaches to HRM. It is clear that favourable market conditions such as high market share allow organisations greater scope to adopt more benign HRM practices, such as attractive high pay and attractive fringe benefits. Thus, organisations which operate from a strong product market position (e.g. high market share, growing market, stable demand) have greater scope to adopt sophisticated human resource policies in areas such as employee development, job tenure commitments and management-employee communications. In contrast, firms under high levels of market pressure (contracting market share; high levels of price competition) may have considerably less scope for choice and be forced to adopt a more traditional cost reduction and labour control approach. The characteristics of an organisation's product market will be influenced by a variety of factors such as the cost of entry, nature of competition, technology, and the customer base. The impact of product market conditions on organisational approaches to HRM is further considered in chapter two.

There are a number of important aspects of *public policy* that impact upon HRM in Ireland, most particularly in the areas of industrial relations and employment law. In the industrial relations area, the traditional approach of successive Irish Governments was grounded in the 'voluntarist' tradition. This meant that the state only intervened to a minimal degree in management-employee relations, allowing employers and employees (or their representative bodies) considerable scope to determine the substantive and procedural terms of their relationship in areas such as pay increases, working conditions and the extent of consultation rights afforded to employees (Hillery 1994). However, this approach has been considerably diluted over recent years as we have seen greater state intervention in industrial relations: see chapter ten on employee relations (also see Roche 1989, 1997b).

Recent Governments have been strong advocates of centralised agreements on pay and other aspects of social and economic policy involving negotiations with the main employer and trade union federations. A more established aspect of public policy is the constitutional guarantee of freedom of association, which gives individuals the right to join trade unions. However, there is no corresponding onus on the employer to recognise a trade union. Indeed the issue of trade union recognition has been an area of some contention in regard to public policy as an increasing number of organisations choose to pursue a non-union strategy (see, for example, McGovern 1989a; Gunnigle 1995; also see chapter ten for greater detail).

An obvious manifestation of the influence public policy has on HRM is in the area of labour legislation. The period since the 1970s has witnessed the passing of several important acts, particularly in the area of individual employment rights such as dismissals and employment equality. A particularly important influence in the area of employment legislation is the impact of the European Union (EU). The 1987 Single European Act, aimed at strengthening economic cohesion, placed a strong emphasis on the integrating of social policy throughout the EU (Hourihan 1997). In 1989 a Charter of Fundamental Social Rights of Workers, the Social Charter, was signed by all member states except the United Kingdom. The Social Charter (subsequently renamed the Social Chapter) and attendant Social Action Programme comprise of forty-nine legally binding directives and recommendations designed to realise the aims of the Social Charter.

A final important aspect of public policy relates to approaches to industrial development. Since the mid-1960s Irish Government policy has been to actively encourage foreign investment in Ireland. In our earlier historical review we noted the extensive role which multinational companies (MNCs) play in the Irish economy. Ireland's strong public policy stance on promoting MNC investment has significantly shaped the development of HRM in the country. We noted earlier that MNCs have been an important source of innovation in HRM, particularly in the application of new HR approaches and in expanding the role of the specialist HRM function (Gunnigle and Flood 1990). However, it would also seem that MNCs pose particular and unique challenges in the sphere of employee relations, particularly in their ability to switch the locus of production and the recent and increasing trend of union avoidance (Kelly and Brannick 1988, McGovern 1988, 1989a and b; Gunnigle 1995).

THE INTERNAL ENVIRONMENT

While factors in the external environment will impact on management practice and decisions, factors in an organisation's *internal environment* will largely determine unique organisational responses to external factors. Such factors include the characteristics of the current workforce and established HRM and employee relations practices.

Organisation structure and size are clearly important factors impacting upon HRM. Irish organisations are generally smaller in scale and employment numbers than is the case in countries such as the US or Germany. Numerous studies have noted that trade union recognition and greater specialisation in HRM are positively correlated with organisation size (Brown *et al.* 1981; Purcell and Sisson 1983; Thomason 1984).

In the Irish context, Gunnigle and Brady (1984) found that management in smaller organisations veer towards a unitarist frame of reference and adopt less formality in employee relations than their counterparts in larger organisations. In relation to organisation structure, Purcell (1990) argues that senior management in highly diversified organisations are primarily concerned with financial issues, with the consequence that HRM considerations are not a concern of corporate decision-making, but rather an operational concern of management at the business-unit level. A corollary of this argument is that 'core business' organisations, whose operation relies on a narrow product range, are more likely to integrate HRM issues into strategic planning, whereas highly diversified organisations are more likely to adopt differing HR strategies and policies suited to the needs of different constituent divisions and establishments (Gunnigle, McMahon and Fitzgerald 1999).

Several writers identify the locus of HR strategy formulation as a key issue in influencing the nature of establishment-level HRM (Purcell and Sisson 1983; Kochan *et al.* 1984, 1986; Poole 1986). For example, Poole (1986) argues that, in the employee relations sphere, the growth of large multinational enterprises presents management with the opportunity to develop policies at corporate level 'where they are relatively unrestricted by intervention by Government or plant-level agreements with labour'. Of course the scope of such unfettered management prerogative is dependent both on public policy (e.g. which may place constraints on management decisions) and the distribution of power between the various parties in employee relations.

Managerial values and ideology are also seen as having a significant influence on variations in organisational approaches to HRM. Management values and ideology incorporate the deeply held beliefs of senior management, which guide decisions on various aspects of workforce management (Poole 1986; Purcell 1987; Gunnigle 1995). They are particularly important in interpreting developments in the external and internal environment, and making decisions about the organisation's overall approach to workforce management.

Clearly, all organisations are characterised by particular values and philosophies on workforce management and employee relations. As discussed earlier, such values/ideology may be explicit in some organisations, as demonstrated in statements of corporate mission or philosophy. In others, they may be implicit and, therefore, must be inferred from management practice in areas such as supervisory style, reward systems and communications. Two cases may be highlighted to emphasise the key role of management values in impacting upon HRM at organisation level (Gunnigle, McMahon and Fitzgerald 1999). Firstly, in a number of organisations the role of influential founders has had a determining influence on their organisations corporate values and general HRM approach. Prominent international examples include Marks and Spencer, Hewlett-Packard and Wang. The influence of entrepreneurial founders is also prominent in Irish indigenous firms and HR approaches adopted by organisations such as Dunnes Stores, SuperQuinn and Ryanair seem to be heavily influenced by the values and philosophy of particular chief executives.

A second instance of the impact of managerial values on HRM relates to the notion that managerial ideology is related to broader ethnic and cultural values. Of particular significance is the suggestion that in the sphere of employee relations (see chapter ten), managerial opposition to pluralism (i.e. accepting that a conflict of interest exists between employers and workers) and particularly to trade unions is characteristic of the value system of American managers, whereas certain HRM-type approaches, which emphasise individual (rather than collective) management-employee relations, direct communications and merit-based rewards are very much in line with this value system (Bendix 1956; Kochan *et al.* 1986).

This interpretation is very significant in Ireland where our economy is heavily dependent on foreign investment and where the bulk of such investment is American. In analysing the broad links between ideology and management practice, Poole (1986) finds support for the suggestion that managerial ideologies differ between countries, particularly in relation to the achievement of control over labour. In relation to Japan, Poole (1986, 47) suggests that while culture is not solely responsible for 'benevolent paternalism' in the Japanese system of industrial relations, the 'modified Confucian world-view which prevailed in the late nineteenth century' was a significant influence in encouraging 'employers to evoke moral appeals to authority and to stress the efficiency of benevolence'. Poole argues that it also helped 'shape personal objectives (the desire of private industrialists and managers to be good moral citizens) and economic goals (such as public reputation as well as greater profits and efficiency and faster expansion)' (also see Dore 1973). Poole argues that in the US context, the effects of values and ideologies are most obviously manifest in trade union avoidance practices, a pronounced 'unitary' perspective and deployment of sophisticated HRM approaches. Both Poole and Kochan *et al.* (1986) note that while managerial preferences have fluctuated over time, many US employers have embraced a non-union approach against a more general trend in the developed world towards a tacit acceptance of trade unions. Several writers identify the origins of this approach to the concept of 'individualism' in the wider US culture, coupled with prevalent private enterprise commitments (Rothenberg and Silverman 1973; Foulkes 1980; Poole 1986; Guest 1989b).

Looking specifically at the Irish context, we find that a traditional criticism of business culture in Ireland is that it has not always encouraged enterprise and innovation. This trait was attributed to Ireland's relatively late independence, which created, what some have termed, a 'dependence mentality'. However, this culture would seem to have been effectively laid to rest over recent decades. Levels of productivity and export performance have increased dramatically and compare very favourably with international standards. Recent studies have noted the flexibility of the Irish workforce and the relevance of coherent and strong corporate culture formation (Kakabadse 1990).

Another major internal factor impacting upon HRM is an organisation's *competitive strategy*. In our preceding historical review we identified increased competitive pressures on organisations as an important influence on changes in HRM over recent decades. In this more competitive environment, the notion of competitive strategy and advantage have become particularly significant. Competitive strategy is concerned with achieving sustainable competitive advantage in a particular industry or industry segment. The notion of competitive advantage is primarily associated with the work of Michael Porter and encompasses the means (i.e. competitive strategies) by which competing firms seek to gain market advantage over one another. This is normally achieved by an organisation either pricing its product more competitively or, alternatively, differentiating it from competitors along some dimension that will make it more attractive for customers (such as added features or better reliability). Porter (1987) labels these alternative competitive strategies as (i) cost leadership and (ii) product differentiation. Porter maintains that the organisation's choice of strategy helps define the overall approach to market competition and thus establishes the context for policies and actions in other key areas of organisational management, such as HRM. In particular it is argued that different business strategies require particular HR strategy configurations and that HR specialists can play an important role in helping to develop HR approaches which are effective aligned with the overall competitive strategy. The issue of business strategy and the linkages between strategy and HRM are explored in considerable detail in chapter two.

Other important factors that affect organisational approaches to HRM are *characteristics of the current workforce and established HR practice.* These factors will be particularly important in impacting upon the efficacy of change initiatives in areas such as organisation redesign or employee involvement (Gunnigle, McMahon and Fitzgerald 1999). They will also influence workforce competencies. For example, an organisation's workforce will have a particular age and skill profile. An ageing workforce may require specific training in areas such as computing while a younger workforce may have very different requirements, such as a need for experiential placements in different sectors of the organisation to build understanding and competence. Past practice also impacts on the viability of certain change initiatives. For example, many organisations have experimented with job enrichment initiatives over recent years. However, research in the field such as that of Hackman and Oldham's (1980) found that employees may necessarily react favourably to proposals for enriching jobs and quality of work life. Rather it was found that employees characterised by a strong desire for achievement, responsibility and autonomy, were most positively disposed to and motivated by such initiatives. Such employee characteristics may in turn have been conditioned by traditional past practice in HRM. For example, if internal mobility and individual initiative have traditionally been discouraged, it may be difficult to effectively implement a comprehensive internal promotion and development policy. These issues are addressed in more detail in chapter five dealing with employee motivation and the design of work.

Key Areas of HR Policy Choice

The above discussions have outlined the major influences on variations in organisational approaches to HRM. The manifestations of such variation will be evident in key areas of HR policy choice, particularly the work system, employee relations, rewards, recruitment and internal flow policies and the role of the specialist HR function.

The *work system* incorporates the way various organisational tasks are structured and affects issues such as organisational structure and job design. We have already noted that the final decades of the twentieth century have seen an increased emphasis on improving competitiveness in many Irish organisations. This is often manifested in work redesign initiatives aimed at restructuring work systems to facilitate greater flexibility and improve performance and quality levels. Decisions on the work system are primarily a managerial responsibility. The approach chosen is a valuable indicator of management beliefs regarding HRM. Traditional approaches to the organisation of work have been dominated by a desire to maintain control over the work process whilst maximising the productive efficiency of the organisation's technical resources. Choices on the organisation of work and the design of jobs were seen as primarily determined by the technical system (Gunnigle and Flood 1990). Management's role was to ensure that other resources, including employees, were organised in such a way as to facilitate the optimal utilisation of the technical system. This approach often resulted in bureaucratic structures, elaborate procedures and systems, top-down supervisory control with minimal employee involvement. It also encouraged the fragmentation of jobs into simple, repetitive and measurable tasks, which gave post-holders little autonomy. In contrast, it is suggested that an increased emphasis on improving quality, service and overall competitiveness has led to work redesign initiatives aimed at restructuring work systems to increase employee autonomy, motivation and performance (Beer 1984; Guest 1989; Morley *et al.* 1998; Walton 1985). Much of this focus has been on restructuring organisations and jobs to incorporate greater scope for intrinsic motivation and to facilitate greater employee involvement. The consequent management emphasis was on developing broadly defined, challenging jobs within a more organic, flexible organisational structure. At the same time there is also evidence of the adoption of 'harder' approaches as evidenced by job and work design initiatives, which seek to tightly prescribe performance targets and objectives, accelerate the pace of work and closely monitor individual employee performance (Gunnigle 1995). These contrasting work systems are an important indicator of preferred organisational approaches to workforce management.

A second important area of HR policy choice is employee relations. *Employee relations* involves issues such as collective bargaining, communications, grievance handling, dispute resolution and discipline administration. It may also encompass related areas such as health, safety, welfare and employee services. Traditionally there has been an emphasis on industrial relations, with collective bargaining as the central activity.

However, in recent years the term employee relations has become synonymous with a more individual approach to workforce management, and the pursuit of a non-union strategy. Differences in managements approach to this HR policy dimension tend to focus on the range of communication mechanisms used and level of senior management involvement in, and commitment to, these mechanisms. An emerging development in HR practice in Ireland is an increasing focus on direct communications with employees (Gunnigle 1991, 1995; Gunnigle, McMahon and Fitzgerald 1999). The Cranfield-University of Limerick (CUL) study of HR practice in Ireland found that there had been a significant increase in direct oral and written communications with employees (Gunnigle, Flood, Morley and Turner 1994; Gunnigle, Morley, Clifford and Turner 1997).

An organisation's *reward system* is a critical indicator of organisational approaches to HRM. High or low pay, the range of fringe benefits and the mechanism for determining reward levels provide valuable insights into an organisation's general approach to HRM. Significant considerations in the design of reward systems are the role of pay, the degree to which pay increases are based upon measures of employee performance, and the compatibility of the reward system with business strategy and other areas of HR activity, such as recruitment. In the Irish context basic pay levels have traditionally been based on the 'going rate' concept, namely what is the rate for similar jobs in other organisations and sectors. Pay increases in recent years have, in most instances, been determined at national level through centralised agreements. These apply to almost all unionised employees but also have 'knock-on' effects for many non-union employees. Increases for managerial and other professional and technical categories are generally agreed at enterprise level. This may normally occur as a result of annual performance reviews based on a range of criteria such as individual performance, section or company performance and comparisons with pay increases in other organisations.

An interesting trend in the Irish context is the growing incidence of performance related pay (PRP). PRP based on a formal performance appraisal of employee performance is more generally seen as a significant indicator of a preference for a more individualist (as opposed to collectivist) approach to employee relations. A study of recently established 'greenfield' companies found that the incidence of PRP for all employee categories was most common in non-union American-owned firms (Gunnigle 1995; Gunnigle, Turner and D'Art 1998). The area of reward systems is addressed comprehensively in chapter six.

Another important area of HR policy choice is *recruitment and internal flow practices*. This area incorporates the nature and sophistication of recruitment and employment practices. The latter dimension embodies the management and deployment of workers once they have taken up employment and incorporates key HR issues such as employee development, succession planning, appraisal and career counselling. In this broad area we can again point to some significant developments in the Irish context. Firstly, our economic boom and high levels of job creation up to the turn of the millennium meant that firms found it increasingly difficult to fill vacant positions. This clearly encouraged employers to place a greater emphasis on sourcing and retaining labour.

Another element has been an increase in the use of performance management techniques, particularly performance appraisal. An important issue for organisations is the relative emphasis placed on using either internal or external labour market sources. This concerns the degree to which management seeks to fill vacancies from within the organisation via the current pool of employees (i.e. the internal labour market), or alternatively, rely on sourcing labour from outside the organisation (i.e. the external labour market). It seems that in some organisations there is an increased desire to focus on the internal rather than the external labour market as a means of filling vacancies. Such an internal labour market emphasis is in line with so called 'strategic' HRM approaches and is often linked to a range of supportive HR policies in areas such as employee development, appraisal, and career counselling (Beer *et al.* 1994; also see chapter two). In contrast, a preference for using the external labour market implies less internal mobility, and demands less sophisticated employee development practices. Recent research evidence identifies an increased use of 'atypical' workers such as sub-contracted labour, temporary and part-time employees (Gunnigle, Morley, Clifford and Turner 1997). These issues are discussed further in chapters two and three.

THE SPECIALIST HR FUNCTION

A particularly significant aspect of HR policy choice concerns the role of the specialist HR function. Organisational approaches to workforce management influences the role of the HR function. For example, it is suggested that an essential feature of the so called 'strategic' HRM is that the major responsibility for HR be assumed by line managers. However, Guest (1987) notes 'the well established professional structure of HRM' in Britain whereby 'professional' HR specialists undertake responsibility for a range of HR issues, and possess valued expertise in core HR areas such as selection, training, pay and employee relations. It would seem that the issue of whether HR issues are best managed by a specialist HR function or by line managers is a matter of emphasis since, in most larger organisations, both will be involved in various aspects of HRM practice. For example, the 'professional'

HRM model involves a major role for the HR function in handling HR activities, with a heavy reliance on systems and procedures, and a strong emphasis on employee relations. Guest feels that this approach is most appropriate in stable, bureaucratic organisations. On the other hand, we have already noted that more contemporary approaches place a greater emphasis on role of line management in HR activities and greater top management involvement in developing HR strategies and policies (Guest 1987, 1989). Recognising the considerable differences that may arise in the role which the HR function may play in organisations, Tyson and Fell (1986) developed a three broad models role of the HR function, as outlined in table 1.5 (also see Tyson 1987).

Table 1.5 Models of the specialist HR function

1. Administrative/support role: Within this model personnel management is a low-level activity operating in a clerical support mode to the line management. It is responsible for basic administration and welfare provision.

2. Systems/reactive role: Within this model personnel management is a high-level function with a key role in handling industrial relations and in developing policies and procedures in other core areas. The role is largely reactive, dealing with the personnel management implications of business decisions. This model incorporates a strong 'policing' component, where the personnel department is concerned with securing adherence to agreed systems and procedures.

3. Business manager role: Within this model personnel management is a top-level management function involved in establishing and adjusting corporate objectives and developing strategic personnel policies designed to facilitate the achievement of long-term business goals. Personnel management considerations are recognised as an integral component of corporate success, with the personnel director optimally placed to assess how the company's human resources can best contribute to this goal. Routine personnel activities are delegated, allowing senior practitioners to adopt a broad strategic outlook.

A study by Shivanath (1987) considered the relevance of Tyson's role models for HRM practice in a cross-section of large organisations in Ireland. In relation to the *administrative and support* model, the survey evidence found that the vast majority of Irish HR practitioners were not limited to this role. While HR departments were, of necessity, concerned with routine clerical and administrative tasks, these were generally delegated allowing senior practitioners to deal with more strategic matters. The description of the HR practitioner within the *systems and reactive* model seemed to most accurately reflect the roles of the majority of Irish practitioners. Employee relations was identified by the bulk of respondents as the most crucial area of their work. The study also found that the *business manager model* was prominent in a number of organisations.

In a similar vein, but using a two-dimensional model, Storey (1992) categorises the HR function along (i) strategic/tactical and (ii) interventionary/non-interventionary continuum as outlined in figure 1.4.

The 'tactical/strategic' dimension measures the level at which the HR function operates in making decisions or providing support in organisations. This provides a useful addition to the Tyson model as it points out that the HR function may act at a strategic level, but in an advisory capacity, and thus may exhibit the strategic input of the business manager model but with the discretion of an administrative/support model. Turning to the 'interventionary/non-interventionary' dimension, this raises a key issue in the HR literature in recent times, namely the suggestion that the HR function is adopting a less 'hands on' approach in the management of the employment relationship (Mackay and Torrington 1986). Whether or not this approach is a result of a conscious policy decision, there is certainly an evident trend towards reassessing the level of intervention that HR departments engage in. Consequently, this dimension represents an informative measure of the role of the HR function in organisations. Storey (1992) uses this two-dimensional model to produce a categorisation of four HRM function types:

(i) advisors
(ii) handmaidens
(iii) regulators
(iv) change-makers

Advisors essentially provide support to line and general management. While this function is carried out at a strategic level it is reactive and non-interventionary providing specialist skills but in a consultancy capacity. *Handmaidens* represent a 'subservient, attendant relationship' with HR operating in a low-level and non-interventionary capacity reacting to the needs of line managers in response to day-to-day operational problems. Storey suggests that this HR type is indicative of a clerical and welfare role and was characteristic of subsidiaries where the HR personnel presence had been depleted or reduced.

Regulators operate in an interventionary mode but rarely at the level of strategy formulation. This approach is representative of a traditional typical 'industrial relations' orientation with the senior HR practitioner responsible for devising and negotiating policies and procedures to ensure the smooth operation of the organisation. This bears many similarities with the systems/reactive model. The rationale behind this category is that even where line managers wish to undertake this role many are not competent enough to do so or are not trained adequately. In this model the HR contribution is significant at an operational level (in ensuring the smooth running of the organisation) rather than at a strategic level.

In contrast *change-makers* act as specialists and are highly interventionist and strategic in perspective. This represents the highest level of the operation of the HR function and bears marked similarities to Tyson's business manager typology. In this model senior HR practitioners are aware of both the 'soft' and 'hard' elements of HR practice. The two roles may exist in part side by side: the calculated, quantitative rational approach of the business oriented specialist and the 'softer' approach of realising the full potential of the 'human' side of the organisation.

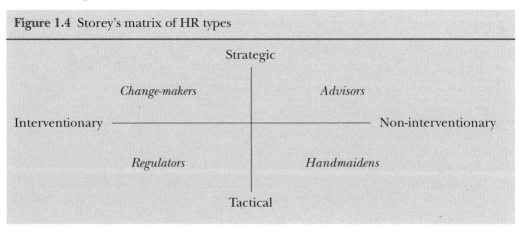

Figure 1.4 Storey's matrix of HR types

Source: Storey (1992).

There is now a widespread consensus that the management of people is an area of immense importance for advanced economies. However, there remains a widespread debate on practice and theory in the field. Many commentators argue that investment in people and commitment to the effective management of human resources can enhance organisational performance and lead to sustainable competitive advantage. On the other hand we find that economic growth and development raise fundamental questions in relation to the distribution of wealth, social cohesion and the maintenance of competitiveness.

In assessing developments over the past decade, we find that the period has been typified as one of both 'continuity and change' in HRM (see Monks 1992; Gunnigle, Flood, Morley and Turner 1994; Turner and Morley 1995; Gunnigle, Morley, Clifford and Turner 1997). The continuity dimension is evident in the fact that the core HRM activity areas (recruitment, development, employee relations, etc.) have remained more or less constant. We similarly find that the continuing presence of a specialist HR function in Irish organisations and an ongoing emphasis on employee relations as a key aspect of the HR role. The Cranfield-University of Limerick (CUL) found that over 90 per cent of organisations employing greater than 200 had a specialist HR function compared to just over half in those employing between fifty and 200 employees (Gunnigle, Morley, Clifford and Turner 1997).

However, this literature also identifies important areas of change in HRM. Thus, while the core areas of HRM have remained fairly constant, the specific manifestation of these issues and the current challenges in each area are changing radically. In Ireland, for example, such change is being driven by changes in technology, expansion of the services sector, strong economic growth, greater female participation in the workforce, expanding employment and changes in social and political life. Internationally, the globalisation of business activity, increased competitive pressures and political integration in Europe have stimulated change in the broader business environment and in HRM practice (see, for example, Sparrow and Hiltrop 1994). We find, for example, evidence of the strategic integration of the HR function, some movement away from traditional industrial relations and collective bargaining to a more individual approach, a growth in atypical forms of employment and greater emphasis on other aspects of HR activity, particularly human resource development.

Looking firstly at the area of strategic integration, we find some evidence of a trend towards a 'strategic business manager' mode. In some Irish organisations it appears that HR practitioners are adopting a more strategic role, devolving operational activities to line and staff managers. Data from the CUL study found that just over half (53 per cent) of organisations reported that the head of HR was a member of the Board of Directors while over 8 per cent of practitioners reported involvement in formulating overall business strategy, 'either from the outset or on a consultative basis' (Gunnigle, Morley, Clifford and Turner 1997). However, the picture is not completely positive and one must be circumspect in evaluating the strategic influence of HR. Questions that addressed specific areas of HR activity present less sanguine findings. For example, although a large number of respondent organisations in the CUL study claimed to engage in HR planning, the actual nature of such planning appeared to be very basic in nature and covered short time horizons. As such it did not appear particularly strategic in nature. Overall the available evidence appears to confirm a trend towards a greater strategic role for HR. However, there is also evidence of considerable variation between organisations. We return to this issue in chapter two.

Turning to the relative emphasis on different HR activity areas, we find evidence of change here also. As noted earlier, HRM in Ireland has traditionally been associated with a collectivist, 'industrial relations' emphasis, involving a primary focus on collective bargaining between employers and trade unions as the primary means of handling employee relations interactions at enterprise level. However, we earlier identified evidence of a trend towards direct management-employee communications, augmenting, if not replacing, traditional collective bargaining. Many commentators have also noted increased employer opposition to trade union recognition (McGovern 1988, 1989a and b; Gunnigle 1995). This issue is further considered in chapter ten. Recent research also identifies training and development as an increasingly important area in the work of the HR function (Heraty *et al.* 1994). An additional area of change in Irish employment practices has been the growth in atypical employment forms. As previously mentioned, atypical employment is any form of employment which deviates from full-time, permanent employment, including temporary, part-time, and the self-employed. The development of atypical employment and its implications for HRM in Ireland is considered in chapter three.

Overall, the available evidence points to high levels of variation in the nature and role of HR and of the specialist HR function in organisations. The HR role adopted in a particular organisation will be influenced by factors in that organisation's internal and external context.

This chapter has provided an overview of the nature and development of HRM in Ireland. We have seen that the concept of HRM has both a generalist and specialist dimension. At the generalist level HRM refers to that aspect of organisational management concerned with the management of an organisation's workforce and incorporates the work of all managers, supervisors and team leaders who have responsibility for managing people. At the specialist level, HRM refers to the role of the specialist HR function. We have seen that the historical emergence of a specialist HR function in organisations is a relatively recent development in Ireland with much of the growth occurring since the 1970s. HRM practice in Ireland has historically been associated with a strong industrial relations emphasis and ancillary involvement in areas such as recruitment and training. More recently we find robust evidence of a re-orientation of the role of the HRM function in many organisations. It is also clear that many organisations are investigating and experimenting with different modes of workforce management. In particular, increasing attention has focused on so called 'strategic' forms of HRM approaches, and on developing coherent linkages between business strategy and HRM practice. This theme is considered in our next chapter on HRM and business strategy.

2

Business Strategy and Human Resource Management

One of the most notable characteristics of management literature over the past decade has been the increased interest in achieving a closer alignment between business strategy and human resource management (HRM). (See for example Fombrun 1984; Schuler 1987, 1992; Schuler *et al.* 1993; Guest 1992; Salaman 1992; Tyson 1992; Huselid 1995; O'Brien 1998; De Cieri and Dowling 1999). Indeed, there are many who take the view that this desire to bring about the alignment of business strategy and people management policies and practices provided the wellspring for both the transition from personnel management to HRM in the first instance, and the more recent evolution towards 'strategic' HRM.

The concept of strategic HRM refers to the development of a strategic corporate approach to workforce management, whereby HRM considerations become integral to strategic decision-making as organisations seek to establish a corporate HR philosophy and strategy that complements their business strategy (Mayrhofer *et al.* 2000; Lundy and Cowling 1996; Fombrun *et al.* 1984; Buller and Napier 1993; Guest 1987; Purcell 1989). Referred to as 'matching' by Boxhall (1992), and often alluding to the messages advanced in the resource-based view of the firm (Barney 1995), and human capital accumulation theory (Garavan *et al.* 2001), the alignment of business strategy, organisational configuration and HR policies and practices in order to achieve valuable, rarer, less imitable sources of competitive advantage becomes the core objective. Though complex, it is, as Monks (2001) notes, a literature that is now well established.

It also seems likely that this strategic focus will continue since HRM considerations have been a neglected area within strategic management thinking generally (Beer *et al.* 1984; Fombrun *et al.* 1984; also see Schuler and Jackson 1987; Huselid 1995; MacDuffie 1995; O'Brien 1998). Arguably, part of this prediction is based on the premise that this field is, at present, marked with a serious hiatus. For example, Beattie and McDougall (1998) note that much of the literature in the field is 'either normative (written mainly by those in consultancy roles), or conceptual (written by academics)', and in their view there have been few attempts to integrate the conceptual with the normative in generalist HRM literature. Similarly, Ferris *et al.* (1999) point to the gap between the science and the practice of HRM in this area. They refer to Buckley *et al.* (1998) who characterise the hiatus as 'a disconnect' and the note that:

It is a disconnect in that scientists and practitioners seem to have segregated along these lines. This is a relatively recent phenomenon because until the relatively recent past, the study of HRM was problem driven (e.g. the Hawthorne studies are a shining example of significant scientist/practitioner collaboration). Our zest to develop a theory of HRM may have been instrumental in driving a wedge between scientists and practitioner . . . managers are relatively familiar with the research in HRM, but they fail to see many practical implications coming from said research.

Thus, despite an extensive and growing body of literature addressing the concepts of strategy and a strategic approach to the HRM, there remains limited consensus as to the substance, nature and implications of these concepts. Indeed Mayrhofer *et al.* (2000) note that 'some of this literature [strategy in HRM] is flawed by rather simplistic notions of strategy, while more of it points to the complex, multidimensional nature of the concept of strategy'. Here they quote Mintzberg (1987) who notes that strategy has been used in at least five different ways, namely as a plan, a ploy, a pattern, a position and a perspective. It would seem that diversity of meaning continues to be the order of the day. Chadwick and Cappelli (1999) recently argued that scholars have varying goals with respect to their particular research in the strategic HRM area with the result that there is considerable variation in the use of the term 'strategic'. Similarly, Luoma (2000) notes that:

> The concepts of strategy and HRM are both somewhat ambiguous. What is the outcome when we put these two together? The result is a strict definition of strategic HRM or a more general idea of valuing people as key elements in a company's business – or something in between . . . . It all depends on the way we view these terms.

Consequently many methodological problems arise when seeking to unearth the linkages between business strategy and HRM because of these differences in meaning associated with the concept of 'business strategy', not to mention 'HRM strategy', the nature of HRM itself and the highly problematic notion of 'integration' and 'measurement' (Tyson *et al.* 1994; Buller and Napier 1993; Whittington 1993; Tyson 1992; Blyton and Turnbull 1992, 1994; Gunnigle, Morley, Clifford and Turner 1997; Delery and Doti 1996; Guest 2001).

This chapter considers the debate on linking decisions in the HRM sphere with broader decisions on business strategy. It attempts to synthesise key aspects of the debate on the relationship between business strategy and HRM and examines efforts at integrating evolving strategy and HRM initiatives. It considers the nature of strategic management with a particular emphasis on competitive strategy at the level of the enterprise. It also explores the impact of product market conditions on HRM. Finally, the chapter explores the emergence of *human resource management* as a distinctive approach to workforce management, contrasts it with traditional personnel management and assesses its relevance for contemporary people management practice in Ireland.

THE CONCEPT OF STRATEGIC MANAGEMENT

There is extensive literature on the concept of business strategy with the consequence, according to Lundy and Cowling (1996, 16), that anyone trying to reach some understanding of the current state of knowledge of the strategy process will likely experience a 'perplexity'. Numerous writers dealing with managerial and business decision-making have used the term 'strategy' to describe a particular set of choices taken over a period of time to achieve given business objectives. Thus, *strategic management* is concerned with policy decisions affecting the entire organisation with the overall objective being to best position the organisation to deal effectively with its environment. This conception for strategic management implies that in an organisational setting there is a hierarchy of decision choices and that key decisions on business strategy will steer more specific operational decisions on short-term problems and issues (Thurley and Wood 1983).

More recent evaluations of strategic management have attempted to identify the various components of the strategy concept, and the levels and types of strategy that may occur. Hofer and Schendel (1978) identify three levels of strategy: corporate, business and functional levels. *Corporate level strategy* is essentially concerned with the question 'what business should we be in?' Business level (competitive) strategy addresses the question, 'how do we compete in this business?' Finally, *functional level strategy* focuses on how the activities of particular functions (such as HRM) come together to support the business level strategy (Hofer and Schendel, 1978). These differing strategy levels are illustrated in figure 2.1.

Figure 2.1 Levels of strategic decision-making

CORPORATE STRATEGY   *Multi-Business*
(what business should we be in?)

BUSINESS/COMPETITIVE STRATEGY   *Single/Related*
(how to establish competitive advantage)   *Business(s)*

FUNCTIONAL STRATEGY
(Contribution of various functional parts of the organisation)

Production Operations	Marketing	Finance	HRM

In addition to identifying different levels of strategy, Hofer and Schendel (1978) found it useful to distinguish between strategy process and content. *Strategy process* concerns the activities involved in the formation of a strategy. These activities include analysing competitors and scanning the environment to identify threats and opportunities. *Strategy content*, on the other hand, refers to the actual policies chosen by the organisation and the methods and activities used to implement these policies.

While these distinctions help to clarify the concept of strategic management, there remains some difficulty in relation to implementing the strategy concept in such a way that it reflects the reality of organisational life/activities. For example, there is an inherent assumption that an organisation's strategy is formed after key organisational leaders have analysed all relevant information, developed a number of possible options, and rationally chosen the option that maximises organisational performance. In addition, it is often assumed that implementing these strategic policies is not problematic because there is goal congruity between the parties. Consequently decisions made by top managers will be followed by individuals and groups at lower levels with little resistance. Clearly, such assumptions run contrary to evidence on the actual practice of organisational decision-making and implementation.

Recognising the difficulties, Mintzberg (1978, 1988) distinguished between '*realised*' and '*unrealised*' *strategies*, and between '*intended*' and '*emergent*' *strategies*. 'Deliberate' strategies are those that are both intended and realised in the organisation. This is the concept of business strategy that appears most frequently in the literature. In addition to deliberate strategies, there may be intended strategies that for some reason are never implemented. These are 'unrealised' strategies. Finally, according to Mintzberg, realised strategies (patterns of decisions) may 'emerge' without the conscious intentions of the strategists. These are termed 'emergent' strategies. Mintzberg's categorisation goes beyond that of a deliberate strategy, in the sense of the traditional planning oriented view of the term, to that of an emergent strategy, which is conceived as patterned responses that may not have been planned by the actors and may develop in an incremental and opportunistic manner. Strategies can therefore develop in an organisation without being consciously intended. Indeed, Mintzberg suggests that for a strategy to have been intended exactly as realised would be a 'tall order'.

STRATEGIC DECISION-MAKING AND HUMAN RESOURCE MANAGEMENT

The preceding discussion has highlighted the increasing emphasis on strategic management as organisations strive to accommodate an increasingly turbulent and competitive business environment. As we have seen, strategic management is concerned with long-term policy decisions affecting the future of the organisation. Strategic decision-making incorporates strategy formulation, strategy implementation and evaluation and control; it emphasises the monitoring and evaluation of environmental opportunities and constraints as well as the strengths and weaknesses of the organisation. Corporate, business and functional strategy represent different levels of strategic decision-making in an organisation. Each level involves decisions that are strategic in nature. However, decisions at higher levels, such as those at corporate or business unit level, will guide subsequent decisions on functional strategy.

Purcell (1989) emphasises this point by differentiating between *upstream* and *downstream* strategic decisions. Upstream or first-order decisions concern the long-term direction and nature of the organisation. Downstream decisions deal with the implications of first-order decisions for organisational structure (a downstream decision). Purcell argues that HR policy choices are made in the context of downstream strategic decisions on organisational structure. Such choices are strategic in nature since they establish the basic approach to workforce management. However, Purcell's argument suggests that HR policy choices are third-order strategic decisions since they will be heavily influenced by first- and second-order decisions and by broader environmental factors (see figure 2.2).

Using British data Purcell examined how trends in first- and second-order strategy, particularly diversification and decentralisation, affect management decision-making. He identified the growth in size and influence of the diversified firm as giving greater prominence to decision-making at the corporate level. Within this business form, portfolio planning is commonly used to evaluate the performance of constituent business units and aid resource allocation and investment/divestment decisions. Within the portfolio planning approach to corporate strategy, the organisation is seen as a collection of different businesses that should pursue different strategies to suit particular market conditions. This implies that different functional strategies, including HRM, need to be applied at the business unit level to suit particular business strategies. Key decisions on resource allocation (first-order decisions) are taken at corporate level and it is the responsibility of business unit managers to deal with the implications of such decisions and take appropriate

Figure 2.2 Upstream and downstream strategic decision-making

	UPSTREAM	
FIRST-ORDER	Long-term direction of the firm	E
	Scope of activities, markets, location	N
		V
		I
SECOND-ORDER	Internal operating procedures	R
	Relationships between parts of the	O
	organisation	N
		M
		E
THIRD-ORDER	(e.g.) Strategic choice in HRM	N
		T
	DOWNSTREAM	

Source: Purcell (1989).

operational decisions to satisfy corporate requirements. Thus, first-order decisions, while not necessarily incorporating HRM considerations, significantly influence HR policy and practice within particular business units.

Second-order decisions concern areas such as organisational structure, operating procedures and control of business unit performance. Purcell (1989) notes that diversified organisations tend to prefer decentralised structures with a clear differentiation between strategic and operational responsibilities. He also notes that such organisations normally view HRM decisions as an operational responsibility at business unit level. An important consideration in examining second-order strategy is the approach of corporate head office to managing its constituent business units. Goold and Campbell (1987) identify three alternative approaches as follows:

1. *Strategic planning organisations:* which place a major emphasis on achieving maximum competitive advantage from a small number of core businesses using co-ordinated global strategies. Ambitious long-term goals are pursued and financial performance is normally strong with fast organic growth and little strategy ownership by business units.
2. *Financial control organisations:* which are more concerned with financial performance than competitive position. Expansion is achieved through acquisition and merger; profit is the key success criteria at business unit level.
3. *Strategic control organisations:* which attempt to balance competitive and financial considerations. Growth in strategically sound businesses is encouraged but there may be divestment from other areas, and long-term focus and considerable emphasis on the motivation of business unit managers.

Purcell suggests that a critical issue in considering second-order strategies is the period over which profits are expected and who stands to gain from profit generation. It is suggested that strategic planning organisations are most likely to have a defined sense of purpose that includes broader concerns than solely financial considerations. Consequently they are seen as having a greater capacity to develop a co-ordinated culture and management style. Guest (1987) suggests that only strategic planning organisations have the capacity and commitment to develop more integrated and 'strategic' approaches to HRM. On the other hand, Purcell feels that tight financial control approaches, and a short-term financial return ethos, prohibits the long-term consideration of HRM considerations and considerably reduce the likelihood of HRM policy being an issue of strategic concern. Purcell (1989) argues that in Britain and the US a short-term stock market emphasis is a primary characteristic of first-order strategies. Since economic performance values are the key yardstick for strategic decision-makers, Purcell argues that less concrete values, such as HRM considerations, do not exert a strong influence on strategic decisions. He suggests that examples of strategic planning companies with integrated HR (such as IBM, Motorola and Marks and Spencer) are the exceptions rather than the norm. Purcell's analysis raises an important contrast between highly diversified organisations operating in a variety of business sectors and 'critical function' organisations whose main activities are restricted to a core industry or sector. Purcell argues that a strategic planning style conducive to more integrated and strategic approaches to HRM is more likely to occur where there is a high level of vertical integration (interdependence between business units). However, it appears that organisations that emphasise long-term strategic objectives, core values and vertical linkages are becoming less common as the trend towards diversification and out-sourcing gathers increasing momentum. Purcell argues that this trend will increasingly place the corporate focus on performance control and financial return with less weight being placed on long-term strategic planning. Where the corporate value system emphasises short-term financial return and tight performance control it is more difficult to develop an integrated approach to HRM.

Purcell concludes that current trends in corporate strategy in many diversified organisations prohibit the development of strategic approaches to HRM. Consequently, he is pessimistic about the likelihood that the ingredients for strategic HRM will find favour with the majority of diversified organisations whose corporate strategy is dominated by a concern with short-term financial criteria.

MODELS OF BUSINESS STRATEGY-HR LINKAGES: FRAMEWORKS OF STRATEGIC HRM

A key factor influencing the upsurge of interest in linking business strategies and HRM is the quest for *competitive advantage*. The idea of competitive advantage has been championed by Michael Porter (see, for example, Porter 1987, 1990) and can be described as any factor(s) that allow an organisation to differentiate its product or service from its competitors to increase market share.

In contrast to the prominence given by Purcell to the corporate decision-making, Porter argues that corporate strategy has failed 'dismally' and suggests that the focus of strategic decision-making should be on the development of appropriate competitive strategies at the level of individual business units. *Competitive strategy* is concerned with achieving sustainable competitive advantage in particular industries or industry segments. Price and quality are common mechanisms by which organisations attempt to achieve competitive advantage. Porter identifies three generic strategies for achieving competitive advantage.

Cost leadership (sometimes called *cost reduction*) involves positioning the organisation as a low cost producer of a standard 'no frills' product for either a broad or a focused market. To succeed with a cost leadership strategy it is suggested that the firm must become *the* cost leader and not one of several firms pursuing this strategy. Cost leadership requires an emphasis on tight managerial controls, low overheads, economies of scale and a dedication to achieving productive efficiency.

On the other hand, a *differentiation* (sometimes called *product innovation*) strategy requires that an organisation's product or service becomes unique in some dimension that is valued by the buyer, to the extent that the buyer is willing to pay a premium price. The basis for a differentiation may be the product or service itself or other aspects such as delivery or after-sales service.

The third generic competitive strategy, *focus*, involves choosing a narrow market segment and serving this either through a low-cost or a differentiation focus. An organisation's choice of generic strategy specifies the fundamental approach to competitive advantage that the firm seeks to achieve and provides the context for policies and actions in each key functional area, such as HRM. While there are criticisms of Porter's work there is no doubt that it clarifies the nature of some of the basic strategies that are available to organisations given varying external contextual factors.

Porter suggests that each generic competitive strategy warrants different skills and requirements for success. Of particular significance is the need to match personnel selection, workforce profile and employee relations practice with the desired competitive strategy. Porter further contends that different organisational cultures are implied in each strategy and that HR policy choice is a key influence in establishing and maintaining 'appropriate' corporate cultures. In the differentiation strategy, it is suggested that culture might serve to encourage innovation, individuality and risk-taking; in cost leadership, culture might encourage frugality, discipline and attention to detail. Porter suggests that there is no such thing as a good or bad culture. Rather, he suggests that culture is a means of achieving competitive advantage and should match the organisation's business strategy; culture is a means to an end, not an end in itself.

Turning to the specific links between business strategy and HR policies, it is argued that organisations will experience severe problems in strategy implementation if it is not effectively linked with appropriate HR policy choices (Galbraith and Nathanson 1978; Fombrun *et al.* 1984; Fombrun 1986; Tomlinson 1993; O'Brien 1998). Numerous authors have identified models of suggested business strategy-HR policy linkages (Miles and Snow 1984; Fombrun *et al.* 1984; Schuler *et al.* 1987; Porter 1987). These models are based on the view that organisations need to achieve a 'fit' between their business strategy, product market position and their internal HRM strategy and policies (Beaumont 1993; O'Brien 1998) in order to achieve sustainable competitive advantage. Generally arguing that strategic HRM concerns the close alignment between competitive strategy and HR practices, Horwitz (1999) highlights that fit models distinguish between internal and external fit. He notes that:

> The notion of external fit deals with how an organisation mobilises its resources to compete in the external environment. Internal fit usually concerns implementing espoused strategic goals and policies, and the degree of alignment between stated intent (vision and mission), actual behaviour and policy performance at operational level.

These 'fit' models of business strategy and HR linkages have sought to advance mutually reinforcing strategy and HR typologies that are appropriate against the backdrop of different competitive circumstances, namely cost-leadership, differentiation and focus. Predominantly US based, the rationale underpinning the emergence of these strategic/HR fit typologies was that such fit was underdeveloped but highly desirable in the context of achieving sustainable competitive advantage over rivals. Some of the more prominent examples of these typologies are reviewed below.

Strategy/HR Fit: Miles' and Snow's Typology

A commonly used competitive strategy typology is that of Miles and Snow (1978, 1984). Miles and Snow advance three generic strategy types, namely 'defenders', 'prospectors' and 'analysers'. *Defenders* seek stability by producing only a limited set of products directed at a narrow segment of the total potential market. Within this limited niche, defenders strive to prevent competitors from entering the market. Organisations do this through standard economic actions such as competitive pricing or the production of high quality products. *Prospectors* are almost the opposite of defenders. Their strength is in finding and exploiting new product and market opportunities. Innovation may be more important than high profitability. The prospector's success depends on developing and maintaining the capacity to survey a wide range of environmental conditions, trends and events and maintaining a high degree of flexibility. *Analysers* try to capitalise on the best of both the preceding types. They seek to minimise risk and maximise opportunity for profit. The strategy here is to move into new products or new markets only after viability has been proven by prospectors. Miles and Snow suggest that successful organisations possess a consistent strategy that is aligned with and supported by complementary organisational structures and management practices. They also suggest that organisations which do not possess this *environment-strategy-structure* alignment (*reactors*) are not as successful as the other three categories. Difficulties in developing appropriate HRM policies are seen as a major barrier to the effective implementation of appropriate business strategies and structures.

Miles and Snow (1984) suggest that these three basic types of strategic behaviour can be associated with particular HR policy configurations as outlined in figure 2.3. To emphasise the need to align HR policy choice and business strategy, Miles and Snow identified organisations in each of the three strategic categorisations, namely defenders (Lincoln Electric), prospectors (Hewlett-Packard) and analysers (Texas Instruments), and suggested relevant HRM policy configurations for each strategy. In defender organisations, the emphasis is on building the organisation's own human resources through recruitment at entry levels and promotion through the ranks. The key HR activities are: selection, placement, training, development, appraisal and ensuring a fit between the reward system and job design. Defender organisations are characterised as lean and hard-working, and demand predictable, planned HR policies and regular maintenance of these policies. Prospector organisations experience rapid change demanding considerable human resource re-deployment. The major HR focus is on sourcing and deploying high-quality personnel. The HR management objective is entrepreneurial, acquiring and developing critical staff. There is little opportunity for long-term planning or sophisticated HRM techniques. In analyser organisations, the emphasis is on developing appropriate organisational structures and management approach with the HRM focus on co-ordinating policies and allocating personnel optimally across the organisation.

Strategy/HR Fit: Schuler's Strategy-Employee Role Behaviour Model

Possibly the most extensive work on linking business strategy and HRM has been conducted by Randall Schuler in the US. Schuler suggests that business strategies are most effective when 'systematically co-ordinated with human resources management practices' (Schuler 1989, 1992, 1995; Schuler and Jackson 1987a and b, 1996; Schuler *et al.* 1987). He further argues that a key objective in HR policy choice is to develop employee behaviours which 'fit' the organisation's particular strategy. Schuler identifies three strategic types, all largely based on Porter's generic strategies. A *cost reduction strategy* is based on becoming a leading low-cost producer. *Differentiation* (or *product innovation*) is based on the development of

Figure 2.3 Linking business strategy and HR policy

| | STRATEGIC TYPE | | |
	DEFENDER	PROSPECTOR	ANALYSER
PRODUCT and MARKET STRATEGY	Limited, stable product line Predictable markets	Broad, changing product line Changing markets	Stable and changing product line Predictable and changing markets
RESEARCH and DEVELOPMENT	Narrow; product improvement	Broad; new product development	Focused; 'second to market'
MARKETING	Sales emphasis	Market research emphasis	Extensive marketing campaigns
HR STRATEGY	Maintenance	Entrepreneurial	Co-ordination
RECRUITMENT and SELECTION	'Make'; internal	'Buy'; external	'Make and Buy'; mixed
MANPOWER and PLANNING	Formal, extensive	Informal, limited	Formal, extensive
TRAINING and DEVELOPMENT	Extensive; skill building	Limited; skill acquisition	Extensive; skill building
APPRAISAL	Process-oriented; identify training needs individual/ group performance evaluation	Results-oriented; identify staffing needs; corporate/division performance evaluation	Process-oriented; identify training and staffing needs; individual/group/ divisional performance evaluation
REWARDS	Based on level in hierarchy; internal equity; pay-oriented	Based on performance; external equity; incentive-oriented	Mostly based on level in hierarchy; internal and external comparisons; pay and incentive-oriented

Source: Adapted from Miles and Snow (1984).

products or services, which differ from competitors and, consequently, command a premium price. A common differentiation strategy is that based on quality enhancement i.e. improving product or service quality. A *focus strategy* is based on serving a narrow market niche.

Schuler proposes that for these strategies to be successful, they have to be supported by particular patterns of employee behaviour. It is further suggested that these behaviour patterns are shaped by the organisation's HR strategies, policies and practices. He identifies three alternative HR strategy types, each designed to develop particular employee

Figure 2.4 Linking business strategy and HRM

BUSINESS STRATEGY	HR STRATEGY	DESIRED EMPLOYEE BEHAVIOURS		HRM POLICY AND ACTIVITY FOCUS
Cost Reduction	Utilisation	Relatively repetive and predictable behaviour	Recruitment	Explicit job analysis; Mostly internal recruitment/labour market focus
		Mostly short-term focus; High concern for quantity	Appraisal	Short term focus; individual criteria; results oriented criteria
		Moderate concern for quality	Rewards	Hierarchical pay, few incentives
		Major emphasis on results	Training and Development	Narrow career paths; limited training
		Comfortable with stability	Employee Relations	Little employment security; low employee participation; traditional industrial relations
Differentiation	Facilitation	Long term focus	Recruitment	Implicit job analysis; external recruitment/labour market focus
		Creative job behaviour; High level of independent co-operative behaviour	Appraisal	Long term focus; process and results criteria; some group criteria
		Moderate concern for quality	Rewards	Egalitarian pay; numerous incentives
		Moderate concern for quantity	Training and Development	Broad career paths; extensive training
		Equal concern for focus and results; Tolerance of ambiguity	Employee Relations	High employee participation; co-operative labour management relations; some employment security
Focus	Accumulation	Relatively predictable and repetitive behaviour	Recruitment	Explicit job analysis; some external recruitment
		Long/medium term focus; High concern for quality	Appraisal	Long term focus; process and results criteria; some group criteria
		Moderate concern for quantity	Rewards	Egalitarian pay; numrous incentives
		Concern for process and results	Training and Development	Broad career paths; development extensive training
		Commitment to organisation goals	Employee Relations	High employee participation; co-operative labour management relations; some employment security

Source Adapted from Schuler (1987, 1989, 1996); Schuler and Jackson (1987a and b) behaviour patterns, which facilitate the achievement of the desired business strategy. These he terms (i) accumulation; (ii) utilisation and (iii) facilitation. Schuler argues that organisations following a focus strategy require an *accumulation* strategy, which emphasises careful personnel selection based on personality rather than technical fit. Emphasis is placed on training, egalitarian pay structures and lifetime employment. Organisations following a cost-reduction business strategy require a *utilisation* strategy, which involves selecting individuals mainly on the basis of technical ability and emphasises cost minimisation in terms of training, etc. Organisations following a differentiation business strategy require a *facilitation* strategy, which focuses on the ability of individuals to work together in a reciprocal relationship. Cross-functional work teams are frequently employed while the use of job rotation and career planning are used to help foster a collaborative work climate. This business strategy employee behaviour-HR policy model is outlined in figure 2.4.

Strategy/HR Fit: Fombrun's Strategy implementation model

A similar model linking business strategy, organisation structure and HRM policies is that developed by Fombrun *et al.* (1984). They contend that integrating HRM considerations into strategic decision-making represents 'a true frontier' in workforce management, but suggest that while many organisations wish to include HR issues in strategic decision-making, the traditional approach has been to consider these issues only after strategic decisions have been taken. Fombrun suggests that very often the major emphasis in strategic planning has been on strategy formulation, with very little thought being given to strategy implementation. He feels that this has resulted in the failure of strategic planning at the operational level. This lack of attention to strategy implementation is seen as a major challenge to organisations, and serves to give a central role to HRM policies in ensuring that employees work to make strategies happen. It is suggested that HRM policies have a crucial role to play in effective strategy implementation, since they are the key to implementing strategic choice and to achieving better alignment between strategic direction and HRM practices. This view is echoed in the work of Butler (1988) and Purcell (1989). As we have seen, Purcell views HRM policy choice as an important 'downstream' strategic choice which serves to implement, effectively, 'upstream' strategic decisions on competitive strategy.

Fombrun *et al.* (1984) suggest that strategic management involves the consideration of three key issues:

- *Mission and strategy*: Identification of an organisation's purpose and plan for how this can be achieved.
- *Formal structure*: For the organisation of people and tasks to achieve mission and strategy.
- *HRM systems*: Recruitment, development, evaluation and reward of employees.

This framework is represented in figure 2.5 and is seen to differ from traditional approaches to strategic management by incorporating HRM considerations as an integral component of strategic decision-making.

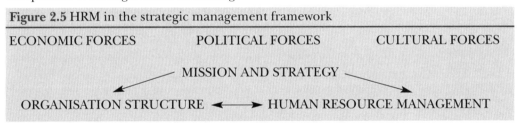

Figure 2.5 HRM in the strategic management framework

ECONOMIC FORCES   POLITICAL FORCES   CULTURAL FORCES

MISSION AND STRATEGY

ORGANISATION STRUCTURE ⟷ HUMAN RESOURCE MANAGEMENT

Source: Adapted from Fombrun *et al.* (1984).

Fombrun *et al.* (1984) suggest that an organisation's HRM policies and practices symptomise managerial assumptions about employees and 'appropriate' workforce management practices. Fombrun (1986) identifies four key aspects of organisational approaches to workforce management that give valuable insights into the managerial approach to employees:

1. *The nature of the psychological contract:* This may vary from, at one extreme, a managerial perspective which views employees in instrumental terms and emphasises high levels of control of both employees and the work environment to, at the other extreme, an approach which sees employees as intelligent and committed beings who should be afforded challenging and meaningful work in a benign work environment.
2. *Level of employee involvement:* Here organisational approaches may vary from those with high levels of employee involvement in decision-making to those where decisions are solely a management prerogative.
3. *Internal/External labour market:* This addresses the relative emphasis on internal versus external recruitment and related differences in emphasis on employee development.
4. *Performance evaluation:* This factor addresses the relevant managerial emphasis on group versus individual performance evaluation.

Fombrun suggests that HRM systems need to become more flexible so as to 'fit' strategic choice. He identifies four key areas of HR policy choice: selection/promotion/placement, appraisal, rewards and employee development, and evaluates each in relation to its 'fit' with business strategy.

Overall, despite the advances that models such as these have brought, according to Ferris *et al.* (1999) the linking of HRM with business strategy remains 'troublesome', principally because of the measures of strategy used in the studies to date. In their review they rightly note that:

> Recent conceptual pieces have been critical of researchers in this area, suggesting that they have incorporated antiquated notions of firm strategy. Most studies have utilised such typologies as those of Porter (1980) or Miles and Snow (1978). These generic categorisations have little in common with the realities of the modern competitive environment with which organisations are confronted. First, categorisations are exclusive, assuming that organisations pursue a certain strategic goal while ignoring other strategic concerns. Second, they depict the competitive environment, and consequently organisational strategy, as being static instead of dynamic.

In light of this, they suggest that future tests of the HRM-strategy relationship must view strategy along a broader continuum involving a broader range of strategic factors and must conceptualise it as a dynamic, rather than a static phenomenon. Finally they suggest that the almost exclusive focus on deliberate intended strategy, to the detriment of the emergent or realised strategy remains problematic. It, they suggest, represents a flawed reality in the context of the omnipresent unstable, dynamic environments that we have all become accustomed to.

THE PARTICULAR IMPACT OF THE PRODUCT MARKET ON HR CHOICES
In the preceding chapter an organisation's *product market* position was identified as a key influence on strategic decision-making with important knock-on implications for HR policy choice. Indeed, Kochan *et al.* (1986) identify increased product market competition as a

critical factor in instigating significant changes in both competitive strategy and organisational approaches to workforce management. An organisation's product market incorporates the nature of the market into which an organisation sells its products or service and its competitive position within that market. Product market position is commonly measured on the twin criteria of market share and market growth. An organisation's product market position will be influenced by a variety of factors such as the cost of entry, nature of competition, technology, and the customer base.

An organisation's business strategy will be developed within the context of a particular product market. Thurley and Wood (1983) argue that broad strategy objectives can be linked to the product market objectives, the enterprise's position in that market, the organisational characteristics and the political, social and economic influences in the community where the enterprise operates (expressed through government policy and legislation, and interest-group pressures). These factors will impact upon the HRM management strategies and policies in the organisation. Kochan *et al.* (1986) identify product market changes as leading to a variety of strategic decisions that may profoundly affect HR policies and practices. This *strategic choice framework* is illustrated in figure 2.6. It helps explain how changes in external environmental (particularly product market conditions) lead to critical strategic choice decisions on a number of different levels: long-term strategy making at the top; HR/employee relations policy at the middle; and workplace and individual/organisation relationships at the shop floor level.

Figure 2.6 Product market change, business strategy and HRM

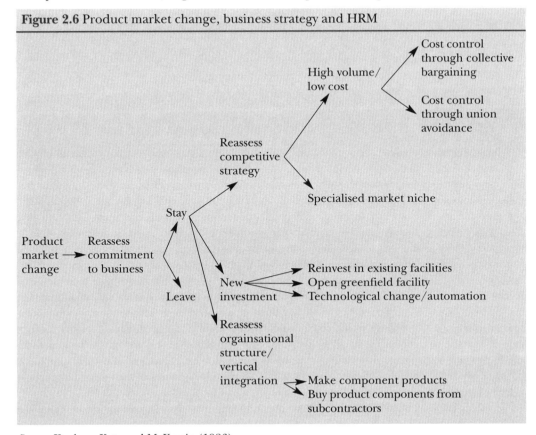

Source: Kochan, Katz and McKersie (1986).

Marchington (1990) evaluates an organisation's product market position along two critical dimensions: (i) monopoly power and (ii) monopsony power (also see Marchington and Parker 1990). *Monopoly power* refers to the degree to which an organisation has power to dictate market terms to customers. An organisation may have high monopoly power as a result of factors such as the cartel arrangements, regulated (e.g. state) monopolies, high barriers to entry, or unique product or technology. In such situations, organisations have considerable power to dictate market terms, particularly price, to customers and therefore act as *price makers*. In contrast, *monopsony power* refers to the extent to which customers exert power over the organisation. High monopsony power may occur as a result of high levels of market competition (numerous competitors) or because of the existence of powerful customers who can exert considerable control over price and other factors (e.g. credit terms, service). In such situations, supplying organisations may be forced to accept the market terms, particularly price, dictated by customers: i.e. become *price takers*. These relationships are illustrated in figure 2.7

Figure 2.7 Product market conditions and HR choice

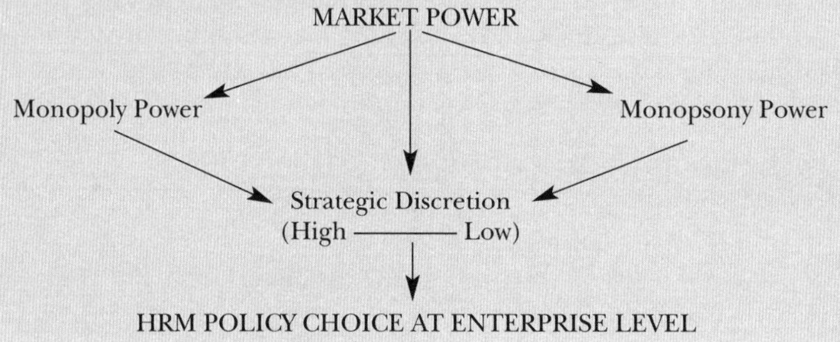

Source: Adapted from Marchington (1990).

Marchington argues that relative levels of monopoly and monopsony power, which an organisation experiences provide a measure of the power of the market over employers, and consequently influence the degree of management discretion in making strategic policy decisions in all functional areas such as HRM. Where market power is low, senior management will have considerable discretion to make a broad range of HRM policy choices. Such favourable market conditions (high market share, growing market, stable demand) allow organisations greater scope to adopt 'investment-oriented styles', and are more conducive to the application of more benign HRM practices such as comprehensive employee development policies, tenure commitments and gain-sharing. This does not imply that employers will always adopt resource-type policies in favourable product market conditions. Rather, such conditions provide management with greater scope to choose from a range of HRM policy choices; actual choice will be further influenced by factors internal to the organisation, particularly management values and competitive strategy. On the other hand, organisations operating under high levels of market pressure may have considerably less scope for choice, and a more traditional cost and labour control approach may be appropriate.

Schuler and Jackson (1987a) are more prescriptive in suggesting that different market and cost considerations influence the appropriateness of different HR policy choices. They use *product life-cycle phases* to evaluate product market influences on both business strategy and HRM policy choice. In the *growth phase*, the attraction of high-calibre employees is seen as the main priority. The key organisational need is for technical talent to transform ideas into saleable products or services. The major source of personnel is the external labour market. The organisation attracts employees by differentiating itself using 'innovative' HR policies such as employment tenure and high levels of employee participation. Various categories of part-time, temporary or sub-contract labour may be used to buffer full-time employees during economic downturns. Employee relations issues are handled through various communications and participatory mechanisms. Wages are normally high and tied to profitability and/or employee skills. This phase is felt to run closely parallel to the dynamic growth strategy. In the *maturity phase*, the organisation has a large internal labour market, and the emphasis is on retaining personnel. Jobs tend to be more narrowly defined, and wages tend to be based more on grade definitions than profitability or skills. There is less employee participation and downturns in profitability may result in lay-offs. Employee relations issues are handled through collective bargaining. This phase is felt to run closely parallel to the extract profit strategy. In the *decline phase*, the organisation needs cuts in both costs and employee numbers. There is downward pressure on wages and a need to agree criteria on which to base redundancy decisions. While this phase is not seen as running parallel to a turnaround strategy, it is clearly a precipitating factor. In such a crisis situation, the future direction of the organisation is uncertain.

Schuler and Jackson then examined policy-choice decisions in four specific areas (job design, performance appraisal, rewards, and training and development) in organisations pursuing three distinct business strategies (i.e. dynamic growth, extract profit and turn-around). They concluded that there are predictable relationships between business strategy and HRM policy choice. However, they found no proof that these choices were systematically selected to fit particular strategies. They also found no conclusive evidence that HRM policies, which fit business strategies, contribute to greater organisational effectiveness. They suggest that fitting HRM policies is an important variable in contributing to effectiveness, but that other factors such as leadership and culture must also be taken into consideration.

Schuler and Jackson argue that as organisations strive to achieve greater fit between business strategy and HRM strategies and policies, this will lead to continuous change in HRM, with employees being exposed to a range of different practices in the course of employment. Thus, employees may be expected to exhibit different characteristics and work under different sets of employment conditions at different stages in their working lives. This implies that multi-business (diversified) organisations are likely to have considerable variation in HR policies to fit with their different business conditions and strategies. This conclusion is similar to that of Purcell (1989) and Armstrong (1988, 1994), who suggest that in diversified organisations strategic decision-making will primarily concern financial issues with decisions on HRM policy devolved to business unit management.

THE DISTINCTIVE CONCEPT OF HUMAN RESOURCE MANAGEMENT AS IT EMERGED IN THE US IN THE 1980s

While in this text we use the term *human resource management* (HRM) in generic terms to encompass that aspect of organisational management which is concerned with the management of an organisation's workforce, it originally entered the management vocabulary as a term which described a distinctive and seemingly novel approach to workforce management. In this section we review the emergence of HRM as the field has developed in the US since the early 1980s. We seek to identify particular conceptions of HRM, which identify a greater strategic role for HRM.

In the earlier sections of this chapter we noted the growing interest in more closely aligning business strategy and HRM. Indeed it appears that this interest in developing a strategic perspective of HRM is set to continue, since many commentators have identified the field as a neglected area of strategic management, and because of the potentially critical role of HRM in the implementation of organisational change (McGrath and Geaney 1998; Beer *et al.* 1984; Fombrun *et al.* 1984). Towards the end of chapter one we noted that the 1980s was a period of reappraisal for the personnel/HR field. Increased competitive pressures forced many organisations to review their approach to workforce management. Increasingly organisations investigated different approaches to workforce management in areas such as job design, reward systems, and employee relations. However, by far the most widely debated development during this period was the emergence of *human resource management* as a distinctive approach to workforce management. HRM was seen by many as a new development that contrasted with 'traditional' *personnel management*. Its apparently proactive stance was viewed as a major departure from the traditionally reactive 'industrial relations' focus associated with established approaches to 'personnel management'.

> The new approaches to industrial relations which adopted a managerialist rather than a pluralist stance, the restructuring possibilities, and the reduction in trade union power and influence were the back drop to what is now perceived as a new paradigm on which to base employment relationships. In the eyes of some commentators, human resource management (HRM) came to represent the new paradigm, and the critical distinction drawn was the notion that HRM placed initiatives on people management at the strategic heart of the business . . . The new flexibility agreements, new working practices, reorganisations, delayering activities, the flatter organisations, direct communications with the workforce, and stronger corporate cultures . . . could be understood as a new, more coherent approach . . . If this was propaganda, it was propaganda that managers themselves started to believe as the 1980s came to a close . . . The real challenge is to try to discover what real attempts at strategic integration there are.
>
> Tyson, Witcher and Doherty (1994)

The conception of human resource management as a distinctive approach to workforce management and the associated emphasis on a greater role for HRM stems from two contrasting sources in the US literature. The first source emanates from the 'human resource' literature and is based on the 'human capital approach' of the Harvard Business School (HBS) model (Beer *et al.* 1984, 1985). This model focuses on the individual employee as the key organisational resource that management must nurture and develop to maximise its contribution to the organisation. Consequently employers are encouraged to employ a coherent range of pro-employee ('soft') HR policies to ensure the attraction, retention and development of committed, high-performing employees. This model is thus the basis for the 'soft' or benign approach to human resource management whereby senior management acknowledge that people are the organisation's 'most valuable' resource.

The second literature source advocating increased strategic consideration of HRM emanates from the broader business strategy literature, specifically the work of Fombrun (see, for example, Fombrun *et al.* 1984). This approach suggests that organisational performance can be substantially improved by integrating HRM considerations into strategic decision-making to ensure that HR policies complement business strategy. In contrast to the HBS model, this approach does not prescribe either a 'hard' or 'soft' approach to workforce management. Rather, it suggests that top management adopt the policies that best suit its particular circumstances and complement strategic purpose.

However, because its focus is overtly managerial, encouraging employers to employ the HR policies that will yield the best returns in terms of organisational performance it has tended to become associated with the concept of 'hard' HRM, see figure 2.8.

Figure 2.8 Hard and soft HRM	
Human Resource Management	*Human Resource* **Management**
HR Strategy as:	**HR Strategy as:**
Series of policy choices	Fit to corporate/business strategy
• Total HR/management philosophy	Emphasis on alignment and coherence
• General management perspective	Key to strategy implementation
• Multiple stakeholders	
• Evaluation through commitment, competence, congruence and cost effectiveness	
Primary emphasis on management philosophy (approach to HRM)	*HR as source of competitive advantage*

The Nature of Human Resource Management[1]

As mentioned above, the most influential early work on HRM as a distinctive approach to workforce management was conducted by Michael Beer and his colleagues at the Harvard Business School (Beer *et al.* 1984). The *Harvard Business School (HBS) model* presents a broad causal map of the determinants and consequences of HRM policy choices as outlined in figure 2.9. Beer and his colleagues describe HRM in generic terms as 'involving all management decisions and actions that affect the nature of the relationship between the organisation and its employees — its human resources'. Thus, those in top management, and particularly the chief executive, are seen as having the primary responsibility for aligning business strategy and HR policy choice. Four key components comprise the HBS model: (i) stakeholder interests; (ii) HRM policy choice; (iii) HRM outcomes and (iv) long-term consequences.

Presented as an open systems perspective 'in that HRM policy choices can affect each of the other components and be affected by them' (Lundy and Cowling 1996, 51), the central contention of the HBS model is that HR outcomes are affected by policy choices made in four key areas: (i) reward systems; (ii) human resource flows; (iii) work systems and (iv) employee influence. Each of these policy areas is seen as a key element of strategic choice, which profoundly impacts upon employee behaviour and attitude towards the organisation. Strategic choice in these areas is influenced by broader contextual factors: (i) situational constraints (including workforce characteristics, business strategy, management philosophy, labour market, etc.); and (ii) stakeholder interests (shareholders, management, employees, government, etc.). Decisions made in these policy areas are seen as affecting HR outcomes in the areas of employee commitment, congruence of employee and management interests, employee competence, and cost-effectiveness. These outcomes are also seen as having broader long-term consequences for individual employee wellbeing, organisational effectiveness and societal wellbeing.

On this side of the Atlantic, Guest's (1987) 'hard-soft, tight-loose' framework of HRM is possibly the most widely referenced (see figure 2.10). The 'hard-soft' dimension refers to a continuum ranging from a resource-based ('soft') managerial perspective, characterised by benign pro-employee policies, to a more calculated ('hard') management

Figure 2.9 HBS model of human resource management

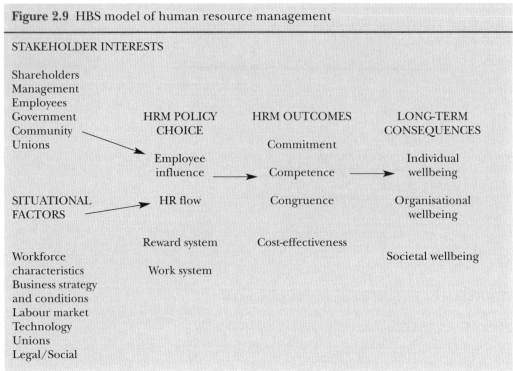

STAKEHOLDER INTERESTS

Shareholders
Management
Employees
Government
Community
Unions

HRM POLICY CHOICE

HRM OUTCOMES

LONG-TERM CONSEQUENCES

Commitment

Employee influence

Competence

Individual wellbeing

SITUATIONAL FACTORS

HR flow

Congruence

Organisational wellbeing

Reward system

Cost-effectiveness

Workforce characteristics
Business strategy and conditions
Labour market
Technology
Unions
Legal/Social

Work system

Societal wellbeing

Source: Beer *et al.* (1984).

perspective where policy choice is driven by the need to complement business strategy and meet financial criteria. The 'tight-loose' dimension refers to a continuum ranging from, at one extreme, HRM merely involving a retitling of traditional personnel management ('loose') with no real change in HR practice, to, at the other extreme, HRM becoming a clearly defined and articulated approach to workforce management with an explicit and strong ('tight') theoretical underpinning.

Figure 2.10 Definitions of human resource management

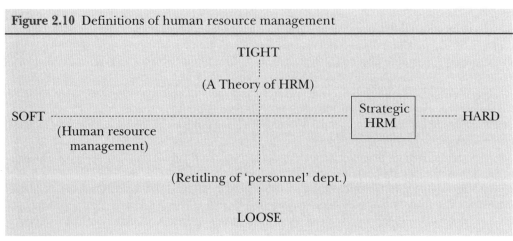

TIGHT

(A Theory of HRM)

SOFT

(Human resource management)

Strategic HRM

HARD

(Retitling of 'personnel' dept.)

LOOSE

Source: Guest (1987).

Guest then proceeded to develop a more fully blown theory of HRM as outlined in figure 2.11. He argued that firms would be more successful if they pursue four key HRM goals: (i) strategic integration; (ii) employee commitment; (iii) flexibility; and (iv) quality. He suggested that these HRM goals can be optimally achieved through coherent HRM policy choices in the areas of organisation and job design, management of change, recruitment, selection and socialisation, appraisal, training and development, rewards and communications. Guest identified five necessary conditions for the effective operation of HRM:

1. Corporate leadership, to ensure that the values inherent in HRM are championed and implemented.
2. Strategic vision, to ensure the integration of HRM as a major component of the corporate strategy.
3. Technological/production feasibility – Guest warned that heavy investment in short-cycle, repetitive production assembly-line equipment mitigates against the job design principles and autonomous teamworking necessary for HRM.
4. Employee relations feasibility – he suggested that multi-union status, low-trust management-employee relations and an adversarial employee relations orientation mitigate against the implementation of HRM.
5. Management capacity to implement appropriate policies.

(This section on Human Resource Management draws primarily from material in Gunnigle, McMahon and Fitzgerald [1999].)

Figure 2.11 A theory of human resource management

HRM POLICIES	HR OUTCOMES	ORGANISATIONAL OUTCOMES
Org./Job design		High job performance
Management of change	Strategic integration	High problem-solving, change and innovation
Recruitment, selection and socialisation	Commitment	
Appraisal, training, development	Flexibility/ adaptability	High cost-effectiveness
Reward systems	Quality	Low turnover, absence, grievances
Communications		
↑	LEADERSHIP/CULTURE/STRATEGY	↑

Source: Guest (1987, 516).

What's New in HRM: Contrasting HRM with Traditional Personnel Management

When HRM is contrasted with more traditional personnel management, as in figure 2.12, a number of key differences do emerge. Firstly, it is argued that workforce management considerations are fully integrated with strategic decision-making in the HRM model, whereas in the traditional personnel model the 'personnel' input is less pronounced and issue-specific. A second contrast is that HRM is seen as essentially proactive and long-term, while the traditional personnel management approach is more reactive and adopts a shorter-term perspective. In terms of the desired mode of psychological contract, HRM is seen as facilitating employee commitment, while the traditional personnel management model is seen as a mode of managerial control over employees (Walton 1985). A specific contrast in the employee relations sphere is that HRM is seen as essentially unitarist in perspective, involving no apparent conflict of interests between employers and employees. In contrast, 'traditional' personnel management is seen as grounded in the pluralist tradition and the acceptance that a conflict of interest exists between employers and workers. Much 'personnel' activity is consequently devoted to managing the adversarial relationship between employers and workers. A related factor is that HRM is seen as focusing on relations between (line) management and the individual worker, while the traditional model is seen as operating primarily through collectivist relations between management and employee representatives. Another area of contrast is that HRM is seen as operating most effectively in organic, fluid company structures, while 'personnel management' is felt to characterise more bureaucratic and rigid company structures. As we have seen, HRM is seen to operate primarily through line management, while in the traditional personnel management model primary responsibility is vested in the specialist personnel function. The final perceived difference relates to the criteria utilised to evaluate effectiveness. HRM is seen as essentially focused on maximising the contribution of human resources to company effectiveness. In contrast, traditional 'personnel management' is seen as having more pragmatic objectives – the maximisation of cost-effectiveness. Despite

Figure 2.12 Personnel management and HRM compared

	Traditional Personnel Management	**HRM**
Input into corporate planning	Issue specific	Integrated
Time and planning perspective	Short-term; reactive; marginal	Long-term; proactive; strategic
Psychological contract	Compliance	Commitment
Employee relations	Pluralist; collective low trust; adversarial	Unitarist, individual High trust
Organisation structures/ systems	Bureaucratic, mechanistic; Centralised; formally defined roles	Organic, fluid; Devolved; Flexible roles
Principal delivery Mechanism	Specialist personnel Management function	Line management
Aims	Maximise cost-effectiveness	Maximise HR utilisation

Source: Adapted from Guest (1987).

these argued contrasts between HRM and traditional personnel management, Guest cautions that this does not necessarily imply that HRM is better than 'traditional' personnel management. Rather, he suggests that traditional personnel management approaches may be more appropriate in certain organisational contexts, such as large bureaucratic organisations or heavily unionised organisations with adversarial collective bargaining traditions, while HRM may be appropriate in organisations with more organic structures and characterised by more individualist, high-trust management-employee relations.

Are There Contradictions and Inconsistencies in HRM?

In its relatively short history, HRM has attracted a good deal of attention with respect to its theoretical pedigree, empirical foundations, and practical implications. Several authors have identified a number of inherent contradictions and inconsistencies in HRM, particularly the 'soft' variant advocated by the Harvard Business School model (Legge 1989; Keenoy 1990; Blyton and Turnbull 1992; Cradden 1992; Hart 1993). For example, Legge (1989) highlights the apparent paradox between the traditional commodity status of labour under the capitalist framework and the essentially unitarist perspective of HRM which sees no inherent conflict of interests between management and employees. It has generally been accepted that in the capitalist framework there is an inherent conflict of interest between management and employees over the price of labour. Indeed, this conflict of interest is the very basis for the existence of employee relations as a key concern of workers and management. However, the HRM perspective appears to ignore the 'inherency' of a conflict of interests, but rather focuses on the achievement of congruence of management and employee interests and on achieving high levels of employee commitment. For example, Flood (1989) suggests that HRM emphasises the needs for organisations to focus on the extrinsic and intrinsic needs of employees and to develop employment practices which increase employee commitment. In a similar vein, Walton (1985) advocates that organisations adopt policies, which emphasise the mutuality of employer and employee interests to ensure employee commitment to achieve organisational goals. This focus on employee commitment not only seems incongruent with the pluralist perspective of the organisation (discussed above) but also appears to conflict with another basic tenet of HRM, namely that HR policies should be integrated with and complement business strategy. Clearly, many decisions that complement business strategy may not develop employee commitment. If, for example, an organisation's business strategy is to maximise short-term returns to owners and shareholders, this may well involve decisions which do not develop employee commitment; for example, replacing labour with technology, contracting out certain tasks and/or making employees redundant. A related issue on this theme is the suggestion that HRM involves the simultaneous achievement of higher levels of individualism and teamwork. These twin goals clearly have tremendous potential for conflict. For example, performance-related pay based on individual employee performance may indeed conflict with teamwork, as can individual communications/negotiations.

High levels of flexibility are seen as a core objective of HRM. Guest (1987) suggests that increased flexibility involves the creation of structural mechanisms in organisations to ensure responsiveness to changing environmental conditions. Guest suggests that such flexibility should encompass both functional and numerical flexibility. However, several authors have noted the difficulties in achieving congruence in different flexibility forms, viz. numerical, functional and financial flexibility. It is clearly difficult to achieve high levels of functional flexibility (e.g. multi-skilling) where employees have a tenuous relationship with the organisation, for example, as a result of attempts to improve numerical flexibility (Blyton and Morris 1992; Gunnigle 1992b).

Another contradiction in the HRM argument that HR policies must be internally consistent arises in relation to job security. A prominent theme in the extant literature is that for HRM to be effective, management must provide implicit job tenure guarantees for employees (Beer *et al.* 1984, Guest 1987, 1989; Walton 1985). For example, Guest (1989) argues that job tenure commitments are a 'necessary' precondition in achieving a 'mutuality of management and employee interests', which he suggests is a key policy goal of HRM. However, it is patently evident that high levels of competition and volatility in product markets have made job security increasingly difficult to achieve. Indeed, job security may itself be incompatible with broader business goals attributed to HRM, such as increased flexibility in responding to rapid changes in demand. In practice, it would appear that some organisations seek to achieve such flexibility by policies that actually reduce the likelihood of job tenure commitments – for example, using atypical employment forms. On the issue of the practicability of achieving a 'fit' between business strategy and HRM policies (e.g. job tenure commitments), Blyton and Turnbull (1992, 10) comment:

> This is particularly problematic in highly competitive or recessionary conditions where the 'needs of the business' are likely to undermine any internal 'fit' with ('soft') HRM values: shedding labour for example will severely challenge, if not destroy, an organisation's HRM image of caring for the needs and security of its employees.

Another apparent inconsistency in HRM is the focus on achieving greater individualism in management-employee relations. As we have seen, employee relations in the Republic of Ireland have been characterised by extensive reliance on collectivism as manifested in, for example, relatively high levels of trade union density and low-trust management-employee relations (Whelan 1982). The 'soft' HRM approach, as outlined by the HBS model and Guest, places the managerial emphasis on achieving high-trust relations between management and employees, and appears to have a preference for pursuing this goal in a non-union environment. Within the 'soft' HRM model, high-trust relations are pursued through managerial initiatives to increase individual employee involvement and motivation, and the adoption of techniques such as performance appraisal and performance-related pay. Thus, such organisations attempt to create close management-employee ties and break down the traditional management-worker dichotomy, of which collective bargaining is seen as the principal manifestation. Such initiatives are indicative of a unitarist management perspective, albeit a very sophisticated variant, and have potential for significant conflict with the pluralist perspective, characteristic of employee relations in Ireland. This unitarist perspective is described by Guest (1989, 43):

> HRM values are unitarist to the extent that they assume no underlying and inevitable differences of interest between management and workers . . . HRM values are essentially individualistic in that they emphasise the individual-organization linkage in preference to operating through group and representative mechanisms . . . These values . . . leave little scope for collective arrangements and assume little need for collective bargaining. HRM therefore poses a considerable threat to traditional industrial relations and more particularly trade unionism.

HRM IN THE IRISH CONTEXT
There is little doubt that 'traditional' approaches to HRM and employee relations in Ireland have come under increasing challenge over recent decades. There is also general

agreement that the main sources of such challenge originate outside the sphere of HRM itself (Beaumont 1995) but can be traced to changes in the broader business environment (see, for example, Sparrow and Hiltrop 1994). In evaluating the Irish context, Roche and Gunnigle (1998, 445–6) identify developments in the wider business context as the source of significant change in 'traditional' approaches to HRM management in Ireland. In commenting specifically on the implications for industrial relations they note that:

> Never before has the analysis of industrial relations practices and policies been so closely tied to an appreciation of commercial and national and international political pressures. In the past the worlds of industrial relations practitioners and academics alike tended to be much more introverted and preoccupied with the internal dynamics of industrial relations systems, agreements and procedures . . . Currently, these concerns, though not altogether displaced, often take second place to such issues as company performance, the union's role in contributing to business success, mission statements and quality standards, business units, employment flexibility and so on.

In essence, changes in traditional approaches to HRM can be traced to increased competitiveness. Increased competitiveness in product and service markets may, in turn, be explained by a number of factors, particularly:

- the globalisation of competition in product, service and capital markets;
- improved communications and transport infrastructures;
- greater liberalisation of world trade;
- more intense price competition;
- competitive strategies based on quality, product innovation and price;
- diffusion of new production techniques to reduce cycle time, control costs and improve quality;
- growth of, and competition from, emerging economies;
- increased product and service customisation;
- changes in the public/semi-state sector.

It is often suggested that these changes in the global, and especially the European, business environment tend to have particularly significant implications for Ireland. This is a result of Ireland's status as a small, open economy, which is heavily reliant on export performance and also on the attraction of mobile, direct foreign investment (i.e. foreign multinational companies). Such reliance on international trade exposes Irish businesses to volatility in the international economy. The impact of increased competitive pressures has been to focus attention on both cost *and* product innovation and quality as factors impacting on competitive positioning and to create a 'flexibility imperative', whereby companies have to be increasingly responsive to consumer demand on dimensions such as customisation, delivery and support services. The overall implication of these developments seem to have all but diluted the concept that companies compete on either a price (low cost) or a product differentiation (premium price) basis (see Marchington and Parker 1990).

Increasingly, it appears that all companies, and not just the low-cost producers, must tightly control their cost structures. The need for tight cost control also extends to labour and pay costs. While the need to control these costs may be more intense in labour-intensive sectors it is also important in less labour-intensive sectors as product and service market competition increases and profit margins are tightened. This conclusion finds support in a recent analysis of payment practices in Irish multinational companies (Roche and Geary 1994). Roche and Geary noted that a significant trend during the 1970s and early 1980s was for foreign-owned companies to concede 'above-the-norm' pay increases. However, the authors note the abandonment of this approach since the mid-1980s with most such companies settling within the norm. By and large, foreign-owned companies in Ireland are more capital-intensive and have lower relative labour costs than their indigenous counterparts (Foley 1990). Extrapolating the logic of Roche and Geary's analysis, it appears that foreign-owned companies could absorb 'above-the-norm' pay increases in previous years because of a combination of less intense competitive pressures and lower relative labour costs. However, in the face of significantly increased competitive pressures, labour costs have now become a focus of management control in foreign-owned companies to a degree only previously experienced in high-labour-cost companies, primarily of indigenous ownership.

Roche and Gunnigle (1997) further note that these competitive trends outlined above are increasingly penetrating the state-owned sector. A major reason for this development is the erosion of state monopolies as a result of developments at European Union level (O'Connor 1995).

An early example of a state company having to deal with increased competitiveness was that of Aer Lingus. Deregulation in the airline industry meant that the company was faced with increased competition on key routes. Resultant restructuring led to significant changes in employment numbers, employment patterns and reward systems. For example, the ESB is currently grappling with EU sponsored initiatives aimed at deregulating the electricity and telecommunications markets. Such changes are likely to have profound effects on HRM strategies, policies and practices in these companies. The conditions imposed by the Maastricht Treaty for entry to the third phase of Economic and Monetary Union on issues such as interest rate convergence and the debt/GDP ratio created considerable challenges for Government, not least the issue of public sector expenditure. The completion of the internal market and removal of trade barriers also serves to expose many Irish organisations to increased international competition with attendant implications at the HRM level of the enterprise. Reviewing the impact of the European Union on Irish industrial relations, Hourihan (1997) argues that EU membership has significantly impacted on the nature of national level collective bargaining in recent years. He argues that 'we may be seeing a new facet to the decision-making process affecting industrial relations, with the European Commission being afforded a validation role which directly affects the conduct of national level bargaining.' Hourihan suggests that access to EU funding is being firmly tied to the acceptance or validation of policy decisions achieved at national level bargaining by the European Commission, and also that the use of EU funds may be linked to the adoption of labour market reforms put forward by Brussels. He suggests that such approaches imply a new dimension, which affords the European Commission an 'unheralded place' in the formation of labour market policies within member states.

Beyond these macro developments, and despite the fact that the theoretical literature places much emphasis on the strategic nature of HRM, the empirical evidence on the extent to which strategic approaches to HRM are actually adopted in practice is, at best, mixed. Recent research on high performing British organisations by Tyson, Witcher and Doherty (1994) sought to examine whether organisations attempt to achieve a fit between the business and HRM strategy, and if so, how. This work discovered three distinct approaches to corporate and business strategy formation and found common elements in the HR strategies adopted by the sample companies in the fields of management and employee development, employee relations and organisation development. However, the integration of HR and business strategies occurs more naturally where there are core values and explicit mission, thus suggesting, according to the authors, that integration is 'easier in more simple businesses'. At the strategic level, the study failed to find any distinctive approach to human resource management, but it did find that all these financially successful companies, in different ways, took human resource issues seriously. Thus, according to Guest and Hoque (1994, 44), while the link between practices and outcomes is tenuous:

> The key is strategic integration. What this means is that personnel strategy must fit the business strategy; the personnel policies must be fully integrated with each other; and the values of the line managers must be sufficiently integrated or aligned with the personnel philosophy to ensure that they will implement the personnel policy and practice . . . Where this can be achieved, there is growing evidence that a distinctive set of human resource practices results in superior performance.

As indicated in chapter one, HRM practice in Ireland has traditionally been associated with a strong industrial relations emphasis. In this model relations between management and employees were grounded in the pluralist tradition with a primary reliance on adversarial collective bargaining (Gunnigle and Morley 1993). As such, 'personnel management' practice was seen as essentially reactive, dealing with various problematic aspects of workforce management (Shivanath 1987). Thus, HR policies and activities tended to focus on short-term issues with little conscious attempt to develop linkages with business policy. An important manifestation of the pluralist tradition at establishment level was a primary focus on 'industrial relations', with collective bargaining and related activities being the key role of the specialist 'personnel' function (Gunnigle, McMahon and Fitzgerald 1999).

However, we have also seen that the 1980s were a decade of reappraisal for HRM both in Ireland and abroad. In Ireland, the onset of recession lessened the need for many core HR activities such as recruitment and, particularly, employee relations (Gunnigle 1992a). The proportion of workers in membership of trade unions fell significantly during the 1980s (see chapter ten) and industrial unrest also declined significantly over the decade (Kelly and Brannick 1988b and c; Brannick and Doyle 1994; Gunnigle, McMahon and Fitzgerald 1999). At the same time we have seen that increased market competition forced many organisations to seek ways of establishing competitive advantages including improved approaches to HRM. Looking at contemporary developments, it appears the past decade has witnessed continuing change of HRM practice, a greater devolution of HRM activities to line management and the emergence of a greater strategic role for HRM issues among some prominent Irish organisations, including some of the major banks and larger multinational corporations (Turner and Morley 1995).

However, practice seems to indicate there are numerous variants of HRM in practice (Keenoy 1990). In the Irish context we can identify four broad variants of HRM as follows (Gunnigle, Morley and Foley 1995):

A. *Traditional Industrial Relations*: In this model HRM considerations rarely concern strategic decision makers, relations between management and employees are grounded in the pluralist tradition with a primary reliance on adversarial collective bargaining.

B. *'Soft' HRM*: This approach emphasises the *human resource* aspect of the term 'human resource management'. This is probably the most visible variant of HRM in Ireland as practised by firms such as IBM and Digital. It is characterised by a resource perspective of employees incorporating the view that there is an organisational pay-off in performance terms from a combination of HRM policies that emphasise consensualism and mutuality of management and employee interests. It also tends to be associated with trade union avoidance, normally in the form of 'union substitution'. This involves firms providing very competitive pay and conditions for their employees and supporting this with a management regime based on rigorous personnel selection, the prompt and effective handling of employee grievances, and extensive management-employee communications, all designed to mitigate the likelihood that employees might be prompted to join trade unions.

C. Neo-Pluralism: This second type of HRM involves moves towards greater consensualism and commitment in unionised companies. It is characterised by what might be termed a 'dualist' approach, involving the use of HRM techniques such as extensive management-employee communications and performance related pay systems alongside established collective bargaining procedures. It is indicative of management approaches in a number of Irish organisations, such as the Electricity Supply Board, Aer Rianta and Analog Devices. While possibly less visible and certainly less analysed than 'soft HRM' this is an increasingly common form of HRM in Ireland.

D. 'Hard' HRM: This variant is characterised by the integration of human resource considerations into strategic decision-making to ensure maximum contribution to business performance. The emphasis here is on the management aspect of the term 'human resource management'. In this approach the organisation's human resources (incorporating not only employees but also subcontracted labour) are treated in a similar vein to any other resource. Thus, human resources should be procured and managed in as cheap and effective a fashion as possible to ensure achievement of the organisations 'bottom line' objectives. Examples of this approach are most obvious in the adoption of 'atypical' employment forms, particularly extensive use of sub-contracting and the use of temporary and part-time employees, to improve cost effectiveness while meeting required performance standards.

Strategic human resource management has proliferated much of the current literature (Ferris *et al.* 1999), but as Luomo (2000) notes while it is often said that a company's HRM practices should fall in line with the strategy of the company, and while nobody denies the importance of such a connection, the deeper nature of this relationship receives amazingly scant attention.

This is a complex area, built upon two diverse literatures beset by definitional disagreements and characterised by empirics derived from differing notions of what should be, or indeed what is worth, measuring. This chapter has attempted to explore core aspects of this literature and unearth some of the linkages between business strategy, product market conditions and HRM. In so doing, it has placed a particular emphasis on the conventional notion of business and competitive strategies, and an increased emphasis on more closely aligning business strategies and HRM policy choice.

We also considered the development of human resource management (HRM) as a distinctive approach to workforce management. We saw that this development can be traced to two contrasting sources in the US literature. The first emanates from the 'HRM' literature and is based on the 'human capital approach' of the Harvard Business School model (Beer *et al.* 1984). This model is the basis for the 'soft' or benign approach to workforce management; whereby senior management acknowledge that people are the organisation's 'most valuable' resource and consequently seek to implement strategic decisions to optimally utilise this resource by adopting a range of HRM policies designed to increase employee commitment and involvement (Guest 1989; Storey 1989; Blyton and Turnbull 1992).

The second source emanates from the business strategy literature (specifically Fombrun *et al.* 1984) and equates to what has come to be termed 'business or hard' approach to HRM (Storey, 1989, 1992; Keenoy 1990). This approach rationalises the strategic importance of HRM considerations on colder economic criteria by suggesting that economic returns from an organisation's workforce can be substantially improved by integrating HRM considerations into business strategy formulation. Blyton and Turnbull (1992) suggest that this approach is 'avowedly unitarist in outlook: a form of "utilitarian-instrumentalism" which provides a singular endorsement of managerialist views'. This view would seem to be confirmed by the proliferation of somewhat prescriptive 'strategy-HRM policy' configurations, briefly discussed in this chapter. These seem to imply that there is a 'best policy' or universalist menu to suit an organisation's particular business strategy and product market conditions and it is up to senior management to find and implement this HRM policy *carte du jour*. However, it is increasingly acknowledged that optimal HRM policy choice is linked to the unique characteristics of the individual organisation. Consequently, it is suggested that organisations need to achieve a 'fit' between HRM policy choice and broader strategic considerations, particularly business strategy and product market conditions.

In the Irish context there has been limited investigation of the linkages between business strategy, product market conditions and developments in HRM. In evaluating current developments, we often run the danger of confusing prominent exemplars of 'soft' HRM with the widespread pervasiveness of such approaches. As we have seen, much of the evidence and support for HRM approaches emanates from the US. However, the context of such developments in the US is considerably different from Ireland and it seems inappropriate to simply extrapolate from the US experience and infer similar trends here. Differences in cultural and political traditions, industrial and employment structure, employee relations institutions and practice are just some of the unique factors influencing approaches to HRM in the Republic of Ireland. We now go on to look more specifically at the practice of HRM beginning with a review of the labour market context.

Note

1. This section on Human Resource Management draws primarily from material in Gunnigle, P., McMahon, G.V. & Fitzgerald, G. *Industrial Relations in Ireland: Theory and Practice*, Dublin: Gill & Macmillan 1999.

3

Human Resource Management and the Labour Market

Much of the theory and debate surrounding the operation of human resource management has focused, to a considerable degree, on the development of policies and practices that allow for the most effective utilisation of an organisation's human capital – its employees. Successive studies have sought to identify key indicators of strategic practice in an effort to prescribe a set of core managerial principles upon which effective human resource management might be based (Guest 1989; Beer *et al.* 1984; Storey 1995; Schuler and Jackson 1999; Way and Johnson 2001). However, one critical component of the equation appears absent all too often, that is, the workings of the labour market within which such practices are located.

Elliott (1991, 3) defines the labour market as the context within which the buyers and sellers of labour come together to determine the pricing and allocation of labour services. He further suggests that, of the many markets that exist in a modern economy, the market for labour is the most important one. It is from selling their services in this market that most families derive their income; it is also in this market that they spend the largest part of their waking hours. When not working, many individuals devote a large part of the remaining time to acquiring the skills necessary for effective performance in this market. The education and training individuals undertake during their lives is chiefly designed to equip them with skills, which enhance their performance in the labour market. The link then, between human resource management and the labour market is clearly demonstrated particularly where HRM is concerned with managing this labour in the most effective means possible.

This chapter proposes to examine the operation of HRM within the context of the labour market. Various theories of the labour market are examined, and the reality of how labour markets operate is set down. The link between labour market theories and human resource management is discussed and finally a profile of the Irish labour market is presented.

THEORIES OF THE LABOUR MARKET

The labour market is comprised of all the buyers and sellers of labour, the buyers being the employers and the sellers being the workers. It has long been recognised, however, that labour markets differ from other markets in the economic system. Marshall (1928) held that labour differed from other commodities because workers are inseparable from the services that they provide, that is, they carry their history, their culture and their social norms into their place of work. Similarly, Keynes (1936) recognised that the employment relationship differs from other contractual relationships because of its frequently long and indeterminable duration, which provides time for customs and norms, particularly those concerned with fairness to build up around it. Marsden (1986) notes that several economists have attempted to develop economic theory in such a way as to take account of such influences. While accepting that pressures of supply and demand, of competition and of substitution are active in the labour market, they feel that customs, social norms, group pressures and institutional rules are also active in shaping wage structures, labour mobility patterns and other aspects of labour market behaviour.

In a broad sense, the behaviour of labour markets can perhaps be best understood by reflecting on the overlap between the three social sciences of labour economics, industrial relations and industrial sociology. Each of these different disciplines make, to some extent, different predictions about human behaviour under similar circumstances, and stress different causes for observed patterns of behaviour. Thus, while labour economics examines the behaviour of employers and employees in response to the general incentives of wages, prices, profits and non-pecuniary aspects of the employment relationship, such as working conditions, the greater part of industrial relations and industrial sociology deals with group activities, the internal dynamics of organisations, social norms and the processes of rule making both within and outside the organisation. It is for this reason that there is no one single theory of the labour market, but rather a number of differentiated and often competing approaches. Three of the most prevalent perspectives shall be examined here:

1. The competitive approach, relating to a market approach to demand and supply.
2. The institutional approach, referring to the critical role of institutions as the determinants of labour market operation.
3. The normative or radical approach, focusing on the traditional class struggle between owners of production and the workers.

The Competitive Model of the Labour Market

In the standard competitive model of the labour market, derived from neo-classical economics, it is presumed that individuals are rational economic maximisers, that is, that they make rational choices to maximise the economic benefit to themselves. It is assumed that individuals have a set of preferences and will organise their time and effort so that they will achieve the highest rate of return possible to themselves. In the context of employment, an individual will weigh up the marginal benefits of working as opposed to not working and thus will take into account factors such as wages, time, leisure and so forth when making the decision to work. In this manner the equilibrium wage and the associated level of employment are determined by the intersection of labour supply and labour demand. This intersection produces a market-clearing wage with the result that, at that wage, the quantity of labour willingly supplied exactly equals the quantity of labour willingly demanded.

Marsden (1986) and Beardwell and Holden (2001) identify a number of key presumptions that underpin this model of the labour market.

- The labour market is comprised of a large number of employers and employees each with their own set of preferences based on utility or wealth maximisation.
- All other forms of labour market organisation develop out of competitive conditions.

- There are no constrains on entry to the labour market, that is, that new organisations and new workers can enter the labour market at any time.
- Jobs in most organisations can be done by a fairly large number of workers provided they have the appropriate skills – in its most extreme form (homogenous labour) all jobs can be done by all workers.
- The organisation can be treated as a transmission mechanism between markets, that is, that in-house training and work experience are of equal benefit to all firms and are thus transferable.
- The only cost to the organisation of hiring labour is the wage, thus there is no marginal gain in retaining existing workers rather than hiring new ones.
- There is perfect information. All workers and all organisations know the state of the market and are instantly aware of any changes in the market.
- Technology is the chief link in the derived demand for labour since it determines the skills that will be required from the labour market and the elasticities of substitution between different factors of production.

In the competitive model, adjustments to changes in product markets or production methods are made through the price mechanism that is, as costs increase, the price of labour decreases. In this way both employers and employees are price takers – organisations will only employ as many individuals as is economically viable, bearing in mind the law of diminishing marginal returns. Workers will only choose to work where the cost of not working (or leisure) outweighs the benefits of being employed. In such a scenario, unemployment does not exist since wages are flexibly adjusted in line with labour supply.

The Institutional Model of the Labour Market
The debate over the validity of economic theories of the labour market has raged over the last number of years with many sceptics arguing that organisational and institutional factors and social norms have a greater influence on the behaviour of labour markets than pure labour market economics. Specifically, the tendency of employees to collectively represent themselves through the operation of trade unions has, in many organisations, led to a situation where the managerial prerogative to manage has been much diluted.

Perhaps the key variable that serves to differentiate the institutional model from the neo-classical model is that institutionalists do not concur that individuals behave independently of others. Rather, they perceive that individuals formulate choices and preferences with reference to perceived choices and preferences made by others. In this way the notion of perceived equity and fairness enters into the equation. In a similar vein, organisations are, to some degree constrained by the choices made by other organisations operating in a given product and service market. Beardwell and Holden (1994) suggest that other goals may be pursued other than profit maximisation i.e. market share, organisational growth or a target rate of return on capital present within the organisation. Institutionalists place a considerable emphasis on the role of group norms, customs and collective power in shaping labour market conditions such as wage rigidities, structured internal labour markets and efficiency wages.

The Radical Model of the Labour Market
The radical approach is based on the traditional class struggle between workers and the capital as presented by, among others, theorists such as Marx and Engels. As a theory of social change, Marxism has been concerned with the conditions under which the working

class could develop sufficient unity and consciousness to challenge and then replace capitalism. Thompson (1983), in discussing the nature of work, indicates that the capitalist labour process is subject to a number of identifiable tendencies, whose critical features are deskilling, fragmentation of tasks, hierarchical organisation, the division between mental and manual work, and the struggle to establish the most effective means to control labour. Similarly, Braverman (1974) argues that deskilling is an inherent tendency of the capitalist labour process and that Taylorism, or scientific management, was an effort to relieve workers of their job autonomy and craft knowledge. Hence, the radical perspective envisages an inevitable conflict between workers and the managers, as the owners of production, where the division of labour is perceived as a means of constraining workers' power while greater specialisation of tasks serves to subordinate the worker.

Within this perspective, the workers' capacity to resist exploitation and alienation lies in the development of collective representation through trade union organisation. Resistance to specialisation and standardisation is not limited to the jobs that workers do but rather extends to forms of work organisation and work structuring that are seen to segment the workforce and workforce solidarity. Hence the adoption of elements of workforce flexibility that results in the creation of core and periphery labour markets is seen as a covert managerial technique to further exploit labour.

The Operation of Labour Markets in Practice

Outside of pure prescriptions or theories of labour market functioning exist a number of core realities or features of labour markets that shape the way labour markets operate in practice, and subsequently influence or constrain the range of choices available to those engaging and managing human resources.

UNEMPLOYMENT

A notable feature of most labour markets is the persistently high levels of unemployment and, contrary to the presumptions of the competitive model, not all of those that are seeking employment can find it. Labour is not homogenous – rather it is highly differentiated and so it is a remarkable peculiarity of labour markets that unemployment can exist alongside wage inflation and job vacancies.

WAGE RIGIDITIES

One of the key presumptions underpinning competitive models of labour markets is that wages can be flexibly adjusted in line with demand for labour, that is, that organisations can reduce wages as their demand for labour falls. In fact, wages are more likely to move upwards more readily than they move downwards and often this downward wage rigidity is offered as a critical explanation for the nature and extent of current high levels of unemployment. More often, organisations resort to recruitment freezes (see for example the cutback in recruitment in the public sector in the early 1990s), reductions in overtime, and ultimately lay-offs or redundancy as short-term reactions to demand for labour. Wage levels are also externally influenced by social partnership agreements (i.e. PESP, PCW, PPF), Joint Industrial Councils, Government interventions and so forth.

OCCUPATIONAL SEGREGATION

Mainstream neo-classical theory usually starts from the presumption of an otherwise homogenous market divided up only by the technical limitations on the substitutability of different skills and abilities, and possibly by the constraints imposed by the need to certify the quality of skills. The labour market is structured into sub markets by the restrictions on the substitutability between different kinds of labour. While competition between workers on different sub markets may be very limited, each sub market itself remains a zone of competition, in which normal market relationships apply. Institutional writers have argued that institutional rule, such as demarcation and apprenticeship rules, arising out of collective bargaining and company recruitment practices can also play a major role in defining the limits of sub markets.

In its most realistic form, the labour market is divided into a number of occupational labour markets. Two discrete types of labour market can be said to exist – labour markets for unskilled or casual labour, and occupational labour markets involving transferable skills. In other words, in the context of rational choice, individual workers seeking to maximise their net advantages will focus on searching for information about advantages in other firms and on obtaining access to different occupational labour markets through investment in education and training.

INTERNAL LABOUR MARKETS

Doeringer and Piore (1971) define internal labour markets (ILMs) as internal administrative units within which the pricing and allocation of labour are governed by a set of administrative rules and procedures. A distinction is drawn between what are termed specific or non-transferable skills, for which there is no market outside of the employing firm, and general skills that can be applied in any organisational context. From an organisational perspective, investment in general skills is a rather more risky venture since these skills are valuable to most organisations and so the potential loss of their investment through labour turnover is high.

Investment in specific skills might well be the preferred option since these skills are not readily transferable; however, individual workers are more likely to be interested in the acquisition of more general skills that will improve their employability. Specific skills are necessary for the individual organisation yet investment in them can reduce employee mobility. Individuals seek general training to enhance their career and job prospects within the labour market and so are attractive for 'poaching' and 'headhunting'.

The development of structured internal labour markets can be seen as a means of managing these competing interests where a system of job hierarchies is designed that provides mobility chains or career progression up through the organisation hierarchy. Formal patterns of progression between jobs are regulated through rules and customs and provide a sense of stability within organisations. Labour mechanisms working within internal labour markets are governed by administrative rules, rather than open market competition, and adjustments within these markets are typically through management-driven techniques such as job evaluation, job design, wage and salary administration and so forth. The use of personnel policies has the cumulative effect of building barriers to labour mobility since accumulated rights are inextricably linked with tenure.

Organisations use ILMs in order to minimise costs of investment in enterprise specific skills or 'human capital'. ILMs are seen to determine wage and employment structures different from, but within the constraints set by, competitive market forces. Williamson (1978) argues that ILMs are developed less to reduce the costs of investing in training, but rather that the offer of more stable employment and of internal labour market conditions creates a situation in which it is in the workers own self-interest to promote the longer-term prosperity of the firm and hence to adopt a co-operative attitude.

FLEXIBILITY

The notion of labour market flexibility within organisations emerged as a key debate in the HRM literature sometime during the mid-1980s. Set against the backdrop of global recession, many of the arguments for labour market flexibility called for structural changes to both the design of organisations and work to overcome 'institutional rigidities' (Boyer 1988); to offset competitive pressures and low productivity (Sparrow and Hiltrop 1994); or to manage the shift towards service sector employment (Morley *et al.* 1994). The basic premise underpinning these arguments was that organisations could pursue two opposing strategies of labour market utilisation, either rely heavily on the external labour market and low levels of employee involvement, or favour internal mobility and the development of multiple skills amongst existing employees.

To date, the flexibility debate has focused on the contribution that various employment strategies might make, both to organisational adaptability and performance and increased opportunities for employees (Brewster *et al.* 1993; Marginson 1991; Berg 1989; Gunnigle and Daly 1992). These adaptability and performance improvements and increased employee opportunities are seen to be brought about through the development of numerical, pay/cost and functional flexibility (Atkinson 1984; Curson 1986; Pollert 1988 and 1991; Green, Krahan and Sung 1993).

The flexible firm model as advanced by Atkinson (see figure 3.1) involves a reorganisation of firms' internal labour markets and their division into separate components, in which the worker's experience and the employer's expectations of him/her are increasingly differentiated (Atkinson and Meager 1986). This hierarchical restructuring allows radically different employment policies to be pursued for different groups of workers. Within this framework, the 'core' is composed of full-time staff, enjoying relatively secure challenging jobs with good pay and employment conditions. Two sets of 'periphery' workers can be created: the first set are highly skilled, often technical or professional employees who are contracted into the organisation on fixed term contracts and who enjoy relatively good conditions of employment. The second 'periphery' is composed of an amalgam of temporary, part-time and contract groups with less favourable pay and employment conditions and less job security or training and promotion opportunities.

The flexible firm scenario suggests an attempt by organisations to increase flexibility in three key areas.

1. *Numerical flexibility* incorporating the use of non-standard employment forms, which allows the organisation to hire and/or shed labour flexibly in line with business demands.
2. *Financial/pay flexibility* whereby pay rates are linked to labour and product market conditions and pay increases for individual employees are variable and contingent upon performance.
3. *Functional flexibility* incorporating multi-skilling, which is defined as the expansion of skills within a workforce or the ability of organisations to reorganise the competencies associated with jobs so that the job holder is willing and able to deploy such competencies across a broader range of skills.

The extant literature reveals several strands within the flexibility debate. It is argued that competitive pressures are increasingly forcing organisations to increase their capacity to employ or shed labour more rapidly in order to achieve a better fit between workforce size and fluctuations in the demand for goods and services (Marginson 1991; Berg 1989; Boyer

Figure 3.1 The flexible firm

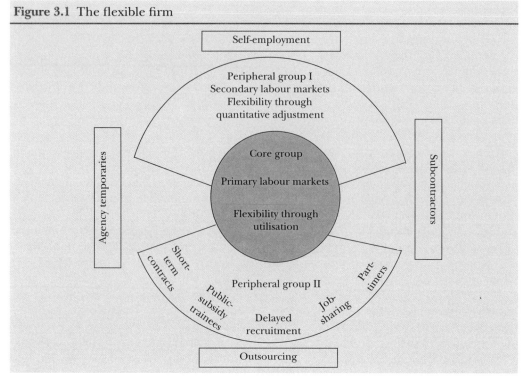

Source: Atkinson (1984).

1988; Dineen 1988). Consequently, non-standard employment in the form of temporary and casual workers, fixed term contracts, home working and subcontracting is seen to follow (Brewster *et al.* 1993; Hegewisch and Bruegel 1992; McGregor and Sproull 1992; Blackwell 1990; Meulders and Tytgat 1989; Lane 1988). Functional flexibility concerned with the relaxing of demarcation lines and the adoption of broader job descriptions (Hunter and McInnes 1992; Blyton and Morris 1991) is also seen as a mechanism for achieving greater organisational adaptability. Finally, while previous research does suggest that flexibility is on the increase, this may simply be occurring in reaction to depressed labour and product market conditions, rather than as a systematically planned emergence of the totally flexible firm. However, such apparently expedient responses to environmental conditions may well be sustained when the environment changes, as organisations become more anxious to retain the advantages of certain flexibility forms (Hakim 1991).

Criticisms of the flexibility scenario are widespread. Pollert (1991) indicates that prophesies of a 'new' or 'radical break' in the nature and the 'future' of work have driven the whole flexibility debate into a 'post-industrial futurology', one in which new types of work, and new employment relations are being heralded as the novel and indeed path-breaking developments of the new era. Similarly, Green *et al.* (1993) note that, despite some evidence of growing reliance on non-standard workers, it is not at all clear that employers are deliberately moving into flexible employment practices for the long-term strategic reasons that Atkinson identified.

Despite concerns regarding the utility of the flexible firm model, the debate concerning labour market segmentation continues. Drawing on the theoretical frameworks of transaction cost economics (Klein *et al.* 1978), human capital theory (Becker 1964;

Flamholtz and Lacey 1981), and the resource-based view of the firm (Barney 1991; Prahalad and Hamel 1990), Lepak and Snell (1999) have developed a human resource architecture that depicts four particular modes of employment: internal development, acquisition, contracting and alliance. The premise for this architecture is based on the recognition that not all employees possess knowledge and skills that are of equal strategic importance and so organisations make decisions on whether to internalise or externalise the employment relationship. Internalisation refers to the continual internal development of employees who are felt to possess unique skills and capabilities that are highly valued by the organisation and which are not readily available from outside it. Externalisation refers to a deliberate strategy of sourcing skills and competencies outside of the organisation – these skills and competencies are neither unique nor firm specific and so they are rather more readily available in the external labour market. Snell *et al.* (1996, 65) note that

> If the types and levels of skills are not equally distributed, such that some firms can acquire the talent they need and others cannot, then (*ceteris paribus*) that form of human capital can be a source of sustained competitive advantage.

Lepak and Snell (1999) suggest that a strong internalisation focus might be reflected in jobs that are rather loosely defined to allow for change, in extensive training opportunities including career development and mentoring arrangements, skills-based payment systems and developmental performance appraisal systems. Indeed this combination of HR practices is similar to those depicted in the high-performance, work systems literature (Huselid 1995; Lawler *et al.* 1995).

HUMAN RESOURCE MANAGEMENT AND LABOUR MARKET THEORIES
The first two chapters of this book examined the nature and scope of HRM to manage the employment relationship in line with the various external market conditions that impact on their operations. The foregoing discussion on labour market functioning provides for varying perspectives on the role that HRM policies might play in determining the nature of this employment relationship. However, rather than ascribing an ideal version of HRM, labour market theories serve to explain why individual organisations may vary the nature of their personnel policies in line with the prevailing economic climate they find themselves operating in. It is within this context that we now discuss how each of the various labour market perspectives might view the role played by HR policies in terms of their effect on established internal labour market structures.

HRM and the Competitive Perspective
The competitive model assumes that, as organisations face increased competition in their product markets, they will continually seek new and better ways of reducing costs. Within this perspective, one can argue that the primary goal of HRM is cost minimisation and particularly, to reduce the labour costs. Given the existence of wage rigidities implicit in the model, one would expect that organisations would seek to reduce such wage rigidities by implementing structures and systems that allow for the more flexible deployment of labour. There are two particular labour pools associated with the competitive model – the unskilled labour market and the skilled labour market.

Taking the unskilled labour market first, the model assumes that labour turnover is high and that the wage rate tends towards the market rate. Since there is a ready supply of unskilled labour available in the external labour market, it is relatively easy and cost-efficient to hire such employees. Furthermore, as these employees do not have specific job knowledge or training, it is assumed that they will only leave the organisation when higher wages are offered elsewhere. For this reason, organisations will accept high levels of labour turnover since it is relatively easy to replace such workers and the costs of replacement are lower than the costs of providing incentives to retain them. Within such a scenario, it is unlikely that companies would adopt a 'soft' HRM approach.

The competitive model also envisages a second labour pool of skilled workers. In this instance structured internal labour markets will exist since, as organisations contribute to the costs of training employees, they will have a vested interest in retaining them. In this situation, it is more cost-effective to develop structured, internal labour markets that typically provide employment security, progressive wage increases based on tenure and opportunities for internal promotion, rather than the costly alternative of recruiting and training.

The competitive model therefore suggests two possible scenarios that HRM might enact. The first scenario envisages a 'no frills' employment strategy, which offers low-skilled work, little if any training, and pays the market rate for labour. The second scenario suggests the development of structured internal labour markets for skilled employment, which may be linked to functional and financial flexibility. In both cases, the primary driver of HRM policies is cost minimisation.

HRM and the Institutional Perspective

The institutional perspective focuses on the process by which the employment relationship is regulated and, in particular, highlights the role played by various interest groups in the development of employment strategies and policies. While the competitive model focuses particularly on cost reduction, the institutional model is more concerned with reducing inefficiencies in the utilisation of labour. Specifically, it suggests that the actors in the labour process play a significant role in determining labour efficiency and advocates the use of various HRM policies that seek to alter the nature of power within organisations. In practice then, the institutional approach would perceive that the central role of HRM is to develop a unitarist perspective of the firm whereby policies are introduced that seek to co-opt employees into the managerial vision of the organisation. One might therefore expect some elements of 'soft' HRM in evidence such as employee involvement, Total Quality Management (TQM), single union agreements in exchange for greater flexibility and productivity agreements. Two scenarios are possible within the institutional framework – the first might involve the co-opting of unions in order to secure agreement through participative decision-making, while the second scenario might result in greater individualising of the employment as a means of marginalising trade union power and influence. In any event, the dominant ethos espoused by the institutional model is the modification of existing power structures, through changing existing norms and behaviour patterns, in order to reduce inefficiencies.

HRM and the Radical Perspective

The radical approach also focuses on organisational processes of regulating the employment relationship but it differs from the institutional approach in that it presumes that all managerial activities are geared towards the creation of greater profits at the expense of the workers. In particular, HRM policies are viewed as deliberate means of exploiting labour and weakening the collective power of employees. Within this framework, the adoption of, for example, the core/periphery employment model, is seen to be a particular example of a divide and conquer policy, where management co-opt a select number of core workers (who receive all the attendant benefits of security, training promotions, incentives), at the expense of the majority for whom flexibility results in increased work intensification, greater direct control, diminished employment security and possibly lower pay.

The radical perspective views all policies and strategies that seek to individualise the employment relationship as further evidence of management's covert objective to reduce collective resistance. Within such an organisation the purpose of HRM, from the radical perspective, is not the reduction of costs or inefficiencies, but rather the exploitation of labour through the extension of managerial control over the employment relationship.

Having explored the various labour market theories and their perspectives on the role of HRM, the latter section of this chapter provides details on the current nature of the Irish labour market as a pre-requisite for later chapters that explore the dynamics of HRM at a more operational level.

PROFILE OF THE IRISH LABOUR MARKET

An editorial in *The Economist* in May 1997 suggests that foreign companies cite a number of specific attractions for choosing Ireland as a European base. These include the combination of having English as the spoken language, with a recognised pro-European outlook, and of a well-educated workforce, particularly at the upper end. Over the past decade the Irish workforce has become increasingly better educated and a higher proportion of young people are remaining in further education and training. Arguably, these and related labour market characteristics have a significant explanatory power in accounting for the recent successes witnessed in the Irish economy, and they are examined in detail here.

Demographic Trends

In 1999, Ireland's population stood at 3.7 million people, which is its highest level since the census of 1881 when a figure of 3.8 million was recorded. Figure 3.2 demonstrates that Ireland has a relatively young population; the most populated age groups are those between ten and thirty years. Overall, 47 per cent of the population is aged twenty-nine and under, which is ten percentage points more than the average of the EU-15. This reflects the historically high birth rates that this country experienced in the 1970s and 1980s.

Figure 3.2 Males and females in Ireland in 1999 by age group (000s)

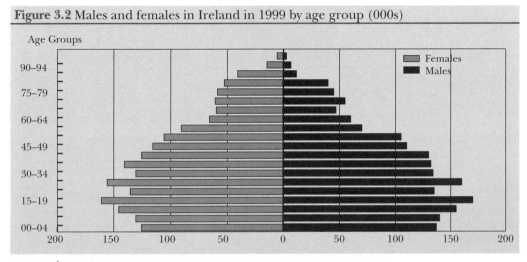

Source: FÁS 2000, Eurostat, Labour Force Survey (1999).

Recent labour market profiles (FAS 2001) indicate that Ireland's population is forecast to reach about 4.3 million by 2029. Figure 3.3 highlights the percentage of the population accounted for within each age group currently and anticipated for 2029.

Figure 3.3 Age structure of Ireland's population in 1999 and projected for 2029

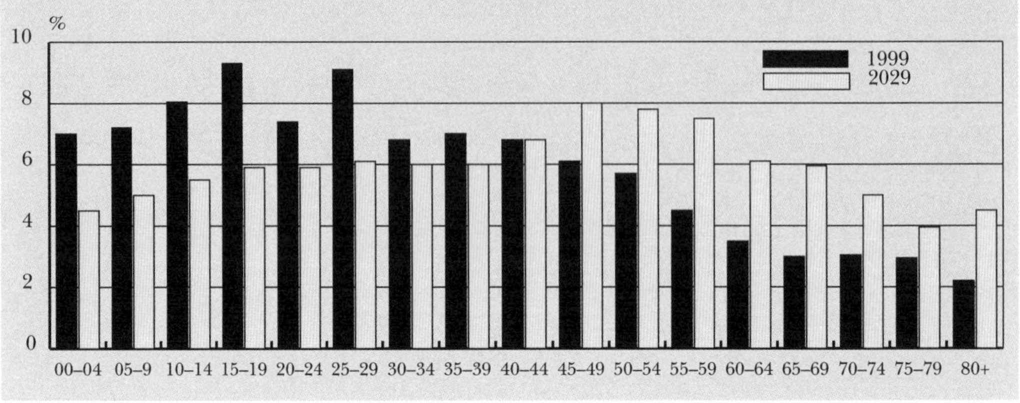

Source: FÁS Labour Market updates: Eurostat, Labour Force Survey 1999 and CSO Population and Labour Force Projections.

Although Ireland continues to have an above EU average birth rate, the overall birth rate has started to decline. Since 1991, the overall decrease in the 0–15 age category is recorded at 34 per cent and, if the population forecasts hold true then:

• The population below age fifteen will decline from present levels (a 20 per cent drop by 2029).
• Overall, in 2029, a significantly higher proportion of the population will be above forty-five, and a significantly lower proportion will be below that age, than the situation today (2001).
• The number of people aged over sixty-five will nearly double over the period.

The Irish workforce will continue to expand in the medium term as those currently of school-going age enter the labour market. However, as in many other EU countries there is evidence of some ageing of the population beginning to emerge i.e. the average age of the population is increasing. An overall fall in the Irish birth rate will impact on the dependency ratio, which is estimated at about 54 per cent and is expected to fall to between 45 and 50 per cent over the next ten years (CSO 1995). It has implications for some increases in overall living standards i.e. fewer individuals in the economically inactive age group depending on those who are economically active. This is unlikely to have any impact in the short-term but, as the average age of the working-age population moves closer to the sixties, then this will have significant implications for personnel policies, particularly in terms of succession planning, training and retraining, rewards and so forth. Furthermore, as the population ages, and, where the birth rate continues to fall, the dependency ratio will increase as greater numbers depend on the shrinking economically active cohort. The figures here suggest, however, that a significant ageing (or 'greying') of Ireland's workforce will not occur for at least another twenty years.

Migration
Migration understood as the difference between emigration from and immigration to Ireland, and the performance of Ireland's labour market are inextricably linked; this

Figure 3.4 Overall net Irish migration flows 1986–2000*

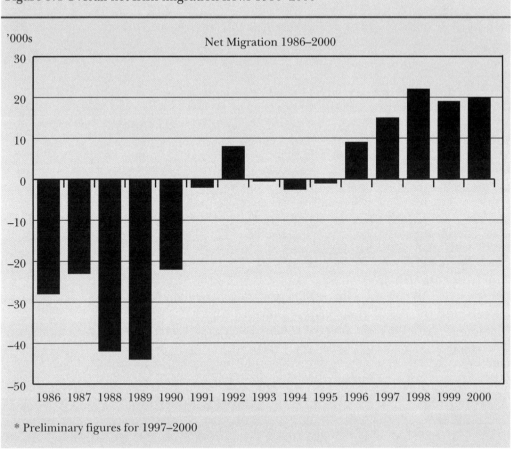

Net Migration 1986–2000

'000s

* Preliminary figures for 1997–2000

Source: FÁS (2000) Central Statistics Office, Population and Migration Estimates, various releases.

relationship has been particularly evident in recent years. Net outward migration has traditionally constituted an integral feature of the Irish labour market. More than 1.2 million people have left Ireland since the foundation of the state in 1921. While the 1970s witnessed a periodical reversal of this trend, net emigration resumed through the 1980s, rising from 9,000 in 1984 to 46,000 in 1989. However, this situation has reversed throughout most of the 1990s (see figure 3.4).

Migration flows can be grouped into three key periods. The first period spans 1986–90 when approximately 160,000 more people left the country than entered it. Net outflows peaked at 40,000 per annum in 1988 and 1989. The second period encompasses 1991–5 when 1,600 more people entered Ireland than left it. Recession in the world economy, particularly in the US and the UK, stemmed the outflow in the early 1990s, and the commencement of the upswing in the Irish economic environment reduced the numbers migrating abroad. The final period represents the years since 1996, which have witnessed historically large net inward migration. Net inflows have averaged around 20,000 per annum for each of the last three years. Analysis of migration flows in recent years indicates that, in addition to being the most popular destination for emigrants from Ireland, the highest proportion of immigrants also came from the UK (FÁS 2000). A total of 45 per cent of the 217,000 immigrants to Ireland since 1996 came from the UK, about two in ten immigrants over the same period came from the rest of the EU, about one in ten came from the USA and a little over 20 per cent were from other countries. Analysis further suggests that over 100,000 Irish persons returned to Ireland over the 1996–2000 period, which accounts for close to half of all immigrants. UK nationals were the second largest group accounting for nearly a fifth of inflows. Nationals from the EU accounted for about one in seven immigrants, about one in fourteen were USA nationals and the remaining 12 per cent were from other countries.

Overall economic buoyancy has resulted in a reversal of external migration – it is estimated that, in the absence of external migration, the Irish labour force has the capacity to expand by between 20,000 and 25,000 persons each year (1.5 per cent of the total labour force). Sweeney (1998) suggests that, since the 1990s, there have been many non-Irish people seeking work in Ireland and also seeking that 'quality of life' which has often been cited as compensation for lower living standards. He indicates that this ephemeral 'quality of life' – meaning the good social life, proximity to countryside and local amenities – is often given as the reason for staying in a country that traditionally offered few opportunities for well qualified people to change jobs.

The Irish Labour Force

While aggregate changes in the Irish labour force over the past fifteen years have been at times erratic, the overall trend has been upward. Figure 3.5 presents the size of the Irish labour force since 1994, as measured by the LFS (annual Labour Force Survey) up to April 1997, and the QNHS (CSO's Quarterly National Household Survey) from the fourth quarter (Q4) 1997. The figure shows that within any year the labour force is highest in the third quarter (Q3) between June and August.

Figure 3.5 Labour force growth April 1994 to Q3 (Jun.–Aug.) 2000

Source: Central Statistics Office (CSO), Quarterly National Household Survey (QNHS).

Over the period 1993–2000 Ireland's labour force grew from 1.4 million to 1.81 million – an increase of close to 25 per cent, which indicates an average annual increase of close to 4 per cent per year. In the first three-quarters of 1999 alone, the labour force increased by almost 120,000 or 7 per cent. The Central Bank of Ireland in its 'Winter 2000 Bulletin' estimated that the labour force grew by an annual average of 3.6 per cent, suggesting that while the labour force continued to grow in 2000, it did so at a slower rate than in previous years. Most of the increases in the labour force are attributed to increased 'domestic labour' supply, supplemented by net immigration. One significant feature underpinning this growth has been increased female labour force participation which has risen from 34.1 per cent of the 15–64 age cohort in 1992 to 49.4 per cent in 2000 (see figure 3.6).

Figure 3.6 Trends in the labour force participation rates by gender, April 1988 to Q3 (Jun.–Aug.) 2000

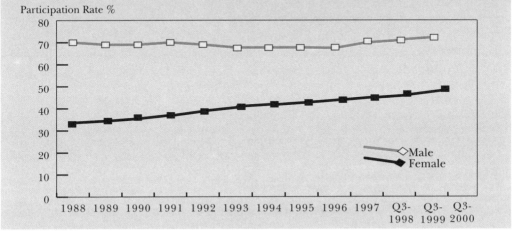

Source: Central Statistics Office (CSO), Quarterly National Household Survey (QNHS), FÁS (2000).

In 1989, the male participation rate was 69.4 per cent, while in 1999 it was 70 per cent. Analysis by FÁS (2000) suggests that this relatively small increase reflects the fact that participation rates of males in the 30–44 age cohort were in excess of 90 per cent for the last number of years. There has been and remains little scope for participation to increase further for these groups. Male participation rates exceed EU rates and have increased relatively little for most age groups over the last number of years.

Female labour force growth has been more rapid than male labour force growth over the last number of years, although these growth rates have started to converge more recently. Overall females accounted for 60 per cent of the 380,000 increase in the labour force over the last decade and the current rate of almost 50 per cent has surpassed the overall EU female participation rate of 46.6 per cent. Overall employment expansion in the 1990s has thus precipitated very rapid growth in the numbers of women working in Ireland. Speculation on the causes of this increased participation has focused on factors such as smaller family size, changing structure of employment demand, institutional factors, and improvements in educational attainment. FÁS (1998) note the emergence of changes in the occupational pattern of women's jobs in Ireland, where within the professional occupations, for example, women's share has increased most rapidly in the business professions and (from a much smaller base) in engineering and science. Their share has also risen, but more slowly, in education and has declined sharply among religious professionals. However, while female participation continues to increase in Ireland, recent labour market analysis by FÁS (2000) suggests that there remains some scope for increased participation in the labour force by females, particularly women aged forty and over. Participation rates among the age group 40–59 are considerably lower than the average EU rate.

Employment Trends

In the third quarter of 2000 employment stood at 1.738 million, which represents an increase of about 4.1 per cent over corresponding figures for 1999. Although still higher than expected, this does represent some slow down in overall employment growth, which averaged out at about 9 per cent at the close of the 1990s. Employment growth has been spread across most sectors of the Irish economy although figures in table 3.1 affirm the continuing trend of significant services sector growth in the years 1999–2000.

Table 3.1 Employment levels and trends by sector Q3 1999 to Q3 2000

	1999	2000	Change 1999–2000	%Change 1999–2000
Agriculture, forestry & fishing	142,300	130,700	–11,600	–8.2
Other production industries	321,300	326,400	5,100	1.6
Construction	150,900	175,500	24,600	16.3
Wholesale & retail trade	236,400	253,400	17,000	7.2
Hotel & restaurants	116,700	118,300	1,600	1.4
Transport, storage & communication	99,900	105,900	6,000	6.0
Financial & other business services	208,000	218,800	10,800	5.2
Public administration & defence	77,800	78,800	1,000	1.3
Education & health	219,000	232,500	13,500	6.2
Other services	97,000	97,600	600	0.6
Total	1,669,200	1,737,800	68,600	4.1

Source: FÁS Labour Market Update 2000, CSO, QNHS.

Employment trends are inexorably linked with the occupational structure of the labour market which tends to be associated with technological developments, product market variations, sectoral composition, and the general nature of employment practices (in terms of work structuring, composition of employment, flexibility and so forth). In 1997 a report on occupational employment forecasts to 2003 was completed jointly by FÁS and the ESRI (Duggan *et al.* 1997). This was in an effort to determine the changing pattern of occupational segregation in the Irish labour market and to identify possible variations in skill requirements across fourteen broadly identified occupational classifications. Over the period 1997–2003 they predicted significant changes in broad occupational groupings to occur, which would have appreciable impact on the distribution of overall employment. Their data predicted that agricultural employment will continue to fall over the intervening years to 2003 and that the largest increases in employment would occur in managerial and professional occupations (categorised in the report as those workers who hold degree level qualifications). Strong growth was also forecast for associate professions (diploma/sub-degree qualification level), for sales and personal services type employment, and for clerical work. Projected growth was also featured for skilled manual workers (both those involved in maintenance and in core production). The forecasts indicated however that jobs that do not require prior specialised qualifications, and that rely more on on-the-job training, or are unskilled, are less likely to experience the same level of growth as those occupations that are qualification based and driven.

In their most recent research on occupation forecasts and human resource requirements, Sexton *et al.* (2001) confirm the trend of growth in professional, managerial and skilled occupation categories (see table 3.2).

Table 3.2 Total human resource requirements in 1989–97 and 1997–2005

Occupation	Total Human Resource Requirement (THR)			THR Annual Averages		
	1989–97	1997–2005 (000)	Change	1989–97	1997–2005 (000)	Change
Agricultural occupations	11.7	3.3	–8.4	105	0.4	–1.0
Managers	22.9	33.6	10.7	2.9	4.2	1.3
Proprietors in services	4.3	9.9	5.6	0.5	1.2	0.7
Professional occupations	40.7	78.3	37.6	5.1	9.8	4.7
Associate professionals	27.4	31.4	4.0	3.4	3.9	0.5
Clerical occupations	48.2	65.1	16.9	6.0	8.1	2.1
Skilled maintenance	16.9	29.3	12.4	2.1	3.7	1.5
Other skilled workers	25.3	46.4	21.1	3.2	5.8	2.6
Production operatives	39.5	37.2	–2.3	4.9	4.6	–0.3
Transport/communication	10.9	11.4	0.5	1.4	1.4	0.1
Sales workers	32.9	61.2	28.3	4.1	7.6	3.5
Security workers	4.9	17.8	12.7	0.6	2.2	1.6
Personal service workers	26.5	27.1	0.6	3.3	3.4	0.1
Unskilled labourers	8.1	17.9	9.8	1.0	2.2	1.2
TOTAL	320.2	470.0	149.8	40.0	58.7	18.7

Source: Sexton *et al.* (2001).

Female employment is predicted to continue to rise over the next number of years by as much as 35 per cent, which represents a rate of expansion more than double that forecast for men. There is evidence to suggest that female participation in employment is extending out from the traditional occupations of clerical work and health associated professions and into more business and commercial professions where they have been, and continue to remain, under-represented.

Although the data presented here represent forecasts of likely changes over the next few years we have already witnessed some of the impacts that will be more keenly felt in times to come. Skills shortages are being reported in many technical fields, in the construction trade, in marketing/sales and in the tourism/hospitality sector. Skilled crafts-persons are in considerable demand, and participation in third level and professional education remains buoyant.

At the end of November 2000, there were 136,962 people on the Live Register, which is equivalent to a standardised unemployment rate of 3.7 per cent. There is considerable evidence of a shift in economic performance, particularly towards the latter half of 2001. The slowdown in the global economy, and the considerable downturn in world markets following the terrorist attacks on the US in September, will likely have appreciable effects on performance of the Irish economy in the next year. Already we are witnessing considerable job losses in certain service sectors (particularly aviation) and in manufacturing, and economic forecasts predict an overall slowing down of the Irish economy. As discussed in earlier chapters, economic performance and policy development inextricably shape the nature of the labour market and it is likely that the Irish labour market will undergo considerable change in the next few years.

Participation at Third Level

The Irish education system has undergone significant change in the past thirty years due, in no small part, to the strongly interventionist role adopted by the Irish state in pursuit of economic development from the early 1960s onwards. In recognition of the fundamental value of a good education system to the economic and social development of a nation, free second-level education was introduced in 1966, and compulsory schooling was extended from fourteen to fifteen years of age.

Following the publication of the White paper on Education (1995), which echoed a persistent concern regarding the general suitability of the Leaving Certificate cycle for all students, a decision was taken to restructure the Leaving Certificate programme into three components: the established Leaving Certificate programme, the Leaving Certificate Applied Programme and the Leaving Certificate Vocations Programme. However, the majority of senior cycle students continue to follow the mainstream Leaving Certificate Programme, which retains an emphasis on general academic education and continues to prepare students for entry to the labour market or to third level education.

Participation at third level is determined by a points system based on Leaving Certificate examination results and, while entry to some programmes of study is more difficult in terms of the number of points required, in general demand for third level education far outstrips the limited supply of places available at third level institutions. This high demand has led to the relatively recent addition of a further tier to the educational system. Private commercial colleges (post-Leaving Certificate colleges) now also provide a range of state certified programmes in a number of disciplines, as well as their other programmes, many of which are not state certified. The total number of full-time students at third level has increased significantly over the last number of years (in excess of 40 per cent since 1990) and a number of factors are seen to have contributed to this general upsurge in participation. These include the provision of post-Leaving Certificate courses; the abolition of fees for undergraduate students in publicly-funded third level colleges in 1995, which provided wider access to third level education; greater investment in education and increased number of third level places.

The past thirty years have been marked by increased expenditure on education, coupled with greater numbers in education and higher participation rates. Young people are staying in the education system for longer across all levels of education, and, in a comparison of those who have completed third level education in the OECD countries, it would appear that Ireland fares positively against many of her EU counterparts. Here again there is evidence of increased participation among the younger age categories, perhaps as a result of the policy changes discussed earlier.

Today, with close to one million students participating in education in Ireland, there is little room for complacency in relation either to Ireland's educational system or indeed educational participation rates more generally. The link between education and employment is well documented where the attainment of educational qualifications critically impacts upon one's ability to successfully gain and retain employment. The recent OECD report on education (1997) argues that many of the benefits of education cannot be quantified and that social cohesion, rather than narrow economic gain, is the greatest prize for societies in which all citizens use learning to become more effective participants in democratic, civil and economic processes. Indicators from the OECD (1995) Education report associate higher levels of education with higher earnings, a lower chance of unemployment and more skills that yield social advantage. This link is evidenced in the most recent Irish labour force survey which suggest that individuals who possess no post-primary qualification are six times more likely to be unemployed than are those with a third level qualification. In the case of those who do find employment, the remuneration they receive is very often far lower than those with higher qualifications. Education and earnings are thus positively linked, and so the earnings advantage of increased education would appear to outweigh the costs of acquiring it.

Flexibility in Ireland
The CUL survey (Cranfield University of Limerick Survey, 1995) represents broad trends in organisational usage of different flexible work practices. Data suggest that there is some evidence that organisations are making more use of some forms of flexible labour, and that they are seeking changes in working practices, which allow for easier deployment of employees across tasks. However, Gunnigle *et al.* (1997) caution that there is no evidence to support the propositions that the use of workforce flexibility today is of any notable difference to its use in the past. Any proliferation in the use of certain labour categories and work practices appears to be less of a deliberate organisational strategy to adopt the flexible firm model, and more an emerging, incremental strategy, which can be accounted for by organisational, sectoral and structural changes.

Growth in Non-Standard and Flexible Employment in Ireland
The growth of non-standard work forms has been observed in Ireland, since the mid to late 1970s (Gunnigle *et al.* 1997). The Irish Labour Market Study (1997) indicated that while the incidence of part-time work, as a proportion of total employment in the Irish economy, is relatively low when compared with other EU countries, it has increased significantly in recent years. From 1983–93, virtually all employment creation related to part-time work, which is, perhaps, reflective of the shift to service sector employment during this period. Part-time work remains much more common among women than men (just over 5 per cent of employed males were working part-time in 1997). Just under a quarter (23 per cent) of all women in employment work part-time, and part-time work has accounted for about one-third of the increase in female employment in recent years. Almost 50 per cent of females engaged in part-time work are to be found in service type occupations, with a further 20 per cent engaged in clerical work. Nearly all of the additional part-time jobs for women have been in three sectors – personal services, distribution, and health and education. The increase has been more limited in sectors such as manufacturing, building and transport. The Labour Force Survey (1997) indicates that almost nine out of every ten people working part-time are not looking for full-time work.

The current proportion of part-time work in Ireland is 12.3 per cent indicating that part-time working is still less prevalent here than in many other EU member states. In 1996, for example, almost 70 per cent of women workers in the Netherlands, and 45 per cent of those in the UK, were working part-time. However, since 1993, the unprecedented growth in the Irish economy has resulted in the creation of mainly full-time jobs. This about-turn may be as a result of the expansion of manufacturing employment and the current 'boom' being experienced in the building and construction industry. Overall, the increased propensity towards part-time employment may be indicative of increased flexibility in the Irish labour market. However, it remains exceptionally low by EU standards and there remains continued scope for an upward trend to continue. Temporary work, as a proportion of overall employment, currently stands at just 7 per cent.

The contention that organisations are consciously restructuring their workforce on a core-periphery basis is largely unsupported however. The CUL (1995) survey results showed a general increase in organisational usage of most forms of atypical employment in Ireland (see tables 3.3, 3.4 and 3.5). (For more detailed information see Gunnigle *et al.* [1995], much of the data on flexibility in Ireland presented here is abridged from this source.) Shift work and overtime appear to be the most stable forms of flexible work arrangements, with over 40 per cent of respondents reporting that there had been no change in the levels of either since 1992 (see table 3.3). However, it should be noted that these forms of non-standard employment practices most often occur in the core workforce, and are seldom considered in discussions on atypical employment (Gunnigle *et al.* 1994).

Table 3.3 Change in organisational use of flexible work arrangements over the last 3 years – core workforce

	Increased	No Change	Decreased	Not used	N
Weekend work	25% (60)	40% (94)	5% (13)	30% (71)	238
Shift work	24% (57)	44% (106)	2% (5)	30% (72)	240
Overtime	24% (60)	44% (111)	25% (63)	6% (16)	250
Annual hours	5% (11)	15% (34)	4% (9)	76% (168)	222
Job sharing	29% (68)	15% (34)	0	56% (131)	233
Flexible working time	25% (56)	31% (70)	1% (2)	43% (97)	225

Source: Cranfield University of Limerick Survey, 1995.

On the other hand, there seems to be substantial increases in the number of organisations reporting the use of forms of atypical employment which are associated with the peripheral workforce (see table 3.4). The most significant increase is in the temporary and casual work category. This category also shows the greatest growth (10 percentage points) in the number of organisations reporting an increase since 1992 (39 per cent of organisations reported an increase in 1992). An interesting finding from the data is that only 10 per cent of respondent organisations do not use temporary contracts, a significantly smaller number than for any other category of atypical employment in the peripheral workforce.

Table 3.4 Change in organisational use of flexible work arrangements over the last 3 Years – peripheral workforce

	Increased	No Change	Decreased	Not used	N
Part-time work	40% (97)	29% (69)	6% (15)	25% (59)	240
Temporary/casual	49% (120)	35% (85)	6% (15)	10% (24)	244
Fixed term contract	47% (109)	29% (67)	2% (5)	23% (53)	234
Sub-contracting	41% (98)	23% (54)	2% (5)	34% (80)	237

Source: Cranfield University of Limerick Survey, 1995.

Tele-working and home-based work are the least popular forms of non-standard contract (see table 3.5), with 77 per cent and 74 per cent of organisations, respectively, reporting that they do not use these flexibility types. In a European context, Brewster *et al.* (1994, 190) suggest that the low levels of usage here may be accounted for by, '. . . the social elements involved in work: the value of face to face meetings and the psychological benefits of interactions with colleagues which are largely lost in home working'.

Table 3.5 Change in organisational use of flexible work arrangements over the last 3 years					
	Increased	**No Change**	**Decreased**	**Not used**	**N**
Home-based work	6% (13)	5% (11)	0.5% (1)	89% (193)	218
Tele-working	6% (13)	3% (6)	0	91% (201)	220

Source: Cranfield University of Limerick Survey, 1995.

On further analysis of the CUL (1995) data, organisational size appears to be an influential factor in determining the forms of non-standard contract that are adopted. The data suggest that a greater proportion of small organisations (organisations employing less than 200 employees) reported an increase in the adoption of flexibility in certain areas that are generally associated with the core workforce, such as overtime and weekend work. This may be indicative of an emerging trend, where smaller organisations are adopting flexible working practices, which enable them to utilise their current workforce more effectively, rather than increasing the size of the workforce. However, although small organisations are reporting increases in those flexible work practices associated with core employment, it is important to note that a greater number of large organisations (organisations employing more than 200 employees) are still more likely to employ all forms of flexibility. An organisation's size was found to have no significant bearing on the organisation's use of annual hours' contracts.

The main finding pertaining to non-standard contracts and unionisation since 1992 was that non-union organisations in particular, have significantly increased their utilisation of most atypical forms of employment, principally overtime, shift work, weekend work, fixed term contracts and subcontracting. These overall findings may be an indication that organisations which do not wish to recognise trade unions in Ireland are adopting a variation of the flexible firm scenario, and seem to be more intent upon developing a workforce that will adapt to changing economic circumstances.

Differences between organisations of different national origins were also analysed. A greater proportion of organisations originating in the US reported increases in shift work, overtime and weekend work. Conversely, organisations originating within the EU were most likely to have reported a decrease in their use of these forms of employment. The only form of flexibility which shows a significant decrease across the board was overtime (20 per cent or more of organisations originating in each geographical area reported a decrease in its use).

A very high proportion of indigenous Irish and UK-owned organisations reported increases in the use of part-time work (over 47 per cent), while a high percentage of US- and EU-owned organisations reported increases in temporary and casual work, 56 per cent and 54 per cent respectively (see figures 4.1 and 4.2). There is a growth in the number of organisations reporting increases in fixed-term employment across the board and these findings reflect closely the findings in relation to changes in temporary work. There are also significant increases in the number of organisations using subcontracting, particularly in US- and EU-owned organisations.

Respondents to the CUL (1995) were asked what *proportion*, if any, of their workforce was working on a non-standard contract. The results that emerged were quite surprising in the context of previous findings, which indicated increases in flexible working practices across Europe. While 73 per cent of organisations that responded to the CUL (1995) survey use part-time employees, 49 per cent have less than 1 per cent of their workforce on such contracts. However, since 1992 the number of organisations reporting between 1–10 per cent of the workforce on part-time contract has increased slightly. The same trend can be identified in the use of temporary and fixed-term contracts. Annual hours' contracts, while accepted as a cost-effective way of dealing with excessive amounts of overtime and having taken a firm foothold in countries such as Germany, Finland, the Netherlands and the UK, are not popular methods of flexible working in Ireland.

In analysing changes that have occurred in the area of *functional flexibility* over the past three years, a clear trend towards wider, more flexible jobs is apparent. Although the broad picture is still quite stable, a greater percentage of jobs in all categories have been made wider to encompass broader duties and responsibilities. When compared to the results of the 1992 survey, it is clear that a significantly greater number of respondents in 1995 feel that jobs have become more flexible for all categories of workers in their organisations (see table 3.6).

Table 3.6 Changes in job specification (1992–95)

	Management		Prof / technical		Clerical		Manual	
	1995	1992	1995	1992	1995	1992	1995	1992
More specific	22%	24%	15%	17%	10%	12%	9%	12%
No major change	35%	38%	40%	49%	40%	52%	42%	56%
Made wider	44%	38%	45%	34%	50%	36%	49%	32%
	N=249	N=226	N=233	N=207	N=240	N=214	N=192	N=191

Source: Cranfield University of Limerick Survey, 1992 and 1995.

However, when the figures are disaggregated to determine the effect of ownership on the degree of functional flexibility, it was found that indigenous Irish organisations were more likely to have made no changes whatsoever to the specification of jobs for all employee categories. Conversely, US-owned organisations tend to expand job specifications for all levels of the hierarchy, with the exception of clerical workers. Similarly, UK-owned organisations were likely to have broadened job specifications. Change was less likely to take place in public sector organisations across all job categories. A greater proportion of jobs have been made more flexible in the private sector. The overall picture that emerges from the data is one of change in the private sector and stability in the public sector.

Considering organisational size as an influencing factor, the CUL (1995) found that change in the specification of jobs is less likely to occur in smaller organisations. This may be due to the fact that jobs in smaller organisations tend traditionally to be less specific and therefore, as a result, required no change. In larger organisations, a greater percentage of jobs in all staff categories have become more flexible.

Overall, the CUL (1995) survey results show that although non-standard employment practices are being adopted on a piecemeal basis by some organisations more than others, there has not been a radical movement toward the adoption of the flexible firm model of employment practices since 1992. Similar to the results of the 1992 Price Waterhouse Cranfield Project (see Brewster *et al.* 1994; Morley and Gunnigle 1994), there is still a substantial proportion of organisations not adopting specific flexible work practices. Nonetheless, the CUL data also illustrated the importance of the flexibility phenomenon in modern day organisations, with flexibility playing an increasing role in manpower and cost reduction strategies. As Nollen and Gannon (1996, 296) noted:

Companies must accept continuous readjustment as turbulent product markets, rapid changes in technology, and global competition force them to accept flexible workforce arrangements . . . The cost of production must be continuously reduced even as quality must be increased.

This chapter has sought to provide some insight into how labour markets function and how this might likely shape the nature of HRM in organisations. The Irish labour market has undergone considerable change in recent years, and, in association with considerable capital investment in the Irish labour market, this has resulted in sustained employment creation combined with falling rates of unemployment and an appreciable rise in the overall standard of living. The demographic profile of the Irish population is favourably disposed towards high labour market participation, and it is unlikely that Ireland will experience the level of ageing of the labour force that will shortly be evidenced in many EU countries. More recently however, educational attainment and human capital investment are being viewed as critical determinants of positive economic growth and development.

Tansey (1998) indicates that each step up the educational ladder yields a significantly positive rate of return in terms of higher lifetime earnings. Thus the benefits of increased educational attainment are spread across the whole of the economy in terms of increased productivity, increased employment and a widened tax base for the state. The educational profile of the Irish labour force has changed considerably over the last number of years, particularly as a result of direct policy intervention to widen the provision and scope of second and third level education. Today the quality of the Irish labour force compares very favourably with those of other EU and OECD countries, particularly with respect to those holding a third level qualification.

Projections of occupational trends over the next five years suggest that unskilled and semi-skilled jobs will be displaced and that educational attainment and qualifications will increasingly become the criterion upon which employability is determined. There is thus a considerable danger that those who drop out of the education system before completing their formal education will become increasingly marginalised and unemployable.

As business becomes increasingly knowledge-based, there is considerable pressure on the organisation to ensure that its internal capability can match external environmental requirements. The onus is increasingly being placed on the personnel/HR function or practitioner to ensure that the firm's labour pool has both the skills and abilities to meet organisational requirements, and furthermore, the capacity to deal with possible changes that the external environment might demand. The following chapters explore these and other issues in greater detail.

4

Human Resource Planning, Recruitment and Selection

Thomas and Ray (2000) argue that, in the face of increasing global competition, the ability to attract, hire and develop the most capable talent is the single most important determinant of an organisation's effectiveness. Selecting individuals with good technical skills is no longer sufficient to ensure effective job performance. Graves and Karren (1996) suggest that employees must be able to work as team members, have knowledge of automated process and be IT literate, be flexible to manage varied workloads and be able to cope with changes as they occur. The question for most organisations is how to find the 'right' candidate with the required qualifications as quickly as possible at the lowest costs possible, what Heraty and Morley (1998) refer to as 'the search for good-fit'.

Human resource management encapsulates a number of core events that, in practice, occur simultaneously but which are presented here as a cycle of events to aid our understanding of each phase. The first phase depicts the organisation determining the nature and calibre of employees required for effective functioning (human resource planning phase) and establishing the employment relationship (recruitment and selection phase) and the psychological contract. Once the employment relationship has been established, the organisation then develops a range of procedures and practices that facilitate the retention of those recruited. This latter phase typically involves such practices as monitoring performance (performance appraisal and management); facilitating performance improvement and learning (employee development); determining the scope of the effort-reward bargain (reward practices); designing an effective system of work (job design); and finally managing the employment relationship (employee relations). However, while the practice of human resource management can be perceived as a cycle of events, this does not infer that each phase in the process is independent of the other. Rather, there is considerable interplay between all stages in the creation and development of an effective workforce. In this chapter, however, we will concentrate on the first two phases of the employment cycle and focus specifically on human resource planning, recruitment and selection.

THE PURPOSE OF HUMAN RESOURCE PLANNING

Many companies address all aspects of managing the workforce through human resource planning, directly linking human resource actions to strategic business issues or priorities (Bechet and Walker 1995; Bratton and Gold 1999; Tansey 1998; Grundy 1997). Human resource planning can be said to be the basis for effective management since it involves forecasting human resource needs for the organisation and planning necessary to achieve these needs. Boerlijst and Meijboom (1989) argue that European organisations now appreciate that their survival depends on the quality of their people and that their human resource management requires a conscious and specific direction of effort in both the short- and long-term. Although recent work, by Finn and Morley (2001) on the selection process employed in Irish firms that were establishing international subsidiaries, revealed the recruitment and selection process to be short-term, informal and often unstructured. In addition, the selection process tended to focus on a narrow range of personal skills, such as technical expertise and past performance whilst paying less attention to broader business skills.

At its most basic level human resource planning is concerned with ensuring that the organisation employs the right quantity of staff with the necessary skills and knowledge that are required for effective organisational functioning. Reilly (1996) defines human resource planning as a process in which an organisation attempts to estimate the demand for labour and evaluate the size, nature and sources of supply, which will be required to meet that demand. For many organisations this constitutes a difficult process since planning, by its nature is fraught with considerable tensions and unpredictability. The process is further complicated as Beardwell and Holden (1994) indicate:

> Human resources are considered the most valuable, yet the most volatile and potentially unpredictable resource, which an organisation utilises. If the organisation fails to place and direct human resources in the right areas of the business, at the right time, and at the right cost, serious inefficiencies are likely to arise creating considerable operational difficulties and likely business failure.

Lundy and Cowling (1996) dismiss the perception that since fewer organisations operate as bureaucratic and hierarchical structures, the frequent restructuring experiences make the forecasting and planning of internal manpower movements largely irrelevant. They argue that, rather than nullifying the requirement for careful human resource planning, new developments in the form of flatter organisation, or high-performance work systems, have attached increased importance to the process to facilitate the emergence of more flexible planning scenarios. A further argument in favour of human resource planning is proposed by Walker (1980) who outlines a number of benefits attached to the process of human resource planning.

- Reducing personnel costs through the anticipation of shortages or surpluses of human resources, which can be corrected before they become unmanageable and expensive.
- Providing a basis for planning employee development to make optimum use of workers' aptitudes.
- Improving the overall business planning process.
- Providing equal opportunities for all categories of employees.
- Promoting greater awareness of the importance of sound personnel management throughout all levels of the organisation.
- Providing a tool for evaluating the effects of alternative personnel policies.

In calculating the additional unnecessary costs of poor recruitment and selection, Hacker (1997) documents the costs of a poor hiring decision as re-advertising, training a replacement, potential customer loss, decreased productivity, low employee morale. Sandico and Kleiner (1999) reinforce this point:

The obvious bad hires are the ones who leave the job soon after they are hired. Other poor hires are not as apparent because the problem does not become noticeable until later: they are the clock-watchers, the incapables who get their work done by others, or the marginal workers who have found a way to beat the system. These are the 'false positive' employees – the people who were hired but should not have been.

Ross (1981) cautions that because human resource planning is future oriented, there must be an explicit link coupling human resource planning with other organisational functions such as strategic planning, economic and market forecasting and investment planning. Human resource planning is based on identified future plans of the organisation and involves major policy decisions that can only be taken by top management. Gunnigle and Flood (1990) further indicate that, at the operational level, human resource planning involves catering for the human resource implications of operational business decisions such as the termination of a particular product line. They suggest that operational plans may then form the basis for short-term action plans in a range of HR areas from recruitment to termination. These may encompass the design of training programmes to upgrade operator skills, recruitment schedules for graduate trainees and forecasts of salary budgets for the next quarter.

Thus, human resource planning facilitates organisational functioning by evaluating current human resource utilisation and the human resource implications of change. Effective human resource planning helps avoid major discontinuities in human resource availability. It helps determine future HR strategies, anticipate human resource related problems and take positive action to ensure adequate human resources. It is a central component of a proactive role whereby HR practitioners can make a valuable contribution to strategic decision-making.

THE HUMAN RESOURCE PLANNING PROCESS

Human resource planning has traditionally started from the premise that a balance needs to be achieved between the supply and demand for human resources. The central assumption underpinning models of human resource planning is that demand for labour is derived from corporate plans, while labour supply is derived either internally – from current stocks of employees, or externally – from potential employees in the external labour market (Taylor 1998; Bratton and Gold 1999; Iles 1999). Thus, the reconciliation of the imbalances between demand for, and supply of, human resources leads to the development of plans related to the functional activities of HR management. A model of the human resource planning process is depicted in figure 4.1.

The planning process outlined in figure 4.1 identifies four key stages in the human resource planning process namely stocktaking, forecasting, planning and implementing. As indicated at the start of this chapter, each of these stages are interlinked and thus form a cycle whereby human resource planning affects, and is affected by, the range of personnel policy choices that the organisation has available to it. Hendry (1995) advocated this view of HR planning as a cycle of events arguing that change can be initiated at any point in the cycle (responding to external market fluctuations for example) and so the HR plan is more flexible as a result.

Stocktaking

The first stage in the development of human resource plans involves the identification of a range of variables that impact upon organisational operations. The model depicts two

Figure 4.1 Human resource planning process

	External environment	Internal environment	
		Corporate Objectives	*HR Systems*
Stocktaking	• labour market	• sales targets	• work practices
	• Government policies	• production	• employee development
	• education/training	• profits	• employee relations
	• legislation	• product/service market	• reward systems
	• technology		• workforce profile
	Supply of labour	**Demand for labour**	
Forecasting		**Estimate of imbalance**	
		Develop action plans for	
		• recruitment	
Planning		• training and development	
		• redundancy/lay off	
		• redeployment	
		• employee relations	
		• organisation development	
Implementing		**Implement and review**	

Source: Adapted from Gunnigle and Flood (1990) and Beardwell and Holden (1994).

particular categories of influencers: the external environment within which the organisation operates, and the internal organisational environment itself. In chapters one and two, much of the discussion focused on external factors that impact upon organisational functioning (such as Government policies, economic considerations and product market conditions) while, internally, the link between business planning and HR management was explicated. In addition to this, chapter three outlined particular labour market considerations that have relevance to the operation of HR management; while chapter thirteen details aspects of the legislative environment that directly affect the employment relationship. Rather than reiterate the discussions of these chapters, it is proposed that the readers review their contents for a holistic understanding of their relevance to human resource planning.

Sisson and Timperley (1994), in reviewing approaches to human resource planning, suggest that stocktaking involves analysing current human resources, that is, developing an accurate human resource profile, where the workforce is evaluated and classified according to factors such as age, experience, skills and abilities. Gunnigle and Flood (1990) suggest that stocktaking provides information on human resource capabilities and potential, which help in both succession planning and scheduling training and development programmes. Furthermore, Mayo (1991) advocates the use of job analysis to determine the knowledge and skills required for each job type; a skills audit to identify core competencies required and to develop a skills inventory of current employees; and a performance review to identify potential as well as future training needs. Bramham (1988) similarly suggests that human resource planning can aid in the assessment of the strengths and weaknesses of the current workforce. They might be analysed on criteria such as age, sex, experience, skills/qualifications and potential while, Beardwell and Holden (1994) further infer that the analysis of current manpower resources leads to the development of:

- recruitment plans – to avoid unexpected shortages;
- the identification of training needs – to avoid skill shortages;
- management development plans – to avoid managerial shortages or avoid bottlenecks in the system;
- industrial relations plans – to avoid industrial unrest resulting from changes in the quantity/quality of employees.

A particular requirement of the stocktaking stage involves the accurate profiling of the existing workforce. Specifically, the organisation needs to gather details on the current skills mix of its workforce in terms of education level, training level, job knowledge and ability. Information of this kind should be readily available from existing HR records, which will include reference data from employees' curriculum vitaes, performance reviews, job descriptions and any job analyses that have been conducted. A skills' profile should be read in tandem with existing work practices, technological processes utilised, and corporate business strategy in order that it provide an accurate depiction of the current competency mix within the organisation.

Forecasting

The forecasting stage of the human resource planning model involves forecasting both the supply of labour and demand for labour. This is probably the most difficult aspect of human resource planning, because it involves the organisation in the making of predictions about how many employees will be required for the future (demand analysis based on past trends and likely future business functioning); and determining where future employees are likely to be sourced (supply analysis). Planning is, by nature, a speculative process that relies heavily on past experience and the development of certain hypotheses concerning the future.

FORECASTING DEMAND FOR LABOUR

As indicated earlier, a preliminary step in developing human resource plans involves the identification of clearly defined organisational objectives, which indicate strategic purpose and direction. These may then be supplemented by more detailed operational plans which outline the role of each function in facilitating the achievement of strategic goals. Cowling and Walters (1990) argue that demand for labour can only be forecast with any degree of accuracy in the very short-term and that while most managers will be aware of what their current requirements are, the issue of predicting requirements for the future is far more problematic. Bennison and Casson (1984) comment that:

> The notion that it is possible to estimate future manpower needs, with the precision necessary to match policies of supply, is quite fallacious. Demand is particularly susceptible to changes in the outside world: wars, commodity prices . . . foreign exchange difficulties too can cause problems in managing economies which, in turn, can affect the growth rate of organisations.

However difficult the process, and imprecise the results, some forecasting is required in order that the organisation can make more informed decisions. Sisson and Timperley (1994) suggest that demand forecasting involves determining the general pattern of trading and production, product demand, technology and administrative changes, capital investment plans, market strategies, acquisitions, divestments, mergers, product diversification and centralisation-decentralisation. Coupled with these demand factors, one can also argue that an organisation's demand for labour will also be affected by current legislative provisions; prevailing economic climate, and the range of flexible choices available to organisations (see details on the flexible firm discussed in chapter three). Mayo (1991) further suggests that knowledge of the following aspects of organisational functioning will facilitate improved demand forecasting:

- changes in requirements for management, geographically or in 'new business areas';
- new subsets of the organisation that may be required as the plan progresses, and those that will no longer be required;
- changes in the number of particular types of jobs;
- the knowledge, skills, attitudes and experiences that will be required of particular types of job;
- requirements for joint ventures and collaborative management; and
- changes needed in career structures.

FORECASTING SUPPLY OF LABOUR
Internal Supply
The forecasting of internal labour supply constituted the central preoccupation of human resource planning throughout the 1960s and 1970s and resulted in the development of a number of mathematical models to predict labour attrition in a given time period (Armstrong, 1992). Sisson and Timperley (1994) provide a summary of the various types of models developed:

- 'Renewal' or 'pull' models, where people are assumed to be 'pulled through' as a vacancy occurs through wastage or promotion and where vacancies in any grade are defined by outflows (wastage or promotion).
- 'Linear programming' models for recruitment and deployment.
- 'Camel' models based on assessing promotion chances in a hierarchy, using age distribution and estimates about the future size of the human resource system.
- 'Markov' or 'push' models that are based on predictable wastage patterns that are determined by length of service and an individual's career.

Lundy and Cowling (1996) suggest that such quantitative approaches to the internal supply of human resources have focused on three key supply indices namely wastage, absenteeism and the age profile of the workforce.

Wastage/Labour Turnover
Wastage (or labour turnover) refers to the proportion of an organisation's employees that leave within a specified time period (usually calculated over twelve months) and therefore need replacing in order to maintain a constant number of employee resources in the organisation (Beardwell and Holden 1994). Employees may leave an organisation for many reasons such as better opportunities elsewhere, dissatisfaction with the job, unrealistic job expectations, retirement, redundancy, dismissal and so forth. An ability therefore, to predict labour turnover is an important aspect of human resource planning. It can facilitate the creation of personnel policies that seek to improve retention rates particularly for those employees that the organisation has a vested interest in retaining (i.e. those who are highly skilled or those in whom the organisation has invested considerable training).

Measuring labour turnover is therefore a necessary prelude to planning and remedial action. One of the simplest methods of calculating wastage is through a turnover analysis:

$$\frac{\text{Number of employees who leave in one year}}{\text{Average number employed in the past year}} \times 100 = \%$$

Beardwell and Holden (1994) suggest that a turnover rate of 25 per cent is perfectly respectable in modern large-scale organisations, but that anything approaching 30–35 per cent should give some cause for concern. The turnover index has the advantage of being easy to calculate, and gives some indication of whether losses are high or low. However it is a relatively crude measure, because it does not provide details of the types of employees who are leaving, or in which departments most losses are occurring.

A calculation of the labour stability index can provide additional information about labour turnover. This stability index is calculated as:

$$\frac{\text{Number of employees with more than one year's service}}{\text{Total number employed one year ago}} \times 100 = \%$$

The stability index provides details on whether the organisation is retaining experienced employees since it calculates and emphasises those that stay with the organisation. However, indices alone will not provide specific details on why the organisation is experiencing particular levels of wastage and thus many organisations are adopting the use of the 'exit interview' to help explain turnover. While organisations vary in their design of exit interviews, the purpose of such interviews is to provide details on why an employee has chosen to leave the organisation. It may ask the employee to rate the organisation against a list of predetermined criteria, such as attractiveness of reward package, satisfaction with job, supervisory arrangements and so forth. Combined with turnover and stability indices, the information received from the exit interviews can provide some useful indicators of potential problems with respect to various personnel procedures and practices.

Hill and Trist (1955), in conjunction with the Tavistock Institute (UK), conducted a number of studies of labour turnover and developed what had become known as the 'survival curve' (see figure 4.2). The evidence from their studies suggested that the propensity to quit employment is highest during the early stages of employment but this tapers away as employees settle down in the organisation.

Gunnigle et al 202

Figure 4.2 The survival curve

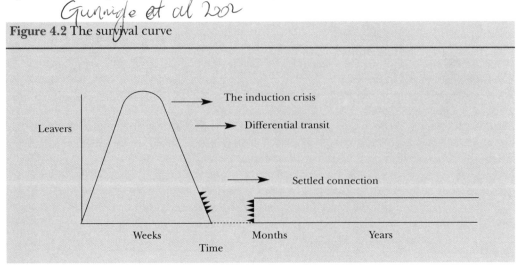

Hill and Trist explained the survival curve in terms of a social process that involves three distinct phases. The first phase they labelled the 'induction crisis' at which time wastage/turnover is very high. Many reasons have been cited for the existence of the induction crisis and generally it is thought to arise because new employees find that the job is not what they imagined it would be; or employees find that they are unhappy with the work environment; or perhaps employees find alternative work elsewhere that is perceived to be more attractive. The period of time covered by the induction crisis can vary considerably between organisations, and between job categories, and, in some cases, can last up to two years. However, it is generally assumed to reach its peak after the first six weeks of employment. The second period is termed the 'differential transit' where, as the employee begins to feel more comfortable in his/her position and settles into company life wastage begins to decrease. The final stage is called 'settled connection' and Hill and Trist (1955) suggest that employees who remain with the organisation for this period of time tend to be viewed as 'quasi-permanent'. At this stage there is a perceived greater incentive in staying with the organisation rather than leaving to go elsewhere. The survival curve is, in many ways, indicative rather than definitive and while it does not take into account personal motivation or career expectations it suggests that there are inherent predictabilities in the process, which allow organisations to forecast wastage with some reliability.

Absenteeism

Forecasting the stock of human resources requires an organisation to gather information on current levels of absenteeism and likely future trends. The Federation of Irish Employers (1980) has defined absenteeism as 'all absence from work other than paid holidays'. Steers and Rhodes (1978) developed a model of employees' attendance that suggests, among other things, that an employee's attendance at work is a function of two particular variables: ability to attend and motivation to attend. Ability to attend is chiefly concerned with illness or some incapacity that prevents an employee from attending work – in most cases this is involuntary absenteeism. Motivation to attend, on the other hand, is explicitly linked with the employee's feelings about the organisation and the job itself, and whether the employee feels a pressure to attend work (see figure 4.3)

Steers and Rhodes found a clear correlation between absenteeism trends and labour turnover trends. Interestingly, when employees are unhappy with their work situation (for whatever reason) and would like to leave but are unable to find alternative work, absenteeism rates tend to increase. However, when alternative work is more readily available, absenteeism rates are less likely to increase but labour turnover becomes more frequent.

At the organisational level information on absenteeism is typically gathered from attendance sheets, time cards, medical records and other personnel files. The most common formula used to calculate absenteeism is as follows:

$$\frac{\text{Total absence (days/hours) in a particular time period}}{\text{Total possible time (days/hours)}} \times 100 = \%$$

This index calculates the percentage of the total time available in a specified period that has been lost because of absence. Cowling and Walters (1990) suggest that there is a significant correlation between the nature of the job and absenteeism, pointing to job satisfaction as an important component of motivation to attend.

It is important, therefore, that organisations maintain accurate records of absenteeism and plot absenteeism on a regular basis to discover any upward trends. High levels of

Figure 4.3 A model of employee absenteeism

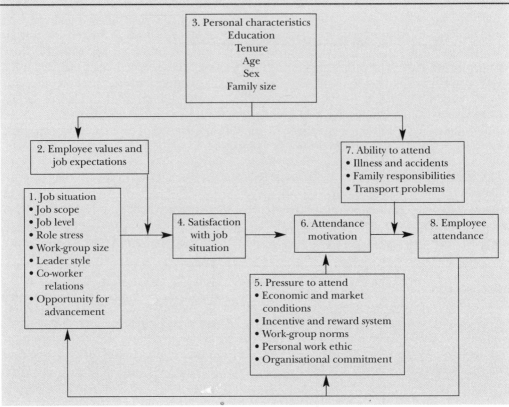

Source: Steers and Rhodes (1978). *Gunnigle et al (2002)*

absenteeism might point to inconsistencies between many of the personnel activities and thus might require an organisation to rethink its strategy. in respect to, for example, selection, supervision, job design, performance appraisal, discipline, rewards and so forth.

Age Analysis

The third supply index that an organisation requires concerns an examination of the age distribution of each category of employee to determine, for example, imminent retirement patterns, plan recruitment policies, and identify career and succession paths for those with future potential within the organisation. Lundy and Cowling (1996) suggest that plotting the age structure of a workforce throws into quick relief whether, for example, a large proportion of employees are reaching retirement age, or whether the cadre of key executives is young and likely to be jostling each other for promotion in the near future.

A predominantly 'mature' age profile would suggest the need for a strong recruitment drive to fill the vacancies left by those about to retire. A predominantly 'middle-aged' workforce might indicate potential (or existing) bottlenecks in the promotion system, which, if unresolved, can create dissatisfaction and possible absenteeism or turnover problems (this can also be a feature of a young age profile). An age distribution that is heavily weighted at the young end and at the 'mature' end might lead to complications in terms of engendering cultural norms and cohesive group dynamics. A balanced mix of ages is, of course the ideal scenario where the organisation can develop and structure its internal labour market around progressive succession planning.

EXTERNAL SUPPLY

Chapter three drew attention to the importance of external labour market trends and the changing demography of the labour force. In terms of human resource planning, the organisation will be particularly interested in, for example, current levels of unemployment (most especially in local geographic area); the changing structure of the workforce and its effects on recruitment and supply (i.e. the increasing propensity to complete third level education leads to fewer young people entering the labour force); the trend towards flexible employment choices with the concomitant increase in female participation rates; and the current levels of education and training provision that determine the skills' mix of the external labour market. All of these factors serve to determine the outcome of the essential 'make or buy' question, that is, is it more effective to source prospective employees outside of the organisation (buy decision) or should the organisation develop its own internal labour market (make decision)? These decisions are made in view of forecasted labour demand, strategic corporate plans and external environmental considerations.

Planning

Once the organisation has forecasted likely demand for, and supply of, labour it can then estimate whether there are any imbalances between the two, that is, whether the organisation is faced with a labour shortage or a labour surplus. Where a shortage exists, or is predicted to occur, the organisation can decide to plan for recruitment or retraining as is appropriate. A labour surplus requires that an organisation make plans for redundancy, redeployment, retraining, or perhaps lay-off or short-time. Regardless of the particular options open to it, the organisation's eventual decision will have consequences for the general nature of employee relations, the structuring of work, the reward package offered, and the structure of its internal labour market. For this reason the organisation needs to carefully weigh the attendant costs and benefits of whichever strategy it decides to employ.

Implementation

On completion of the human resource plans, the organisation operationalises its decision and the cycle is once again set in motion. Since both internal and external environments are subject to considerable change over time, it is advised that human resource plans are monitored and reviewed on a regular basis and amended or redirected as required.

The human resource planning process identifies a range of options that are available to an organisation depending on whether it forecasts a shortage or surplus of labour occurring in the future. The remainder of this chapter explores the process of recruitment and selection as a response to a perceived shortfall in required human resources.

RECRUITMENT AND SELECTION

Terpstra (1996) indicates that, as companies downsize, 'delayer' (reduce hierarchy) and try to boost productivity with fewer people, those that remain are being asked to assume more tasks, roles and responsibilities. He suggests that, as this trend continues, companies will be asking fewer employees to know, do, change and interact more. Thus interest is increasingly focused on identifying the recruiting sources that are most likely to yield high-quality employees and the selection methods that best predict future job performance. Organisations can be said to deal with two different kinds of uncertainty – uncertainty about job demands and uncertainty about candidate's suitability – job analysis seeks to cope with the first while selection deals with the second.

A study commissioned by the CIPD's Recruitment Forum (Kilibarda and Fonda 1997) highlighted a number of common failings in the recruitment and selection process. Included among these failing were:

- No obvious link with HR strategy, resourcing strategy and broader business and organisational goals.
- A lack of job analysis and, therefore, inappropriate job descriptions and person specifications.
- Important details missing from recruitment advertising.
- Little use of referencing for short-listing.
- An unclear use of structured interview design and application.
- An insufficient use of occupational psychology, where psychometric testing is employed, together with a lack of feedback and counselling.
- An increasing use of invalid prediction methods.
- A lack of widespread monitoring and lack of remedial action in those organisations that did monitor recruitment.
- A lack of validation of situation specific selection procedures.

The recruitment and selection process is essentially concerned with finding, assessing and engaging new employees. As such, its focus is on matching the capabilities and inclinations of prospective candidates against the demands and rewards inherent in a given job (Plumbley 1985; Herriot 1989; Heraty *et al.* 1994; Heraty and Morley 1998). Montgomery (1996, 94) highlights this notion of fit as the key to job success:

> Think back in your career and ask yourself, of all the people you know who failed in a job and were terminated, how many of them failed because they lacked the right educational degree, the right job experience, or the right industry background? In all likelihood, most of them failed because of inadequate interpersonal skills, an inability to communicate, or because they just didn't fit in with the culture; in other words – bad chemistry!

Much of the literature on HRM has emphasised the necessity for the recruitment and selection of employees that are committed to the goals of the organisation. It suggest that the profitability and even the survival of an enterprise usually depends upon the calibre of the workforce (Schuler and Jackson 1999; Storey 1992) and that human resources represent a critical means of achieving competitiveness (Prahalad and Hamel 1990; Plumbley 1985). It has been argued that the recruitment and selection decisions are the most important of all decisions that managers have to make since they are a prerequisite to the development of an effective workforce; while the costs of ineffectual commercial viability can often be attributed to decades of ineffective recruitment and selection methods (Russo *et al.* 1995; Redman and Mathews 1995; McMahon 1988; Plumbley 1985; Smith and Robertson 1986; Lewis 1984).

There are two distinct phases involved in this matching process; that of recruitment which is concerned with attracting a group of potential candidates to apply for a given vacancy, followed by selection, which denotes the process of choosing the most suitable candidate from a pool of candidates identified through recruitment. The recruitment and selection process is outlined in figure 4.4.

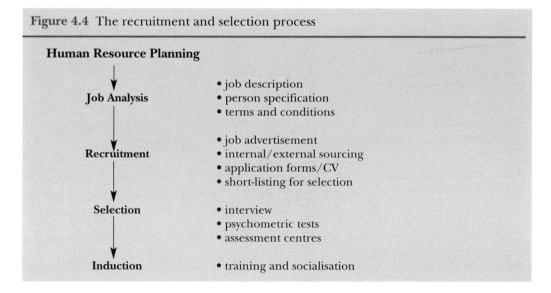

Figure 4.4 The recruitment and selection process

Human Resource Planning

Job Analysis
- job description
- person specification
- terms and conditions

Recruitment
- job advertisement
- internal/external sourcing
- application forms/CV
- short-listing for selection

Selection
- interview
- psychometric tests
- assessment centres

Induction
- training and socialisation

The Job Analysis Phase

When an organisation makes the decision to fill an existing vacancy through recruitment, the first stage in the process involves conducting a comprehensive job analysis. This may already have been conducted through the human resource planning process, particularly where recruitment is a relatively frequent occurrence. Schneider and Schmitt (1986) define job analysis as a means of identifying the human behaviour necessary for adequate job performance; in other words, it provides an indication of the knowledge, skills and abilities (KSAs) about all kinds of work activity. Based on the identification of such behaviours, theories about the kinds of people that the job requires, in terms of knowledge skills and abilities, can be formulated and procedures for the identification of such people can be developed. While a number of different methods of job analysis have been developed over the years, many of which involve considerable statistical modelling, figure 4.5 outlines nine of the most common job analysis techniques that are used in organisations today.

A job analysis has a variety of uses that extends beyond the selection process. Among others, it can be used for promotion and career development purposes, for job transfers, for learning and training programmes, for salary review, for work restructuring and for the introduction of new technology. Once a job analysis has been conducted, the organisation has a clear indication of the particular requirements of the job, and where that job fits into the overall organisational structure. The job analysis then forms the basis for developing three critical recruitment and selection tools namely the *job description*, the *person specification* and the *terms and conditions of employment*.

JOB DESCRIPTION

In the past, there was a tendency to couch job descriptions in vague or loose terms to allow for any changes that may occur in the main job purpose over time. Furthermore, in many organisations, job descriptions were discussed in general terms at the selection interview but were not formally recorded, or written down. This practice has largely dissipated in recent years, particularly since the Terms of Employment Act 1994. The Act requires all employers to furnish their employees with written details of the terms and conditions pertaining to their employment, or to refer such employees to where their job details are

Figure 4.5 Advantages and disadvantages of nine methods of job analysis

1. Questionnaire method

Advantages   Good for producing quantitative information and can produce objective and generalisable results; cheap.

Disadvantages   Substantial sample needed; substantial foreknowledge needed to be able to construct questionnaire; respondents must be able and willing to give accurate replies.

2. Check-list method

Similar to questionnaire method, but, since responses are either 'yes' or 'no', the results may be cruder or require larger sample; they tend to require fewer subjective judgments.

3. Individual interviews

Advantages   Very flexible; can provide detailed information; easy to organise and prepare.

Disadvantages   Time-consuming; expensive; difficult to analyse.

4. Observation interviews

Similar to individual interviews but give additional information, for example visual or auditory information; these contextual clues make it more difficult for the analyst to be misled; the methods may expose both the analyst and the worker to increased safety hazards.

5. Group interviews

Similar to the individual interview but less time-consuming for the analyst, and some claim that richer information is obtained, since interviewees stimulate each other's thought. They are more difficult to organise, and there is the danger that a group is over-influenced by one person.

6. Expert analysis

Advantages   Quick, cheap, and can be used for jobs that do not yet exist. Can avoid restrictive practices.

Disadvantages   The experts may not be true experts, and an unrealistic analysis may result.

7. Diary method

Advantages   Cheap, flexible, and requires little advance preparation. Useful for non-manual tasks, where observation is of limited value. Can also be used in jobs requiring a wide variety of tasks.

Disadvantages   Needs co-operation from respondents; tendency to keep incomplete logs, so frequent but minor items are often omitted.

8. Work participation method

Advantages   Can produce very realistic analyses.

Disadvantages   Expensive, time-consuming, and can only be used for jobs requiring short training and no safety hazards.

9. Critical incident method

Advantages   Focuses on the aspects of a job that are crucial to success.

Disadvantages   Often produces incomplete data that is difficult to analyse.

Source: Smith and Robertson (1993).

specified (i.e. company handbook or notice board). For this reason organisations are paying careful notice to the development of job description that are up-to-date, complete and inclusive of all job requirements. While job descriptions vary according to job classification or type, they typically conform to a set framework (figure 4.6).

Figure 4.6 Elements of a job description

Job title
Department
Location
Reports to
Purpose
Main tasks
Liaison and main contacts
Staff responsibilities
Special features
Rewards and conditions

The job description is essentially a broad statement of the purpose, scope, duties and responsibilities that are attached to the job, and as such are the basis for the contract of employment. Furthermore, since job advertisements normally detail the job description, it is critically important that organisations have a precise understanding of the nature of the job vacancy and that this realistic preview of the job then be used to attract the most suitable candidates. Russo *et al.* (1995) suggest that an effective job description could include information on the following:

- *Job identification:* in particular job title, department, division, company name and location.
- *Relationship with others:* notable vertical relationships (supervision and monitoring) or horizontal relationships (liaison with others, co-operation).
- *Job content:* especially the actual tasks of the job, the level of responsibility of the task, frequencies of performance, the importance of the task.
- *Working conditions:* for instance physical environment (noise, heat), social environment (working in a group, night shift), economic environment (salary, fringe benefits).
- *Performance standards/objectives:* expressed in quantitative terms (i.e. level of output or sales, time limits to me met), or in qualitative terms (i.e. maintenance of a quality standard within a group).
- *Human requirements:* such as physical and psychological characteristics of the job holder/applicant that would comply with the demands of the job (person specification).
- *Other important information:* for example, training and career opportunities, firm's performance in its market (image-related information).

A job analysis can perform a variety of purposes that extend beyond the role remit of recruitment.

PERSON SPECIFICATION

Once the job description has been drawn up, the organisation can then develop a person specification. The person specification is essentially a description of the ideal person that will fit the job and should include details on the qualifications, knowledge, specific skills and aptitudes, experience and personal attributes that are required to do the job effectively. The person specification has a number of very important functions within the recruitment and selection process since, not only does it describe the person required for the job, but it also determines where the organisation should concentrate its search and advertising efforts. It can facilitate systematic short-listing and will form the basis upon which selection criteria are determined. It is therefore of critical importance that the person specification exactly matches the job description so that the most suitable potential job candidates can be attracted for selection.

Since, by their nature, personnel specifications describe the ideal candidate or job holder, it is often advisable to further discriminate between essential characteristics and desirable ones that are required for the job. This process further facilitates the assessment of suitability when the eventual selection is made. Both Rodger (1952) and Munro Fraser (1954) have developed somewhat similar categorisations that are deemed useful for specifying the personal characteristics that can aid effective recruitment and selection. Both of these schemes are detailed in table 4.1.

Table 4.1 Person specification categories

Rodger (1952)
- Physical make-up: physique, health, appearance, speech
- Attainments: education, training, experience
- General intelligence: fundamental intellectual capacity
- Special aptitudes: dexterity, numeracy, verbal, other
- Interests: leisure, intellectual, practical, physical, social, artistic
- Disposition: acceptability, interaction, impact on fellow-workers and management, dependability, stability
- Circumstances: domestic, family, mobility, flexibility

Munro Fraser (1954)
- Impact on others: first impressions, appearance, verbal ability
- Qualifications: education, training, experience
- Innate abilities: comprehension and capacity, conceptual ability, aptitude, intelligence
- Motivation: objectives commitment, ambition, initiative
- Emotional adjustment: coping with stress, working with others

Both of the frameworks outlined here are useful in that they establish general guidelines around which the person specification can be built. However, they are also heavily reliant on personal judgement to determine the kinds of human qualities associated with successful performance and so are neither politically nor socially neutral. The organisation must then take into account the nature of existing equality legislation in order to ensure that the person specification is not discriminatory in any way (this equality legislation is discussed fully in chapter thirteen). Using the frameworks outlined above, figure 4.7 illustrates a sample person specification that might be used for a position as a HR officer in a unionised foreign multinational.

The characteristics specified in figure 4.7 can be weighted if required e.g. for a graduate position, greater importance might be attached to educational attainments and skills rather than work experience, which a graduate might not yet have gained. By attaching weights to the various criteria outlined, the process of eventual selection is facilitated, particularly where two or more candidates appear to be similarly suitable. A clear focus on the job content will indicate the types of behaviours that are required to do the job, and these behaviours can also be weighted to differentiate between candidates.

In summary then, a person specification must meet four particular requirements:

1. It must relate to a particular job and thus closely match the job description.
2. It must be specific and detail exactly what is required to complete the job effectively i.e. 'extensive management experience' gives no indication of the quantity or quality of experience that is deemed necessary for the job.

Figure 4.7 Sample person specification – HR officer

	Essential requirements	Desirable requirements
Education	Degree/diploma in business studies or related discipline	Specialisation in personnel/HRM or training; membership of CIPD
Experience	One's year's experience in computerised HR department with knowledge of selection, reward systems, and training	Two or more years experience at HR/training officer level in a manufacturing environment
Skills	Computer literate in use of excel, access, CBT; interviewing skills; negotiation skills	Knowledge of dedicated HR software packages; French language fluency
Motivation	Ambitious to succeed in HR; commitment to continuous professional development	Ability to motivate and influence others
Disposition/ Circumstances	Outgoing personality; ability to work as team member; adaptable	Flexibility in working patterns; available to travel abroad as required

3. It must allow the organisation to differentiate between individual applicants and so ideally, the specification should be weighted or scaled to facilitate an accurate measurement of individual characteristics.

4. It must allow the organisation to assess whether a candidate meets the specification, i.e. all of the characteristics specified must be capable of being measured and assessed. As an example, many person specifications require individuals who are 'highly motivated' yet motivation is inherently difficult to assess, particularly in an interview. We shall return to this later in the chapter.

TERMS AND CONDITIONS

While often included in the job description, in practice the terms and conditions of employment refer specifically to the effort-reward relationship and so include details on the hours to be worked, methods of payment, job entitlements (holidays, bonuses, allowances) and other attendant benefits. Since terms and conditions are often the most visible attributes of the job, they play an important role in the attraction of suitable candidates. Furthermore, as with person specifications, care must be taken to ensure that the terms and conditions of employment meet the requirement of the various employment law statutes (again, please refer to chapter thirteen for details on relevant employment legislation).

The Recruitment Phase

Once the job analysis stage has been completed, the organisation begins the process of recruitment to attract suitable candidates for the particular vacancy. Anderson and Shackleton (1986) indicate that the quality of new recruits depends upon an organisation's recruitment practices, and that the relative effectiveness of the selection phase is inherently dependent upon the calibre of candidates attracted. Indeed Smith, Gregg and Andrews (1989) argue that the more effectively the recruitment stage is carried out the less important the actual selection process becomes. Recruitment can be seen to have three important functions:

1. To attract a pool of suitable applicants for the vacancy.
2. To deter unsuitable candidates from applying.
3. To create a positive image of the company.

The decision to recruit will normally involve the development of a job advertisement. This job advertisement should include the job description, person specification and details on the terms and conditions of employment. It is probably the most effective tool available, which if completed correctly, can meet the three key objectives outlined above. The advertisement itself should be striking so that it can be noticed and the key information pertaining to the job should dominate so that it will attract those who might be suitable for the position.

Perhaps the most immediate decision facing recruiters is whether to recruit internally from those already employed by the organisation, or to source the external labour market. The decision to access the internal labour market brings with it a number of distinct advantages. It is cost-effective, both in terms of eliminating the need for external advertising or sourcing and also in terms of reducing the induction or settling in period. It is also considered to be good HR practice, as not only may it be viewed as a positive motivator by current employees, but the quality of the internal labour market is continuously upgraded and maintained through high quality recruitment, selection, promotion, career development and multi-skilling. However, the organisation limits its potential range of candidates by limiting its search to the internal labour market, and often, the introduction of 'new blood' can provide a rewarding stimulus and facilitate organisational dynamics.

There are a number of alternative recruitment methods available to an organisation, the more salient of which are described briefly in table 4.2.

Table 4.2 Recruitment methods

Method	Comments	Advantages	Disadvantages
1. Internal: existing employees	Internal advertising may be requirement for some companies under union-negotiated agreements.		
1.1 Self-applicants		Inexpensive, quick. Motivation factor.	Can be indirectly discriminatory. No new talent into company.
1.2 Supervisor/manager recommendations		Know applicant's strengths, weaknesses and behaviour well.	Records of existing and acquired skills and experience need constant updating.
1.3 Succession planning		Training and development already in place, therefore succession smoother.	Information may be subject to bias.

⟶

Table 4.2 Recruitment methods (cont.)

Method	Comments	Advantages	Disadvantages
2. Using existing contacts			
2.1 Unsolicited enquiries	Write-ins, personal enquiries on spec. NB: Should be handled courteously or may affect success of other external methods.	Less expensive. Know applicants are already interested.	Needs system implementation to cope. Need to review 'hold' file after certain period (six months?). May be indirectly discriminatory.
2.2 Previous applicants	Maintain forms of unsuccessful applicants for given period and assess against new vacancies as they arise.	Can enhance company image if handled well. May speed process considerably.	As 2.1.
2.3 Previous employees	Particularly retired, or others leaving to unpaid job (e.g. new mothers or carers for elderly or ill dependants) in the 'would re-employ' category.	By changing terms of employment (especially by increasing flexibility or reducing hours). Could re-attract to part-time, flexible or temporary working to meet peak organisational demands. Known work behaviour.	Inbuilt flexibility requirement for employee not always feasible in given situations. Requirements for peaks of job may be outside remit of person.
2.4 Existing employee contacts	Existing employees encourage family, friends or contacts to apply for vacancies.	Employee may well know others with similar skills, knowledge, and attitudes. May have passed on knowledge of culture and job requirements.	May well be in-directly discriminatory if not combined with other methods. May be 'weaker' employees who recommend, whose attitudes etc. company does not wish to have reinforced through peer recruitment.
3. External contacts			
3.1 Union referrals	Register kept by union of members seeking employment. Usual in some sectors (e.g. printing) where closed shop and/or custom-and-practice arrangements are traditional.	Confidence in skills. Cost.	Indirectly discriminatory. Overlooks those in work.

$\longrightarrow$

Table 4.2 Recruitment methods (cont.)

Method	Comments	Advantages	Disadvantages
3.2 Professional referrals	Registers as above, particularly for professions, e.g. lawyers, doctors, accountants, engineers, linguists.	As 3.1.	As 3.1.
3.3 Employment exchange	Government provision. Network covering most towns and cities, acting as agents for and employees. Particularly concerned with manual and junior positions.	Variety of free services, which can be provided at national level. Speed. Perceived as potential employers service within a secure, non-profit-making framework. Extremely valuable if effort made to cultivate contact.	Unemployed rather than employed are registered, reinforcing labour exchange stereotype. As socially responsible with all agencies, results reflect quality of job description supplied.
3.4 Out-placement consultants	Providing practical help to redundant employees, enforced early retirees, etc.	Actively seeking to place, and may provide training required.	Available when recruitment needs reduce, and vice versa, reflecting economic situation.
3.5 Private selection consultants—local	Deal mainly with clerical, junior administration, shop staff, etc.	Reduce administration for employer. 'Normal' method in many places.	Employer pays for recruits. No guarantee against recruit leaving quickly. Some poor practice has led to employer distrust on occasions.
3.6 Management selection	Usually recruitment plus initial stages of selection of managerial, professional and specialist staff.	Specialist knowledge, objectivity, selection skills (especially when unusual recruitment need for company).	Payment by employer. May lack cultural awareness of company. Exclusion of internal applicants.
3.7 Search consultants ('headhunters')	Informal network of contacts keeping track of those likely to be in constant demand, especially senior management. Promising candidates sought out and approached directly.	Possibility of joining can be discussed without commitment. Concentrates on those in employment.	Potential candidates outside head-hunters network excluded. Recruit may be headhunted again by same consultant! Cost (because labour intensive).
3.8 Schools and career service	Guidance and some testing of young people under 18. In-depth knowledge of potential applicants.	Useful source of 'raw' recruits to be developed by the company. Can assist in image enhancement. Cost.	Some 'guidance' of higher quality than other methods. Possibility of indirect discrimination if recruitment concentrated on one or two institutions.

Table 4.2 Recruitment methods (cont.)

Method	Comments	Advantages	Disadvantages
3.9 Colleges	Recruitment of college leavers after conclusion of variety of courses. Tendency to recruit in local colleges in catchment area.	Work experience placements offer opportunity to preview. Increased employer impact on training provided, which can be very work-specific.	Tends to be once-yearly process. Recruits lack experience. Possible indirect discrimination.
3.10 Universities	Traditional 'milk round' by large national and inter-national employers. Ad hoc enquiries by leavers. Frequently appointment boards provide full-time careers advisory service.	Can build strong relationship with those offering specialisms, prestige, etc. Sandwich and other work placements offer opportunity to preview potential.	Travel and accommodation costs can be high. Takes recruiters away from company for long periods.
3.11 Government training schemes	Government-funded initiatives aimed at specific skill shortages and/or disadvantaged groups.	Many skills provided at Government cost can be integrated with on-the-job experience. Opportunity to preview before offering permanent employment. Financial incentives.	Perception of 'cheap labour' can reduce company image unless well managed. Administration heavy. Training commit-ment required.
3.12 Temporary agencies	Provision of short-or longer-term cover (an alternative to recruiting permanent employees).	Provide cover for coping with unexpected absence (e.g. illness), peaks in work loads, one-off or temporary requirement for skills (installation of new, specialist machinery), or transitional developments in work organisation.	Time scale often makes integration into company culture difficult. Quality can vary. Cost.
4. Advertising, media	An overlap between advertising and previous methods discussed frequently exists. Recruitment agencies can provide external expertise.		Essential for monitoring cost-effectiveness.
4.1 Press	Local and national papers, trade and professional journals.	Expensive, especially television and national press. Must be aimed at identified groups.	Only reach those using that medium.

→

Table 4.2 Recruitment methods (cont.)

Method	Comments	Advantages	Disadvantages
4.2 Television	Includes teletext (Aertel) and view-data (Minitel).	Can provide non-recruitment advantages through increased customer awareness. Sound and vision used.	
4.3 Radio	Local, occasional national broadcasts.	Cheaper than television.	
4.4 Cinema		May be useful for 17 to 25-year-old groups, where several recruits needed; targets likely to have some prior knowledge.	

Source: Beardwell and Holden (1994).

The choice of recruitment method is often determined by the nature of the position being advertised and whether the skills required for the job are in short supply or otherwise. Thus, for entry-level jobs, for example, it may be sufficient to advertise in local papers or to allow news of the position to be spread by word-of-mouth. However, where the position requires considerable experience and/or qualifications of a particular type, the organisation might have to consider recruitment at national level or beyond, through the newspaper media, trade and professional journals, or employ the services of recruitment agencies or consultants.

Concomitant with decisions on the choice of recruitment method, the organisation must take account of the application process for vacancies. The most common methods involve the application form or the curriculum vitae (CV). The CV is probably the most common method of job application and it generally tends to conform to a set standard: name, contact address, contact telephone number/email, education and achievements, employment history, professional associations and references. Most CVs are accompanied by a covering letter that seeks to 'sell' the applicant's suitability for the position. Increasingly, however, organisations are developing in-house application forms that seek to elicit job specific information in a uniform fashion that can enable comparisons to be made between separate applications. Application forms elicit much the same information as is generally presented in a CV, but they also require the applicant to supply additional information in support of his/her application. In practical terms this requires the applicant to again 'sell' his/her skills and highlight the positive contribution he/she could make to the organisation. Also of increasing significance in the recruitment arena is *e-recruiting*.

E-RECRUITING

In an *Irish Times* special feature on web recruitment (McMahon 2001) it was estimated that over 300 million people are now online worldwide and that close to one million people in Ireland are online. If we consider that the Internet is a very recent phenomenon – it only dates back to the late 1980s – it is easy to see that its use will become an ever more pervasive feature of everyday life, which will inevitably change the way individuals and organisations do business. Already we are seeing evidence of this in the recruitment sphere. Thomas and Ray (2000) comment that recent strong economic growth in many countries has produced a demand for both a quality and quantity of employees that local or regional labour markets have not been able to satisfy. For many companies, online recruiting has represented one response to their staffing challenge and they are seeking to utilise one or more of the major techniques available to them for recruitment purposes: general commercial sites, specialised job sites, chat rooms or newsgroups and company websites.

- *General job sites* are commercial, all purpose sites such as www.monster.com or www.careermosaic.com worldwide or www.irishjobs.ie or www.jobfinder.ie – these services are often offered free to applicants but charge employers a fee, depending on the type of subscription.
- *Specialised job sites* come in many forms (e.g. www.jobtrack.com) and can include newspaper classified ads reproduced on the websites (i.e. the *Irish Times*), or professional associations can host their own careers pages or vacancy slots (the Academy of Management in the US regularly advertises lectureship/research positions).
- *Chatrooms and newsgroups* vary considerably and allow a ready access to a specialist audience i.e. HRNet which is a newsgroup for HR professionals.
- A *company web page* uses the firm's own web page as a recruiting tool – here the marginal costs are low and the company can control the content and provide any amount of information it feels is relevant to attract candidates. One downside is that only those who are already familiar with the company name or what it stands for (brand) are likely to be viewing the jobs pages.

It is suggested (Internet Business Network, 1999) that many visitors (up to two thirds) to commercial job sites are not actively seeking employment, but that individuals who actively seek out company websites are more likely to be actively seeking jobs.

For the most part, convenience and speed are the two distinct advantages offered by the Internet. E-recruiting lowers recruiting costs and levels the playing field. Menagh (1999) suggest that e-recruiting may cost less than half that of conventional advertising; it is faster and reaches more applicants than more conventional forms of recruitment. However, it does require that other organisational systems be in place to support it (i.e. to screen and short-list applications efficiently).

Those attracted to the net tend to be relatively well educated and computer literate (Thomas and Ray 2000) and so e-recruitment is particularly useful for graduate recruitment. However, e-recruiting has a limited ability to attract some types of job seekers i.e. it might not be able to target, for example, the local labour market or those with no Internet access. That said, McMahon (2001) reports the following figures for Ireland:

- The Marlborough Group has more than 2000 jobs posted on its website at any one time and can update its site daily.
- Calibre Consultants claims that 95 per cent of the CVs it receives now arrive by email.

- Richmond Recruitment estimate that three quarters of IT appointments arrive via the Internet.
- A survey by Una Mann at DIT suggests that the high-tech sector is the greatest user of Internet advertising in Ireland, with the financial services and services sectors next.

SCREENING AND SHORT-LISTING

Once applications have been received, organisations must devise means of analysing their contents and suitability for selection. In this respect the person specification becomes an invaluable tool for identifying suitable and unsuitable applicants. Dale (1995) suggests that there is an inherent tendency to compare applicants against each other rather than against the job requirements, and the biases and heuristics of the short-lister provide the underlying rationale that determines suitability. Using the example of a vacancy for an office manager, she identifies a short-listing matrix, based on the person specification, that can facilitate more informed decisions (see table 4.3).

Table 4.3 Short-listing matrix for position of office manager

Criteria	Candidate			
	1	2	3	4
Attainment				
Successful completion of further education course	Yes	Yes	Yes	Yes
Some job-related management training	Yes	No evidence	No evidence	Yes
Experience				
IT office applications	No evidence	Yes	No evidence	Yes
Customer service	Yes	Yes	Yes	Yes
Staff training and supervision	Yes	No evidence	No evidence	Yes
Record maintenance	No evidence	Yes	Yes	Yes
Abilities				
Communication skills	Untidy application	Yes	Application badly produced	Yes
Leadership skills	Trainer with no supervisory responsibilities	No evidence	No evidence	Yes
Planning and organisation	Poor organisation of information on form	No evidence	Application badly produced	?
Training and instructional skills	Yes	No evidence	No evidence	Yes

→

Table 4.3 Short-listing matrix for position of office manager (cont.)

Criteria	Candidate			
Aptitudes				
Customer-focused	No evidence	Yes	No evidence	Yes
Accuracy	No evidence	?	Application badly produced	Yes
Concern for quality	Untidy application	Yes	Application badly produced	Yes
Interests				
Involved with people	Yes	Solitary interests	No evidence	Yes
Learning and self-development	No evidence	Yes	No evidence	Yes

Source: Dale (1995).

The matrix can be used as a means of eliminating applicants who fail to achieve the minimum essential criteria as set down in the job description. Individuals are scored according to how well they meet the particular job and behavioural requirements (rather than on how they appeal to the individual doing the short list) and those that score lowest are dropped from the process. The short-listing matrix will only work effectively where there is a well-detailed, measurable job description – incomplete or inaccurate information will render the process largely redundant. Those that score high on the short-listing matrix are deemed more likely to be suitable and they can then be progressed to the next phase i.e. selection.

The Selection Phase

While the calibre of candidate is determined by the value of the recruitment process, the selection decision remains a difficult one. Dale (1995) proposes that:

> Most mistakes are caused by the fact that managers generally give little thought to the critical nature of the decisions. Employers are surprised and disappointed when an appointment fails, and often the person appointed is blamed rather than recognising the weaknesses in the process and methodology . . . even the soundest of techniques and best practice (in selection) contain scope for error. Some of this is due to the methods themselves, but the main source is the frailty of the human decision-makers.

There are a number of alternative selection techniques that can be used to determine the suitability of a job applicant. Before these are discussed however, it is important to understand terms such as 'suitability', 'validity' and 'reliability' as they apply to the selection decision.

Suitability is largely determined by the nature of the job and the responsibilities that are attached to it and how well the candidate's knowledge, skills and abilities match these job requirements (Adkins *et al.* 1994). While the job description and person specification will largely determine specific job criteria, one can distinguish four generic criteria that can help to evaluate the relative suitability of an applicant.

1. The organisation requires an individual who has the capacity to perform the tasks associated with a position to an acceptable standard. Previous work experience, educational attainments, and the skills' profile of the applicant will all provide a reasonable indication of work ability.

2. The organisation requires an individual who has the ability to develop new knowledge and skills and can 'grow' with the job. Increasingly, as the nature of work changes and becomes more demanding, there is a strong orientation towards continuous development and competency upgrading. An individual's previous history of skills' development and educational and training records can provide some useful indicators in this respect.

3. The organisation requires an individual who will 'fit' into the organisation's culture and has the capacity to work effectively within its structures and systems. The extent to which an individual will 'fit' into the organisation is largely indeterminable, but some inference may be drawn from experiences in previous work environments and a determination of his/her ambitions and expectations.

4. The organisation requires an individual who will work productively, is intrinsically motivated and can establish co-operative relationships with other workers. While past behaviour is not the most reliable predictor of future intent, organisations typically conduct reference checks to establish some idea of previous work behaviour.

Validity, in terms of the selection decision, refers to the extent to which the selection method used, measures what it is supposed to measure. Thus, can the organisation be assured (in so far as is possible) that there are no intervening factors or biases that are distorting the result that has been achieved. Reliability, on the other hand, refers to whether the same selection decision reached would again be reached if other individuals made it, i.e. that it is consistent. To illustrate the relevance of both validity and reliability it is useful to use the example of the selection interview. If the interview is a valid selection technique then it should predict, with a high degree of accuracy, the expected work behaviour of a job applicant (validity). Were it a reliable selection technique then, regardless of who makes the selection decision, the end result will be the same, i.e. if five managers were independently asked to interview a number of candidates, they would all choose the same candidate.

There are a considerable number of alternative techniques available that can aid the selection decision and research studies completed on the reliability, validity and utility of these different methods (Gatewood and Fields 1998; Terpstra *et al.* 1999). Gilliland (1993) suggests the use of organisational justice theory as a means of understanding applicants' reactions to selection procedures and proposes that four procedural justice dimensions may form the basis for fairness reactions:

1. Perceived job relatedness
2. Opportunity to demonstrate one's ability
3. Interpersonal treatment
4. The propriety of the questions

Studies have found that the predictive validity of the structured interview is quite high (Campion *et al.* 1988; Weisner and Cronshaw 1988); that cognitive ability tests are among the most valid predictors available to organisations; that work samples and assessment centres are highly valid selection devices (Hunter and Hunter 1984; Reilly and Warech

1993). The sole selection device that appears to have limited usefulness is the unstructured interview. Selection affects the emergence of a psychological contract between employees and organisations, therefore organisations should be just as much concerned with the social validity of a selection method (its acceptability to the candidate) as with its predictive ability.

Newell (2000) cautions that while attempts have been made to improve the selection process through developing a more systematic approach, it could be argued that some of the current trends in organisations (with their emphasis on sharing and creating knowledge) make the 'best practices' model somewhat problematic. She particular notes that:

- Best practices associated with a thorough job analysis and person specification may be difficult or inappropriate particularly where the job requires flexibility and there is no fixed job role *per se*.
- Best practice tends to highlight the importance of 'fit' with the current organisational culture, yet many jobs call for innovative and creative individuals – this may be counter to the prevailing culture.
- Issues surrounding diversity should be taken into account in terms of the selection techniques applied, to ensure no disadvantage to particular groups of individuals.

Individuals tend to assume that a device that is widely used must be valid and it is perhaps for this reason that the interview continues to enjoy considerable popularity across organisations. For many jobs, organisations utilise a series of interviews ranging from the initial meeting through to the second and often third interview. While interviews can be conducted either on a one-to-one basis, or be panel based, the principles underpinning effective interviewing apply to both (these are discussed in the following pages). Anderson and Shackleton (1993) provide an interesting comparison of some of the more commonly used selection techniques (see tables 4.4 and 4.5). However, they describe the selection

Table 4.4 Different functions of the interview

Interview function	Appropriate stage in selection procedure	Interview functioning	Interviewer's objectives	Interviewee's objectives
1. Mutual preview	Phase I/II. Early stages of selection procedure probably following initial screening of written applications but preceding administration of main assessment techniques.	Informal, open-ended discussion to explain selection procedures and to offer career guidance counselling to interviewee by providing detailed and realistic job preview (RJP).	• To meet and 'set the scene' for applicant. • To inform applicants of company's selection procedure.	• To establish what will be involved at each stage in selection procedure. • To visit company 'on site'. • To obtain preview of job to allow self-assessment and self-selection.
2. Assessment	Phase II, one of a battery of candidate assessment techniques.	Formal, structured interaction guided by detailed job analysis and pre-formulated strategy.	• To record answers to critical incident-type questions. • To probe and feed back results of other selection methods (particularly testing).	• To survive! • To obtain feedback and ensure accuracy of results of other methods.

Table 4.4 Different functions of the interview (cont.)

| 3. Negotiation | Phase III. Final stage of selection procedure, immediately before, or after, offer of employment has been made. | Negotiation of outstanding points of difference, both interviewer and interviewee-directed and led. | • To ensure acceptance of job offer.
• To facilitate job role transition.
• To identify follow-up personnel procedures. | • To discuss contractual and non-contractual terms and conditions.
• To facilitate job role transition.
• To initiate the job change process. |

Source: Anderson and Shackleton (1993).

Table 4.5 Main techniques of candidate assessment

Technique	Description	'Fit' with interview	Contribution to selection system
Psychometric testing	Standardised test of performance attitudes or personality. Major types: • cognitive ability • personality • attitudes and values • career choice and guidance	Can precede or follow interview stage. Results can form basis of further interview questions, or interview can be used to feed back test results. Personality tests are particularly useful in this respect and can facilitate probing questions at interview.	*Ability tests* • High predictive accuracy for aspects of cognitive ability. • 'Normed' results allow candidate to be compared with many similar people. Longer-term relevance, i.e. job role may change over time; ability remains relatively constant. *Personality tests* • Indications of interpersonal or managerial style that can be followed up at interview and/or compared with exercises in an AC. • 'Faking' scales built in to tests may detect high level of impression management and biasing of self-presentation.
Work examples	Pre-designed and constructed samples of work performance designed to tap aspects of critical job performance usually monitored and observed by trained experts, who rate candidates on job-relevant dimensions.	Usually following initial interview and often conducted as part of an AC. Can therefore provide dynamic and highly job-relevant data for discussion at follow-up interview stage.	• High predictive accuracy. Directly relevant job tasks as samples of future behaviour. • Rated by observers on critical dimensions of job performance, sometimes identical to those used for staff appraisal. • If constructed properly can add a sample of directly relevant candidate behaviour on segments of the job itself. →

Table 4.5 Main techniques of candidate assessment (cont.)

Technique	Description	'Fit' with interview	Contribution to selection system
Assessment centres (ACs)	Multiple-method design, usually incorporating testing, interviews, and work sample exercises, where candidates are tested by observers on job-relevant dimensions. Can last from one to five days.	Usually the final stage of assessment to reach outcome decisions. Because of cost of running ACs interviews usually conducted as integral part of an AC.	• All the above, as well as: • Opportunity to observe candidates over longer period in formal and informal situations. • Multiple assessments by several assessors over several exercises can eliminate some individual biases associated with one-to-one interviews (see chapter 3).
Reference letter	Varies from very brief factual check (e.g. 'Did candidate hold this position between these dates, as claimed?') to extensive rating of abilities, personality, and attitude to work.	Commonly used as final check on candidate after conditional offer of employment has been made. Interview can throw up specific issues to be checked with previous employers by reference letter.	• Best used as factual check only. • Most appropriate as final check: references taken up with existing employer before offer of employment will not be popular with candidates!

Source: Anderson and Shackleton (1993).

interview separately since the interview forms the basis of almost all selection decisions, and they suggest that the techniques outlined in table 4.5 should, in fact, be used to augment the interview decision.

THE EFFICIENCY OF THE SELECTION INTERVIEW

Over the years considerable research concerning both the validity and reliability of the selection interview have been undertaken, often with conflicting results (Anderson 1992; Hunter and Hunter 1984; Wiesner and Cronshaw 1988). In reviewing this body of research, Anderson and Shackleton (1993) suggest that, in terms of validity and reliability, the overall efficiency of selection interview decisions has, in fact, been much maligned in recent years and they highlight a number of points that merit attention.

- Interviews can be much more accurate than many recruiters may believe.
- Structured interviews that are built around a pre-planned format are more valid and reliable than unstructured, non-directed conversations (Wiesner and Cronshaw 1988).
- Interviews are significantly more accurate if based upon detailed job analysis techniques, where the interview decision reached is based on the application of both the job description and person specification.

- The interview is an appropriate and fairly reliable method for assessing job-relevant social skills (Wagner 1949; Avery *et al.* 1987).
- Interviewer accuracy varies and recruitment decisions should always be validated, that is, that interviewers should check their decisions against subsequent job performance.

Errors and Biases in Selection

While the central question of whether 'interviewers are born, not made' remains unanswered, there is considerable evidence to suggest that the process of interviewing is, all too often, subject to a number of underlying biases and errors that adversely affect the selection decision (Anderson and Shackleton 1993; Wareing and Stockdale 1987; Macon and Dipboye 1988; Anderson 1992; Dale 1995). While it is untrue to suggest that all interviews are biased or error-prone, based on existing research Anderson and Shackleton (1993) have classified some of the more common errors and biases, a number of which are considered below.

- Expectancy effect – interviewers can form either a positive or negative impression of a candidate based on the biographical information from the application form/CV and this tends to have a bearing on all subsequent decisions (often termed gut instinct or snap decision).
- Information seeking bias – based on their initial expectations, interviewers can actively seek information that will confirm this initial expectation.
- Primacy effect – interviewers may form impressions about a candidate's personality within the first five minutes of meeting him/her and tend to be more influenced by what is said early in the interview.
- Stereotyping – stereotypes can often be ascribed to particular groups of individuals and can occur based on gender, race, family circumstances, and are in contradiction of the current equality legislation.
- Horns/halo effect – based on information received an interviewer may rate a candidate either universally favourably or universally unfavourably. Furthermore, negative information tends to be more influential than positive information, and thus, even where there is a balance between positive and negative information, the overall impression will tend to be negative.
- Contrast and quota effects – interviewer decisions can be inherently affected by decisions made about earlier candidates, and pre-set selection quotas. Thus, where a number of candidates have been selected for interview, those who are interviewed later are invariably compared with those who went before them (rather then being assessed specifically against pre-determined criteria).

However rigorous the process, interviewing remains essentially a selective process and thus the interviewer needs to ensure that, as far as is possible, the errors or biases described above are eliminated from the process. The operation of panel interviews or successive interviews can obviate many of the inherent problems associated with interviewing and can facilitate greater validity and reliability in the final decision analysis. Furthermore, attention to effective interpersonal interaction such as active listening and attendant non-verbal behaviour; competent questioning; and a facilitative interview environment (free from noise and other distractions) can further ensure that the interview is as productive as possible. Evenden and Anderson (1992) suggest that the choice of questions, and appropriate use of them can ensure greater balance and flow to the interview itself (see table 4.6).

Table 4.6 Types of interview questions

1. **Direct or closed**
These have the effect of yielding short answers such as 'yes,' 'no,' or 'sometimes': 'How did you travel?'

2. **Leading**
These lead the interviewee to give the answer the interviewer expects or wants to hear: 'We are always in flux. You do like change, don't you?'

3. **Topic-changing**
Moving the interview on to a new topic: 'Thanks for the information on your qualifications. Would you tell me how you chose your career route?'

4. **Probing and developing**
These enquire more fully into an area, or encourage building on an answer already given: 'Why did you say you prefer jobs that involve travel?'

5. **Open-ended**
These encourage full answers: 'Would you tell me about how you spend your leisure time?' 'Why did you apply for this particular job?'

6. **Reflecting back**
Reflecting back to the person what they have said by restating their reply: 'Promotion is very important to you, then?' 'Are you saying you're frightened by computers?'

① They are useful for the purpose of getting facts, but too much use leads to a staccato interview, and a short one if the applicant is nervous.

② There is no value in this type of question, unless the interviewers have self-deception in mind. Most interviewees would follow the lead.

③ Necessary to control the move through your plan and your timing. Helpful in creating a smooth flow in the interview.

④ Very important in seeking evidence and testing the interviewee's knowledge, experience, feelings and attitudes.

⑤ The interviewee is given the opportunity to answer at length and to choose what to select to talk about. Very useful in getting the person talking and involved in the interview. Good for shy people if allied to gentle persistence.

⑥ These are important in making sure that your understanding is clear and accurate. It also shows that you are listening and interested in what the interviewee is saying.

Source: Evenden and Anderson (1992).

Testing

The use of selection tests can be used to improve the validity and reliability of the selection process, but are not used alone. Rather they tend to be used in tandem with other selection techniques, such as the interview. While a range of tests is available, the most commonly used tests, for selection purposes, include cognitive ability tests, personality tests, and performance or work sample tests. A range of cognitive tests has been designed and standardised; they are primarily used to measure an applicant's capability to perform a job (i.e. measure mathematical reasoning for IT software/programming jobs) and they have a fairly high predictive ability. Personality tests are designed to measure personality dimensions such as extroversion, conscientiousness, emotional stability, openness to new experiences and ability to get on with others and while some have high predictive ability, over-reliance on their outcomes is not advised. Performance or work sample tests require job applicants to perform some of the tasks that make up the job being applied for. They provide a fairly immediate assessment of the skills and abilities of the applicant i.e. computer technician asked to diagnose a problem with a server; an artist asked to provide a portfolio or produce a sketch.

Placement, Induction and Follow-up
When the selection decision is made, a job offer is made to the chosen candidate and the unsuccessful applicants are notified. Where the selection process involved a number of internal applicants, due care should be taken in communicating the selection decision to them, particularly where they have been unsuccessful. A letter of offer can constitute a legally binding document since they usually form part of a legal contract of employment. When the offer has been accepted, it is customary to offer a period of induction for the successful candidate, which is designed to facilitate the smooth transition to work in the organisation. Induction periods vary from company to company and can last as long as three months. It is similarly common to find that the new recruit is 'on probation' for the first three months of employment to determine whether the events work out as expected (this largely depends on the job position).

As discussed earlier in this chapter, labour turnover tends to be highest during the induction period and thus organisations can reduce the induction crisis through a carefully managed socialisation process. This can involve furnishing the new employee with a company manual, explaining the nature of the business in greater detail, outlining the structure and hierarchy of the organisation, and providing a liaison to 'show him/her the ropes' as it were. (Coaching, mentoring, facilitation, training and development, as socialisation techniques are further discussed in chapter nine.) Positive reinforcement and feedback are critical considerations throughout the induction period. They can be facilitated by some form of interim performance appraisal, and can aid in the establishment of behaviour norms that are desired by the organisation.

RECRUITMENT AND SELECTION IN IRELAND
With respect to the current state of play in recruitment and selection in Ireland, the 1999 round of the Cranet E./University of Limerick is instructive. In the survey, questions in the area of recruitment and selection focused on whether respondents were experiencing difficulties in staff recruitment and retention, the methods employed in recruitment and retention, how managerial vacancies were filled and the selection methods most commonly employed.

Turning to issue of difficulties in recruitment and retention, which is an indicator of the current state of the labour market, the 1995 round of the survey reported that some two thirds of Irish organisations had a staff turnover level of 5 per cent or less. The situation is somewhat different in the 1999 survey and is reflected in the number of organisations reporting difficulties in recruitment and retention, as shown in figure 4.8.

Across the employee grades of manual, clerical, professional, information technology and managerial a large number of respondents reported that they were experiencing problems in this area. The most profound difficulties lay in attracting and keeping professional and IT staff, which can be attributed to skills shortages in these areas concomitant with strong growth in the IT sector in Ireland as a result of direct foreign investment.

Figure 4.8 Difficulties in staff recruitment and retention in Ireland

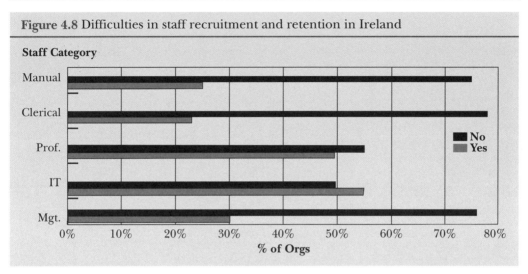

Source: Cranet E./University of Limerick Survey (1999).

In response to the problems of recruitment and retention respondents were asked what methods, if any, they had adopted in relation to this area. The most common method found was to increase pay and benefits, quoted by 56 percent of respondents. Retraining of existing employees was a method adopted by 53 percent of respondents. The impetus for this arguably stemming from either the need to meet the development requirements of employees to aid retention or from the need to look to internal recruitment as a means of filling hard to fill vacancies.

Figure 4.9 Methods adopted in relation to recruitment and retention

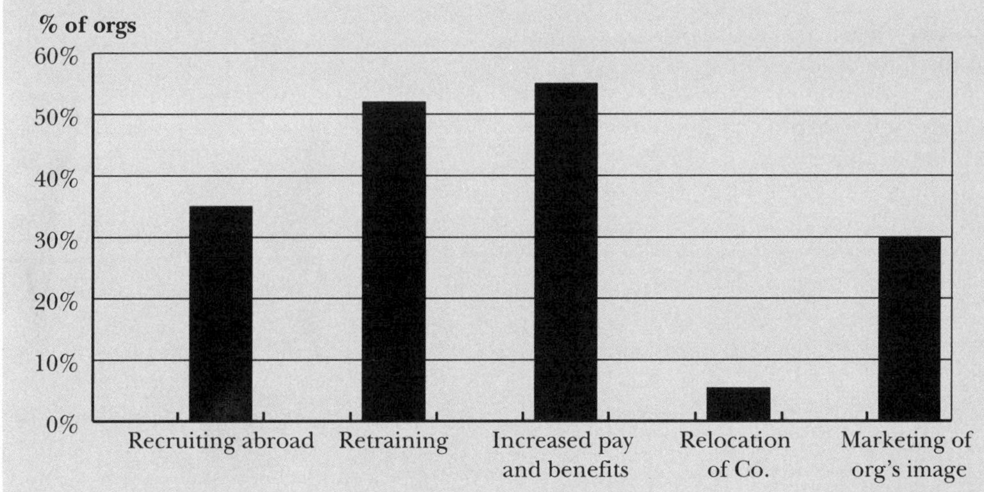

Source: Cranet E./University of Limerick Survey (1999).

The filling of managerial vacancies is an important area of recruitment, and may have significant implications for organisational performance and the managing of human resources within a firm. The 1999 survey found that most Irish organisations chose to recruit internally for all levels of management. However other methods such as recruitment agencies, advertisements etc. are still commonly used, particularly in the recruitment of senior managers (see figure 4.10).

Figure 4.10 Filling of managerial vacancies

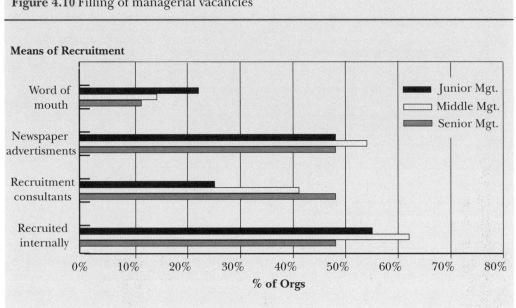

Source: Cranet E./University of Limerick Survey (1999).

As identified earlier, selection tools available to organisations range from the more traditional methods of interviews, application forms and references, through to the more sophisticated techniques such as psychometric tests and assessment centres. The selection methods used can determine whether or not the right person is matched to the right job, which in turn has knock on effects for the firm's performance. Storey (1992) suggests that developments in the realm of selection lend some support to those who propound the HRM thesis, where a major feature has been the increase in testing designed explicitly to assess behavioural and attitudinal characteristics. He further indicates that the extent to which these more sophisticated and systematic approaches can be, and are, deployed, depends to a large degree, on the sector circumstances and on the wider employment-management policies being pursued.

The data generated by the Cranet E./University of Limerick survey indicates that less use is being made of what are considered the more 'sophisticated' selection techniques. The picture emerging from the data suggests that the application form, the interview panel and reference checks are the most commonly used selection methods, while more sophisticated and reliable techniques such as psychometric testing and assessment centres are used in a smaller number of cases. The 1999 data reveals that interview panels, one-to-one interviews and application forms still remain the most popular methods of selection, with application forms being used in every appointment by 56 per cent of respondents. Reference checks are also used by 73 per cent of companies in all appointments (see figure 4.11).

110

Figure 4.11 Selection methods used in Ireland

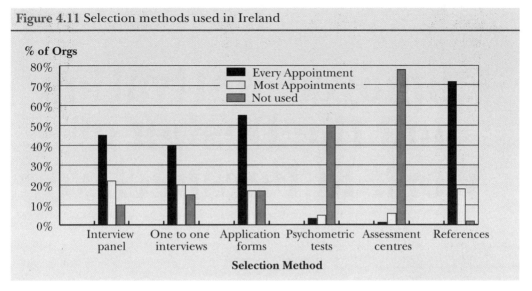

Source: Cranet E./University of Limerick Survey (1999).

This chapter has focused on human resource planning, recruitment and selection. The nature of the human resource planning process in terms of stocktaking, forecasting, planning and implementation was set down and the benefits of engaging in the HR planning process were presented. With respect to the recruitment process, job analysis, and the general advantages and disadvantages attached to it were outlined. The nature of the job description and the person specification were presented and the importance of outlining the terms and conditions attached to the job being recruited for were discussed. The large array of recruitment options available to an organisation and their particular advantages and disadvantages were also presented. The selection options and errors and biases commonly associated with different approaches were set down. Finally, current practices in Ireland as revealed by the 1999–2000 round of the Cranet E./University of Limerick survey were presented.

In this way the chapter has presented a cyclical or processual understanding of the HR planning and recruitment and selection process. However, as with any planning process, the dynamic interplay between all aspects and all pieces of information of the process cannot be underestimated. Indeed, as Newell (2000) has recently highlighted, our traditional understanding of recruitment and person-job fit is being challenged by the dynamic environment now confronting many firms. She notes that:

> The traditional view of selection and assessment presents a very static picture of the job. It underestimates the degree of change within organisations. Jobs continuously change in response to changes in the environment so that the 'square hole' today may well be the round hole next year, requiring very different knowledge, skills and attitudes. This view also presents a static view of the individual. It overestimates the personal criteria that influence job criteria and underestimates the role of situational demands. Recognising the dynamic nature of jobs and the interactions between the individual and the situation is imperative if organisations are going to achieve long-term sustainability within this knowledge-intensive age.

5

Employee Motivation and the Design of Work in Perspective

In 1971 Thomas Fitzgerald, writing in the Harvard Business Review, argued that motivation theory does not work and we should discard the dismal vocabulary of motives, motivators, and motivation and think about becoming a society of persons. His argument was based on the premise that the proposed remedies advanced by prominent motivation theorists were inadequate; because the seriousness of the motivation problem had been underestimated, and in some respects misunderstood; and because the problem of employees' motivation is rooted in certain fundamental conditions of industrial society and its solution requires costly and extensive changes in our interdependent, closely linked systems. Truth, he argued, is sometimes damaged in the process of analysis and reconstruction, and concepts can easily become more real than the reality from which they were cut.

> When transplanted from the laboratory, the language of motivation may become subtly elitist by suggesting that the employee resembles a captive rodent in a training box equipped with leavers, trick doors, food pellets, and electric grids . . . When a man gets up in the morning, we can say that this act is a conditioned response to the stimulus of an alarm, but that doesn't tell us anything important.
>
> Fitzgerald (1971, 12)

Thirty years later, the vocabulary prevails, promulgating concepts such as needs, wants and desires as central aspects of the human condition. However, it is recognised that effective management depends on a knowledge and understanding of human motivation that goes beyond any 'common sense conventional wisdom' (Litwin and Stringer 1968). While motivation, as a concept, is a complex phenomenon, 'frequently used', according to George and Jones (2001), 'but often poorly understood', any management practices that wish to make inroads in this area must be based on systematic knowledge about motivational processes that have *relevance* to the individual and the workplace. Managers confronted with organisational ills such as persistent absenteeism and turnover, low morale, expressed job dissatisfaction, poor job and organisational commitment and unacceptable quality, productivity and performance want, as Herzberg (1968) put it 'the surest and least circumlocuted way of getting someone to do something'.

In this chapter we explore the concept of motivation and examine the relationship between motivational processes and – that other important organisational factor – job design. Linking both motivation and job design helps to establish the important of job context in generating goal directed behaviour and to avoid the mistake that motivation is the only important determinant of work performance (Griffin and McMahan 1994). Definitional aspects of the concept are considered and the scope of motivation is examined. Various content and process theories of motivation are presented and evaluated. The main job design schools of thought are synthesised in an attempt to maximise our understanding of the main issues involved and to give a flavour of the interdependent, symbiotic nature of both motivation and job design as potential mechanisms for the delivery of sustained performance. This is considered important against the backdrop of a situation where, as Martin (2001) notes, 'increasingly the formal design of jobs is being seen as a means of improving levels of employees' motivation, quality and commitment to the objectives of the organisation'.

MOTIVATION: ROLE AND DEFINITION

Motivation at work has been the object of sustained attention since the emergence of industrial society as a result of the industrial revolution. Steers and Porter (1987) advance a number of factors that account for the status of motivation as a crucial point of interest. Firstly, they suggest that managers and organisational researchers cannot avoid a concern for the major behavioural requirements of the organisation. The necessity of attracting the right calibre of employee and engaging them in such a way as to ensure high-performance remains a central concern of the productive process and productive effort. Secondly, they argue that the all-encompassing nature of the concept itself has resulted in it remaining as a central line of inquiry. As a complex phenomenon it impacts upon a large number of factors and any worthwhile understanding of organisations requires a deal of attention to be focused on this collection of factors and how they combine to create certain outcomes. Thirdly, competitive trends of the business environment, coupled with increased business regulation, has forced organisations to seek out any mechanisms which might improve organisational *effectiveness* and *efficiency*. The ability to direct employees' efforts towards these twin goals of effectiveness and efficiency are seen as crucial. A fourth reason for the sustained interest in motivation concerns the issue of technological advancement, which is particularly evident in the job design debate. Organisations must continually ensure that its workforce is capable and willing to use advanced manufacturing technologies to achieve organisational goals. A final reason, according to Steers and Porter, centres on the issue of planning horizons. Taking a longer-term perspective of the human resource in an attempt to build up a pool of well-skilled enthusiastic employees has brought the concept of motivation centrefold. Dessler (2001) highlights that it remains a central plank of current management practice and spans the range of techniques used in building a performance-oriented organisation. These include the use of performance-related pay, merit pay, on the spot rewards, skill-based pay, recognition, job redesign, empowerment, and the use of goal setting methods, of positive reinforcement and life-long learning.

Nevertheless it is an extremely difficult area in which to apply accurate measurement. Furnham (1997, 293) notes that there are major problems in measuring job motivation. Asking people, he notes, is problematic, both because some people find it very difficult to report their motives accurately as they do not have sufficient insight into themselves, as well as the fact that there are pressures put on people to give socially desirable, rather than truthful answers. Furnham suggests that it is equally difficult to try and infer motivation from actual behaviour, 'because although it is true that efficient performance is a function of hard work, it may be impaired by a range of other activities such as the group norm of production, machine breakdown, or the non-delivery of crucial items'. He goes on to note that:

> Measuring job motivation, involvement and commitment is not very problematic in terms of theory. The major problem lies in either people dissimulating their answers (usually lying about how motivated they are to get the job, and demotivated they are on the job) or not being able to report on their motivational patterns accurately. Motivation is complex and many workers are unable to articulate what features of their job are motivating or not.
>
> Furnham (1997, 295)

However, despite such quantification difficulties, or perhaps because of them, motivation remains a central area of inquiry. The study of motivation at work has and continues to be largely based on analysing employees' behaviour at work and thus motivation theory is essentially concerned with explaining why people behave as they do, or why people choose different forms of behaviour in order to achieve different ends.

Figure 5.1 Elements of work motivation

Element	Definition	Example
Direction of Behaviour	Which behaviours does a person choose to perform in an organisation?	Does an engineer take the time and effort to convince sceptical superiors of the need to change the design specifications for a new product to lower production costs?
Level of Effort	How hard does a person work to perform a chosen behaviour?	Does an engineer prepare a report outlining problems with the original specification, or does he/she casually mention the issue when bumping into a supervisor in the hall and hope that the supervisor will take the advice on faith?
Level of Persistence	When faced with obstacles, roadblocks, and stone walls, how hard does a person keep trying to perform a chosen behaviour successfully?	When the supervisor disagrees with the engineer and indicates that a change in specifications is a waste of time, does the engineer persist in trying to get the change implemented or give up despite his/her strong belief in the need for a change?

Source: George and Jones (2001).

Westwood (1992) notes that the concept of motivation is comprised of seven key features.

- It is an internal state experienced by the individual. While it is subject to external contextual influences, an individual's motivational state develops within and is unique to oneself.
- The individual experiences a motivational state in a way that gives rise to a desire, intention or pressure to act.

- Motivation brings with it an element of choice i.e. the individual experiencing a state of arousal as a result of an internal or external stimulus responds through choosing to act in a way and at a level of intensity that they determine.
- Action and performance are, in part, a function of motivation.
- Motivation is a multifaceted phenomenon best characterised as a complex process with multiple elements and the possibility of multiple determinants, options and outcomes.
- Individuals differ in terms of their motivational state and the factors that affect it and the motivational state of an individual is variable across time and situations.

Traditional approaches to employees' motivation have relied heavily on extrinsic factors, particularly pay. However, the motivation of individual employees and perceived job satisfaction will be influenced by a myriad of factors. Some will be related to individual employees and their personal characteristics. Others, such as supervisory relations or discretion, will stem either from the working environment or the job itself.

Figure 5.2 Factors influencing employees' motivation

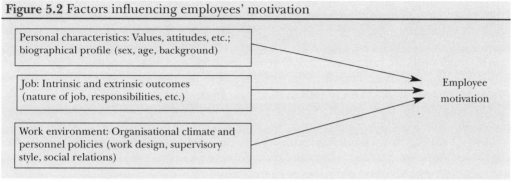

Source: Gunnigle and Flood (1990).

In relation to individual factors, it is important that organisations select employees whose motives and work values 'fit' the organisational environment, management approach and reward package. On the other hand the organisational climate, management style, and design of work should facilitate good performance by providing adequate opportunity for employees to satisfy their varying needs. Management must be keenly aware of the need to motivate employees through both extrinsic and intrinsic outcomes. Extrinsic outcomes are tangible and visible and include things such as a pay increase or a company car. Intrinsic outcomes relate to the satisfaction of personal wants and desires and include elements such as increased autonomy, responsibility and feedback.

However, there is no simple answer to the crucial question: How do you motivate people? Herzberg (1968), perhaps best demonstrates the complexity attached to this question:

> What is the simplest, surest, and most direct way of getting someone to do something? Ask him? But if he responds that he does not want to do it, then that calls for a psychological consultation to determine the reason for his obstinacy. Tell him? His response shows that he does not understand you, and now an expert in communication methods has to be brought in to show you how to get through to him. Give him a monetary incentive? I do not need to remind the reader of the complexity and difficulty involved in setting up and administering an incentive system. Show him? This means a costly training programme.

This remains a vital area of inquiry in an attempt to achieve and maintain high levels of motivation, especially in competitive industry, primarily because, according to Pettinger (1994),

> There is a correlation between organisations that go to a lot of trouble to motivate their staff, and profitable business performance . . . The ability to gain the commitment and motivation of staff in organisations has been recognised as important in certain sectors of the business sphere. It is now more universally accepted as a critical business and organisational activity, and one that has highly profitable returns and implications for the extent of the returns on investment that is made in the human resource.

The word motivation was originally derived from the Latin word *movere* meaning to move. Modern interpretation of motivation is somewhat more all encompassing, expressing various understandings about how we view people and organisations. Thus while Vroom (1964) conceptualises of motivation as a process governing choices made by persons or lower organisms among alternative forms of voluntary activity, DuBrin (1978) suggests that motivation centres on the expenditure of effort toward achieving an objective the organisation wants accomplished. Arnold *et al.* (1995), using a mechanical analogy, suggest that the motive force gets a machine started and keeps it going and argue that motivation concerns the factors that push or pull us to behave in certain ways. Bennet (1991) suggests that an employee's motivation to work consists of all the drives, forces and influences – conscious or unconscious – which cause the employee to want to achieve certain aims.

Most of the early work on motivation was centred around getting more out of the employee, although many of the theorists were also concerned with finding an answer to the problem that was consistent with the essential dignity and independence of the individual. Motivation theory bases its analysis of employees' performance on how work and its rewards satisfy individual employees' needs. Numerous theories have been developed over the years to aid management in identifying employees' motives and needs, the most influential of which will be discussed here.

The study of motivation at work has been based on analysing employees' behaviour at work. People react in different ways to different stimuli and various theories of employees' motivation at work seek to identify factors that induce good or bad performance and suggest how management might apply these effectively at organisational level. Here we briefly examine some of the more influential theories on employees' motivation and work design and evaluate their application in practice.

Motivation theory bases its analysis of worker performance on how work and its rewards satisfy the individual employees' needs. The general conclusion is that if these needs are satisfied employees will be motivated to work at high-performance levels but, if not, their performance will be less than satisfactory. Of course motivation is only one factor affecting performance. Other factors, particularly technology, training, and individual ability, will have a major influence on performance levels.

A central management concern is how to get employees to perform at the height of their abilities. If this can be achieved, management will have gone a long way towards creating a successful organisation. The understanding of human needs at work and the creation of a working environment that satisfies those needs is a key task of senior management.

When discussing motivation theory, it is useful to distinguish between content and process models of motivation as they differ in their relative focus. Content models focus on the wants and needs that individuals are trying to satisfy or achieve within the situation, or *what* motivates human behaviour. They are dedicated to an exploration of individual needs, wants, desires and aspirations. The content approaches discussed here are the *hierarchy of needs theory, ERG theory, acquired needs theory* and *dual-factor theory*. Process models attempt to show how the external context drives individuals to behave in a particular fashion and on how managers can change the situation to better link need satisfaction to performance, or *how* the content of motivation influences behaviour. The process approaches discussed here are *theory X, theory Y, expectancy theory* and *equity theory*.

Maslow's Hierarchy of Needs

Maslow, who was a clinical psychologist, suggested that human motivation was dependent on the desire to satisfy various levels of needs. Maslow's *hierarchy of needs* is perhaps the most publicised theory of motivation. It seeks to explain different types and levels of motivation, which are important to individuals at different times. It is based on the principle of the existence of a series of needs that range from basic instinctive needs for sustenance and security to higher-order needs, such as self-esteem and the need for self-actualisation. Lower-order or fundamental needs, according to this theory, must be satisfied before higher-order needs can be set in motion and dealt with.

Figure 5.3 Maslow's Hierarchy of Needs

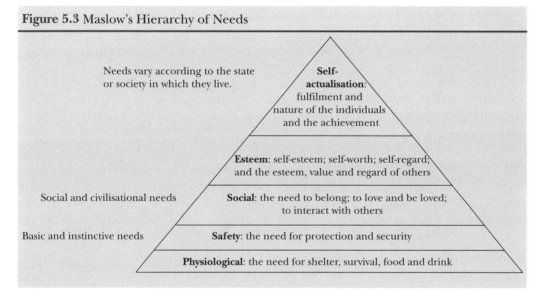

Source: Maslow (1943).

Maslow suggests that there are five levels of needs, ranked in the order shown, as this is the order in which they will likely be activated by the individual in order to satisfy them. The chronological order of needs from the lowest to the highest order is important. Firstly it suggests that it is the next unachieved level that acts as the prime motivator. Thus people without the basic necessities of life such as food and shelter will be motivated by basic physiological and, later, security needs. Only when these have been satisfied will higher-order needs become important. And, then, only when all the lower-order needs are satisfied, do higher level needs act as a motivator – first esteem needs and ultimately self-actualisation.

The second inference arising from this ascending order of needs is that once a particular needs' category is satisfied it ceases to have a major impact on motivation. Thus any level of needs only motivates while it remains unachieved. Once achieved it is the next level in the hierarchy that dominates the individual's priorities.

Physiological needs include such elements as food, shelter, clothing and heat. These basis needs must be satisfied for the person to survive. In modern society it is employment and the income it generates that allows the individual to satisfy such needs.

Safety needs refer to things such as security at home, tenure at work and protection against reduced living standards. Only when physiological needs have been satisfied will the individual concentrate on safety needs.

Social or love needs refer to people's desire for affection and the need to feel wanted. Our need for association, for acceptance by others and for friendship, companionship and love might also be included here.

Esteem needs cover one's desire for self-esteem and self-confidence and also one's need for recognition, authority and influence over others. Self-actualisation refers to the need for self-fulfilment, self-realisation, personal development and fulfilment of the creative faculties (see figure 5.3).

Hierarchy of needs theory states that a need that is unsatisfied activates seeking or searching behaviour. Thus the individual who is hungry will search for food or the one who is unloved will seek to be loved. Once this seeking behaviour is fulfilled or satisfied, it no longer acts as a primary motivator: needs that are satisfied no longer motivate. This clearly illustrates the rational for arranging these needs in a hierarchy. The sequential ascending order implies that it is the next unachieved level that acts as the prime motivator. However, need propensity means that higher-order needs cannot become an active motivating force until the preceding lower-order need is satisfied. However, individuals will seek growth when it is feasible to do so and have an innate desire to ascend the hierarchy. Self-actualisation is the climax of personal growth. Maslow (1943) describes it as the desire for self-fulfilment. The desire to become more and more what one is, to become everything that one is capable of becoming.

Figure 5.4 The self-actualising person

1. Perceives people and events accurately, without undue interference from their own preconceptions.
2. Accepts self and others, including imperfections, but seeks improvement where possible.
3. Is spontaneous, especially in their thoughts and feelings.
4. Focuses on problems outside self, rather than being insecure and introspective.
5. Is detached, so that they are not unduly thrown off course by awkward events.
6. Is autonomous, and remains true to self despite pressure to conform.
7. Appreciates good and beautiful things, even if they are familiar.
8. Has peak experiences of intense positive emotions of a sometimes mystical quality.
9. Has close relationships, but only with a few carefully chosen people.
10. Respects others, avoids making fun of people, and evaluates them according to their inner qualities rather than race or class.
11. Has firm moral standards and sense of right and wrong, though these may be different from many other people.
12. Is creative; this is perhaps the most fundamental aspect of self-actualisation and is seen as the result of the other aspects listed above. By being open-minded and open to their experience the self-actualising person sees things in novel ways and can draw novel conclusions from established information.

Source: Sugarman (1986).

Maslow's theory has been the subject of much interpretation and criticism. Firstly, Maslow's work was based on general studies of human behaviour and motivation and, as such, was not directly associated with matters central to the workplace. Arising from this the theory is extremely difficult to apply because of the illusive nature of the needs identified, particularly in the context of the workplace. Researchers have also found little support for the concept of exclusive pre-potency. A more realistic scenario is that individuals have several active needs at the same time, which implies that lower-order needs are not always satisfied before one concentrates on higher-order needs. Another criticism of this approach is that career advancement may be the true factor underlying changes in need deficiencies. Research demonstrates that as managers advance in organisations, their lower-order needs diminish. Simultaneously they experience an increased desire to satisfy higher-order needs. Finally, it has also been suggested that the theory attempts to demonstrate an imputed rationality in human actions that may not necessarily exist. The conceptualisation of our needs in such a logical, sequential fashion, while useful as a frame of reference to which we can all compare ourselves, has not resulted in convincing evidence among researchers.

Other inconsistencies which research have thrown up include the fact that needs do not often group together in the ways predicted, the restricting of the concept of a need to a purely biological phenomenon remains problematic and needs, while often generally described, are done so with insufficient precision.

Overall, Maslow's hierarchy of needs appears to be a convenient way of classifying needs, but it has limited utility in explaining work behaviour. Its primary value has been the fact that it highlights in a general way the importance of human needs.

Existence-Relatedness-Growth (ERG) Theory

ERG theory, as developed by Alderfer (1972), reduces Maslow's fivefold needs category into a threefold taxonomy. A second major difference, stemming from criticisms of Maslow's approach, is that less emphasis is placed on a hierarchical order of lower- and higher-order needs inferring that all needs levels may be influential at the same time.

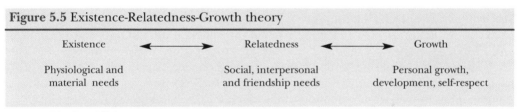

Figure 5.5 Existence-Relatedness-Growth theory

Source: Alderfer (1972).

Another important variation is the proposition that an already satisfied lower-order need may be reactivated as a motivator when a higher-order need cannot be satisfied. Thus an employee who has satisfied basic material and social needs may be concerned with his personal growth and development (e.g. promotion). If there is no scope for such development he may revert back to a preoccupation with previously satisfied needs (e.g. social or financial). The other implication, referred to above, is that more than one needs category may be important at any one time. Robbins (2001, 161) summarises the contribution of ERG theory in the following way:

> ERG theory argues, like Maslow, that satisfied lower-order needs lead to the desire to satisfy higher-order needs; but multiple needs can be operating as motivators at the

same time, and frustration in attempting to satisfy a higher-level needs can result in regression to a lower-level need. ERG theory is more consistent with our knowledge of individual differences among people. The evidence demonstrating that people in other cultures rank the need categories differently – for instance, natives of Spain and Japan place social needs before their physiological requirements – would be consistent with ERG theory. Several studies have supported ERG theory, but there is also evidence that it does not work in some organisations. Overall, however, ERG theory represents a more valid version of the need hierarchy.

Acquired Needs Theory

An alternative approach, developed by McClelland (1961), concentrated on identifying motivational differences between individuals as a means of establishing which patterns of motivation led to effective performance and success at work. He distinguishes three basic needs in addition to physical drives:

- Need for achievement [nAch]: desire to consistently want challenging tasks demanding responsibility and application.
- Need for power [nPow]: need for control over people.
- Need for affiliation [nAff]: need for good social and personal relations with people.

McClelland suggested that these needs are acquired and developed over one's life. Depending on which needs are dominant, these will exert varying influences on work performance. People with a high need for achievement tend to have a strong motivation to take on challenging tasks and do them better. This, combined with a moderate to high need for power and a lower need for affiliation, has been suggested as a good indicator of success in senior management (McClelland and Boyatzis 1982). An important implication of this approach is that, if such needs are acquired, then they may be developed through appropriate environmental conditions that facilitate the emergence of the desired needs profile.

McGregor's Theory X, Theory Y

Unlike previous approaches that concentrated on analysing the motivations of people at work, McGregor (1960) examined managerial assumptions about employees and the resultant implications of such assumptions for managerial approaches to issues like control, job design and remuneration systems. He identified two very differing sets of assumptions about employees' behaviour and motivation which were termed theory X and theory Y.

Figure 5.6 Theory X, theory Y

THEORY X	THEORY Y
Employees are inherently lazy, dislike work will do as little as possible.	Employees like work and want to undertake challenging tasks.
Consequently, workers need to be corrected, controlled and directed to exert adequate effort.	If the work itself and the organisational environment is appropriate, employees will work willingly without need for coercion or control.
Most employees dislike responsibility and prefer direction.	People are motivated by needs for respect, esteem, recognition and self-fulfilment.
Employees want only security and material rewards.	People at work want responsibility. The majority of workers are imaginative and creative and can exercise ingenuity at work.

Source: Gunnigle and Flood (1990).

Approaches by organisations to workforce management differ considerably and these two contrasting frameworks are useful in helping to analyse and explain management styles. Both classifications represent extreme styles and approaches to people management. In practice, organisations may adopt elements of both approaches but, often, with a particular leaning that indicates a preference for one or other approach.

Traditional autocratic management approaches were clearly based on theory X assumptions. Despite considerable academic and practical support it would seem that theory Y has not got the whole-hearted backing of many senior managers. Consequently its application has often been restricted to once-off initiatives designed to deal with particular problems or issues rather than reflecting a change in corporate approaches to the way employees are managed.

Dual-Factor Theory

Figure 5.7 Herzberg's dual-factor theory of work motivation: factors affecting job attitudes

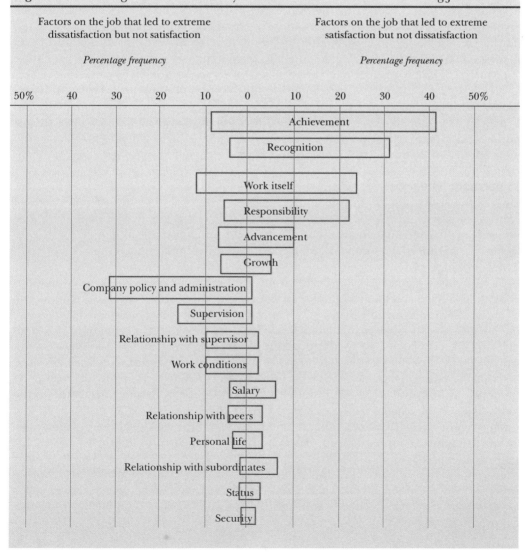

Source: Herzberg (1968).

Herzberg (1968) was equally concerned about the impact of work and job design on motivation. He saw the key to improving employees' motivation in terms of job satisfaction. Herzberg felt that by identifying the factors at work, which produced the greatest levels of satisfaction (or dissatisfaction) it would be possible to design jobs that provided job satisfaction, thereby encouraging higher levels of performance. His approach concentrated on identifying which factors contributed most to employees' satisfaction at work (called 'motivator' factors). He also sought to identify those factors that influenced levels of employees' dissatisfaction ('maintenance/ hygiene' factors). Herzberg concluded that these two sets of factors were inherently different in terms of their impact on motivation and performance.

A central aspect of Herzberg's dual-factor theory is that only by varying motivator factors can management improve performance and motivation. Varying maintenance factors will reduce levels of dissatisfaction but will never act as a motivator.

The implication here is that management can only stimulate employees' motivation by designing jobs to incorporate the motivator factors (i.e. jobs that encourage and facilitate responsibility, advancement and recognition). Herzberg believed that high levels of job satisfaction could be achieved by altering job content to allow for personal growth and development while also ensuring that the job context (pay, working conditions, etc.) were appropriate. This process became known as job enrichment (see job design).

Herzberg's approach has gained considerable recognition, particularly for differentiating between the impact of intrinsic and extrinsic factors on employees' motivation. Criticisms have tended to focus on its reliability of application to all types of jobs (not just professional/white collar) and the view of job satisfaction as being almost synonymous with motivation.

Expectancy Theory

Most of the approaches discussed above represent attempts to identify a general set of employees' needs, which cause workers to behave in a certain way. The belief is that by identifying such needs management can provide for their ease of achievement thus facilitating improved performance. Many of these approaches rank such motives or goals in a hierarchical order with self-actualisation as the ultimate motivator.

However most managers will probably point out that employees differ markedly in terms of motivation. One may find two employees, similar in terms of age, sex and background, one of whom will strive to achieve high-performance levels, undertake additional tasks, etc. while the other is content to get by doing the minimum acceptable to the organisation. How does one explain such variations? One approach that avoids attempts to find a definitive set of employees' motives, but seeks to explain individual differences in terms of goals, motives and behaviour is expectancy theory. Associated with Vroom (1964), expectancy theory focuses on the relationship between the effort put into the completion of particular activities by the individual and the expectations concerning the actual reward that will accrue as a result of expending the effort. Expectancy theory attempts to combine individual and organisational factors that impact on this causal effort/reward relationship. Broadly this theory argues that individuals base decisions about their behaviour on the expectation that one or another alternate behaviour is more likely to lead to needed or desired outcomes. The relationship between one's behaviour and particular desired outcomes is affected by individual factors such as personality, perception, motives, skills and abilities, and by organisational factors such as culture, structure and managerial style (the context in which one is operating).

Thus, expectancy theory avoids attempts to isolate a definitive set of employees' motives, but rather seeks to explain individual differences in terms of goals, motives and behaviours. It postulates that employees' motivation is dependent on how the employer perceives the relationship between effort, performance and outcomes.

Figure 5.8 Expectancy theory

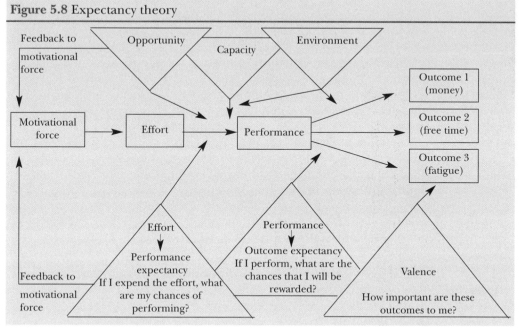

Source: Umstot (1988).

Mabey and Salaman (1995, 191) note that expectancy theory has been developed from Vroom's early specifications to be expressed very clearly as a combination of three factors, namely expectancy, instrumentality and valence.

Expectancy is the probability assigned by the individual that work effort will be followed by a given level of achieved task performance (value = 0 to 1). It refers to the perceived probability that a particular level of effort will lead to desired performance levels. If the desired outcome (e.g. bonus pay) demands a given level of performance (production goals), the individual employee must believe that level is achievable or he will not expend the necessary effort. (If I tried, would I be able to perform the action I am considering?)

Instrumentality is the probability assigned by the individual that a given level of achieved task performance will lead to various work outcomes (rewards) (value = 0 to 1). Thus expectancy theory suggests that employees' decisions on how they perform are based upon their perception of desired outcomes, whether performance targets are achievable and an evaluation of the likelihood that by achieving these targets they will realise their desired outcomes. (Would performing the action lead to identifiable outcomes?)

Valence is the value attached by the individual to various work outcomes (rewards) (value = −1 to +1). It is thus a measure of the strength of attraction which a particular outcome or reward has for the individual employee. (How much do I value these outcomes?)

The motivational appeal of a given work path is drastically reduced whenever any one or more of the factors approaches the value of zero. Thus the model suggests that the individual's level of effort (motivation) is not simply a function of rewards. The individual must feel that they have the ability to perform the task (expectancy), that this performance will impact on the reward and that this reward is actually valued. Only if all conditions are satisfied will employees be motivated to exert greater effort in the performance of a job. It is critical that individuals can see a connection between effort and reward and that the reward offered by the organisation will satisfy employees' needs. However there is no simple formula, since individuals possess different preferences for outcomes and have different understandings of the relationship between effort and reward. They may well be motivated in very different ways. Among the criticisms levelled at the theory are the difficulties associated with testing the theory empirically, and the fact that it assumes a type of rationality with respect to how the individual thinks and behaves, which may not exist. This approach suggests that employees will expend a high level of effort if they believe this will result in performance levels that will be rewarded by valued outcomes. These valued outcomes may vary between individuals. One may value money, another promotion, and yet another recognition. However, it is not only the outcome that is important, but also the belief that valued outcomes can be achieved through improved effort and performance.

In relation to the implications of expectancy theory for management Vroom (1964) suggests that managers must seek to understand the goals and motives of individual employees, ensure these are clearly and positively linked to desired performance levels which in turn are achievable from the employee's perspective. Lawler (1978) goes a little further and highlights specific areas for management action:

- need to establish what are valued outcomes;
- need to specify desired and achievable performance levels;
- ensure there is a clear link between effort, performance and desired outcomes;
- ensure adequate variation of outcomes available;
- ensure equity and fairness for the individual employee.

Expectancy theory does not attempt to identify a universal set of motivational factors. Rather it highlights the importance of a range of potential motivational factors. These may be either intrinsic or extrinsic. Intrinsic outcomes are those originating from doing the job (sense of achievement, satisfaction) while extrinsic outcomes are those provided by other people, particularly management, and include pay and promotion.

Equity Theory

The concept of a fair day's work for a fair day's pay is often utilised to express how the parties to the labour process wish to perceive the employment relationship. Equity theory, sometimes referred to as justice theory resembles expectancy theory in that it sets down the individual's cognitive process that determines whether or not he/she will engage in the effort-reward bargain within the framework of the social exchange process.

Developed by Adams (1965), the equity theory of motivation is based on the comparison between two variables: inputs and outcomes. Inputs refer to that which the individual brings to his/her employment and include things such as effort, experience and skills. Outcomes describe the range of factors the employee receives in return for his/her inputs i.e. pay, recognition, fringe benefits and status symbols. Adams suggests that individual expectations about equity correlation between inputs and outcomes are learned during the process of socialisation in the home or at work and through comparison with the inputs and outcomes of others. Adams' (1963) suggests that individuals can:

- change inputs i.e. can reduce effort if under paid;
- try to change their outcomes i.e. ask for a pay rise or promotion;
- psychologically distort their own ratios by rationalising differences in inputs and outcomes;
- change the reference group to which they compare themselves in order to restore equity.

Huseman *et al.* (1987) enumerate the core propositions of equity theory as follows:

1. Individuals evaluate their relationships with others by assessing the ratio of their outcomes from, and inputs to the relationship against the outcome-input ratio of another comparable individual.
2. If the outcome-input ratios of the individual and the comparable other are deemed to be unequal, then inequity exists.
3. The greater the inequity the individual perceives (in the form of either over-reward or under-reward), the more distress the individual experiences.
4. The greater the distress an individual experiences, the harder he/she will work to restore equity. Among the possible equity restoration techniques the individual might use are, distorting inputs or outcomes, disregarding the comparable other and referring to a new one, or terminating the relationship.

Thus, employees will formulate a ratio between their inputs and outcomes and will compare this ratio with the perceived ratios of inputs and outcomes of other people in the same or a similar situation. If these two ratios are not equal then the individual will take action in an attempt to restore a sense of equity.

Considerable research interest has been generated in testing the relationships advanced by Adams, particularly those relationships that focus on employees' reactions to pay.

Table 5.1 Equity theory research on employees' reactions to pay

Study	Equity condition	Method of induction	Task	Dependent variables	Results
Adams (1963)	Overpayment; hourly and piece rate	Qualifications	Interviewing	Productivity, work quality	Hourly overpaid subjects produced greater quantity; piece-rate overpaid subjects produced higher quality and lower quantity than equitably paid subjects
Adams and Jacobsen (1964)	Overpayment; piece rate	Qualifications	Proof-reading	Productivity, work quality	Overpaid subjects produced less quantity of higher quality
Adams and Rosenbaum (1962)	Overpayment; hourly and piece rate	Qualifications	Interviewing	Productivity	Hourly overpaid subjects produced more quantity, while piece-rate overpaid subjects produced less quantity
Anderson and Shelly (1967)	Overpayment; hourly	Qualifications, importance of task	Proof-reading	Productivity, work quality	No differences were found between groups

$\longrightarrow$

125

Table 5.1 Equity theory research on employees' reactions to pay (cont.)

Study	Equity condition	Method of induction	Task	Dependent variables	Results
Andrews (1967)	Overpayment and under-payment; piece rate	Circumstances, previous wage experiences	Interviewing, data checking	Productivity, work quality	Overpaid subjects produced higher quality and under-paid subjects produced greater quantity and lower quality
Arrowood (1961)	Overpayment; hourly	Qualifications, work returned	Interviewing	Productivity	Overpaid subjects had higher productivity
Evans and Simmons (1969)	Overpayment and under-payment; hourly	Competence, authority	Proof-reading	Productivity, work quality	Underpaid subjects produced more of poorer quality in competence condition; no difference found in other conditions
Friedman and Goodman (1967)	Overpayment; hourly	Qualifications	Interviewing	Productivity	Qualifications induction did not affect productivity; when subjects were classified by perceived qualifications, unqualified subjects produced less than qualified subjects
Goodman and Friedman (1968)	Overpayment and under-payment; hourly	Qualifications, quantity v. quality emphasis	Questionnaire coding	Productivity, work quality	Overpaid subjects produced more than equitably paid subjects; emphasis on quantity v. quality affected performance
Goodman and Friedman (1969)	Overpayment; piece rate	Qualifications, quantity v. quality emphasis	Questionnaire scoring	Productivity, work quality	Overpaid subjects increased productivity or work quality, depending on induction
Lawler (1968b)	Overpayment; hourly	Qualifications, circumstances	Interviewing	Productivity, work quality	Overpaid (unqualified) sub-jects produced more of lower quality; subjects overpaid by circumstances did not
Lawler, Koplin, Young and Fadem (1968)	Overpayment; piece rate	Qualifications	Interviewing	Productivity, work quality	Overpaid subjects produced less of higher quality in initial work session; in later sessions subject's perceived qualifications and produc-tivity increased; the need for money was related to productivity for both groups
Lawler and O'Gara (1967)	Underpayment; piece rate	Circumstances	Interviewing	Productivity, work quality	Underpaid subjects produced more of lower quality and perceived their job as more interesting but less important and more complex
Pritchard, Dunnette and Jorgenson (1972)	Overpayment and under-payment; hourly and piece rate	Circumstances, actual change in payment	Clerical task	Performance satisfaction	Circumstances induction did not result in performance differences for piece rate, but some support was found for hourly overpay and under-pay
					Changes in pay rate supported hourly predictions; some support found for piece rate overpayment prediction but not for underpayment ➤

Table 5.1 Equity theory research on employees' reactions to pay (cont.)

Study	Equity condition	Method of induction	Task	Dependent variables	Results
Valenzi and Andrews (1971)	Overpayment and under-payment; hourly	Circumstances	Clerical task	Productivity, work quality	No significant differences found between conditions; 27% of underpaid subjects quit; no subjects in other conditions quit
Wiener (1970)	Overpayment; hourly	Qualifications, inputs v. out-comes, ego-oriented v. task-oriented	Word manipulation		Outcome-overpayment subjects produced more; input-overpaid subjects produced more only on ego-oriented task
Wood and Lawler (1970)	Overpayment; piece rate	Qualifications	Reading	Amount of time reading, quality	Overpaid subjects produced less, but this could not be attributed to striving for higher quality

Source: Mowday (1987).

Overall, the research highlights support for Adams' theory about employees' reactions to wage inequities. Mowday concludes that the research support for the theory appears to be strongest for predictions about under payment inequity. Furthermore, equity theory appears to offer a useful approach to understanding a wide variety of social relationships, which may occur in the workplace.

WORK DESIGN

The nature of work organisation and design will significantly influence the degree to which work is intrinsically satisfying for employees and promotes high levels of motivation. Indeed, early concern with job design, according to Brooks (1999), focused almost exclusively on attempts to improve individual motivation and it remains that organisations should carefully consider their approach to work organisational design and choose the approach which best suits their particular needs.

The study of individual tasks in organisations has long been accorded a high degree of importance in organisation and management literature and theory. Investigation in the area has attempted to describe strategies for changing or refining jobs so as to enhance variables such as effort, performance, motivation, satisfaction, commitment, absenteeism and so forth. Historically and presently the focus within job design has been on results and outcomes (Janson 1979). There is a body of opinion that sees at least some of the roots of the industrial and indeed social problems of modern societies in the nature of poorly structured work (Kopelman 1985). The central view of the various schools of thought, according to Kelly (1980) consists of the view that the organisation of work on the basis of task fragmentation is counterproductive. It is suggested that the situation can be remedied by reversing the division of labour and meeting the social needs of individuals at work, as well as the economic needs of employers. The central issue therefore in Lupton's (1976) words is 'how to design for best fit'. Over the years the field of job design has been characterised by shifts from one theoretical perspective to another. According to Griffin (1987), the primary shifts have been from task specialisation (e.g. Taylor 1911), to job enlargement (e.g. Walker and Guest 1952), to job enrichment (e.g. Herzberg 1968), to socio-technical systems theory and the quality of working life (QWL) movement (e.g. Cherns and Davis 1975) to high-performance work design (e.g. Hackman 1987; Buchanan and McCalman 1989; Morley 1994).

Figure 5.9 Historical development of job design

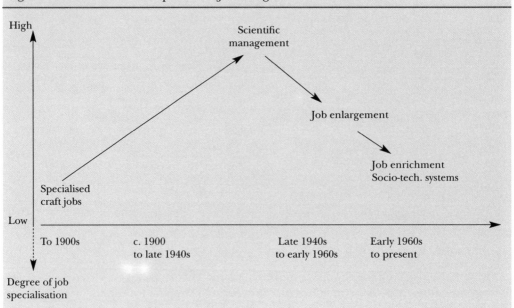

Source: Adapted from Moorhead and Griffin (1989).

Broadly conceived, work organisational design refers to the way the various tasks in the organisation are structured and carried out. It reflects the interaction of management style, the technical system, human resources and the organisation's products or services. Davis (1966) defines the process of job design as that which is concerned with the ' . . . specification of the contents, methods, and relationships of jobs in order to satisfy technological and organisational requirements, as well as the social and personal requirements of the job holder'. Concurring with this definition, the following table demonstrates that the reasons that employers restructure jobs are a mix of improving productivity, reducing or eliminating organisational problems and providing satisfying work for employees.

Cherns and Davis (1975) identify three parties with an explicit interest in job restructuring, employees' motivation and satisfaction and work performance. The first, they claim, is labour, primarily represented by unions and other organised bodies. Unions are seen to be interested in 'the conditions of work, learning and adaptability, reward and satisfaction, and future structures of formal relationships with management'. The second part to the process is management; they are interested in the efficient use of their human resources through the development of appropriate work methods. Finally there is the state. Government is seen to be concerned with matters related to labour and management because of the integral part they play in the successful running of the economy. Manpower planning, training and education, income policy, unemployment and the enhancement of industrial democracy projects are, argue Cherns and Davis (1975) typically regulated by the institutions of the state.

The design of individual jobs is seen to particularly impact upon employees since it influences job content, employees' discretion, degree of task fragmentation and the role of supervision. Gunnigle and Flood (1990) suggest that decisions on the organisation of work are primarily a management responsibility and the particular approach chosen will

Table 5.2 Reasons for introducing job changes

	Birchall and Wild		Reif and Schonerbek		Total
	Blue-collar	*White-collar*	*Blue-collar*	*White-collar*	
System output					
Productivity	12	9			21
Costs	5	3	21		29
Quality	7	5	13		25
Down time	1				1
Inventories	1				1
Skills	2	2			4
Flexibility	3	3			6
Specialisation			14		14
System changes					
Introduction of automated equipment	2	1			3
Introduction of new plant	3	2			5
Personnel problems					
Labour turnover	6	5		6	17
Absenteeism	4	1			5
Attract labour	1				1
Improve labour relations	2	2			4
Concern for employee					
Worker morale	10	7	15		32
To give meaning to work	4	4			8
Monotony			11		11
Eliminate social problems	3				3
Others	8	3	4	6	21
Total	74	47	78	12	211

Source: Birchall (1975).

be a good indicator of corporate beliefs about how employees should be managed, jobs structured and the role of supervision. It will also reflect the organisation's approach to many aspects of personnel management as manifested through attitudes to recruitment, employees' development, motivation, rewards and management/employee relations.

Task Specialisation

Kopelman (1985) notes that task specialisation, standardisation and work simplification are three of the key implementing concepts of what is often referred to as the classical approach to job design. Variously referred to as task specialisation, scientific management or Taylorism, the traditional approach to the organisation of work was dominated by a desire to maximise the productive efficiency of the organisation's technical resources. Choices on the organisation of work and the design of jobs were seen as determined by the technical system. Management's role was to ensure other organisational resources, including employees, were organised in such a way as to facilitate the optimal utilisation of the technical system. This efficiency approach is based on scientific management principles and has been a characteristic of employer approaches to job design since the turn of the century. Jobs were broken down into simple, repetitive, measurable tasks whose skills could be easily acquired through systematic job training.

Figure 5.10 Traditional approach to job design

Characteristics	Outcomes
Bureaucratic organisation structure	Tight supervisory control
Top-down supervisory control	Minimal need for employee discretion
Work planning separated from execution	Work measurement
Task fragmentation	Reliance on rules and procedures
Fixed job definitions	Job specialisation
Individual payment by results	Reduced job flexibility
	Short training time
	Little employee influence on job or work organisation

Source: Gunnigle and Flood (1990).

The rationale for this approach to work and job design was based on 'technological determinism' where the organisation's technical resources were seen as a given constraint and the other inputs including employees had to accommodate the technical system. It also reflected managerial assumptions about people at work. Close supervision, work measurement and other types of controls indicate a belief about employees akin to McGregor's theory X. It suggests that employees need to be coerced to work productively and that this is best achieved by routine, standardised tasks.

Figure 5.11 The three main objectives of Taylorism

High productivity: through the identification of the best way of doing each task and of applying the use of monitory incentives workers would be encouraged to produce efficiently. This would benefit both company and employee financially and in other ways.
Standardisation of work activity: through the application of work-study techniques the best way would be identified and each employee would be carefully selected to match the needs of the task. This would standardise both work activity across employees and the performance they achieved (through the application of incentive payments).
Discipline at work: he also attempted to introduce an improved hierarchical approach to authority, which would allow the decisions of managers to be effectively cascaded throughout the organisation. This would allow a more effective control of workforce activity, channelling it in the desired directions, which the scientific management designed jobs would then convert into a highly cost-effective output.

Source: Martin (2001).

This traditional model of job design has undoubtedly brought positive benefits to many organisations. It helped improve efficiency and promoted a systematic approach to selection, training, work measurement and payment systems. However, it has also led to numerous problems such as high levels of labour turnover and absenteeism and low motivation. Thus short-term efficiency benefits were often superseded by long-term reductions in organisational effectiveness. Many behavioural scientists argued that the effectiveness of organisations could be increased by recognising employees' abilities and giving them challenging, meaningful jobs within a co-operative working environment. The consequence, according to Newell (1995, 22) in her treatise on the 'healthy organisation' was that:

> Taylor had a limited perspective on human needs and motivation. He saw a worker as no different from a machine. With a machine, output depends on the amount of fuel put in. Likewise, with a worker, output was seen to depend on the amount of fuel put in: however in this case the fuel needed was money. No account was taken of the individuals psychological needs for interesting work with some degree of challenge and autonomy. Nor was account taken of the psychosocial needs of workers for friendship and support. Indeed, Taylor explicitly tried to prevent the formation of work groups, seeing these as a potential threat to managerial control, and so to efficiency.

More recently the increased emphases on improving quality, service and overall competitiveness have led to the emergence of other schools of thought aimed at restructuring work systems to increase employee motivation, commitment and performance. Much of the focus of work of the successors to task specialisation has been on the restructuring of jobs to incorporate greater scope for intrinsic motivation. Subsequent schools questioned traditional management assumptions about why employees worked. The traditional approach saw employees as essentially instrumental in their attitudes to work. Jobs were seen as a means to an end and it was these extrinsic rewards that motivated employees. Consequently employers created work systems with closely circumscribed jobs, supervised work and rewarded quantifiable performance.

Job Enlargement

Regalia (1995, 13) suggests that, in the European context at least, there is no doubt that demands for greater employee say and participation in the organisation of their work as well as worker commitment and interest in productive goals have had a long history. Job enlargement and job enrichment as alternative mechanisms of work structuring differ in their relative emphases; the former makes one's job 'bigger', while the latter adds some element to the job that is dedicated to increasing the employees' psychological growth. Job enlargement grew from the arguments of humanitarians in the 1950s that production methods prevalent at the time created poor working conditions that led to high levels of job dissatisfaction. The proposed solution was job enlargement, which, when introduced, would lead to more variety and less routine work. This assumption was drawn upon by Walker and Guest (1952) in their study of automobile assembly lines. They studied 180 workers and identified six main characteristics of mass production technology: (i) repetitiveness, (ii) low skill requirement, (iii) mechanically paced work, (iv) little alteration of tools or methods, (v) low requirement for mental attention and (vi) minute sub-division of product.

In concluding that the solution to eliminating the ills of mass-production technology, lay in job enlargement, their proposals have generated some debate. The disputed issues centre on meaning and methodology. Walker and Guest viewed job enlargement as 'the combination of more that two tasks into one'. However this did not in any way distinguish it from 'job extension', which could possibly be nothing more than the addition of more meaningless tasks (Wall 1982). It has been argued that there is no explicit theory on which the concept of job enlargement can become a model of job restructuring. There is no motivation theory, according to Buchanan (1979), on which job enlargement stands. Aldag and Brief (1979) note that job enlargement experiments failed to use a conceptual framework of how the structuring of jobs should be actually executed. Furthermore,

Buchanan (1979) argues that job enlargement studies have largely ignored external variables and people's differing attitudes towards work.

Job Enrichment

Largely attributed to Herzberg (1968) job enrichment was developed for the advancement of the dual-factor theory of work motivation. The job enrichment approach suggested that employees gain most satisfaction from the work itself and it was intrinsic outcomes arising from work which motivated employees to perform well in their jobs. In his celebrated article 'One more time: how do you motivate employees?' Herzberg establishes the concept of *vertical loading* as a means of moving away from the addition of 'one meaningless task to the existing (meaningless) one'. Vertical loading, dedicated to the addition of more challenging dimensions to the job remains the mainstay of job enrichment.

Figure 5.12 Principles of vertical job loading

Principle	Motivators involved
A. Removing some controls while retaining accountability	Responsibility and personal achievement
B. Increasing the accountability of people for their own work	Responsibility and recognition
C. Giving a person a complete natural unit of work (module, division, area, etc.)	Responsibility, achievement, and recognition
D. Granting additional authority to an employee in their activity; job freedom	Responsibility, achievement, and recognition
E. Making periodic reports directly available to the worker rather than to the supervisor	Internal recognition
F. Introducing new and more difficult tasks not previously handled	Growth and learning
G. Assigning people specific or specialised tasks, enabling them to become experts	Responsibility, growth, and advancement

Source: Herzberg (1968).

In a similar treaties of intrinsic outcomes and job satisfaction Hackman and Oldham (1980) enumerate three basic conditions necessary for promoting job satisfaction and employees' motivation.

- Work should be *meaningful* for the doer.
- Doers should have *responsibility* for the results.
- Doers should get *feedback* on the results.

This approach suggested that it was the design of work and not the characteristics of the employee that had the greatest impact on employees' motivation. Hackman and Oldham identified five 'core job characteristics' that needed to be incorporated into job design to increase meaningfulness, responsibility and feedback.

1. Skill variety: extent to which jobs draw on a range of different skills and abilities.
2. Task identity: extent to which a job requires completion of a whole, identifiable piece of work.

3. Task significance: extent to which a job substantially impacts on the work or lives of others either within or outside the organisation.
4. Autonomy: freedom, independence and discretion afforded to the job holder.
5. Feedback: degree to which the job holder receives information on their level of performance, effectiveness, etc.

Having identified the factors necessary to promote satisfaction and intrinsic motivation, the next stage is to incorporate these characteristics into jobs through various job redesign strategies. Hackman and Oldham suggest five implementation strategies to increase task variety, significance, identity, and create opportunities for greater autonomy and feedback.

1. Form natural work groups: arrange tasks together to form an identifiable, meaningful cycle of work for employees, e.g. responsibility for single product rather than small components.
2. Combine tasks: group tasks together to form complete jobs.
3. Establish client relationships: establish personal contact between employees and the end user/client.
4. Vertically load jobs: many traditional approaches to job design separate planning and controlling (management functions) from executing (employee's function). Vertically loading jobs means integrating the planning, controlling and executing functions and giving the responsibility to employees (e.g. responsibility for materials, quality, deadlines and budgetary control).
5. Open feedback channels: ensure maximum communication of job results (e.g. service standards, faults, wastage, market performance and costs).

Figure 5.13 Designing enriched jobs

How does management enrich an employee's job? The following points, which we have just alluded to in the text, are derived from the application of the Job Characteristics Model and they seek to specify the types of changes in jobs that are most likely to lead to improving their motivation potential score.

Combine Tasks: Management should seek to take existing and fractionalised tasks and put them back together to form a new and larger module of work. This effort increases both skill variety and task identity.

Create Natural Work Units: The creation of natural work units means that the tasks that an employee does form an identifiable and meaningful whole. This increases employees' ownership of the work and improves the likelihood that employees will view their work as meaningful and important rather than irrelevant and boring.

Establish Client Relationships: The client is the user of the product or service that the employee works on (and may be an internal customer within the organisation or an external one beyond the organisation). Wherever possible, managers should try to establish direct relationships between workers and their clients. This has the impact of increasing skill variety, autonomy, and feedback for the employee.

Expand Jobs Vertically: Vertical expansion gives employees responsibilities and control that were formally reserved for management. In particular it seeks to close the gap between the 'doing' and the 'controlling' aspects of the job, and it increases employees' autonomy. ⟶

Open Feedback Channels: By increasing feedback, employees not only learn how well they are performing their jobs, but also whether their performance is improving, deteriorating, or remaining at a constant level. Ideally, this feedback about performance should be received directly as the employee does the job, rather than from management on an occasional basis.

Source: Hackman (1977).

Figure 5.14 Model of job characteristics

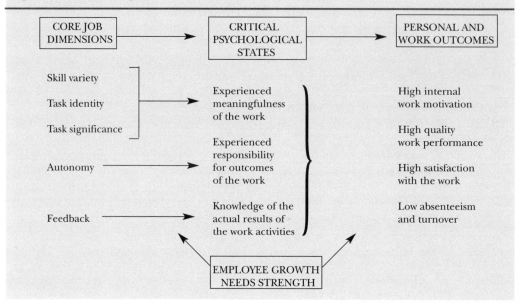

Source: Hackman and Oldham (1980).

Having proven to be 'by far the most popular approach to task design' (Roberts and Glick 1981), the espoused advantages of redesigning jobs along the lines of Hackman and Oldham's job characteristics model have been summarised thus,

> By redesigning jobs to increase variety, identity, significance, autonomy and feedback, the psychological experience of working is changed . . . individuals experience the work as more meaningful, they feel more responsible for the results, and they know more about the results of their efforts. These psychological changes lead to many improved work outcomes, which have been observed following the redesign of work.
>
> Beer *et al.* (1985, 576–7)

Hackman and Oldham thus argued that changes have positive long-term benefits for both the organisation and the individual employee, such as increased motivation and improved performance. However, their theory also posits that not all workers are expected to respond favourably to job enrichment initiatives (Hackman *et al.* 1975) 'Employee growth needs strength' is considered the most important source of variation in this respect: only those workers with a strong desire for achievement, responsibility and autonomy will be motivated by increased intrinsic satisfaction and hence motivated to perform better (see figure 5.16). For other workers, these changes may be a source of anxiety and lead to resentment and opposition to job redesign and other changes in the work system.

The utility of job enrichment has been tested in a variety of work contexts such as banking, medicine and telecommunications. In evaluating the results, Schermerhorn *et al.* (1985, 213) concludes that while the results have been promising, further research is necessary to refine and support the concept.

> At the moment, researchers generally feel that job enrichment is not a universal panacea for job performance and satisfaction problems. They also recognise that job enrichment can fail when job requirements are increased beyond the level of individual capabilities and/or interests.

In the Irish context, support for the job enrichment approach is to be found in Blennerhasset's study of motivation among civil service executives (Blennerhasset 1983). This study found that respondents identified the work itself as the most important potential source of job satisfaction and motivation. However, Blennerhassett also found that respondents rated their jobs very poorly on the core job characteristics of skill variety, identity, significance, etc. and generally felt their jobs allowed little scope for satisfaction, motivation or involvement. Since the study population were executive and higher executive officers, these findings raise serious question marks about the design of jobs in the civil service, and possibly beyond.

The 'Quality of Working Life' Movement

While job enrichment has the potential to positively impact on how employees experience work, its focus on job content has certain limitation. Clearly, many factors beyond job content impact on how employees experience work, such as working conditions, employees' involvement and autonomy, work intensity and the nature of supervision.

The 'quality of working life' (QWL) approach has its origins in the US during the 1960s and 1970s (see, for example, Walton 1973; Skrovan 1983). Focusing on the overall quality of employees' experiences in the workplace it embraces both job design and broader issues such as autonomy, employees' participation, justice, working conditions and job security, as critical factors impacting on the quality of working life. A particular stimulus for the QWL approach was a desire to improve the quality of working life for employees by avoiding what were seen as characteristics of a low quality of working life (Morley, Moore, Heraty and Gunnigle 1998). Figure 5.15 summarises some of the main characteristics of low and high quality working life as identified in the extant literature (see for example Steers and Porter 1987; Schermerhorn *et al.* 1985; Schuler and Jackson 1996).

Figure 5.15 High and low quality working life: indicative characteristics

Low Quality of Working Life	*High Quality of Working Life*
• Jobs characterised by low levels of task significance, variety, identity and feedback	• Adequate and fair reward systems
• No or little employee involvement	• Safe and healthy working conditions
• Top-down communications	• Opportunity to use personal capabilities
• Inequitable reward systems	• Opportunity for personal growth and development
• Inadequate job definition	• Integration into social system of organisation
• Poor employment conditions/Hire and fire approach	• High labour standards/employee rights
• Discriminatory HR policies	• Pride in relevance and value of work
• Low job security	• Balance between work and non-work roles

Source: Morley, Moore, Heraty and Gunnigle (1998).

Beyond the job enrichment initiatives mentioned earlier, the QWL movement seeks to increase employees' influence and involvement in work organisation and job design. Again this challenges some traditional management assumptions about employees. It involves recognising that employees can and want to make a positive input into organisational decision-making. It assumes that such involvement is valued by employees and results in increased commitment, responsibility and performance.

Increased employee influence in work system design also addresses the issue of employee supervision as an aspect of the management role. If employees are to be involved in making decisions about the organisation of work and responsible for the subsequent execution of such decisions much of the 'control' aspect is removed from the supervisory role. It necessitates a change in attitude to workforce management. Supervisors become less concerned with monitoring and controlling employees' performance and more involved in advising and facilitating employees in carrying out their jobs.

This approach requires high levels of commitment and trust from both management and employees. Management must feel confident that employees have the required competence and will use their greater levels of influence positively and to the benefit of the organisation. Employees must be happy that their increased commitment and sense of responsibility will not be abused or exploited by employers.

There are various mechanisms available to encourage increased levels of employees' participation in the design and operation of work systems. Possibly the best known approach is quality circles. These are small groups of employees and managers who meet together regularly to consider means of improving quality, productivity or other aspects of work organisation. They are seen as having played an important role in the success of Japanese organisations and have been successfully applied in Western economies including Ireland.

There are numerous other participative and consultative mechanisms that may be established and can work effectively in the appropriate organisational environment. Creating such an environment has become an important concern for organisations. Past experience in applying various techniques to improve employees' motivation and involvement have demonstrated that these operate best where there is a change in the overall corporate approach. The issue for senior management is how to create a corporate culture whose values, beliefs and practices establish an organisational environment within which employees are highly committed to and work towards the achievement of business goals.

High Performance Work Systems (HPWS)

Recent commentators such as Buchanan and McCalman (1989) suggest that the heretofore limited impact of job design theories is a weakness that needs to be remedied. 'It (job design) has tended to be regarded as an isolated management technique aimed at local organisational problems and at individual jobs rather than realising that it must form part of the whole company philosophy, through all levels, if it is to be really successful' (Buchanan and McCalman, 1989). The motive behind high-performance work systems (HPWS) is rooted in the desire and the need to improve the overall competitive position of the organisation. As Buchanan and McCalman comment, 'the new strategic imperatives require new work organisation strategies'.

The notion of HPWS is very much associated with the new high-tech companies of the 1980s, and especially those that located to greenfield sites in attempts to establish a fundamentally different type of organisation and organisation culture. The essence of HPWS appears to lie in the adoption of a culture of continuous improvement and innovation at all levels in the organisation and the implementation of a range of work and human resource practices to sustain and develop this culture; in particular team-working, quality consciousness and flexibility (Morley *et al.* 1998). They are also felt to reflect an increased management emphasis on developing broadly defined, challenging jobs within more organic, flexible organisation structures:

> The high-performance work organisation has a distinctive structure which is designed to provide employees with skills, incentives, information and decision making responsibilities that will lead to improved organisational performance and facilitate innovation . . . The main aim is to generate high levels of commitment and involvement of employees and managers.
>
> Tiernan *et al.* (1996, 113)

High performance work systems are thus seen as embracing much more than a change in the nature of jobs. Rather, they appear to embrace fundamentally different assumptions about organisational structure and orientation, so that all aspects of organisational management are altered to embrace a new culture designed to improve performance and responsiveness through developing a more committed, flexible and skilled workforce (see for example, Buchanan 1994).

As a means of distinguishing high-performance work design from previous movements Mooney (1988) draws upon the differences between system and value changes within organisations. As the concept implies, a system change simply encompasses changes of methodology or ritual, he argues. Many of the previous job design schools were built on principle. On the other hand, value changes, according to Mooney, run deeper, involving a refocus on fundamental business tenets. Thus while the HPWS school involves system changes to accompany the new emphasis, they are driven and sustained by value changes dedicated to the creation of a new order in workplace relations, and a revised understanding of them.

As noted earlier, a primary driver of HPWS is increased pressure on organisations to improve organisational competitiveness. This indeed may explain its prevalence in high technology sectors, especially electronics and software, which tend to be characterised by high levels of market volatility and product innovation. In relating the experience of the Digital Equipment Corporation (possibly the most prominent early exemplar of high-performance work systems), Perry (1984, 191) notes how the company's Connecticut (Enfield) plant sought to respond to increased competition and product change.

> The goal at Enfield was flexibility: the capacity to respond quickly and effectively to an uncertain environment. Traditional ways to handle uncertainty had included the introduction of new procedures, changing the structure, employing more people, and tightening management controls. These strategies simply increased overheads, increased the complexity of the organisation and generated more uncertainty. To deal with these issues, management decided to introduce a more participative style of decision-making, multi-skilled operating teams, an innovative rewards system, and systematic career planning and development. The plant manager's review of these changes revealed a 40 per cent reduction in product manufacturing time; a sharp increase in inventory turnover; a reduction in the level of management hierarchy to three; a 38 per cent reduction in standard costs; a 40 per cent reduction in overhead and equivalent output, with half the people and half the space.
>
> Buchanan (1994, 102)
> [Summary of more detailed review by Perry (1984)].

HPWS are also closely linked to the idea of benchmarking performance against external standards: the idea that organisational performance should be disaggregated and compared to valid external standards such as cycle time, re-work, labour costs and productivity (Vaill 1982). The external comparators may be other similar companies or simply other plants with the organisation's portfolio. The growth of total quality management and, particularly, quality accreditation schemes have been an important catalyst in this regard. For example, companies who trade internationally often seek to achieve ISO 9000, which is a worldwide standard. In Ireland the Quality Mark Scheme, introduced in 1982, is an increasingly important goal.

Clearly, an important dimension of HPWS entails the development of new or different approaches to the management of employees as well as in regard to the structure of jobs and systems. These themes pervade both what is termed the high-performance literature (Vaill 1982; Perry 1984; Lawler 1986; Buchanan and McCalman 1989), and indeed the excellence literature (Peters and Waterman 1982; Moss Kanter 1983; Quinn Mills 1991). Almost all contributors highlight the need to empower employees in an attempt to make the organisation more effective. While commentators may differ on detail, there is overwhelming support for the use of team-based work systems as a means of developing a highly skilled, flexible and motivated workforce within a leaner, flatter more responsive organisation structure.

Some of the most important early work on high-performance work systems was undertaken by Ed Lawler in the United States (Lawler 1978, 1982, 1986). He paid particular attention to newly designed plants that opened on greenfield sites and which were viewed as representative of a new departure in terms of work systems and management practice and style. Lawler sets out a list of organisational design features, which he suggests significantly increase employees' involvement in the workplace and help to improve organisational performance. While Lawler (1982) feels that this list is an ideal and not characteristic of any particular organisation, he argues that it most closely approximates to the configuration of employment practices adopted by companies that located to (or sometimes relocated to) greenfield sites in the United States, during the late 1970s and early 1980s. Lawler argues that such new plants were especially likely to embody high involvement work systems and employment practices comprising mutually reinforcing arrangements and practices such as autonomous work groups, quality circles, and gain-sharing arrangements.

In evaluating the impact of HPWS, it is necessary to consider the extent to which this development represents a fundamentally new approach to the design of jobs and work systems. Huczynski and Buchanan (1991) address this issue and identify the following distinctions between the high-performance work systems (HPWS) approach of the 1990s and the quality of work life (QWL) approach of the 1960s and 1970s:

1. *More strategic focus*: it is argued that the HPWS approach seeks to improve organisational competitiveness through increased flexibility and quality, while the QWL approach primarily concentrated on achieving reductions in absenteeism and turnover.
2. *Focus on performance rather than job experience*: the HPWS approach has a strong focus on performance criteria; increased employee autonomy is seen as leading to increased employee competence and skills, better decision-making, greater flexibility and adaptability and better use of technology. In contrast, the major rationale of the QWL approach was based on improving the job experience of employees; increased autonomy was seen as leading to increased worker satisfaction and a better job experience.
3. *Major change in management style*: the HPWS approach is seen as requiring a fundamental overhaul of management style, requiring major cultural change and redefinition of the

Figure 5.16 Organisational characteristics of high-performance, high involvement work systems

Organisational Structure	Flat and lean
	Enterprise-oriented
	Team-based
	Participative structure; councils, fora
Job Design	Job enrichment
	Autonomous teams/work groups
Information System	Open flow
	Work/job focus
	Decentralised – team/group-based
	Participatively established goals/standards
Career System	Career tracks/ladders/counselling
	Open job posting
Selection	'Realistic' job preview
	Team/group-based
	Potential- and process-skill-oriented
Training	Strong commitment and investment
	Peer training
	'Economic' education
	Interpersonal skills
Reward System	Open
	Skill-based
	Gain-sharing/share ownership
	Flexible benefits
	All salary/egalitarian
Personnel Policies	Employment tenure commitments
	Participatively established through representative group(s)
Physical Layout	Based on organisational structure
	Egalitarian
	Safe and pleasant

Source: Adapted from Lawler (1982).

role of management, from top management down. The QWL approach appeared to be more limited, involving only a re-orientation in the role of first line supervisors.

4. *Long term comprehensive strategy:* the HPWS approach is seen as a major change initiative affecting the whole organisation and involving a long-term commitment by all parties. The QWL approach tended to be more of a 'quick fix applied to isolated and problematic work groups' (Huczynski and Buchanan 1991: 86).

5. *Representative of strategic human resource management:* consistent with the argument that the 1980s and 1990s witnessed a move from 'reactive/operational' personnel management to 'strategic' human resource management (HRM), it is argued that HPWS is a key element of strategic HRM while QWL is more of a personnel administration technique.

In Ireland, the first prominent examples of organisations that sought to develop high-performance work systems along the lines described above, came from the ranks of firms which had previously experimented with such systems elsewhere. These were mostly US high-tech companies such as Digital, Apple and Amdahl. More recently we have seen greater diversity in the range of companies undertaking such initiatives. One of the mostly widely quoted examples is that of Bord na Mona (see O'Connor 1995; Magee 1991). Here we find a semi-state company, which, by the 1980s, faced severe competitive problems, particularly in relation to (high) costs, (poor) productivity and a pressing need to improve quality, performance and employee relations (Magee 1991). In an attempt to deal with these issues, the company undertook a number of radical initiatives. Firstly, a new multi-disciplinary and team-based management structure was established. The initial challenge was to reduce costs, which was addressed by a major redundancy programme which saw 2500 workers (out of approximately 5000) leave the company. After this, management initiated a more fundamental overhaul:

> It was recognised by everyone concerned . . . that cost-cutting through redundancy would not be enough. We had to change our work practices at the same time. We knew that a fundamental restructuring of how we did our business had to be undertaken to create flexibility in adapting to changing markets, to improve productivity and to improve our competitive position. After extensive negotiation, the 'enterprise scheme' was introduced with the full agreement and co-operation of all parties. The Bord na Mona enterprise scheme allows our staff to form their own autonomous enterprise units, which are team-based and where the unit's earnings are directly related to performance and productivity. *Our workers have become their own bosses.*
>
> O'Connor (1995, 116)

The introduction of autonomous work groups (AWGs) meant that instead of working in isolation, the workers became team members. Leaders were selected for these AWGs, which then assumed responsibility and authority for the completion of tasks (Tiernan *et al.* 1996). In addition to the establishment of AWGs, Bord na Mona also reduced the number of levels in the management hierarchy. It seems that the results of these various changes have been extremely positive. Edward O'Connor, then managing director of the company, summed up the experience as follows:

> The spirit of enterprise this has brought into Bord na Mona has increased productivity per workers in a way that is truly amazing. Our productivity has increased by 75 per cent. Our people now make their own decisions and take their own risks. The series of work groups or enterprise units that have been set up have different structures, but essentially Bord na Mona supplies them with services and they produce quality peat, at a price that is agreed in advance. These are people who, formerly, did what they were told to do, got paid whether or not peat was produced, whether the sun shone all summer or whether it rained all the time . . . The new work practices and systems we have introduced amount to nothing less than a fundamental restructuring of the organisation.
>
> O'Connor (1995, 117)

This section (pages 136–40) has drawn substantially on material in Morley, Moore, Heraty & Gunnigle (1998, chapter 11).

HPWS and Working Life

In evaluating the impact of HPWS, an issue of particular significance is their effect on the work experience of employees. It is particularly important to address the coupling of initiatives to improve direct employee involvement with the application of management techniques designed to improve quality and productivity, especially Just in Time (JIT) and Statistical Process Control (SPC) systems. Just in time (JIT) approaches focus on reducing waste, with particular emphasis on eliminating inventories (of materials, work in progress and finished goods). Statistical process control (SPC) approaches seek to apply rigorous statistical analysis of quality and performance levels to improve performance.

The introduction of these initiatives is generally rooted in the premise that increased direct employee involvement and autonomy is consistent with the use of JIT, SPC or related techniques. Indeed the arguments that direct employee involvement/autonomy mutually complements the use of SPC and JIT is often a key selling point in encouraging employees (and their trade unions) to co-operate in the introduction of such approaches. However, this is not necessarily the case. In her incisive review of the implications of techniques such as JIT and SPC for employees and their work experience, Klein (1989, 60) argues that such changes in production systems do not necessarily make for a more empowered workforce,

> In Japan . . . where JIT and SPC have been used most comprehensively, employees are routinely organised into teams, but their involvement in workplace reform is typically restricted to suggestions for process improvement through structured quality control circles or kaizen groups. Individual Japanese workers have unprecedented responsibility. Yet it is hard to think of them exercising genuine autonomy, that is, in the sense of independent self-management.

Using examples from both the US and Japan, Klein argues that increased pressures and constraints on workers are a common by-product of such manufacturing reforms. While allowing for greater employee involvement and autonomy than traditional assembly line systems, they are not conducive to the high levels of employee empowerment often thought to accompany a shift towards high-performance work systems:

> True, under JIT and SPC, employees become more self-managing than in a command and control factory. They investigate process improvements and monitor quality themselves; they consequently enjoy immediate, impartial feedback regarding their own performance . . . They also gain a better understanding of all elements of the manufacturing process.
>
> On the other hand, the reform process that ushers in JIT and SPC is meant *to eliminate all variations within production* and therefore requires strict adherence to rigid methods and procedures. Within JIT, workers must meet set cycle times; with SPC, they must follow prescribed problem-solving methods. In their pure forms, then, JIT and SPC can turn workers into extensions of a system no less demanding than a busy assembly line. These systems can be very demanding on employees.
>
> Klein (1989, 61)

This analysis challenges the thesis that high-performance work systems necessarily contribute to an improved work experience for employees. In particular, Klein points to important aspects of the work experience that may regress or be lost as a result of reforms using SPC and JIT.

1. *Individual autonomy* may be reduced due to the elimination of inventories under JIT, resulting in less slack or idle time which in turn limits the opportunity for workers to discuss issues, evaluate changes and make suggestions.
2. *Team autonomy* may be reduced because of the greater interdependency between groups due to the absence of buffer inventories, with resulting work pressures reducing the time available to consider broader changes in the work system.
3. *Ability to influence work methods* may be reduced because SPC sets strict guidelines for working methods and procedures.

However, this analysis does not necessarily mean that high-performance work systems incorporating JIT and SPC cannot positively impact on the job experience of workers. Rather, it points to the fact that these techniques and systems may be applied in differing ways. Thus, the issue of management choice is important. Equally important one could argue is the role of workers and trade unions in influencing management choice as to the nature of deployment of these new systems. It is plausible to argue that unfettered management prerogative in introducing so called high-performance work systems, can contribute to a regression in employment conditions and the work experience of employees. Klein (1989) argues that the key to improving employees' involvement and autonomy while instigating high-performance work systems is to provide for *greater collaboration between teams* and to allow *greater opportunity for teams and individuals to propose and evaluate suggestions* for changes in the work process and in the conduct of different jobs. It would appear that the optimal means of facilitating workers' influence on the application of new work systems is through some combination of direct and indirect participation.

A final and critical human resource consideration for organisations considering the adoption of high-performance work systems, is the issue of employees' expectations. It is important to avoid the common pitfall of promising more than can be delivered in terms of employees' involvement and autonomy (which can quickly lead to widespread disillusionment among employees). One approach, suggested by Klein, is to introduce SPC or JIT approaches before worker participation programmes. It felt that this may remove confusion and reduce the likelihood of unrealised worker expectations:

> If, for example, worker participation programs are implemented after JIT, there will be less confusion: workers will then not be invited to imagine greater freedom just when the new process takes freedom away. Even if some workers participate in the design of the system, this doesn't necessarily mean the plant will be operated by worker teams from the start. Besides, it is the task of managers, as always, to prepare the ground. They ought not to promise workers autonomy when they mean them to deliver an unprecedented degree of co-operation.
>
> Klein (1989, 66)

Lean Production

A contemporary development very much associated with HPWS is the focus on lean production. As Legge (2000) notes, lean production systems rest on the principle of eliminating anything that does not add value to the end product. It is, she notes, characterised by the absence of indirect workers, buffer stocks and the rework typical of mass production, and by the presence of re-skilled, multi-tasked workers using flexible equipment, organised on cellular lines for small-batch, just-in-time, right-first-time production with rapid changeover. Much of the literature in this field emanates from the automobile manufacturing sector and merits brief review here.

In 1990 researchers at the Massachusetts Institute of Technology (MIT) published the results of one of the largest studies undertaken in the automobile or any other industry (Womack, Jones and Roos 1990). The study looked at ninety assembly plants in seventeen countries. This study concluded that the industrial world is experiencing the most revolutionary change since the growth of mass production, as Japanese inspired 'lean production techniques begin to replace conventional means of mass production' (European Industrial Relations Review 1992, 13).

The focus on Japanese 'advantage' in the automobile industry sector began in the 1960s and was largely attributed to lower labour costs that gave a (low) cost advantage to Japanese cars. However, the significant impact of Japanese competitors in the auto industry has been their ability to develop and sustain cost and quality advantages over time and, most particularly, in foreign-based plants in countries such as the US and UK. The fact that these Japanese plants are located in the same regions as European and US auto manufacturers served to focus attention on Japanese production methods and work systems, such as just-in-time and kaizen (continuous improvement).

In their attempt to discern the source of Japanese advantage, the MIT study concluded that their success was due primarily to what they termed 'lean production'. This term was used to indicate that it involved using 'less' of almost everything when compared to mass production: half the human effort, half the manufacturing space, half the investment in tools and half the engineering effort (Womack, Jones and Roos 1990). Additional advantages noted in the study included the need to carry lower inventory (less than half of that associated with conventional mass production), a lower level of defects and greater product variety. The development of lean production is attributed to Eiji Toyota. It is reported that after a visit to a Ford assembly plant in Detroit, Eiji concluded that the methods used were excessively wasteful and that none of the indirect workers added value to the product. Together with his chief engineer, Taiichi Ohno, they set about developing the system that became known as lean production. The MIT study identified the mean characteristics of lean production or 'Toyotism' as follows:

- Workers are organised into teams with a leader who, unlike the mass-production foreman, undertakes assembly work and fills in for absent workers. Teams are given responsibility for the functions previously carried out by indirect workers such as simple machine maintenance, quality control, materials ordering and clearing up the work area.

- There is a 'zero defect' approach to production, involving an effective system for immediately detecting defects and problems, and tracing them to their root cause to make sure they do not recur. As the process is perfected, almost no 'rework' is necessary.

- 'Lean' product development techniques, involving strong design team leadership, personnel continuity of development teams, and an emphasis on communications and 'simultaneous development', drastically reduce the time and effort involved in manufacturing.

- Production in small batches, in order to eliminate the costs of high inventories of finished parts required by mass production systems. Cars are built to specific order, with the assistance of flexible machinery, and parts are delivered on a just-in-time basis.

- An absence of vertical integration. Instead, production of parts and components is rationalised in a hierarchy of suppliers. Thus, 'first tier' suppliers are responsible for working as an integral part of the development team, while 'second tier' suppliers are responsible for making the components required for the first tier supplier.

In evaluating the job experience of workers under lean production we find some divided opinions. The authors of the MIT study argue that while lean production requires very high effort levels from workers, it represents a more positive work experience than conventional mass production. The essence of the MIT argument is that lean production contrasts the 'mind numbing stress' of mass production by providing workers with the skills to exercise greater control over their work environment. This, they argue, leads to 'creative tension' at work which requires high effort levels but also gives workers numerous ways to deal with work problems and challenges (Womack, Jones and Roos 1990; European Industrial Relations Review 1992). The MIT study also compares lean production to what they term the 'neocraftmanship' model associated with some Swedish assembly plants. Again, they posit that lean production systems provide a more rewarding and challenging work experience than that found in plants such as Volvo's Uddevalla facility, which the MIT study categorises as a very limited form of job rotation. In the Irish context, Mooney (1988) argues that work systems modelled around lean production principles represent a jettisoning of traditional approaches towards a more positive perspective on employees as 'human assets'.

Not everyone agrees with this benign analysis of the work experience under lean production. Delbridge and Turnbull (1992), in investigating one of the cornerstones of lean production, namely just-in-time (JIT) manufacturing systems, suggest that such systems can negatively impact on the job experience of employees.

> Evidence from both Britain and America suggest that the experience of work under a JIT system involves work intensification, very little autonomy for the individual, a more complete system of management control and a concomitant decline in trade union (and worker) bargaining power. Team working, job rotation and flexibility are not the means of releasing the untapped reserves of 'human resourcefulness' by increasing employee commitment, participation and involvement . . . Rather they are the tools of work intensification and heightened management control. The emphasis is almost exclusively on the management, or more precisely the maximisation, of human resources, involving an instrumental approach which is coherently integrated into corporate business strategy . . . this is not so much a question of choice as necessity, since the JIT system increases the dependency of management on the workforce by removing all elements of slack or waste in the system.
>
> Delbridge and Turnbull (1992, 58)

In a review based on the experiences of the Swedish automobile industry, Berggren (1990) challenges the MIT argument that lean production is fundamentally different to mass production. This study compares Japanese lean production systems with Swedish 'whole car' manufacturing systems. Berggren argues that lean production essentially represents another stage in the evolution of mass production, since it entails many of the core characteristics of that system: pre-defined work processes, short job cycles, repetitive tasks and intense supervision. He also points to the intense demands which lean production places on workers in areas such as working time, flexibility, effort levels and attendance. Based on his research of five Swedish plants with different work systems, Berggren concludes that the further one moves away from assembly line work systems towards 'whole car systems' the greater the improvements in terms of the job experience of workers (on dimensions such as job satisfaction, challenge, stress and employee involvement). He thus argues that moves towards 'whole systems' correlate with worker preferences (for variety and development rather than repetitive tasks). Clearly such 'whole car' systems are very different from assembly line systems in their rejection of task fragmentation and job specialisation.

This latter argument in relation to whole job systems versus assembly systems brings us to a traditional dilemma in the area of job and work system design, namely that concerning quality of working life considerations with a regard to costs and profits. We have earlier noted that the 1990s have been characterised by increased competitive pressures on organisations, such as the need to concurrently reduce costs and improve quality and service, the need to reduce cycle times and speed to market and the need to be more responsive to market trends. All these pressures combine to encourage management to seek improvements in their internal operating systems on dimensions such as costs, speed, quality and flexibility. While on occasion these pressures may serve to improve the job experience of workers in areas such as job content and employee involvement, it is probably more likely to lead to greater job pressures on workers. This is particularly the case in highly competitive sectors where labour costs represent a high proportion of total production costs. In Berggren's study of the automobile industry, he concedes that the long term viability of the Swedish 'whole car' manufacturing system is dependent not on the quality of the job experience but rather on the extent to which it can be reconciled with profitability. If lean production systems can provide cars at lower cost and equal or better quality, then 'whole car' systems cannot compete with assembly line systems.

This chapter has explored the principles of motivation and work design. Definitions were set down and the pedigree of both concepts in the management cannon were established. In relation to motivation, hierarchy of needs theory, ERG theory, acquired needs theory and dual-factor theory were all examined under the umbrella of *content* approaches to understanding motivation at work. Theory X, theory Y, expectancy theory and equity theory, as process theories of motivation were also examined. Finally, the importance of work organisation and job design as a critical determinant of employee satisfaction and motivation at work has been presented and the various schools of thought have been synthesised.

The issues raised in this chapter are related to broader corporate choices about the nature and role of the organisation. Employee performance will be influenced by a variety of factors relating to both the individual and the work context. The work environment is seen as particularly important. As information technology becomes more flexible in its application, employers have possibly greater scope to introduce changes in work organisation. Apart from the necessity for management commitment and positive beliefs about people at work, these changes have broader implications for other HRM policy choices. In particular it is important that any changes in work organisation complement decisions taken in other HR areas especially in human resource planning, selection, employee development, employee relations and remuneration.

Decisions on work organisation and job design represent a critical aspect of human resource management in organisations. It influences key areas such as organisational structure, management style, employees' motivation and reward systems. While environmental factors exercise a key influence, top management still retain considerable discretion in making choices on the nature of work systems. Indeed, the growth in sophistication and flexibility of information technology may allow employers greater scope to introduce changes in work organisation

Employees' selection and development are particularly significant since corporate choices on work and job design need to dovetail with workforce needs and motives. The degree of congruence between the work system, job design and employees' needs will be a major influence on employee relations.

6

Reward Management

Reward management, which according to Smith (1992) has become the means to describe the administration of pay and the reward package offered, represents a central tenet of any organisation's approach to human resource management. In today's business environment, its importance should not be underestimated. It has been highlighted (Morley and McCarthy 1999) that the quantity of evidence on the apparent significance of reward policies and practices and their links to organisational outcomes, though controversial, is beginning to grow. This is largely as a result of the recognition that compensation practices must be relevant in a world where there is increasing competition and awareness of the contribution of the human asset to overall organisational performance (Miller and Lee 2001; Morley *et al.* 2001; Benchley 2001; Bloom and Milkovich 1998).

Reward management has become especially important in helping to attract and retain employees and also in influencing performance and behaviour at work (Allen 2001). As Sanfilippo and Weigman (1991) put it 'in the 1990s there is a recognition that compensation practices must be relevant to a world where there is unrelenting competition at every level and more awareness that labour productivity is a key dimension of making a profit'. While Lawler (2000) in his treatise on 'Rewarding Excellence' argues that strategic success is heavily dependent on how well the organisations reward systems support the organisation's strategic intent. Viewed in this way, it becomes obvious that pay, incentives and benefits are of central importance to employees and organisations alike. Subsumed under the label 'reward management' are numerous objectives relating to human resource plans and business strategies, high-performance and continuous improvement, the satisfaction of individual needs and wants, cultural maintenance and the promotion of teamwork. High or low pay, the nature of incentives and the range of fringe benefits in existence provide a valuable insight into the corporate approach to human resources. How the reward package is structured and applied may have a major impact on employee performance and it represents 'a major mediating mechanism between the requirements of those planning the organisation and the desires and interests of the employees' (Bowey 1975, 57).

This chapter explores the concept of reward management. Pay, incentives and benefits as possible components of the overall reward package are defined and the objectives and scope of reward management are examined. During the course of the chapter, it will become obvious to the reader that the management of rewards is more than just direct wages and salaries paid. Additional direct payments in the form of bonuses and other incentives are used extensively. A growing cost for many employers are employees' benefits, which represent indirect reward because employees receive the value of the benefits without getting direct cash payments (Mathis and Jackson 1994). The reward package is often one of the largest costs faced by employers with many having labour costs as high as 50 per cent of all operating costs. It will also become clear that although the total cost of a reward system is reasonably straightforward to calculate, the value derived by employers and employees is much more difficult to identify and quantify. In order to help clarify where added value might accrue, issues in the design of an effective reward system are considered and the meaning, purpose and methods of job evaluation are set down. The choice of pay, incentive and fringe benefits available to an organisation are presented and examined. Finally, the debate on pay as a motivator is briefly examined.

THE SCOPE OF REWARD MANAGEMENT

As with the design of the work system, an organisation's reward system is a powerful indicator of its philosophy and approach to people management (Gunnigle and Flood 1990). Three aspects of the reward package are worth distinguishing at the outset, namely *pay*, *incentives* and *benefits*. Pay refers to the basic wage or salary that an employee receives. An incentive refers to the rewarding of an employee for effort that results in higher performance that goes beyond normal performance expectations. Benefits refer to indirect rewards such as health insurance cover and pension entitlements associated with organisational membership. In relation to incentive schemes that emphasise differential rewards based on performance as a means of increasing motivation, it is not axiomatic that higher motivation will follow. Such schemes have numerous drawbacks in terms of design, operation and negative side effects. For this and other reasons many organisations use standard pay rates that do not vary according to performance. In establishing a remuneration system an organisation must weigh up the motivational aspects of a performance-related scheme against its drawbacks in terms of operational and other difficulties. It must be established in the context of the organisation's strategic needs and manpower profile, and be part of the overall human resource approach encompassing other motivational factors appropriate to the organisation and relevant to the workforce.

Schuler (1995) outlines a number of core objectives underlying an organisations reward package.

- It serves to attract potential employees: in conjunction with the organisation's human resource plan and its recruitment and selection efforts, the reward package and its mix of pay, incentives and benefits serves to attract suitable employees.
- It assists in retaining good employees: unless the reward package is perceived as internally equitable and externally competitive, good employees may potentially leave.
- It should serve to motivate employees: the reward package can assist in the quest for high-performance by linking rewards to performance i.e. having an incentive element.
- It contributes to human resource and strategic business plans: an organisation may want to create a rewarding and supportive climate, or it may want to be an attractive place to work so that it can attract the best applicants. The reward package can assist these plans and also further other organisational objectives such as rapid growth, survival or innovation.

Thus the reward package is important to the organisation because it helps to attract and retain employees and influence performance and behaviour at work, though the extent to which reward management actually achieves performance improvements remains somewhat disputed (Smith 1992). Concomitantly it is important to employees because it provides the means to satisfy basic needs and may also allow them to satisfy less tangible desires for personal growth and satisfaction.

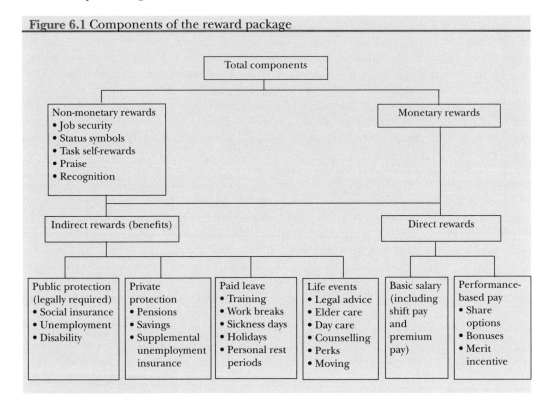

Figure 6.1 Components of the reward package

Source: Adapted from Schuler (1995, 384).

Overall, regardless of how it is constituted, and clearly employers do have choices in this area, the reward package is centrally important to the organisation. It serves to attract potential employees, something that may be more or less difficult, depending on the nature of the external labour market. In conjunction with the organisation's human resource plan and its recruitment and selection activities, the reward package and its mix of pay, incentives and benefits serves to attract suitable employees. It also assists in the retention of good employees, provided that the reward package is perceived to be both internally equitable and externally competitive. In relation to internal equity, rewards must be seen as fair when compared to others in the organisation. The criteria for the allocation of rewards should be equitable and clear and should be relatively easily understood. These should be communicated and accepted by all parties and applied consistently throughout the organisation. In terms of external competitiveness, the package must be seen as fair when compared to those offered for comparable work outside the organisation. More broadly, it constitutes a core aspect of the human resource and business planning process. Concomitantly, it is important to employees because it provides the means to satisfy basic needs for survival, security and may also allow them to satisfy less tangible desires for personal growth and satisfaction.

TOWARDS AN EFFECTIVE REWARD SYSTEM

Important considerations in the design of an organisation's reward system will be the relative emphasis on extrinsic versus intrinsic rewards, the role of pay and whether it is contingent upon individuals' performances and its compatibility with the organisation's business goals and other human resource policies. This latter issue is particularly significant since the organisation's reward system must complement overall business objectives and other human resource policy choices. Decisions on the organisation's cost structure and market strategy will influence the reward strategy. A high-volume, low-cost strategy may constrain the organisation's ability to provide expansive rewards. On the other hand a product innovation strategy may require a comprehensive reward system that attracts and retains high calibre staff. The reward system must also 'fit' other HR decisions. Recruitment and selection will provide a particular workforce profile and the reward system must cater for their various needs. The reward system also complements HR practices in areas like employee development and promotion.

The design and implementation of an effective reward system has proven a difficult task for many organisations. Beer *et al.* (1985) suggest that many employee grievances and criticisms of reward systems actually mask more fundamental employee relations problems. Because extrinsic rewards are a tangible outcome of an employee's relationship with an organisation, they are an obvious target for discontent within the employment relationship. Dissatisfaction with elements of this relationship, such as the supervisory style or opportunities for personal development, may manifest themselves in dissatisfaction with aspects of the reward system. Consequently, organisations experiencing problems with their reward system should examine decisions taken on other human resource policy issues such as selection, employee relations or work design, rather than making piecemeal changes to the compensation package.

Another potential problem concerns suggestions that pay should be contingent on individual performance. Support for contingent payment systems is based on the concept that it is fair and logical to reward individual employees differentially, based on some measure of performance. While this principle is rarely a source of contention, problems may arise in attempting to develop reliable and acceptable mechanisms for evaluating employee performance. These include the limited criteria used (e.g. work-study), inconsistency of application (e.g. performance appraisal), or bias and inequity in employees' evaluations. A more fundamental issue may be resentment towards the exercise of managerial control via performance measurement and reward distribution, which is inherent in many 'reward-for-performance' approaches.

In attempting to develop an effective reward system Lawler (1977) highlights the following essential characteristics.

- Reward level: the reward package must satisfy basic needs for survival, security and self-development.
- Individuality: apart from satisfying basic needs the reward system must be flexible enough to meet the varying individual needs of the organisation's employees.
- Internal equity: rewards must be seen as fair when compared to others in the organisation; criteria for the allocation of rewards should be equitable and clear; these should be communicated and accepted by all parties and applied consistently throughout the organisation.
- External equity: rewards must be seen as fair when compared to those offered for comparable work outside the organisation.

- Trust: management and employees must believe in the reward system; employees accepting that certain rewards will be forthcoming when the relevant criteria are met; management trusting that employees will perform at an appropriate level in return for such rewards.

Thus the objectives of an effective reward system encapsulate the identification of prevailing market trends, balancing individual and groups needs with organisational needs and/or constraints, ensuring fairness and equity, inducing and rewarding higher levels of performance and working within the law.

DETERMINING THE RELATIVE VALUE OF JOBS

Of primary importance is the establishment of basic pay levels for various jobs. Here again the organisation must be aware of the need to establish pay equity. This initially applies to *external comparisons* with pay levels in other organisations. Comparable pay rates influence an organisation's ability to attract and retain employees. Suitable comparable organisations should be chosen to both maintain pay competitiveness while keeping wage costs at reasonable levels. Pay levels will be influenced by factors in the broader business environment such as:

- Economic climate: here factors like levels of inflation, disposable income and industrial activity will exert both direct and indirect influences on payment levels by affecting employment levels, demand, consumer price indices, etc.
- Labour market: the state of the labour market will be influenced by general economic factors. It will also depend on labour supply and demand for certain skills and local factors like the level of company closures, emigration, etc. Information on local and national pay rates may be obtained through wage surveys of comparable organisations.
- Government policy: Government will exert considerable influence on pay levels both indirectly (fiscal policy) and directly through what it pays its own employees (state, semi-state sector), national pay guidelines, minimum pay levels (Joint Labour Committees), and legislation (e.g. equal pay).
- Trade unions: through collective bargaining trade unions will seek to improve or, at least, maintain their members' earning levels. Such claims will generally be based on comparability, differentials and cost of living increases.

They will also depend on factors relating to the organisation itself. Managerial philosophy and style in managing employees will impact upon approaches to the supervision, development and payment of employees. The organisation's competitive position will influence its ability to reward employees. These factors help determine the organisation's position as a low, high or average payer, which in turn will influence the choice of comparable organisations for pay purposes.

Organisations must also strive to maintain *internal equity* in determining differential pay rates for various jobs. The establishment of an internal pay structure involves deciding the relative value of jobs within an organisation and results in the creation of a hierarchy of job grades. The perceived equity of internal job grades will impact upon employees' performance and commitment. Grading can equally be a source of grievance and conflict, which requires careful handling.

Establishing fair and consistent pay rates and differentials between jobs is an important step in developing an effective compensation system. Management will want to ensure that jobs that contribute most to the organisation are rewarded appropriately. They will also be keen to ensure that conflict over pay and job grading is kept to a minimum by establishing an equitable and consistent system for grading jobs and determining differentials. Aspirations for pay equity can be partially satisfied by ensuring pay rates are competitive in comparison with other organisations. Before this, however, the organisation should establish an acceptable mechanism for internally grading and evaluating jobs.

The initial stage in establishing the relative worth of jobs is an analysis of job content. This will often be achieved through systematic job analysis that should provide detailed information on the duties, demands, responsibilities, and skills of the various jobs in the organisation. Such information may then be used to establish the organisation's grading structure and decide related pay levels through some method of job evaluation.

Approaches to Job Evaluation

Job evaluation is often described as being concerned solely with the techniques used to establish the comparative worth of jobs within an organisation, but is also, according to Armstrong and Baron (1995) about making decisions on what people should be paid for the work they do. Gunnigle and Flood (1990) suggest that it is a technique for determining the relative worth of jobs within an organisation so that differential rewards may be given to jobs of different worth. It operates by examining job content and placing jobs in a hierarchy according to their contribution to the attainment of corporate objectives. Fowler (1996) notes that:

> Selecting the right job evaluation system is crucial if the resulting pay frameworks are to be consistent with an organisation's structure, style and values. There is no one best scheme. Each organisation needs to assess its own requirements and set these against the range of available methods.

Armstrong and Baron (1995) cite the following key purposes of job evaluation:

- to provide a rational basis for the design and maintenance of an equitable and defensible pay structure;
- to help in the management of the relativity existing between jobs within the organisation;
- to enable consistent decisions to be made on grading and rates of pay;
- to establish the extent to which there is comparable worth between jobs so that equal pay can be provided for work of equal value.

Job evaluation schemes are commonly classified into *non-analytical schemes* and *analytical schemes*. Non-analytical schemes involve the making of comparisons between whole jobs without analysing them into their constituent parts or elements. Among the main schemes here are *job ranking, job classification* and *paired comparison*. Analytical schemes involve jobs being broken down into a number of critical factors that are then analysed and compared, using a quantitative measure. Among the main analytical methods are *points rating, Hay method* and more recently, *competence-based* job evaluation. We now turn to a description of the non-analytical and analytical schemes mentioned.

Job Ranking

Ranking is the simplest method of job evaluation and according to Armstrong and Baron (1995) 'is almost intuitive'. It aims to judge each job as a whole and determine its place in a job hierarchy by comparing one job with another and arranging them in perceived order of importance, their difficulty, or their value to the organisation. No attempt is made to quantify judgements. A ranking table is then drawn up and the jobs thus ranked are arranged into grades. Pay levels are then agreed for each grade. Sometimes a single factor such as skill is used; alternatively a list of factors such as skill, responsibility, complexity and physical demands is used. Armstrong and Baron (1995) list the following advantages and disadvantages of job ranking.

Advantages
- It is in accord with how people instinctively value jobs.
- It is simple and easily understood.
- It is quick and cheap to implement, as long as agreement can be reached on the rank order of the jobs without too much argument.
- It is a way of checking the results of more sophisticated methods to indicate the extent to which the hierarchies produced are felt fair – but this may simply reproduce the existing hierarchy and fail to eliminate the gender bias.

Disadvantages
- There are no defined standards for judging relative worth – and therefore no rationale to defend the rank order – it is simply a matter of opinion.
- Ranking is not acceptable as a method of determining comparable worth in equal-value cases.
- Evaluators need an overall knowledge of every job to be evaluated, and ranking may be more difficult when a large number of jobs are under consideration.
- It may be difficult, if not impossible, to produce a felt-fair ranking for jobs in widely different functions, when the demands made upon them vary significantly.
- The division of the rank order into grades is likely to be somewhat arbitrary.

Overall, job ranking as a method of job evaluation is most useful for small organisations with a limited range of jobs to evaluate.

Job Classification

Job classification is more complex than job ranking in that classes or grades are established and the jobs are then placed into the grades. Thus, it begins, not by ranking jobs, but by agreeing a grading structure. Initially the number of job grades and particular criteria for these grades are agreed, so that for each job grade there is a broad description of its key characteristics. The number of grades is usually limited to between four and eight, between each of which there are clear differences in the demands made by any job in its respective grade. In establishing the grades, benchmark jobs considered to be particularly characteristic of each job grade are chosen, and using detailed job descriptions, all other jobs are evaluated by comparison with both the benchmark jobs and the criteria for each job grade. Evaluated jobs are then placed in their appropriate grades. Job classification advantages include:

- Its simplicity and the ease with which it can be understood.
- Greater objectivity than job ranking.
- Standards for making grading decisions are provided in the form of the grade definitions.

Key disadvantages include:
- The basis of the job evaluation is either one factor or an intuitive summary of many factors.

- It is difficult to apply with more complex jobs where duties and skills do not fit neatly into one grade but overlap with other grades.
- It may not be able to cater for a wide range of jobs or for senior jobs where grade descriptions have to be very general.
- Because it is not an analytical system it is not effective as a means of establishing comparable worth and is unacceptable in equal value cases.

Paired Comparison

More sophisticated than the previous two methods, the paired comparison approach is based on the premise that it is more reasonable to compare one job with another than to consider a larger number of jobs together. The method requires the comparison of each job individually with every other job, until one builds up a rank order of jobs. When a job is deemed to be of higher worth than the one to which it is being compared, it is awarded two points. If it is deemed to be of equal worth it receives one point; if it is found to be of less worth it receives no points. The points are then totalled for each job and a rank order is produced.

The main advantage of this approach is that it is easier to compare one job with another at a time, which results in greater overall consistency. The main disadvantages are that it relies on whole or complete job ranking, which is difficult, and there is a limit to the number of jobs that can be ranked.

Points Rating

Points rating is a widely used method of job evaluation. It involves breaking down each job into a number of component job factors and then analysing these separately defined factors, which are assumed to be common to all jobs. Gunnigle and Flood (1990) suggest that it is based on the assumption that the degree to which differences in the job factors arise will accurately reflect the actual difference between total jobs. The selection of the job factors is critical. Benge (1944), who first promulgated the method, suggested that it should be limited to the following five factors, which he believed were the universal factors found in all jobs: skill requirements, mental requirements, physical requirements, responsibility and working conditions. Each of these job factors may then be broken down into a number of sub-factors. The sub-factors of responsibility might well include financial, quality, equipment and materials, training and others. Once the factors and sub-factors have been agreed, point values are then allocated (see table 6.1).

Table 6.1 Points rating job evaluation

| | LEVEL | | | | |
Factor	1 Minimum	2 Low	3 Moderate	4 High	Total points
Responsibility					
(a) Financial	10	20	30	40	
(b) Quality	10	20	30	40	
(c) Equipment	10	20	30	40	
(d) Training	10	20	30	40	
(e) Other	10	20	30	40	200
Working conditions					
(a) Hazardous	15	30	45	60	
(b) Unpleasant	10	20	30	40	100

Source: Gunnigle and Flood (1990).

In the example shown here, responsibility is twice as important as working conditions, while in relation to working conditions, hazardous conditions get more points than those that are simply rated as unpleasant. The various jobs may then be evaluated and placed in their appropriate grades. Gunnigle and Flood (1990) suggest that this can be done by either taking one factor and evaluating its significance in all jobs under consideration, or taking each job and evaluating it in terms of all job factors. The former approach is recommended as it concentrates on the comparable worth of jobs in terms of a specific factor and this information can be brought together at the end to give a total picture of relative job worth.

Among the advantages of points rating are:
- It is systematic and analytical in the sense that it compares jobs on a factor by factor basis.
- The standards of comparison are clearly defined.

Frequently cited disadvantages include:
- It is complex and difficult to understand.
- It can be time consuming and expensive.
- Although analytical, it still relies on a deal of subjective judgement.
- It may be impossible to put numerical values on different aspects of jobs, since skills are not always quantifiable in this way, particularly when comparing the skills demanded by jobs of often disparate demands and responsibilities.

Hay Method
The Hay method or plan is one of the most widely used job evaluation methods in the world and is generally classified as a points-factor rating. Traditionally associated with managerial and professional jobs, it is becoming more widely used for technical, clerical and other positions. The method relies on three primary factors, namely know-how, problem solving and accountability (see figure 6.2).

It combines aspects of points rating and factor comparison. Values are established for each job using the factors set out in the table and jobs are compared to one another on each factor. Points-factor schemes of this kind are popular because people generally feel that they work.

Among the frequently quoted advantages are:
- the wide acceptance of the approach;
- evaluators are forced to consider a range of factors and thus avoid over simplifications;
- a higher level of objectivity than other approaches;
- many external comparisons are available because of the widespread adoption of the method.

Disadvantages include:
- the degree of complexity;
- because of its standardised nature, it may not reflect an organisations real needs;
- despite the impression of objectivity, human judgement is required in the process.

Competence-Based Job Evaluation
Variously referred to as competence-based, skill-based or knowledge-based, the emphasis is on an evaluation of the individual who performs the job and his/her competencies and performance abilities rather than on job title or grade. Thus if the previously described job evaluation methods had at their core the principle of 'paying for the job', competence-based evaluation has as its central tenet 'pay for the person'. Armstrong and Baron (1995) argue that competence-based job evaluation is growing in importance because much greater significance is now attached to knowledge work in organisations, and more

Figure 6.2 Primary factors in the Hay method

PROBLEM-SOLVING (MENTAL ACTIVITY)	KNOW-HOW	ACCOUNTABILITY
The amount of original, self-starting thought required by the job for analysis, evaluation, creation, reasoning, and arriving at conclusions.	The total of all knowledge and skills, however acquired, needed for satisfactory job performance (evaluates the job, not the person).	The measured effect of the job on company goals.
Problem-solving has two dimensions:	Know-how has three dimensions:	Accountability has three dimensions:
• The degree of freedom with which the thinking process is used to achieve job objectives without the guidance of standards, precedents, or direction from others.	• The amount of practical, specialised or technical knowledge required.	• Freedom to act, or the relative presence of personal or procedural control and guidance, determined by answering the question, 'How much freedom has the job holder to act independently?'—for example, a plant manager has more freedom than a supervisor under his or her control.
• The type of mental activity involved; the complexity, abstractness or originality of thought required.	• Breadth of management, or the ability to make many activities and functions work well together; the job of company president, for example, has greater breadth than that of a department supervisor.	• Dollar magnitude, a measure of the sales, budget, value of purchases, value added or any other significant annual money figure related to the job.
Problem-solving is expressed as a percentage of know-how, for the obvious reason that people think with what they know. The percentage judged to be correct for a job is applied to the know-how point value; the result is the point value given to problem-solving.	• Requirement for skill in motivating people. Using a chart, a number can be assigned to the level of know-how needed in a job. This number—or point value—indicates the relative importance of know-how in the job being evaluated.	• Impact of the job on dollar magnitude, a determination of whether the job has a primary effect on final results or has instead a sharing, contributory or remote effect. Accountability is given a point value independent of the other two factors.

Note: The total evaluation of any job is arrived at by adding the points for problem-solving, know-how, and accountability. The points are not shown here.

Source: Schuler (1995).

emphasis is being placed on flexibility, multi-skilling individuals and team autonomy and empowerment.

Armstrong and Baron (1995) highlight three approaches to developing competence-based job evaluation:

1. Take an existing analytical scheme and modify the factor plan to make it more competence-related by reference to an existing competence framework.
2. Take existing competence frameworks and adapt them to develop a competence-based scheme.
3. Conduct a special analysis of generic and job specific abilities to produce a competency framework and develop a scheme from this analysis.

Among some of the abilities likely to be examined or considered in any of these approaches are interpersonal and communication skills, reasoning and critical thinking ability, technical and business knowledge, decision-making ability, team working and

Figure 6.3 A comparison of conventional job evaluation and competence-based job evaluation

COMPONENT	SKILL-BASED EVALUATION	JOB-BASED EVALUATION
1. Determination of job worth	Tied to evaluation of skill blocks	Tied to evaluation of total job
2. Pricing	Difficult because overall pay system is tied to market	Easier, because wages are tied to labour market
3. Pay ranges	Extremely broad: one pay range for entire cluster of skills	Variable, depending on type of job and pay grade width
4. Evaluation of performance	Competence tests	Performance appraisal ratings
5. Salary increases	Tied to skill acquisition as measured by competence testing	Tied to seniority, performance appraisal ratings, or actual output
6. Role of training	Essential to attain job flexibility and pay increases for all employees	Necessitated by need rather than desire
7. Advancement opportunities	Greater opportunities: anyone who passes competence test advances	Fewer opportunities: no advancement unless there is a job opening
8. Effect of job change	Pay remains constant unless skill proficiency increases	Pay changed immediately to level associated with new job
9. Pay administration	Difficult, because many aspects of pay plan (training, certification) demand attention	Contingent on complexity of job evaluation and pay allocation plan

Source: Adapted from Schuler (1995).

leadership skills, resource management capabilities and planning, organising and problem-solving abilities. The advantages of competence-based job evaluation include:

- It provides a framework for relevant ongoing employee development.
- It can assist in making the organisation more flexible through an ever-expanding focused skill base.
- There is a clear focus on the person.

The following disadvantages are frequently cited:
- The competence movement has been accused of being vague in its terminology.
- It can be as complex and difficult as any other form of job evaluation.
- It can lead to too much emphasis being placed on the skills and knowledge that the person brings to the job and not enough on the outputs from that job.

CRITICISMS OF JOB EVALUATION

Fowler (1996) suggests that:

> Job evaluation, once a highly regarded management tool, has come under fire in recent times. Its critics say that because it assesses the job rather than the job holder, it fails to recognise the contribution of the individual. It has also been argued that the detailed job descriptions involved in some schemes serve to inhibit flexibility.

Edwards *et al.* (1995) enumerate a number of weaknesses associated with traditional job evaluation. They suggest that it leads to an inappropriate focus on promotion where by people are led to believe that a job is more important than the individual in the job. Secondly, they highlight its inability to reward knowledge workers on the basis that traditional job-based pay systems that reward position in the hierarchy do not work well for knowledge workers whose performance is based on specialised applied learning rather than on general skills. Thirdly, they point to its inability to keep pace with high-speed organisational changes and emergent employee roles.

Gunnigle and Flood (1990) cite the potential for error in human judgements that form a central part of the process as perhaps one of its greatest drawbacks.

> Despite some of the obvious benefits of job evaluation . . . it is not infallible. It attempts to create a consistent and equitable system for grading jobs. However, it depends on the judgement of people with experience and training, requiring them to make decisions in a planned and systematic way, and the results do not guarantee total accuracy.

Choosing and Introducing the Job Evaluation Scheme

Introducing job evaluation will have a tremendous impact on company pay structures and employee relations generally. Therefore any decisions should only be taken after careful deliberation. Fowler (1996) suggests that a job evaluation scheme needs to be determined primarily by setting the characteristics of different methods against the organisation's circumstances and objectives. In this respect he suggests that the following questions are useful:

1. Is the principal aim to meet the requirements of equal pay legislation?
2. How many different jobs are there to be evaluated?
3. How complex is the pay structure?
4. What are the factors or characteristics to which the organisation wishes to allocate monetary value within the pay structure?
5. Is the scheme intended for making market comparisons?
6. Is there an advantage in using a computerised system?

Gunnigle and Flood (1990) highlight the necessity for advice and participation. They argue that the introduction of job evaluation can be a complex process and thus it is often useful to seek expert advice and guidance at the initial stages. This expert would usually be responsible for advising on the technical aspects of the scheme and assisting with decisions on the type of scheme to use, the establishment and composition of overseeing committees, the training of job analysts and communicating the details of the scheme to all concerned.

In relation to participation, they suggest that at all stages in the process staff should be kept adequately informed. It is vital that those who will be most directly affected by the scheme should know its objectives, its content and how it will operate. Middle management and supervisors are critical here. They will play a vital role in implementing the scheme so it is imperative that they understand it and appreciate their role in its operation.

THE REWARD PACKAGE: PAY AND INCENTIVES

Determining the worth of a job and the setting down of basic pay levels are critical aspects of the process of establishing a pay system. Choosing the actual payment system is the other critical aspect.

The choice of system is an important consideration for organisations. It will partially reflect the corporate approach to human resource management and impact on areas such as employee relations, supervisory style and employees' motivation. The particular package offered will be determined by a variety of factors related to the organisation, the general business environment and the workforce. In relation to choices of payment schemes Mooney (1980) feels these are related to the characteristics of the organisation and product. In particular he identifies the significance of:

1. Company ownership: Mooney feels that a continuing influx of foreign companies will increase the utilisation of performance-related bonus schemes.
2. Size: performance-related schemes are more common in larger organisations, while small firms tend to rely on a flat rate only.
3. Technical system: organisations operating large batch production techniques – which are common in Ireland – are more likely to use performance-related payment systems.
4. Labour costs: Mooney feels this is the most important factor influencing the choice of payment system. Flat-rate-only or company-wide schemes dominate in capital cost-intensive organisations, while individual or group incentive schemes are popular in high labour cost organisations.

Overall, as with other aspects of human resource management, the corporate approach to compensation should complement the organisation's strategic business goals, human resource philosophy and other HR activities.

There are numerous options in the type of pay and incentive and benefits package an organisation might adopt. The more common types of payment systems are presented below. Statutory and non-statutory benefits available in Ireland are then considered.

Flat Rate Systems

FLAT RATE ONLY

A traditional approach to reward, flat-rate-pay schemes pay a person for the time spent on the job and no incentive is provided for actual performance. They are popular because of their simplicity and ease of administration. They are particularly useful for managerial and administrative jobs where specific performance criteria are difficult to establish. They help attract employees to join the organisation but there motivational potential in encouraging good performance is thought to be limited. In Mooney's (1980) study of wage payment systems in Ireland, he found the flat rate system by far the most popular, particularly for indirect employees. However, he also found that the utilisation of approaches that combine the flat rate with incentive payments based on some measure of performance were on the increase.

ANNUAL HOURS CONTRACT

As with the flat-rate-only system, the annual hours contract is based on the premise that one is paid for the time spent on the job. However, in this instance working time is organised on an annual rather than a weekly basis. Thus the annual hours contract will specify the number of hours to be worked in the year rather than the week. Originally developed in Scandinavia, O Sullivan (1996) notes that it is increasingly being regarded as an important alternative to the standard 39-hour week plus overtime in Ireland.

O'Sullivan cites a number of advantages to be gained from this approach: from the company's perspective, there will often be an improvement in unit costs and productivity, the elimination of large scale overtime, a closer match between output and demand and a reduction in absenteeism. From the employee's perspective, the benefits include

Figure 6.4 Methods for calculating the annual hours' contract

There are two ways of calculating the contract, which produce the same result:

(1) Standard working week formula

Calendar year:	52.18 weeks (inc. leap year)
Annual leave:	4 weeks
Public holidays:	1.8 weeks
Average working week:	46.38 weeks $\times$ 39 hours
Annual hours:	1,808.82 (net basic working hours)

(2) Annual working formula

In a complete calendar year there are an average of 365.25 days, which comprise 8,766 hours.
Example:
Employee works 39 hours a week.

$$\frac{39 \times 365.25}{7} = 2,035 \text{ hours a year}$$

Less annual and public holidays:	2,035
20 days' annual leave:	7.8 $\times$ (20)
9 public holidays:	7.8 $\times$ (9)
	$- 226.2$
Employee available to work:	1,808.8 hours per year

Source: O'Sullivan (1996).

improved basic pay, stability of earnings and increased leisure time. The disadvantages cited by O'Sullivan include the necessity to recoup monies owing to the company if an employee leaves during the year; the necessity for re-organisation and cultural and value changes that are congruent with this approach.

Performance-Based Incentive Systems

The use of incentives is not a new phenomenon with performance-related pay schemes having formed a significant part of the traditional remuneration package in many organisations. McBeath and Rands (1989) define performance-related pay 'as an intention to pay distinctly more to reward highly effective job performance than you are willing to pay for good solid performance', the objective of which should be to develop a productive, efficient, effective organisation (Hoevemeyer 1989).

Kessler and Purcell (1992) argue that the very mechanics of such schemes involve a fundamental restructuring of the employment relationship, which often results in greater managerial control over staff by isolating the individual from the work group and forcing the personalised design and evaluation of work. Support for performance-based incentive systems is based on the concept that it is fair and logical to reward individual employees differentially, based on some measure, or combination of measures, of performance. 'In fact, the principle of [such] pay is so logical that it seems almost ludicrous to criticise it' (Meyer 1975, 39). Since if 'two individuals are performing the same job and one is substantially more effective than the other, the person with the superior contributions should surely be paid more' (Lowery *et al*, 1996, 27). Bowey and Thorpe (1986) suggest there is a positive correlation between individual performance and incentive payments with improvements in costs and quality. However, they also point to potentially adverse affects on attitudes to work and employee relations. A continuing problem in such approaches is finding an acceptable mechanism to assess equitable and consistent performance. Otherwise performance-based payments can lead to problems as a result of resentment towards managerial control or inequity and inconsistency in performance evaluation. An important factor seems to be the extent of employee involvement with schemes that require extensive consultation; they have greater chances of success. Armstrong and Murlis (1988) outline six factors that underpin such successful systems.

1. An equitable mechanism for performance measurement incorporating performance appraisal.
2. Consistency of rewards among individual employees.
3. Managerial flexibility to link reward decisions to organisational needs to attract and retain employees.
4. Simple to understand and apply.
5. Good basic compensation package.
6. Clearly defined employee development policy.

It is important that management clearly outline key performance criteria and reward employees accordingly. Employee acceptance will depend on perceived equity in performance evaluation. It demands a climate of trust and fairness – the main responsibility for whose development lies with management. In this context, performance-based incentive schemes in an organisational environment will be much more likely to fulfil their core functions.

- To ensure an adequate supply of skilled and trained employees in response to fluctuating labour demands. While choice is more repressed in turbulent economic circumstances individuals making an employment decision will look not only at the terms of employment, but also at the total remuneration package, including variable and incentive pay.
- To elicit from employees, both individually and collectively, performance which reinforces the strategic direction of the organisation. Thus one of the key underlying assumptions is that pay has the potential to motivate.
- To serve as vehicle for organisational change.

Kelly and Monks (1997), in their trawl of the research literature, discovered that performance-related pay schemes often have the realisation of change objectives at their core.

The growth of performance-based incentive systems in Ireland has been inexorably linked to the broader HRM trend towards relating pay more closely to performance. It is evident that performance-based incentive systems might take a number of forms and the question facing most organisations is not which type of scheme to pick but rather, which package of methods will be most successful in fulfilling the organisation's strategic goals. Morley *et al.* (1999) report that in the area of performance-based incentive pay, Irish private sector organisations were, in recent years, far more likely to have introduced such schemes for several grades, than formerly. They found that performance-related pay was the most popular incentive used, with 59 per cent of private and 25 per cent of public sector companies implementing it at managerial level. However, this figure declines rapidly as one descends the hierarchy, a factor that has not changed to any significant degree since the early 1990s. Thus the established practice of differentiating between manual and managerial employees in the application of such performance-based incentive schemes remain very much in evidence. Arguably this may be rationalised in a number of ways. A traditional explanation for such treatment has been the difficulty of disaggregating the impact of the individual's effort and performance on effectiveness at the lower echelons of the organisation, and thus, performance-related pay was generally considered to be applicable principally to managerial levels. In recent times, this problem has been overcome in many organisations, by assessing the individual within the confines of his/her particular task or job.

A second explanation is the opposition of trade unions, which may often be opposed to payments based on individual performance preferring collective increases achieved through management-union negotiations. Grafton (1988) feels that schemes that operate increases in addition to general salary awards are less likely to cause employee opposition as they operate as a discretionary element, which does not cut across the collective bargaining role of the trade union. In an appropriate organisational climate performance-based incentive pay can be effectively used to augment negotiated pay and benefit increases and stimulate improved employee and organisational performance.

The penetration of foreign multinational companies (MNCs), particularly US-owned MNCs, into Irish industrial structures is significant here in accounting for the performance-based incentive pay trend in Ireland. While McMahon *et al.* (1988) feel that MNCs have adapted to accommodate local practices, this need not necessarily result in an abandonment of foreign management philosophy, but rather, the pursuit of such within existing frameworks and customs. In the case of US multinationals, successive research has repeatedly emphasised the prevalence of linking pay to a measure of performance (Hay Associates 1975; Locker and Teel 1977; Eichel and Bender 1984). The perceived importance of performance-related schemes amongst US organisations is maintained in their subsidiary plants in the Irish context, with many managerial, professional and clerical employees being covered by such schemes. In more recent years, Britain has also seen a change of emphasis in relation to performance approaches. Much of the effort traditionally was directed at assessing future labour requirements and labour training needs (Gill 1977).

However, more recently, according to Long (1986), there has been a greater emphasis on organisational survival and the assessment of current performance. Such emphasis has resulted in a large growth in performance-related pay as a method of improving such performance.

In the section that follows here, we provide a description of several variants of 'shorter term and longer term' (Fierro 2001) performance-based incentive schemes.

FLAT RATE PLUS INDIVIDUAL PBR SYSTEM

Many commentators suggest that individually rewarding performance has a strong motivational impact. Payment is related to the employee's contribution, required performance levels and related financial rewards are specified and these are achievable immediately after these performance criteria have been met. Despite the popularity that individual PBR schemes have achieved in the recent past they do, according to Appelbaum and Shapiro (1991), potentially have a number of flaws. Firstly, they result in a preoccupation with the task at hand and do not relate individual performance to the larger company objectives. Secondly, they work against creating a climate of openness, trust, joint problem-solving and commitment to organisational problem-solving. Thirdly, they can divide the workforce into those supporting the plan and those not in favour of the plan, which may create adversarial relationships.

FLAT RATE PLUS GROUP/TEAM-BASED PBR

The greatest problem therefore associated with individual PBR schemes is not that they will not work, but rather, they will focus the attention and effort in a direction that does not aid the achievement of the strategic goals of the organisation. In recognition of these, and related problems, many organisations have turned to group/team bonus schemes. Payment systems which pay a flat rate plus an incentive based on group/team or sectional performance are used where it is difficult to measure individual performance or to avoid some of the harmful side-effects of individual-based schemes, while providing some incentive which is related to a measure of performance. Daly (1989) defines Group Bonus Schemes as 'The application of payment by results schemes to a group or team where the bonus payments are divided among team members on a pre-agreed basis.' As with individual schemes there are a wide range of schemes from which an organisation may choose, but Ost (1990) feels that all incentives based on group or team work are subject to a number of guiding premises:

1. They always have one or more explicitly stated unit or firm-level performance goals that can only be achieved through team work;
2. A team based incentive system always contains a reward component that is contingent on the successful achievement of those goals;
3. The reward must be perceived by the employee as resulting from contributions that he/she has made;
4. The reward must be perceived as a fair reward;
5. The behaviours and the rewards offered must clearly signal what is meant by good performance.

Piecework

Piecework involves payment solely by performance. While it remains popular in specific areas (e.g. seasonal work in agriculture, outworkers) it is unacceptable to many employees and their organisations since it provides no guarantee of a minimum income to satisfy basic requirements for both individual and societal well being.

Gain-sharing and Share Ownership Schemes

Gain-sharing and share ownership schemes incorporate arrangements that reward employees for improvements in corporate performance through profit sharing, share ownership or some other compensation mechanism. Gain-sharing schemes differ from more traditional profit sharing arrangements insofar as it links rewards based on corporate performance to changes in managerial philosophy and style, which incorporate greater employee influence, involvement and participation.

The direct effects of such schemes on employee motivation are believed to be poor because of its weak relationship with individual performance and lack of immediacy. However, they are seen as having important long-term benefits in increasing employees' participation, awareness and commitment.

Most gain-sharing schemes involve either profit sharing or employee share ownership. Profit sharing is a scheme under which employees, in addition to their normal remuneration, receive a proportion of the profits of the business. Profit sharing may take a number of forms and it is largely at the discretion of the employer and employees to decide to what measure of profit the incentive should be tied, what percentage should be allocated and how it should be administered to employees.

Employee share ownership schemes involve the allocation of company shares to employees according to an agreed formula. Interest in Ireland in employee share ownership schemes has traditionally been relatively low (Long 1988). The growth, small though it has been, is rooted in the finance acts of 1982–4, which were driven by governmental commitment to 'ensuring the success and efficiency of Irish industry and the prosperity and security of Irish workers for the future', by developing employee shareholding. More recent changes however have served to further undermine the already narrow base of share ownership in Ireland. Bertie Ahern, the then Minister for Finance, removed tax incentives for employee share schemes. While resultant action was a dilution rather than removal, employees and employers may be more reluctant to adopt such schemes in what could be described as 'an atmosphere of uncertainty'.

Gain-sharing arrangements incorporating either profit or equity sharing are generally linked to organisational attempts to increase employee involvement and commitment. Armstrong and Murlis (1988) enumerate a number of objectives underlying such schemes:

- to encourage employees to identify themselves more closely with the company by developing a common concern for its progress;
- to stimulate a greater interest among employees in the affairs of the company as a whole;
- to encourage better co-operation between management and employees;
- to recognise that employees of the company have a moral right to share in the profits they helped to produce;
- to demonstrate in practical terms the goodwill of the company to its employees;
- to reward success in businesses where profitability is cyclical.

Such schemes have become particularly popular in Britain and the US and have been linked to corporate successes on such criteria as market share, profitability and quality.

COMPETENCE OR SKILL-BASED PAY

The concept of skill-based pay is not particularly new. However, it has recently been revived in the context of 'a move towards person-based pay, rather than job-based pay as the tasks people do at work change so rapidly' (Sparrow 1996). According to O'Neill and Lander (1994), while relatively limited in application, it has been used for years under names such as pay for knowledge, competency pay, pay for skills and multi-skilled pay. While there may be slight technical differences in these terms they are generally used interchangeably. Skill-based pay is a payment system in which pay progression is linked to the number, kind and depth of skill that individuals develop and use. Ricardo and Pricone (1996) view skill-based pay as an innovative reward system that promotes workforce flexibility by rewarding individuals based on the number, type and depth of skills mastered. Armstrong (1995) highlights that it involves paying for the horizontal acquisition of the skills required to undertake a wider range of tasks, and/or for the vertical development of the skills needed to operate it at a higher level, or the in-depth development of existing skills. In this way competence or skill-based pay is directly linked to competence or skilled-based job evaluation described earlier. In terms of operation, there will usually be a basic job rate for the minimum level of skills. Above this level, individuals will be paid for new skills acquired that assist them in performing their job as individuals or members of a team. O'Neill and Lander (1994) cite four major reasons for the increasing adoption of skill-based pay:

- The need to develop and maintain productive efficiencies through increased output, often combined with a leaner workforce and fewer levels of supervision.
- The need to make more flexible utilisation of the existing workforce to cover absenteeism, turnover and production bottlenecks.

- The need to support new technologies such as computer-aided manufacturing, and new value systems such as total quality management.
- The need to build higher levels of involvement and commitment, increased teamwork, and provide more enriched jobs that provide greater reward opportunities for employees.

BROADBANDING

A concept that is closely related to competence or skill-based pay is broadbanding. Broadbanding has been defined by Tyler (1998) as the elimination of all but a few, usually between three and ten, comprehensive salary bands. It therefore represents a compensation management strategy that involves consolidating several salary grades into fewer, wider pay bands. The bands have minimum and maximum monetary amounts. Hequet (1995) claims that broadbanding is one of the fastest growing compensation schemes in the US. He cites a study carried out by the American Compensation Association that found that 78 per cent of the 116 respondents used broadbanding. Merrick (1997) notes an increasing trend towards broadbanding in Europe also. One of the reasons for its growth is the trend towards de-layering and flatter organisational structures (Sheehan 1997). Examples of companies who are using broadbanding in Ireland include IBM and Nortel. Merrick notes that IBM Europe has dedicated itself to replacing its twenty-five traditional grades with ten bands. The IBEC survey reports that 11 per cent of the companies surveyed have skill-based, competency-based or broadbanding pay systems in operation (IBEC 1998).

Overall, it is evident that incentive or performance-based schemes may take a number of forms and the question facing most organisations is not which type of scheme to pick but rather, which package of methods will be most successful in fulfilling the organisations strategic goals. In implementing incentive schemes Balkin and Mejia (1987) highlight a number of issues which must be addressed: the number of different forms to offer, the relative importance of each form and the proportion of the workforce to which each form may be applicable. The responses to these questions will be determined by the objectives of the performance-based incentive system itself and whether the organisation sees enhanced performance, cost containment or employee retention as the overriding objective of the system. It must be realised however that while performance-based incentive schemes represent a potentially effective tool, they are not a panacea for all organisational ills. Incentive schemes will only fulfil their true potential if existing barriers to individual, group and organisational effectiveness have been removed. Such schemes do not represent a mechanism for compensating wage differentials, nor for overcoming inadequacies in the production system.

Performance-based incentive schemes seem to be becoming more popular in Irish organisations, but on a gradual incremental basis. Drawing upon data from the Cranfield E./ University of Limerick *Study of HR Practices in Ireland*, we can view some evidence of the increased popularity of incentive schemes in many Irish organisations. There is remarkable consistency between the results from the 1992 round of this survey and the 1995 and 1999 subsequent rounds. The use of profit sharing and share options appears to have changed little during the three rounds of this survey. A higher percentage of respondents report the utilisation of group bonus schemes in the most recent round of the survey, especially for managerial grades and professional and technical grades. Merit or performance-related pay continues to be used primarily among higher-level employee grades, though the 1999 results do show a slight decrease here. The use of merit/PRP for manual grades appears stable.

The growth of incentive schemes in Ireland has been inexorably linked to the trend towards relating pay more closely to performance. However, the take up of incentive schemes is correlated with the organisational ownership. Thus, in the Irish context, US

Table 6.2 Use of incentive schemes in Ireland

	Management 1999 1995 1992			Prof/technical 1999 1995 1992			Clerical 1999 1995 1992			Manual 1999 1995 1992		
Share options	21.5	23.0	22.8	13.9	13.8	13.6	11.2	11.5	9.2	9.0	9.6	8.8
Profit sharing	17.9	19.2	15.8	13.9	13.4	12.3	12.1	12.6	10.5	10.5	10.0	10.1
Group bonus	24.2	21.1	14.9	20.0	15.7	12.7	17.3	16.1	11.0	16.8	15.3	14.0
Merit/PRP	44.4	51.3	49.1	38.6	44.8	42.5	30.0	36.8	29.4	17.7	15.3	13.2

Source: Cranet E./University of Limerick Surveys (1992, 1995, 1999).

owned organisations on the whole appear far more likely to utilise incentives than their counterparts, particularly Irish indigenous organisations who demonstrate a lower take-up across the range of incentives (Gunnigle *et al.* 1994; Morley *et al.* 1999).

THE REWARD PACKAGE: FRINGE BENEFITS
In general, fringe benefits (both statutory and voluntary) are estimated to constitute an additional 25–30 per cent on top of basic weekly pay for manual grades. For clerical, administrative and managerial categories, a figure of 15–35 per cent may be appropriate. However, the percentage add-on is primarily related to the level of fringe benefits voluntarily agreed at company level, particularly items such as company cars, pensions, health insurance cover, and sickness benefit and can, therefore, vary considerably between organisations.

The nature of fringe benefits provided to employees varies considerably between organisations and are normally the result of voluntary agreements either between employees (or their representatives) and management. Major differences also exist between blue- and white-collar workers. Some general guidelines on the nature of fringe benefits in Irish organisations are outlined below (see also chapter thirteen on Employment Law).

Maternity/Paternity/Adoptive Provisions
Female employees are entitled to a minimum period of fourteen weeks unpaid maternity leave in accordance with the terms of the Maternity Protection of Employees Act 1981 and the Worker Protection (Regular part-time employees) Act 1991, during which a social welfare benefit is available. Amendments to the maternity legislation in the form of the Maternity Protection Act (1994) were introduced to satisfy Ireland's obligations under EC Directive 92/85. While many of the entitlements provided by the Maternity Protection Act 1994, already existed under the Maternity Protection of Employees Act 1981, there were significant changes with regard to who is covered by the Act; provision for payment for the time off for natal care visits, and health and safety leave provisions under certain circumstances. In terms of leave coverage, any individual under a contract of employment is entitled to protection under the Maternity Protection Act 1994. This includes apprentices, employees on probation and employment agency workers. The act entitles a pregnant employee to fourteen weeks consecutive leave, with a minimum of four weeks; leave before the last day of the expected week of confinement and a minimum of four weeks leave after the last day of the expected week of confinement. There are exceptional provisions for early, late and stillbirths.

The Adoptive Leave Act 1995 entitles female employees and, in certain circumstances, male employees to employment leave for the purpose of child adoption. It provides for a minimum of ten consecutive weeks of adoptive leave. Notice of at least four weeks must be given in writing to the employer of the employee's intention to take adoptive leave. The employee is entitled to additional adoptive leave for a maximum period of four consecutive weeks commencing immediately after the end of the adoptive leave.

The Parental Leave Act 1998 was introduced to implement Council Directive 96/34/EC of June 1996 on the framework agreement on parental leave concluded by UNICE, CEEP and the ETUC. According to this act, an employee who is the natural or adoptive parent of a child shall be entitled to leave from his/her employment for a period of fourteen weeks. The child for which leave is being sought must be born or adopted on or after the 3 June 1996. Parental leave must be taken before the child in question reaches his/her fifth birthday. Notice of intention to take parental leave must be given in writing at least six weeks before the anticipated commencement date.

The Parental Leave Act 1998 also makes provision for *force majeure* leave with pay where the employee is entitled to employment leave because of urgent family reasons such as injury or illness of a family member. An employee is entitled to *force majeure* leave if the person who is ill or injured is: a person of whom the employee is a parent or adoptive parent; the spouse of the employee or a person with whom the employee is living as husband and wife; a person to whom the employee is in loco parentis; a brother or sister of the employee. With regard to *force majeure* leave, the employee must give notice to the employer that he/she has taken *force majeure* leave as soon as possible after taking the leave. This leave can consist of one or more days on which, but for the leave, the employee would be working in the employment concerned, but will not exceed three days in any period of twelve consecutive months or five days in any period of thirty-six consecutive months.

Carer's Leave

Provision for temporary unpaid leave to care for individuals who are in need of full-time care is made for under the Carer's Leave Act 2001. Individuals who satisfy the conditions established in the Act are entitled to take leave to personally provide care for a 'relevant person' who is deemed to need such care. An employee is entitled to a maximum of sixty-five weeks in respect of any one relevant person. The 65-week entitlement may be taken as one ongoing period, or in separate block periods. Individuals may continue to work for up to a maximum of ten hours per week during the period of their carer's leave. In order to qualify for leave, the employee must have been in the continuous employment of the employer from whose employment the leave is to be taken for at least twelve months before he/she can commence the leave

Childcare Facilities

A small number of Irish organisations provide childcare facilities for staff. Currently there are about fifty state-financed nurseries sponsored by local health boards, mostly for families with special needs. There are four semi-state nurseries in Dublin and approximately ten in third level educational institutions. The percentage of respondents offering workplace childcare in the 1999 round of the Cranet E./University of Limerick Survey was 2.5 percent, while only 1.1 percent reported offering childcare allowances.

Career Breaks

Historically, provision for career breaks was relatively rare in Irish private sector organisations. However, career break schemes were and are becoming increasingly widespread in the public sector. These provide for unpaid leave up to a maximum of three years. Where schemes exist in the private sector, they are normally shorter – generally one to two years. The Cranet E./University of Limerick Survey of 1999 reported 33.9 per cent of respondents offering a career break scheme to employees. Approximately 47 per cent reported offering education/training breaks.

Holidays

Holiday entitlements are provided for under the Organisation of Working Time Act 1997. The great majority of organisations provide annual leave entitlements greater than the statutory minimum of fifteen days. This may vary from eighteen to twenty-three days with the average being twenty days per annum. Legislation provides for eight public holidays per annum. Some companies also grant Good Friday, which is not a public holiday, as a privilege day off.

Additional Holiday Pay and Bonuses

Practice varies enormously on this issue. However, many larger private sector companies make such payments. These are typically in the form of either additional holiday pay (from one to several weeks pay), end of year bonus (Christmas bonus – one to several weeks pay) and discretionary payment/gifts for special occasions (service, marriage). An IBEC (1998) survey found that 37 per cent of respondents had a system of pay bonuses that were related to overall company performance, while approximately 4 per cent had Christmas and/or annual bonuses in operation.

Managerial Incentive Schemes

A large number of organisations operate incentive bonus schemes for managerial grades. However, there are considerable variations in the level of payment and the grades involved. Typical criteria for basing incentive payment upon include company performance (particularly profitability), sales or output.

Sickness Pay

There is no legal obligation on organisations to provide sickness pay to employees. However, a large number of organisations provide some kind of sick-pay scheme during defined periods of absence from work due to illness or injury. A 1990 survey carried out by the Federation of Irish Employers found that of the 515 companies questioned, 351 (68 per cent) had sick pay schemes for full-time manual workers and 424 (82 per cent) had schemes for white-collar grades. Of the 168 companies who employed part-time workers, sixty-two (37 per cent) extended their sick pay schemes to cover these employees.

Sick pay schemes normally provide that once a particular service requirement is fulfilled, employees receive full pay (inclusive of social welfare payments) for a finite period (which may vary from a few weeks to a year). It is normal practice for employers to take into account the total benefit payable to employees from social welfare, as well as income tax rebates, in calculating how much the company should pay to make up the total employee benefit during periods of absence due to illness or injury. This may be achieved by either paying the total benefit through payroll and recovering social welfare cheques from employees or by paying a 'top up' element with the employee retaining social welfare benefits.

Health Insurance

The state provides free health care to persons on very low incomes via the 'medical card' system. There is no legislative requirement on employers to provide employees with the coverage of a private medical employment scheme. However, health insurance is available to individuals through the Voluntary Health Insurance Board (VHI) or BUPA Ireland or indeed other providers. The VHI is a semi-state body that provides health insurance to members in line with member contributions. It is wholly financed by member contributions and provides a range of insurance cover, depending on one's level of contribution. The

VHI is self-funded with over one million members and historically it was the monopoly provider of health insurance. Health insurance contributions are fully deductible for income tax purposes. It has been estimated that over 75 per cent of private sector companies have such health insurance schemes in operation for employees. Over half of the white-collar schemes and one third of the manual grade schemes incorporate an employer contribution to the cost of such schemes.

Canteen Facilities

There are no statutory requirements for the provision of canteen facilities. However, the Safety in Industry Act 1980 requires that 'where more than five people are employed, there must be adequate provision for boiling water and taking meals'. In practice, the majority of larger employers provide some form of canteen facilities. These may be subsidised by up to half the economic costs of meals. Tea/coffee facilities may also be provided at a subsidised rate.

Sports and Recreation Facilities

These are typically restricted to larger organisations that may contribute towards some of the cost of their operation.

Company Cars

The majority of larger organisations provide company cars for senior management and, in some instances, for sales staff. The cost of such cars varies considerably according to range but is normally from €14,000 to €33,000. Where cars are supplied, the company normally pays for insurance, tax, petrol and service. When employees use their own cars on company business firms normally pay a mileage allowance, typically varying from 32–76 cent per mile depending on engine size. Company cars are taxed as benefits in kind as a cash equivalent of 20 per cent of original market value. This is reduced where the employee pays the cost of fuel (3 per cent), insurance (2 per cent), service (2 per cent) and tax (0.5 per cent).

Pension Schemes

Most larger organisations have pension schemes, particularly for managerial grades. A total of 87.8 percent of respondents to the Cranet E./University of Limerick (1999) survey reported having a pension scheme in operation. The majority of these schemes are contributory. Most schemes are based on a normal retirement age of sixty-five, although some are based on retirement at sixty. Company pension schemes are governed by the Pensions Act 1990. In Ireland the state provides a basic pension at age sixty-five. This is related to means, but is independent of income and is non-contributory. There is no incomes' related state pension scheme. Private occupational schemes provide earnings related pensions to supplement state entitlements; the state actively encourages the introduction of such schemes through various tax concessions. The Pensions Act of 1990 is designed to protect the rights of members of private occupational pension schemes. It provides for the control of private schemes through a regulatory body, the Pensions Board and deals with funding, benefits and information disclosure in relation to private occupational pension schemes.

Other Benefits

Some companies give employees a discount on the company's products or services or occasionally provide them free of charge. Other popular benefits are death in service benefits in conjunction with the pension scheme, free or subsidised health insurance, and share option schemes. Few companies provide employees with low interest or interest free loans.

PAY AS A MOTIVATOR

The utility of using pay to motivate and promote performance has been a subject of debate for many years with empirical and theoretical support for both sides of the argument. Most managers instinctively believe that money is a motivator, even though empirical evidence to support this is far from conclusive (Kelly and Monks 1997; Fowler 1991; Goffee and Scase 1986). Indeed, failure of such schemes, in some instances, to fulfil their potential has been attributed to a flawed theoretical base (Pearse 1987), which in many cases serves to undermine effectiveness by demotivating employees (Sargeant 1990). The propensity of pay to motivate has been the subject of much academic debate which has done little to clarify our thinking, a problem intensified by the fact that empirical evidence has failed to establish a tangible link between incentive pay and enhanced performance (Bevan and Thompson 1992).

Perhaps the key point that may be drawn from the available evidence, both academic and empirical, is that pay is a complex, multi-faceted issue that serves as both a tangible and intangible motivator, offering intrinsic and extrinsic rewards. Thus, the applicability of pay related incentive schemes across a wide range of organisational contexts is difficult to generalise on and is largely dependent on organisational circumstances and prevailing conditions.

Not withstanding the reservations expressed however pay and benefits are increasingly becoming areas of extreme importance in determining the effectiveness of the organisation.

In his treaties on how to motivate employees Herzberg (1968) wrote 'a KITA' which he suggests stands for a kink in the pants, produces movement, but not motivation. Kohn (1993) argues the same is true of rewards. 'Punishment and rewards', he argues, 'are two sides of the same coin. Rewards have a punishment effect because they, like outright punishment, are manipulative. 'Do this and you'll get that' is not very different from 'Do this or here's what will happen to you'. In the case of incentives, the reward itself may be highly desired, but by making that bonus contingent on certain behaviours, managers manipulate their subordinates, and that experience of being controlled is likely to assume a punitive quality over time.

Herzberg has further argued that just because too little money can irritate and demotivate does not mean that more and more money will bring about increased satisfaction, much less, increased motivation.

Pay is important to employees. It provides the means to live, eat, and achieve other personal or family goals. It is a central reason why people hold down and move between jobs. However, a key question is not the importance of financial incentives as such but whether they motivate employees to perform well in their jobs.

Once an employee has been attracted to the organisation and the job the role of money as a motivator is debatable. Clearly money – or the lack of it – can be a source of dissatisfaction and grievance. However, if the employee is reasonably happy with his income, does that income induce him to perform at high levels of performance? Many of the theoretical prescriptions suggest that money is important in satisfying essential lower order needs. Once these are out of the way it is factors intrinsic to the job which are the prime motivators, especially self-actualisation. Others suggest that money is important at all levels and, as expectancy theory indicates, may be a prime motivator where it is a valued outcome and where there is a strong link between effort, performance and the achievement of greater financial reward.

During the 1960s and 1970s many organisational behaviourists emphasised the importance of job enrichment and organisational development and it became somewhat popular to discount the importance of money as a motivator (Biddle and Evenden 1989). The current emphasis on performance, productivity and cost reduction have tended to focus on primary job values like employment security, benefits and – particularly – the pay package. Most managers will agree that remuneration – especially the money element – has an important role in motivating employees. However, it is only one factor in the total motivational process. Clearly many people are not primarily motivated by money, but by other factors such as promotion prospects, recognition or the job challenge itself. All employees do not have a generalised set of motives. Rather, an organisation's workforce will be comprised of people with varying sets of priorities relating to different situations and work contexts resulting in differing employee motives and goals. These motives and goals will vary both between employees and with individual employees over time. For example a young single person may prioritise basic income and free time and the job itself may not hold any great interest. Later that person, now married and with a mortgage, may be more concerned with job security and fringe benefits such as health insurance and pension.

Morley and McCarthy (1999, 381) suggest there are four key issues that should be considered when exploring the extent to which employees are motivated by pay:

1. Firstly, it is clear that employees must value financial rewards. If people are paid at a very high level, or simply not concerned with financial rewards, higher pay will have little incentive value for employees. At this stage other factors related to the job and work environment must have the potential to motivate employees.
2. Secondly, if money is a valued reward, employees must believe that good performance will allow them to realise that reward. This suggests that pay should be linked to performance and differences in pay should be large enough to adequately reward high levels of performance. This approach obviously rejects remuneration systems that reward good, average and poor performance equally, such as regular pay increments based on seniority.
3. Thirdly, equity is an important consideration. Employees must be fairly treated in their work situation especially in terms of the perceived equity of pay levels and comparisons with fellow employees. They will be keen that rewards (pay, incentives and benefits) adequately reflect their input (effort and skills). Should employees feel they are not being treated fairly on these criteria performance levels may fall.
4. Finally, employees must believe that the performance levels necessary to achieve desired financial rewards are achievable. The required performance criteria and levels should be clearly outlined and communicated to employees.

Organisations must also ensure that employees have the necessary ability, training, resources and opportunity to achieve such performance levels. Otherwise, employees will either not be able, or else not try, to expend the necessary effort.

From the motivational perspective effective payment systems should have the following characteristics:

• Be objectively established.
• Clarify performance levels required and rewards available.

- Reward the achievement of required performance levels adequately and quickly.
- Ensure employees have ability, training resources and opportunity to achieve required performance level(s).
- Recognise that financial incentives are only one source of motivation and design jobs to ensure employees can satisfy other needs through their work (e.g. achievement, challenge).
- Take regular steps to identify employee needs and ensure these can be satisfied within the organisational environment.

Even where these characteristics are present success is not guaranteed. For example an incentive scheme based on production figures may be established to encourage employees to achieve high-performance levels. However, unofficial norms established by the work group may dictate 'acceptable' performance levels and ensure this is not exceeded through various social pressures. Equally such an approach may signal to employees that management are clearly in charge and may either lessen employee feelings of control and competence or encourage conflict over the standards set.

It should always be appreciated that while pay is an important source of employee motivation it is not the only one. To motivate effectively, financial incentives should be structured in such a way as to highlight the link between effort, performance and reward; adequately reward good performance and be equitable in the eyes of employees. The remuneration system should be viewed as part of a total motivational process that allows for individual differences and provides motivational opportunities through additional extrinsic and intrinsic factors, particularly self-fulfilment.

This chapter has focused on the area of reward management. An organisation's reward package is seen to consist of pay (base wages), various incentives (performance-related incentives and rewards) and fringe benefits. Organisations will provide various mixes of these three components in order to attract, retain and motivate their employees. While developing an effective reward package can prove a rather difficult task, if the reward package satisfies basic needs as well as being flexible enough to meet individual employee needs and has equity, fairness and trust as its central tenets, it can be effective.

Job evaluation is the most common method of determining the relative worth of jobs and a variety of analytical and non-analytical schemes are available. With the exception of competence-based approaches, job evaluation techniques focus solely on the job, rather than on the individual performing it.

Numerous options are available to organisations in the types of pay, incentive and benefits packages it might adopt. While flat rate systems still prevail, various individual, group and team incentive schemes have grown in popularity in recent years, largely in response to competitive pressures. Additional direct payments in the form of bonuses and other incentives are used extensively.

Turning to the actual payment approaches employed there has been an increase in variable pay in Ireland in recent years. A total of 41.1 per cent of respondents to the 1999 round of the Cranet E./University of Limerick Survey on HR practices in Ireland reported that they had increased their use of variable pay in the three years previous. Concomitantly, only 1 per cent of respondents reported that they had decreased their use of variable pay during the same period. The general increase is consistent with the European trend and it serves not only to allow employees enjoy periods of success, but also helps spread risk in times of difficulty. Zalusky (1991) suggests however that this growth in variable pay is limited as the banks that hold mortgages do not adjust monthly bills to fit changes in workers' income. This is particularly relevant in Ireland, given the open nature of the economy (Foley *et al.* 1996; Morley and McCarthy 1999).

The cost of employee benefits is also on the increase for many employers. These benefits represent a type of indirect reward because employees receive the value of the benefits without getting direct cash payments. More broadly, the complete reward package is now often one of the largest costs faced by employers with many organisations having labour costs at or above 50 per cent of all operating costs (Morley and McCarthy, 1999). The recent 'Employee Participation in Organisational Change Survey' reports the findings of an investigation carried out across ten countries of the EU. It is reported that public service organisations have very high labour costs, as 40 per cent of the respondents indicated that labour costs constituted over 75 per cent of total costs. Private firms indicated that their labour costs were a smaller proportion of overall costs, 45 per cent reported that labour costs were between 25 and 50 per cent of overall costs (European Foundation for the Improvement of Working and Living Conditions 1999).

7

Managing
and Appraising
Performance

The management of performance in organisations is a key variable in organisational effectiveness and growth. In view of the strategic pressures driving organisations, it is becoming increasingly evident that organisations will need to carefully monitor performance if they are going to realise improvements in productivity and growth, and to do so through the institutionalisation and consistent application of a 'goals oriented approach' (Scott-Lennon 1995). Pulakos (1997, 291) in her treatise on the 'ratings of job performance' puts it thus:

> Rewarding and promoting effective performance in organisations, as well as identifying ineffective performers for developmental programmes or other personnel actions, are essential to effective human resource management in organisations. The ability to perform these functions relies on assessing employee performance in a fair and accurate manner.

Sparrow and Hiltrop (1994) highlight a number of key organisational and social variables that impact upon performance priorities. Included in these are the propensity towards organisational delayering with its concomitant widening of spans of control; devolvement of accountability and responsibility; changing career and job expectations; the increased use of more flexible working arrangements; and the greater individualising of the employment relationship. All these factors are effecting the nature of the employment relationship and are placing increasing importance on the managers' abilities to manage the performance of their staff. However, effective performance management does not operate in a vacuum and thus must take cognisance of the related human resource policy choices of job design (see chapter five), reward management (see chapter six) and the principles of effective employee development (discussed in chapter nine).

The emphasis in this chapter is on exploring the dimensions of performance management and outlining a range of considerations pertaining to the development and operation of effective performance appraisal systems. The chapter concludes with an examination of recent developments in the area of performance management and explores current performance appraisal practices in Ireland.

THE NATURE OF PERFORMANCE MANAGEMENT

The extant literature on managing job performance reveals several terms that are often used interchangeably, such as performance appraisal, performance assessment, performance evaluation and job appraisal. However, in general terms, they are invariably all concerned with measuring an individual's performance in a given job against pre-determined work standards and involve designing a formal system to facilitate observation, monitoring, analysis, feedback and target setting. Armstrong (1995) indicates that performance management, as a concept, emerged in the late 1980s as a result of a growing recognition that a more continuous and integrated approach was needed to manage and reward performance. He further notes that many of the more recent developments in performance appraisal have been absorbed into the concept of performance management, which is 'a much wider, more comprehensive and more natural process of management' (Armstrong 1995, 431).

Sparrow and Hiltrop (1994) suggest that performance management is essentially a strategic management technique that links business objectives and strategies to individual goals, actions, performance appraisal and rewards through a defined process. They further stress that the most important feature of an effective performance management system is its ability to be seen as a method of continuously securing improvements in the performance of teams and individuals against pre-defined business strategies and objectives (Sparrow and Hiltrop 1994, 553). Lockett (1992) indicates that the core objectives of performance management are:

1. The continuous improvement of business performance in terms of customer service, product quality and market leadership.
2. The continuous development of organisational capability through the design of effective production systems, the development of organic structures; the enhancement of employee performance in line with business demands and the expansion of product and service lines.

Philpott and Sheppard (1993), from their analysis of performance management in operation, outline a number of characteristics that are associated with effective and ineffective performance management systems (see table 7.1).

In a similar vein, Fletcher and Williams' (1992, 47) research suggests that, not only were most of the organisations studied a long way from operating sophisticated personnel management, but, for most of them, performance management was synonymous with performance appraisal, or performance related pay, or both. They commented that:

There is, of course, much more to it than that. The real concept of performance management is associated with an approach to creating a shared vision of the purpose and aims of the organisation, helping each individual employee understand and recognise their part in contributing to them, and in so doing manage and enhance the performance of both individuals and the organisation.

The various definitions of performance management outlined suggest that it is essentially a management process of linking individual, group and organisational performance with the main strategic mission and values. As such it is an organisation-wide activity that is concerned with the continuous assessment and review of performance against pre-determined strategic objectives. There are a number of marked similarities between the performance management system and management by objectives (MBO),

Table 7.1 Characteristics of good and bad performance management systems

Good	Bad
• Tailor-made to fit the particular needs and circumstance of the organisation	• Lack of strategic direction, with no clear objectives
• Congruent with the existing culture insofar as they support the achievement of high performance standards but will help to change or reshape that culture if necessary	• Rivalry and territorialism between departments
	• Persistent failure to meet objectives and deadlines
• Support the achievement of the organisation's mission and the realisation of its values	• Lack of clear accountabilities and decision-making
• Define the critical success factors which determine organisational and individual performance	• Confusion over roles in organisation
	• Middle managers feel unable to influence events
• Clarify the principal accountabilities of managers and staff so that they are fully aware of their objectives, the standards of performance expected of them, and the quantitative key performance indicators which will be used to measure their achievements	• Absenteeism, sickness and/or overtime out of control
	• Work-force and middle managers resistant to change
	• High turnover amongst key posts
	• Staff appraisal lacks credibility
	• PRP scheme regarded as ineffective
• Enable systematic review of performance against agreed criteria in order to establish and act on strengths and weaknesses, identify potential, plan and implement career development and training programmes and provide a basis for motivation through intrinsic and extrinsic rewards	• Lack of detailed information on costs and contributions
	• Poor budgetary control and plan
	• Outdated or inadequate management information systems
• Develop PRP systems which provide incentives and rewards as motivators for improved performance	• Lack of structural career and succession planning process
• Provide an integrated approach to increasing motivation and commitment, which combines the impact of results-orientated performance appraisal and PRP systems with the actions that management and individual managers can take, such as career development and succession planning programmes to develop attitudes and behaviours which lead to better performance	

Source: Philpott and Sheppard (1993). Copyright © L. Philpott and L. Sheppard, 1993. Reprinted with permission.

since both systems set objectives, require the identification of performance measures and involve continuous appraisal and feedback. However, Fowler (1991) suggests that performance goes further than MBO, in that it is applied to all staff (not just managers as was traditionally the case with MBO). It includes greater qualitative performance indicators, and focuses more on corporate goals and values than on individual objectives. In a similar vein, Armstrong (1995) differentiates performance management from traditional performance appraisal, indicating that it does not represent an activity that is imposed on managers and that it is primarily owned and driven, not by the personnel department, but by line managers.

THE PROCESS OF PERFORMANCE MANAGEMENT

A central tenet of effective performance management is that a participative approach is taken to the system design. This implies involving all organisational actors in jointly determining the nature and scope of the system. The system should have the full commitment of top management, yet not be viewed as a top-down affair (Wright and Brading 1992). Armstrong (1995) suggests that performance management be regarded as a flexible process and presents a conceptual framework of the performance management cycle (see figure 7.1).

175

Figure 7.1 A conceptual framework for performance management

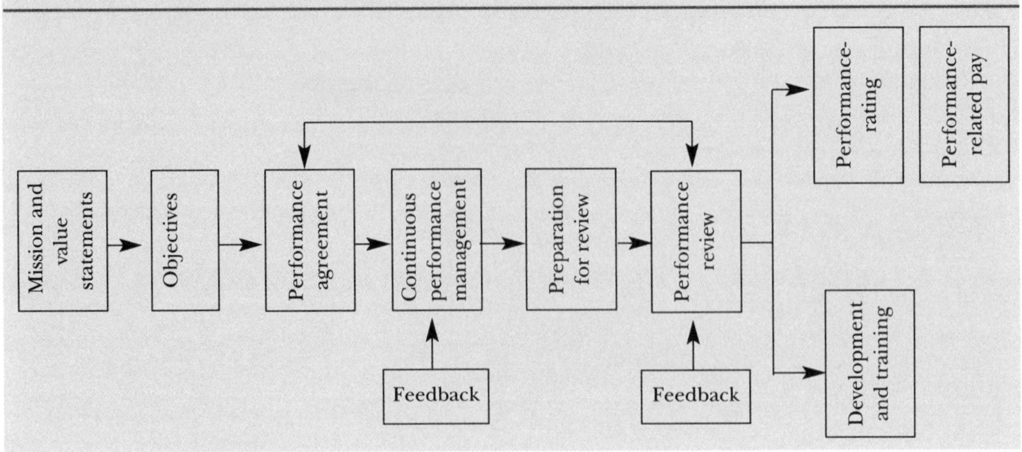

Source: Armstrong (1995).

   This model is based on the premise that all work performance is driven by a range of corporate strategies and objectives, which are broken down and translated into key functional or departmental objectives. A performance contract is developed that outlines the tasks, knowledge, skills and competencies that are required to achieve these key objectives. Built into the model is the requirement for continuous feedback on performance, with the possibility of interim reviews. The system further prescribes the operation of one formal review per year, when employees and managers constructively evaluate performance and identify a new performance contract. This review typically takes the form of an annual performance appraisal, which will be described in the next section. Continuous employee development is an inherent aspect of the process where specific training requirements are identified at the review stage, and informal training and learning through coaching, mentoring and self-development is encouraged throughout the year. The model identifies two further components, namely performance rating and performance-related-pay. Armstrong suggests that these are not inevitably associated with performance management, *per se*, while Wright and Brading (1992) argue that formal ratings of performance should be avoided if possible and the focus brought closer to qualitative outcomes. However, while there is an increasing tendency to link rewards with performance (see chapter six), it is recommended that decisions on pay be separated from the performance review to facilitate the developmental nature of performance management (Armstrong 1995; Gunnigle and Flood 1990; Evenden and Anderson 1992).

PERFORMANCE APPRAISAL

Over the past fifty years, Grote (1996, ix) notes that performance appraisal has become such a commonplace in organisational life that virtually every company has an appraisal system. Gunnigle and Flood (1990) describe performance appraisal as a systematic approach to evaluating employee performance, characteristics and/or potential, with a view to assisting decisions in a wide range of areas such as pay, promotion, employee development and motivation. Outlining the purpose of performance appraisal, they suggest that the performance management loop provides the framework within which systematic appraisal can take place (see figure 7.2).

Figure 7.2 The performance management loop

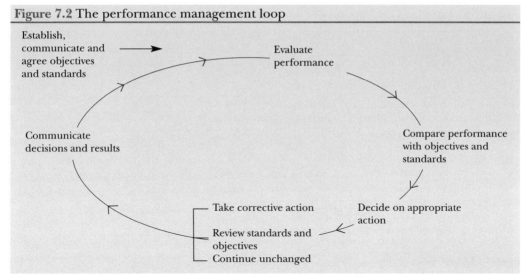

Source: Gunnigle and Flood (1990).

Appraisal of performance is likely to take place on a daily basis, often on a very informal basis i.e. through casual meetings, informal discussions between supervisor and staff, team briefing and so forth. However, the establishment of a formal appraisal system is a necessary prerequisite to effective performance management since it provides a dedicated period of time for managers and supervisors to meet with their staff and discuss a range of factors pertaining to work performance.

Table 7.2 Why should you appraise: employer and employee viewpoints

The employer's perspective:
Appraisals are conducted for a number of reasons, not least to help the organisation to:
1. Assess the performance of individuals
2. Set individual objectives
3. Assess how well objectives are being attained
4. Confirm what jobs/tasks are actually being done
5. Determine who should be promoted or transferred
6. Determine who needs training and of what sort
7. Assess who should be considered for advancement

The employee's perspective:
If the process is well handled and the appraisal system is effective, the employee should see the process and its constructive engagement as:
1. A career development exercise
2. A way of assessing career and other wants and needs, and how the organisation can actually provide them
3. A way of clarifying the job, its duties, objectives etc.
4. A way of becoming aware of their own potential, and how that potential can be realised and fulfilled

Source: Hunt (1992).

Similarly, Evenden and Anderson (1992) identify a range of perceived benefits associated with effective performance appraisals, some of which are presented in table 7.3.

Table 7.3 Benefits of performance appraisal

Benefits to managers
- Opportunity to learn about employees' hopes, fears, anxieties and concerns relating to both their present job and their future
- Chance to clarify and reinforce important goals and priorities
- Mechanism for measuring changes in employee work performance
- Opportunity to motivate staff by recognising achievements
- Clarification of overlap or ambiguities that may exist in the work structure

Benefits to employees
- Opportunity to receive feedback on how performance is viewed in the organisation
- Opportunity to communicate views about the job
- Opportunity to discuss career options
- Recognition of tasks carried out well and objectives achieved
- Basis for identifying training and development needs

Benefits to the organisation
- Assistance with succession planning and the identification of future potential
- Facilitation of human resource planning through competency analysis
- Method of ensuring harmony between business objectives and employee performance
- Generally improved communications throughout the organisation
- Opportunity to improve performance

Source: Evenden and Anderson (1992).

The performance appraisal system can be seen to have many interrelated functions including performance evaluation and target setting, the establishment of work standards, identification of skills gaps, and the facilitation of communications and motivation. However, only an effective appraisal system will result in the realisation of many of these outcomes. Hunt (1992, 10) notes that appraisals are characteristically inefficient. Among the reasons for this are an unclear definition of the appraisee's job; unclear objectives; one or both parties being unaware of the format and aims of the appraisal interview; untrained appraisers and/or appraisees; a high degree of subjectivity surrounding the process; and biased or incomplete data being gathered and used for determining process outcomes. Furthermore, in some cases, the process of evaluation can become the overriding consideration of the appraisal process, and often the motivational and developmental aspects are given little consideration. Given that the annual appraisal may represent the only formal meeting the manager or supervisor has with his/her staff (on a one-to-one basis), there is a considerable onus on the manager or supervisor to ensure that adequate attention is paid to all aspects of the appraisal process. However, in spite of their perceived benefits, performance appraisal schemes are not a general panacea for poor management or fundamental weaknesses in the organisation's structure or design, and thus, as indicated earlier, the organisation must take cognisance of the range of policies, systems and procedures that affect work performance.

Randell (1994) suggests that an examination of an organisation's appraisal scheme can show a great deal about how the organisation views its staff and how they should be managed and developed. Adopting the approach that beliefs about human behaviour at work can be broadly classified, he suggests that appraisal systems are developed according to what those who design them view as the causes of work performance:

- Where the past is seen as a reasonable determinant of present and future work behaviour, the performance appraisal scheme will focus on a comprehensive assessment of past strengths and weaknesses. This view is largely connected with reinforcement theories of motivation, whereby good performance is rewarded in the hope that it will be repeated, while poor performance is discouraged or punished to decrease the likelihood of it occurring in the future.
- Where the 'here and now' is seen as the critical determinant of work behaviour then the appraisal system will focus on factors such as employees' understanding and learning. This approach draws heavily on cognitive psychology and equity theories of motivation where employees' perceptions of the work situation are seen to determine subsequent behaviour.
- Where the 'pull' of future events desired by employees is seen as the prevailing influence on work behaviour, appraisal systems will emphasise rewards and opportunities. This approach draws upon expectancy theories of motivation and focuses on self-fulfilment to encourage desired work behaviour.

There are two underlying principles associated with all three perspectives, namely a desire to add to the individual's capacity for doing an existing job, and a need to maintain and/or improve motivation.

Methods of Performance Appraisal

There is considerable variety in the range of performance appraisal techniques that can be used by organisations. A summarised description of the most commonly used techniques are presented in table 7.4. A number of these techniques will be examined in closer detail.

Table 7.4 Performance appraisal techniques

Method	Characteristics	Strengths	Weaknesses
Rating	Appraiser specifies on a scale to what degree relevant characteristics (normally related to job-related behaviour or personality) are possessed by appraisee	Ease of comparison; range in complexity from very simple to very involved, using descriptions of behaviour or performance	Subjective; personality or behavioural traits difficult to measure
Ranking	Appraiser ranks workers from best to worst, based on specific characteristics or overall job performance	Simple; facilitates comparisons	Little basis for decisions; degrees of difference not specified; subjective
Paired comparison	Two workers compared at a time and decision made on which is superior, resulting in a final ranking order for full group	Ease of decision-making; simple	Difficult with large numbers together with weakness attributed to ranking
Critical incident	Appraiser or supervisor observes incidence of good and bad perform-ance. These are used as a basis for judging and assessing or discussing performance	Job-related; more objective	Needs good observational skills; time-consuming

$\longrightarrow$

Table 7.4 Performance appraisal techniques (cont.)

Method	Characteristics	Strengths	Weaknesses
Free-form	General free-written appraisal by appraiser	Flexible	Subjective; difficulty of comparison
Performance or objectives-oriented systems	Appraiser evaluates degree to which specific job targets or standards have been achieved	Job-related; objective; participative	Needs measurable targets; danger of collusion
Assessment centre	Appraisees undergo a series of assessments (interviews, tests, simulations, etc.) undertaken by trained assessors	Range of dimensions examined; objective	Expensive; not necessarily job-specific
Self-assessment	Appraisees evaluate themselves using a particular format or structure	Participative; facilitates discussion; promotes self-analysis	Danger of lenient tendency; potential source of conflict between appraiser and appraisee

Source: Gunnigle and Flood (1990).

The *free form* appraisal technique is completed unstructured and essentially involves the appraiser writing a narrative discussion of the employee's performance. While it allows considerable discretion to the appraiser, who is not constrained by set criteria, this discretion can result in some inconsistencies and does not allow for effective comparisons.

Rating usually involves the appraiser rating the employee's performance and behaviour against a pre-determined scale. These ratings, based on a sequential scale, can be made against a series of relatively standard headings that tend to include generalised performance characteristics or particular personality traits. Rating scales are often used in conjunction with results-oriented schemes, which measure performance against a set of objectives. In such cases, rating scales are used to indicate the extent to which an employee was successful in achieving the objective. Two examples of the use of rating scales in results-oriented schemes are illustrated in tables 7.5 and 7.6 which contain extracts from performance plans used in a large manufacturing organisation in Ireland.

Table 7.5 Extract from performance appraisal plan for managers – manufacturing firm

Employee name:
Job title:
Appraiser:
Appraisal period:
Date of appraisal:

Section one: this section outlines the key roles and competencies that managers must demonstrate to perform their jobs effectively. Using the rating scale below, evaluate the extent to which the managers named above demonstrates effectiveness in each of the areas identified. Enter N/A for those areas that are not relevant to the manager's current position.

⟶

	Rating
1. Planning	____

1. Planning
   - manages systems and processes
   - sets measurable goals and targets
   - assigns tasks responsibly

2. Production
   - motivates others positively
   - demonstrates personal commitment
   - facilitates co-operative environment

3. Teambuilding
   - manages conflict
   - facilitates participation
   - develops interaction

4. Coaching
   - develops others
   - communicates effectively
   - understands interaction

5. Innovation
   - divergent thinking
   - challenges processes
   - stimulates change

Rating scale
1. *Negative results, did not achieve objectives*
2. *Mixed results, achieved some objectives*
3. *Good results, achieved most objectives*
4. *Very good results, achieved all objectives*
5. *Strong results, achieved all and exceeded some objectives*
6. *Excellent results, exceeded most objectives*
7. *Outstanding results, exceeded all objectives*

Table 7.6 Extract from performance appraisal form for employees – manufacturing firm

Employee name:
Job title:
Appraiser:
Appraisal period:
Date of appraisal:

Section one: this section outlines the key roles and competencies that employees must demonstrate to perform their jobs effectively. Using the rating scale below, evaluate the extent to which the employee named above demonstrates effectiveness in each of the areas identified. Enter N/A for those areas that are not relevant to the employee's current position.

1. Quality of work: the extent to which the quality of work is accurate and thorough ____
2. Dependability: the extent to which the employee can be relied upon to do a good job ____
3. Judgement: the extent to which the employee makes rational choices ____
4. Organisation: the extent to which the employee can plan and structure work ____

→

5. Communications: the extent to which the employee can transmit and receive information in a comprehensive manner ____
6. Adaptability: the extent to which the employee can cope with change and uncertainty ____

Rating scale
1. *Negative results, did not achieve expectations*
2. *Mixed results, achieved some expectations*
3. *Good results, achieved most expectations*
4. *Very good results, achieved all expectations*
5. *Strong results, achieved all and exceeded some expectations*
6. *Excellent results, exceeded most expectations*
7. *Outstanding results, exceeded all expectations*

Armstrong (1995) and Gunnigle and Flood (1990) argue that, while rating scales are a convenient means of comparing employees and arriving at an evaluation, they tend to ignore the complex set of variables that determine work performance, and are a highly subjective method of assessment. Furthermore, it is particularly difficult to achieve any great level of consistency with rating scales because, as indicated, they are highly subjective and some appraisers will be more generous than others, while others will be harder on their staff (Armstrong refers to these as 'the swan effect' and 'the goose effect' respectively). A further problem associated with both rating and ranking methods concerns the error of central tendency, that is, that there is a particular tendency to veer towards the mid point on such scales and so ascribe average values to performance.

One means of improving consistency might be to require the appraiser to make a forced distribution of assessment that involves plotting overall evaluation against the normal distribution curve. An example of this might be where, if there are twenty employees in a particular department, the overall distribution of performance should appear as follows:

Excellent:	5%
Good:	15%
Average:	60%
Poor:	15%
Unsatisfactory:	5%

A major problem with this technique is that there is no rule that suggests that performance or ability should be normally distributed and, to assume so, ignores the myriad of variables such as culture, production norms, supervisory arrangements and personal motivation that can impact on work performance.

An alternative to forced distribution might be the forced choice technique, which seeks to avoid the error of central tendency. Again appraisers are asked to rate performance against a pre-determined scale, but this technique does not have a middle or average value. Gunnigle and Flood (1990) use the example of measuring initiative to demonstrate the forced choice technique (see table 7.7).

Table 7.7 Example of forced choice appraisal technique

Criterion	Evaluation choices (tick as appropriate)			
Initiative	Takes responsibility and uses it well	Keen to take on new tasks	Needs direction	No initiative
	____	____	____	____

Results-Oriented Schemes

Results-oriented schemes are based on the underling principles of management by objectives (MBO), which include the specification of objectives, participation in agreeing objectives, measurement of performance against objectives, and finally feedback and monitoring. In the results-oriented system, performance is measured against previously agreed targets or key result areas. As with MBO, there is a particular requirement for targets to be jointly set between manager and employee to ensure commitment to the process and allow for re-negotiation as required. Hunt (1992) uses the example of targets for a sales person. They might include the total number of sales, number of new customers, number of repeat customers, average size of orders, proportions of different products sold, plus whatever is deemed to be relevant to the organisation. In this schema, numerical figures can be put side by side with actual performance, and successes and areas for improvement can be straightforwardly determined (see table 7.8).

Table 7.8 Performance against previous objectives scheme: sales personnel

Appraisee's name: _____

Position: _____

Appraiser's name: _____

Date: _____

Length of time in the post (years): _____

	TARGET	ACTUAL
Number of customers:	_____	_____
Total value of sales:		
Average value of sale per customer:	_____	_____
Number of new contacts:	_____	_____
Number of new customers:	_____	_____
Proportion of contacts turned into customers:	_____	_____
Size of territory:	_____	
Number of potential new customers:		

Source: Hunt (1992).

This type of appraisal scheme requires managers to have a comprehensive understanding of the nature and scope of the employee's job and demands high levels of vigilance in observation, target setting, feedback and future planning. As with all appraisal systems, it is highly dependent on a responsible appraiser. Although a useful technique, it can pose difficulties when the job is subject to considerable variation, or when it is largely dependent on the performance of other jobs. Furthermore, there is a strong emphasis on measurable and quantifiable criteria, which might overshadow more qualitative criteria, such as work behaviour and interaction.

Critical Incident Technique

When jobs are difficult to quantify in measurable terms, the critical incident technique might prove useful. This technique was advanced by Flanagan (1954), who viewed it as a procedure for gathering certain important facts concerning behaviour in defined situations. Anderson and Wilson (1997, 89) define it as a technique consisting of 'a flexible set of procedures for collecting and analysing reports of incidents – instances of actual behaviour – that constitute job performance at various levels of effectiveness'.

This technique requires the appraiser to identify three or four critical components of the job, and assess performance based on how well these tasks were completed. Anderson and Wilson (1997) note that critical incident reports that are at the core of this technique, are obtained from persons who are in a position to observe those performing the activity in question. They suggest that such a critical incident report must include three important pieces of information:

1. A description of the situation that led to the incident;
2. The actions or behaviours of the focal person in the incident; and
3. The results or outcomes of those actions.

Based on these three pieces of information, an interpretation of the effectiveness of the actions can be made.

Table 7.9 An example of a critical incident report

SITUATION:	A contractor was assigned a project that would involve de-terminating and removing several hundred wires, removing the conduit from the gear, relocating the gear, reinstalling the conduit and wire, and finally re-terminating the wire. The work had to begin at 11.00 p.m. on Thanksgiving and it had to be completed by 7.00 a.m. the following day, which seemed nearly impossible.
ACTION:	The foreman chose seven of the best wiremen employed by the company to do the work. Through skilful planning and hard work, the crew worked through the night without stopping for a break and got the job done on time and with no problems.
OUTCOME:	The customer was extremely impressed that they got such a project completed in such a short amount of time with zero errors. As a result, the customer has chosen this contractor to do almost all of its work.

Source: Anderson and Wilson (1997).

The critical incident technique can be costly to perform, particularly as it may involve considerable observation, which may generate negative feelings from employees who might feel threatened by the process. When the appraisal takes place on an annual basis, it can be difficult to constructively discuss key incidents that took place more then six months ago.

Behaviourally anchored rating scales (BARS), particularly associated with the early work of Smith and Kendall (1963), were developed to reduce rating errors and they include a number of performance dimensions that represent major requirements of the actual job, such as teamwork. Armstrong (1995) provides the following example of BARS in operation (see table 7.10).

Pulakos (1997) notes that the development of BARS relies on input from job incumbents and/or their supervisors. These stakeholders, referred to as 'subject matter experts' in the developmental process, are charged with the task of providing the detailed information that is necessary to construct the actual rating scales. These scales, Pulakos notes (1997, 298), are the rating dimensions and the behaviours that define different levels of effectiveness for each performance dimension of the job. With respect to how the relevant behaviours are gathered, she highlights that:

Table 7.10 Example of BARS

A. Continually contributes new ideas and suggestions. Takes a leading role in group meetings but is tolerant and supportive of colleagues and respects other people's points of view. Keeps everyone informed about own activities and is well aware of what other team members are doing in support of team objectives.

B. Takes a full part in group meetings and contributes useful ideas frequently. Listens to colleagues and keeps them reasonably well informed about own activities while keeping abreast of what they are doing.

C. Delivers opinions and suggestions at group meetings from time to time but is not a major contributor to new thinking or planning activities. Generally receptive to other people's ideas and willing to change own plans to fit in. Does not always keep others properly informed or take sufficient pains to know what they are doing.

D. Tendency to comply passively with other people's suggestions. May withdraw at group meetings, but sometimes shows personal antagonism to others. Not very interested in what others are doing or in keeping them informed.

E. Tendency to go own way without taking much account of the need to make a contribution to team activities. Sometimes uncooperative and unwilling to share information.

F. Generally uncooperative. Goes own way, completely ignoring the wishes of other team members and taking no interest in the achievement of team objectives.

Source: Armstrong (1995).

The behaviours are derived from critical incidents [see technique mentioned earlier] . . . After the critical incidents are collected from subject matter experts and edited by psychologists, subject matter experts are then asked to sort the critical incidents into dimensions and rate them on an effectiveness rating scale. Often, a 7 point rating scale is used. The percentage of subject matter experts sorting each incident into a particular dimension and the means and standard deviations of the effectiveness ratings for each incident are computed.

One of the main advantages of such an approach is that the behavioural anchors settled on for measurement purposes can be particularly effective for generating comparisons. However the drawback document in the literature is that those conducting the appraisal often report difficulties in rating the individual's performance to the specific scale anchors that are generated and used in the rating assessment. By way of example, look at the BARS rating scale shown in table 7.10 and you will get some indication of the potential difficulties that an appraiser might experience in trying to compare the individual's performance to the specific scale anchors illustrated in the table.

360-Degree Feedback

360-degree feedback is a relatively new appraisal technique that has gained popularity in recent years. Also known as multi-rater assessment and multi-sourced assessment, Ward (1995) and Garavan, Morley and Flynn (1997) suggest that it is designed to provide a complete multi-dimensional overview of an employee's performance. McCarthy and Pearson (2001) define it thus:

360-degree, or multi-rater, feedback is the practice of collecting perceptions of an employee's performance from sources such as subordinates/direct reports, peers/colleagues, and supervisors. What makes 360-degree feedback revolutionary is that the perspectives of many stakeholders are included in the evaluation of an employee's performance and workplace behaviour. In traditional appraisal systems, it is only the observations and opinions of the boss that are considered important and are therefore the only source of evaluation included in the appraisal.

Nowack (1993) identifies five major reasons for the increasing use of 360-degree inventories as follows:

1. A need for cost-effective alternatives to assessment centres.
2. The increasing availability of assessment software capable of summarising data from multiple sources into customised feedback reports.
3. The need for continuous measurement in continuous-improvement efforts.
4. The need for job related feedback for employees affected by career plateauing.
5. The need to maximise employees' potentials in the face of technological changes, competitive challenges, and increased workforce diversity.

Waldman *et al.* (1998), add that a further key purpose driving the present spread and use of 360-degree feedback is the legitimate desire to further management or leadership development. In this important regard they note that:

> Providing feedback to managers about how they are viewed by direct subordinates, peers, and customers/clients should prompt behaviour change. Many managers have not received as much honest feedback as is necessary for an accurate self-perception.

The appraisal takes into account skills, competencies and work behaviour and information is typically sourced from records, reports, work colleagues and the individual being appraised. McCarthy and Pearson (2001) observe that while some organisations restrict the stakeholder groups used in the evaluation process to peers or subordinates, others take a broader approach and include additional raters, such as customers, suppliers, cross-functional team members, managers-once-removed, and subordinates-once-removed. Structured questionnaires are designed and administered to relevant assessors, they are completed anonymously and then returned to the employee. This technique is particularly comprehensive and provides a multi-faceted assessment of work performance, taking into account a range of variables that might not be considered when one manager conducts the appraisal. However, as this technique provides such a broad range of information, there may be a need to train employees in its interpretation and provide counselling where required.

Most appraisal techniques require some element of target setting for their effective operation. Objectives and target setting can help to provide clarity, realism and precision and allow both parties to focus upon the same criteria during discussion. Evenden and Anderson (1992) suggest that, in order to improve the motivational aspects of appraisal, each job should be broken down to its key areas and then objectives for each area be developed. They describe key areas as the main tasks that need to be done, so that effective contributions can be made to departmental and, through them, company objectives. In identifying targets and objectives, Evenden and Anderson (1992) suggest the use of a few ground rules to facilitate the target-setting process:

- Should not set too many
- Should be set jointly by the manager and employee
- Should be related to agreed personal objectives (of employee)
- Should be revisable and not too rigid

Figure 7.3 Who is using 360-degree feedback?

Fifteen years ago, 360-degree feedback was virtually unheard of, but since then it has become extremely popular, especially in the United States. The majority of Fortune 500 companies have embraced it. The Trends in Ireland indicate that 360-degree is also becoming popular here. A survey conducted at the University of Limerick and in conjunction with IMI reports that 43.2 per cent of companies that have introduced competencies also use 360-degree feedback. Organisations such as Allied Irish Bank, Pfizer Tablet Plant, Intel Ireland, Eircom, Boston Scientific, First Active and Ulster Bank Markets all use 360-degree feedback.

Philip Anderson, Head of Management and Staff Development at AIB declares, 'The process has worked very well at the Bank and has been very well received by the management population'. He highlights the importance of follow-up and that feedback recipients at AIB are currently being afforded the opportunity to go through the 360-degree feedback programme a second time. One of the managers who participated in the programme at AIB heralds it as 'one of the best courses I have ever undertaken'. Another forwards that the process 'offered an opportunity to reflect on my areas of strength and weakness and more importantly offered an avenue to address those weaknesses'. In terms of the perceived changes that have resulted from receiving the 'all round' feedback, one manager at AIB asserts, 'the feedback highlighted a couple of areas for attention which improved my focus and commitment. This in turn led me to attaining a highly accomplished performance rating at my annual performance review'.

Pfizer Tablet Plant introduced, from start up, a paperless, face-to-face 360-degree feedback programme. The process differs from the more typical 360-degree feedback approach since feedback is given in a group setting, with a facilitator present and thus, anonymity is not part of the system. The same feedback process is used by all colleagues throughout the plant, no matter what their role. Eileen O'Riordan, Team Development Facilitator with Pfizer, explains, 'The drive in the tablet plant is to improve and develop high performance teamwork. We had to create a process that could only become a reality if teams truly believed they could influence their effectiveness. A 360-degree paperless feedback process provides a much more appropriate way of doing this than more conventional approaches. It is not about dumping your opinion on anyone. It is about development and growth. It is about building mutual support and trust'. One of the feedback recipients at the Tablet Plant claims 'The process is a great learning tool . . . it is honest, open feedback on performance, relationships etc.' Another recipient stated, 'You know that the feedback on performance is genuine, because it's in their own words.'

Source: McCarthy and Pearson (2000).

- Should be clear, concrete and challenging
- Should identify constraints that may affect achievement
- Should identify time scales, review dates and milestones on the way
- Should link target-setting into the action plans

The Appraisal Interview

Some of the principles of effective interviewing were outlined in chapter four (see selection interviewing) and many of these have application here. Of particular importance is the preparation for the interview itself. Most formal appraisal interviews take place once a year, even though there may be ongoing reviews throughout the year. For this reason both managers and employees need to set time aside to think carefully about the appraisal process: the targets that were previously identified, work performance over the period, particular variables that may be affecting successful completion of work tasks, and the range of developmental opportunities that might have application in developing action plans for the future. Adequate notice of the appraisal interview is a major consideration in facilitating thorough preparation. An employee needs to determine, not only how he/she has performed over the past year, but what his/her main expectations, in terms of career and skills development, might be. Equally, the manager needs to be assured that he/she is familiar with all aspects of the employee's performance so that constructive, motivational feedback can be provided. A key 'rule of thumb' associated with appraisal interviewing is to focus on behaviour, which the employee can change if required, rather than personality, which is rather more constant and very difficult to modify. It is in this respect that pre-determined key objectives and associated standards and targets come into play.

The appraisal interview is perhaps the most difficult interview that a manager has to conduct, because the twin goals of performance evaluation and motivation facilitation are not necessarily compatible. Evaluation requires a manager to act as 'judge' and yet the developmental aspect demands a more facilitative 'supportive' approach. When these are combined with the inherent pitfalls that are associated with the interviewing process (see chapter four), the result can often lead to interaction that is stressful and demanding for both the manager and the employee being appraised.

There are three particular interview styles that are often associated with the appraisal interview: the tell-and-sell approach; the tell-and-listen approach and the problem-solving approach. The *tell-and-sell* approach is directive and authoritative in nature and involves the manager telling the employee how he/she has evaluated performance, and then attempting to convince the employee of the fairness of the assessment. This approach is invariable uni-directional, from the manager to the employee, and provides very little opportunity for the employee to participate in the evaluation process. The likely response from the employee is a defensive one, and, where he/she has no input into setting action plans for the future, there is likely to be little commitment to follow-up action. Bearing in mind the key perceived benefits of appraisal outlined earlier it is unlikely that this approach will facilitate their attainment and is thus not recommended as good practice.

The *tell-and-listen* approach is similar in some respects to the one just outlined, but there is some attempt made to involve the employee in the process. In this approach, the manager again communicates his/her evaluation of performance to the employee, and then actively encourages the employee to respond to the evaluation given. However, given the exigencies of human nature (particularly in respect to being told, rather than being asked), it is unlikely that this approach is any more effective than the first one.

The *problem-solving* approach is based on the premise that the appraisal process is one that is jointly conducted by the manager and the employee. Here, the manager first asks the employee to discuss his/her performance against agreed targets and to express any problems that might be affecting work behaviour. Rather than being given an evaluation, the employee is free to comment and highlight particular aspects of performance, and the manager provides feedback on performance. This approach advocates that an evaluation be conducted after the interview has been completed and takes account of the contribution made by the employee towards his/her own evaluation.

Evenden and Anderson (1992) identify a set of guidelines that can facilitate effective appraisal interviewing:

- The interview should commence with a clear statement of the purpose of the meeting, which will ensure both parties are aware of the rationale for the interview.
- The managers should attempt to establish rapport and put the employee at ease. While this is a difficult process and is heavily dependent on the nature of the relationship

between both parties, it can be facilitated by ensuring that adequate notice of the interview has been given to the employee and he/she has had time to prepare for it.

- Discuss the main tasks and responsibilities undertaken by the employee and invite comments. This stage should take account of any self-appraisal that has been conducted and should focus on the objectives and key tasks of the job.
- Ensure that a balanced discussion takes place. The manager is required to praise the employee for good performance, but also to be frank in discussing any perceived weaknesses. As indicated earlier, the focus should be on the attainment of work targets and standards.
- Encourage the employee to talk frankly about any frustration in the job and any problem areas. Questioning style is particularly pertinent here, especially if the employee is unsure about, or unwilling to admit to problems or difficulties.
- Encourage the employee to develop self-analysis and self-discovery particularly in relation to developing action plans for the future. Greater commitment to new objectives and plans is likely where the employee has an input into determining them.
- Bring the interview to a close with a summary that clarifies what action is expected for the coming appraisal period.

Once the interview has been conducted and feedback given to the employee, it is important to ensure that the focus on performance is not neglected until the next appraisal interview. The performance management cycle requires a continuous alignment of work targets with key business objectives and thus performance should be reviewed throughout the year. Expectations created at the appraisal interview, in terms perhaps of promotion prospects or training initiatives, should be acted upon to ensure the motivational aspects of performance appraisal are not disregarded. Above all, however, a genuine commitment to the process of performance management is required of all managers and employees if the process is to be effective.

THE ETHICS OF APPRAISAL

Banner and Cooke (1994) in their contribution on ethical dilemmas in performance appraisal suggest that despite the fact that performance appraisal involves the passing of a judgement on another individual using often rather subjective mechanisms, an organisation can morally justify the use of appraisal. This justification derives from the greater good principle that positive outcomes for both the organisation and the appraisee can accrue from an engagement of the process. In their paper, the authors do point to a number of possible ethical dilemmas that may sometimes arise during the course of the appraisal process:

1. The problematic use of trait oriented and subjective evaluation criteria;
2. Difficulties in the preparation and writing of performance standards and measurement indicators;
3. The deployment of different systems of performance appraisal within the same organisation;
4. Issues around how the results of the performance appraisal will subsequently be used;
5. Issues surrounding who actually determines the so-called objective standards.

Banner and Cooke conclude that despite these issues, as long as the performance appraisal procedure is fair, is consistent, and is evenly applied to all, it is a morally justified device and serves a legitimate function in advancing the objectives of the organisation and the individual.

Beyond the moral justification, and despite strong efforts to maintain a fair, objective and impartial approach in the preparation of appraisal assessments, errors of judgement do occur, where, as Grote (1996, 137) puts it 'one individual observes and evaluates another. Grote's extensive research and trawl of the extant literature has led him to identify nine common appraisal errors: contrast effect, first impression error, halo/horns effect, similar-to-me-effect, central tendency, negative and positive skew, attribution bias, recency effect and stereotyping. The following table, extracted from Grote's (1996) *Guide to Performance Appraisal*, defines and provides an example of each error.

Table 7.11 Common errors in the appraisal process

ERROR	DEFINITION	EXAMPLE
Contrast Effect	The tendency of a rater to evaluate people in comparison with other individuals rather than against the standards for the job.	Think of the most attractive person that you have known. Rate this individual's attractiveness on a scale of 1 to 10. Now think of your favourite glamorous movie star. Re-rate your acquaintance. If you have rated your friend lower the second time around, contrast effect is said to be at work.
First Impression Error	The tendency of a manager to make an initial positive or negative judgement of an employee and allow that first impression to colour or distort later information.	A manager new to a work group noticed one employee, who was going through a divorce, performing poorly. Within a month, the employee's performance had returned to its previously high level, but the manager's opinion of the individual's performance was adversely effected by the initial negative impression.
Halo/Horns Effect	Inappropriate generalisations from one aspect of an individual's performance to all areas of that person's performance.	Jeff was outstanding in his ability to get delinquent customers to pay up. His excellence in this most important area caused his manager to rate him highly in unrelated areas where his performance was actually mediocre.
Similar-to-me-Effect	The tendency of individuals to rate people who resemble themselves more highly than they rate others.	Carol, a single mother of four small children, had prevailed in her efforts to succeed and had been promoted to manager. She unwittingly rated several women who were also single mothers higher than their performance warranted.
Central Tendency	The inclination to rate people in the middle of the scale even when their	Out of an erroneous belief that the law required all companies to

→

ERROR	DEFINITION	EXAMPLE
Central Tendency (cont.)	performance clearly warrants a substantially higher or lower rating.	treat all employees the same and a conscious desire to avoid confrontation, Harold rated all seven of the employees in his work group as 'Fully Meets Standard'.
Negative and Positive Skew	The opposite of central tendency: the rating of all individuals as higher or lower than their performance actually warrants.	Susan rates all of her employees higher than she feels they actually deserve, in the misguided hope that this will cause them to live up to the high rating that they have been given. Carlos sets impossibly high standards and expectations and is proud of never having met a subordinate who deserved a 'Superior Rating'.
Attribution Bias	The tendency to attribute performance failings to factors under the control of the individual and performance successes to external causes.	Harriet, a manager with a mixture of excellent and mediocre performers in her work group, attributes the successes of the former group to the quality of her leadership and the failings of the latter group to their bad attitudes and inherent laziness.
Recency Effect	The tendency of minor events that have happened recently to have more influence on the rating than major events of many months ago.	Victoria kept no formal records of the overall performance or critical incidents of her work group of twelve people during the course of the year. When she began writing their appraisal, she discovered that the only examples she could provide for either positive or negative performance had happened in the last two months.
Stereotyping	The tendency to generalise across groups and ignore individual differences.	Waldo is quiet and reserved, almost meek – about as far from the conventional cliché of a salesman as can be imagined. His sales record, however, is one of the best in the company. But his boss rated his performance lower than that of other salespeople since he didn't fit the mould, ignoring the results that Waldo had produced.

Source: Grote (1996, 138–9).

Knowing that many of these errors can and do occur, Longenecker and Ludwig (1990, 75) argue that the organisation has the right to demand accuracy in performance appraisal, but they also have a number of core obligations that they must observe and fulfil in order to improve accuracy and fairness in the process. Longenecker and Ludwig advance four such obligations that the organisation must meet:

1. The organisation must provide a sound procedure for managers to use in the execution of performance appraisal.
2. Training in performance appraisal must be provided for managers. This training should formally address the issue of intentional inaccuracy, and should deal not only with managers' ability, but willingness and motivation to execute accurate ratings.
3. Organisations must provide leadership from above. Middle and lower level managers cannot be expected to provide accurate ratings if intentional inaccuracy is practised higher up in the organisation.
4. Like any procedure, the performance appraisal process must be audited to ensure the accuracy of the data generated and the overall integrity of the process.

PERFORMANCE APPRAISAL IN IRELAND

Empirical data on performance appraisal in Ireland is relatively scarce. Earlier evidence provided by McMahon and Gunnigle (1994) confirmed performance appraisal as a regular feature in most organisations. Among the key objectives for performance appraisal identified by this study were the improvement of future work performance, the provision of feedback on performance and the identification of training needs. The Cranet E./University of Limerick's *Study of HR Practices in Ireland* (1999), supplies more recent evidence on performance appraisal in Ireland. The survey focused on three key areas, namely the existence of an appraisal system for management, professional/technical, clerical and manual employees, the contributors to the appraisal process and finally the purpose for which the appraisal system is used.

Table 7.12 The existence of an appraisal system for employee categories (N=446)

	Yes	No	Missing
Managerial	62.6%	33.9%	3.6%
Professional/Technical	59.9%	35.2%	4.9%
Clerical	55.2%	39.9%	4.9%
Manual	38.6%	49.3%	12.1%

Source: Cranet E./University of Limerick Survey (1999).

The data from the survey reveal that managerial employees are covered by an appraisal system in 62.6 per cent of cases, as are 60 per cent of professional employees. By comparison, it appears a relatively less common provision for manual employees. Just over one third of respondents indicate that they operate such a scheme for manual workers.

Turning to the issue of who is involved in the process, our survey asked HR managers to indicate that when they operated a performance appraisal system who contributed directly to the process.

Table 7.13 Direct contributors to the appraisal process (N=446)

	Yes	Missing/No
Immediate Superior	66.4%	33.6%
Next Level Superior	38.3%	61.2%
Employee	56.3%	43.7%
Subordinates	5.8%	94.2%
Peers	6.3%	93.7%
Customers	8.1%	91.9%

Source: Cranet E./University of Limerick Survey (1999).

Here the data portrays a relatively traditional picture of involvement and participation in the appraisal process. External stakeholder participation in the form of customer feedback is relatively uncommon as is upward and lateral participation. In the majority of instances boss and individual appraisals dominate suggesting more limited support for multi-source/multi-rater schemes.

Table 7.14 Uses of the appraisal systems (N=446)

	Yes	Missing/No
Individual training needs	61.2%	38.8%
Organisational training needs	40.8%	59.2%
Promotion potential	49.3%	50.7%
Career development	52.9%	47.1%
Individual performance-related pay	39.9%	60.1%
Organisation of work	32.5%	67.5%

Source: Cranet E./University of Limerick Survey (1999).

Thus, in Ireland it emerges that the most commonly used appraisal systems are training, career development and promotion. This confirms the dual remit of improved work performance and individual development and advancement.

Hunt (1992, 11) argues that there are many potential problems with appraisal systems. They are, he notes, often poorly designed, over-ambitious, inadequately resourced, or any combination of these factors. Too often, he suggests, they consist simply of unstructured interviews, with neither party, appraiser nor appraisee, being fully aware of the purposes of the encounter. This is clearly unfortunate because the organisation that pays careful attention to the process of performance management and utilises a range of performance appraisal schemes to facilitate work performance will probably reap some dividends. However, with respect to ensuring that whatever system is put in place works, it must be seen to be 'procedurally fair and just' (Cropanzano 2001), and above all ethical (Longenecker and Ludwig 1990). Grote (1996) believes that performance appraisal done well, in an organisational context that takes the procedure seriously, can have a major and positive impact on the corporate culture. He notes that:

> The creation or renovation of a performance appraisal procedure can transform an
> enterprise from a best-effort environment to a results-driven climate. If a company is

going to survive, let alone prevail, in the competitive climate that all face, performance appraisal, more than any other technique, has the power to generate incredible and sustained change throughout the organisation. More than any other action that management can take, the development or redevelopment of a performance appraisal procedure can focus the attention of every stakeholder on exactly those ends that must be achieved for the enterprise to survive . . . Do you want culture change? Serious and major change? Then look to your performance appraisal system. It can be the source of the most significant organisational redirection possible.

Grote (1996, xi)

Given the requirement for high performance work organisation (as described in chapter five) one might have expected somewhat greater utilisation of performance appraisal systems. However, as the pressures for competitive functioning intensify, it is likely that organisations will pay more, rather than less, attention to performance management in the future.

8

Training and Development: Policy and Context in Ireland

It has been argued (Sappey and Sappey 1999) that some industrialised societies may have been impeding their own economic development by ignoring the necessity for a more skilled workforce. A central objective of modern economies concerns how to create the conditions for rapid and sustained productivity growth and superior competitive advantage (see for example Doyle and Young 2000; Porter 2000; Scarbrough *et al.* 1999; Leadbeater 1999; Boisot 1999; Prahalad and Hamel 1994). A nation's standard of living is ultimately determined by the productivity of its economy, which tends to be measured by the value of goods and services (products) produced per unit of the nation's human, capital, and natural resources. Horst Sieberg, President of the Kiel Institute of World Economics in Germany emphasised at the World Economic Forum (2000) that improvement of national systems for human capital formation was a major determinant of economic growth. Human capital encompasses not only the level of education but also the work experience of the labour force and managerial expertise. The capital stock of an economy includes not just the accumulated physical capital in machinery, structures and physical infrastructure (roads, ports and telecommunications), but also the level of education, workforce skills and attitudes, and managerial talent.

Abramovitz and David (1996) suggest that the most rapidly growing factor of production has been human capital, while Baldwin *et al.* (1997) argue that in the new business reality, individuals need to be able to learn their way out of problems rather than try to apply known solutions to them. In this way learning and knowledge have emerged as essential competitiveness levers (Fulmer *et al.* 2000; Olian *et al.* 1998; Hallier and Butts 1998; Berry 1990) or indeed 'the new organisational wealth' (Sveiby 1997; Heraty and Morley 2002).

The last few years have witnessed considerable efforts to improve the national system of training and development in Ireland (Heraty and Morley 1998; Tansey 1998; Walsh 1998). Since the mid-1960s, Government policy has focused on attracting foreign direct investment (FDI) to Ireland (using generous tax and financial incentives) and on building the physical and human-capital support infrastructures. At the macro level, up until the mid-1990s the single greatest challenge facing the Irish economy was the need to effectively tackle the persistently high level of unemployment. Despite a pervasive feeling that the fundamentals of the Irish economy were sound (low inflation, stable currency, balance of payment surpluses, good industrial relations and solid GNP growth), the country had increasingly struggled to provide jobs for its young, well-educated workforce. However, since 1994 the Irish economy has experienced six straight years (1994–2000) of unprecedented economic performance (discussed earlier in chapters one and three). This growth has been reflected in considerable employment gains, impressive labour productivity growth, consistent decreases in the level of Government debt and positive trade surpluses (OECD 1999).

Much of this renewed focus on training and development has been instigated by heightened international competition, technological advancements leading to the emergence of skill gaps in certain industries, and renewed pressure to provide increased incentives for organisational level training. The focus has switched to educational attainment and human capital investment as critical determinants of positive economic growth and development. The combined effect has been the dilution of the essentially voluntarist nature of the state's role in training and development towards a more interventionist approach. The dimensions of training and development in Ireland are explored both in this chapter and the next one. The frame of reference for this chapter is essentially policy-based and examines training and development at a macro, national level, while organisational level training and development, focusing on procedures and practices, is discussed in the following chapter.

To start with, this chapter describes the evolution of the national system of training and vocational education in Ireland and provides a basic 'map' of Ireland's training framework. In particular it examines the historical development of Ireland's training infrastructure and highlights the major statutory and institutional reforms that have shaped the training system currently in operation. National policy decisions are analysed, critical commentaries expressed by various actors in the training arena are discussed, and the leading providers of training and development services in Ireland are reviewed. The chapter concludes with a discussion on the economic value of training and likely future developments of the national training system.

HISTORICAL OVERVIEW OF TRAINING AND DEVELOPMENT
The development of a national training and development framework can best be viewed as a series of distinct phases that originated with the guild system around the eleventh century and developed with considerable statutory reform in the last century. Table 8.1 provides a chronological overview of the stages in this development. In order to trace and fully understand the origins of the national training system in Ireland, it is necessary to consider the beginnings of vocational education, since it was from initiatives in this area that vocational education and training, as we now know it in Ireland, gradually evolved.

The Guild System
The history of training in Ireland can, like Britain, be traced back as far as the guild system. The Norman conquest of Britain in the eleventh century brought with it the guild system from mainland Europe, merchants settling in Britain used it to control and regulate trades. This system was also to follow the invaders into Ireland and commence the British influence on trade and training in this country.

The guilds became self-contained and self-perpetuating through a process of controlled apprenticeships, which provided each craft with a ready supply of trained craftsmen, but

Table 8.1 Development of Ireland's National Training Infrastructure

1898	Agricultural and Technical Instruction (Irl) Act	First form of regulated apprenticeship in Ireland, it specified that all training should be on-the-job.
1930	Vocational Education Act	Established VECs to provide a nation-wide system of technical and continuing education with emphasis on vocational education.
1931	Apprenticeship Act	Set up apprenticeship committees to regulate apprenticeship training, including duration, wages and training courses.
1959	Apprenticeship Act	Established An Cheard Comhairle to co-ordinate and regulate the apprenticeship system.
1967	Industrial Training Act	Established AnCo to promote training and to assume responsibility for industry and commercial training, including apprenticeships.
1970s and 1980s		Industrial expansion and development followed by recession.
1987	Labour Services Act	Established FÁS to provide, co-ordinate and promote training activities. Evidence of change in policy direction.
1988	Galvin Report	Highlighted the inadequacies of existing management development initiatives and the necessity for greater investment in such initiatives at organisational level.
1990	Culliton Report	Recommended the reorganisation of FÁS and the redirecting of resources to providing training for those at work and preparing for work.
1992		Apprenticeship system revisited and reorganised along the lines of competency-based standards.
1997	Government White Paper on Human Resource Development	Focus on the state's role in assisting industry to create a learning environment with a view to upgrading the quality of Ireland's human resources.

Source: Adapted from Heraty, Morley and McCarthy (2000).

in numbers that left the power and control of each guild in the hands of a few. Training became an integral feature of these apprenticeships. The apprentice was viewed as his master's property, bound by contract to serve his master faithfully for seven years, while simultaneously learning his trade. The origins of craft apprenticeships may be traced to this era.

Industrial Development
The gradual decline of the guilds in mainland Europe and Great Britain coincided with the rise of the factory system of production in the late eighteenth century. Over time, this

system of production was further developed through the application of scientific techniques for controlling and measuring work, which were aimed at eliminating inefficiency. A net result of such application lay in the introduction of the concept of division of labour, combined with the mechanisation of the production process. The rapid growth of industrialisation, and its increased utilisation of the division of labour, organised work into particular skills, crafts and tasks. It gave rise to a form of work classification that still exists today and is taken to be synonymous with the existing distribution and nature of occupational work categories. Groups within the labour force became broadly categorised as managerial, clerical, technical, skilled, semi-skilled and unskilled employees. These categorisations also reflected the growing organisation of trade unions around particular groups of workers, e.g. the skilled in craft unions, the semi-skilled and unskilled in general unions, clerical and technical staff in white-collar unions. In overall terms, a recognisable training entity was most associated with craft apprenticeships, and this system was to become the central focus of the earliest initiatives in vocational education and training.

Statutory Reform
In an attempt to formalise and regulate technical and scientific education, the City and Guilds of London was established in 1878. Through an examination system it initiated the development of courses and formulated recognised standards of attainment. Around this time, some significant developments had taken place in the large urban areas in Ireland such as Bolton Street College in Dublin and the Crawford Institute in Cork.

The British Government responded to this change of emphasis by enacting the Technical Instruction Act of 1891. This act made provision for funding by local authorities for technical education in schools, and was seen as a new departure towards satisfying the training needs of industry, which heretofore had been largely privately funded. This was soon followed in Ireland by the enacting of the Agricultural and Technical Instruction (Irl) Act of 1898, which introduced the first form of regulated apprenticeship in Ireland and specified that all training and instruction for apprentices should be given on the job.

Following the establishment of the Free State in 1922, it became clear that the system of apprenticeship training could be classified as aspirational in nature and was proving of little value to apprentices. Irish independence set the development of the Irish economy in motion, and a government-appointed Commission on Technical Education in 1926 was heavily critical of the educational system, particularly concerning its inability to meet the development needs of trade, industry and agriculture. In particular major statutory reform was recommended to alleviate the inconsistencies of the previous system.

The Vocational Education Act 1930 introduced a new structure by establishing thirty-eight Vocational Education Committees (VECs), which were responsible for the provision of a suitable system of continuing education and technical education in committee areas. An emphasis was placed on vocational training, which was defined in terms of full-time, second-level training in literacy and scientific subjects, augmented by some concentration on manual skills. However, despite these new initiatives, the overall picture of apprenticeship training remained much the same, as there was no compulsion on the employer to send apprentices on any of the courses organised by the VEC, and many continued their practices unchanged.

Arising from the recommendations of the 1926 commission, the Apprenticeship Act 1931 attempted to achieve the reorganisation of the apprenticeship system. This represented the first systematic effort at regulating the Irish apprenticeship system. The main provisions of the Act centred around the formation of apprenticeship committees with responsibility for regulating apprenticeship training in the designated areas, e.g. construction, electrical, and so forth. These committees formulated rules governing the length of an apprenticeship, age limits for entry and educational requirements, wage levels, the number of working hours and the regulation of training courses. Employers were obliged by statute to release apprentices for these courses, providing such a course was held within three miles of the workplace and took place during normal working hours.

This Act is now perceived as being largely ineffective, as it merely laid down ground rules for the co-ordination of the apprenticeship system. There was evidence of considerable variation in the standard of training programmes available to apprentices and, in some cases, abuse of the apprenticeship system. To compound these difficulties, certain trades were in demand by industry, e.g. engineering and construction, while others were in decline. The organisation of apprenticeship schemes was very much scattered amongst the thriving industries, e.g. transport, steel, textiles and footwear, leaving other sections lagging behind.

In an effort to mitigate these problems, a new Government Commission on Youth Employment in 1943 recommended the establishment of a National Apprenticeship Committee to control and co-ordinate apprenticeship training at national level. Such a committee would have overall responsibility for all trades and so replace the existing committee system. There was general recognition that the origination of apprentices on a committee basis was ineffective and led to quality problems and other inconsistencies.

Statutory reform continued in the form of the Apprenticeship Act 1959, which attempted to address the problems caused by the multiple responsibilities allocated under the 1931 Act. Under its terms, a national apprenticeship board, An Cheard Comhairle, was set up to co-ordinate the apprenticeship system. This body was vested with the authority to examine the methods used by any trade for the recruitment and training of apprentices. It had a number of specific objectives including the setting down of appropriate education qualifications, ensuring the release of apprentices to technical colleges, providing on-the-job training, and establishing a system of examination on the practice and theory of each trade. While this board was successful in its aims to a large degree, outside of the apprenticeship system however, there was little recognition of the need for, or value of, training.

Economic Stagnation

The Irish economy about this time was inward focused, with the policies adopted by Éamon de Valera and successive Fianna Fáil Governments concentrating on the imposition of trade barriers and the preservation of ownership of industry at national level. The manufacturing industry was still in its infancy when compared to agriculture and commerce, and it merited little attention in national planning terms. Indeed, foreign ownership of industry was barred, and there was little emphasis on export markets and foreign trade. With the exception of the statutory reform on the apprenticeship front, no coherent training policies were pursued at national level.

Ireland remained slow to recognise the need for training outside of the apprenticeship system. At national level, the Government adopted an essentially voluntaristic approach. Training was held to be the preserve of joint negotiation between both sides of industry, with the Government's role defined in purely advisory and facilitative terms. The Irish industrial sector was largely left to its own devices to provide the skills necessary for its growth and development. De Valera's philosophy of keeping Ireland for the Irish, with little emphasis on export markets and foreign trade left marginal opportunity for the expansion of indigenous industry, and even less for the importing of new technologies and systems from abroad.

Ireland experienced a shortage of skilled labour in the early 1950s, especially in the engineering field. However there was little coherent response at a policy level. By the end of the 1950s, there was no shortage of criticism of the training system in operation. Suggested reforms included direct financial aid from Government to companies, in respect of apprenticeship training, and the introduction of some system of statutory training levy, whereby companies which did not themselves train might contribute to the training costs of others.

Significantly, perhaps, this lack of progress towards reform was marked by the fact that neither side of industry was motivated to press for major change in the voluntarist structure of training provision. Employers, though pressed in some sectors by skill shortages, were prepared to pay the wages necessary to poach the skilled labour they required from their competitors. Trade unions concentrated on consolidating the apprenticeship system, following the logic that maintaining defensive control over conditions of entry led to skilled labour attracting a good price. The principle of voluntarism, and the maintenance of the status quo, therefore appeared to suit everybody.

Movement towards Institutional Reform

As the 1960s dawned it seemed increasingly clear that the voluntarist approach to training was failing to meet national needs. There were insufficient skilled workers and the lack of training outside the apprenticeship systems, combined with the narrow content of apprenticeship training itself, resulted in Ireland lagging behind most of her mainland European competitors in terms of the average skill levels and educational qualifications of her workforce. However, if the diagnosis of Ireland's training illness was clear, agreement on a possible cure was altogether more contentious. The Department of Labour and the educational establishments were somewhat more advanced than industry in recognising the need for reform. Employers and trade unions remained unconvinced and, to a large degree, unconcerned that there was a major problem with a voluntarist system that allowed both sides to pursue their different interests in relative harmony, through the apprenticeship framework. Skilled labour could attract a good price. Employers were left to train or not to train according to their short-term cost criteria, while negotiation between both sides of industry and the Government remained a purely facilitative one. Relative, if fragile, economic security allowed this complacency to flourish.

It was to take the perception of harsher economic conditions in the early 1960s, and a new determination on the part of the Government led by Seán Lemass, to inspire attempts at major reform. There is considerable agreement that this Government was responsible for dragging the Irish economy into the twentieth century. Ireland had joined the International Monetary Fund (IMF) in 1957 and shortly afterwards the World Bank. The Economic Development Report of 1958 added its impetus to the liberalisation of trade and commerce, and a more outward looking economic focus began to emerge. Controls on foreign ownership of Irish industry were removed in 1963, import tariffs were removed over the period 1962–4, and in 1965 the Anglo-Irish Trade Agreement on Tariffs and Trades (GATT) was signed. These initiatives reflected Government policy aimed at creating a more open economy with the emphasis on attracting foreign investment to Ireland.

A cornerstone of this policy was the encouragement given to foreign companies to locate here, through tax incentives, capital investment grants, advance factories, and so forth. With the arrival of these companies vocational and skills training took on a new impetus, although the skill base remained very weak. It is worth noting that the influx of these multinational companies, many of whom espouse the training and development of employees as a fundamental priority investment, represents a landmark influence on training in this country, which has persisted to the present day.

Meanwhile, tourism and agriculture were also targeted for development with a view to reaching foreign markets. The Farm Apprenticeship Board was set up in 1963 to provide training for young farmers, and the Council for Education, Recruitment and Training (CERT) was established by the Tourist Board, to handle education and training in the tourist and hospitality sector. This change in economic policy led to a considerable slowdown in emigration and actually resulted in many emigrants returning to Ireland to work or to establish their own businesses.

In response to an International Labour Organisation (ILO) report on vocational education in 1962, a Dáil committee was set up in 1963 to tackle the problem of retraining the unemployed. The bulk of those unemployed were unskilled and in dire need of training so that the kind of workforce necessary for attracting foreign companies would be more readily available. The mid-1960s represented a watershed in national training policy, when the recognition of a number of significant issues was instrumental to the subsequent change of direction. The general conclusions reached were that

- the voluntarist system facilitated the perpetuation and enhancement of familiar problems and allowed them to continue untackled;
- there was no effective national body to keep apprenticeship and other training activities under review;
- there was an insufficient number of skilled workers to meet the growing demands of the developing Irish economy;
- a small number of employers trained well, e.g. Guinness and Bewleys, and their skilled workers were often poached by those who invested little in training;
- the state itself provided a poor example in this regard with inappreciable investment in training in the public sector;
- training methods were also poor, with few formal qualifications, and the training situation was in considerable need of improvement.

In response, the Government White Paper of 1965 adopted many of the recommendations of the ILO Report and set about establishing a national Industrial Training Authority.

The period from 1967 to 1980 is characterised by significant upheaval and reform of the training system at national and organisational level. The Industrial Training Act of 1967 repealed the 1959 Act and established An Comhairle Oilun – AnCo. This body was empowered by the Act to assume full responsibility for all industrial training, including apprenticeships, and its functions included the provision of training at all levels of industry and the provision, facilitation, encouragement, assistance, co-ordination and development of training initiatives. The activities of AnCo were designated into three key areas:

- *Training Advisory Service:* Through this service, trained advisors (including the ID, SFADCo, and Udaras na Gaeltachta) acted as consultants to industry. Their activities incorporated the assessment of company training needs, the drawing up of training plans and programmes and the sanctioning of grants to industry.
- *Training for Individuals:* Training centres were established to provide a range of courses aimed at unemployed or redundant workers, those seeking retraining for new skills, school leavers, and in assisting some community-based initiatives.

- *Apprenticeship Training:* AnCo was empowered to make detailed provisions for the training of apprentices; statutory designated areas included construction, engineering, metals, electrical, motor, furniture, printing and dental craft work.

AnCo was funded mainly by the Government, but the Act also allowed for the imposition of a levy/grant scheme to underwrite training costs and to heighten awareness of the economic benefits of investment in training. The scheme itself considered several factors, including company size, gross payroll levels, and the amount of training provided. The levy amounted to between 1 per cent and 1.25 per cent of annual gross payroll. Varying portions of the levy could be recovered e.g. companies with less than fifty employees could claim back 90 per cent, while those employing between 51–500 could claim back between 50 per cent and 90 per cent. An upper limit of £50,000 (€63,487) was payable to any one company or £2,800 (€3,555) in respect of any one employer. The general purpose of the scheme was to tax prime industry into accepting its responsibility for its own training, while simultaneously fostering a systematic approach to training and development.

The 1967 Act represented a significant change in Government policy, reflecting an interventionist strategy aimed at sweeping away the concept of voluntarism. It also heralded an institutional role for a National Training Agency.

The early 1970s saw a considerable upsurge in economic activity in Ireland with the influx of foreign multinationals creating valuable employment for skilled and semi-skilled employees. This buoyancy was short-lived, however. The Irish economy drifted into crisis from the mid-1970s onwards due to the recession brought about by the oil price shocks and the resultant escalating unemployment. High levels of Government borrowing for current expenditure led to a soaring foreign debt. Spending on education and training was severely curtailed during this period and companies, faced with rising costs and shrinking markets, cut back on non-essential spending. Consequently, training and development activities were severely curtailed.

The economic conditions of the late 1970s focused considerable attention on AnCo. The multiplicity of agencies seeking resources, paralleled by the growing scarcity of funds, was now a major problem. The perception of widespread duplication of functions precipitated severe criticisms of AnCo, the more salient of which were the following:

- Considerable doubt was expressed about the quality of the training and the competency of AnCo to provide such a wide range of training activities.
- There was considerable evidence to suggest an over-dependence on AnCo as a supporter of training.
- AnCo's concept of training was felt, by many employers, to be overtly concerned with paperwork, which was seen to create a situation where training specialists were ultimately judged on their ability to recover the levy paid, rather than the innovativeness or the relevance of their training activities.
- Considerable resentment was building up over AnCo's access to European Social Fund monies. Accusations were made concerning the duplication of courses that were already available in many of the technical colleges; the redirection of funding away from education and towards AnCo; and the lack of any coherent, integrative policy on management training.
- The lack of a strategic focus, and the industry-based nature of training schemes militated against the development of an economy-wide strategy for training.

In 1985, in the midst of a sea of criticism, the Confederation of Irish Industry carried out a comprehensive analysis of the Irish training system and called for an extensive review of the levy scheme. Their main arguments are worth recording, and may be summarised as follows:

- In a period of rapid technological and market changes, education and training are crucial factors in the struggle to improve competitiveness and achieve further employment.
- The Government is responsible for ensuring the provision of basic education and transferable skills that are necessary for entering employment.
- Enterprises are responsible for the provision of relevant specialised training that is necessary for their economic development.
- Irish industry recognises the need to provide for retraining and the continuing education of its existing workforce, particularly in technical fields.
- Both employers and employees have a mutual interest in availing of education and training.
- Employees should be willing, in their own interests, to invest in further education and training, outside of working hours if necessary.
- Recognition was given to the historical position of apprenticeship in Ireland in the sphere of education and training of craftspersons, and it was pointed out that the decreasing role of craftspersons within the manufacturing industry must be recognised, together with an increasing demand for technicians and skilled operatives.

White Paper on Manpower Policy (1986)
A White Paper on Manpower Policy was published in September 1986, which examined the role of all actors involved in Manpower Policy and cited a number of proposals for action.

1. While the primary responsibility for providing training rested with employers, Government intervention was necessary to ensure that the quality and quantity of training available conformed to policy objectives.
2. The multiplicity of agencies responsible for training could be addressed through the amalgamation of a number of agencies into one authority.
3. The levy-grant scheme to be re-organised and based on a more selective approach (i.e. linked to approved company development plans and concentrated on key skill areas).
4. The apprenticeship system to be revised and modernised with a view to developing a system based on standards achieved, to ensure a satisfactory balance between supply and demand, and a reduced cost to the state while still maintaining quality.
5. Deficiencies in management training to be identified under the auspices of an advisory committee.

While the White Paper caused considerable consternation among the actors involved in training at the time, it also provided the impetus for the Government to make significant institutional reform and to streamline the training system in Ireland.

Labour Services Act (1987)
The Government's response to the White Paper was the enactment of the Labour Services Act 1987, which represented the first attempt in twenty years, at state level, to reform the training system and bring it into alignment with economic objectives pursued by the Government. This Act provided for the establishment of FÁS (Foras Aiseanna Saothair),

an amalgam of the National Manpower Service, AnCo and the Youth Employment Agency into one body. CERT was excluded largely because of the tourism lobby who argued that because of the skill shortages, and the importance of tourism as an employment growth sector, CERT should remain independent and provide a specialised service. The Act set out a number of important functions for FÁS, including the provision of training and retraining for industry and the management of particular employment schemes to assist in the reduction of unemployment in Ireland. Specifically, the mantra ascribed to FÁS was that it should adopt a customer-centred approach, regionalise its operations and give a high priority to meeting the needs of the long-term unemployed.

The Minister envisaged FÁS as a labour intensive service, doing invaluable work for the economy and the community, and offering job satisfaction to its own employees. He did not, however, visualise any major dismantling of the existing services of the NMS, YEA or AnCo, but instead saw them being adapted over time to achieve a more regionally-based and integrated service. His aspiration was for FÁS to move towards the provision of more effective services at local level. The period between 1987 and 1991 therefore represented a time of significant change for FÁS. In the immediate aftermath of the Act, a meaningful shift in its activities was seen, away from company-based facilitation activities towards an increase in community and youth employment type training programmes.

Advisory Committee on Management Training (1988)

A review of statutory and institutional reform over the years highlights a consistent focus on apprenticeship training, youth employment schemes, training for the unemployed and so forth. However, little attention was given to management training and development and it was not until 1986 and the White Paper on Manpower Policy that explicit reference was made to the importance of management development. Under the direction of Paddy Galvin, the Advisory Committee on Management Development was set up to evaluate the quantity and quality of existing provision for the development of managers. The committee reported in 1988 and noted that economic performance is significantly influenced by the quality of organisational management. A number of key strengths of the management training and development system were identified including the quality of the main providers, the standard of general education, the wide choice of provision and experimentation with different delivery systems. The report further highlighted a number of specific weaknesses and made recommendations for action. The most salient finding concerning both the weaknesses identified and the recommendations made are summarised in table 8.2.

In particular, the committee reported that over one fifth of the top companies spent nothing on management development, while one half of them spent less than £5,000 (€6,349) on management development activities. In its recommendations, the committee highlighted the strategic importance of management training and development and stressed the necessity for it to be closely integrated with the strategic business objectives of the organisation. While the report was criticised on the basis that it was overtly prescriptive and that its case analysis was highly selective, it is recognised that its proposals represent a progressive development in highlighting the need for investment in training and development at all levels of the organisation.

PROVISION OF TRAINING AND DEVELOPMENT SERVICES

As a result of many of the initiatives discussed earlier, the provision of training and development services has grown considerably in recent years. In this section we consider the role of the key actors currently operating in the Irish scene.

Table 8.2 Summary findings of the advisory committee on management development

Issue to be addressed	Recommendations
Insufficient level of commitment and expenditure on management development initiatives	Increased commitment an urgent national priority; establish action group on management development to promote management training
Lack of understanding of what is involved, or what constitutes good practice, in management training and development	Develop a set of national guidelines on management development to be used as a code of practice
Lack of a common core of relevant business knowledge and skills	Adjustment of business education to reflect business needs; broadly common curriculum to be offered by providers of business education
Difficulties experienced by small businesses in implementing management development policies	Provision of incentives for small firms to draw up and implement management development programmes
The ambiguity and inconsistency of the state's role in funding post-experience management training	State funding to be redirected away from the providers of training and towards the users of training; closer alignment of utilisation of funds with economic policy
Separate training for public and private sector managers is not in the national interest	Merger of management training activities of the IMI and IPA

FÁS: The National Training Agency

While a considerable amount of FÁS's activities are directed towards reducing unemployment and fostering community-based initiatives, it also provides a number of services to industry. These services now operates on a regional basis (ten regions comprising of twenty training centres and fifty-six employment offices), using a network of training advisors. There are also industry experts at national level who oversee the development of FÁS's activities in relation to the various industrial sectors, by liaising with the Industrial Training Committees which supervise the overall identification and planning of training in their respective sectors.

The *Training Support Scheme* (TSS) was introduced by FÁS in 1990 to encourage and promote training in small and medium-sized organisations. The scheme is available to companies involved in manufacturing, internationally traded services and physical distribution. While the TSS provides graduated grant aid to eligible companies to purchase their training in the marketplace, over half of the allocation for TSS is targeted at firms employing less than fifty employees. In 1995, 2,500 organisations were granted aid under the TSS – 32,400 employees were involved and the average duration of training amounted to just under eight days per trainee (Labour Market Study: Ireland, 1997).

Training grants are administered by the state development agencies (Forbairt and SFADCo) and are directed at skill needs arising from location of overseas investment in Ireland. Grants of up to 100 per cent of eligible costs are provided to carry out approved training for new employees. These training programmes are developed in conjunction with FÁS. Average coverage of such training is about 4,500 employees per year.

The *Management Development Grants* scheme is a further indication of a strong national commitment to training and is operated by the development agencies and supported by the state. Grants are available to improve the management performance of firms particularly in aspects of management information systems and strategic and business planning. The size of grants awarded varies between £2,500 (€3,174) and £35,000 (€44,410) and approximately 600 companies participate in the scheme each year.

In 1995, FÁS introduced it's *Training Awards Scheme* and a new training quality standard *Excellence Through People* which is designed to reward and encourage high training standards and to demonstrate the link between training investment and improved business performance. In conjunction with FÁS's efforts, a new national certification authority, TEASTAS, has been established to facilitate progression to more advanced levels of education and training, as benchmarked against best practice in the international arena.

The apprenticeship system operated today is competency-based. It combines both on-the-job and off-the-job training with the latter provided by a combination of FÁS and third level institutes of technology. Apprentices who successfully complete the programme are issued with a National Craft Certificate, a qualification that is recognised not only in Ireland but also in other EU and non-EU countries. This competency-based or standards-based model of apprenticeship consists of seven distinct phases (there is one trade exception) and is based on the achievement of certain pre-set standards of skill and competence rather than on time served. This system facilities the progression of successful apprentices to further educational qualifications and to continue to technical level at a recognised national and international standard.

Participation in the apprenticeship system continues to be male dominated. FÁS operates a policy that is designed to promote and encourage the entry of women into apprenticeship and has established a number of measures to facilitate female participation in apprenticeships. One such measure sees FÁS offer a bursary to both private and public sector employers who recruit female apprentices under the Standards-Based Apprenticeship system in the currently designated trades. Up to £2,100 (€2,666) is paid to the employer for each female apprentice recruited. FÁS, in conjunction with the education system, further provides training for females where required to prepare them to train and work in what has been a traditionally male work environment.

The number of apprenticeships declined quite considerably in the 1990s. This decline in recruitment can be attributed both to demand constraints in terms of curbed public sector recruitment and industrial restructuring on the one hand, and to the increased incidences of subcontracting and outsourcing on the other (*Labour Market Study: Ireland,* 1997). However, since 1994, there has been renewed interest in apprenticeships as it becomes an increasingly popular career choice for school leavers where recent economic buoyancy and increasing skill shortages have created significant opportunities for qualified craft and trade occupations. At the end of 2000, there were almost 20,000 people registered in the apprenticeship system – 8,100 were recruited into the system in 2000. A recent evaluation of the apprenticeship system (ESF Evaluation Unit, 1999) suggests that the educational profile of apprentices in recent years has demonstrated higher qualifications among participants than had hitherto been the case, again reflecting the growing attraction of craft qualifications in Ireland.

Figures from the *FÁS Annual Report* (2000) indicate that in 2000 about 95,200 unemployed job-seekers or other individuals completed FÁS programmes, and, at the end of the year, 52,000 persons were on FÁS programmes. FÁS also provided financial support for the training of an estimated 8,700 employees in about 1,800 companies. FÁS expenditure in 2000 amounted to £576 million (€731 million). Complete details on the range of services provided by FÁS can be found on its website (www.fas.ie).

While FÁS has a strong institutional role to play in the provision of training services, both to industry and to the unemployed, there are numerous other actors involved in the training arena. The more widely recognised of these are listed below.

Irish Institute of Training and Development (IITD)

The IITD is a professional body that caters for those concerned with training and development in business, industry, consultancy and the community. Founded in 1969, the institute's mission is to provide for the growth of those involved in training and development and, by doing so, to become the Irish voice for the development of people at both organisational and individual level in Ireland. Membership of the institute currently stands at about 1,500 and members are organised through a national council and ten chapters around the country. It provides a range of services including local meetings, a bi-monthly journal (*Arena*), seminars and workshops, an annual conference and a mechanism for the representation of membership views to Government and other institutions. The IITD also runs its own certificate and diploma in training and development, and continuing professional development programmes at centres throughout the country. See the website www.iitd.ie for further information.

The Irish Management Institute (IMI)

The Irish Management Institute is a leading provider of management training in Ireland with a defined mission of providing leadership in the development of Irish management competence. Established in 1957, the IMI is a user-owned organisation (circa 1,400 corporate members and 700 individual members) that provides a range of advanced management and specialist programmes, both open and customised, that are dedicated to raising the level of corporate performance. Details on the range of services it provides can be found on its website (www.imi.ie).

Chartered Institute of Personnel and Development (CIPD)

The Chartered Institute of Personnel and Development is a professional body for those concerned with personnel management and development. Established in the UK, the CIPD now operates in a number of countries worldwide and has more than 100,000 members. CIPD Ireland is a branch member of CIPD UK and has about 5,000 members in Ireland. The CIPD operates an integrated education scheme that is designed to prepare individuals for a career in personnel/HR management. In Ireland, a number of universities, colleges and ITs around the country run programmes that are recognised as 'exempted' by CIPD. Students of these programmes, who opt to register with CIPD, are recognised as student (licentiate) members of CIPD (level of membership varies with the level of qualification achieved). Exempted programmes in Ireland tend to be undergraduate business (or related) degrees; diplomas in personnel/HR management and, for associate memberships, Certificate in Personnel Practice and Certificate in Training and Development. CIPD also provides an information and advisory service to members, arranges a number of conferences, workshops and seminars throughout the year, and publishes a range of journals (*People Management* in the UK and *CIPD News* in Ireland), books and monographs in the human resource management and human resource development fields. Further information can be found on its website (www.cipd.co.uk).

Institute of Public Administration (IPA)

The Institute of Public Administration provides a range of education, training and development services that are designed to meet the changing demands on public servants in Ireland. In particular, it offers a wide range of courses on general business services, sectoral programmes for specific public sectors, and professional education services, including courses that are accredited by the HETAC, and programmes accredited by the institute itself.

Other Institutions

A considerable range of undergraduate, graduate and post-experience programmes are provided by the various universities, colleges, and privately-funded educational establishments throughout the country, and a number of institutes have been established that cater for professional development in select disciplines. The large growth in private-sector employment in recent years has also seen a considerable increase in the numbers of consultants who provide expertise in a range of training and development activities.

THE ROLE OF THE EUROPEAN UNION

A recent EU White Paper on the 'Learning Society' highlights the necessity of increasing investment in education and vocational training. It posits a number of critical short-term objectives that have application for member states, including the necessity to encourage the acquisition of new knowledge, to bring the school and the business sector closer together and to treat capital investment and investment in training on an equal basis.

Ireland has recorded significant gains from membership of the European Union; in recent years these gains have spilled over into the general areas of education and training provision. The EU Commission supports a number of specific initiatives that are designed to improve initial and continuing vocational education and training and to strengthen the links between the education and training systems and the enterprise and industry sectors. Four programmes, in particular, have relevance to the discussion here.

The first is the LEONARDO DA VINCI Vocational Training Programme. Its aim is to help member states devise national policies on vocational education through, for example, fostering university and industry co-operation, development of language skills, vocational guidance, and improved access to education and training. Between 1995–99 close to £12 million (€15 million) had been received to support Irish-led projects.

Secondly, the SOCRATES Programme focuses on improving the quality and relevance of education and supports initiatives, such as student and staff exchanges, a system of credit and mutual recognition of qualifications between member states, curriculum development, language training, open and distance learning. Between 1995–99 it is estimated that Ireland received about £11 million (€14 million) under this programme.

Thirdly, the EU EMPLOYMENT Initiative targets individuals with particular difficulties in relation to employment in the workplace, including people with disabilities, those who are disadvantaged, equal opportunities for women (NOW), and employment initiatives for young people from disadvantaged backgrounds. A total of £62 million (€79 million) has been made available over the lifetime of this programme.

Fourthly, ADAPT is a Human Resources Community Initiative supported by the European Social Fund which operated in all member states of the European Union (EU) until the end of 1999. A key objective of the ADAPT initiative was to heighten awareness of the need for industry to adapt swiftly to changing work environments. It was designed therefore to support innovative training and human resource development projects in organisations interested in introducing progressive human resource development practices and policies that will enhance the technical and skill levels and career development opportunities of their employees.

The cumulative effect of these programmes has been to heighten awareness of the critical link between education and economic and social wellbeing. It highlights the need for a more cohesive approach to developing education, vocational education and training systems that provide mutual gains to all stakeholders – students, participants, employees, employers, the economy and wider society. These EU-sponsored initiatives go some way towards fostering this learning society.

NATIONAL TRAINING POLICY IN REVIEW

There is a growing recognition that training policy, at national level, has resulted in a number of inconsistencies and there is a perceived need for a re-orienting of training policy to take greater cognisance of industry's needs. Over the years, a number of criticisms have been levelled at the current national training system that are worth reporting here.

The Culliton Report

In 1992 the Culliton Report was published which made two specific recommendations about training and development at national level.

1. The provision for training at work is inadequate. New structures are needed to remedy the situation. An institutional reorganisation of FÁS should be adopted to reflect the sharp distinction between support activities for the unemployed and industry-relevant training. These two activities should at a minimum be separated into two distinct divisions. In the longer term a more radical approach may be necessary.
2. A greater proportion of FÁS resources and activities should be allocated to industry – relevant training directed towards those at work and preparing for work.

While acknowledging the role of the Labour Services Act (1987) in shifting emphasis away from in-company training to schemes such as the social employment scheme and other youth employment initiatives, these recommendations clearly espouse an interventionist approach on the part of the state. The report pointed out that about 90 per cent of FÁS's budget was absorbed on activities that could not generally be described as training. Roche and Tansey (1992) argued that FÁS is a very complex organisation, with a set of multiple objectives both economic and social, coupled with a wide span of activities and programmes. They also suggested that FÁS is deserving of closer analysis due to its position and the national resources it has responsibility for managing.

IBEC's Analysis of Industrial Training (1994)

IBEC carried out a comprehensive review of industrial training in 1994, which identified a number of perceived weaknesses in our national training system. A summary of the issues identified is recorded below.

- National policy on training is seen to be primarily driven by the state with the result that employers have only a consultative role and are not directly represented on important bodies.
- The training support scheme is held to be inadequate, with insufficient state support for industrial training.

- Training provision is overtly fragmented between state agencies, educational institutions, consultancies, private training organisations and industrialists.
- Companies need to invest more in training but the real problem in many small firms may be less to do with increasing their investment in training and more to do with the need to get a better return on any investment made.
- There is a major imbalance of resources allocated between support for training for the unemployed and training for those in employment. The report cited an expenditure figure of £280m for the unemployed and £1.8m for those in employment.

The report, while acknowledging the passive role played by employers to date and the consequent inadequate provision that resulted, concluded with a number of recommendations that would facilitate a greater contribution from employers.

Table 8.3 IBEC recommendations for industrial training

- The development of national training policy for the employed and the co-ordination of Government services to support industry.
- The researching of industry training needs to clearly articulate the training needed in key business growth areas to support business development. Direct consultation and the development of pilot projects would be a key part of this function.
- The promotion of truly effective and cost-efficient training that supports organisational objectives and improved performance.
- The development of a national framework of vocational qualifications both for off-the-job and in-company training.
- The generation of greater awareness of the contribution that well structured training can make to business competitiveness.
- The development of appropriate initiatives to satisfy the training and development needs of small business.
- The securing of direct financial support for training initiatives that meet criteria and standards laid down, with the actual training to be carried out by approved trainers, of whom FÁS would be one option. In this way, company-relevant training would receive a greater level of support.
- The improvement of the quality and design of training programmes for those in employment.
- The promotion and establishment of a quality training mark for companies with the objective of developing company accreditation as a requirement for the future availability of grant-aided training.
- The development of initiatives to meet gaps in training provisions particularly in the service sector.
- The representation of industry's interests on sectoral and educational bodies in the planning and organisation of education and training for industry.

Source: Garavan, Costine and Heraty (1995).

Trade Unions and Training

There are indications that a broadening of the trade union view of training and development is occurring. For instance, the ICTU has highlighted the fact that in the area of raising the skill levels of existing employees, Irish firms lag well behind their European counterparts (Duffy 1993). In outlining an argument for improving this situation, Duffy referred to several deficiencies in the Irish training scene, including:

- the need for companies to engage in greater consultation with trade unions in the area of training and development;
- the focus on very job-specific training without any element of personal development;
- the tendency of firms to design their training with a view to maximising grant recovery, rather than focusing on the needs of individuals being trained;
- the absence of formal training agreements.

Duffy goes on to state that training requirements fall into two broad categories: the need to continue upgrading existing skills, and the need to meet the challenges of a total change in work practices brought on by changes in technology. These general themes were also embraced in a report commissioned in 1993 by the ICTU, entitled *New Forms of Work Organisation: Options for Trade Unions*, in which the need to ensure adequate skills training, as well as providing opportunities for personal development, is associated with the introduction of new work organisation strategies. In addition, William A. Attley (1994) (then Joint General President SIPTU) stated his belief that the success of the Irish economy depends in large measure on high levels of skills and knowledge, and that it is the intention of trade unions to press for its vision of a highly skilled and flexible workforce.

Garavan *et al.* (1995) suggest that, from an overall perspective, a number of inconsistencies exist in the area of national training and development policy. A summary of these inconsistencies is presented below.

- The state has handled its own training badly. It exhorts private enterprise to develop and implement corporate training plans, and yet the state itself does not operate such a process.
- During the last ten years or so the Government has invested heavily in training, almost to the point where organisations have become dependent on such funding, with very uneven results. The cumulative effect of all state intervention has served to represent training to employers as something that is essentially provided by external agencies. Studies carried out by FÁS have highlighted the prevalence of inadequate levels of training provision, a fact reinforced more recently by the 'Industrial Training in Ireland' report prepared by Roche and Tansey (1992). Indeed, it is their contention that employers are reluctant to provide anything more than the basic minimum level of training for their employees.
- Since the mid-1980s there has been a preoccupation in Ireland with training to reduce mass unemployment (particularly youth unemployment). This, in turn, has switched the emphasis of national training strategies away from the existing business enterprise and its needs, towards the creation of a network of non-business organisations. Because of this, the value of training for organisational improvement has been diminished in the eyes of many employers.
- With regard to providing the critically required impetus to the concept of continuing training in this country, the Labour Services Act (1987) seems less than effective legislation. It does not make a significantly positive statement about the role of training within organisations and the need to allocate more resources and commitment in this vital area. Among the specific issues it fails to embrace are the following:

1. The stipulation that a minimum amount of total labour costs be allocated towards training. It is suggested that, in order to respond effectively to initiatives in other countries, an initial level of 2 per cent should be included, with tax relief applicable to additional expenditure over and above this statutory minimum.

2. The necessity for organisations to draw up an annual training plan, which would include details such as the use of training for technological and other major organisational changes; the types of general training activities to be undertaken and the resources being committed to them; and the qualifications of the training specialist charged with implementing the training plan. Such a planning process would encourage organisations to treat training as a strategic activity, rather than perceiving it as an operational activity with a limited contribution to make to business success.

3. The need to focus on the quality of training at national and organisational levels. Those responsible for the allocation of funds for training purposes should satisfy themselves as to the nature of the training requirements, the quality of the delivery mechanism, and in particular the qualifications and credibility of the trainers who provide it. This stipulation should be equally applicable both to in-house specialists and external consultants. Furthermore, multiple assessment criteria should be utilised – evaluation only in terms of numbers trained should not be considered sufficient.

White Paper on Human Resource Development

In response to continued criticism of the state's role in Ireland's training infrastructure, the Government produced a policy document entitled 'Human Resource Development White Paper' in May 1997. This White Paper represents a significant departure from the traditional programme-led interventions that have typified previous governmental responses, and which have resulted in ad-hoc interventions that lack overall strategic coherence. Instead, the emphasis is on clear objective-driven solutions and calls for significant change in the approach to training and human resource development by business, individuals and the providers of training services. Three critical pillars of developing effective human resource development strategies are identified:

- the promotion of investment on the development of skills and knowledge of the workforce;
- the promotion of gainful employment by helping people to develop their knowledge and skills to their full potential;
- the achievement of high levels of efficiency, effectiveness and value-for-money in the delivery of state interventions which yield permanent benefits to clients.

The White Paper further outlines a number of structural- and policy-based changes that are required if the Government is to achieve these strategic pillars. The more salient of these proposals are briefly attended to here:

1. The 'Service to Industry' division of FÁS (including the regional advisory component) is to be transferred to a new body, Forbairt, while FÁS will then be responsible for the delivery of training for those individuals who seek to enter or re-enter the labour market.

2. The development of a revitalised National Employment Service.

3. The development of a new training networks' programme, which provides for state support to encourage the development of best practice strategies.

4. The industrial training grants to be reviewed and grant-aid support maintained to those firms that provide the training necessary to enable newly-recruited workers attain the requisite level of expertise and productivity.

5. The establishment of a Future Skills Identification Group, comprising representatives of business and trade unions, as well as representatives of Government, state development agencies and education and training providers, with a view to identifying skill needs and making recommendations for the education and training system.

Although there has been a change in Government since this policy document was published the present administration supports many of the provisions contained therein and have taken steps to enact many of the changes detailed. Developments have taken place in the interim, including increased training provision for the unemployed (i.e. FÁS traineeship programme) and the establishment of a training network operated by FÁS. Much of the current debate has raised expectations of a major re-organisation and restructuring of FÁS in the near future to separate training for the unemployed and new labour market entrants from continuing training for those in employment. It is unclear at the present time whether an entirely new body will be created that will have a specific remit for continuing training, although critics of the current system (Garavan *et al.* 1995) have argued along these lines for years.

Tansey (1998) highlights the continuing importance of economic training to encourage the delivery of high-quality training as a national priority. In particular, he highlights an essential set of benefits that are seen to be associated with strategic economic training.

- It promotes national economic development by ensuring that the potential for national economic growth is maximised. Insufficient training, or a poor level of training, can lead to skill shortages that can inhibit the growth of the economy.
- Economic training improves individual productivity.
- Economic training has the potential to improve an industry's adaptability and its capacity to absorb changes in product and process technologies.
- Extensive economic training facilitates the introduction of more advanced physical capital.
- The existence of a pool of highly-skilled labour at all levels is used as a mechanism for attracting foreign industry to Ireland.
- A skilled labour force becomes a significant differentiation factor within a single market.

This chapter has concentrated on the evolution of the national system of training, development and vocational education in Ireland. Here our concern has been with training and development at a macro, national level, while organisational level training and development, focusing on procedures and practices in the workplace, is the subject of focus in the next chapter.

In this chapter we have endeavoured to provide the reader with a route map through Ireland's national system of training and development, past and present. In this regard we traced the historical development of Ireland's training infrastructure and set down the major statutory and institutional reforms that have shaped the training system that we see in operation today. In establishing the route map, we reviewed core national policy decisions in conjunction with the critical evaluations proffered by the actors in the training arena in Ireland on the direction that policy was taking. Finally we presented a summary of the economic value of training and the likely future developments of the national training system.

Having established the nature of the enveloping national training framework, and the economic necessity of training and development, it remains to investigate training and development at the micro or organisational level. The following chapter discusses training and development at the level of the firm and examines the process by which organisations seek to achieve efficiency returns on their training investment.

9

Learning, Training and Development in Organisations

Aseries of social, organisational and technological developments over the last forty years have had a considerable impact on how organisations function and how they choose to manage and develop their workforce. More than ten years ago, Block (1990) argued that strict controls, greater pressure, more clearly defined jobs and tighter supervision had run their course in their ability to give organisations the productivity gains required to compete effectively in the marketplace. Today, we live in the post-industrial era, the 'knowledge society' or the 'information age' each of which have likely implications for the array of knowledge, skills and abilities that are required to work in them. Here, DeGeus (1997, 28) postulates that 'within companies, our success depends on our skill with human beings: building and developing the consistent knowledge base of our enterprise'. While Iles (1994) cautions that the importance of people to an organisation's success is easily acknowledged in rhetoric, Walton (1999) argues that the way development activities are conducted and co-ordinated is a telling index of how an organisation views and values its staff.

This chapter examines the nature of learning, training and development (LT & D) in organisations. The rationale for increased attention to LT & D systems and processes is first explored and two core frameworks prompting this increased attention are reviewed. Learning as an organisational process that underpins all training and development activity is next discussed and a number of learning principles are highlighted. The process of formally managing learning through training and development activities is presented. The chapter concludes with a summary review of current training and development practices in Ireland.

THE ORGANISATIONAL REQUIREMENT FOR LEARNING, TRAINING AND DEVELOPMENT

There is an ever-increasing volume of material that argues that effective learning, training and development is a core means of leveraging organisational competitiveness. Much of this literature suggests that heightened global competition, the internationalisation of business, borderless economies, and widescale technological advancements are leading to the realisation that the primary source of competitive advantage in the future is sharply focused on creating new knowledge that is disseminated through the company and which, in turn, leads to continuous innovation (Nooteboom 1999; Probst and Buchel 1997; Nonaka and Takeuchi 1995; West 1994; Porter 1990; Senge 1990; Stata 1989). Porter (1990), in his prominent study on the competitiveness of nations, argued that to sustain competitive advantage an organisation must have a commitment to improvement, innovation and change. Important sources of these qualities, which cannot easily be replicated by competitors, are superior human resources and technical capability. As Gee *et al.* (1996, 19) suggest, 'gone are the workers hired from the neck down and simply told what to do'. Rather, as McEwan *et al.* (1988, 47) argue:

> If the people in the company are not mobilised to produce the right quality product or service, on time and every time, then the enterprise will fail. Thus people must be considered a factor of equal importance to finance, marketing, production and so forth in the business planning equation, because they are the medium through which plans are turned into successful reality.

Some of the most recent literature emphasises mechanisms that promote the development of learning and knowledge, which will enhance the strategic capability of the organisation. It tends to focus on issues such as organisational delayering, employees' empowerment, process re-engineering, and the adoption of some elements of functional flexibility, all of which require a culture of continuous development and competency upgrading. Barrow and Loughlin (1992), for example, propose that organisations seek employees who:

- have the ability to learn new skills and adapt to changing circumstances;
- can conceptualise the contribution of their role to organisational effectiveness;
- are capable of working in flatter structures and without supervision;
- have the ability to manage the interface between customers and the organisation;
- possess capabilities such as problem-solving, creative thinking and innovativeness.

The core of the argument is that organisations that can improve on their capability for learning (through increased knowledge, skill accumulation and application) are in a better position to compete. Saul (1997) argues that although work practices in many organisations still reflect the hierarchical, fixed horizontal and vertical relationships, where many workers have narrowly defined job duties and responsibilities characteristic of fordism; nevertheless, there is a movement towards teamwork and flatter hierarchies where workers at various levels participate in decision-making, and different backgrounds, experiences and perspectives are understood to enhance the productive potential of teams.

Boud and Garrick (1999, 4) sum up many of the core arguments that highlight the importance of this 'people' dimension.

> Distinctions between life and work, learning and production, community and enterprise are becoming less firm. No longer are the pools of knowledge and expertise acquired in initial education sufficient for the new work order . . . Modern organisations ignore learning at the cost of their present and future successes.

All of these requirements place considerable responsibility on the organisation's human resource department to ensure that employees are equipped to meet the demands required of them for this competitive agenda.

DEFINITION OF TERMS

There are a number of terms in common parlance within the field of LT & D: learning, training, development, education, knowledge, human resource development, strategic human resource development, employee development, competency development, organisational learning, knowledge management, the learning organisation. Much of these variations arise when different authors seek to focus on, or highlight, particular elements of the field of study, but it is probably true that some of the terms are used interchangeably. Some useful classification can be made relatively easily between for example, education, learning, training and development, although learning, as a construct, underpins each activity (see table 9.1). Meaningful differentiation between some of the other terms is somewhat more problematic since it essentially comes down to a matter of interpretation i.e. can organisations learn of themselves (the learning organisation) or is organisational learning anything more than the sum of individual learning that occurs in organisations? However, in an attempt to show the thinking behind them, a broad differentiation of each term is provided.

Table 9.1 Distinctions between learning, training, development and education

	Learning	Training	Development	Education Informal	Education Formal
Focus of activity	On values, attitudes, innovation, and outcome accomplishment	On knowledge, skills, ability, and job performance	On individual potential and future role in work-place	On personal development and the experience of life	On structured development of individual to specified outcomes
Clarity of objectives	May be vague and difficult to identify	Can be specified clearly	Objectives stated in general terms	Objectives are unique to individual and may not be clearly articulated	Objectives stated in general terms
Time-scale	Continuous	Short-term	Long-term	Lifelong	Specified period: e.g. ten years
Values that underpin activity	Assumes continuous change; emphasises breakthrough	Assumes relative stability; emphasises improvement	Assumes continuous change; emphasises maximising potential	Assumes incremental change; emphasises improvements	Often assumes stability; emphasis on breakthrough
Nature of learning process	Instructional or organic	Structured or mechanistic	Instructional or organic	Instructional or organic	Structured or mechanistic
Content of activity	Learning how to learn, values, attitudes relevant to work	Knowledge, skills and attitudes relevant to specific job; basic abilities	Interpersonal, intrapersonal, and life skills	Life experience provides basis for education	Imposed and specified curriculums
Methods used	Informal learning methods, learner-initiated methods	Demonstration, practice, feedback	Coaching, counselling, guidance mentoring, peer learning	Experience, observation, experimentation, and reflection	Lectures, guided reading, debate, self-managed learning

$\longrightarrow$

Table 9.1 Distinctions between learning, training, development and education (cont.)

Learning	Training	Development	Education Informal	Education Formal
Outcomes of process	Individuals learn how to learn and create own solutions	Skilled performance of tasks that make up job	Improved problem-solving, decision-making, intrapersonal, interpersonal competence	Personal outcomes internal to individual	External specified outcomes
Learning strategy used	Inductive strategies	Didactic, tutor-centred	Skill-building and inductive strategies	Inductive strategies	Combination of didactic, skill-building and inductive strategies
Nature of process	Inside-out: seeks to do for self	Outside-in: done by others	Combination of outside-in and inside-out	Inside-out: seeks to do for self	Largely outside-in: done by others
Role of professional trainer	To facilitate and guide	To instruct, demonstrate, and guide	To guide, instruct, coach, counsel, and mentor	Minimal: largely individual-directed	To act as expert, instruct, facilitate, and guide to learning resources
Document trainer philosophy	Existentialism; self-managed process	Instrumentalism: transferring knowledge using formal methods and measuring results	Existentialism: one-to-one learning, self-managed learning	Existentialism: totally self-managed	Combination of instrumentalism and existentialism
Type of need emphasised	Individual and organisational needs	Organisational needs	Organisational and individual needs	Individual needs	Institutional and individual needs
Process of evaluation	Continuous evaluation	Evaluation against specific job performance standards	Evaluation of skills and effectiveness	Evaluation against life goals and personal development	Evaluation in terms of pass v. fail levels
Link with corporate aims and strategies	Directly aligned with company's vision and requirements for success	Not necessarily linked to company's aims and goals	Directly aligned with company's aims and requirements for future but depends on type of development	No link to company's aims and goals	Not necessarily linked to company's aims and goals
Pay-back to company	Immediate and continuing	Almost immediate in form of skilled performance	Medium to long-term pay-back	No direct pay-back	Long-term at most

Source: Garavan, Costine, and Heraty (1995, 4–5).

Education: Educational objectives have traditionally been couched in general or abstract terms and are often perceived as person rather than job oriented. In its true sense, education refers to the assimilation of knowledge and understanding that can be far broader than the work context within which an individual may operate. When we speak of education, we typically refer to formal programmes of study, many of which are accredited, and which generally occur outside of a workplace. A core purpose of an education system, for example, is to provide and improve general skills (e.g. ability to read, to write and to reason).

Training: While no standard definition of training exists it is generally expressed in behavioural terms and, in a narrow sense, refers to the planned acquisition of knowledge, skills and abilities (KSA) required to perform effectively in a given role or job. Each training intervention requires some change in performance and, for the most part, new performance requires some form of learning to occur. Training is vocationally based i.e. its purpose is to improve specific skills or abilities that will (hopefully) result in better work performance.

Learning: For the most part learning is perceived as a process through which individuals assimilate new knowledge and skills that results in relatively permanent behavioural changes. Learning can be conscious or unconscious, formal or informal and requires some element of practice and experience. Effective learning requires the ability to question habits and methods, to challenge one's assumptions and mental maps. As learning underpins all LT & D activity in an organisation, it shall be treated separately in the next section.

Development: By its nature development is a broad concept that is future oriented and is concerned with the growth and enhancement of the individual. In organisational terms it refers to the acquisition of skills and abilities that are required for future roles in the organisation. In this way, development can be seen as a vehicle of career enhancement (career development), for succession planning (with an internal labour market – refer back to chapter three), for determining managerial potential (management development/ assessment centres) or for reasons of personal development (lifelong learning). To ensure commitment to the principles of development, individuals must recognise and understand the prerequisites and conditions for 'success' in their company, and how their contribution fits within this.

Human resource development: This concept has largely developed alongside the strategy literature (it first emerged at a conference in 1969) and generally refers to the development of a strategic organisational approach to managing LT & D at work. It advocates the strategic linking of training and development activities to corporate business objectives and a central role for line managers in developing employees. It refers to learning at the individual, group and organisational levels to enhance the effectiveness of human resource utilisation. It is the explicit link with strategy formulation and business objectives that serves to differentiate the term HRD from training and development more generally.

Competencies: While there is considerable confusion surrounding a definition of competence or competencies, two streams of work can be identified. The first is vocationally based and it examines the competencies demanded by the job. Here the emphasis is on breaking the job into its various components parts and describing behavioural characteristics and standards of performance that need to be attained by the job holder (Harrison 1997). The second focuses on the nature of the skills and abilities that the individuals bring to the job (Boyatzis 1982). Organisations are increasingly adopting competency frameworks to help them identify the types of behaviours they wish to promote to assist the performance of individuals and organisations.

Knowledge management: Snyder (1996) suggests that an organisation's knowledge consists of three essential elements: skills, cognitions and systems. An organisation's skills include the technical, professional and social expertise of the organisation's members – the know-how of the organisation. Cognitions refer to the information, ideas, attitudes, norms and values shared by the organisation's members – including the know-why of the organisation. An organisation's systems include the structures, procedures, and policies related to performing tasks, co-ordinating resources and managing external relationships. All three components are inextricably interrelated and their configuration has variously been referred to in the management lexicon as core competencies (Pralahad and Hamel 1990), organisational capability (Ulrich and Lake 1991), knowledge or intellectual capital (Zeleny 1990), or strategic capability (Lenz 1980).

The learning organisation: The literature on the learning organisation as a distinct concept is relatively new, and again, while there is no agreement on what exactly constitutes a learning organisation, it is generally described as a participative learning system, which places an emphasis on the exchange of information and being open to enquiry and self-criticism. It promotes continuous development and improvement, a willingness to take risks and a work system that actively facilitates learning at work. A fuller description of the learning organisation and organisational learning is provided later in this chapter.

Finally, in recent years the term *employee development* became increasing popular with both HR academics and students when the Chartered Institute of Personnel and Development (CIPD) used the term to refer to the specialist element of their professional programme that deals with the management of organised learning interventions at work. This term has now been replaced by CIPD with Learning and Development, but employee development is still in common parlance. Within this text, we have connected the terms learning, training and development to form LT & D that we use to describe deliberate organisational interventions that seek to expand the range of knowledge, skills and competencies of individuals at work. In this way LT & D is broader than skills' acquisition. Rather, it is about how, what and where individuals learn and how an organisation can facilitate this learning. It requires that we understand that individuals can and do learn outside of the often narrow scope of his/her job; that individuals' contributions need not be bound within the confines of their job; and that the challenge for organisations is as much about creating work systems that facilitate and capture this, as it is about designing training interventions.

LEARNING AS AN ORGANISATIONAL PROCESS

All organisational activities, including training and development, involve some form of learning. Garavan, Costine and Heraty (1995) describe this learning as a complex process of acquiring knowledge, understanding, skills, and values in order to be able to adapt to the environment in which we live. This adaptation generally involves some recognisable change in behaviour, though this is not always the case. Barnett (1999) suggests that in our complex world today we are constantly challenged to reappraise or review the way we interpret the world and the underlying frameworks that we adopt to make sense of this world. He further notes that:

> The learning challenge that we all face at work requires not only that we learn new techniques, or new ideas or new practices. They require us to change or at least widen the frameworks through which we interpret the world. In this way we are being called upon to change who and what we are.

The field of individual psychology has informed much of what we know about individual learning. Early behavioural psychologists concentrated on cause-effect models of behaviour (stimulus-response) to demonstrate how learning can occur. Pavlov's experiments with dogs demonstrated how it was possible to prompt a reflexive, involuntary response through classic conditioning. Skinner's (1938) work focused on reinforcement (operant conditioning) and showed how more complex, voluntary behaviours could be shaped through the achievement of a desired reward, or the prevention of an undesired punishment. In an organisational scenario, the use of praise and encouragement by trainers or line mangers can be seen as examples of promoting operant learning.

Further work by cognitive theorists focused on the 'thinking' part of human learning and is most closely associated with the process of experiential learning. Kolb's (1984) experiential learning cycle suggests that learning occurs in a sequential or cyclical manner. We experience something new (new information or knowledge), we reflect on that new experience and try to make sense of it, we generalise about it (i.e. what would happen if ...) and then we test it out (try doing something new or adopt a different approach). The result of this experimentation leads us back to the start of the cycle, where this new result represents the something new or new experience that acts as a catalyst for further learning. Experiential learning suggests that learners must have time to experiment and try out new ideas if meaningful learning is to take place i.e. practice or trial-and-error.

Bandura (1986) introduced a social dimension to learning and suggested that much of our experiences are picked up either directly, or indirectly, through observing other people. This social aspect to learning points to the necessity to have a supportive learning environment, which, in a work situation, would include superior or boss, work colleagues, or friends and family outside of work.

Each of these theories of learning provides important starting points for LT & D systems. If we understand how individuals learn then we can build this into how training courses and development programmes are designed and delivered. In this context of workplace learning, Revans' (1982) ideas on adult learning are worth noting. He suggests that adult learning is most effective if:

1. They are motivated to learn of their own volition and not solely at the will of others – it must be something they want to achieve.
2. They can identify themselves with others who may not only share their needs, but who may also satisfy some of these needs – they seek support from their peers and colleagues and learn more effectively with this group support.
3. They can try out any new learning in actions of their own design – learning should be more than the acquiring of information but should involve some action.
4. That, within a reasonable lapse of time, they can attain first hand knowledge of the results of their trials – constant reinforcement and feedback on their performance.

Boud and Garrick (1999, 1) emphasise the critical importance of a thorough understanding of work-based learning and note that:

> In the complex enterprises of the new millennium, learning has moved from the periphery – from something that prepared people for employment – to the lifeblood which sustains them. There are few places left for employees at any level who do not continue to learn and improve their effectiveness throughout their working lives. There is no place for managers who do not appreciate their own vital role in fostering learning.

Arising from much of the theory of individual learning, it is possible to isolate a number of key learning principles that can be applied to the design and delivery of training or development programmes at work.

- *Motivation to learn*: The employee must want to learn and thus, in order to be committed to the process, must perceive that the learning event will result in the achievement of certain desired goals.
- *Involvement of the learner*: The training or learning should be seen as an active, rather than a passive process. Briscoe (1987) and Pont (1991) suggest that adults learn more effectively when they are actively involved in the learning process. Getting individuals involved in discussing the course, what they hope to achieve from it, and seeking opinions and contributions throughout can make the learning more meaningful. Individuals need to 'own' the learning i.e. if they are actively involved in coming up with solutions to problems or thinking up ideas the learning is internalised more easily. Where learning is off-the-job, the use of work problems and case studies workshops are useful means of creating ownership of learning.
- *Reinforcement of learning*: Employees should be given an opportunity to practice what they have learned. This facilitates continuous improvement and employees can engage in goal setting to heighten the learning process. In tandem with this, the training event must allow employees sufficient time both to absorb the material and practice or test new knowledge and skills.
- *Feedback*: Learners need constant and immediate feedback on their performance. This feedback should be both realistic and constructive if it is to reinforce behaviour or encourage further learning
- *Meaningfulness of the material*: The nature of the training/learning intervention must be seen to be relevant to the employee's work i.e. it must be something that he/she can use or will be able to use sometime in the future. Wexley and Latham (1991) suggest that, to increase meaningfulness, learners should be provided with an overview of the material to be learned; the material should be presented using examples, concepts and terms familiar to the learner; the material should be sequenced in a logical manner; and simpler skills be introduced as a basis for the attainment of more complex intellectual skills.
- *Communities of practice*: Communities of practice evolve as people united in an organisational setting develop a shared history as well as particular values, beliefs, ways of talking and ways of doing things. Since individuals both shape and are shaped by their social contexts, they bring to the workplace a variety of knowledge, experience and insights that can be capitalised upon. They learn to construct shared understanding amidst confusing and conflicting data and begin to rely on each other for mutual assistance. The context then within which LT & D is organised has a powerful influence on the learning that occurs and should be structured and managed in order to allow for information to be exchanged and applied.

There is a danger here of presenting an over-simplification of the learning process. Although it is argued that learning is as natural as breathing, it is also an inherently complex process. Work-based learning is particularly complex since individuals at work do not represent a completely homogenous group. They may share some common attributes, and work within a shared culture, but essentially employees represent a diverse group of individuals that happen to be working in the same organisation. As such, each individual brings a unique set of experiences and expectations to the learning event that can shape the level of learning that takes place and the degree to which the learning becomes a significant aspect of subsequent behaviour. A number of pertinent factors have been identified by Buckley and Caple (1990) as having a significant influence on learning. These factors include: the employee's age (which affects attitudes, motivations and interests), his/her levels of intelligence and ability (affects preferences for structured vs. unstructured learning events); his/her background and psychological disposition (predetermined perceptions of the value of training, previous experiences of training/schooling, concerns or anxieties surrounding learning); his/her learning style and preference (for reflective, practical, or conceptual approaches); and finally his/her trainability or motivation to learn (affects aptitude for improved performance and expectations of training outcomes).

An understanding of learning styles is particularly important since the training method chosen by an organisation must take cognisance of particular learning preferences that individual employees might express. For example, some individuals may learn more effectively in a structured training environment using concrete examples that they can relate to, whereas others might prefer a more informal conceptual framework that draws on various scenarios that are not necessarily work based. Mumford (1986) suggests that a failure to take account of different learning styles can have seriously negative implications for the training process while Garavan *et al.* (1995) quoting Arment (1990) indicate that:

1. By the time we reach adulthood, each of us has developed our own method of learning, reflected in a unique and well-established learning style.
2. Trainers also have well-established learning styles and preferences.
3. The more compatible the style of learning with the approach to training adopted, the more likely it is that a positive learning experience will occur.

FRAMEWORKS FOR MANAGING, LEARNING, TRAINING AND DEVELOPMENT AT WORK

Thus far our discussion has centred on learning at the individual level and the need for organisations to understand some of the guiding principles underpinning effective individual learning. However, the approach that the organisation adopts with respect to how it manages the range of human resource activities that underpin its activities will have an enormous influence on how LT & D is enacted, its role and function and, ultimately, its effectiveness. While there are a wide variety of organisational frameworks and approaches to choose from, here we look very briefly at two frameworks that have been widely debated in recent years and explore their likely implication for the management of LT & D within organisations. These frameworks include the *resource-based view of the firm* and the *learning organisation*. Each of these approaches has its own view on what is seen as permissible learning at work and what the underlying rationale for LT & D is – maximising resource potential or individual self-actualisation through lifelong learning.

The Resource-Based View of the Firm

The resource-based view (RBV) of the firm is rooted in an economic perspective of competitive functioning and it suggests that organisational assets that demonstrate a number of core characteristics allow a company to attain a sustainable competitive advantage. The RBV is most widely associated with Barney (1991) who argues that any number of a firm's attributes can be considered as resources, including all assets, capabilities, competencies, organisation processes, information and knowledge. However, only resources that meet the four criteria of value, rareness, inimitability and non-substitutability can deliver sustainable competitive advantage. The RBV essentially argues that an organisation's human resources can deliver sustainable competitive value provided that the organisation ensures that it delivers value, it is rare, it is difficult to imitate and cannot be easily substituted (Flood *et al.* 1996). Where an organisation adopts the RBV, we can envisage a number of core objectives for LT & D :

1. To ensure that human resources are valuable i.e. add value to the organisation. Here LT & D would focus on activities that would differentiate employees from others in the competitive field in terms of their knowledge, skills and productivity levels. In chapter three, we demonstrated how, over a period of time, internal labour markets can become highly differentiated; that investment in an organisation's specific, rather than general skills increases the value of employees to the one organisation (although this might not be as attractive to employees who seek general skills and therefore greater employ-ability). Increased investment in specific skills that are non-transferable, but which are required by the organisation can result in a highly differentiated workforce.
2. To ensure that human resources are rare. The extent to which a resource is rare depends on the quality and availability of that resource. This is somewhat more difficult to envisage unless there is a very tight labour market where needed skills are in short supply and difficult to source. It is plausible that economic growth in recent years has made some types of employees very rare indeed, i.e. those with particular expertise in software development for the telecom market, and knowledge workers more generally. However, it is also possible to argue that the nature of business today demands particular sets of abilities and behaviours (e.g. flexibility, adaptability and autonomy) and these attributes are not that readily available on the open market.
3. To ensure that human resources cannot be imitated. How an organisation manages its workforce is probably as much to do with serendipity as with conscious choice. An organisation's culture, values, ways of being, managerial style, co-worker relationships, communities of practice – each of these evolve over long periods of time and combine to make each organisation's environment unique. It is this combination of factors that make the calibre of human resources, and the human resource systems themselves, difficult to imitate. The LT & D system permeates all organisational knowledge systems and so directly contributes to the inimitableness of human resources.
4. To ensure that human resources are non-substitutable. In the long run it is doubtful whether any one individual cannot be replaced, either from within the external labour market, or from other companies. However, substitution in the short-term can be more problematic, costly and risky, particularly where the skills or knowledge are valuable and rare. Moreover, as work processes are becoming team- and project-based, the breath of knowledge required might not actually exist outside of the company and so substitution might not be an option.

The resource-based view suggests a broad canvas for LT & D within organisations. However, it is a strongly resource-oriented approach and it appears to suggest that organisations should only be concerned with resources that are capable of delivering sustainable competitive advantage. This approach could increase the pressure to deliver LT & D that is organisation specific, that is immediately visible or that can demonstrably add value. It is difficult to determine whether there is any role for learning activity that has no immediate tangible results, but which nevertheless might be highly valuable. Furthermore, resources by their nature probably have a limited lifespan of sustainable competitive value – there is less clarity on what occurs to the human resource dimension in those circumstances.

The Learning Organisation

Conceptualising about and researching the dimensions of the learning organisations has become a significant academic activity in recent years (Heraty and Morley 1995). However, there is relatively little agreement on a definition of the learning organisation other than it is an organisational process that seeks to highlight the supremacy of learning as a core competitive strategy. It has been described as an organisation that facilitates the learning of all its members and consciously transforms itself (Pedler, Boydell and Burgoyne 1989). It is a place where:

> . . . people continually expand their capacity to create the results they truly desire, where new and expansive patterns of thinking are nurtured, where collective aspirations are set free, and where people are continually learning how to learn together.
>
> Senge (1990)

Solomon (1999, 122) describes a learning organisation thus:

> While learning has always been a feature of working, learning at work has a new status in contemporary workforce discourse as learning is considered a part of everyday work. Learning becomes a cultural practice that is affirmed through the development of a mission and value statements, an identification of workers with corporate aims and the conceptualisation of an organisation as a site on ongoing learning.

Field and Ford (1995) describe a learning organisation as one with a well developed capacity for that which Argyris and Schön (1978) refer to as double-loop learning: where there is ongoing attention to learning how to learn and where key aspects of organisational functioning support learning. Nonaka (1991) argues that a company is not a machine but a living organism and that the learning organisation represents a shared understanding of what the company stands for, where it is going, what kind of world it wants to live in, and most importantly, how to make that world a reality.

West (1994) indicates that the learning organisation concept is embedded in the notion that innovative organisations should be designed as participative learning systems that place an emphasis on information exchange and being open to enquiry and self-criticism, while Pedler *et al.* (1989) propose that a learning organisation is one that:

- has a climate in which individuals are encouraged to learn and develop to their full potential;
- extends its learning culture to include customers, suppliers and other significant stakeholders;
- makes human resource development strategy central to its business policy so that the process of individual and organisational learning becomes a major business activity.

The learning organisation literature suggests that, rather than interpreting the environment as a force to be reckoned with, organisations have the potential to shape and develop their environmental context. Calvert *et al.* (1994, 40) maintain that learning organisations use learning as a means of attaining their goals and create structures and procedures that facilitate and support continuous learning and development. They propose that:

- all organisations learn, hence learning is continuous;
- all organisations learn at different levels of proficiency and at different paces;
- to become a 'learning organisation' an organisation must find ways to make learning more intentional and more systematic, deliberate learning is more effective than learning that is left to chance.

There is an attempt made to link individual and organisational performance, which is often reflected in the reward choices, made by the organisation. However, the process of becoming a learning organisation is not easily realised since it requires fundamental changes to how individuals think and interact and involves a comprehensive evaluation of deeply held assumptions and values. As with any change of process, the move towards adopting the learning mantle is often perceived with suspicion and mistrust by those that are averse to changing all that has traditionally been stable and consistent, and moving towards a situation where they are required to take responsibility for their continuous development and competency improvement.

Garavan *et al.* (1995) propose that the LT & D remit within a learning organisation involves:

- attending to the requirements of all members and groups, and building a sense of cohesion and group purpose and support;
- identifying and satisfying individual motivational and developmental needs;
- harnessing the efforts of all members to meet the desired goal.

It is arguable that some of the literature on the learning organisation is overtly prescriptive and aspirational, since, by definition, organisations never reach the stage at which they can be said to have fulfilled the criteria required to become a learning organisation. Notwithstanding this, the principles upon which the concept is founded represent a set of ideals to which most organisations would aspire: the creation of an organisational climate that facilitates continuous development, a system that rewards continuous improvement, and a structural design that promotes on-going learning.

It is possible to identify a range of LT & D systems and activities that would fit within the learning organisation paradigm. For example, the promotion of learning for the sake of learning (not tied to specific jobs or roles within the organisation); the development of facilitative structures that would promote learning and development such as mentoring and coaching arrangements; identified developmental pathways through the organisation for career progression; a commitment to the principles of lifelong learning in whatever guise they present themselves.

THE PROCESS OF LEARNING, TRAINING AND DEVELOPMENT IN ORGANISATIONS

The process of learning, training and development is presented here as a series of key stages that commence at the strategic or business level of the organisation and work sequentially down from there. In practice, LT & D probably occurs much more intuitively and spontaneously that this sequence of activities suggests, but the sequencing is useful here to illustrate the interconnected nature of LT & D activity. In most organisations planned learning events are converted into training and/or development programmes and so, when we use the term training here i.e. training policy, training needs analysis, training budget, it is to reflect this operationalisation of work-based learning.

Training Philosophies and Policies

A training policy reflects the organisation's philosophy towards LT & D and governs the priorities, standards and scope of its training activities. As such it provides the framework within which all planned interventions take place. An organisation's philosophy towards LT & D can be expressed along a continuum where, on the one hand, training is viewed as an expense and only occurs as the need for it arises, and, on the other, employees are

Table 9.2 A comparative summary of employee development models

Model	Characteristics	Focus	Limitations
Unsystematic model	Unplanned approach; lack of training policies; individuals largely responsible for own development investment	Operational	Ad-hoc; reactive; training viewed as a cost rather than as an an investment
Problem-centred model	Identification and prioritisation of performance problems coupled with generation and evaluation of results	Operational	Highly reactive; high risk of inaccurate identification of priority problems
Systematic model	Grounded in systems theory; highly structured; rational means of directing resources; cyclical process from identification of needs through evaluation of outcomes	Operational	Very simplistic; low applicability in times of uncertainty; does not recognise individual differences; ignores context
Cycle of training model	Adopts a stakeholder approach; views training as a total organisational process; considers wider organisational implications	Semi-strategic	HR considerations not linked with business planning; does not consider line management role in training and development
Effectiveness improvement model	Advocates close relationship between line and staff managers; utilises performance audits as evaluation tool	Semi-strategic	No incorporation of HR considerations into strategic business planning; organisation's culture and role of top management not considered
Business focused strategic model	Related training needs to business requirements; identifies external triggers for change; highlights top and line management support	Strategic	Inadequate consideration of the training context; ignores nature of individual as learner

Source: Heraty (1992).

seen as a potential source of competitive advantage and so training and development is a central organisational concern. In this respect, all organisations have an LT & D policy whether explicit or implicit, positive or negative. The extent to which organisations develop explicit training policies is contextually bound and influenced by a number of factors. For example, prevailing employment legislation (i.e. equality, health and safety); state of the labour market (whether skilled labour is readily available, or can be contracted in or out); available resources that can be allocated to LT & D; prevailing views on the value of training (particularly at senior and strategic levels); nature of the product or service market (see chapter two for further clarification); and, in some cases, the expectations of employees themselves. Furthermore, organisations can differentiate themselves as 'desirable' employers by providing a range of employee and career development opportunities that are designed to attract and retain the required calibre of employee. Such an approach requires a high level of co-ordination between LT & D and the range of other human resource policy choices, such as recruitment and selection, performance appraisal, reward systems and employee relations.

Within the extant training literature there exists a myriad of training models that have developed over the years ranging from the reactive, ad-hoc varieties to those that seek to describe training and development in strategic terms. A select number of these models are presented in table 9.2 which illustrate the range of approaches that organisations can adopt towards LT & D.

The LT & D model adopted by an organisation presents a useful indication of its training philosophy and thus the training policy that it will employ. Moreover in an organisation that adopts the unsystematic framework, one would expect little integration of employees' considerations into strategic decision-making or broader business issues. The converse holds true for organisations that adopt the more strategic models, where LT & D considerations play a critical role in the formulation of strategic business plans.

Once the training policies have been developed the organisation needs to translate the key training objectives into action. At this stage a training plan is drawn up that seeks to merge individual and organisational requirements into a clear course of action. A model of the training process is presented in figure 9.1.

Figure 9.1 Model of a training process

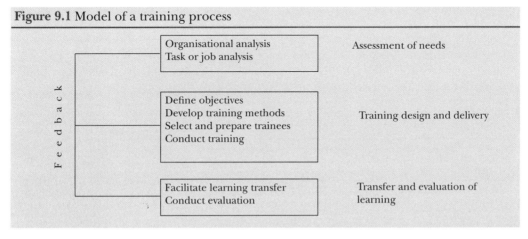

The first stage in the training process is the identification of training needs or training needs analysis (TNA). In an organisational context, a need is a discrepancy or 'gap' between 'what is' and 'what ought to be', i.e. desired performance as against actual performance. Thus, training needs refer to any shortfall between current knowledge, skills, attitudes etc. and the level required now, or in the future. This 'training gap' is represented in figure 9.2.

Figure 9.2 The training gap

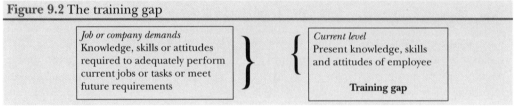

Source: Armstrong (1987).

Training needs can be either current or in the future, or both. Current needs arise where inconsistencies emerge in the present training system and the organisation must act to remedy the situation. Garavan *et al.* (1995) view this as a reactive needs analysis which usually provides a short-term solution. Future needs, on the other hand, arise from organisational changes and are usually diagnosed by proactive needs identification. They are prompted by internal and external factors such as strategy change, work restructuring, product or service diversification, introduction of new technology; skills' inventories matched against future requirements, and so forth. Such needs are usually more developmental in nature, and there can be a temptation to dismiss them and deal only with immediate needs. In such circumstances, it is difficult to envisage how employee development can make a strategic contribution to effective organisational functioning.

Identifying Training Needs

Needs analysis is a central component of the training process as it ensures that training and development occurs only where there is a valid need for it. Many organisations invest considerable resources in training, but often fail to examine how effectively training can meet the business objectives. It can thus be viewed as a systematic process of determining and ordering training goals, measuring training needs and deciding on priorities for training action.

Needs manifest themselves in a number of ways. Although there is much focus on identifying the needs of individual employees, needs can occur at three levels (see table 9.3). All these groups influence each other – organisational needs highlight needs for particular groups and thus carry implications for individual needs.

Table 9.3 Level of training needs analysis

LEVEL	CONCERN
Organisational	What does the organisation need to achieve its goals? Does it have the capability? Are there any strategic long-term objectives to consider?
Job or Occupational	Special skills, knowledge or attitude training needs for particular jobs
Individual	Where individual skills fall short of those required

Source: Boydell (1983).

A review of the organisation is undertaken to systematically uncover and analyse its long-term training and development needs. Wexley and Latham (1991) suggest that the analysis of an organisation involves an examination of how it interfaces with the external environment. The environment in which an organisation operates can be a critical factor in determining whether training and development should be conducted, specifically:

- If the training and development function is to survive it must be supported financially by the organisation. The level of this support is determined by the overall profitability of the organisation.
- The environment in which an organisation operates can impact upon training and development needs. It can influence the way employees do their jobs, how decisions are made and the types of skills and levels of flexibility required.

Sparrow and Bognanno (1993) refer to the development of a competency profile for the organisation as a whole and suggest that there are four different categories of competency that an organisation needs to recognise.

1. Emerging competencies: those that will require greater emphasis as the organisation pursues its particular strategic path.
2. Maturing competencies: those that are becoming less relevant – perhaps due to technology or work restructuring;
3. Transitional competencies: those required of individuals during any change process such as a high tolerance of uncertainty or an ability to manage stress and conflict.
4. Core competencies: those that are central to an organisation's performance and so have persistent relevance.

By compiling a competency profile, the authors suggest that the organisation can attach a 'shelf life' to its existing range of skills, knowledge and abilities and can therefore estimate where training gaps exist.

A comprehensive job analysis provides information about the duties required of, and the responsibilities attached to, various jobs. Priority areas for individual training and development can then be identified to bridge the training gap. Performance standards in these areas may be specified in terms of criterion behaviour – what the employee is expected to be able to do at the end of the training. A range of data sources is available to an organisation that can be utilised to compile a training needs analysis. This range is presented in table 9.4.

Design and Implementation of Training Programme

Once a needs analysis has been completed the organisation can then set particular training objectives. Arising from the prioritising of training objectives, the organisation will then choose the categories of employees that require the particular training and then select the most appropriate training method. However, in many organisations the training method is chosen before the individual participants are identified and thus problems can arise when the particular methods chosen are inconsistent with the learning styles and preferences of the trainees.

The choice of training methods available to organisations is considerable. Organisations, when deciding on the most appropriate method to use, must take cognisance of the principles of learning discussed earlier, the needs of the employees to be trained and the

Table 9.4 Data sources for training needs identification

LEVEL	SOURCE	TRAINING NEED IMPLICATIONS
Organisational	Corporate objectives	emphasise direction training must take
	Manpower plans	current capability versus future needs
	Skills inventories	areas needing development
	Org. statistics (absenteeism, etc.)	identifies trends and problem areas
	System changes	new equipment/systems call for training
	Management requests	may apply in other areas too
	Exit interviews	may identify problems like poor supervision, etc.
Operational	Operational manpower plans	profiles future requirements, indications, etc.
	Job analysis/job description	indicates exact requirements of each job
	Task analysis	very detailed job analysis
	Person specifications	profiles skills/characteristics job holders need
	Training surveys	up to date information on needs
	Performing the job	shows trainer the needs of a new recruit
	Observe output	this may be delegated to line manager
	Review literature	journals, guidelines, approaches of other orgs.
	Ask questions	of the job holder, the supervisor, the manager
	Working groups	combine several viewpoints
	Analyse operating problems	differentiate environmental problems etc.
Individual Job	Appraisal, career development, etc.	identifies weaknesses and development needs
	Interview	self-analysis involves the worker, increasing motivation
	Questionnaire	gives employee time to consider his needs
	Individual job analysis	compared with job description
	Tests	of knowledge, skill, achievement
	Attitude surveys	determining morale and motivation
	Training progress charts	up to date records
	Assessment centres	intensive assessment
	Manager's recommendation	the manager can identify individual needs

Source: Garavan, Costine and Heraty (1995).

logistics of training that affect every organisation. Table 9.5 provides a comparison of some of the more commonly recognised training interventions and, while this table is not exhaustive, it seeks to highlight key characteristics of each approach that merit some consideration.

All training methods have their own particular strengths and can be modified to suit the organisation's requirements. The most important criteria in determining the choice of training method is the extent to which it meets the particular objectives that have been established. Once the training method and targeted trainees have been identified, the organisation can then conduct the actual training or learning event. On completion of this stage of the training process, the next phase involves evaluating the impact of the training itself.

Transfer of Learning

The term learning transfer refers to the extent to which skills and abilities acquired during a training session are applied to the actual work situation or to the learning of a new, but related, skill. Reid *et al.* (1992) distinguish between two types of positive learning transfer:

Table 9.5 Training and development methods

Method	Advantages	Disadvantages
On-the-Job Methods		
Sitting by Nellie; learn job from co-worker	Inexpensive; natural learning; high transfer of learning;	May pick up bad habits; often time-consuming; feedback may not be supportive/constructive
Coaching; supervisor guides and develops employee	Job relevant; facilitates succession planning and employee relations	Adversely affected by time constraints and work pressures; individual attention may be limited
Mentoring; manager guides, counsels and encourages development	Flexible; useful for socialisation, succession planning and management development	Contact may be infrequent; manager may not have the required mentoring skills or be committed to the process
Job rotation; range of placements within company	Relatively inexpensive; provides exposure to many situations; facilitates inter-departmental relations	May be unsettling; may lack direction; may be inconsistent; difficult to monitor
In-house courses	Can be tailored to meet specific organisational needs; range of techniques i.e cases, projects etc. can be based on real problems	High opportunity costs due to absence from work; participation may be quota based; can become an exercise in head count i.e quantity vs. quality of courses
Off-the-Job Methods		
External courses educational/skills-based	Exposure to broader range of knowledge and views; promotes networking; useful for specialised knowledge/skills acquisition	Learning transfer may be difficult; can be very expensive and time consuming; may raise employee expectations
Workshops, active discussion	Particularly suitable for managers; group-based approach facilitates problem solving; high learning transfer	Requires advance notification and preparation by participants; may be difficult to manage
Computer-based training	Individually focused; self-paced learning; performance is easily monitored; large numbers can be readily trained	Expensive to design; some employees may have a 'phobia' about computers; learning situation is contrived
Open/distant learning	Facilitates career development; useful for self-motivated employees; participants direct pace of learning	Very expensive; high drop-out rate; time consuming; can be difficult to balance work load and learning
External Placements	Provides useful external perceptions; builds external networks; facilitates attitudinal change	Learning transfer may be limited; can be very costly; may be perceived as a 'junket'; difficult to manage and control learning

Source: Adapted from Garavan *et al.* (1995) and Gunnigle and Flood (1990).

vertical and lateral. *Vertical transfer* occurs when one subject area acts as a basis for another i.e a foundation course in general business forms the basis upon which students or learners can progress to greater specialism or diversification, where students can apply the general principles learned at foundation level. In training terms this involves the acquisition of additional knowledge or skills that builds upon existing skills and abilities.

Lateral transfer occurs where the same type of stimulus requires the same response. In this respect, training simulates a particular type of task and allows the learner an opportunity to practice in a 'safe' environment. Reid *et al.* (1992) use the example of training simulations that are used to train aircraft pilots. Buckley and Caple (1990) indicate that positive transfer will have taken place if the trainee is able to apply on the job what has been learned in training with relative ease (lateral), or is able to learn a new task more quickly as a result of earlier training on another task (vertical).

In some circumstances negative transfer occurs and this may be as a result of past learning experiences that contradict present practice, or perhaps the learning experience creates inhibitions that impede the acquisition of new skills. An illustration of the former might be where an individual who learns to drive on one side of the road might find it difficult to drive on the opposite side while abroad – this is particularly so in cases where the driver is distracted or stressed. The particular choice of training method, style of trainer, or indeed the training situation might, individually or combined, serve to inhibit the learning process and this result in negative learning transfer.

As an addendum to the above, two further sets of factors may also play a part in determining the scope of learning transfer namely, organisational and social factors. Latham and Crandall (1991) identify pay and promotion policies as key organisational variables that influence the level of training transfer because they affect training outcome expectations. Bandura (1986) suggests that trainees may believe that they are capable of performing a specific behaviour, but may choose not to do so because they believe it will have little or no effect on their status in the organisation. This highlights the necessity that employee development practices take cognisance of the key learning principles discussed earlier.

Two significant social variables that affect transfer are peer group influences and supervisory support. Garavan *et al.* (1995) indicate that peer interaction can provide support and reinforcement not only for the learning but also for the application of learning to the job. Failure to achieve this support can result in alienation during and after training. Supervisory support is a critical factor. Good supervisory support increases trainee outcome expectations that the learning skills will be valued by the organisation.

EVALUATION OF TRAINING

Evaluation of training and development activities ensures that control is maintained over the training process and allows for assessment of the outcomes, methods and overall impact of any training and development programme. Buckley and Caple (1992) describe evaluation as the process of attempting to assess the total value of training, that is, the cost benefit and general outcomes that benefit the organisation as well as the value of the improved performance of those who have undertaken training. Easterby-Smith (1986) outlines three general purposes of training evaluation:

- Summative – testing to determine whether training and development was effective and achieved its objectives.
- Formative – qualitative analysis of training as it is occurring to determine whether improvements or adjustments are required.

- Learning – assessing the extent to which the trainee can transfer the learning acquired back to his/her job performance.

The systems approach to training evaluation as proposed by, among others Hamblin (1974) and Kirkpatrick (1959) delineates the contributions that training makes at different levels within the organisation and requires that data be quantifiable and based on pre-determined objectives. Such models propose a hierarchy of evaluation where each level requires a different evaluation strategy and is seen as a measure of the progressive transfer and application of training content. This hierarchical approach to training evaluation is presented in table 9.6.

Table 9.6 Levels of training evaluation

Level	Description	Methods	Assessment
1. Reaction	Seeks opinions of trainees	Questionnaires at end of training	Easy to collect; subjective; does not evaluate learning or learning transfer
2. Learning	Seeks knowledge, principles and facts learned by trainees before training	Tests, exams, projects, after training is completed	Evaluates level of learning; does not measure impact of learning on job performance
3. Behaviour	Seeks to determine positive changes in behaviour	Observation, measurement before start; after return to job	Objective assessment of impact of training on job performance; can be difficult to assess in some jobs
4. Results	Seeks to determine contribution to organisational objectives	General indicators (profits, turnover etc.) Specific indicators (absenteeism, accidents)	Evaluates return on investment of training expenditure; difficult to quantify

Evaluation constitutes the final stage in the learning, training and development process and, while difficult to measure, provides information that is critical to effective organisational functioning. Lack of training evaluation can result in inappropriate training that is wasteful of both financial and human resources. The difficulty for most organisations lies in identifying a set of measurable criteria that can facilitate the effective evaluation of employee development interventions. In particular, many of the perceived key benefits of employee development such as improved morale, increased job satisfaction, improved employee relations are, by their very nature, difficult to demonstrate in quantitative terms, and thus many organisations limit their activities to a level one (reaction) evaluation.

Learning, training and development is not solely limited to the provision of a number of formal training interventions. As the term itself implies, it is an on-going process and learning can be viewed as an inherent process that spans the individual's employment with the organisation. For this reason, many organisations are developing a range of continuous development initiatives and putting in place a number of planned structures that facilitate an individual's lifelong learning experience. A number of these initiatives are now discussed.

MANAGEMENT DEVELOPMENT

Managerial competence has been advanced as one of the keys to unlocking the potential of other core factors of production (Drejer 2001; Docherty and Nyhan 1997; Burack *et al.* 1997; Capelli and Crocker-Hefer 1996; Hall and Foulkes 1991; Prahalad and Hamel 1990; Storey 1989) where the ability of managers is, to a great extent, what influences the return an organisation gets from its investment in human and material capital. Management development is now viewed as an 'enabler', which leverages organisational flexibility and efficiencies (O'Connell and Lyons 1995; Lippitt 1981) and builds competence among those responsible for formulating and implementing strategies and policies designed to effectively manage the firm's resources (Hales 1986; Hambrick 1987; Lees 1992; Baird *et al.* 1994; Black and Boal 1994; Cannon 1995; Sveiby 1997). However, as Kamoche (2000, 748) notes, while there seems to be some evidence that management training and development can positively impact on organisational performance, the 'difficulty of establishing such a linkage has led some to accept the value of management training and development as an act of faith'.

Definitions of management development abound, but the main difficulty with defining the concept lies in the debate on what exactly constitutes management and managerial work. Seminal work by both Stewart (1976, 1991) and Mintzberg (1973) reveal managerial work to be fragmented and disparate, which is conducted within complex social networks and with short time horizons.

There are various views on the rational for management development itself. Some theorists view management development as a means of engendering organisational change; as a tool in facilitating quality and excellence; or as a means of establishing core company values and strong corporate culture. As Cannon (1999) puts it:

> Management competence is without doubt a key factor in developing strategies to further an organisations mission, in achieving an organisation's objectives and in improving performance, whether this means competitiveness in global markets or delivering a better public service. Developing that competence among managers whose daily routines are frequently fragmented and reactive has become a quest of Herculean proportions for companies and business schools alike in the increasingly unpredictable and often precarious environment of the modern organisation.

Similarly, Thompson *et al.* (2001, 1) note that:

> Without adequate development of the management cadre, it has been accepted by policy makers, companies, and perhaps most important of all, managers themselves, that a modern industrial economy cannot maintain its competitiveness, that organisations cannot be sufficiently flexible to respond to the rapidly changing circumstances of the late twentieth and early twenty-first centuries, and that managers cannot adjust to career patterns considerably removed from the expectations of their predecessors.

In defining management development Mumford (1986) describes it as an attempt to improve managerial effectiveness through a planned and deliberate learning process, while Molander (1986) views it as 'a conscious and systematic process to control the development of managerial resources in the organisation for the achievement of goals and strategies'. Armstrong (1992) adopts a broader perspective in suggesting that management development incorporates any attempt to develop the effectiveness of the management pool and to equip managers to deal with change and future jobs requirements.

Table 9.7 The many agendas of management development

Type	Characteristic	Assumptions	Questions and problems
Functional-performance: 'a garage'	Knowledge, skills or attitudes to improve performance, bring about change, and increase national stock of managers	• Training needs can be objectively identified and matched against training	• Overlooks other factors influencing the impact of MD on performance
Political-reinforcement: 'a cascade'	MD acts as extension of company's political order	• Top team's perception of how organisational performance is to be improved is correct	• MD dogmas are frequently dependent on one or two key figures; what happens when they go?
	Programmes (e.g. culture change) propagate skills and attitudes believed by top team to be necessary to turn company around	• 'Recipe for success' can be translated into an MD programme and cascaded down the company	• Approach leaves little opportunity to be questioned, and career costs of doing so may be high; such a climate defies genuine commitment
Compensation: 'a reward'	MD activities are offered as compensation for deprivations of employment: e.g. • as welfare substitute • as alternative focus to alienating work-place • to promote self-development	• Such activities encourage employees to acquire a habit of learning	• This approach deflects attention from causes of alienation, offering a palliative instead • It is deceptive – and morally dubious – to 'use' education in this manner
Psychic defence: 'a displacement'	MD provides a safe situation in which to discharge anxieties by giving access to or participation in more strategic matters	• Managers need a social system for defending their psyche against persecutory anxiety arising from their competitive career drives • Apparently fair appraisal systems, target-setting and ordered management succession help reduce fear of disorder and chaos if latent competition were to leak out	• Would greater self-development and self-determination in the work-place necessarily lead to unbridled and selfish anarchy? • Only a few MD activities would typically provide an opportunity for such displacement

Source: Mabey and Salaman (1995, 147–8).

Storey (1995) differentiates between two divergent models of management development. The first model views management development as a highly structured, top down event with a strong emphasis on structured training programmes, which all managers must progress through in order to rise up the ranks. The opposite approach, according to Storey, is far more decentralised and places the emphasis on self-development where the individual manager devises his/her own development plans and, in effect, owns the process. Within these two models, a variety of management development approaches may be adopted, ranging from educational programmes (MBA route is most common in Ireland), through mentoring, coaching, action learning and natural learning.

Gunnigle and Flood (1990) suggest that management development activities are based on the premise that an organisation can develop and improve its managerial talent over time and thus a strong linkage with a performance appraisal system is essential to identify current levels of performance and assess performance over time. Garavan *et al.* (1995) propose that the development of essential managerial qualities involves three main areas of training.

1. The acquisition of knowledge, which includes professional, technical, organisational and business environment information that is required for all managerial tasks.
2. The acquisition of skills in areas such as problem-solving, communication, motivation and negotiation that are necessary for effective managerial functioning.
3. The development of aptitudes and attitudes, such as judgement, creativity, flexibility, initiative, self-reliance and respect for ethical standards that are required for high performance.

Mabey and Salaman (1995) outline a number of different organisational 'agendas' for investing in management development. These are presented in table 9.7.

CAREER DEVELOPMENT
While both organisations and individuals are paying increasing attention to the planning and management of careers, the concept of career is becoming much more difficult to define. Accelerated economic change, organisational delayering and an increase in the use of outsourcing have combined to challenged the traditional perceptions of not only a job for life, but also of the existence of established, easily identifiable career paths and development initiatives. The concept of career is essentially perceptually based and there is no complete agreement about what it is. Greenhaus and Callanan (1994) describe the career as the pattern of work-related experiences that span the course of a person's life. From an employee's perspective this will encapsulate the sequence of jobs that individuals pursue throughout their working life. In organisational terms career development is a systematic process in which the organisation attempts to assist employees in the analysis of their abilities and interests and to guide their placement, progression and development while with the organisation (Gunnigle and Flood 1990).

The process of career development requires an understanding of both the stages of career development and the various careers that individual employees might pursue. Driver (1982) differentiates between four different types of career:

1. Steady state – a career choice represents a lifetime commitment to a particular occupation.
2. Linear – the employee moves 'up the ladder' in one particular occupation.
3. Spiral – the employee remains in a particular occupation for a lengthy period of time (7–10 years) and then chooses another occupation, which builds on acquired skills and abilities.
4. Transitory – the employee's choice of career changes frequently with each move signifying a change in direction.

Career development can further be understood in terms of an individual's life-cycle: as an individual progresses through the various stages in his/her life, different needs, concerns and aspirations take priority. Table 9.8 summarises the relationship between an individual's life stages and career cycle.

Table 9.8 Life and career stages

Stage	Characteristics
1. Childhood	Focus on ego-identification; development of concept of self; search for values and roles; formulation of interests and capabilities
2. Early adulthood (growth/ exploration)	Self-identification through role and occupational analysis; closer identification of needs, identification interests and capabilities; potential conflict between need to establish identity vs feeling of losing autonomy
3. Adulthood (establishment)	Focus on establishing self in work and life situations; clear career pattern; search for stability and personal security
4. Late adulthood (maintenance)	Emphasis on acceptance and consolidation of position; possible review and modification of life/work role; concern with providing for and guiding new generation
5. Maturity/Decline	Conclusion of career role; acceptance of life/career pattern; preparation for post-work challenges

Source: Gunnigle and Flood (1990).

Nicholson and West (1988) propose a transition cycle model of job change in organisations, and identify a set of strategies that organisations might adopt to facilitate the smooth transition from one job to another. They can include both the transition from education to work, and relocation within the organisation including transfers, promotions, and moves to group-based work design.

Figure 9.3 The transition cycle

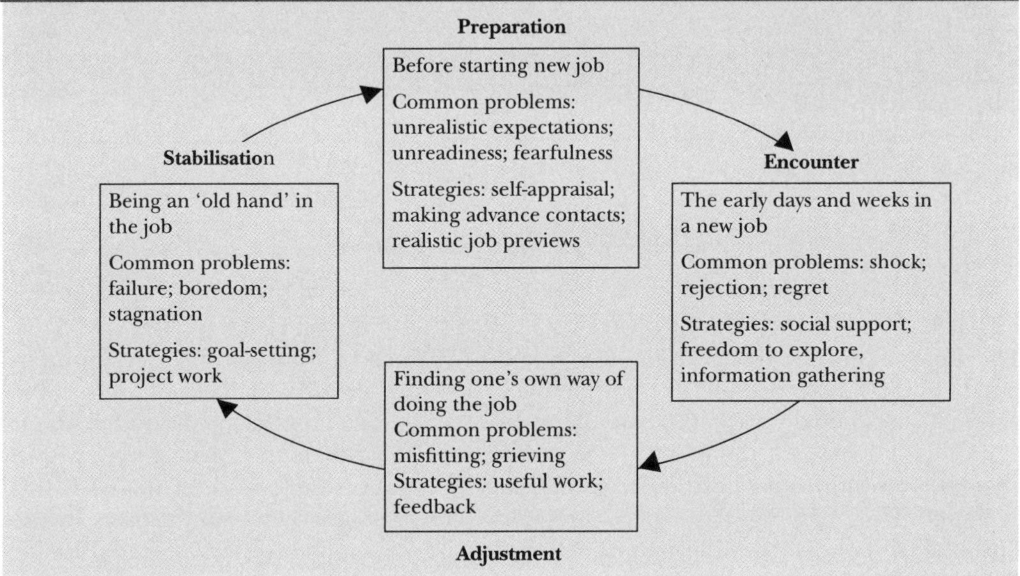

Source: Arnold, Robertson and Cooper (1995).

One major problem experienced by many organisations is the mismatch of employee expectations about the job and career prospects and the reality of the situation. This, in part, may explain the 'induction crisis' experienced by many organisations, when several new employees leave the organisation within the first six weeks of starting employment. Organisations can reduce this crisis by developing a 'realistic job preview', which attempts to describe the job and the company as seen by those who work there. In this way potential job applicants can self-match their skills, abilities and aspirations against the realistic job description provided.

Socialisation of employees in new work roles is critical and can be facilitated further through the establishment of informal support networks. Once employees become comfortable with their role and develop an understanding of the work environment, the organisation needs to concern itself with providing challenging work and feedback on performance. The danger exists that employees can become dissatisfied with the work or developmental opportunities available – for this reason career management is a central concern at every stage of the employment relationship.

Nicholson and Arnold (1989) identify four common shortcomings of organisational career development systems:

- Restricted: while some restrictions are inevitable, organisations can often create unnecessary ones such as non-promotional transfers between functions;
- Political: where career opportunities can be blocked by managers who perhaps seek to advance their own interests at the expense of individual employees;
- Mechanistic: where career moves are controlled by rules and procedures that do not allow for exceptions and fail to take account of changing circumstances;
- Neglected: where possible career paths are simply not identified and no one can see the way forward.

Mayo (1991) and Iles and Mabey (1993) variously defined career development or career management intervention as any effort by organisations to assist individuals in managing their careers. Several such interventions have been identified over the years, with the more salient of these outlined in table 9.9.

The establishment of formal career management techniques is a useful managerial tool that can be used to build an effective internal labour market. Similarly it is of benefit to employees where the system used takes cognisance of individual career aspirations and creation of a range of opportunities that facilitates and encourages continuous development.

LEARNING, TRAINING AND DEVELOPMENT PRACTICES IN IRELAND

The final section of this chapter examines the nature of training and development practices in Ireland. Chapter eight demonstrated how institutional actors such as the national educational system, professional associations, government interventions in labour market skill formation (i.e role of FÁS) and trade unions shape the environment within which organisations do business and ultimately impact on the nature of their LT & D activities. The challenge facing Irish organisations, as with their counterparts in the European Union, is the mobilisation of human resources as a necessary prerequisite for the tight, efficient and productive operation of business strategies. The question is to what extent Irish organisations are actively meeting this challenge? Here, recent evidence from a CIPD (Ireland) sponsored survey on training and development in Ireland conducted by

Table 9.9 Career development techniques

Technique	Description
Succession Planning	The organisation identifies or 'earmarks' employees who are deemed suitable for key positions in the future and provides the necessary experiences, training and so forth to enable such employees to take up these positions.
Career Counselling	The organisation appoints an external counsellor (in some cases an internal manager may adopt the role) to assist individual employees to clarify their ideas about self and work. Psychometric tests are often used to identify career opportunities for individual employees.
Skills Inventories	The organisation develops detailed records on the skills, experiences, qualifications and expertise accumulated by each employee, coupled with information on individuals' career preferences and objectives.
Mentoring Programmes	The organisation develops systems whereby an older, more experienced worker acts as a role-model for a younger employee and supports, guides and counsels this employee through his/her time with the organisation.
Educational Opportunities	The organisations overtly promotes continuous development and provides information and financial support on both internal and external courses/training/conferences.

Heraty and Garavan (2001) is instructive. For the purposes of this chapter, five key pieces of evidence are drawn from that survey: the forces that trigger training among Irish organisations, the level of expenditure on training and development activity, the volume of training activity undertaken, the methods utilised to identify training needs and the evaluation strategies employed.

Respondents identified a wide range of factors that they perceived to be influencing the training and development in their organisation. Three factors in particular were considered to be significant triggers: the requirement to ensure the effective utilisation of human resources, the use of training and development to facilitate the implementation of new technology and organisational change. Other organisational-level triggers reported, included the development of an appropriate organisational culture, the implementation of multi-skilling strategies, and the maintenance of quality standards. It emerges that training and development investment may also be used to achieve a number of human resource type objectives, including the retention of employees, the attraction of high-quality candidates to the organisation, the management of employee career expectations and psychological contract.

In relation to the issue of expenditure on training and development, unlike some of their European counterparts, Irish companies are not required to invest a minimum proportion of annual turnover on updating the skills and knowledge of their employees, nor are they obliged to declare the amount they spend annually on the training and development function (Heraty and Morley 1994).

Fox (1987) argues that problems continuously arise in drawing up statistics on training and development as organisations have differing perceptions of what constitutes training, and since many companies tend to rely on informal training strategies and mechanisms,

Table 9.10 Factors influencing or driving the provision of training and development in organisations

Factor	Mean	Std. Dev.	N.
To ensure the effective utilisation of human resources	4.02	1.07	207
Facilitation of the implementation of new technology	3.96	0.94	213
Facilitation of the implementation of organisational change	3.88	0.86	208
Meet employee career expectations and demands for learning	3.71	0.92	210
Foster the development of an appropriate organisational culture	3.70	0.97	206
Meet statutory requirements such as health and safety	3.70	1.05	212
A strategy to foster employee commitment to business objectives	3.65	0.89	205
Create a work environment that encourages individuals to learn	3.67	0.93	206
Enhance establishment ability to attract good candidates	3.64	1.07	204
Enhance the retention of employees	3.51	1.11	213
Facilitate the implementation of multi-skilling strategies	3.45	1.07	203
Secure or retain international quality standards	3.23	1.36	208
Facilitate product innovation and development	3.16	1.29	201
Improve the market share of the business	3.13	1.30	198
Manage the employee psychological contract	2.96	1.08	198

Source: Heraty and Garavan (2001).

the problem of quantifying training expenditure are further compounded. Here 78 per cent or 174 organisations provided details of their expenditure on training as a percentage of their total payroll for 2000 (see table 9.11).

Table 9.11 Training and development expenditure as a percentage of payroll

Training Expenditure	%	No.
No details provided	21	47
< 0.5%	8	17
0.5 – 1%	9	19
> 1% – < 2%	26	57
> 2% – < 4%	26	57
> 5%	10	24
Total	100	221
Average	3.85	
Median	2.8	

Source: Heraty and Garavan (2001).

The data here reveal that the spending average on training amounts to 3.85 per cent of payroll with the median expenditure standing at 2.8 per cent. A ballpark percentage figure of training expenditure is useful to the extent that it allows for comparison and illustrates trends in expenditure over time.

The survey asked respondents to estimate the number of days training per employee per annum (for 2000) that they provided. Their responses are presented in table 9.12 by occupational category.

Table 9.12 Number of days formal training provided per employee

Occupational Category	None	AVERAGE NUMBER OF DAYS TRAINING					
		< 1 day	1–3 days	4–7 days	8–12 days	12+ days	Total
Semi-skilled/Unskilled	4.05	5.78	36.99	40.46	10.40	2.31	173
Supervisors	3.80	12.50	38.04	36.96	6.52	2.17	184
Craft/Technician	6.08	6.08	42.57	36.49	6.76	2.03	148
Clerical/Admin.	3.09	4.64	40.72	39.69	9.79	2.06	194
Senior Management	4.37	12.62	35.92	35.44	7.28	4.37	206

Source: Heraty and Garavan (2001).

The data is interesting in a number of respects. Very few organisations indicate that they provide no training at all to employees. They are more likely to provide training for senior management personnel than for any other employee category. The mean number of days training for manager grades is 5.25. Establishments are less likely to provide training and development for professional and technical job categories. Only a small percentage of establishments provide more than eight days of formal training per employee in any one year. Almost 4.5 per cent of establishments indicated that they provide twelve days or more training. The mean number of days training for all job categories is 5.61 days.

Needs analysis is considered a central component of the training and development process, primarily because it helps ensure that an appropriate training and development solution is selected to match the identified needs. There is evidence that many organisations invest considerable resources in training and development activities, but they often do not consider whether such an intervention represents an appropriate response to the performance problem identified. The data reveals a high level of awareness of the necessity to systematically identify training and development needs before investing in training and development. Eighty-one per cent of establishments indicated that they conduct a systematic training needs analysis. This figure suggests that training and development needs identification is a relatively common practice in establishments in Ireland.

A broad range of methods are used to identify training and development needs (see table 9.13).

Table 9.13 Methods used by Irish establishments to identify training and development needs

Method Used	Weighted Score
Line manager requests	913
Data from performance management appraisal systems	840
Employee requests for training	662
Training and development audits	625
Performance training	249
Competency profiling	206
360° feedback processes	143
Psychological testing	57
Work study processes	54
Work sample tests	44

Source: Heraty and Garavan (2001).

The data reveal that respondents tend to rely on what may be described as the more traditional methods to identify training and development needs. In order of usage these are line manager requests, data from performance management appraisal systems, employee requests for training and the use of training and development audits. There is some evidence to indicate an increased usage of more progressive and innovative identification methods of training needs, however the data suggest that these are more commonly utilised by larger organisations.

The evaluation of training and development is considered a critical component of the training cycle since it provides an indication of the extent to which learning occurred. Two questions were included in the survey to derive a snapshot of current training and development evaluation practices in Irish establishments. Table 9.14 presents the data.

A total of 78 per cent of respondents indicated that they evaluated training and development activities while 22 per cent suggested that they do not have any evaluation systems in place. Organisations utilise a broad range of quantitative and qualitative criteria to evaluate the effectiveness of training and development. Some of the more quantitative criteria used include the total number of days training undertaken per period, the level of exam pass rates for certified programmes and measured job performance both immediately and some months after training. Seventy-seven percent of establishments indicated that they utilise the informal feedback of line managers as a source of feedback. This is ranked the second most important criterion used by establishments. The highest ranked criterion, that of meeting the objectives set out in the training and development plan, is a rather narrow one and is more akin to training validation rather than training evaluation *per se*.

Table 9.14 Ranked criteria used by Irish establishments to evaluate training and development

Criterion	% used	No.	Priority Weighting	Rank
Informal feedback from line managers	77	127	162	2
Meeting the objectives set out in the training and development plan	75	124	183	1
Informal feedback from employees	64	104	102	4
Measured job performance some months after training	50	83	108	3
Total number of days training per period	39	65	72	5
Exam pass rates for certified programmes	39	64	36	7
Measured job performance immediately after training	36	59	56	6
Enhanced promotability of employees	26	43	35	8

Source: Heraty and Garavan (2001).

Seventy-five percent of establishments reported that they evaluate training on whether it meets the objectives set out in the training and development plan. The majority of the criteria utilised by establishments operate at the level of the job itself and dimensions of the training programme. However, 26 per cent of establishments indicated that they consider the enhanced promotability of employees to be an important criterion, but it is accorded the lowest priority of all the evaluation criteria reported by establishments.

This chapter has focused on learning, training and development within organisations. It has been highlighted that recent social, organisational and technological developments have combined to heighten the overall significant of LT & D in organisational life. Building and continuously developing the knowledge base of the enterprise has gained a strong currency in the armoury of competitiveness, globally and locally (Tregaskis, Heraty and Morley 2001).

This chapter has sought to unpack some of the arguments being advanced for according a 'new status' to LT & D and set down the typical systems being established by organisations in the training domain. We have reviewed some of the core reasons for the increased attention being paid to LT & D systems, examined learning processes and outlined some of the conditions necessary for effective learning to take place. We have also presented the core aspects of the cycle of training and reviewed particularly important initiatives beyond that cycle, namely, management development and career development. Finally, drawing upon recent survey evidence, we have provided a contemporary portrait of organisational-level training and development in Ireland.

10

Employee Relations: Institutions and Actors

Employee relations is one of the most significant aspects of the HR role in organisations. Indeed, in the past the traditional role of the average personnel or HR manager in Ireland could perhaps more appropriately be described as industrial or employee relations manager, given their primary concern with collective bargaining and trade union interactions. While the last decade has undoubtedly witnessed some diminution of this *industrial* relations emphasis and a concomitant broadening of the HR role, *employee* relations remains a most critical area of HR activity.

This chapter sketches the nature of employee relations, describes the Irish context, and considers the parties involved in employee relations interactions. Particular focus is placed on the role of trade unions and state institutions in employee relations. The role of employers and employer organisations in employee relations is discussed in chapter eleven.

THE NATURE OF EMPLOYEE RELATIONS

As has often been noted, the very nature of employee relations is a source of some confusion (Tiernan *et al.* 1996). Traditional definitions have focused on the concept of *industrial* rather than *employee* relations. Such an approach reflected an emphasis on the formal regulation of the employment relationship through collective bargaining between organised *employees* and employers. This perspective remains significant as employers, trade unions and Government seek to develop rules and norms to govern *employment relations* at organisational, industrial, national and supranational levels. However, as the nature of employment has changed, the term employee relations has achieved increased prominence. The concept of employee relations is seen as embracing a broader scope than *industrial relations*. In this text the term *employee relations* is adopted as a generic concept, which embraces all employer, employee and state interactions on employment matters. It focuses on the nature of the relationship between the parties to the labour process, embraces both collectivist and individualist approaches and encapsulates both state and organisational level arrangements. It primarily involves the following issues: (i) collective bargaining, (ii) communications policy and practice, (iii) grievance handling, (iv) discipline administration, (iv) joint decision-making and problem-solving, (iv) the management of change and (v) aspects of social responsibility. In most of these issues trade unions can play an important role. However, they are not a prerequisite and employee relations is a critical HRM concern in non-union as well as in unionised organisations.

EMPLOYEE RELATIONS IN IRELAND

Employee relations practice in the great majority of medium and large organisations in the Republic of Ireland has traditionally been associated with a strong collectivist emphasis. In this model, employee relations considerations rarely concern strategic decision-makers; relations between management and employees are grounded in the pluralist tradition with a primary reliance on adversarial collective bargaining:

> Over a wide range of industries and services, employers and unions have conducted their relations on the basis of the premise that their interests were in significant respects different and in opposition ... These differences of interest were reconciled on an ongoing basis through what is sometimes known in the academic literature as 'collective bargaining pure and simple'.
>
> Roche (1990, 22)

This so called pluralist tradition is manifested in relatively high levels of union density, a heavy reliance on collective bargaining in handling employee relations issues, and employee relations as the key role of the specialist HR function (Gunnigle and Morley 1993).

As has been the case in many developed countries, the 1980s witnessed considerable change in the environment and practice of employee relations. From an employer's perspective, economic recession lessened the emphasis on hitherto core workforce management activities, such as recruitment and, particularly, employee relations. Trade union membership fell significantly in the period for much of the decade, and industrial unrest also declined significantly (Roche and Larragy 1989; Roche 1997a and b; Brannick *et al.* 1997). At the same time, many companies sought to establish competitive advantage through improvements in quality, service and performance. Consequently, it is argued that we began to witness significant change and innovation in employee relations practice, particularly in areas such as work systems, rewards, management-employee communications and employee development (Murray 1984; Flood 1989; Garavan 1991).

In terms of Government approaches to employee relations, a number of significant issues emerge. At a general level, Irish Governments have adopted an essentially benign approach to trade unions and organised labour. Traditionally, the approach of successive Governments to employee relations in the Republic of Ireland has been grounded in the 'voluntarist' tradition. This meant that employers and employees (or their representative bodies) were largely free to regulate the substantive and procedural terms of their relationship with a minimum of intervention from Government or its agencies (Hillery 1994; Breen *et al.* 1990; Roche 1997b).

An important aspect of public policy in employee relations is the constitutional support for the concept of freedom of association. Article 40.6.1. of the Irish Constitution supports the right of individuals to form or join associations or unions. However, there is no statutory provision for trade union recognition in Ireland. This means that although workers have constitutional support to join trade unions, there is no legal obligation for employers to recognise or bargain with trade unions. The issue of trade union membership and recognition is addressed later in this chapter.

Another important aspect of public policy relates to approaches to industrial development. Since the 1960s, Irish Government policy has actively encouraged direct foreign investment in Ireland. There are now over 1,200 overseas companies operating in Ireland which employ approximately 120,000 people with a particular focus on electronics, pharmaceuticals, software and 'teleservices' (Hannigan 2000). Employment in multinational companies (MNCs) accounts for roughly one third of the industrial workforce. These foreign-owned companies account for 55 per cent of manufactured output and some 70 per cent of industrial exports (Tansey 1998). The main sources of direct foreign investment (DFI) in Ireland are the US, the UK and Germany. Firms owned by US companies have a particularly strong presence in Ireland: over 400 such firms employ around 50,000 people. Recent years have also witnessed significant growth in the scale of direct FDI in Ireland. The decade 1987–97 saw a 50 per cent increase in the number of foreign multinationals investing in the Irish economy (OECD 1999). In terms of investment, OECD data reveals that there has been a threefold increase in FDI inflows to Ireland since 1990, with the US now accounting for almost 85 per cent of all such inflows (OECD 1997, 1999).

In regard to employee relations it certainly appears that MNCs have been a source of innovation in management practices, particularly in the application of new HR and employee relations approaches and in expanding the role of the specialist HR function (Gunnigle, McMahon and Fitzgerald 1999; Gunnigle and McGuire 2001). However, it would also seem that MNCs pose unique challenges in the sphere of employee relations. In particular, their ability to switch the locus of production and also to adopt employee relations styles that challenge the traditional pluralist model, most particularly in regard to union avoidance (Kelly and Brannick 1988b; McGovern 1988; Gunnigle 1995; Gunnigle, Morley and Turner 1997).

A critical initial step in grappling with the study of employee relations in Ireland is an appreciation of the range and nature of the actors and institutions involved in our employee relations system. The key parties or 'actors' involved in employee relations include individual workers, trade unions, worker representatives, employers, managers, Government and Government agencies. The interaction of these parties in employee relations will be heavily influenced by context so that economic conditions, historic and political factors and developments in technology will significantly influence employee relations activities. Table 10.1 outlines the main parties involved in employee relations. In employee relations terms the critical parties are employers and employees, both of whom may seek to form and use associations to represent their interests, namely, employers' association and trade unions. The state also plays a critical role in employee relations. The respective roles of trade unions and state are reviewed below while employers' approaches are considered in the next chapter. Before this, we briefly consider the main means through which employers and unions (and sometimes, Government) interact in employee relations, namely via collective bargaining.

Figure 10.1 Employee relations: the main parties

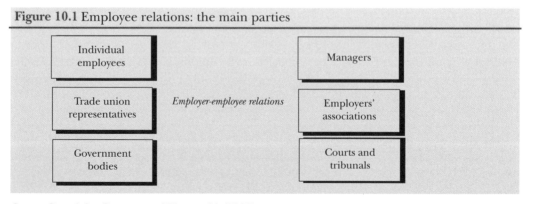

Source: Gunnigle, Garavan and Fitzgerald (1992).

COLLECTIVE BARGAINING

Collective bargaining has traditionally been seen as the primary means of regulating interactions between unions, employees and employers in Ireland (Turner 1988; also see chapter twelve). It refers to the process through which agreement on pay, working conditions, procedures and other negotiable issues are reached between organised employees and management representatives (Gunnigle and Flood 1990). Collective bargaining represents a mechanism through which divergent interests of employees and employers can be reconciled through an orderly process involving negotiation and compromise. Its principal feature is that employees do not negotiate with their employers on their own behalf, but do so collectively through representatives, and that various aspects of a worker's contract of employment are determined not individually but collectively (Gunnigle, McMahon and Fitzgerald 1999).

For collective bargaining to operate effectively a number of conditions are necessary. Workers must have the freedom to join together in trade unions, which are not in any way under the control or influence of employers (i.e. freedom of association), while employers must be prepared to recognise and deal with trade unions for collective bargaining purposes (also see more detailed discussion of employee relations practice in chapter twelve). Additionally, we have also noted that the Irish 'system' of collective bargaining is essentially voluntary. There is no legal obligation on trade unions and employers to engage in collective bargaining on pay or any other issue at any level. The system relies on the moral commitments of the participants, with collective agreements regarded as being 'binding in honour only'. The Report of the Commission of Inquiry on Industrial Relations (1981) noted that the Irish system reflects the view that collective bargaining, not the law, should be the primary source of regulation in the employment relationship based on the assumption by all parties that recourse to the law will be avoided.

While collective bargaining has been the primary means of managing employee relations in most industrialised nations, it is not the only method of dealing with issues such as pay and working conditions. Indeed, even where collective bargaining predominates, it generally operates concurrently with other mechanisms, including individual bargaining between employer and employee, regulation by the state, the unilateral imposition of terms of employment by employers or similarly – if much less likely – the imposition of unilateral terms by trade unions.

Individual bargaining refers to the situation whereby individual workers negotiate on a one-to-one basis with their employer to arrive at an 'individual contract' that sets outs the terms and conditions of each individual's employment.

Collective bargaining may take place at differing levels (see figure 10.1). The most obvious, of course, is bargaining between union and management representatives at the level of the individual workplace or establishment i.e. *establishment level bargaining*. However, we also know that many organisations have multiple establishments, such as banks, restaurant chains or manufacturing firms. Thus, collective bargaining may also take place between unions representing workers and a number of establishments and corporate level management, i.e. multi-establishment level bargaining. Both establishment level and multi-establishment level bargaining are focused on one employer. However, employers with common interests may also choose to form employers' associations. Often these common interests come from operating in the same industrial sector or geographical region and, consequently, such an employer grouping may seek to bargain with trade unions representing workers in the relevant industrial sector or region, i.e. multi-employer bargaining. In Ireland, for example, this has occurred in sectors such as the construction industry, where the Construction Industry Federation, representing employers and a grouping of trade unions representing workers in the construction sector, have regularly concluded collective agreements dealing with pay and working conditions. Over recent decades we have also seen that *national level bargaining* involving representatives of employers, Government and trade unions, has become the principal means of dealing with pay, in addition to numerous other aspects of economic and social affairs.

This tendency towards so called 'centralised bargaining' essentially refers to institutionalised negotiations between trade unions (via the Irish Congress of Trade Unions), employers' association (primarily the Irish Business and Employers Confederation and some other employers' association, see next chapter), Government and certain other societal groupings (e.g. farming organisations, and the community and voluntary sector) over wages and various other economic and social issues.

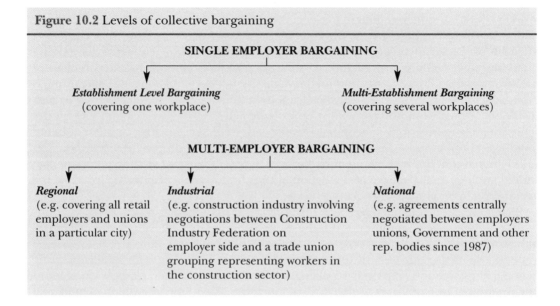

Figure 10.2 Levels of collective bargaining

SINGLE EMPLOYER BARGAINING

Establishment Level Bargaining
(covering one workplace)

Multi-Establishment Bargaining
(covering several workplaces)

MULTI-EMPLOYER BARGAINING

Regional
(e.g. covering all retail employers and unions in a particular city)

Industrial
(e.g. construction industry involving negotiations between Construction Industry Federation on employer side and a trade union grouping representing workers in the construction sector)

National
(e.g. agreements centrally negotiated between employers unions, Government and other rep. bodies since 1987)

After Ireland achieved independence in 1922, collective bargaining has oscillated between national and establishment level bargaining (including levels in between), with a general trend towards centralised (national) bargaining over recent decades. Indeed, we have previously noted that in latter years centralised bargaining has become the dominant bargaining form. Since 1970 pay determination has predominantly been decided through some form of centrally bargained agreement between employers' association and the trade union movement (except for the years 1982–6). Since 1987 we have had five major agreements involving unions, employers and Government, namely the *Programme for National Recovery* (PNR), the *Programme for Economic and Social Progress* (PESP), the *Programme for Competitiveness and Work* (PCW), *Partnership 2000*, and the most recent *Programme for Prosperity and Fairness* (PPF). A summary background on these agreements is provided later in this chapter and in chapter twelve (see also Gunnigle, McMahon 1999)[1].

Even in the presence of centralised bargaining however, collective bargaining may still take place at various other levels. This is particularly the case in regard to workplace bargaining. National agreements generally set out agreed, broad national level guidelines for wage increases and other related issues, while also allowing scope for supplementary bargaining between unions and employers in individual firms, such as on issues of productivity, organisational change and working time.

We now turn to the role of trade unions in employee relations.

TRADE UNIONS

As we have seen in chapter one, the historical development of HRM is inextricably linked to the growth of organised labour through the trade union movement. Modern trade unionism has its roots in the 'factory system' and the dramatic changes brought about by the industrial revolution, which began in Britain in the eighteenth century and later spread to Europe and North America. The growth of the factory system heralded a change from a largely peasant society based on agriculture and craft production to an industry-based society characterised by new social divisions, where people worked together in much larger numbers and relied on wages for their existence (Gunnigle, McMahon and Fitzgerald 1999). In the face of authoritarian management styles and poor working conditions, these new factory workers were poorly positioned. Lacking in economic or political power, it was not until the growth of organised labour, through the trade union movement, that employee concerns could command the attention and action of factory owners and management.

Despite Ireland's relatively recent history of industrialisation, trade unions were well established in many industries in Dublin, Belfast and Cork by the early 1900s (McNamara *et al.* 1988; Gunnigle, McMahon and Fitzgerald 1999). The development of trade unionism in Britain profoundly influenced events in Ireland. The passing of the Trade Disputes Act of 1906, often referred to as the 'Bill of Rights for Workers', provided legal immunity for unions involved in strike activity and authorised peaceful picketing. Increased conflict between employer and trade union interests characterised this period and eventually came to a head in the Dublin lockout of 1913. An important effect of this turbulent period was that it served to encourage the organisation of employees into trade unions and employers into employers' association. It also served to increase employer emphasis on employee relations as an increasingly significant management task. Over time, the fledgling union movement was reluctantly accepted and employers began to take initial steps to accommodate its role. This was often achieved through multi-employer bargaining via employers' association, and through the employment of labour relations officers to deal with HR and employee relations matters at organisation level.

Trade Union Objectives and Legal Status

Essentially unions are organisations who aim to unite workers with common interests, while seeking to define those interests, express them, safeguard and advance them through their interactions (particularly collective bargaining) with individual employers, employers' association, Government, Government agencies and other parties (Gunnigle, McMahon and Fitzgerald 1999). A trade union's basic strength rests with its ability to organise and unite workers. Through joining trade unions, it is argued that workers provide themselves with the collective means to redress the imbalance in bargaining power, which is otherwise perceived to exist between individual workers and their employer. While workers may join trade unions for numerous reasons, the most common reasons include a desire to influence pay claims, to have protection against management actions, and because of an ideological belief in the role that trade unions play in a democratic society (Tiernan *et al.* 1996). The Webbs, who wrote the first comprehensive history of trade unions and early collective bargaining, came up with what was long accepted as the most comprehensive definition of a trade union (Webb 1920, 1), 'A continuous association of wage earners with the objective of improving or maintaining conditions of employment'.

Although this definition accurately embraces the workplace role of trade unions, it does not capture their broader societal role in advancing worker interests in the political arena (Salamon 1998; Gunnigle, McMahon and Fitzgerald 1999). Thus, trade unions may be most appropriately viewed as permanent associations of organised employees whose primary objectives are to:

- Replace individual bargaining by collective bargaining thereby redressing the balance of bargaining power in favour of employees and reducing management prerogative in employment related matters.
- Facilitate the development of a political system where worker interests have a greater degree of influence on political decisions resulting in an economic and social framework which reflects the interests of wage earners.
- Achieve satisfactory levels of pay and conditions of employment and provide members with a range of services.

The main legislation dealing with the formation and operation of trade unions in Ireland are the Trade Union Acts of 1941 and 1971 and the Industrial Relations Act 1990. Trade unions are defined under the 1941 Trade Union Act as bodies carrying on negotiations for fixing wages or other conditions of employment. This legal definition of trade unions is very broad ranging and extends to employer organisations (Kerr 1997; Kerr and Whyte 1985). This legislation stipulates that, apart from certain 'exempted' bodies, only 'authorised' trade unions holding negotiating licenses are permitted to engage in collective bargaining on pay and working conditions. The legislation also specifies the conditions that a trade union must fulfil before it will be issued with such a licence. Trade unions may only be granted a negotiating licence when they register with the Registrar of Friendly Societies and meet specified criteria, particularly the following:

- *Notification:* Unions must notify the Minister for Enterprise and Employment and the Irish Congress of Trade Unions at least eighteen months before applying for a licence.
- *Membership:* A minimum of 1,000 members.
- *Financial deposit:* Ranging from IR£20,000 (€25,395) for up to 2,000 members to IR£60,000 (€76,184) for 35,000 or more members.

It should be noted that financial deposits are not required when a new trade union is formed as a result of the amalgamation of two or more unions. Furthermore, while trade unions with headquarters outside the Republic of Ireland are not required to adhere to these requirements, they must be legally recognised trade unions in their country of origin and meet some prescribed guidelines in relation to their controlling authority. Otherwise such unions must meet the notification, membership and deposit requirements set out above.

The legislation also provides for the operation of a number of 'excepted' bodies. These excepted bodies are not required to hold a negotiating licence to engage in collective bargaining and include work-place ('staff' or 'house') associations and unions, some civil service associations and teachers' associations (Kerr and Whyte 1985). Examples of excepted bodies include the Irish Hospital Consultants Association and the Irish Dental Association. A number of organisations which now hold a negotiation licence and operate as a trade union were originally 'excepted bodies', such as the Irish Nurses Organisation (Von Prondzynski and Richards 1994).

The major piece of legislation governing trade union operation is the Industrial Relations Act 1990. This Act deals with trade disputes, immunities, picketing, secret ballots, injunctions and trade union rationalisation. The 1990 Act provides for the protection of persons who organise or engage in trade disputes from civil liability. The Act further provides for the protection of trade union funds against actions for damages and for the legalisation of peaceful picketing in trade disputes. The Act requires trade unions to conduct secret ballots of all union members who could be reasonably expected to take part in the strike prior to engaging in industrial action. The 1990 Act only provides for secondary picketing (i.e. picketing an employer other than the primary employer involved in the dispute) where it is reasonable for workers to believe that the second employer was acting to frustrate the industrial action by directly assisting the primary employer.

Trade Union Types

Irish trade unions are normally organised on an occupational basis. This means that workers tend to join a particular union because of the particular job or trade in which they are employed. Trade unions in Ireland have traditionally being grouped into three broad categories: craft unions, general unions and white-collar unions. It should be noted that it is extremely difficult to categorise unions as 'pure' craft, general or white-collar since many unions deviate from a tight definition of their union category on some dimension. For example, general unions may have white-collar and craft workers in membership; not all 'craft' unions operate an 'exclusive' membership system based on the completion of a recognised apprenticeship programme. Thus, the categorisation of trade unions as craft, general or white-collar should be interpreted as broadly indicative of unions types in Ireland. Other countries may be characterised by different union classifications. In Japan, for example, one finds a proliferation of so called 'enterprise unions'. These are company-based unions comprised of different employee categories (manual, administrative, etc.) whose sole membership comes from the enterprise in which it operates. Even in the UK, which has a similar union classification to Ireland, Turner (1962) suggests that a more appropriate categorisation of union types is one based on whether union membership is 'open' to employees regardless of occupation or 'closed' to all employees except those working in a defined trade requiring a prescribed apprenticeship or training period. However, the craft, general, white-collar categorisation provides a convenient benchmark upon which to analyse Irish trade unions as discussed below.

CRAFT UNIONS

Craft unions cater for workers who possess a particular skill in a trade where entry is restricted to workers who have completed a prescribed apprenticeship programme or equivalent. Prominent examples of occupational categories which are organised in craft unions are electricians and fitters. Craft unions probably represent the earliest form of union organisation and have their origins in the early unions, which emerged in Britain at the start of the nineteenth century. These 'model' unions, as they became known, confined their membership to skilled categories such as printers and carpenters who had served a recognised apprenticeship in their particular trade. The first British craft union to organise in Ireland was the Amalgamated Society of Engineers, which established branches in the early 1850s (Boyd 1972). While the early craft unions only represented a small proportion of the labour force, the organisation of workers into craft unions was critical in establishing trade unions as legitimate institutions representing worker interests to employers and Government.

Craft unions have traditionally sought to protect their trades by ensuring that full members of the relevant craft union are allowed to carry out particular types of skilled work. This is the basis of the concept of 'demarcation', which relates to the delineation of skilled work among different craft categories. It is suggested that craft unions, by controlling entry to the craft, have traditionally held considerable negotiating power. This strategy is often criticised as being a source of restrictive work practices and demarcation disputes. Increased mechanisation and consequent de-skilling has had a detrimental impact on the membership and power of craft unions as reflected in the reduction of their share of union members from a high of 17 per cent in 1940 to approximately 10 per cent by the mid-1990s (Roche and Ashmore 2000). Indeed some older craft unions have ceased to exist, as their traditional craft was rendered obsolete by developments in technology and work practices.

However, craft unions remain an important part of Ireland's employee relations landscape. In recent years this was made apparent by the number of disputes by craft workers in the construction industry. Figures from the Irish Congress of Trade Unions suggest that the three main engineering craft unions, Amalgamated Engineering and Electrical Union (AEEU), the Technical, Electrical and Engineering Union (TEEU) and the National Union of Sheet Metal Workers of Ireland (NUSMWI) have 6 per cent of ICTU members, while the major building unions, the Union of Construction and Allied Trades and Technicians (UCATT), the Building and Allied Trades Unions (BATU) and the Operative Plasterers and Allied Trades Society of Ireland (OPATSI) account for just under 4 per cent of total ICTU membership (Gunnigle, McMahon and Fitzgerald 1999).

GENERAL UNIONS

Unlike the restrictive recruitment strategies of craft unions, general trade unions adopt a more open approach taking into membership all categories of worker, broadly regardless of skill or industry. Despite this open recruitment approach, however, general unions have traditionally catered for semi-skilled and unskilled workers. In more recent years, some general unions have attracted white-collar and some craft categories into membership.

The origins of general trade unions are rooted in the increased number of unskilled or general workers employed in the large factories and other major organisations that characterised late nineteenth- and early twentieth-century Britain. These new unions tended to be more militant than the more traditional craft unions of the period. They initially organised categories such as general labourers and dock workers and were noted for both their aggressive bargaining style in attempting to improve pay and working conditions of their members, as well as for their greater political consciousness in attempting to advance working class interests.

Whereas general unions catering for unskilled workers such as labourers and dockers existed in Ireland from the 1860s, they came to play a more active role in Irish industrial and political life in the early 1900s (Gunnigle, McMahon and Fitzgerald 1999). A major development was the establishment of the Irish Transport and General Workers Union (ITGWU) in 1909 led by Jim Larkin. The ITGWU and some other general unions organised categories such as dockers, carters and railway workers and became engaged in series of disputes culminating in the Dublin lockout of 1913. While this dispute initially dealt a severe blow to the general unions they slowly recovered and reorganised and by the early 1920s membership had recovered dramatically (Boyd 1972; McNamara *et al.* 1988).

In 2001, general unions were typically the largest union types and were commonly found in all types of organisations and industrial sectors. General unions account for approximately 46 per cent of all trade union members in the country (Roche and Ashmore 2000). The best known general union in Ireland is the Services, Industrial, Professional and Technical Union (SIPTU) with a membership of 230,000 (Department of Enterprise and Employment 1998). SIPTU is by some way the country's largest union itself accounting for approximately 40 per cent of total trade union members. It was created in 1990 as a result of the merger of the, then, two largest trade unions in the country, the Irish Transport and General Workers Union (ITGWU) and the Federated Workers Union of Ireland (FWUI). Other prominent examples of general unions in Ireland include the Amalgamated Transport and General Workers Unions (ATGWU) and the Marine Port and General Workers Union (MPGWU).

WHITE-COLLAR UNIONS

White-collar unions primarily cater for professional, supervisory, technical, clerical and managerial categories. These unions have experienced significant growth in membership since the late 1960s. The share of workers in white-collar unions increased from 24 per cent in 1940 to 42 per cent in the mid-1990s (Roche and Ashmore 2000). In the period 1966–76 white-collar unions increased their membership by 71 per cent as compared to an overall growth in union membership of 30 per cent over that period (Roche and Larragy 1989). The dramatic growth in employment in the services sector (particularly the public sector) was a significant factor contributing to increased white-collar unionisation. However, Kelly (1975) identifies a number of factors that served to increase the propensity of white-collar workers to unionise. In particular, he noted the impact of negative circumstances at work, especially poor job design and general quality of working life, as important factors encouraging white-collar unionisation. One can also point to changing attitudes of white-collar workers to trade unions, a development accelerated by the emergence of unions designed to cater for the specific needs of white-collar workers. The British based Association of Scientific Technical and Managerial Staffs (ASTMS) attracted a large number of Irish insurance workers and other professional staff into its membership. The Irish Transport and General Workers Union became the first general union to explicitly develop a white-collar section under the now sitting TD Pat Rabitte.

Another significant factor in white-collar unionisation was the significant advances in pay and conditions secured by blue-collar unions, which encouraged hitherto more conservative white-collar workers to unionise. White-collar categories thus represented a relatively 'greenfield' opportunity for union membership drives in the 1960s and 1970s.

In 2001, white-collar unions accounted for some 42 per cent of all trade union members in the country (Roche and Ashmore 2000). In evaluating union membership statistics it is difficult to differentiate between white-collar and blue-collar workers. However, the major areas of concentration of white-collar workers are the public sector and in financial and professional services. Recent figures from the Irish Congress of Trade Unions (ICTU) suggest that the five largest public sector unions, the Irish Municipal Public and Civil Trade Union (IMPACT), the Communications Workers Union (CWU), the Irish Nurses Organisation (INO), the Civil and Public Services Union (CPSU) and the Public Services Executive Union (PSEU) account for almost 17 per cent of ICTU members while the three major teachers' unions, the Irish National Teachers Organisation (INTO), the Association of Secondary Teachers of Ireland (ASTI), and the Teachers Union of Ireland (TUI) account for over 8 per cent of ICTU members. Turning to the financial services sector we find that the two major unions, the Irish Bank Officials Association (IBOA) and the Manufacturing Services and Finance union (MSF) account for another 8 per cent of ICTU membership. As noted earlier, many white-collar workers are also members of general unions such as SIPTU.

Trade Union Structure

Turning to the actual operation of trade unions in Ireland, three different levels may be identified: (i) workplace level, (ii) branch level and (iii) national level. This structure is illustrated in figure 10.3. The ultimate decision-making authority in a trade union is vested in the membership and executed through resolutions passed at the Annual Delegate Conference (ADC). It is the responsibility of the union executive to carry out policy decisions reached at the ADC. The primary role of the trade union official is to carry out the operational aspects of the union's role, servicing the membership through assistance and advice.

Figure 10.3 Trade union structure

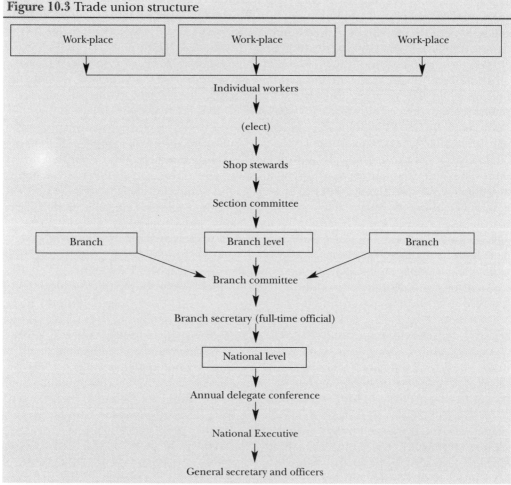

Source: Gunnigle, McMahon and Fitzgerald (1999, 120).

The *shop steward* is the key trade union representative in the workplace. They are selected by fellow trade union members at elections, which normally take place once a year. A number of shop stewards may be elected to represent different sections within the workplace. The shop steward's role is to represent the interests of union members on workplace issues, liaise with union officials, and to keep members well-informed about union affairs. Salamon (1998, 175) describes the role of the shop steward as 'an employee who is accepted by management and union as a lay representative of the union and its members with responsibility to act on their behalf in industrial relations matters at the organisational level'.

Shop stewards may become involved in workplace bargaining involving local grievances or disputes. On more major issues, their role is to support the trade union official and give feedback to the membership. Shop stewards are also employees of the organisation and, as such, must perform their normal job. It should be noted that the Code of Practice (under the Industrial Relations Act 1990) issued in 1993 in respect of Employee Representatives states that such representatives should be afforded 'reasonable' time off to perform their representative duties. Equally, trade union representatives are charged with representing their members in a fair and equitable manner. It has become custom and practice in a number of organisations for shop stewards to be given time-off to perform their union role and have access to requisite facilities (e.g. secretarial and telephone). However, these are often minimal and it is extremely rare for shop stewards to be given substantial leave to perform their union duties. This may be because the small scale of most Irish organisations does not facilitate such resources being afforded to shop stewards.

The *section committee* consists of group of elected shop stewards. The section committee allows stewards representing various sections or groupings in the organisation to meet regularly, discuss common problems and decide on policy. Such a committee is generally called a Shop Stewards Committee. All of the shop stewards are members of the same trade union. However, one can also have a section committee of shop stewards who are members of different trade unions. In this instance it is called a Joint Shop Stewards Committee. Joint Shop Stewards Committees can regulate conflict between unions, and support and – if necessary – sanction individual stewards. They also constitute a more powerful and unified body for negotiating with management.

The *branch* is the basic organisational unit in a trade union and may be organised on either a geographic (catering for several companies) or establishment basis (Gunnigle *et al.* 1995). In Ireland, a trade union branch normally comprises of a group of trade union members from different companies located in the same geographic area. Occasionally, a branch may comprise of union members from one large business enterprise. A union branch manages the internal affairs of the union in their particular area or constituency and strives for improvements in the terms and working conditions of branch members.

The affairs of the branch are managed by the branch committee. This committee is elected at the Annual General Meeting of the branch, which is also the forum for electing delegates from the branch to attend the Annual Delegate Conference of the union. Both the Branch Committee and the Branch Members are served by a Branch Secretary. In larger unions, this individual is normally a permanent employee of the union. If so, they are described as a Full-time Branch Official, whose role is to administer the affairs of the branch and negotiate terms and conditions for all branch members with management.

At *national level*, the election of union officers takes place at the ADC. It is here that motions concerning trade union policy are discussed and voted upon. Such motions usually emanate from branch level. If approved by the ADC a motion then becomes a resolution of the conference and ultimately union policy. The ADC comprises of branch delegates and the union's National Executive. The National Executive is responsible for carrying out the decisions of the ADC and appointing branch officials and other union staff. The

General Officers of the union are usually full-time union employees and normally consist of a General President, a General Secretary, a General Vice President and a General Treasurer.

IRISH CONGRESS OF TRADE UNIONS (ICTU)

The Irish Congress of Trade Unions (ICTU) is the central co-ordinating body for the Irish trade union movement. It is estimated that some 95 per cent of Irish trade unionists are in membership of unions affiliated to Congress (Roche and Ashmore 2000). However, important unions not affiliated to the ICTU are the National Bus and Rail Workers Union (NBRU), the Psychiatric Nurses Association (PSA), the Dairy Executives Association (DEA)] and the Association of Secondary Teachers, Ireland (ASTI).

Although Congress acts as the representative of the collective interests of the Irish trade union movement, individual unions retain a large degree of autonomy and the ICTU relies on the co-operation of affiliated unions in promoting its overall goals (Gunnigle *et al.* 1999). The ICTU plays an extremely important role at national level, representing union views to Government and other institutions. The ICTU role is particularly significant in centralised pay negotiations. Along with the other social partners (i.e. Government, employer and farming representatives), it is party to national negotiations on pay and other aspects of social and economic policy. It is the vehicle through which trade unions decide on participation in centralised pay bargaining, approve any agreement thus concluded, and ensure affiliated unions adhere to the terms of such agreements. The ICTU also represents trade unions on several national bodies and provides union nominees for conciliation and arbitration services.

Ultimate decision-making power within Congress is vested in the Annual Delegate Conference, where delegates from affiliated unions consider various resolutions presented by union delegates and those adopted become ICTU policy. The executive is responsible for policy execution as well as general administration. A number of important committees operate under the auspices of the ICTU. A Disputes Committee deals with inter-union disputes in relation to union membership. The Demarcation Tribunal deals with inter-union disputes in relation to work boundaries. The Industrial Relations Committee has the particularly important responsibility of granting an 'all-out picket' in industrial disputes. An 'all-out-picket' requires that all union members employed in the organisation with which the dispute exists, do not pass the picket, provided that the picket is peaceful, at the place of work of the employer and 'in contemplation or furtherance of a trade dispute'. Furthermore, a secret ballot of all union members must be held and the aggregate majority must be in favour of such industrial action. Individual unions can only sanction a 'one union picket', whereby only members of the union in dispute are obliged not to pass.

TRADE UNION MEMBERSHIP

A major indicator of the role of trade unions in a country is the level of trade union membership. Ireland now has forty-six unions, which in 2000 catered for a total membership of over 560,000 people. The most commonly used indicator of trade union penetration is *trade union density*, which gauges the proportion of 'unionisable' workers currently in membership of trade unions. It is normally based on two measures.

1. *Workforce density:* This measures the percentage of the total civilian workforce (i.e. including those employed and those seeking employment) who are trade union members.

2. *Employment density:* This measures the percentage of civilian employees in the labour force (excluding the self-employed, security forces and assisting relatives) who are trade union members.

Table 10.1 outlines trends in trade union density in Ireland over the period 1925–99. This data indicates that aggregate trade union membership increased, more or less progressively, from the 1930s right up to 1980[2]. We then witnessed a significant decline in union membership from 1980 to the end of the decade. This decline in union membership in the 1980s is principally attributed to macro-economic factors: economic depression, increased unemployment, changes in employment structure involving the decline or stagnation of employment in traditionally highly unionised sectors (such as areas of the public sector and 'traditional' manufacturing e.g. textiles) and growth in sectors traditionally more union averse, such as private services and areas of 'high technology' manufacturing such as electronics (see Roche 1997b; Roche and Larragy 1989; Roche and Ashmore 2000). In addition to these factors, it is also likely that developments at enterprise level also contributed to this decline, most notably changes in management approaches to industrial relations. Of particular significance in this respect was the growth in union avoidance strategies on the part of employers (Gunnigle, O'Sullivan and Kinsella 2001; McGovern 1989).

Table 10.1 Trends in trade union density in Ireland 1925–99

Year	Membership	Employment Density %	Workforce Density %
1925	123,000	21.2	18.7
1930	99,450	20.0	20.0
1935	130,230	22.6	18.6
1940	151,630	26.2	23.0
1945	172,340	27.7	25.3
1955	305,620	45.7	41.6
1965	358,050	52.4	48.8
1975	449,520	60.0	53.2
1980	527,960	62.0	55.3
1985	485,040	61.3	47.5
1990	474,590	57.1	45.0
1995*	518,708	53.2	41.5
1999*	561,800	44.5	38.5

*Figures for 1995 and 1999 are estimates derived from the annual affiliated membership of the Irish Congress of Trade Unions and also from the Department of Enterprise and Employment (Gunnigle, O'Sullivan & Kinsella 2001).

Source: Figures for 1925–1990 are derived from the UCD DUES Data Series (Roche 1992; Roche 1997b, Roche and Ashmore 2000).

Table 10.2 outlines more detailed data on recent trends in trade union membership in Ireland. Here we find that union membership increased from 500,000 in 1994 to almost 562,000 in 1999 (Roche and Ashmore 2000). This increase in membership clearly reflects the progressive and significant increase in employment levels over this period. However, when we look at trends in trade union density we find a much less positive picture. In 1999 employment density was 44.5 per cent and workforce density was 38.5 per cent. This represents a fall in employment density of almost 10 per cent since 1994, in a period when the numbers at work in Ireland has increased by a third. Historically, employment growth has positively impacted on trade union density in Ireland. Clearly this has not been the case in the boom years of the 1990s and represents a very worrying trend for Irish trade unions. Taking a longer-term perspective, these figures for employment density represent a fall of 17 per cent since the high point of 1980, when employment density reached 62 per cent.

Table 10.2 Recent trends in trade union density in Ireland

Year	Total Union Membership	Total Employed	Total Labour Force	Employment Density	Workforce Density
1994	499.7	1221	1432	54.3%	41.7%
1995	518.7	1282	1459	53.2%	41.5%
1996	539.1	1329	1508	52.4%	41.1%
1997	538.4	1380	1539	50.2%	40.6%
1998	545.3	1494	1621	46.5%	38.9%
1999	561.8	1591	1688	44.5%	38.5%

Source: Gunnigle, O'Sullivan and Kinsella (2001).

In comparison to other countries however, we find that levels of union density in Ireland are reasonably high. As illustrated in table 10.3, the level of trade union density in Ireland compares favourably with union density in the UK (33 per cent) and is considerably higher than in the US where employment union density is just 14 per cent. The Nordic and Scandinavian countries tend to be the most highly unionised countries.

Table 10.3 International employment union density 1995

Australia	35%	Japan	24%
Austria	41%	Luxembourg	43%
Belgium	52%	Netherlands	26%
Canada**	37%	New Zealand	24%
Denmark*	80%	Norway	58%
Finland	79%	Portugal	26%
France	9%	Spain*	19%
Germany	29%	Sweden*	91%
Greece	24%	United Kingdom	33%
Italy*	44%	United States	14%

  * Figures based on 1994 data.
** Figures based on 1993 data.

Source: International Labour Organisation, World Labour Report (1997–8).

When we look at the distribution of trade union membership in Ireland by size of union we find considerable imbalance as illustrated in table 10.4. At one extreme, we find that a small number of large unions account for the majority of union membership in Ireland, while at the other, we find a large number (thirty-one) of small unions which together cater for just 10 per cent of total union membership in Ireland. This may be a vindication of Government policy in the Industrial Relations Act 1990 to encourage the reduction of small unions (see discussion below on trade union mergers).

Table 10.4 Trade union membership by size of union 1999

No. of Members	No. of Unions	% of Total Membership
Less than 1,000	15	0.7%
1,000–4,999	14	6.7%
5,000–9,999	2	2.6%
10,000–19,999	8	19.0%
20,000 or over	7	71.1%

N.B. This table only refers to trade unions holding negotiating licences under the Trade Union Acts and excludes a number of other representative bodies who do not hold such a licence but who operate as trade unions.

Source: Department of Enterprise, Trade and Employment.

A related and important development in regard to Irish trade union structure over recent decades has been the increase in trade union merger activity. This relates to situations where two or more unions join together. The aggregate number of trade unions in the Republic of Ireland has declined dramatically in recent years, falling from eighty-six unions in 1980 to forty-six unions in 1999, see table 10.5. The merger of the two largest trade unions in the country, the Irish Transport and General Workers Union (ITGWU) and the Federated Workers Union of Ireland (FWUI), in 1990 to form SIPTU (Services, Industrial, Professional and Technical Union) was probably the most significant trade union merger in Ireland. It is estimated that SIPTU, the largest union in the state, caters for approximately 40 per cent of all trade union members in the country.

Table 10.5 Number of trade unions in Ireland 1980–99

Year	Number of Unions	Year	Number of Unions
1980	86	1994	56
1985	77	1995	56
1990	67	1996	56
1991	62	1997	55
1992	59	1998	47
1993	59	1999	46

N.B. Figures presented here are based only on trade unions holding negotiating licences.

Source: Labour Relations Commission Annual Report (2000).

TRADE UNION MEMBERSHIP AT ORGANISATION LEVEL

While national statistics provide us with an overall picture of trade union density, it is necessary to look at union membership levels at organisation level to gain insights into the operational role and impact of trade unions. The levels of trade union membership and the extent of trade union recognition are key indicators of the nature of enterprise level employee relations.[3]

The CUL study conducted in 1992, 1995 and 1999 investigated human resource management (HRM) and industrial relations practices in large and medium sized Irish organisations.[4] Respondents were asked to indicate the proportion of the workforce in their organisation that was in membership of a trade union. These findings are summarised in figure 10.4. If we take a point-in-time perspective, one might argue that this data indicates that union density levels among larger organisations in Ireland are reasonably high: in 1999 over half the organisations reported that 50 per cent or more of their employees were trade union members.[5] It should also be noted that the CUL study covers organisations employing fifty or more employees and thus provides insight into industrial relations and HRM among larger organisations in Ireland. However, much of Ireland's business activity takes place among firms employing less than fifty workers. It is well established in the literature that union penetration is lower in smaller organisations (Gunnigle 1989; Gunnigle and Brady 1984; McMahon 1996).

However, if we look at the trend in regard to union density we find a pattern of progressive decline. In the first survey (1992), two thirds of organisations reported that 50 per cent or more of their workforce were trade union members: by 1999 this had fallen by some 13 per cent.

Figure 10.4 Proportion of workers in membership of a trade union

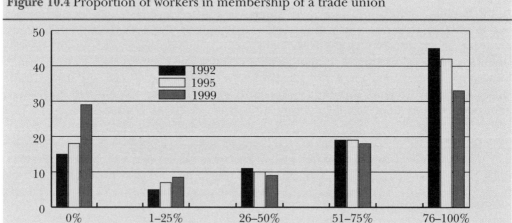

Source: Cranfield-University of Limerick (1992, 1995, 1999).

As in the previous phases of the CUL survey, the 1999 data reveals that levels of union density remain particularly high in the public sector. The difference in union density is clearly outlined in figure 10.5, which compares union membership levels in private and state or semi-state organisations. While only a small fraction of state or semi-state organisations report low or zero levels of union membership, some 40 per cent of private companies report no union members with a further 20 per cent reporting membership levels of 50 per cent or less. In contrast state or semi-state companies account for by far the greatest proportion of highly unionised organisations. Eight in ten public sector companies reported union membership levels of between 76 and 100 per cent: the equivalent private sector figure was just two in ten. These findings are in line with other studies: for example,

Hourihan (1996) estimated that union density in the public service is approximately 80 per cent but only around 36 per cent in the private sector.

Figure 10.5 Proportion of workers in membership of a trade union: private versus state sector

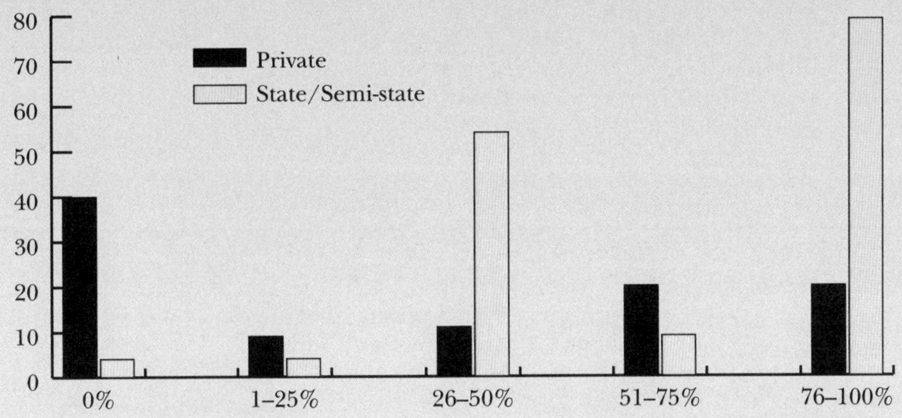

Source:

Trade Union Recognition

Trade union recognition represents a critical barometer of 'collectivism' in industrial relations. This is particularly the case in Ireland, which has no mandatory legal procedure for dealing with union recognition claims (see the discussion later in this chapter on the Code of Practice on Voluntary Dispute Resolution and the Industrial Relations [Amendment] Bill 2000). As we noted earlier, while the Irish Constitution supports the right of workers to join trade unions, there is no legal obligation on employers to recognise or bargain with such unions, with the exception of the Protection of Employment Act 1977, in cases of collective redundancies. Thus the granting of recognition remains largely an issue to be worked out voluntarily between employers and trade unions and ultimately depends on whether or not employers agree to recognise and bargain with a trade union representing all or a proportion of its workforce. In addition to data on trade union density therefore, trends in regard to trade union recognition thus provide another important indicator of trade union penetration.

Salamon (1998, 175) defines trade union recognition as 'the process by which management formally accepts one or more trade unions as the representative(s) of all, or a group, of its employees for the purpose of jointly determining terms and conditions of employment on a collective basis' and describes it as ' . . . perhaps the most important stage in the development of an organisation's industrial relations system . . . it confers legitimacy and determines the scope of the trade union's role'. By securing recognition an employer acknowledges the right of a trade union to represent and protect their members' interests in the workplace and to become jointly involved in regulating key aspects of the employment relationship. As Torrington and Hall (1995, 492) specifically comment, trade union recognition represents ' . . . an almost irrevocable movement away from unilateral decision making by management'.

Turning to empirical evidence, data from the 1999 CUL study finds what at first might seem a reasonably healthy picture of trade union recognition in Ireland (see table 10.6).

In the 1999 survey, some 69 per cent of participating organisations recognised trade unions for collective bargaining purposes. However, when we look at the trend in regard to trade union recognition, we find that the proportion of organisations which recognise trade unions fell from 83 per cent in the first survey (1992), to the current level of 69 per cent, a fall of 14 per cent over a seven-year period. We should also add the important caveat that the CUL study covers only larger organisations, excluding those with less than fifty employees. Moreover, we know that much of Ireland's business activity takes place among small firms employing less than fifty workers. It is well established in the literature that union penetration is lower in smaller organisations; consequently, union recognition in the small firm sector is likely to come in well below the CUL figures presented in table 10.6.

Table 10.6 Trade union recognition in larger organisations 1992–99

Trade Union Recognition	1992	1995	1999
Yes	83% (186)	80% (205)	69.2% (296)
No	17% (38)	20% (50)	30.8% (132)

N.B. Actual numbers in parentheses.

Source: Cranfield-University of Limerick (1992, 1995, 1999).

By and large, the national statistics and data from the CUL study present a mixed picture of trade union penetration in Ireland. Looking at trends in regard to aggregate levels of trade union density we find a picture of steady decline since 1980. A similar picture emerges from our review of trade union membership levels within organisations. However, while there is some decline in the numbers of workers in membership, the evidence also indicates that most of the larger organisations are characterised by reasonably high levels of union penetration. In the 1999 CUL study, seven in ten organisations recognised trade unions for collective bargaining purposes, while over one third report that 75 per cent or more of their workforce are trade union members. Thus, whilst the evidence indicates a decline in union penetration, the case remains that reasonably high levels of trade union recognition and density characterise most of Ireland's larger organisations. We have already seen that union penetration tends to be strongest in the public service and in 'traditional' manufacturing. It is therefore useful to look outside these sectors to better inform our understanding of trade union penetration.

Some of the most interesting evidence on trends in trade union recognition emerges from research on newly established greenfield companies in Ireland. Looking first at the international literature, we find that a significant aspect of the debate on change in enterprise-level employee relations has focused on developments in greenfield sites (Beaumont 1985). Two particular facets of this debate are noteworthy. Firstly, we find that a recurrent theme in analysis of employee relations in greenfield sites is the suggestion that employers and management have assumed a dominant role in establishing the parameters of employee relations practice at workplace level (Gunnigle 1995). Secondly, we have the contention that the decision of many corporations to establish at, or re-locate to, greenfield sites has led to increased union avoidance (Kochan *et al.* 1986; Beaumont and Harris 1994; Foulkes 1980).

In reviewing developments in Ireland we can draw on survey and interview data from a representative sample of firms in the manufacturing and internationally traded services sectors, which were established at greenfield sites over a ten-year period 1987–97. (The study excluded firms with less than 100 employees and used qualitative semi-structured interviews with senior managers, and statistical analysis of a questionnaire completed by the senior manager responsible for industrial relations.)

The data set was gathered in two distinct phases. Phase one covered all qualifying greenfield site firms established in the manufacturing and internationally traded services sectors over the period 1987–92 (Gunnigle 1995; Gunnigle, Morley and Turner 1997). This phase covered a study population of fifty-three firms. The second phase relied on the same definitions and methodology but focused on a sample of twenty-three companies (33 per cent) from a total of seventy qualifying firms (Gunnigle, MacCurtain and Morley 2001). Altogether, the greenfield site data set draws on information from seventy-six greenfield firms. Of the total, forty-four (58 per cent) were owned by US companies, with the remainder comprising of thirteen Irish (17 per cent), ten European (13 per cent), and nine (12 per cent) other foreign-owned firms. These seventy-six firms employed some 22,900 workers at the time of investigation. As one might expect, there was a concentration of firms in 'high technology' sectors, with the largest numbers in office and data processing equipment manufacture and in software.

Given the profile of the greenfield site population and, particularly, the prevalence of both US and 'high-technology' firms, one would anticipate a high incidence of non-union firms. As can be seen from figure 10.6, this was certainly the case with over 65 per cent of firms not recognising trade unions. This evidence is indicative of significant growth in union avoidance among large greenfield start-ups in Ireland. Given that the incidence of non-union approaches was significantly higher in the latter (second) phase of the study than in the first, the findings also reflect the progressive diminution of union penetration in greenfield firms over the ten-year period studied (91 per cent of firms were non-union in the second phase while the corresponding figure for the first phase was 53 per cent).

Non-unionism is clearly most prevalent amongst multinationals of US origin in high technology industries. This factor is commonly attributed to both the prevalence of a unitary managerial ideology among US-owned companies as well as to the competitive nature of the technology sector and the consequent managerial preference for maintaining high levels of numerical and functional flexibility (see Roche and Gunnigle 1997; Toner 1987).

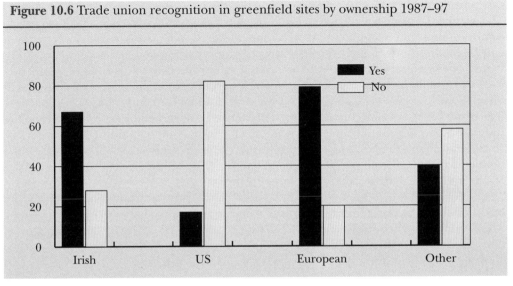

Figure 10.6 Trade union recognition in greenfield sites by ownership 1987–97

Looking at the longitudinal pattern of union recognition in greenfield sites, it appears that non-union approaches began to take off in the early 1980s, became significantly more commonplace as the decade progressed, and are now characteristic of the majority of greenfield site firms in the manufacturing and internationally traded services sector in Ireland (Gunnigle 1995; Gunnigle, MacCurtain and Morley 2001). While the early non-union firms were predominantly US-owned and located primarily among 'high-tech' firms (mostly electronics, software and internationally traded services), more recent evidence from the early 1990s points to the broader diffusion of union avoidance to embrace both Irish and other foreign-owned firms, and a broader range of industrial sectors. It is all the more revealing that this decline in union penetration in new firms has occurred during an era when the trade union movement has exerted significant influence in shaping economic and social policy and when economic growth and employment creation have been exceptionally high.

Alternatives to Trade Unions

Before completing our discussion of trade unions, it should be noted that while trade unions have been the most conspicuous means of representing employee interests, there are a number of alternative approaches that workers may adopt.

Workers may deal with employers on an individual basis (*individual bargaining*). This may be attractive to workers who are in a strong bargaining position, especially those in possession of particular skills or knowledge that is highly valued by employers. This may particularly be the case when certain categories of labour are in short supply and where workers in such categories and possessing valued skills can command favourable terms and conditions of employment through direct dealings with employers. Individual bargaining may be also attractive in organisations where management place a high priority on individual employee needs and provide attractive pay and conditions of employment. More generally, however, it is felt that individual workers are at a severe disadvantage in bargaining terms *vis-à-vis* employers and, consequently, individual bargaining is not an optimal approach for most workers. Indeed, this has been a traditional selling point of trade unions: that collective employee representation through trade unions serves to counter-balance employer bargaining power and thus redresses the perceived bargaining disadvantage of the individual worker.

Another alternative for workers is to form work-based staff associations or groups to represent their interests to employers. Company-based *staff associations* usually represent employee interests through consultation with senior management on employee relations issues. They have traditionally been associated with white-collar grades, particularly professional and managerial categories, who are not trade union members. The use of staff associations is often seen as an improvement on individual bargaining. By joining together, it is argued that workers can present a more united front to employers and redress the perceived bargaining imbalance associated with individual bargaining. An important consideration, particularly among some employers, is that staff associations provide for a modicum of collective employee representation without the introduction of a 'third party' (trade union) into management-employee relations.

Employees may also prefer to join staff associations on occasion. For example, the traditional perception of trade unions as catering for blue-collar workers may create a 'snob' value that encourages employees to join or remain in staff associations. Employers may also perceive staff associations as less difficult to deal with and less likely to engage in confrontational or adversarial employee relations approaches. Employers may thus see staff associations as 'easier' bargaining partners. However, work-based staff associations have been criticised because of their lack of independence from the organisation. Another disadvantage is the absence of an external organisational structure and resources with which to provide bargaining expertise or legal advice.

Traditional trade unionists generally take a cynical view of staff associations, viewing them as a poor apology for real trade union organisation. These factors may often combine to limit the bargaining power of staff associations in their interactions with management. Some of the major contrasts between trade unions and staff associations are summarised in table 10.7. It is important to note that these generalisations may not characterise all trade unions or staff associations.

Table 10.7 Trade unions and staff associations: contrasts

	Trade Unions	**Staff Associations**
Objectives	1. Replace individual bargaining with collective bargaining 2. Pay and employment conditions 3. Political objectives	1. Similar but less ideological commitment 2. Yes 3. No
Controlling authority	Union headquarters; normally strong role for ICTU	No external authority
Rules/ Procedures	Detailed constitution often with strong political dimension	None or brief constitution; oriented to firm
External resources	Access to external expertise and resources. Influence on national issues (e.g. via centralised agreements on pay and other social/economic issues)	None except by contracting in external expertise. No explicit means of influence on national issues.
Methods	Collective bargaining, often with adversarial orientation	More consultative orientation
Use of sanctions	Prepared to use strike weapon	Most unlikely
Services to members	May have range of services	None or limited range

ROLE OF THE STATE

This section considers the role of the state in Irish employee relations. It focuses on the four main methods by which the state may intervene in employee relations:

1. in terms of overall employee/industrial relations policy;
2. as a provider of dispute resolution machinery;
3. as a legislator; and
4. as an employer.

Policy: State Approaches to Employee Relations[6]

Before reviewing the Irish context let us first consider the range of options that Governments may pursue in the employee relations sphere. Crouch (1982) provides a useful framework of four policy alternatives or approaches which may be pursued by the state, namely: (i) market individualism, (ii) liberal collectivism, (iii) corporatism and (iv) bargained corporatism. Crouch sees these alternative approaches as expressions of the inter-relationship between the dominant political and economic ideology *vis-à-vis* employee relations, the relative power and autonomy of trade unions and the nature of employer-employee relations (see table 10.8).

Table 10.8 State approaches to employee relations			
	Political ideology	**Trade unions**	**Employer-employee relationships**
Market individualism	laissez-faire	weak and regulated	exploitative or paternalistic
Liberal collectivism	liberal	strong and autonomous	voluntarist, free collective bargaining
Corporatism	corporatist	weak and regulated	subordinated and controlled, trade unions agents of control
Bargained corporatism	interventionist	strong and autonomous	voluntarist and tripartite

Source: Adapted from Rollinson (1993).

With *market individualism* the dominant political and economic philosophy is that of *laissez-faire*. This philosophy sees the market forces of supply and demand as the ultimate arbitrator of the competitive interests of capital and labour. Labour is seen as a commodity to be bought or sold at a price to be determined by the market mechanism. Trade union interventions in the form of collective bargaining are seen as distorting the operation of the market and are treated with open hostility by employers favouring such a strategy. The *laissez-faire* option means mitigating trade union strength other than by means of compromise and agreements, typically by increased legislation aimed at placing legal limitations on trade union freedoms. Hence trade unions under market individualism tend to be weak and regulated. Thus, as Crouch (1982) points out, market individualism subordinates employees to the control and authority of the owner and the relationship between them is at best paternalistic but at worst exploitative. In keeping with the *laissez-faire* doctrine, direct involvement by the state in employee relations matters is avoided. Roche (1997b) refers to this state approach as a 'market control' strategy which sees the Government's role as supporting the re-construction of competitive labour markets and controlling inflation and hence wage settlements by managing the money supply.

Liberal collectivism describes a framework which sees the co-existence of a liberal political ideology and the development of strong autonomous trade unions. Such an accommodation sees the acceptance of autonomous trade unions (by management) which represent, bargain and reconcile conflicting interests with management through the collective bargaining process. However, as Salamon (1998) points out, the dominant interests of management are protected through the establishment of a boundary between issues to be decided by collective bargaining and issues to be determined by managerial prerogative. The concepts of 'voluntarism' and 'pluralism' are central to this state approach. In this approach the parties to employee relations insist on settling their own affairs without state interference. Roche (1997b) classifies this state approach as 'auxiliary state control'. The role of the state is primarily facilitative, confined to providing dispute resolution institutions to aid the reconciliation of conflicts of interests which arise, and legislating to provide employees with a 'floor of rights' or minimum standards, which of course can be improved upon through collective bargaining between employers and trade unions.

Corporatism as an employee relations concept has its origins in a broader model of society, whereby the state would function in co-operation with organised social interest groups. As such it was intended to chart a middle ground between liberal capitalism and state totalitarianism. Roche (1989) defined corporatism

> . . . as a strategy or model of public policy-making in which the state seeks to co-opt the leadership of social interest groups into policy formulation in return for assurances that the latter will seek to deliver their respective constituencies when it comes to the implementation or execution of policies developed in central talks or agreements.

Lehmbruch *et al.* (1982) attribute the following characteristics to a full corporatist system:

1. Interest organisations are strongly co-opted into governmental decision making.
2. Large interest organisations (in particular unions) are strongly linked to political parties and take part in policy formation.
3. Most interest organisations are hierarchically structured and membership tends to be compulsory.
4. Occupational categories are represented by non-competitive organisations enjoying a monopoly.
5. Industrial relations are characterised by strong concentration of unions and employers' association with the government involved.

Two types of corporatism have been identified: (i) state corporatism and (ii) bargained corporatism. *State* or *pure corporatism*, is facilitated by a concentration of powers in government, monopoly forms of capital, and the absence of associations of labour and political systems with a single party. This form of corporatism either involves massive state coercion or sufficient societal unity to make coercion unnecessary. In particular a unity of view must exist among employers, the state and the trade union leadership. The corporate state is one that is often associated with totalitarian regimes of fascist Italy and Germany in the 1930s and 1940s and countries of the former Soviet bloc.

Bargained corporatism, often referred to as societal or liberal corporatism, describes a state approach to employee relations that evolves in the presence of a dominant interventionist political ideology and strong autonomous trade unions. It represents the outcome of centrally organised interest groups and of open political systems. Such an approach involves increased Government consultation, negotiation or political exchange with both employers' associations and organised labour through established tri-partite corporatist forums at national level. This approach involves the Government, in effect, becoming a third party to the collective bargaining process interposed between the trade union movement and employers' association. It is the voluntary nature of bargained corporatism and the consequent lack of compulsion and independence of trade unions which differentiates it from pure corporatism. (This section has drawn primarily on material from Gunnigle, McMahon and Fitzgerald [1999].)

State Approaches in Ireland: a Summary Overview

The dominant state approach to industrial relations in Ireland at the beginning of this century was market individualism. However, the increased 'collectivisation' of employee relations, particularly the increased worker organisation into trade unions prompted a change to liberal collectivism or what Roche (1997b) terms 'auxiliary state control'. This is in line with our earlier observation that, traditionally, Government approaches to employee relations in Ireland were grounded in the so called 'voluntarist' tradition. This is generally taken to indicate an approach in which the role of the state in employee relations was restricted to the establishment of legislative ground rules and the provision of mediation and arbitration machinery, leaving employers and employers' association and employees and trade unions free to develop procedures and terms and conditions to suit particular organisational contexts.

Therefore, Governments tended to adopt a 'hands off' approach in regard to inter-actions between employers and workers or trade unions, who were then left comparatively free to engage in collective bargaining and come to their own agreements on issues such as pay increases and working conditions. The state only tended to become involved when conflict occurred (e.g. by providing conciliation services) or when one party was in a dominant power position (e.g. by laying down basic terms and conditions of employment in a particular industrial sector where trade union organisation was weak: see discussion on Joint Labour Committees below). This approach was largely an historical legacy of the British voluntarist tradition.

In discussing state strategies towards employee relations in the post World War II period, Roche (1989) argues that there has been a drift from auxiliary state control to attempts at greater corporate control. He argues that this has occurred in two fairly distinct phases. The first phase, which occurred during the 1960s, saw trade unions becoming involved in a number of largely consultative bodies such as the Employer-Labour Conference and the National Industrial and Economic Council. Throughout this period, however, liberal collectivism and 'collective bargaining remained inviolate' with any attempt by the state to intervene in pay determination being perceived as hostile by the trade unions, who used the threat of withdrawing from these consultative bodies as a means of repelling such corporatist advances. Roche suggests that it was during this phase that the strategic and institutional basis for further state intervention into employee relations was established.

The second phase involved the negotiation of a series of National Wage Agreements and two tri-partite National Understandings beginning in 1970 and continuing into the 1980s. This period was characterised by more active state involvement in the process of collective bargaining together with trade union participation in the process of government. Liberal collectivism or the auxiliary state re-surfaced for a short period between 1982 and 1986 with a return to decentralised bargaining. However, as we saw earlier, 1987 saw the negotiation of the first in a series of national agreements (the Programme for National Recovery [PNR]) which have continued right up to this text going to press (2001). In evaluating this growth in bargained corporatism in Ireland some background is useful, specifically in relation to developments since the turn of the 1980s.

We have already noted the voluntary tradition of employee relations in Ireland and its roots in the British voluntary framework. Consequently the Irish approach closely reflected the British context. However, by the turn of 1980s it was clear that Government approaches to employee relations in both the UK and Ireland had begun to follow quite different trajectories. In the UK, Conservative Governments from the turn of the 1980s took progressive steps, both legislative and otherwise, to reduce union power, lessen the coverage of collective bargaining, and ensure that wage levels and other industrial relations outcomes were determined by market forces.

In Ireland, the voluntarist tradition also became increasingly diluted over the period. In contrast to the UK, however, this change took the form of greater centralisation in employee relations (Roche 1989; 1997b). We already noted that over the period 1970–82 Ireland had a series of national agreements and understandings on pay and related employment issues. These were initially heralded as important vehicles in delivering wage restraint, reduced industrial conflict and low inflation. However, these agreements failed to deliver, and the period was characterised by high levels of inflation and industrial conflict. Central agreements were abandoned by the somewhat disillusioned social partners (particularly employers) and there was a brief return to decentralised bargaining in the 1982–86 period. With the country locked in a deep recession, the Fianna Fáil administration revived central agreements through the 'Programme for National Recovery' beginning in 1987. This period was characterised by very moderate wage increases and increased economic growth. We have since had four more centralised agreements on pay and aspects of economic and social policy covering issues such as welfare provision, employment creation and tax reform, involving negotiations between the 'social partners' (principally Government, trade unions, employers' association and farming organisations).

This period saw unprecedented levels of economic growth and employment creation (see chapter one earlier and chapter three on labour market changes and employment). Much of the credit for such success has been attributed to centralised agreements, although it is plausible to argue that much of this period would have been characterised by low pay increases and low levels of industrial conflict regardless of whether pay was negotiated centrally or locally. Clearly a range of factors, many related to developments in the world economy, have combined to contribute to Ireland's strong economic performance over this period and one cannot simply attribute this economic success to centralised agreements. Many of these other contributory factors were mentioned in chapter one (such as the growth in foreign direct investment) while others such as monetary and fiscal policy, and the impact of the European Union are beyond the scope of this text (see, for example, Gray 1997; Tansey 1998). Since the turn of the millennium we have seen increased debate on the effectiveness and stability of centralised agreements, particular in the context of high economic growth such as that experienced in the mid to late 1990s. Indeed it has been suggested that

> there is an uncomfortable feeling among unions and employers alike that the type of partnership arrangements which have helped build the economy over the last twelve years, structurally cannot handle the demands of an economy growing at the speed with which ours is at the moment.'
>
> Frawley (2000, 15)

Some groups of public sector employees, in particular, have illustrated their dismay at being 'left out of the loop' of economic prosperity. Notable examples of such groups include the nurses and teachers. Indeed the basis for the pay demands of the Association of Secondary Teachers of Ireland (ASTI) are indicative of the feelings of other public sector employees. These include a fair share in the current economic prosperity and compensation for increases in the cost of living (ASTI website, www.asti.ie). Such sentiments in 1999 led to the highest number of working days lost since 1990, after an eight-year period of relatively low strike activity. Some observers have been highly critical of the wealth distribution effects of 'social partnership' with Allen (2000) claiming that three traditional linkages involving pay (pay and profit, pay and productivity, and pay and inflation) have been removed. At the time of going to press the PPF has, so far, survived the pressures brought upon it with its renegotiation in late 2000 and it remains to be seen what affect the Benchmarking Body, established to reform public sector pay by comparing public sector and private sector jobs, will have on the continuance of the 'social partnership' approach. Its sustainability may also be dependent on Ireland's economic position and there are currently strong indications of an economic slowdown.

The State as a Provider of Dispute Resolution Machinery

In the area of dispute resolution the state provides a number of specific agencies to address employee relations matters: the Labour Relations Commission, the Labour Court, Rights Commissioners, Employment Appeals Tribunal, Equality Authority and Office of Director of Equality Investigations. The passing of the Industrial Relations Act 1990 into legislation introduced a new framework under which some of these institutions must operate. A summary of the provisions of this act is outlined in chapter thirteen. This section briefly considers the role of the various dispute resolution institutions in Ireland and their overall operation is summarised in figure 10.7.

Figure 10.7 State institutions for resolution of disputes

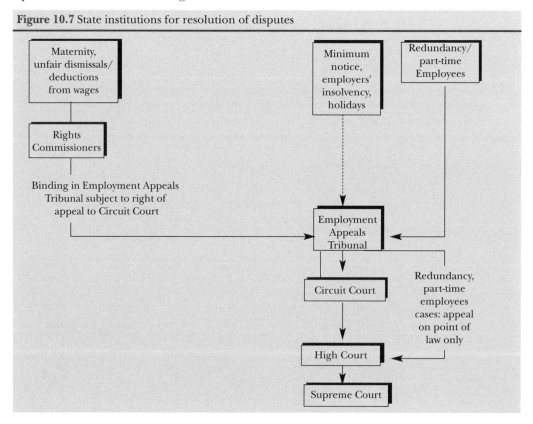

THE LABOUR RELATIONS COMMISSION

The Labour Relations Commission was established under the Industrial Relations Act 1990. It is a tri-partite body with employer, trade union and independent representation and has been charged with the general responsibility of promoting 'good industrial relations'. The Commission provides a comprehensive range of services designed to help prevent and resolve disputes. The main functions provided by the Labour Relations Commission (LRC) are as follows:

- the conciliation service;
- the advisory service;
- the preparation of codes of practice relevant to industrial relations after consultation with unions and employers organisations and the provision of guidance on such codes of practice;
- the selection and nomination of persons for appointment as rights commissioners;
- the commissioning of research into matters relevant to industrial relations;
- the review and monitoring of developments in the area of industrial relations;
- assisting joint labour committees and joint industrial councils in the exercise of their functions.

A critical aspect of the work of the Labour Relations Commission is its *conciliation service*. This service was formerly provided by the Labour Court and, together with the Labour Court (see below), the role of conciliation is to assist resolution of cases referred to them by parties in dispute. These are normally issues where the parties have failed to reach agreement or compromise at local level. The relocation of the conciliation service to the Commission in 1991, was designed to give a new impetus to the role of conciliation and to encourage the conflicting parties to take more responsibility for the resolution of disputes. It was hoped that this would encourage the resolution of disputes at the earliest possible stage of the dispute-settling machinery rather than having issues progress almost automatically to a full Labour Court investigation. The normal pattern for an issue to be processed to conciliation and, possibly, to full Labour Court Investigation is outlined in figure 10.8.

Figure 10.8 Labour Court referral procedure

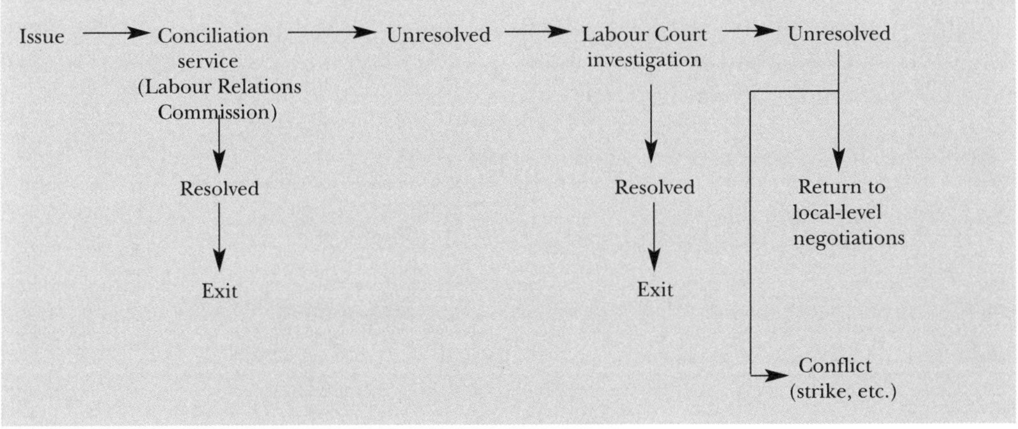

Issue → Conciliation service (Labour Relations Commission) → Unresolved → Labour Court investigation → Unresolved

Conciliation service (Labour Relations Commission) ↓ Resolved ↓ Exit

Labour Court investigation ↓ Resolved ↓ Exit

Unresolved ↓ Return to local-level negotiations

Conflict (strike, etc.)

The conciliation process involves an industrial relations officer (IRO) presiding over a meeting of the conflicting parties. Having listened to the parties in dispute, the IRO may hold separate meetings ('side conferences') with both to get a better idea of the basis for the dispute and what is required to resolve the issue. The IRO can then attempt to guide the parties towards an acceptable solution. Conciliation is essentially voluntary with the IRO acting as a facilitator in the search for an acceptable solution. Success rates in resolving issues at conciliation have fluctuated over the years and there have been frequent criticisms of both the employers and unions abusing the system through their unwillingness to settle at conciliation. However, conciliation generally has a good track record in resolving disputes, as demonstrated in table 10.9.

Table 10.9 Conciliation service referrals, 1971–2000

Year	No. of disputes in which conciliation conferences were held	No. of disputes settled at conciliation (% in parentheses)	Year	No. of disputes in which conciliation conferences were held	No. of disputes settled at conciliation (% in parentheses)
1971	628	429 (68)	1986	1,892	1,268 (67)
1972	713	443 (62)	1987	1,787	1,151 (64)
1973	855	487 (56)	1988	1,571	1,064 (68)
1974	951	646 (68)	1989	1,450	1,019 (70)
1975	1,108	576 (52)	1990	1,552	1,143 (74)
1976	1,071	581 (54)	1991	1,880	1,598 (85)
1977	1,175	638 (54)	1992	1,935	1,451 (75)
1978	1,288	651 (51)	1993	1,844	1,309 (71)
1979	1,301	633 (49)	1994	1,551	1,028 (66)
1980	1,375	693 (50)	1995	1,692	1,184 (70)
1981	1,582	766 (48)	1996	1,487	1,204 (81)
1982	1,855	927 (50)	1997	1,588	1,318 (83)
1983	2,090	1,114 (53)	1998	1,563	1,286 (82)
1984	1,750	1,037 (59)	1999	1,923	1,615 (84)
1985	2,021	1,355 (67)	2000	1,899	1,614 (85)

Source: Labour Court and Labour Relations Commission Annual Reports.

Table 10.10 summarises the work of the conciliation service in the period 1998–2000. The main issues dealt with in that period were pay and remuneration, restructuring and rationalisation and conditions of employment.

Table 10.10 Conciliation service activities, 1998–2000

Year	No. of Disputes Settled Private Sector	Public Sector	Total	Meetings	
1998	1021	419	1563	1946	82%
1999	1362	561	1923	2236	84%
2000	1225	674	1899	2116	85%

Source: Labour Relations Commission Annual Reports.

While the main focus of the conciliation service is to deal with the immediate dispute, the role of the advisory, development and research service (*advisory service*) is to help identify problems which may give rise to employee relations difficulties and to provide direction and advice in resolving such problems. The advisory service represented something of a new departure in the role of Irish dispute resolution agencies when it was introduced. It has as its central brief the task of working with employers, trade unions and employees to develop the 'best industrial relations policies, practices and procedures' in organisations in non-dispute situations. The Labour Relations Commission is also responsible for undertaking or commissioning *research* as well as *monitoring* developments in the general employee relations arena.

Another function of the Labour Relations Commission is to prepare codes of practice on a range of matters in industrial relations (unspecified). While codes of practice are set in a statutory framework they are not directly enforceable in that a breach of the code will not attract any civil or criminal sanction. The codes of practice are intended to give guidance to employers and trade unions on particular issues and are intended to have strong moral authority. To date six codes of practice has been prepared:

1. Code of practice on disputes procedures including procedures in essential services;
2. Code of practice on the duties and responsibilities of employee representatives and the protection and facilities to be afforded to them by their employer;
3. Code of practice on disciplinary and grievance procedures;
4. Code of practice on compensatory rest periods;
5. Code of practice on Sunday working in the retail trade;
6. Code of practice on voluntary dispute resolution.

The Industrial Relations Act 1990 also assigned the LRC with responsibility for assisting *Joint Industrial Councils* (JICs) and *Joint Labour Committees* (JLCs) in the discharge of their functions. The LRC's main role is to provide industrial relations officers to act as chairpersons to a number of JICs and JLCs.

Joint Industrial Councils are permanent voluntary negotiating bodies whose task is to facilitate collective bargaining at industry level in certain industrial sectors. They are composed of representatives of employers and trade unions from within the relevant industrial sector. Joint Industrial Councils may be registered with the Labour Court. At present there are three registered JICs in existence in the footwear and construction industries and one for the Dublin wholesale fruit and vegetable trade (Gunnigle *et al.* 1999). There are a further eleven unregistered JICs in the following industries: bacon curing, bakery and confectionery trade, banks, electrical contracting, flour milling, grocery provision and allied trades, hosiery and knitted garments manufacture, printing and allied trades in Dublin, state industrial employees, woollen and worsted manufacture and Telecom.

Joint Labour Committees are statutory bodies comprised of employer and trade union representatives and independent members which regulate wages and conditions of employment in areas where collective bargaining is poorly established. There are currently nineteen Joint Labour Committees (JLCs) in existence. Joint Labour Committees exist in respect of the following industries: aerated waters, agriculture, brush and broom, catering (excluding Dublin), catering (County Borough of Dublin and Dun Laoghaire), contract cleaning (Dublin), contract cleaning (outside Dublin), hairdressing (Cork), hairdressing (Dublin), handkerchief and household goods, hotels (excluding Dublin and Cork), hotels (Dublin), law clerks, provender milling, retail grocery, security, shirtmaking, tailoring and women's clothing and millinery. JLCs are charged with determining legally binding minimum wages and conditions of employment for those workers represented by it. The JLC submits proposals to the Labour Court for fixing minimum wage rates or for regulating conditions. If the Court accepts the proposals then it makes an Employment Regulation Order (ERO) giving statutory effect to the proposals. Employment Regulation Orders are enforced by inspectors appointed by the Minister for Enterprise, Trade and Employment.

THE LABOUR COURT

The Labour Court is the principal institution in Ireland that facilitates the resolution of trade disputes (Gunnigle *et al.* 1995). It was established under the terms of the Industrial Relations Act 1946 and amended by the Industrial Relations Acts of 1969 and 1976. The Industrial Relations Act of 1990 assigned many of the functions previously held by the Labour Court to the Labour Relations Commission (most notably the conciliation service). The Court has a number of key functions:

- the investigation and issuance of recommendations on cases referred to it by parties in dispute;
- the registration and variation of certain agreements;
- the establishment and servicing of Joint Labour Committees and the ratification of conditions of employment by these committees;
- the provision of chairpersons and/or secretaries for Joint Industrial Councils;
- hearing appeals against a rights commissioner's recommendations and appeals against an equality officer's decision.

The principal role of the Labour Court is to investigate and make recommendations on cases referred to it by parties in dispute. These are normally issues where the parties have failed to reach agreement or compromise at local level. At the first stage of a Labour Court investigation, the parties in dispute are obliged to go through conciliation as discussed above. Should an issue remain unresolved after conciliation, it may be then referred to the Labour Court for investigation. The Industrial Relations Act 1990 provides that the Court may normally investigate a dispute only in one of the following situations:

- if it receives a report from the Labour Relations Commission that no further efforts on its part will help resolve the dispute; or
- if it is notified by the Chairman of the Labour Relations Commission (LRC) that the LRC has waived its function of conciliation in the dispute. In both of the above cases, the parties to the dispute must also request the Court to investigate the dispute. The Court may also investigate a dispute:
- if it is hearing an appeal in relation to a recommendation of a rights commissioner or of an equality officer; or
- if it decides, after consultation with the Commission, that the exceptional circumstances of the case warrant a Labour Court investigation;
- if referred to it under Section 20 of the Industrial Relations Act 1969.

In addition the Court may investigate a dispute at the request of the Minister for Enterprise, Trade and Employment.

The Labour Court currently comprises a chairman, two deputy chairmen and six ordinary members. While all these appointments are made by the Minister, ordinary members are nominated for appointment by organisations representative of trade unions and employer interests. To facilitate speed of operation, the Labour Court normally sits by *division*. A division of the Court comprises of an independent chairman (chair or deputy chair of the Court) and an employer and union representative. A Labour Court hearing is normally presided over by such a division. Hearings are generally held in private, involve written and oral submissions by the parties, and some element of cross-examination. When the Court feels it has adequately investigated the case it will conclude the hearing and set about issuing a recommendation. The recommendations of the Court are generally not legally binding on the parties to the dispute. Consequently such recommendations may be accepted or rejected by the parties. However, there are some important instances where decisions of the Court are legally binding: (i) where the Court hears an appeal of the decision of a rights commissioner or an equality officer; (ii) where workers or their trade unions refer a dispute to the Court for investigation under section 20.1 of the Industrial Relations Act 1969 (i.e., where the trade union refers the dispute on its own and agrees to be bound by the Court's recommendation).

One other instance comes under the Industrial Relations (Amendment) Act 2001. Recommendations by the Court on disputes taken under this Act will be binding with regard to terms and conditions of employment and dispute resolution and disciplinary procedures. It is useful to consider some context in relation to this Bill and its linkages to our earlier discussion in regard to trade union recognition. We noted that while the Irish Constitution supports the right of workers to join trade unions, there is no legal obligation for employers to recognise or bargain with such unions with the exception of The Protection of Employment Act 1977 in cases of collective redundancies. Traditionally, the role of the Labour Court, as the primary dispute resolution body, was to issue non-binding recommendations in union recognition cases that came before it. A trade union also had the option of taking a case to the Labour Court, under section 20.1 of the Industrial Relations Act 1969, whereby any recommendation made would be binding on the union but not the employer. This was used as an attempt to pressure an employer into recognising the union. The lack of statutory provision in relation to trade union recognition has not been a major problem in Irish industrial relations as most medium and large employers have traditionally recognised and concluded collective agreements with trade unions.

However, we have seen earlier that the issue of trade union recognition has in recent years become an extremely contentious issue, due to the fall in trade union density throughout the 1980s and 1990s, and to a number of high profile disputes between unions and employers, such as Pat the Baker and Ryanair. To address the concerns of trade unions, and the Irish Congress of Trade Unions in particular, a High-level Group was established under *Partnership 2000* to examine the issue. The Group issued two reports in 1997 and 1999. These have since been used to create a code of practice on voluntary dispute resolution, promulgated in 2000 by the Minister for Enterprise, Trade and Employment, and an Industrial Relations (Amendment) Act 2001. Where a union recognition dispute exists under the new arrangements, it is intended that a voluntary process would be given precedence as outlined in the code of practice. Under the provisions of the code, the employer and union would negotiate the issue voluntarily with the assistance of the Labour Relations Commission. If this does not resolve the dispute, or bargaining arrangements are non-existent, the provisions of the Industrial Relations (Amendment) Act would come into effect. Under the Act, the Labour Court may investigate the case and issue a non-binding recommendation. Should this, and a subsequent short-term determination fail to resolve the dispute, the Court may issue a second binding determination. It is important to note that the recommendations and determinations of the Court will not decide on union recognition but on terms and conditions of employment, dispute resolution and disciplinary procedures. The Act's provisions mean an enhanced role for the Labour Court and a further departure from its traditional voluntary position. It is unclear as to what effect, if any, the Act may have on increasing trade union penetration among reluctant employers, including those on greenfield sites.

In spite of the generally non-binding nature of Labour Court recommendations, it has had a very satisfactory record with over three-quarters of its recommendations accepted by both parties (Gunnigle *et al.* 1995). Indeed, even where Labour Court recommendations are rejected, their terms may often form the basis for a solution on return to local level negotiations.

The Labour Court was seen to depart from its broad role of promoting collective bargaining and resolving industrial conflict when it was given the role as the determinant of disputes under the Employment Equality Legislation, notably the Anti-Discrimination (Pay) Act 1974, Employment Equality Act of 1977, and more recently, the Employment Equality Act 1998 (Fennell and Lynch 1993; Gunnigle *et al.* 1995). Table 10.11 summarises the range of cases that the Labour Court was involved in during 2000.

Table 10.11 Cases completed by the Labour Court in 2000

Industrial relations	428
Of which	
Referrals by LRC	53
Direct referrals	18
Appeals against rights commissioners' recommendation	18
Complaints of breach of a Registered Employment Agreement	10
Other	1
Equality	18
Organisation of Working Time	49
Total	595

Source: Labour Court Annual Report.

THE RIGHTS COMMISSIONER

The appointment and functions of the rights commissioner were approved under the terms of the Industrial Relations Act 1969. The rights commissioner service was originally attached to the Labour Court, and its function was to intervene in and to investigate industrial disputes with the view to promoting settlement. The rationale underpinning the establishment of the rights commissioner service was to reduce the workload of the Labour Court and to provide a speedy service to parties in dispute over 'less major industrial relations issues' (Kelly 1989). The rights commissioner service is now attached to the Labour Relations Commission. However, rights commissioners operate independently in the performance of their functions. Rights commissioners are appointed by the Minister for Enterprise, Trade and Employment from a panel submitted by the Labour Relations Commission and, under the terms of the Industrial Relations Act 1969, may investigate a trade dispute provided that:

- it is not a dispute connected with the rates of pay, hours or times of work, or annual holidays of a body of workers;
- it is not a dispute concerning persons who do not have access to the Labour Court;

- a party to the dispute does not object in writing to such an investigation;
- the Labour Court has not made a recommendation about the dispute.

Rights commissioners operate individually and meet the parties in dispute. They are available to parties in dispute provided both agree to such a hearing and to accept the commissioner's decision. In practice, rights commissioners mostly investigate disputes concerning individual employees (e.g. discipline or demarcation issues). Hearings are held in private with rights commissioners examining each case on its merits and issuing a written recommendation. A great advantage of this service is its flexibility and accessibility, providing a quick and efficient mechanism for dealing with problems which have proved intractable at local level. An objection to an investigation by a rights commissioner must be notified in writing to the commissioner within three weeks of the date of notification by post that a dispute has been referred.

There are currently five rights commissioners in office. Their role has significantly expanded since 1969 with the enactment of further employment legislation giving them additional functions. They now have a statutory role in investigating cases under a variety

Table 10.12 Rights commissioner activity 1979–2000

Year	Disputes referred	Recommendations issued by rights commissioners*	Appeals to Labour Court (% in parentheses)
1979	1,699	506	36 (7.1)
1980	2,025	661	86 (13)
1981	2,057	639	73 (11.4)
1982	1,931	531	63 (11.9)
1983	1,637	583	100 (17.2)
1984	1,445	687	118 (17.2)
1985	1,431	679	109 (16.1)
1986	1,708	603	107 (17.7)
1987	1,732	630	98 (15.6)
1988	1,477	550	76 (13.8)
1989	1,149	455	91 (20)
1990	1,202	434	64 (14.7)
1991	n.a.	1,106	111** (10)
1992	n.a.	1,191	125 (10.5)
1993	n.a.	1,306	147 (11.3)
1994	n.a.	1,209	147 (12.2)
1995	n.a.	1,154	106 (9.2)
1996	1,807	1,030	101 (9.8)
1997	n.a.	829	117 (14.1)
1998	2,260	906	126 (13.9)
1999	2,996	989	141 (14.3)
2000	3,206	1,623	178 (11)

* In the years 1979–90, the Department of Labour and Labour Court reported on the number of recommendations issued by rights commissioners. Since 1990, the Labour Relations Commission has reported on the number of investigations held by rights commissioners.
** This figure is an estimate.

Source: Department of Labour, Labour Court Annual Reports and Labour Relations Commission Annual Reports.

of acts including the Unfair Dismissals Act 1977–93, the Maternity Protection Act 1994, the Payment of Wages Act 1991, the Organisation of Working Time Act 1998 and the National Minimum Wage Act 2000. A recommendation by a rights commissioner is not legally binding but in practice they tend to be observed by employers and trade unions. However, disputes heard under the Industrial Relations Act 1969 may be appealed to the Labour Court, which can result in a binding order on the parties in the dispute. An appeal against a rights commissioner's recommendation must be notified in writing to the Labour Court within six weeks from the date of the recommendation. Cases in relation to the other acts in which they have a role can be appealed to the Employment Appeals Tribunal. Similarly, an appeal against the recommendation of the rights commissioner under these acts must be made within six weeks.

Table 10.12 summarises the work of the rights commissioner service over the period 1979–2000 and table 10.13 details the legislation dealt with by the service in the years 1997–2000. The number of recommendations which are appealed to the Labour Court has averaged 13 per cent in recent years. In general the rights commissioner service has been received favourably by all sides of industry (Kelly 1989; Gunnigle *et al.* 1999).

Table 10.13 Legislation dealt with by rights commissioners 1997–2000

Category of dispute	1997	1998	1999	2000
Industrial Relations Acts 1969–90	471	363	430	505
Unfair Dismissal Acts 1977–93	178	137	103	238
Maternity Protection 1981–94	4	5	5	3
Payment of Wages Act 1991	234	255	220	494
Terms of Employment Act 1994	42	16	45	66
Organisation of Working Time Act 1997		130	148	288
Adoptive Leave Act 1995			1	
Protection of Young Persons (Employment) Act 1998			37	23
Parental Leave Act 1998				
Protection for Persons Reporting Child Abuse Act 1998				7
National Minimum Wage Act 2000				
Totals	929	906	989	1,624

Source: Labour Relations Commission Annual Reports.

EQUALITY INSTITUTIONS

Equality officers, under the auspices of the Labour Relations Commissions, dealt with issues relating to discrimination on the grounds of sex or marital status arising under the terms of the equality legislation (previously the Anti-discrimination [Pay] Act 1974 and the Employment Equality Act 1977). When a dispute was referred to an equality officer, they would carry out an investigation and issue a recommendation based on the merits of the case. During the course of an investigation the equality officer would meet the parties in dispute and also examine written submissions from both sides. If either party was dissatisfied with this recommendation, they could appeal to the Labour Court within forty-two days. The Court's determination in such circumstances would be final and legally binding on the parties. However, there was a right to appeal the determination of the

Labour Court to the High Court on a point of law. Table 10.14 summarises the pattern of equality officer recommendations over the period 1978–98.

Table 10.14 Equality officer recommendations 1978–98

| Year | Employment Equality Act 1977 | | Anti-Discrimination (Pay) Act 1974 | |
	No.	In favour of claimant	No.	In favour of claimant
1978	5	2	52	n/a
1979	14	8	52	38
1980	14	9	65	48
1981	20	9	55	42
1982	12	2	27	18
1983	22	11	28	12
1984	28	10	27	7
1985	18	7	17	2
1986	8	3	19	8
1987	11	8	14	7
1988	11	5	16	9
1989	12	8	12	5
1990	35	11	13	5
1991	22	16	8	4
1992	22	12	14	4
1993	19	11	11	4
1994	20	9	7	2
1995	17	4	9	1
1996	25	7	11	2
1997	31	6	11	5
1998	22	5	23	4

Source: Employment Equality Agency and Labour Relations Commission Annual Reports.

There have been significant changes to equality legislation in recent years with the Anti-Discrimination (Pay) Act 1974 and the Employment Equality Act 1977 consolidated into a single Employment Equality Act in 1998. This Act prohibits direct and non-direct discrimination against employees in pay and non-pay areas on nine grounds: gender, marital status, family status, sexual orientation, religious belief, age, disability, race and membership of the traveller community. The Equal Status Act introduced in 2000 prohibits discrimination in the provision of goods, services, disposal of property and access to education on the nine grounds mentioned. Employers, and those who provide services, are obliged to abide by the terms of the Acts. Further details about this are provided in chapter thirteen.

The Employment Equality Act 1998 also made some changes to the structure of the state dispute resolution machinery. It provided for a body, the Equality Authority, to replace the Employment Equality Agency. The Equality Authority is responsible for the promotion of equality of opportunity; the elimination of discrimination in employment, the promotion of equal status in education provision, provision of goods, services and accommodation and disposal of property; the provision of information on a number of Acts and for monitoring the operation of employment equality legislation (Equality Authority Annual

Report 2000). The Authority provides advice and also free legal representation to those who take a case under the Employment Equality Act 1998. Also, an office of the Director of Equality Investigations (ODEI) was created in the Department of Justice, Equality and Law Reform to act as the main locus for redress under the Employment Equality Act and the Equal Status Act. It does this by investigating cases and can award compensation or other forms of redress if discrimination is found to have taken place. Should a dispute arise under the 1998 Employment Equality Act, a case may be taken in the first instance to the ODEI, Labour Court or Circuit Court, depending on the issue in dispute (see figure 10.9 and chapter thirteen). Equality Officers were moved from the Labour Relations Commission to the ODEI when it came into operation in October 1999.

Figure 10.9 State institutions for resolution of equality cases

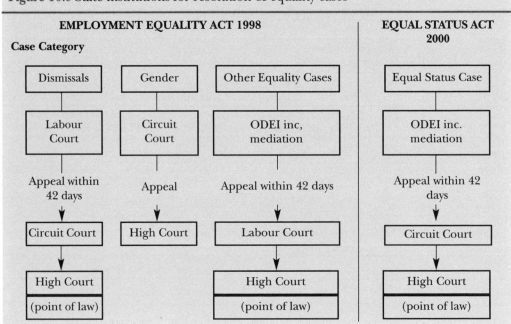

THE EMPLOYMENT APPEALS TRIBUNAL

The Employment Appeals Tribunal (EAT) was originally established as the Redundancy Appeals Tribunal under the terms of the Redundancy Payments Act 1967. The Minimum Notice and Terms of Employment Act 1973 extended the jurisdiction of the Tribunal to claims brought under that Act by dismissed employees for compensation for loss sustained by them by reason of their employer's failure to give them the statutory period of notice. It was later renamed the Employment Appeals Tribunal (EAT) under the terms of Unfair Dismissals Act 1977–93, which further extended its work to incorporate claims for redress for unfair dismissals. The EAT currently adjudicates upon, and interprets a number of other Acts, including the Maternity Protection Act 1994, Protection of Employees (Employers Insolvency) Acts 1984–91, the Payment of Wages Act 1991, the Worker Protection (Regular Part-time Employees) Act 1991, the Parental Leave Act 1998 and the Organisation of Working Time Act 1997. The EAT may also hear appeals of the decisions of rights commissioners. Table 10.15 summarises the number and outcome of claims referred to the EAT under these various pieces of legislation in 1999.

Table 10.15 Summary of appeals referred and the outcome of the appeals disposed of in 1999

Act	Number of appeals referred*	Allowed	Dismissed	Withdrawn during hearing	Withdrawn prior to hearing	Total number of appeals disposed of
Redundancy payments	310	58	74	80	40	252
Minimum Notice and Terms of Employment	1,308	709	173	242	83	1207
Unfair Dismissal (Direct claims)	895	151	113	400	151	815
Maternity Protection (Direct claims)	1	0	2	5	0	7
Protection of Employees (Employers Insolvency)	71	124	5	0	0	129
Worker Protection (Regular Part-time Employees Act)	80	2	22	22	11	57
Organisation of Working Time	135	14	16	28	11	69
Total	2,800	1,058	405	777	296	2,536

* Some appeals referred in 1999 were not disposed of in 1999.
Appeals against recommendations and decisions of rights commissioners are excluded.

Source: EAT Thirty-second Annual Report.

In 1999 the EAT comprised of a chairman, who must be a practising barrister or solicitor, and twenty-one vice-chairmen. The Minister for Enterprise, Trade and Employment appoints these members. The tribunal also consisted of a panel of twenty ordinary members, drawn equally from nominees of employers' association and the Irish Congress of Trade Unions. The tribunal normally sits in divisions. Each division consists of a chairman or vice-chairman and one member from the employer and trade union sides. A clerk, whose function is to offer mainly administrative support to the tribunal, attends each EAT hearing.

Applications to the EAT are made on special forms available from the tribunal or the Department of Enterprise, Trade and Employment. Applicants to the EAT may present their case in person, may be represented by counsel or a solicitor or by a representative of a trade union or employer's association (Fennell and Lynch 1993). Of the 762 claims heard under the Unfair Dismissals Act 1977–93 in 1999, 619 employees (81.2 per cent) were represented (88 by trade unions, 512 by solicitor and/or counsel and 19 by other persons) and 531 employers (69.7 per cent) were represented (69 by employer organisations, 420 by solicitor and/or counsel and 42 by other persons) (EAT Thirty Second Annual Report). Employees must observe the time limits specified by the Act that they apply under – otherwise they may lose their right to bring a claim.

The procedures adopted by the EAT follow, to a certain degree, court procedures but there is a greater amount of informality. Under the various regulations it is possible for parties at an EAT hearing to make an opening statement, call witnesses, cross-examine any witnesses called by any other party, give evidence and address the tribunal at the close of the evidence. Evidence is normally given under oath. Hearings of the EAT are usually held in public, but may be held *in camera* (in private) at the request of either party. The decision ('determination') of the EAT can be given at the close of the hearing, but is more usually issued some time later in written form. Should an employer fail to carry out the terms of an EAT determination, proceedings may be taken by the Minister for Enterprise, Trade and Employment to the Circuit Court in order to ensure compliance. EAT determinations are not subject to the principle of precedence as in a court of law.

For applicants under the unfair dismissals and maternity legislation, the EAT issues determinations that may be appealed to the Circuit Court within six weeks. At the Circuit Court the case is heard *de nova* i.e. there is a full re-hearing of the case. Appeals in relation to the other acts such as redundancy, protection of employees, minimum notice and part-time workers, falling under the jurisdiction of the EAT, can only be made to the High Court on a point of law.

THE STATE AS AN EMPLOYER – EMPLOYEE RELATIONS IN THE STATE SECTOR

Apart from its legislative and facilitative functions, the state plays a significant role as the country's major employer. It accounts for approximately one third of all employees in a range of areas principally composed of the civil service proper, education, local authorities and health boards, security forces, and state-sponsored bodies. Trade unions or staff associations represent the bulk of these state-sector employees. In some public sector areas distinctive employee relations features have developed. However, as the Commission on Industrial Relations (1981) noted, personnel and employee relations issues in the public and private sectors are largely similar and differences which tend to occur are largely in the area of procedural responses (Cox and Hughes 1989).

In relation to the negotiation of pay and conditions of employment, a notable distinction may be drawn between those public sector areas subject to agreed conciliation and arbitration schemes and those which come within the scope of the Labour Court and the Labour Relations Commission. Conciliation and arbitration (C and A) schemes date from the 1950s. Currently, different schemes operate for categories such as the (non-industrial) civil service, teachers, gardai, local authorities and health boards and the Vocational Educational Committees. A unique feature of the civil service scheme is the network of staff panels who evaluate any claims from recognised unions or staff associations before these are forwarded to conciliation. Conciliation consists of joint councils of management and employee representatives, which consider claims before them and issue an agreed report. The composition and specific role of conciliation councils differs between individual schemes and only specific issues may be referred to conciliation. These generally include pay, allowances, working hours, overtime, grading, and policy on recruitment, promotion, discipline, pensions and sick pay. Most schemes exclude issues relating to individual employees.

The vast majority of issues are resolved at conciliation, but those which are not, may proceed to arbitration provided they are arbitrable under the appropriate C and A scheme. An Arbitration Board normally consists of an agreed chairman (often legally qualified) and two representatives from both the management and staff side. Both sides make detailed written submissions and these are supplemented by oral submissions and witnesses may be called as appropriate. The findings of the Board are sent to the Minister for Finance and the other appropriate Minister, who have one month to either approve the report or submit it to the Government. It has the option of accepting the report or moving a Dáil motion to reject or amend it. This latter route is normally seen as an exceptional one. The local authority and health board scheme differs from the above format in that the management or staff side have the option of rejecting the decision of arbitration. In addition to the specific grades in the public sector as discussed above, employees in most state-sponsored bodies have access to the Labour Court. The exception is An Post, which has a separate conciliation and arbitration scheme.

A notable characteristic of public sector employee relations is the key role of the Department of Finance. It acts as the Government's adviser on matters relating to public sector pay and employment related matters. It will critically review pay claims, lay down appropriate policy guidelines and oversee their implementation through direct and indirect negotiations. The Department represents the state as employer at the Employer-Labour Conference and is involved in many of the conciliation and arbitration hearings. Another important actor on the management side in the public sector is the Local Government and Staff Negotiations Board (LGSNB) whose role is to assist local authorities and health boards in employee relations. Representatives of the board act on behalf of management on the appropriate conciliation and arbitration scheme and in major negotiations with non-officer grades.

This chapter has considered the nature of employee relations with particular focus on the Irish context. It also considered the role of trade unions and Government in employee relations. The next chapter considers the role of employers and management in employee relations.

Note

1. For detailed review of collective bargaining in Ireland, including recent centrally negotiated agreements see Gunnigle, P., McMahon, G.V. & Fitzgerald, G., 1999. *Industrial Relations in Ireland, Theory and Practice* (Chapter 6), Dublin: Gill & Macmillan 1999.
2. For a detailed review of trends in trade union membership in Ireland see Roche 1997b, Roche & Ashmore 2000.
3. The Cranfield-University of Limerick (CUL) Study of Human Resource Management in Ireland forms part of the Cranfield Network (*Cranet*) on International HRM, first established in 1989 and currently involving twenty six participating countries. The Irish node of this study is located at the *Employment Relations Research Unit*, University of Limerick and directed by Michael Morley, Patrick Gunnigle and Tom Turner. For a summary of data emanating from the international study see Brewster, C. and Hegewisch, A. (1994), *Policy and Practice in European Human Resource Management: The Price Waterhouse Cranfield Survey*, London: Routledge. For review of the 1992 Irish data see Gunnigle, P., Flood, P., Morley, M. & Turner, T. (1994), *Continuity and Change in Irish Employee Relations*, Dublin: Oak Tree Press, and for the 1995 data see Gunnigle, P., Morley, M., Clifford, N. & Turner, T. (1997), *Human Resource Management in Irish Organisations: Practice in Perspective*, Dublin: Oak Tree Press. Information from the most recent survey (1999/2000) is available from the University of Limerick.
4. It should also be noted that the CUL study covers organisations employing 50 or more employees and thus provides insight on industrial relations and HRM among larger organisations in Ireland. However, much of Ireland's business activity takes place among firms employing less than fifty workers. It is well established in the literature that union penetration is lower in smaller organisations (see, for example, Gunnigle 1989: Gunnigle & Brady 1984; McMahon 1996). Consequently, union density levels in the small firm sector are likely to be well below those indicated in the CUL study.
5. The study excluded firms with less than 100 employees and used qualitative semi-structured interviews with senior managers and statistical analysis of a questionnaire based survey completed by the senior manager responsible for industrial relations.
6. This section draws primarily on material from Gunnigle, P., McMahon, G.V. & Fitzgerald, G., 1999. *Industrial Relations in Ireland, Theory and Practice*, Dublin: Gill & Macmillan 1999.

11

Employer and Management Approaches to Employee Relations

This chapter focuses on the role of employers and management in employee relations. It initially considers employers' objectives in employee relations. The role of employers' associations is then addressed with particular emphasis on the Irish context. Finally, the chapter considers management approaches to employee relations and reviews some contemporary developments.

EMPLOYERS' OBJECTIVES IN EMPLOYEE RELATIONS

The primary concern for organisations operating in a competitive environment is to maximise organisational performance and generate satisfactory returns for the owners and stakeholders of the enterprise (Gunnigle *et al.* 1999). Such returns are often expressed in terms of cost effectiveness and, for the commercial organisation, profitability. Thus, the primary goal of the management is to organise the factors of production, including labour, to achieve these objectives. It is difficult to assess the degree to which employers have specific employee relations objectives or adopt related workplace strategies (Thomason 1984; Gunnigle 1995). Organisations vary greatly and it is apparent that a particular organisation's approach to employee relations will be influenced by a range of environmental factors such as historical development and market conditions. Nevertheless, it is worthwhile considering some general beliefs common among employers. Thomason (1984) identifies the following employer beliefs or objectives in employee relations:

1. *Preservation and consolidation of the private enterprise system:* This has larger political overtones and relates to the concerns of employers to preserve an environment conducive to achieving business objectives at enterprise level. They will be particularly concerned that principles such as private ownership, the profit motive and preservation of managerial authority and control are maintained.
2. *Achievement of satisfactory returns for the owners:* This relates directly to the organisation's primary business goals. For commercial organisations to survive in the long term, satisfactory profit levels must be achieved. Consequently, managerial approaches and strategies will always be influenced by this primary concern. Non-profit making organisations will be equally concerned with cost-effectiveness and quality.

3. *Effective utilisation of human resources:* An organisation's workforce represents a key management resource and its effective utilisation is central to the management process.
4. *Maintenance of control and authority in decision-making:* Employers will strive to ensure effective control and authority in executing its management role particularly in strategic decision-making.
5. *Establishment and maintenance of satisfactory management-employee relations:* Employers will also strive to maintain good working relations with employees but this must be achieved within the operational constraints of the organisation. The scope to agree attractive remuneration levels and conditions of employment will vary according to the organisation's market position and profitability as well as its HRM philosophy. Good employee relations will be a priority since they are an important ingredient in ensuring the organisation achieves its primary business goals as well as being laudable in itself.

THE ROLE OF EMPLOYERS' ASSOCIATIONS

To help achieve the employer and managerial objectives listed above it is clear that employers are likely to combine collectively for purposes associated with employment and labour matters. The major impetus for the growth of employers' organisations was the perceived need to react to and deal with the 'new unionism'. This helps distinguish between employers' associations whose *raison être* was to deal with labour matters, from those where trade and commercial reasons were the major focus and which are normally referred to as trade associations. Oechslin (1985) provides a widely accepted definition of employers' associations as:

> . . . formal groups of employers set up to defend, represent or advise affiliated employers and to strengthen their position in society at large with respect to labour matters as distinct from commercial matters.

A particular and traditional reason why employers have formed representative associations is to prevent harmful economic competition with each other, particularly in relation to pay, and to counter the power of trade unions. Another reason for the development of such associations was the increasingly complex nature of collective bargaining and employment legislation. Employers' associations also provide a forum for the exchange of views among employers (Thomason 1984; Gunnigle *et al.* 1995). The main role of employers' associations is to represent employers' views in employee relations and their objectives may be categorised as political, social, economic and employee relations (see figure 11.1).

Figure 11.1 Objectives of employers' associations

---

1. Political: To effectively represent employers' views to Government, the general public and other appropriate bodies so as to preserve and develop a political, economic and social climate in which business objectives can be achieved.

2. Economic: To create an economic environment that supports the free enterprise system and ensures that managerial prerogative in decision-making is protected.

3. Social: To ensure any social or legal changes best represent the interests of affiliated employers.

4. Employee Relations: To ensure a legislative and procedural environment which supports free collective bargaining and to co-ordinate employers' views and approaches to employee relations matters and provide assistance to affiliated employers.

Employers' associations assume a significant role in representing the interests of employers on national issues. They provide a mechanism through which Governments can solicit the opinions of employers on areas like labour legislation and are important vehicles for influencing public opinion on more general political matters. This political role is most clearly associated with the desire to influence broad economic decision-making. Employers' organisations will generally support what could be termed conservative economic policies, which serve to protect the interests of employers and ensure freedom from an excess of state intervention in business. In the area of social policy the approach of employers' associations will largely be pragmatic. On the one hand they will generally attempt to prevent, or at least lessen, the effects of protective labour or social legislation such as legal moves towards extending industrial democracy or information disclosure. On the other hand, they will accept some degree of social and legislative reform provided their perceived effects on the interests of business are not adverse. An outline of the objectives of Ireland's largest employers' association, the Irish Business and Employers Confederation (IBEC), is outlined in its mission statement in figure 11.2 below.

Figure 11.2 Mission statement – Irish Business and Employers' Confederation

The mission statement of the *Irish Business and Employers' Confederation* is . . .

To influence vigorously the formation of policy at national, European and international levels towards the development of an enterprise culture, the creation of economic and social conditions favourable to the profitable growth and effectiveness of Irish business and employers, and the development of productive employment, whilst having due regard to the interests of the wider community
And
to provide quick response assistance, information, advice and representation for members in protecting their interests and maximising performance.

The specific role of employers' associations in employee relations may be categorised into four broad areas as follows (Gunnigle, McMahon and Fitzgerald 1999):

1. *Exchange of views:* Employers' associations provide a useful forum for opinion exchange and discussion. However, employers may also use associations to develop and agree common policies and strategies in employee relations.
2. *Represent employers' views to Government and its agencies:* Employers' associations provide an important means through which employers may represent their views to Government. For example, they may seek to influence labour legislation and Government policy generally so that the position of affiliated employers is adequately protected. In Ireland this role is executed by the major employers' associations, particularly the Irish Business and Employers' Confederation (IBEC), in representing business and employer views. They represent employers' opinions on bodies such as the National Economic and Social Council, which was established by the Government as a forum for the discussion of the principles relating to the economy; the Central Review Committee which monitors issues arising from centralised agreements; FÁS, the industrial training authority; the Employer-Labour Conference which was established to allow the various interest groups to deal directly with employee relations issues; the National Authority for Occupational Safety and Health which controls the operation

and enforcement of occupational health and safety legislation in Ireland; and the Equality Authority which is the statutory authority with responsibility for the elimination of discrimination and promotion of equality in employment. Employers' associations also provide representatives of employers' interests for appropriate bipartite or tripartite bodies such as arbitration councils, Government commissions, international organisations. In Ireland, IBEC plays the lead role in nominating employers' representatives to such bodies as the Labour Court, the Labour Relations Commission and the Employment Appeals Tribunal.

3. *Representation of Employer Interests to the General Public:* Employers' associations are also involved in representing employers' opinions to the general public on relevant issues such as forthcoming employment legislation.

4. *Provision of Specialised Services to Members:* A major role of employers' associations is the provision of a range of employee relations services to their membership. Sisson suggests the main employee relations services provided by employers' associations are: (i) negotiation of pay and conditions of employment, (ii) operation of disputes procedures, (iii) advisory and consultancy services and (iv) representation. This key role is discussed later in this chapter.

EMPLOYERS' ASSOCIATIONS IN IRELAND

As indicated above employers' organisations in Ireland are classified into two categories, namely *employers' associations* and *trade associations*. While both of these are required to register with the Registrar of Friendly Societies, only *employers' associations* are involved in employee relations and are required to hold a negotiating licence under the terms of the Trade Union Act 1941. In 1999 there were some eleven registered employers' associations in Ireland as defined below (see table 11.1).

Table 11.1 Employers' associations in Ireland 1999

NAME OF ASSOCIATION	MEMBERSHIP
Construction Industry Federation	2,679
Cork Master Butchers' Association	11
Dublin Master Victuallers' Association	106
Irish Business and Employers' Confederation	3,625
Irish Commercial Horticultural Association	361
Irish Hotels' Federation	895
Irish Master Printers' Association	38
Irish Pharmaceutical Union	1,380
Irish Printing Federation	54
Licensed Vintners' Association	632
Society of the Irish Motor Industry	1,664
Total	**11445**

Source: Department Of Enterprise and Employment.

While the number of employers' associations in Ireland is considerably less than their trade union counterparts, there is clearly a considerable diversity in membership composition. For example, table 11.1 provides examples of traditional masters' associations, industry-based associations, and a general association that is national in scope.

The Irish Business and Employers Confederation (IBEC)

The Irish Business and Employers' Confederation (IBEC) is the largest employers' association in Ireland. It was formed in 1993 as a result of the merger of the then Federation of Irish Employers (FIE) and Confederation of Irish Industry (CII). IBEC represents business and employers in all matters relating to employee relations, labour and social affairs. It has a current membership of over 3,500 who employ some 300,000 people or approximately one third of total employment in the country, excluding agriculture, the public service and the self-employed. As the country's major representative of business and employers, IBEC seeks to shape national policies and influence decision-making in a way that protects and promotes the interests of its members. Unlike its predecessors, IBEC's role is not confined solely to employee relations. Rather, IBEC seeks to represent industry in all matters of economic and social policy. A major role of IBEC is to represent employers' interests to Government, other 'social partners' and the general public. It also provides employers' representatives for various national and international bodies. The organisational structure of the Irish Business and Employers' Confederation is outlined in figure 11.3.

Other Employers' Associations in Ireland

The *Construction Industry Federation* (CIF) is Ireland's second largest employers' association. Unlike IBEC, the CIF is essentially an industry-based association dealing with both trade and employee relations affairs on behalf of employers in the construction industry. According to 2000 figures, the CIF had a membership of over 3000 firms, and the Federation estimated that these accounted for approximately 75–80 per cent of the 175,000 workers employed in the construction industry. In the employee relations sphere, the main role of the CIF incorporates the negotiation of national registered agreements, representing members at conciliation and arbitration, and the provision of information and advice to member companies (Pollock and O'Dwyer 1985).

Most of the remaining employers' associations in Ireland are primarily concerned with trade and commercial issues. However, some also have a strong employee relations dimension. The *Irish Hotels' Federation* represents employers' interests on the Hotels Joint Labour Committee and Hotels (Dublin) Joint Labour Committee and provides general employee relations advice to members. However, it does not involve itself in local bargaining. The *Society of the Irish Motor Industry* provides advice and assistance on HRM and employee relations matters to affiliated members. The *Licensed Vintners' Association* represents Dublin-based publicans in negotiations on pay and working conditions with the Irish National Union for Vintners and Allied Trades Assistants. It also provides members with a HRM advisory service.

Other Groups of Employers

It is important to note that employers may establish and combine in less formal groupings for purposes associated with employee relations. Such groups are generally used by employers as a forum for the exchange of views and information on employee relations/HRM matters. They may also facilitate co-ordination of employers' approaches in dealing with particular employee relations issues. Such associations may be organised by industrial sector (e.g. the Electronics Sector) or region (e.g. the Limerick/Shannon Personnel Managers group) and may meet on either a semi-permanent basis or only when a significant issue arises. The Chartered Institute of Personnel and Development (CIPD) in Ireland, which is the major professional association for HRM practitioners, may also act as a forum for representing employers' interests in employee relations.

Figure 11.3 The Irish Business and Employers' Confederation: structure of organisation

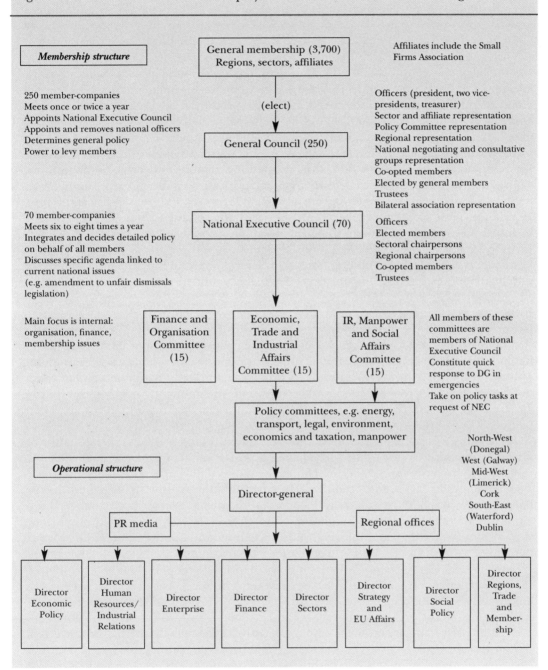

EMPLOYERS' ASSOCIATIONS' SERVICES

The earlier discussion alluded to the range of employee relations services provided by employers' associations in areas such as collective bargaining, research and advice. These services are discussed below.

Research and Advisory Services

In commenting on developments in Britain, Sisson (1983) found that the greatest area of growth in the work of employers' associations was in the provision of research and advisory services. Such services of employers' associations fall into three broad categories: (i) legal, (ii) pay and (iii) specialist consultancy. The growth of *labour legislation* in Ireland since the 1970s has led to a significant increase in employers' demands for specialist legal advice in areas such as dismissal, employment conditions and employment equality. Many larger employers' associations provide a specialist legal section to advise and assist member companies. They may also publish and disseminate guidelines on legislation for their membership. A more traditional service involves the provision of *information and advice* to members on wage rates and levels of wage increases. Many of them provide surveys of wage levels and fringe benefits for differing occupations, regions and size of organisation. Consequently they are able to provide members with up to date information on local, regional and national pay trends and advise such firms on reward issues. Some employers' associations also provide members with specialist advice and assistance. These might include issues such as performance management, productivity schemes and recruitment. In an Irish pilot study Butler (1985) found that advisory and consultancy services are seen by members as the most useful function of the associations and found that those dealing with legislation, pay and redundancy were most widely utilised.

Collective Bargaining

Historically, one of the most important services provided by employers' associations was that of assisting employers in collective bargaining with trade unions. Such bargaining might be of a multi-employer (regional, industry or national) or single employer nature. Multi-employer bargaining on an industry or, more commonly, national basis has traditionally meant a key role for employers' associations in conducting negotiations on pay and related matters on behalf of affiliated employers. In Ireland, they have been particularly prominent in periods of centralised pay bargaining.

IBEC plays a significant role in the Irish context, being the key representative of employers' opinions to the other 'social partners'. However, the Irish experience indicates that even where the locus of collective bargaining moves to the enterprise level, employers' associations still play an important role in advising and assisting management in the bargaining process. This role may incorporate co-ordination of policy on pay and employment related issues; formulating general guidelines for affiliated employers; supplying research data and information for use in negotiations and providing expert personnel to either conduct the negotiations or advise and assist local management (Gunnigle *et al.* 1999). Such involvement may comprise direct participation in employee relations negotiations, but would also cover research and specialist advisory services as well as assistance with the preparation of employment agreements, consultation on particular HRM issues and the provision of premises and facilities for consultation and negotiation.

A particularly important role for employers' associations in collective bargaining is that of *representing affiliated members* in face-to-face negotiations or during third party referrals. They may represent members in enterprise level negotiations with trade unions. They may also represent employers' interests in industry or national level bargaining. An increasingly significant aspect of this representational role applies to mediation and arbitration. Here, officials from employers' associations may represent affiliates in tribunal hearings, conciliation meetings and arbitration hearings such as the Labour Court, Labour Relations Commission or Employment Appeals Tribunal. The extent of such involvement is evident in the summary of IBEC involvement in conciliation, mediation and arbitration outlined in table 11.2.

Table 11.2 FIE/IBEC involvement in mediation, arbitration and negotiations								
	Cases per year							
	1986	*1987*	*1988*	*1989**	*1992**	*1995*	*1996*	*1997*
Labour Court Investigation	538	488	386	394	217	159	169	170
Labour Court/Labour Relations Commission Conciliation	1470	1146	874	1014	684	486	556	546
Employment Appeals Tribunal	396	190	n/a*	216	258	165	159	225
Rights Commissioner	586	429	n/a*	346	266	204	173	247
Equality Officer	28	35	n/a*	72	18	11	6	2
Consultation with Members	6400	6919	6726	5864	4804	4218	4048	3917
Trade Union Negotiations	2928	2842	2702	2540	1286	797	764	1040

(* some figures not available in IBEC annual reviews; 1990, 1991, 1993, 1994 and since 1997).

Source: IBEC Annual Reviews.

Education and Training

An increasingly important service provided by larger employers' associations relates to the provision of education and training programmes for affiliated members. Such provision is often aimed at keeping member firms *au fait* with current developments in employee relations such as employment law, working conditions and EU level matters. They may also focus on developing managerial capacity among members firms by providing training programmes for HRM practitioners in areas such as negotiating skills and employment legislation.

MEMBERSHIP OF EMPLOYERS' ASSOCIATIONS

In analysing the factors impacting on membership of employers' associations, Thomason (1984) notes the impact of *corporate form*. In particular, Thomason (1984) differentiates between entrepreneurs who essentially own and run their businesses and abstract corporate entities that are run by professional management. The corporate business firm has replaced the older entrepreneurial type firm as the prevalent type of organisation in membership of employers' associations. Thomason argues that the change in composition of membership from entrepreneurial owner-managers to corporate business firms run by professional management partly explains the changing role of employers' associations. There is also evidence that *country of ownership* may influence the membership of employers' associations. In Ireland a study of newly established companies in Ireland found that US-owned firms were less likely to join employers' associations than other foreign-owned companies (Gunnigle 1995). This may be related to the corporate approach to trade unions and collective bargaining. Where this involves a preference for non-union status, such organisations may be reluctant to join an employers' association (Purcell and Sisson 1983; Oechslin 1985).

The issue of *public sector organisations* becoming members of employers' associations is a relatively recent phenomenon. While initially it might seem incompatible for public sector organisations to join employers' associations (traditionally a bastion of free enterprise), many have adopted a pragmatic approach by utilising their services in certain areas (Oechslin 1985). In Ireland the Department of Finance and the Local Government Staff

Negotiations Board plays a role in assisting and advising management on employee relations issues in many parts of the public sector. However, some public sector organisations, and particularly those in the semi-state sector, have increasingly taken up membership.

It has also been argued that an *organisation's size* is an important factor impacting on membership and patterns of utilisation of employers' associations. It is sometimes suggested that small firms have more to gain by joining them for reasons related to cost and resource considerations (ILO 1975). When a small organisation becomes involved in formalised collective bargaining it may be particularly attractive to join an employers' association. A small organisation may not be in a position to employ HRM specialists; the owner or managers of such firms may not have either the necessary time or expertise to effectively handle such matters. Since the cost of joining such an association is generally related to size and/or profitability, it may be relatively inexpensive for small firms to join. However, despite the apparent validity of this line of argument there is no conclusive evidence to support the view that small firms are more likely to join employers' associations (Government Social Survey, UK 1968; Gunnigle 1995). In fact the research evidence indicates that employers' associations are not more frequently used by smaller organisations (Brown 1981; Daniel and Millward 1983). Indeed, it seems that larger firms are more likely to join and utilise the services of employers' associations and that membership is positively correlated with the organisation's size, trade union recognition, and the presence of specialist HR function.

Important influences on organisational decisions on whether or not to join employers' associations are the perceived advantages and disadvantages of such membership. Clearly such perceptions will be influenced by issues specific to the individual organisations such as management's desired approach to employee relations. Broader contextual and environmental factors such as industrial sector, size, product market performance and ownership will also be influential (Thomason 1984). Figure 11.4 summarises some of the generally perceived advantages and disadvantages of employer association membership. Clearly the relative significance of these will vary between organisations and across industrial sectors.

Figure 11.4 Advantages and disadvantages of membership of employers' associations

ADVANTAGES	DISADVANTAGES
• Collective approaches and uniform policy	• Cost of membership
• Advice on trade union matters	• Loss of autonomy
• Technical advice and information	• Loss of flexibility
• Skilled negotiators	• Comparisons with other firms
• Expert advisory and consultancy services	• Greater acceptance of role for trade unions
• Standardised pay and employment conditions	• Greater formalisation in employee relations
• On par with regional/industry norms	
• Assistance in employee relations difficulties	
• Influence on Government, national affairs	

Source: Gunnigle, McMahon and Fitzgerald (1999).

The range of employee relations services provided by employers' associations, considered in the preceding section, correlate closely with the perceived advantages of membership of employers' associations (as outlined in figure 11.4). It is therefore appropriate to consider here some reasons why organisations may choose not to join employers' associations. A common argument for not joining an employers' association is the potential reduction of *managerial autonomy* in decision-making. As in any formal association or club, employers' associations will be keen to ensure that members adhere to commonly agreed polices in areas such as pay and conditions of employment. These policies and related guidelines normally reflect the needs of the general membership. However, it is a decision for the individual organisation to assess whether such norms are appropriate to its particular needs.

The issue of *comparability with other firms* is also an important consideration. By joining an association comprised of numerous other companies, a particular firm's pay and conditions will be compared to that pertaining across the general membership. Trade unions often use the terms of collective agreements struck with some member firms as 'leverage' to secure similar terms with other member organisations. Another important consideration impacting on membership of employers' associations is the impact of a firm's desired *employee relations/HRM style*. As we have seen, the legal definition of employers' associations means that they are, in a legal context, trade unions of employers. Traditionally they have had a preference for dealing with their employee counterparts, trade unions, through collective bargaining. However, it is also clear that many firms now pursue employee relations 'styles' which seeks to avoid trade union recognition (Gunnigle and Brady 1984; McGovern 1989a; Gunnigle 1994). Some of these firms place a strong emphasis on dealing with employees on a more individual basis (Gunnigle, Morley and Turner 1997). For such firms, membership of an employers' association (i.e. a trade union of employers) would be totally incompatible with a management approach based on direct contact with the individual.

A more pragmatic reason for non-membership is related to the cost of membership. Normally firms pay the full *cost of membership* regardless of services used. This contrasts with the situation in relation to the use of management consultants where firms normally only pay a fee which is related to services used. Subscriptions to employers' associations are normally related to company size (number of employees). The following examples reflect the cost of membership for IBEC, the full list is shown in table 11.3: £1,712 (€2,173) (75 employees), £6,740 (€8,558) (300 employees), £16,532 (€20,991) (750 employees), £27,452 (€34,857) (1,500 employees).

Table 11.3 IBEC subscription rates in respect of employee relations services (2000)

First Year Minimum Payment	IR£650.00 (€825.00)
Minimum Subscription per Annum	IR£550.00 (€698.00)
and/or	
First 200 Employees	IR£22.82 (€28.98)
Next 800 Employees	IR£21.76 (€27.63)
Next 1000 Employees	IR£10.96 (€13.92)
Remaining Employees	IR£5.40 (€6.86)

MANAGEMENT APPROACHES TO EMPLOYEE RELATIONS

While employers' associations clearly play an important role in employee relations, individual employers are primarily responsible for the development and implementation of employee relations policies and practices within their individual organisations and workplaces. The remainder of this chapter addresses the role of management in enterprise level employee relations and reviews contemporary research on management approaches to employee relations.

Managerial Frames of Reference

In his seminal work, Fox (1968) argues that management approaches to employee relations are largely determined by the frame of reference adopted by managers. A frame of reference is defined by Thelen and Withall (1979) as 'the main selective influences at work as the perceiver supplements, omits and structures what he notices'. Fox suggests that a manager's frame of reference is important because:

1. it determines how management expects people to behave and how it thinks they should behave (i.e. values and beliefs);
2. it determines management reactions to actual behaviour (i.e. management practice); and
3. it shapes the methods management choose when it wishes to change the behaviour of people at work (e.g. strategies/policies).

Fox identified two alternative frames of reference to help evaluate management approaches to employee relations. These were termed (i) the *unitarist* and (ii) the *pluralist* frame of reference. The key features of these two approaches are summarised in figure 11.4.

Figure 11.5 Unitarist and pluralist frames of reference

Unitarist	Pluralist
Emphasises the dominance of common interests. Everyone – management and employees – should strive to achieve the organisation's primary business goals since everyone will benefit	The organisation is viewed as composed of different interest groups with different objectives but linked together instrumentally by their common association with the organisation
There is only one source of authority (management) and it must command full loyalty	Management's role is to achieve some equilibrium satisfying the various interest groups thus helping achieve the organisation's goals
Anyone who does not share these common interests and does not accept managerial authority is viewed as a dissenter/agitator	A certain amount of conflict is inevitable since the objectives of the parties will clash on occasion
Since dissenters endanger organisational success they must either fall into line, appreciate the overriding importance of corporate goals and accept managerial authority, or risk elimination from the organisation	Management must expect and plan for conflict so that it can be handled successfully and not endanger the achievement of the organisation's primary objectives
	Management should not seek to suppress conflicting interests, but rather aim to reconcile them in the organisation's interests.

Source: Fox (1968).

These contrasting frames of reference represent dominant employee relations orientations, which may be adopted by management. In practice one finds that managers do not strictly adhere to one of these approaches but may adopt different approaches in different situations and/or change their approaches over time. Nevertheless the frames of reference approach provides a useful framework for evaluating management approaches to employee relations at enterprise level. For example, Marchington's (1982) analysis considered how management approaches to employee relations might differ depending on the particular frame of reference adopted. In firstly evaluating management approaches to trade unions, Marchington argues that managers holding a unitary perspective, would see no role for trade unions. Such managers would see unions as 'encroaching on management's territory', making unreasonable demands, prohibiting change, flexibility, and, therefore, competitiveness (Gunnigle *et al.* 1999). As a consequence trade unions would be viewed as an externally imposed force which introduces conflict into the organisation and prohibits the development of 'good' employee relations. Furthermore, workers associated with the promotion of trade unionism would be seen as 'disloyal', 'agitators' or 'troublemakers'.

In contrast, managers adopting a pluralist perspective would see a legitimate role for trade unions in representing and articulating employees' views in the workplace. A second area where Marchington identified different approaches was in relation to managerial prerogative. Managerial prerogative refers to areas of decision-making where management see themselves as having sole decision-making authority. Marchington suggests that managers adopting a unitary frame of reference would be unwilling to accept any reduction of management prerogative as a result of trade union organisation. They would see management as the legitimate decision-making authority. On the other hand, managers adopting a pluralist frame of reference would acknowledge the legitimacy of other interest groups in the organisation, such as trade unions. They would also accept the need to allow trade unions a role in decision-making and consequently accept some reduction in managerial prerogative. The final area where management approaches may differ is in relation to industrial conflict. Marchington suggests that managers adopting a unitary frame of reference would view the enterprise very much along 'team'/'family' lines with everyone working together to achieve company objectives. In this context conflict is seen as something of an aberration, only occurring as a result of a breakdown of communications or the work of troublemakers. By contrast, managers adopting a pluralist frame of reference would accept that some degree of industrial conflict is inevitable because the interests of management and labour will clash on occasion. Since the pluralist perspective accepts the legitimacy of conflict, managers adopting this frame of reference will tend to plan for it by, for example, agreeing to grievance disputes and disciplinary procedures.

The Concept of Management Styles

Moving beyond Fox's unitarist-pluralist dichotomy, several commentators have attempted to develop categorisations of management styles in employee relations to explain differences in organisational approaches to employee relations. On of the most widely used management styles typologies is that of Purcell and Sisson (1983), who developed a five-fold categorisation of 'ideal-typical' styles of employee relations management. Their typology is outlined in figure 11.6 and was based on differing management approaches to trade unions, collective bargaining, consultation and communications.

Despite the apparent attractiveness of management style typologies, it appears that in reality it is difficult to categorise organisations into neat 'ideal-typical' groupings (Deaton 1985; Gunnigle 1995). Using data from some 1400 UK organisations Deaton (1985) sought to empirically evaluate the appropriateness of Purcell and Sisson's typology. He firstly attempted to classify management styles in unionised companies as either 'sophisticated' or 'standard modern'. However, Deaton found it difficult to distinguish between these two types of management styles, suggesting that it is rather tenuous to classify firms recognising

Figure 11.6 Management styles in employee relations

Management Style	Characteristics
Traditionalist	'Orthodox unitarism': oppose role for unions; little attention to employee needs
Sophisticated Paternalist	Emphasise employees' needs (training, pay, conditions etc.); discourage unionisation; demand and facilitate employee loyalty and commitment.
Sophisticated Modern	Accept trade unions' role in specific areas; emphasis on procedures and consultative mechanisms; Two variations: (i) Constitutionalists: emphasise codification of management–union relations through explicit collective agreements; (ii) Consultors: collective bargaining established but management emphasises personal contact and problem-solving, playing down formal union role at establishment level.
Standard Modern	Pragmatic approach: unions' role accepted but no overall philosophy or strategy developed; 'Fire-fighting'/reactive approach.

Source: Adapted from Purcell and Sisson (1983).

trade unions into either of these groupings. Deaton also attempted to categorise management styles in non-union companies into 'paternalist', 'anti-union', and 'sophisticated paternalists'. Here Deaton found greater evidence of organisations conforming to Purcell and Sisson's 'ideal-typical' style typologies. He found that 'sophisticated paternalists' and 'anti-union' organisations emerged as 'polar opposites' while 'paternalist' organisations took the middle ground (having some characteristics common to both 'anti-union' and 'sophisticated paternalist' organisations). Deaton concluded that attempts to classify firms into a small number of ideal styles were problematic and that, while the distinction between organisations which recognise trade unions and those which do not is crucial, it may not be possible to sub-divide styles further in organisations where unions are recognised. However, Deaton felt that there was a greater tendency in organisations that do not recognise trade unions to adopt the 'identikit' styles suggested above.

Using more anecdotal evidence to examine variations in managerial styles in employee relations, Poole (1986) suggested that the evidence points to the existence of 'a progressively rich array' of hybrid styles, rather than any convergence towards particular predominant styles or patterns.

INDIVIDUALISM AND COLLECTIVISM AS DIMENSIONS OF MANAGEMENT STYLES

More recent analyses of management styles in employee relations have tended to focus on key dimensions of management styles rather than 'ideal-typical' style categorisations. Purcell (1987) provides us with two widely accepted dimensions of management styles in employee relations, namely individualism and collectivism.

Collectivism in employee relations incorporates the extent to which management acknowledges the right of employees to collective representation and the involvement of the collective in influencing management decision-making (Purcell 1987; Sisson 1994;

Storey and Sisson 1994). This dimension addresses both the level of democratic employee representative structures and the extent to which management legitimise their representational and bargaining role. Thus conceived, the collectivist dimension spans a continuum from a unitarist perspective incorporating management opposition to employee representation, through a middle ground of adversarial or reluctant collectivism, to a co-operative perspective (Purcell 1987; Marchington and Parker 1990). Thus, high collectivism is manifested in the establishment recognition and incorporation of mechanisms for employee representation, particularly trade unions, as a vehicle in the conduct of establishment-level employee relations, while at the other extreme low collectivism is manifested in managerial opposition to collective employee representation (see figure 11.7).

Figure 11.7 Collectivism as a dimension of management styles in employee relations

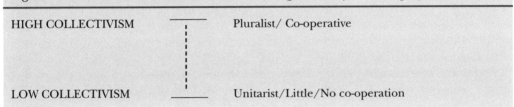

Source: Adapted from Purcell (1987).

Individualism as a dimension of management style in employee relations incorporates the degree to which management adopts an essentially individualist focus in employee relations management (Purcell and Gray, 1986; Purcell 1987; Marchington and Parker 1990). Purcell (1987, 536) describes individualism thus:

> . . . the extent to which the firm gives credence to the feelings and sentiments of each employee and seeks to develop and encourage each employee's capacity and role at work . . . Firms which have individualistically-centred policies are thus expected to emphasise employees as a resource and be concerned with developing each person's talents and worth.

Purcell argues that high individualism is characterised by managements recognising the resource value of employees and adopting comprehensive employee development policies. In contrast, low individualism conceives of employees in utility terms within the overriding goal of profit maximisation. Here the management emphasis is on tight management control, minimisation of labour costs and little concern for broader human resource issues such as job satisfaction, employment security or employee commitment (see figure 11.8).

Figure 11.8 Individualism as a dimension of management styles in employee relations

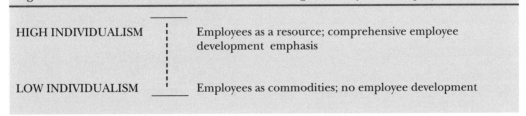

Source: Adapted from Purcell (1987).

The contemporary literature identifies an increased management emphasis on the development of an individualist orientation in management-employee interactions as a significant development in changing patterns of employee relations (Beaumont 1985, 1991; Beaumont and Townley 1985; Kochan *et al.* 1986; Guest 1989; Storey 1992; Bacon and Storey 1993). However, we have also seen earlier that high levels of collectivism, and specifically trade union recognition, membership and influence are integral to the traditional pluralist model, and are considered characteristic of employee relations in Ireland (Roche 1989, 1997b; Brewster and Hegewisch 1994; Roche and Turner 1994; Hillery 1994). Thus, findings on the levels of collectivism and individualism are seen as critical indicators of change in management styles in employee relations (Beaumont 1985).

The so called 'soft' HRM approach has been associated with a move from collectivism to individualism via sophisticated recruitment, rewards and employee development policies (Guest 1987, 1989). However, Purcell (1987) argues that individualism need not necessarily counterpoise collectivism, so that managements can develop policies to increase individualism whilst retaining established collectivist structures, including trade union recognition. Marchington and Parker (1990) suggest that this interpretation makes the dimensions of management style more 'dynamic', allowing organisations to alter their positions along these dimensions over time. In a study of recently established ('greenfield') companies in Ireland, Gunnigle *et al.* (1997) attempted to evaluate management approaches to employee relations on the dimensions of collectivism and individualism (see, for example, Gunnigle, Morley and Turner 1997; Gunnigle, Turner and D'Art 1998). To this end a number of indicators were developed to evaluate the relative management emphasis on individualism and collectivism. These indicators are summarised in figure 11.9.

Figure 11.9 Indicators of collectivism and individualism

MEASURES OF INDIVIDUALISM

1. *Sophistication of the employment and socialisation system:* measured through an evaluation of the degree of sophistication and relative emphasis on individualism in the management of human resource 'flows'.
2. *Communications:* based on an analysis of the level, nature and sophistication of management-employee communications.
3. *Performance-related pay:* measured through an analysis of the incidence of performance-related pay systems and the utilisation of formal performance appraisals to aid performance-related pay decisions among manual/operative grades.
4. *Employee involvement:* measured through an analysis of the extent to which management utilises explicit techniques to facilitate employee involvement in decision-making.
5. *Employee autonomy:* measured through an analysis of the extent to which management seek to facilitate/promote employee autonomy.

MEASURES OF COLLECTIVISM

1. *Trade union presence:* measured through an analysis of levels of trade union recognition and trade union density.
2. *Pattern of trade union organisation:* measured though an examination of the nature of trade union recognition and impact of trade unions on workplace employee relations
3. *Role of trade unions and other employee representative bodies:* measured though an examination of role of trade unions and other employee representative bodies in management-employee communications/interactions
4. *Employers' association membership and utilisation:* measured through an examination of the extent to which greenfield companies are in membership of employers' associations and of the patterns of utilisation of employer association services.

These measures were used to evaluate management styles in a number of Irish organisations on the dimensions of collectivism and individualism. While the findings only apply to recently established firms, they provide some interesting insights into management approaches to employee relations in Ireland (Gunnigle 1995; Gunnigle, Morley and Turner 1997).

Probably the most significant finding of the greenfield-site study was the powerful evidence of changing management approaches to collectivism as a means of managing workplace employee relations. Such a trend was evidenced by policies designed to mitigate attempts to achieve trade union recognition or, where unions are recognised, to prescribe tightly their role in workplace employee relations. As noted in the preceding chapter, this evidence points to a severe erosion in levels of trade union recognition and density in newly established firms. While it might be argued that this differential may be explained by the relative immaturity of greenfield companies, it is important to note that pre-production closed-shop agreements have traditionally characterised large industrial start-ups in Ireland (see, for example, O'Hara 1981; Murray 1984; McGovern 1989). It appears that this is no longer the case and that greenfield companies are increasingly and consciously choosing the non-union alternative rather than pre-production agreements. The trend emerging in greenfield sites indicates a shift from collectivism to individualism. While this development does not mean that collectivist structures are abandoned, it does appear that the strong collectivist traditions characteristic of Irish employee relations are being diluted.

The second critical characteristic of emergent patterns of employee relations management was a greater emphasis on individualist approaches to employee relations. This study found that the most significant indicators of high levels of individualism were performance-based pay systems tied to individual employee appraisals and greater direct communications with employees. An increased management focus on more extensive and direct communications with individual employees was an important feature of employee relations management in many of the companies studied, and predominantly so among the non-union companies. In particular, many companies put an especially strong emphasis on communicating information on company performance to employees. In many of these companies, such information was used to emphasise issues such as market volatility, intensity of competition and requirements for high-quality and low-cost production and service. However, it appears that the rationale for such communications was largely based on utilitarian objectives of facilitating improved employee performance and flexibility, rather than on more altruistic motives such as enhanced employee involvement.

The other critical indicator of individualism identified in the greenfield study was the extent of utilisation of performance-related pay (PRP) systems based on formal appraisals of individual employee performance (Gunnigle 1995; Gunnigle, Turner and D'Art 1998). This study found significant differences between greenfield and longer established ('brownfield') companies in the extent of utilisation of PRP systems based on formal appraisals among non-managerial/white-collar grades. The role of appraisal in aiding PRP decisions among non-managerial and white-collar grades is a crucial differentiating factor since the use of more 'traditional' PRP systems among manual grades is nothing new (Clegg 1979; Mooney 1980).

However, such PRP systems (e.g. measured day work) were based on quantitative evaluations of employee performance and were normally the subject of collective bargaining. As such, quantitative PRP systems were very much integral to the collectivist tradition of Irish employee relations (Mooney 1980; Grafton 1988; Armstrong and Murlis 1994).

By contrast, performance appraisal is essentially an individualist management tool (Beer *et al.* 1984). By linking performance appraisals to incremental pay decisions, managements in greenfield sites are posing a challenge to collectivism in employee relations. The collectivist tradition implies that incremental pay decisions are achieved through collective bargaining and, once agreed, apply 'across the board' to all relevant employee categories. In contrast, PRP decisions based on performance appraisal are normally the subject of a management review of individual employee performance. Consequently, incremental pay decisions are made by management rather than through collective bargaining and vary according to individual appraisals rather than applying equally to all through a collective agreement. Thus, individualism replaces collectivism at two critical phases: (i) the process of appraisal is individualist rather than collectivist (individual appraisal rather than collective bargaining); and (ii) the outcome takes the form of varying PRP decisions among individual employees rather than a fixed amount which applies equally to all employees.

Some commentators have suggested that PRP does not necessarily have negative implications for collectivism, and specifically trade unions (Heery 1992). This argument is based on evidence that PRP systems may co-exist alongside collective bargaining on pay (Casey *et al.* 1992). The evidence from Irish greenfield sites does not support this argument. In these companies, individualism tends to counterpoise collectivism. Furthermore, the strongest component of individualism in greenfield sites is the use of PRP systems based on individual performance appraisals among non-managerial and white-collar grades. The evidence on greenfield sites identifies company ownership and trade union recognition as the major factor impacting on the adoption of PRP systems based on individual performance appraisals. Such systems were predominantly used in non-union and US-owned companies and were largely absent in unionised companies. As mentioned above, these findings indicate that individualism tends to counterpoise rather than complement collectivism in terms of management styles in employee relations.

Another indicator of increased individualism identified in the literature is the adoption of sophisticated and highly individualist employment systems to effectively manage 'human resource flows', particularly in the areas of selection and employee development (Foulkes 1980; Beer *et al.* 1984). A further important indicator of high individualism in the extant literature is the incidence of extensive mechanisms to facilitate employee autonomy and involvement (Lawler 1978, 1982; Beer *et al.* 1984). It was interesting that Gunnigle's study of Irish greenfield companies did not find widespread evidence of sophisticated employment systems or mechanisms to facilitate employee involvement or autonomy in the majority of greenfield companies studied (Gunnigle 1995).

In considering these results it can be argued that while individualism appeared to be an important and significant management strategy in employee relations in greenfield companies, this did not necessarily imply that managements in greenfield companies adopt a 'resource perspective' of employees (Purcell 1987). This Irish study found little evidence of a shift from a utility perspective to a resource perspective in greenfield companies. The aggregate evidence suggests that, while there is a greater emphasis on individualism in greenfield companies than has traditionally been the case with longer established companies, this does not equate to high levels of individualism. Rather it appears that managements in greenfield sites are adopting more individualist approaches in selected aspects of employee relations but are not moving towards a wholly individualist approach equating to the 'soft' HRM model (Beer *et al.* 1984; Guest 1989; Storey 1989).

This chapter has reviewed employers' organisations and approaches to employee relations. It has placed particular emphasis on the role of employers' associations in Ireland. The chapter also considered the issue of management styles in employee relations and reviewed some recent research evidence on developments in management styles in employee relations. The next chapter focuses more specifically on employee relations practice at the level of the workplace.

12

Employee Relations Practice

This chapter considers key aspects of employee relations practice. Particular emphasis is placed on those employee relations activities undertaken at enterprise level such as collective bargaining, grievance handling, discipline administration and employee participation.

COLLECTIVE BARGAINING

We have seen that employee relations is primarily concerned with how issues such as pay, conditions of employment, workplace relations, workplace rules and other such issues are dealt with by employers and employees. In chapter ten we noted that a key institution of employee relations is collective bargaining, whereby pay, conditions of employment, and other employment-related issues are regulated between organised employees and management. Collective bargaining thus represents a mechanism through which divergent employer and worker interests may be reconciled through an orderly process involving negotiation and compromise. A key feature of collective bargaining is that employees do not negotiate with employers on their own behalf, but do so collectively through representatives (normally trade unions, but also through staff associations or employee councils/committees). As noted earlier, some necessary conditions must therefore be fulfilled for collective bargaining to function effectively.

1. Employees must have the freedom to associate, enabling workers to join together in trade unions or other associations which are not in any way under the control or influence of employers.
2. Employers must be prepared to recognise such trade unions and associations and accept the constraints placed upon their ability to deal with employees on an individual basis.

We have also noted that collective bargaining is not the only method of regulating employment matters. Even in countries where it is widely used, such as Ireland, it usually operates alongside other mechanisms such as individual bargaining between employer and employees, regulation by the Government (legislation), the unilateral imposition of terms of employment by management or similarly the imposition of terms unilaterally by trade unions. While such methods can represent alternatives to collective bargaining, there is a traditional and widely held view that collective bargaining is the most satisfactory way for employers and employees to regulate conditions of employment (see for example Donovan 1968; ILO 1975). The International Labour Organisation (ILO) has long argued that collective bargaining offers a number of advantages which make it the most appropriate method of regulating labour issues and which explain its widespread application. Some such advantages of collective bargaining include the following:

1. It is seen as more flexible than other methods (e.g. statutory control).
2. It helps redresses the disparity in bargaining power between the individual employee and his/her employer.
3. It allows workers an opportunity to participate in decisions on the conditions of employment under which they operate.
4. It provides an orderly mechanism for identifying and handling grievances and differences of opinions through negotiation aimed at securing eventual agreement.

The normal end product of the collective bargaining process is a collective agreement. However, this objective does not preclude bargaining situations which may break down and result in a strike or other forms of industrial action, provided of course there was a genuine attempt to reach agreement.

Collective agreements are frequently regarded as covering two different kinds of arrangements, namely those that deal with substantive issues and those that are procedural in nature. The scope of substantive agreements will obviously vary widely from company to company, but substantive terms incorporate the 'hard' terms of collective agreements, such as those dealing with levels of wage increases, hours of work and holidays. In contrast, procedural issues are concerned with the ways (procedures) in which terms and conditions of employment are arrived at and how differences over the application of agreed terms and conditions are settled. Such procedural arrangements normally prescribe how wage claims, disciplinary issues, grievances, disputes and related matters are to be processed or handled by the parties.

Levels of Collective Bargaining

We have seen that collective bargaining requires collective action on the part of employees. However, employers may engage in collective bargaining on an individual basis or collectively through, for example, employers' associations. Thus, trade unions or other representative employee bodies may bargain with one employer, a group of employers or with representatives of employers' associations. As a consequence the *locus* of collective bargaining may vary between organisations and over time. It can occur at a multi-employer or single-employer level (see discussion on levels of collective bargaining in chapter ten, especially figure 10.2).

Multi-employer bargaining normally involves the representation of employers' interests by employers' associations and may take place at national, regional or industry level. *Single-employer bargaining* can also take place at a number of levels depending on the structure of the organisation. A particular organisation may be involved in bargaining at establishment level, (largely referred to as workplace bargaining) and at a multi-establishment level (if the organisation is a multi-site operation). In addition collective bargaining at the level of the single employer might involve negotiations either with an individual union or in a multi-union environment with representatives from a group of unions.

In Ireland we have seen that the primary locus of collective bargaining in recent years has been at a national level involving negotiations between representatives of trade union interests (Irish Congress of Trade Unions) and employers' interests (representatives of employers' associations). Such national level bargaining normally operates alongside supplementary workplace level bargaining on company level issues, such as work practices and productivity. Several commentators have noted the pros and cons of bargaining on either a single- or multi-employer basis. For example, it is suggested that employers may prefer multi-employer bargaining because it removes the need to deal with annual wage negotiations at company level and leaves the management team free to devote their time to other aspects of organisational management. It is also suggested that the standardisation of pay levels and working conditions helps to avoid wage competition between employers, regulating an important aspect of the competitive market. It has also been suggested that organisations in comfortable trading positions may see multi-employer bargaining as a relatively painless way of dealing with employee relations. On the other hand, multi-employer bargaining may have disadvantages for employers. For example, bargaining on a single-employer (individual) basis may allow management greater scope to ensure that wage levels and other conditions of employment more closely reflect their competitive position. This may be achieved by linking concessions on wage levels and working conditions to union and worker commitments to increase productivity, or contribute to other cost reductions in a way that may be more difficult to achieve through multi-employer bargaining.

Collective Bargaining in Ireland

In Ireland the scope of collective bargaining is extensive with the terms of collective agreements becoming implied terms of the individual employee's contract of employment. In chapter ten we saw that collective bargaining has traditionally been the major activity area for HRM practitioners and a major consideration for larger Irish organisations (Shivanath 1987). We further noted that the Irish system of collective bargaining is grounded in voluntary principles, relying on the moral commitment of the participants to adhere to agreements achieved through the bargaining process. A key characteristic of collective bargaining in Ireland over recent decades is a tendency towards high levels of centralisation in the level of bargaining.

As noted earlier, centralised bargaining essentially describes institutionalised negotiations between representatives of trade union confederations (in Ireland the ICTU) and employers' associations (in Ireland primarily IBEC) about wages and other issues. Although the first attempts at centralised pay bargaining took place in 1948 and led to a series of 'wage rounds', it was not until the 1970s that the first (of seven) National Wage Agreements were negotiated. In addition to dealing with basic wage increases these national agreements included arrangements for moving towards equal pay for equal work, for special anomaly claims, for incentive schemes and productivity bargaining and for procedures for resolving disputes.

These early national agreements did not encompass direct Government involvement as a separate party to the negotiations. (However, the Government was involved in its role as an employer). Towards the end of the 1970s, as it became clear that national pay bargaining was closely linked to Government's economic and social policy, the Government became directly involved in negotiations on national agreements in its own right and not simply as an employer. The result was the more ambitious *National Understandings*, of which two were negotiated in 1979 and 1980. These National Understandings embraced policies not just on employment and pay, but also issues such as taxation, education, health and social welfare.

The sequence of centralised agreements ceased at the expiry of the second National Understanding in 1982. The period from 1982 to 1987 witnessed a short period of decentralised bargaining. During this period it appeared that viability and economic performance became a key criterion in shaping levels of wage increases. Settlement levels varied widely between industries and industry sectors, with little convergence towards a wage round norm (see McGinley 1989a and b). The Government at times sought to impose a norm through pay guidelines but these were largely ignored by private sector negotiators and, as Von Prondzynski (1985) argues, were best seen as the Government's opening position in public sector pay negotiations. A notable feature of this period was the reduction over the rounds in the number and range of supplementary cost-increasing claims. Irish wage costs rose by only 7 per cent between 1980 and 1985, compared to an average of 37 per cent in competing countries (Hardiman 1988).

The major factor contributing to a return to centralised bargaining in 1987 was, undoubtedly, the growing crisis in the public finances. The national debt represented 148 per cent of GNP in 1986, while unemployment had risen dramatically and contributed to an apparently disastrous economic outlook. A critical Government concern was the need to control the public sector pay bill. The newly elected Government led by Fianna Fáil announced a number of measures to improve the public finances, including restrictive measures in relation to public sector pay. The Government also indicated its interest in attaining a three-year pay agreement. The ICTU and some prominent union leaders also indicated interest in discussing a national plan for growth and economic recovery. Negotiations for a new agreement eventually concluded towards the end of 1987, with the conclusion of the terms of the Programme for National Recovery (1987–91). Since then, four further such agreements were negotiated, the Programme for Social and Economic Progress (1991–4), the Programme for Competitiveness and Work (1994–7), Partnership 2000 for Inclusion, Employment and Competitiveness (1997–2000) and the Programme for Prosperity and Fairness (2000–03).

A summary of the sequence of centralised wage agreements in Ireland since 1970 is outlined in table 12.1, while table 12.2 summarises the detailed provisions of the most recent Programme for Prosperity and Fairness. The pay terms of this programme were renegotiated in December 2000 due to greater trade union demands as inflation rates escalated after the initial conclusion of the agreement.

Table 12.1 Centralised wage agreements 1970–2003

Seven National Wage Agreements 1970–78

1st National Wage Agreement	1970
2nd National Wage Agreement	1972
3rd National Wage Agreement	1974
4th National Wage Agreement	1975
5th National Wage Agreement	1976
6th National Wage Agreement	1977
7th National Wage Agreement	1978

Two National Understandings 1979 and 1980

1st National Understanding	1979
2nd National Understanding	1980

Programme for National Recovery (PNR)	1987–90
Programme for Economic and Social Progress (PESP)	1991–94
Programme for Competitiveness and Work (PCW)	1994–97
Partnership 2000	1997–2000
Programme for Prosperity and Fairness	2000–2003

N.B. No centralised agreements in period 1982–87.

Table 12.2 Pay terms of the Programme for Prosperity and Fairness, including renegotiated terms

Category	Phase 1 (first 12 months)	Phase 2 (second 12 months)	Phase 3 (next 9 months)	Total
Private Sector	5.5% of basic pay	7.5% of basic pay	4% of basic pay plus 1% lump sum, April 2002	Increase of 17% in basic pay over 2 years and 9 months plus 1% lump sum
Public Service	5.5% of basic pay	7.5% of basic pay	4% of basic pay dependent on specific performance indicators plus 1% lump sum, April 2002	Increase of 17% in basic pay over 2 years and 9 months plus 1% lump sum

N.B. According to the original terms of the PPF, the increases in basic pay for full-time employees must not be less than £12 (€15.24) per week in the first phase; £11 (€13.97) per week in the second phase and £9 (€11.43) per week in the third phase.

NEGOTIATING IN EMPLOYEE RELATIONS

The fundamental constituent of collective bargaining is the negotiations process. Negotiations in employee relations involve discussions and interactions between representatives of employers and employees over some divisive issues with the objective of reaching agreement. Walton and McKersie (1965) identified two dominant forms that negotiations tend to take. Negotiations between unions and management over pay and conditions of employment are normally termed 'distributive bargaining' since they involve bargaining or haggling over issues where a favourable settlement for one party means an element of loss for the other. This 'win-lose' approach represents an adversarial model of collective bargaining, where each party pursues its own specific objectives and hopes to concede minimal concessions to the other party. It is most obvious in pay negotiations where concessions by management inevitably represent both a quantifiable cost and a reduction in profits/dividends. On the other hand negotiations can have a joint problem-solving approach, sometimes referred to as 'integrative' or 'co-operative' bargaining, where both parties are concerned with finding a jointly acceptable solution resulting in benefits for both sides (often referred to as a 'win-win' approach). Inevitably, employee relations negotiations will involve some combination of both approaches.

Phases in the Negotiations Process

Formal employee relations negotiations normally involve one party submitting a claim to the other party and subsequently entering discussions on this claim or issue. Subsequent interactions generally involve the various parties bargaining and haggling over the divisive issues and reporting back to their respective constituents. Such negotiations may conclude either by reaching a mutually acceptable agreement on the issues raised or, possibly, failure to agree resulting in a breakdown of negotiations. Such an impasse may be addressed through further discussion, use of third party mediation or the use of sanctions, such as industrial action. Whether or not the negotiating process reaches a successful conclusion depends on a number of factors. Most importantly, such issues like the willingness to compromise, the bargaining skills of both sides (including their persuasive abilities) and ultimately, the power balance between parties will all have some impact on the final outcome of the negotiation (Hawkins 1979).

It is important to note that negotiating is an ongoing process not limited to one particular issue or time. All parties will generally be concerned with the establishment of enduring and stable relations. The long-term relationship between both parties is often treated as more important than the particular issue upon which a single negotiating process is focused. Frequently, the maintenance of this relationship takes precedence over achieving a short-term 'victory' (Gunnigle *et al.* 1999).

It should be noted that employee relations negotiations may also occur at a more informal level involving line management and employees and/or their representatives. Such negotiations normally involve more minor and/or individual issues such as employees' grievances or minor disciplinary issues. The negotiating process itself will generally follow a number of predictable phases. These may be categorised as (i) preparation for negotiations, (ii) bargaining and (iii) follow-up action as outlined in figure 12.1.

Figure 12.1 Phases in the negotiations process

PHASE	ACTIVITIES
1. PREPARATION	Agree objectives and mandate
	Assess relative bargaining power
	Conduct relevant research
	Choose negotiating team/develop skills
	Make appropriate administrative arrangements
2. BARGAINING	Discover positions
	Expectation structuring
	Compromise and movement
3. POST-NEGOTIATION	Document agreement/disagreement
	Clarify
	Agree action plans
	Communicate
	Review

Source: Gunnigle *et al.* (1999).

PREPARATION

As with all types of managerial activity, careful preparation is an important prerequisite for success in employee relations negotiations. Such preparation requires that negotiators be familiar with the details of the case and have a clear idea of their objectives and mandate before entering the bargaining arena, i.e. negotiators should clarify what they want to achieve from the collective bargaining process in general, and each set of negotiations in particular. Particular objectives vary according to the issue at hand and should involve specific targets, trade-off options, and resistance points. Flexible objectives are generally more appropriate than rigid ones, since information may be uncovered during negotiations that can alter the substance of the management's case. It is important that each party's objectives are clearly articulated and approved by constituents, particularly top management on the managerial side and trade union members or representatives on the union side (Gunnigle *et al.* 1999).

A central issue in agreeing negotiating objectives involves establishing a bargaining range, including the limits within which each party is prepared to reach agreement. In practice this often means establishing an ideal settlement point, a realistic settlement point and a fall-back position, beyond which a party is not prepared to enter agreement. These various positions are illustrated in figure 12.2 in the context of hypothetical negotiations between a trade union and employer on wage increases. Here the process of establishing bargaining parameters facilitates the identification of bargaining objectives, deciding on trade-offs and concessions and provides a benchmark against which to evaluate progress. In this it is clear that agreement between the management and trade union teams is only possible where resistance points (fall-back positions) overlap, that is in the 2–4 per cent pay range. A settlement is not possible outside this range unless one of the parties alters its position. If this does not happen then the parties are in conflict over the issue and industrial action may be used to help resolve this impasse.

Figure 12.2 Management-trade union bargaining range (example of pay negotiations)

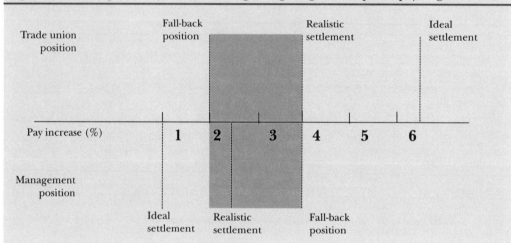

Source: Gunnigle, Garavan, and Fitzgerald (1992).

An important aspect of effective preparations for employee relations negotiations is adequate research. This helps focus negotiations on facts rather than discussing opinions or value judgements (Fisher and Ury 1986). Preparatory research might also incorporate an evaluation of the repercussions of likely settlement options and 'knock-on' effects of different potential outcomes of negotiations, including industrial action. Effective preparation also involves ensuring that appropriate administrative arrangements are made in relation to timing, location and support facilities. The size and composition of the negotiating team largely depends on the issue for negotiation. It is generally suggested that, with the exception of quite minor issues, a negotiating team should comprise of a minimum of two people to facilitate case presentation, record keeping and evaluation of progress (Nierenberg 1968). In larger organisations the HR manager will normally represent management in employee relations negotiations. However, line managers may often handle more minor issues or assist the HR manager during major negotiations.

BARGAINING

Figure 12.3 outlines the typical phases involved in the actual bargaining process: (i) opening, (ii) expectation structuring, (iii) offer, concession, movement, (iv) agreement/disagreement and (v) close.

Figure 12.3 Stages in the bargaining process

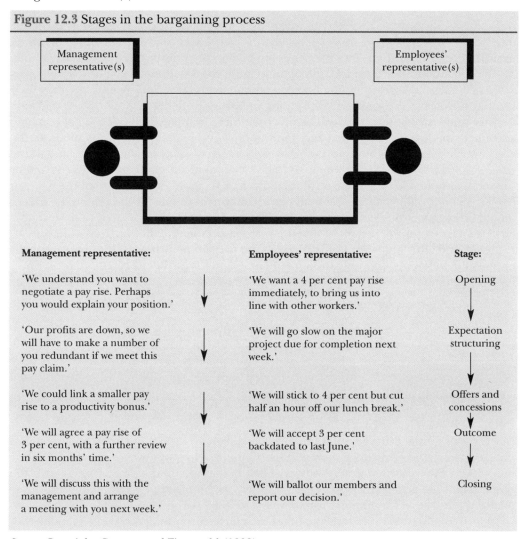

Management representative:		Employees' representative:	Stage:
'We understand you want to negotiate a pay rise. Perhaps you would explain your position.'	↓	'We want a 4 per cent pay rise immediately, to bring us into line with other workers.'	Opening
'Our profits are down, so we will have to make a number of you redundant if we meet this pay claim.'	↓	'We will go slow on the major project due for completion next week.'	Expectation structuring
'We could link a smaller pay rise to a productivity bonus.'	↓	'We will stick to 4 per cent but cut half an hour off our lunch break.'	Offers and concessions
'We will agree a pay rise of 3 per cent, with a further review in six months' time.'	↓	'We will accept 3 per cent backdated to last June.'	Outcome
'We will discuss this with the management and arrange a meeting with you next week.'	↓	'We will ballot our members and report our decision.'	Closing

Source: Gunnigle, Garavan and Fitzgerald (1992).

The opening phase normally involves both parties articulating their respective positions. At this stage both parties normally attempt to find out more about each other's positions and assess the degree to which movement and concession is possible. The next phase of bargaining often involves what is termed 'expectation structuring', where each party attempts to convince the other of the logic of their position and their depth of commitment to that position.

The parties may also highlight what are seen as deficiencies in the other party's position. Each party to the negotiations thus attempts to structure or influence the other party's expectations and tries to convince them to accept whatever concessions are offered. For example, during pay negotiations employers often refer to factors such as increased competition, or the need for re-investment, in an attempt to reduce employee or union expectations. The 'offer, concession, movement' phase generally follows the process of expectation structuring. This stage involves some initial offers and concessions by either party. This is a crucial phase in the overall negotiating process. It is felt that correct timing is absolutely crucial in making offers or concessions and it is normally advisable to take some time before making any major concessions. If such concessions are made too early in negotiations the other party may press for even greater ones during subsequent bargaining. Any movement or offer from a team's opening position should be carefully weighed up in terms of its long- and short-term implications. During this phase adjournments are often used to allow the parties to evaluate their options and progress to date.

After some time both parties will be in a position to evaluate the likelihood of reaching agreement or, possibly, the extent and implications of a breakdown in negotiations. In the event of a breakdown, it is important that neither party walks away from the bargaining table without at least some agreement as to how communication will be re-initiated and by whom. Again, the idea that long-term relations may be more important than the issues at hand is an important principle for both parties to keep in mind. For this reason the parties should be keen to avoid damaging conflict or breakdowns and be prepared to compromise on certain issues for the benefit of that longer-term perspective. Both parties will normally recognise and anticipate the closing phase in the bargaining process. This phase normally involves the following: finalising the agreement, issues for further negotiation, procedures for interpretation of the agreement or details of breakdown.

POST-NEGOTIATION PHASE

At the end of the actual negotiations, the parties involved will usually report back on the outcome, the employee or union side reporting back to the workers they represent and the management team reporting back to senior and, possibly, line management. This post-negotiation phase normally involves reviewing the implementation of any agreement reached and, possibly, a general evaluation of the implications of the negotiations and agreement.

INDUSTRIAL CONFLICT

Given the potential differences of interest, which can arise on employment matters, it is not surprising that some degree of conflict is inherent in employee relations. There are numerous explanations as to why industrial conflict occurs. In the preceding chapter, the pluralist and unitarist frameworks were posited as useful models for explaining employee relations interactions and industrial conflict (Fox 1968, 1974; Marchington 1982).

In the pluralist framework, organisations are seen as comprising of a range of individuals and groups with different interests and priorities. It suggests that the interaction of these competing interests and groups necessitates the development of institutional arrangements, which help manage these competing interests and achieve a level of bargained compromise that allows the organisation to conduct its normal business. Thus, the pluralist framework accepts that conflict in organisations is inevitable because the needs and objectives of various interest groups will clash on occasion.

The unitarist framework provides a different explanation for industrial conflict. The unitarist approach is based on the premise that organisations are essentially cohesive and harmonious units and that all members of the organisation (management and employees) should share common goals. Within the unitarist framework there is only one source of authority, namely management (Fox 1968, 1974; Marchington 1982). Management and employees are seen as having the same interests with conflict occurring only as a result of misunderstandings or due to the efforts of troublemakers. Thus, within the unitarist model industrial conflict is not seen as inevitable and consequently, there is no perceived need for institutional arrangements to deal with conflict.

In practice it would seem that some degree of conflict is inherent in employee relations and that differences will arise between management and workers. These differences are not necessarily harmful and need not necessarily lead to industrial conflict. In some instances such conflicts can have decidedly positive effects by, for example, leading to positive changes in management practice.

Industrial conflict is normally categorised into two broad forms: (i) explicit and organised industrial conflict, and (ii) unorganised and more implicit industrial conflict (Bean 1976). Explicit, overt forms of industrial conflict represent organised and systematic responses and include strikes, go-slows and overtime bans. Implicit reactions include absenteeism, labour turnover, and poor performance and may often reflect low levels of employee satisfaction and morale.

Strike Activity in Ireland

The most visible way in which workers can demonstrate industrial conflict is to go on strike. Strike action can take different forms and arise for a variety of reasons. 'Official' strikes are defined as those that have been fully sanctioned by the union executive. Such strikes normally occur after negotiations have failed to resolve the issue and when all due procedures have been exhausted (Gunnigle *et al.* 1995). In contrast, 'unofficial' strikes are those which have not been sanctioned by the trade union. Such strikes tend to be quite reactive in nature and are often sparked off by a particular event or incident at workplace level, such as the dismissal or suspension of a worker. Unless subsequently granted official approval by the trade union, unofficial strikes normally last for a shorter time and involve fewer workers than official strikes (Wallace and O'Shea 1987; Wallace 1988a and b).

Three key measures are normally used in evaluating the extent of strike activity: (i) strike frequency (number of strikes), (ii) workers involved (number of workers participating in strikes) and (iii) working days lost (number of working days lost due to strike activity). Using these indicators, the pattern of strike activity in Ireland over the period 1922–2000 is summarised in figures 12.4, 5 and 6 and table 12.3. This outline of strike activity in Ireland is based on data from University College Dublin (see, for example, Kelly and Brannick 1983, 1986, 1989a; Brannick and Doyle 1994), the Department of Enterprise and Employment and the Central Statistics Office. This evidence indicates a clear upward trend in strike activity in Ireland during the 1960s and 1970s, followed by a significant decline in strike activity for much of the 1980s and 1990s.

In evaluating the pattern of strike activity in Ireland, Kelly and Brannick (1983) identify two key trends: (i) the disproportionate effect of a few large strikes on Irish strike statistics, and (ii) the different patterns of strike activity between the public and private sectors. In relation to the former, Kelly and Brannick note that over the period 1960–79, forty-three strikes (2 per cent of total strikes in the period) accounted for 57 per cent of all days lost due strike activity and comment thus:

> Clearly, the Irish strike pattern is extremely sensitive to this comparatively small number of large strikes and it has been an enduring feature over the 20 year period. Indeed should these be removed from the Irish strike quantum the result would be a record which would show a comparatively strike-free nation in terms of workers involved and total man-days lost.

Figure 12.4 Strike activities in Ireland: strike frequency, 1922–2000

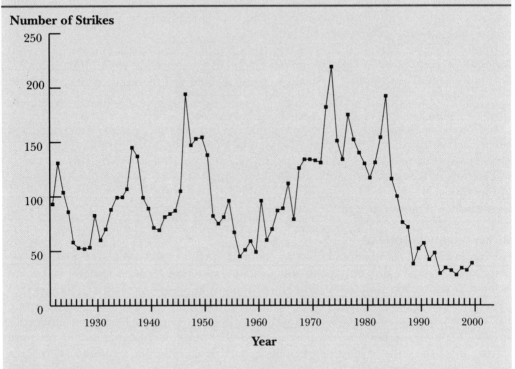

Figure 12.5 Strike activities in Ireland: workers involved, 1922–2000

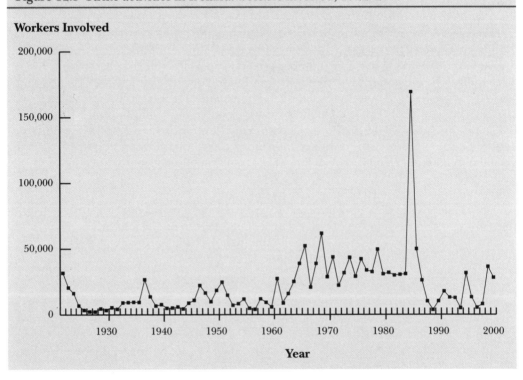

Figure 12.6 Strike activities in Ireland: working days lost, 1922–2000

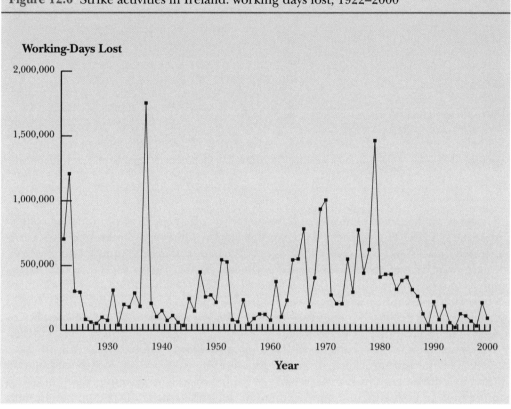

In evaluating patterns of strike activity in the public and private sectors, Kelly and Brannick found that the private sector was the most strike prone sector in the period 1960–86. However, their study indicated that the proportion of strike activity accounted for by the private sector was greatest during the 1960s but has been declining since then. This development has paralleled a marked increase in the proportion of strike activity accounted for by the public sector over the period 1970–89. While the public sector accounted for an increased proportion of strike frequency in the years 1990–98, its share of working days lost fell in the same period (see figure 12.6). In the public sector Kelly and Brannick found that much of the strike activity has been concentrated among a relatively small number of organisations. They identified nine organisations, which accounted for 62 per cent of all strikes, 85 per cent of workers involved and 86 per cent of man-days lost in the public sector during the 1960–84 period.

A number of critical factors which impact on the level and pattern of strike activity have been identified such as the level of economic activity (business cycle), unemployment (tightness/looseness of the labour market), industrial development, inflation (earnings), and unionisation (Brannick and Doyle 1994). In the Irish context, the decline in strike activity during the 1980s is generally explained in terms of the deep recession and rising unemployment (Gunnigle *et al.* 1995).

Table 12.3 Strike activity in the public and private sectors (in per cent)

	Strike frequency		Workers involved		Working days lost	
	Public sector	Private sector	Public sector	Private sector	Public sector	Private sector
1960–69	17.9	82.1	36.5	63.5	24.2	75.8
1970–79	18.3	81.7	22.6	67.4	37.9	62.1
1980–89	29.1	70.9	68.9	31.1	37.7	62.3
1990–98	44.1	55.9			25.3	74.7

Source: 1960–89 data from Brannick and Doyle (1994); 1990–8 data derived from Central Statistics Office.

However, management strategies and practice also influences levels of industrial conflict and strike activity. The impact of a range of factors which may influence patterns is illustrated in Kelly and Brannick's analysis of strike patterns among multinational (MNC) companies in Ireland (Kelly and Brannick 1988a, b and c, 1989b, 1991). In comparing patterns of strike activity in British and US-owned MNCs, Kelly and Brannick found that US companies were the most strike prone during the 1960s. However, levels of strike activity in US companies declined dramatically from the 1970s to a stage where US-owned MNCs now have a low incidence of strike activity.

In contrast, the strike record of British companies deteriorated dramatically over the period. Kelly and Brannick attribute the increase in strike activity to product market difficulties encountered by British-owned companies in Ireland resulting from increased competition. In evaluating the improvement of the strike record of US companies, Kelly and Brannick offer two reasons.

1. The changed industrial composition of US MNCs: most are now high technology companies in the 'newer' industrial sectors, particularly electronics and chemicals (as opposed to labour intensive companies producing standardised products in the 1960s).
2. US MNCs are predominantly based in the electronics sector, which has been at the forefront in developing what are seen as innovative and proactive employee relations and HR strategies and policies.

The relative impact of official and unofficial strikes is another important issue affecting patterns of strike activity. In their study of unofficial strikes in Ireland, Wallace and O'Shea (1987) found that there has been a dramatic reduction in unofficial strikes since the mid-1970s (see table 12.4). In the years 1991–2000, on average 28 per cent of strikes were unofficial, compared with an average of 40 per cent in the period 1980–90 and 66 per cent in the mid-1970s. Looking at the distribution of working days lost, we see an even more dramatic decrease in the impact of unofficial strikes. We find that during the period 1990–2000, approximately 7 per cent of the total working days lost due to strike action were attributed to unofficial strikes. Since unofficial strikes are normally of shorter duration and involve fewer employees this has meant that unofficial strikes now account for a very small proportion of working days lost due to strike activity (Wallace and O'Shea 1987, Wallace 1988a and b).

Table 12.4 Official and unofficial strikes in Ireland (percentage share in parentheses)

	Unofficial strikes	Official strikes	Working days lost, unofficial strikes	Working days lost, official strikes
1980	81 (61.4)	51 (38.6)	184,000 (45.6)	219,500 (54.4)
1981	61 (52.1)	56 (47.9)	131,000 (30)	305,000 (70)
1982	55 (42)	76 (58)	74,000 (16.9)	363,000 (83.1)
1983	58 (38.4)	93 (61.6)	58,000 (18.6)	253,000 (81.4)
1984	75 (39.3)	116 (60.7)	51,000 (14)	313,000 (86)
1985	45 (39.1)	70 (60.9)	43,000 (9.8)	394,000 (90.2)
1986	38 (38)	62 (62)	20,500 (6.5)	295,500 (93.5)
1987	22 (28.9)	54 (71.1)	25,000 (9.6)	235,000 (90.4)
1988	26 (36.1)	46 (63.9)	6,500 (5)	123,500 (95)
1989	13 (31.7)	28 (68.3)	11,600 (28)	29,800 (72)
1990	16 (31.4)	35 (68.6)	6,800 (3.3)	196,900 (96.7)
1991	13 (25)	39 (75)	9,300 (11.2)	73,600 (88.8)
1992	11 (26.8)	30 (73.2)	2,800 (1.5)	186,800 (98.5)
1993	9 (18.8)	39 (81.3)	4,800 (7.3)	60,600 (92.7)
1994	5 (15.6)	27 (84.4)	3,800 (14.9)	21,700 (85.1)
1995	7 (19.4)	29 (80.6)	900 (.7)	129,700 (99.3
1996	6 (18.8)	26 (81.3)	3,000 (2.6)	111,600 (97.4)
1997	6 (21.4)	22 (78.6)	1,000 (1.3)	73,500 (98.7)
1998	15 (44.1)	19 (55.9)	8,600 (23)	28,800 (77)
1999	16 (50)	16 (50)	27,100 (12.6)	188,500 (87.4
2000	12 (30.8)	27 (69.2)	12,000 (12.4)	85,000 (87.6)

Source: Department of Enterprise and Employment and Central Statistics Office.

Other Forms of Industrial Action

Other forms of action, such as overtime bans and working to rule (that is, working to the letter of written terms and conditions of employment) are actually more common than strikes themselves. These other forms of overt action can provide an effective means of achieving bargaining goals, while not entailing the potential hardships of strike action. In particular, actions such as go-slows or overtime bans can place considerable pressures on employers to move towards resolution while not jeopardising employees' income and job security to as great a degree as might be the case as result of strike action (Gunnigle *et al.* 1995). A far less obvious result of poor employee relations is a lack of commitment to the organisation and lack of trust in management. This can have far reaching long-term effects: for example, changes in work practices may be bitterly resisted; if other jobs are available labour turnover may be high; recruitment may be difficult; productivity may fall and absences may be high. It is important that managements are aware of such long-term consequences and have a clear and fair policy on employee relations.

Finally, it is important to note that employers may also instigate industrial action. The major form of industrial action undertaken by management is normally a *lockout*. A lockout by management involves preventing the workforce from attending at work and is the equivalent of strike action by employers.

CONFLICT RESOLUTION: DEALING WITH DISPUTES IN EMPLOYEE RELATIONS

At the level of the enterprise, all parties involved in employee relations have an important role to play in conflict handling and resolution. Line managers, shop stewards and employees have a key role in handling disputes and grievances that arise at shop-floor level. Senior management has overall responsibility for the development of effective policies and procedures to handle employee relations and industrial conflict. Where a specialist HRM function exists, it will normally have responsibility for advising top management on optimal employee relations strategies and developing appropriate procedures and practices. It may also provide training, advice and guidance to line management in handling workplace issues. Trade unions undertake a similar role on the employee side. As mentioned above, industrial conflict should not be viewed as having a necessarily negative impact on employee relations. Industrial conflict can have certain positive effects, allowing employees to highlight and pursue issues of concern, and thus facilitate change and development in the nature of employee relations.

Possibly the most widespread response to conflict in the workplace has been the development of joint mechanisms to discuss and resolve issues of difference (Gunnigle *et al.* 1995). Such institutionalisation of conflict is primarily characterised by the development of procedures to facilitate conflict resolution. This institutionalisation of conflict reflects an implicit acceptance that issues of conflict will arise and is characteristic of the pluralist approach to employee relations discussed earlier (see Fox 1966, 1974; Marchington 1982).

In creating institutions (such as collective bargaining) and procedures for handling employee relations and industrial conflict the parties involved seek to create a framework through which the parties can interact, argue, disagree and agree while allowing for the ongoing operation of the business (Jackson 1982; Gunnigle *et al.* 1995). Grievances, disputes and disciplinary procedures are a characteristic feature of Irish employee relations and represent an important means of dealing with employee relations and industrial conflict at the level of the enterprise (see, for example, Wallace 1989).

Grievance Handling

In employee relations, the term 'grievance' is normally used to describe a formal expression of employee dissatisfaction. Given the nature of industrial organisation, it is inevitable that employees, either individually or in groups, will have grievances that they want management to address. The great majority of such grievances normally involve minor complaints related to the immediate work environment. As such, these grievances can normally be handled at shop-floor level by line management and employees and/or employee representatives. It is suggested that managers should pay particular attention to effective grievance handling and its contribution to the promotion of good employee relations in the workplace. It is also suggested that management should handle employee grievances promptly, since the non-handling of grievances may give rise to frustration which can permeate through to other employees and promote an uneasy working environment in which disputes and poor employee relations can arise (Gunnigle *et al.* 1995). Some summary guidelines for managers involved in grievance handling are outlined in figure 12.7.

An important dimension in grievance handling is the establishment and application of grievance procedures (Thomason 1984). Such procedures normally outline the stages and approaches to be followed in handling grievances in the workplace. The main advantages associated with such procedures include the following: (i) increased clarity in employee relations interactions; (ii) prevention of misunderstandings and arguments over

---

Figure 12.7 Management checklist for grievance handling

- Management should make every effort to understand the nature of, and the reasons for, disputes and grievances.
- All levels of management should be aware of the key influence which grievance handling has on industrial and company performance generally.
- Management should establish a policy, which sets out an orderly and effective framework for handling disputes/grievances.
- Line management, particularly first level supervision, must be aware of their key role in effective grievance handling.

interpretation; (iii) ease of communication and (iv) increased fairness and consistency in application (Hawkins 1979; Wallace 1989, Gunnigle *et al.* 1995).

The main aim of grievance procedures is to ensure that issues raised by employees are adequately handled and settled fairly and as near as possible to their point of origin. Such aims are based on the premise that, operated effectively, grievance procedures embrace a strong preventative dimension in helping thwart the escalation of grievance issues into more serious industrial disputes. Most problems or complaints raised by employees should, ideally, be handled by the immediate supervisor without recourse to a formal grievance procedure.

However, issues that warrant more thorough consideration, may be more appropriately handled through a formal, written and agreed procedure. Grievance procedures should normally be in writing, simple and easy to operate, and aim to handle disputes and

---

Figure 12.8 Sample grievance procedure

STAGE Nature of Grievance	Procedural Level	
	Management	Employees/Trade Union
1. Issue involving local work rules or employment conditions affecting an individual or small work group.	Immediate supervisor	Employee(s)/concerned.
2. (a) Any issue which has remained unresolved at stage 1. (b) Grievance or claim where the issue has direct implications for a group of workers on a departmental or section basis.	Department manager (with relevant supervisor as appropriate)	Employee(s) concerned and shop steward or employee representative.
3. (a) Any issue which has remained unresolved from stage 2. (b) Grievance or claim with company wide implications.	HR manager and line manager(s)	Employee(s) concerned and/or shop steward/ employee reps. (inc. union official)
4. An unresolved issue that has been through the appropriate lower stages and remains unresolved.	Third party investigation: rights commissioner, Labour Relations Commission	
5. Any issue which remains unresolved after stage 4.	Labour Court Investigation: Employment Appeals Tribunal	

grievances fairly and consistently. Formal procedures generally follow an upward path from one organisational level to the next. A sample grievance procedure in a unionised organisation is outlined in figure 12.8.

Since it is not always possible to resolve all grievances at enterprise level, it is generally necessary to make provision for referral of issues to an independent third party for mediation and/or arbitration. The main third party agencies involved in employee relations were outlined earlier in chapter ten. Grievance procedures normally contain a provision that no form of industrial action should be taken by either party until all stages of the procedure have been exhausted, and an agreed period of notice has expired before industrial action is initiated. Effectively operated, this ensures both parties have ample opportunity to settle issues either through direct discussion, or by opting for third party referral.

Handling Disciplinary Issues

Inevitably, situations will also arise in organisations where management seeks to take disciplinary action against employees who failed to conform to the established rules or norms of the organisation. Most organisations will seek to establish and maintain what they consider are acceptable standards or norms in areas such as performance, attendance and conduct at work. Should employees breach such standards management will normally seek to take some form of disciplinary action. Such disciplinary action may range from relatively minor rebukes to more serious forms such as formal warnings, suspension or dismissal.

An important aspect of discipline administration in organisations is the establishment of acceptable rules and standards and the utilisation of disciplinary procedures to deal with breaches of such rules/standards. *Disciplinary rules* set out the standards of acceptable behaviour expected from employees within an organisation and the consequences of not meeting these standards. *Disciplinary procedures* constitute the administrative machinery for applying these rules and executing any resulting action.

A critical concern in the area of discipline administration is the legal context within which discipline should be administered in organisations. For example, the common law concept of natural justice requires that:

1. There should be a basic understanding of what constitutes a transgression, therefore company rules and standards should be clearly outlined and communicated.
2. The consequences of breaching such rules/standards should be clear.
3. Employees not achieving the required standards should be so informed and given opportunity to improve where possible.
4. Employees alleged to have breached discipline should be entitled to fair and consistent treatment, including an opportunity to state their case, have access to representation, and a right to appeal to a higher authority.

These principles combined with the legislative framework surrounding discipline administration indicate that organisations should have some formal disciplinary procedure in operation, ensure employees are familiar with its contents and apply this procedure in a reasonable way. The legal context for discipline administration is summarily outlined in chapter thirteen.[1]

The most significant legislative development affecting discipline administration is the Unfair Dismissals legislation (1977, 1993) which provides guidelines as to what constitutes fair and unfair dismissal, and provides a mechanism for dealing with claims of unfair dismissal and for deciding upon redress for those found to be unfairly dismissed.

A disciplinary procedure is an important aspect of effective discipline administration. It is suggested that disciplinary procedures serve to establish an explicit *modus operandi* for bringing alleged offences to the notice of employees, allow employees an opportunity to respond to such charges and facilitate the imposition of disciplinary action as necessary. A critical initial step in establishing a disciplinary procedure is to outline company rules and standards, and the form of disciplinary action associated with breaches of these rules and standards.

The establishment of explicit workplace rules helps ensure consistency in the treatment of employees. Such an outline of rules and standards should indicate (i) those rules and standards where breaches may lead to dismissal in the first instance (e.g. theft or violence at work); and (ii) those rules and standards where breaches would lead to the operation of a standard disciplinary procedure (e.g. lateness, absenteeism and inadequate work performance). To facilitate the effective administration of disciplinary procedures the golden rules would seem to suggest that such procedures should be (i) agreed between management and employees, (ii) fair, (iii) understood by management and employees and (iv) applied consistently. A sample disciplinary procedure is outlined in figure 12.9.

An important aspect in ensuring procedural fairness and equity in discipline administration is the employee's right to adequate representation (by either a fellow employee or trade union representative as appropriate). Management should also ensure that accurate records are maintained in disciplinary cases.

It is important to note that the Unfair Dismissals' legislation places the burden of proof primarily on the employer. Consequently management must be able to substantiate their case with adequate documentary evidence. Much of this work will be the responsibility of the specialist HR function. In disciplinary cases there is an onus on management to thoroughly investigate the circumstances and establish the facts of the case. If, after a thorough investigation, management decide that disciplinary action is merited a meeting is normally arranged with the employee(s) concerned. The purpose of such *disciplinary interviews* is to assess culpability, decide on appropriate action and attempt to effect the desired change in employee behaviour. The disciplinary interview also provides the employee(s) with an opportunity to present their point of view. In disciplinary cases, employees should be given a reasonable opportunity to explain their position.

Only after a thorough investigation and disciplinary meeting is management in a position to decide on appropriate action. Should the investigation and disciplinary meeting point to a need for disciplinary action, management's position should be explained to the employee(s), who should be made fully aware of their shortcomings and management's concern. The precise nature of any improvement required and the means for its achievement should be outlined, as should the consequences of future transgressions.

There is an onus on management to ensure that employees fully understand the discipline imposed and the right of appeal. After the interview, the details should be accurately recorded and a copy given to the employee(s) concerned (and their representative as necessary). Any commitments entered into should be carried out promptly.

In the longer term the total process should be monitored from a number of viewpoints (e.g. impact on employee behaviour, trends in disciplinary incidents and effectiveness of

Figure 12.9 Sample disciplinary procedure

Preamble

The following disciplinary procedure will be used to deal with all breaches of company rules and standards except where the offences or transgression constitute gross misconduct.

The primary aim of this procedure is to help employees whose conduct or performance falls below company requirements to achieve the necessary improvements. It is desirable both in contributing to company success and the fair treatment of employees. It is company policy to apply this procedure as reasonably as possible and to ensure consistency and order in its application. It will apply to all breaches of company rules or standards not constituting gross misconduct that may typically include, but are not limited to the following:
- bad timekeeping
- unacceptable work performance
- unauthorised absence
- poor attendance
- lack of co-operation
- breaches of safety regulations

Disciplinary Procedure

1. In the first instance the individual will be asked to attend a counselling interview by his supervisor, where the employees' transgression will be made clear, the standard of performance required outlined and the employee verbally reprimanded.
2. In the second instance the employee will receive a verbal warning at a formal meeting with his supervisor and department manager, where details of the misdemeanour and the consequences of further offences will be outlined.
3. In the third instance the employee will receive a final written warning from the HR manager at a meeting with the HR manager, the department manager and, if appropriate, the supervisor. The employee will be informed of the details of the offence, future performance standards required and that further offences will lead to suspension or dismissal.
4. In the last instance the employee will either be suspended without pay or dismissed (depending on the offence). Notice of this will be given to the employee at a meeting with the general manager, when the offence will be outlined both verbally and in writing and the employee advised of his/her right of appeal.

Gross Misconduct

Gross misconduct is conduct of such a serious nature that the company could not tolerate keeping the employee in employment and it is hoped that such instances will not occur. However, for the mutual protection of the company and its workforce, any employee found guilty of gross misconduct may be dismissed summarily. Examples of gross misconduct include:
- violation of a criminal law
- consumption or possession of alcohol or illegal drugs
- threats or acts of physical violence
- theft from another employee or from the company
- malicious damage to company property
- falsifying company records (including clock cards)

Before any action is taken the company will thoroughly investigate the case, during which time the employee will be suspended. After such investigations the employee will attend a meeting with company management where he will have an opportunity to state his case and be advised of his right of appeal. Should the company still feel the employee was guilty of gross misconduct he will be dismissed and given a letter outlining the nature of the offence and reasons for dismissal.

various forms of discipline). The area of discipline administration should be approached by management in a positive vein with the overall objective being to change employees' behaviour. The HR function has an important role to play in establishing disciplinary policy and related procedures and in monitoring their application throughout the organisation. Two key factors, which need to be kept in mind, are the need for reasonableness and consistency in undertaking disciplinary action.

TOWARDS A 'NEW MODEL': PARTNERSHIP v. ADVERSARIALISM

Much of the preceding discussion on employee relations practice and particularly that concerning collective bargaining, is grounded in what is characterised as 'adversarialism'. The adversarial system, based on the premise that the interests of management and labour conflict, relies primarily on bargaining interactions between these parties to achieve 'mutually acceptable compromises'.

As noted earlier, employee relations in Ireland is characterised by a strong adversarial tradition. This system has come in for increasing criticism in recent years, both in Ireland and abroad. A general criticism has been the perceived dominance of distributive bargaining with its emphasis on dividing limited resources (Fisher and Ury 1986). It is argued that this approach leads the parties to develop adversarial positions believing that any gains can only be made by inflicting losses on the other side. Distributive bargaining reflects the very essence of the traditional pluralist and adversarial employee relations model: claims, offers, bluff, threats, compromise, movement, agreement or conflict. However, it is suggested that approaches based on more integrative and co-operative bargaining represent a more attractive alternative with their emphasis on a collaborative approach, exploring common ground and seeking solutions of mutual benefit to both parties.

The so-called 'partnership approach' to employee relations is grounded in such thinking, suggesting that employers, workers and their representative associations should seek to jointly address employee relations problems and develop mutually beneficial solutions (see, for example, Kochan and Osterman 1994; Beaumont 1995).

Based on recent analyses of industrial change, it is widely argued that there is a need for a new 'partnership' model of employee relations that incorporates a strong trade union role (see, for example, Kochan and Osterman 1994). This need emerges from the argued weakness of a traditional employee relations system based on adversarial collective bargaining. It is further argued that this new model allows both sides to break out of the traditional adversarial relationship through the adoption of a 'new industrial relations' model based on 'mutual gains' principles. The essential 'deal' is that employers and trade unions enter into a set of mutual commitments as follows:

1. Employers recognise and facilitate worker rights to information, consultation and involvement.
2. Workers and trade unions commit themselves actively to productivity improvements.
3. The gains of productivity improvements are shared between employers and workers.
4. Productivity improvements do not result in redundancies but rather employers actively seek new markets to keep workers gainfully employed.

In essence the mutual gains argument is that workers and trade unions actively pursue, with management, solutions to business problems and appropriate work re-organisation, in return for greater involvement in business decisions and in the process of work re-organisation.

In evaluating the merits of developing such a new relationship with workers and their trade unions, it appears that both sides face a fundamental choice on the nature of management-employee relations. Should worker/trade union involvement be confined to joint consultation or extended to joint regulation? From a worker/trade union perspective, joint consultation initiatives run the risk of remaining essentially 'symbolic', whereby workers/trade unions have no real influence but become associated with decisions where they possess no right to veto. Employers may be equally reticent to enter into joint regulation initiatives because it may lead to a slowing in the decision-making process.

Some of the difficulties in developing partnership approaches, in the conduct of enterprise-level employee relations, are apparent in recent debates. As noted earlier, a criticism of patterns of social partnership in Ireland is that its operation is restricted to the most senior levels of employer and trade union interests, with little diffusion into enterprise-level employee relations (see Roche 1995). At the enterprise level, a critical aspect of the partnership debate is that concerning employee participation.

EMPLOYEE PARTICIPATION

Partnership approaches to employee relations are invariably associated with initiatives designed to facilitate greater employee participation. Employee participation may be broadly interpreted as incorporating any mechanisms designed to increase employee input into managerial decision-making. Increased employee participation is an important aspect of many recent initiatives in the areas of work organisation (see for example Marchington and Parker 1990; ICTU 1993; Kochan *et al.* 1986; Kochan and Osterman 1994).

Employee participation can take numerous forms and can range from the relatively superficial level, such as management informing employees of decisions that affect them, to consultation with employees on certain decisions or joint participation in the actual decision-making process. Such initiatives may result in a variety of institutional arrangements to facilitate employee participation, such as suggestion schemes, joint consultative committees, works councils, quality circles and board level participation. Employee participation can also be facilitated through collective bargaining, which attempts to lessen the sphere of managerial prerogative and make more issues subject to joint negotiation and agreement.

In particular, we can point to a difference between *direct* and *indirect* forms of employees' influence. With the former approach, workers are directly involved in the decision-making process. Often captured under the rubric of 'employee involvement', direct employee participation may take a variety of forms, such as quality circles, consultative meetings and possibly the most commonly used example – team-working.

In contrast, indirect forms rely on the use of employees' representatives to articulate the views and claims of the larger body of employees and therefore is often termed 'representative participation'. Common examples include trade unions (through collective bargaining) and works councils. Representative participation seeks to reduce the extent of management prerogative and effect greater employee influence on areas of decision-making that have traditionally been the remit of senior management.

It is possible to identify four different forms of participation, each varying in both the level and nature of participation (see figure 12.10): (i) task participation, (ii) equity participation, (iii) representative participation, and (iv) participation through collective bargaining (see Gunnigle *et al.* 1995). Variations in approaches to employee participation may stem from a variety of reasons, such as the structure and development of collective bargaining, the attitude of trade unions or the political philosophy of Government. The variety of institutional arrangements adopted in different countries and by different organisations may also reflect different philosophies and approaches to employee participation. Participation may be supported by the law or may be established through collective agreements and may be minimal or extensive.

Figure 12.10 Forms of employee participation

Task Participation: This encompasses various initiatives to design jobs and work systems, which allow for greater employee involvement in decisions affecting their jobs and immediate work environment. Such initiatives may take a variety of forms such as autonomous work groups, quality circles and consultative meetings and committees.'

Equity Participation: This involves the adoption of mechanisms through which employees can gain an equity share in their organisations through various profit-sharing and share-ownership schemes. Some schemes may have the broad-based objective of increasing employee loyalty, commitment and morale through the closer identification of employee interests with those of the organisation. However, equity participation by itself will not normally allow for a substantial increase in employees' influence, as employees will generally represent a minority of the shareholders. Organisations such as the John Lewis Partnership in the UK and Donnelly Mirrors in Ireland have long been known for their policy of sharing profits with employees, and many companies now offer share options or some other form of profit-sharing.

Representative Participation: This has been the focus of most attention and applies to institutionalised arrangements that give employees input into management decision-making, sometimes with statutory support. The most obvious example is provision for the election of worker-directors to the boards of management. It also applies to lower-level participation, such as joint consultative committees and works councils. The passing of the Worker Participation (State Enterprises) Act 1977 introduced board-level participation to seven semi-state companies and these provisions were extended to a number or other state organisations under the terms of the Worker Participation (State Enterprises) Act 1988. However, board-level representation has largely been confined to the semi-state companies covered by the legislation.

Participation through Collective Bargaining: This has been the most traditional approach to effecting higher levels of employee participation. The growth of workplace bargaining has greatly facilitated this process with trade unions being the key mechanism for representing and extending employees' rights at workplace level. However, as discussed in the text, this approach is seen as essentially adversarial in nature and as such has attracted the criticism that it is not an effective means of promoting a joint problem-solving approach to employee relations issues.

A significant aspect of the debate on employee participation in Ireland concerns the role of trade unions. Traditionally, the Irish trade union movement did not seem particularly committed to representative forms of employee participation, such as worker-directors or works councils (Morrissy 1989). Reactions to participation though equity participation have been mixed, and no discernible trend is evident. Indeed, apart from support for greater disclosure of information, the traditional trade union approach to employee participation has been marked by a considerable degree of apathy. Such apathy has strong links with the doubts many trade unionists harbour about the implications of representative participation for the union's role in collective bargaining.

However the trade union position seems to have altered in recent years. The ICTU policy documents, *New Forms of Work Organisation* and *Managing Change* suggests that trade unions need to take a more proactive role in influencing the planning and implementation of new workforce management strategies (ICTU 1993, 1995). These reports place a particular focus on task participation at enterprise level. They note the importance for trade unions of developing, and actively participating in, employee involvement initiatives at workplace level. They also identify important aspects of employee participation that unions need to address, particularly the joint monitoring of participation initiatives at workplace level, involvement of trade unions in the internal communications processes of organisations, access to and understanding of business information and involvement in high-level business decision-making.

It is often suggested that all parties in employee relations can benefit from increased employee participation (Beer *et al.* 1984). For example, it is suggested that employers need a flexible and committed workforce that will respond to change and perform at high levels of productivity, with minimum levels of supervision and that this can be achieved through employee involvement and participation initiatives. From the employees' perspective, it is suggested that the achievement of an input into decisions that affects their working lives is a very legitimate goal, allowing them greater control and discretion in their jobs (Hackman and Oldham 1980). Even at the macro level, the state and the community at large may benefit from positive workplace relations based on trust, open communications, and employees' satisfaction (Beer *et al.* 1984).

However the achievement of real and effective participation within organisations remains problematic (Marchington and Parker 1990; Salamon 1992). Employers' organisations may, for example, argue that business confidence and discretion in decision-making must be maintained to encourage investment and expansion, while at the same time suggesting that barriers to worker involvement must be removed and employees given a worthwhile say in decision-making. This perspective is commonly used to encourage employees' involvement in shop-floor issues, while legitimising the retention of management prerogative in higher-level decision-making (Gunnigle and Morley 1992).

Indeed it might be suggested that the four forms of participation described in figure 12.10 might be viewed as options in a participative mix, any combination of which may suit a particular organisational context. The imposition of particular models may often prove problematic and it seems important that any legislative measures allow for flexibility in the modes of participation to be adopted. It would appear that effective participation requires a high level of commitment and positive engagement from employers, employers' associations, employees and trade unions. Trust has been identified as a key factor in facilitating effective communications and information disclosure or exchange (Whelan 1982). Indeed it would appear that the existence of high-trust relations is more important than the actual participative form or mechanism adopted.

Task Participation and the Teamworking Debate

Possibly the most widely debated contemporary participation form is task participation, and particularly the issue of teamworking. Geary (1994a) defines *task participation* as follows:

> Task participation is defined as opportunities which management provides at workplace level for consultation with and/or delegation of responsibilities and authority for decision-making to its subordinates either as individuals or as groups of employees relating to the immediate work task and/or working conditions.

Task participation therefore involves the devolution to employees of greater control over work-related decisions; workers' involvement in contributing opinion and solving problems is actively facilitated. Workers are thus required to concern themselves with broader enterprise objectives, such as improving productivity and controlling costs. Two key forms of task participation may be identified (Sisson 1994):

- *Consultative participation*, whereby workers are given the opportunity to become involved in decisions and make their views known; however, management retains the prerogative to make final decision.
- *Delegative participation*, whereby workers are empowered to make key decisions without the need for management approval.

Within the broad parameters of the debate on task participation, the growth in interest in teamworking emerges as a significant theme with far-reaching implications for employee relations and HRM. The concept of teamworking has its traditional roots in notions of improving the quality of working life. While these early developments met with some support in countries such as the US and Scandinavia, they had little impact in Ireland. In recent years there has been a significant increase in employers' interest in work re-organisation and teamworking. However, it appears that employers are now the key instigators of teamworking (Beaumont 1995). This contrasts with earlier initiatives in teamworking that were worker and trade union driven and designed to improve the quality of working life of employees. Teamworking is seen as an advanced form of delegative task participation, where workers make key decisions such as those concerning the selection of team leaders, team members and roles (Geary 1994a and b).

According to Geary (1995a; also see 1994b; 1995b), teamworking is more pronounced in Europe than in Britain or Ireland. In Ireland such initiatives appear to be few and are largely efficiency driven, rather than driven by a desire to improve the quality of working life. Geary further notes that Irish developments have largely involved 'tinkering at the margins' of work practices, and were confined to a handful of foreign-owned companies. While the progress of teamworking in Europe also appears modest, some of the more significant developments appear to have take place in the automotive sector, especially in Germany (Roth 1993; also see Womack *et al.* 1990). In evaluating the European experience in teamworking, Geary identifies five crucial areas:

1. *The regulation of teamwork:* Geary notes that the introduction of teamworking in Europe has been achieved more through agreement with employees' representatives rather than via unilateral imposition. This trend is attributed to the strength of collective employee representation (especially works councils and trade union involvement in industry bargaining) in countries such as Germany and Sweden who have led the way in the introduction of teamworking.
2. *The objectives of teamworking:* Geary identifies achieving a balance between managerial goals of improved economic efficiency and worker goals of improved quality of working life, as a critical issue in facilitating the successful introduction of teamworking. In particular, it appears that trade unions are more willing to engage in teamworking when it is not used solely, or primarily, to achieve managerial aims.
3. *Impact on working lives:* Geary's analysis of the European experience indicates that teamworking has favoured skilled workers and that the 'gender divide' has been left relatively untouched (i.e. a major divide remains with limited opportunities for women). However, specialist categories such as engineers and accountants have been transferred to line positions. Geary further notes that employers have not relied solely on persuasion to introduce teamworking. 'More traditional forms' of management control have also

been utilised, such as increased employee surveillance and more intense work schedules and that, overall, increased skill and effort levels have been a common outcome of teamworking. However, Geary also identifies potential positive changes associated with teamworking, such as improved working conditions and job security, which can lead to productive efficiencies and encourage worker acceptance of teamworking.

4. *Teamwork and management support:* Geary suggests that the European experience indicates that management commitment and support is an absolute pre-requisite for the effective introduction of teamworking. He suggests that if teamworking is introduced as an 'island solution' it has little chance of success and identifies line management 'indifference and resistance' as a key impediment to the effective introduction of teamworking.

5. *Integrating teamworking with other aspects of HRM:* Geary suggests that the evidence from Europe indicates that teamworking is likely to be more successful where it is integrated with complementary changes in other aspects of HR policy. In particular, a number of key policy changes are identified: (i) shift from individual-based pay to team-based pay, (ii) significant investment in training and development, and (iii) maintenance of job security commitments.

Task Participation in Practice

Probably the most important source of information on the extent and nature of diffusion of task participation is the *European Foundation for the Improvement of Living and Working Conditions* (EFILWC) survey conducted in ten EU member states (see EFILWC 1997; Sisson 1997). Generally known as the EPOC (employee direct participation in organisational change) project, this study examined both the incidence of task participation and also the nature of such participation, particularly the scope and extent of autonomy afforded to employees. In Ireland, the EPOC study surveyed a sample of Irish companies, excluding those with less than 25 employees. The study achieved a response rate of nearly 39 per cent (382 organisations), which represented the highest response rate among all the countries involved in the study (EFILWC 1997; also see Geary 1998).

Looking firstly at the diffusion of consultative participation, the EPOC study found that what Geary (1998, 12) labels 'temporary groups', (particularly project groups or task forces) were found in 36 per cent of firms, while 'permanent groups' such as quality circles were present in 28 per cent of firms. Turning to delegative participation, the EPOC study found that team-based structures were present in 42 per cent of respondent firms. Based on these findings, Geary (1998) estimates that task participation is present in around one third of Irish workplaces. Newly established firms seem more likely to use task participation than their longer established counterparts.

In addition to examining the incidence of task participation, the EPOC study considered the nature and intensity of such participation, particularly delegative participation (incorporating teamworking). The EPOC study utilised two measures in this regard: (i) the scope of teamworking, which measured the extent of employees' rights to solely make decisions in relation to their work; (ii) the extent of autonomy afforded to employees to select team members and to decide on which issues the team should tackle (EFILWC 1997). The EPOC findings indicate that just 17 per cent of Irish firms which used teamworking were characterised by a high-level team or group delegation.

In evaluating the implications of the EPOC findings, it appears that while task participation is reasonably well diffused in Ireland, most organisations rely on predominantly traditional forms of work organisation. Of particular note is that fact that the uptake of modes of work organisation, which devolve a high level of autonomy to workers and work teams, is very low. This finding leads Geary (1998, 14) to conclude that task participation 'of an advanced form, is a minority practice in this country'.

Overall, this and other studies such as the Cranfield-University of Limerick (CUL) study provide little evidence of direct employee involvement in Irish organisations. It appears that the predominant focus of direct involvement initiatives is on facilitating the involvement of individual employees and small groups on issues of immediate work relevance. These initiatives seem to be primarily concerned with encouraging a greater employees' 'voice' on issues of immediate job-related interest rather than employees' 'influence' on higher-level management decision-making.

Implications for the Introduction of Teamworking: The Trade Union Dimension

Based on the European experience, Geary (1994a) suggests that a critical issue in teamworking is the development of strategies for dealing with employees' representatives and trade unions. Employers commonly object to the involvement of trade unions in work re-organisation and teamworking on the grounds that it is too time-consuming and serves to slow the process of organisational change. However, Geary points to the offsetting benefits of union involvement, based on the European experience: firstly, trade unions and employees' representatives will have expertise, which can benefit the process and, secondly, they can legitimise the 'necessity of proposed change' to their membership. An additional benefit is that such involvement forces management to integrate HRM considerations more centrally in their decision-making than might otherwise be the case.

On this theme, Geary raises the critical question of how to involve employees' representatives and trade unions in the introduction of work re-organisation initiatives such as teamworking. Since in the Irish and British context such changes are normally discussed in the traditional collective bargaining arena, Geary questions whether new institutional arrangements need to be developed. In particular, it is noted that in many of the European countries that have experimented with teamwork, there is an institutional separation whereby traditional collective-bargaining issues are the remit of union-employer bargaining at industry level, while working arrangements are normally dealt with within the enterprise through works councils (especially in Germany and France). Turning specifically to the Irish context Geary poses a number of questions on this dilemma:

- Can the introduction of teamworking be productively discussed through traditional 'adversarial 'collective bargaining arrangements?
- Is there a need for arrangements of the works council type?
- Are Irish managers ready for this type of joint decision-making?
- Is it better if the structures used to inform employees are employee-based and not strictly union-based?

A final and critical concern for organisations is how can they effectively facilitate such change. Geary's analysis identifies the effective 'managing of managers' as the key to successful teamworking (Geary 1994a, 1995a and b, 1996). He argues that employers must move beyond their traditional concern of 'getting the goods out the door and reducing costs'. Rather he suggests that there is a need to reconcile the management of managers with the objectives of employee involvement. In particular he argues that the reward and appraisal system for managers should reward managers who facilitate effective teamworking.

Finally, it should be noted that increased employee participation and teamworking will not mean an end to 'adversarial' collective bargaining. As Geary points out, pay issues and 'significant changes' in work organisation may still be channelled through 'traditional' collective bargaining.

This chapter reviewed key aspects of employee relations practice with particular emphasis on collective bargaining, grievance handling, discipline administration and employee participation. It also considered the impact of employee involvement initiatives and particularly teamworking for employee relations. The next chapter considers an area of particular interest to HR practitioners, namely that of employment law.

Note
1. This text provides a summary overview of the legal context of discipline administration and is not a legal interpretation thereof. Readers requiring more comprehensive insights into the legal context of discipline administration might refer to Fennel and Lynch (1993) and/or Meenan (1998).

13

Employment Law[1]

This final chapter provides an overview of Irish employment law, but is not a legal interpretation thereof. It explores the legal framework within which human resource management (HRM) takes place. There are two particular aspects of employment or labour law that concern us.

1. Individual labour law, which concentrates on the relationship between the individual worker and the employer.
2. Collective labour law, which is concerned with regulating the relationship between employers and groups of employees – normally trade unions.

The primary emphasis in this chapter is on documenting the various legislative provisions that have particular relevance to the practice of HRM in Ireland. We begin with a brief introduction to the sources of law, which has implications for the employment relationship. The formation of a contract of employment is then examined and various statutes affecting employment are discussed. The chapter concludes with a brief discussion on the reform of collective labour law. We have previously considered the area of employee relations and aspects of 'collective' labour law in chapter ten.

SOURCES OF IRISH LAW

The Irish legal system comprises of a number of sources of law namely the Constitution, statute law and common law.

- The *Constitution* is essentially divided into two distinct parts. Firstly, that which sets down fundamental personal rights that are guaranteed to every Irish citizen and that the state is obliged to protect. Secondly, that which directs the structures and establishment of various institutions such as the Oireachtas, Government and judiciary.
- *Statute law* consists of the various acts that have been passed over the years, collectively referred to as legislation. After the Constitution, statute law is the most important source of law. It can be broadly classified according to its subject matter: family law, company law, land law, criminal law, labour law and so forth. A number of pertinent employment statutes are reviewed later in this chapter.

- *Common law* is an unwritten system that has evolved over the centuries. Often called 'judge-made' law, it consists of the decisions made by the judiciary when cases are decided. In practice, this means that judges refer to similar cases when making their decisions; this is commonly known as following a precedent and it provides for some element of consistency in the interpretation of the law. Common law implies a number of duties into the contract of employment. Employers' duties specify that all employers must reimburse employees for legitimate expenses and must provide a duty of care, a safe place of work, a safe system of work, safe machinery and competent co-workers. As the employment relationship is a contract for services, it is implied that employees will perform the job personally; work co-operatively, obey all reasonable instructions, give fidelity to the employer, employ reasonable care and skill and avoid conflicts of interest.

FORMATION OF A CONTRACT OF EMPLOYMENT

The contract of employment is the legal basis of the employment relationship and is central to the interpretation and application of statutory rights. As with the basic law of contract it requires that there must be 'offer and acceptance'; the offer being made by the employer and the acceptance by the employee when he/she agrees to work for the employer. There must also be 'consideration' or remuneration from the employer for work done, and both parties must intend to create legal relations, that is, both parties must recognise that they have particular rights and obligations that must be observed. The contract of employment may be made either orally or in writing.

Common law attempts to distinguish between a contract *of* service and a contract *for* service. An employee is someone who is employed under a contract of service; this is distinct from an independent contractor who is employed under a contract for services. The distinction is a vital one, for a variety of reasons, not least of which is that only 'employees' can benefit from much of the modern employment legislation granted to workers (Fennell and Lynch 1993). Three tests have been developed to differentiate between contracts of and for service:

1. *The Control Test:* This is based on the principle that the employer has the right to control how work is done. In other words, the employer not only tells the employee what to do but also how to do it. However, this test is difficult to administer in practice, particularly where many contracts of service (employees) have considerable discretion over the work that they do.
2. *The Integration Test:* This is based upon the view that an employee is a person whose work is integrated into the business, whereas independent contractors merely work for the business. This test is also difficult to apply today since it fails to take account of work practices such as home working that can give the appearance of self-employment and thus might be construed as contracts for service.
3. *The Multiple or Economic Reality Test:* Under this test, the entire arrangement between employer and worker is reviewed to determine whether the worker is an employee or an independent contractor. Thus the court would seek information concerning:

   - whether wages, sick and holiday pay are provided and who pays them;
   - whether income tax and social security are deducted under the PAYE and PRSI schemes by the company;
   - whether the worker shares in the profits or losses of the company;
   - whether tools and equipment for the job are provided by the company;

- whether there are specific provisions relating to termination of employment; and finally
- whether the employer is entitled to exclusive service.

If the person is free to work for other companies, provides his or her own equipment, sets his or her own work pace, and can sub-contract the work to others, then it might generally be assumed that he or she is an independent contractor.

However, despite the variety of issues that can be examined in dealing with this question, Fennell and Lynch (1993) suggest that a certain amount of confusion exists about what test should be applied. Figure 13.1 outlines the key differences that can be seen to exist between a contract of service and a contract for service.

Figure 13.1 Key differences between contracts of service and contracts for service

CONTRACTS OF SERVICE	CONTRACTS FOR SERVICE
Employer-employee relationship	Employer-contractor relationship
Usually a continuous relationship	A relationship based on a one-off-piece of work
Duty of care owed to employees	Duty of care arising from occupier's liability
Generally liable for the vicarious acts of employees, e.g. any wrong or injury done by an employee while in the course of his or her work	Generally not liable for the vicarious acts of independent contractors
Protective legislation applies to contract	Protective legislation does not apply (apart from Safety, Health and Welfare at Work Act 1989)
Wage or salary payment	Fee payment
Subject of contract is to carry on continuous work	Subject of contract is one-off

Source: Gunnigle, Garavan and Fitzgerald (1992).

EMPLOYMENT LEGISLATION

There is a considerable body of employment protection legislation in Ireland that provides a basic floor of rights for individual employees. This legislation is marked by several inconsistencies particularly with respect to the differing periods of service required to qualify, and the different adjudicating mechanisms employed (please refer to chapter ten for full details). Several important Acts have been passed since the 1970s, which have increased the number of rights that employees can expect from the employment relationship. A summary of employment legislation and its main provisions is given in figure 13.2.

It is important to note that certain categories of employees are excluded from the protection of some pieces of employment legislation, e.g. the defence forces, gardai, FÁS trainees, those working for a close relative in the home, certain public sector categories and anyone engaging in illegal employment. It is important to consult the particular Act for precise details in relation to excluded categories.

Figure 13.2 Summary of employment legislation in Ireland

INDIVIDUAL EMPLOYEE LEGISLATION

Terms and conditions of employment

Terms of Employment (Information) Act 1994	Provision of a written statement to employees setting out particulars of their conditions of employment
Organisation of Working Time 1997	Hours of work; rest periods; annual leave; public holidays
Worker Protection (Regular Part-Time Employees) Act 1991	Extends the benefits of employment legislation to part-time workers
Protection of Young Persons (Employment) Act 1996	Conditions for employing young persons
Payment of Wages Act 1979–91	Payment by cheque; deductions from pay
National Minimum Wage Act 2000	Right to minimum rate of pay
Pensions Act 1990	Rights in relation to pensions

Employment Equality

Maternity (Protection of Employees) Act 1981 and 1994	Maternity pay and job security, rights to health and safety, and paternal leave in certain circumstances
Adoptive Leave Act 1995	Rights of an adopting mother and a sole male adopter are outlined
Parental Leave Act 1998	Rights of parents to leave for the purpose of caring for their child
Carers Leave Act 2001	Rights of employees to leave to care for person requiring full-time care
Employment Equality Act 1998	Outlaws nine areas of discrimination; establishes Equality Authority

Termination of Employment

Minimum Notice and Terms of Employment Act 1973	Notice and provisions regarding termination of employment
Unfair Dismissals Act 1977 and 1991	Protection against unfair dismissal
Protection of Employment Act 1977	Consultation prior to group redundancies
Redundancy Payments Acts 1967–91	Payment of lump sum on redundancy

Health and Safety at Work

Safety, Health and Welfare at Work Act 1989	Duties on employers, employees and others regarding health and safety issues
Safety, Heath and Welfare at Work Regulations 1993	Specific procedures and regulations for employers

COLLECTIVE EMPLOYEE LEGISLATION

Industrial Relations Act 1946 to 2001	Outlines rights and procedures regarding regulation of trade disputes and industrial relations issues
Transfer of Undertakings Regulations	Right to employment security, seniority and continuity of service on the transfer of a business

INDIVIDUAL EMPLOYEE LEGISLATION

The following is a brief summary of the main individual rights of employees. Most of the statutory rights (i.e. those granted under the various acts) are only available to those who have had a specific period of continuous employment with their company or organisation. Legally, this is known as the 'qualifying period', but unfortunately there is little consistency from one right to another as differing periods of service apply.

Terms and Conditions of Employment

WRITTEN PARTICULARS OF TERMS OF EMPLOYMENT

A contract of employment comes into force as soon as a job offer is made and accepted, whether orally or in writing, and appropriate conditions related to contract formation are adhered to. The Terms of Employment (Information) Act 1994, implements a European Union Directive that requires employers to provide a written statement setting out particulars of the employee's terms of employment within twenty-eight days or to refer employees to where they can find details of their employment. The Act also repeals sections nine and ten of the Minimum Notice and Terms of Employment Act, 1973, as those sections are overtaken by the provisions of this Act.

Information to be included in the written statement includes:

- the full names of the employer and employee;
- the address of the employer in the state or, where appropriate, its principal place of business, or, the registered address of the employer as registered with the Companies Registration Office;
- the place of work or where there is no main place of work, a statement that the employee is required or permitted to work at various places;
- the job title or nature of the work;
- the date of commencement of employment;
- if the contract is temporary, the expected duration of employment;
- if the contract is for a fixed term, the date on which the contract expires;
- the rate of remuneration or method of calculating remuneration;
- whether remuneration is paid weekly, monthly or otherwise;
- terms or conditions relating to hours of work (including overtime);
- terms or conditions relating to paid leave (other than paid sickness leave);
- terms or conditions relating to incapacity for work due to sickness or injury;
- terms or conditions relating to pensions and pensions schemes;
- periods of notice which the employee is entitled to receive and required to give on termination of employment; where this cannot be indicated when the written statement is given, the written statement must give the method for determining the period of notice;
- a reference to any collective agreements that affect the terms of employment; where the employer is not a party to the agreement, the written statement must indicate the bodies or institution that made the agreement.

CONDITIONS OF EMPLOYMENT

The entitlement of employees to holidays, rest periods and the determination of hours of work is governed by the Organisation of Working Time Act 1997. It repeals the Conditions of Employment Acts 1936 and 1944, the Holidays (Employees) Act 1973, and a range of other acts covering working conditions in shops and bakeries. It provides that employees shall not work more than an average of forty-eight hours in each seven-day period. Such an average is calculated over a four-month period, but in certain specified cases, a six-month period is permissible.

The Act contains very specific provisions in relation to rest periods, Sunday working and night-working. An employee is entitled to at least eleven consecutive hours of rest in each period of twenty-four hours worked. They are also entitled to a rest period of fifteen minutes for working four hours and thirty minutes and a rest period of thirty minutes if the working period is six hours long. A weekly rest period of twenty-four consecutive hours is also provided for in the Act. This weekly rest period must include a Sunday, unless otherwise provided for in the employee's contract of employment. Where an employee is required to work on Sunday and this does not form part of the employment contract, the employee is entitled to compensation. This may take the form of the following: time off in lieu, payment of a special allowance, increase in the employee's rate of pay or a combination of these items. Night-work is defined under the Act as work carried out between midnight and 7 a.m. A night-worker is defined as an employee who works at least three hours of their daily working period during night-time and where the number of hours worked during night-time represents at least 50 per cent of the total hours worked during the year. In order to comply with the Act, employees must ensure that night-workers do not work more than an average of eight hours per night, averaged over a two-month period. The Act also sets out quite extensive provisions relating to zero-hour contracts.

In relation to holidays, an employee is entitled to paid annual leave equal to the greater of:

- four working weeks in a leave year in which 1,365 hours are worked
- one third of a working week for each month in a leave year in which 117 hours are worked
- eight per cent of the hours worked in a leave year (to a maximum of four working weeks).

This ensures that all employees (full-time and part-time) are entitled to annual leave/ holiday entitlements. In the case of public holidays, employees are entitled to one of the following:

- a paid day off on that day
- a paid day off within a month of that day
- an additional day of annual leave
- an additional day's pay.

At present, there are nine public holidays.

- New Year's Day
- St. Patrick's Day
- Easter Monday
- May Public Holiday (first Monday in May)
- June Public Holiday (first Monday in June)
- August Public Holiday (first Monday in August)
- October Public Holiday (last Monday in October)
- Christmas Day
- St. Stephen's Day

In addition, the Act states that part-time employees must have worked at least forty hours during the five weeks prior to the public holiday to be entitled to the public holiday.

PART-TIME EMPLOYEES

The Worker Protection (Regular Part-time Employees) Act 1991, extends labour law protection to part-time employees who work more than eight hours a week and who have an appropriate period of service with the same employer. Part-time employees falling under the scope of the Act are afforded certain rights in the areas of unfair dismissals, redundancy payments and minimum notice and terms of employment.

In relation to unfair dismissals, an employee must have one year's service to bring an unfair dismissals claim. However, if the dismissal relates to trade union matters, the period of service required under the Act falls to thirteen weeks.

EMPLOYMENT OF YOUNG PEOPLE

The Protection of Young Persons (Employment) Act 1996 repeals the Protection of Young Persons (Employment) Act 1977, and lays down a number of conditions for the employment of young people. A child is defined under the Act as a person under sixteen years of age whereas a young person is regarded as a person between sixteen and eighteen years of age.

The Act prohibits the employment of children. Young people are allowed to work a maximum of forty hours per week or eight hours in any one day. They must receive a maximum rest period of twelve hours in each twenty-four hour period and a rest period of two days in each seven-day period.

The Act creates exemptions in relation to the employment of close relations of the employer. Specific provisions are also laid down in the Act in relation to rest periods, rates of pay and the complaints procedure to the rights commissioner. Neither children nor young people are permitted to be engaged in night-work.

PAY

The Payment of Wages Act 1991 repeals the Payment of Wages Act 1979 and the Truck Acts 1831 to 1896, and provides that no deductions can be made from an employee's wages without their explicit consent. The Act obliges employers to furnish an employee with an itemised pay statement setting out any deductions from the employee's wages and explaining the nature and amount of the deductions. The Act also allows for the payment of wages, in modes other than cash, provided the employee consents to such arrangements.

The National Minimum Wage Act 2000 introduces a legislative framework establishing the right of employees to a legally enforceable minimum rate of pay for their labour.

Significantly, the provisions of the Act do not apply when the employee is related to the employer, or when the employee is an apprentice. Specific provisions and calculations are also set out under the Act for individuals entering employment for the first time upon reaching the age of eighteen, as well as for individuals undergoing a course of training or study authorised by their employer. However, the provisions of the Act also extend to individuals employed under a contract for services.

The Act also contains detailed provisions to ensure ease of compliance with the Act and ease of determination of employee remuneration, taking into account employee working hours and issues of 'reckonable' and 'non-reckonable' pay.

The national minimum wages have been determined in conjunction with the Programme for Prosperity and Fairness (Section 12) as follows:

- £4.40 (€5.59) per hour from April 1, 2000
- £4.70 (€5.97) per hour from July 1, 2001
- £5.00 (€6.35) per hour from October, 1, 2002

PENSIONS

The Pensions Act 1990 and the Pensions (Amendment) Act 1996 regulate the operation of occupational pension schemes in Ireland. The 1990 Act is a lengthy and complex piece of legislation establishing a legal framework for the regulation and beneficial tax treatment of pension schemes established by employers for the benefit of employees. It provides that members who have the appropriate length of service and who lose their employment before retirement age are entitled to a preserved benefit. The Act also contains provision for a transfer payment for eligible members and lays down specific provisions relating to the disclosure of information in relation to pension schemes and provisions for the equal treatment of men and women in occupational benefit schemes. Furthermore, the 1990 Act establishes the Pensions Board to carry out the following functions:

- to monitor and supervise the operation of the Act and pensions developments;
- to advise the relevant minister on pensions matters;
- to issue guidelines on the duties and responsibilities of pension scheme trustees and establish codes of practice;
- to encourage the provision of appropriate training facilities for pension scheme trustees;
- to publish reports (including an annual report);
- to perform other tasks at the minister's request.

Employment Equality

MATERNITY PROTECTION AND MATERNITY LEAVE

The Maternity Protection Act 1994 applies to all women who work at least eight hours per week and who are insurable for the purposes of the social welfare code. The main purpose of the Act is to provide protection for all pregnant employees and those who have recently given birth or who are breast-feeding. It does this by giving them certain legal rights, the main ones being:

- the right to fourteen weeks paid maternity leave;
- the right to up to four weeks additional unpaid maternity leave;
- the right to return to work;
- the right to take time off from work without loss of pay to attend ante-natal and post-natal care medical appointments;
- the right to health and safety leave in certain circumstances;
- the right to protection of their jobs during maternity leave, additional maternity leave, father's leave, health and safety leave and time off for ante-natal and post-natal care;
- the right not to be dismissed for any pregnancy-related reason, from the beginning of pregnancy until the end of maternity leave;
- the right of an employed father to leave where the death of the mother occurs within fourteen weeks of the birth.

The Act entitles female employees to a period of maternity leave of at least fourteen weeks, if notice is given to the employer in writing at least four weeks before the expected date of birth, together with a medical certificate establishing the fact of pregnancy. There is no qualifying service in order to secure the right. The exact dates of the maternity leave can be chosen by the employee, but the period must cover the four weeks before and the four weeks after the birth.

During the period of maternity leave there is no break in the continuity of employee's service. She is entitled to return to her job after the birth, provided she notifies the employer in writing of her intention at least four working weeks before the expected date of return. Strict compliance with these requirements is essential.

In the event of the death of the mother, within fourteen weeks of the birth of a living child, the father of the child has certain leave entitlements, referred to as, 'leave to which the father is entitled' and 'further leave to which the father is entitled'. Where leave to which the father is entitled has been taken, he may choose to take a period of further leave of four weeks. Notice to take the further leave may be given at the same time as the original notification is given or, if it is later, not later than four weeks before he is due to resume work having taken his original leave entitlement.

ADOPTIVE LEAVE

Under the Adoptive Leave Act 1995, an adopting mother or a sole male adopter who is in employment is entitled to:

- a minimum of ten consecutive weeks' leave from work, beginning on the day of placement of the child, and
- up to four weeks' additional leave.

The ten-week period of adoptive leave will attract a social welfare benefit in the majority of cases.

PARENTAL LEAVE

The Parental Leave Act 1998, gives an employee fourteen working weeks unpaid leave for the purpose of caring for his/her child. The provisions of the Act apply to the natural or adoptive parents of a child, and both the mother and the father of the child qualify for the leave concerned. In addition, one period of leave may be taken in respect of each natural or adopted child of the employee. However, the Act stipulates that periods of leave are not transferable between parents. To qualify for the full period of parental leave, the employee must have completed one year's continuous service with the employer from whom the leave is to be taken.

Employees wishing to take parental leave must give notice in writing to their employer at least six weeks before the commencement of the period of leave. An employer may postpone parental leave for a period of six months where the taking of parental leave would have a substantial adverse effect on the employer's business.

The Act also makes provision for *force majeur* leave, when an employee may avail of paid leave where their immediate presence at home or elsewhere is indispensable because of urgent family reasons owing to the injury or illness of certain persons. Such leave should not exceed three days in any twelve-month period or five days in any thirty-six month period.

CARER'S LEAVE

The Carer's Leave Act 2001 provides an opportunity to employees with twelve months continuous service of taking sixty-five weeks unpaid leave for the purpose of providing full-time care and attention to a person requiring it. It applies to situations where the person involved has a disability, which requires the continual supervision and frequent assistance of the employee throughout the day in connection with normal bodily functions or in order to avoid danger to themselves. To avail of carer's leave, an employee must apply to the relevant minister for a decision by a specially appointed deciding officer. Notice of the intention to take carer's leave must be given in writing to the employer at least six weeks before the commencement of such leave. The notice must state:

- the proposal to take carer's leave;
- that an application for carer's leave has been made to the deciding officer;
- the proposed date of commencement of the carer's leave.

The Act also specifies a set of provisions under which an employee may apply for a second consecutive period of carer's leave.

EMPLOYMENT EQUALITY ACT

The Employment Equality Act 1998 has become the cornerstone of Irish Employment Equality law. It repeals the Anti-Discrimination Pay Act 1974 and the Employment Equality Act 1977 in total and its provisions affect or repeal over thirty other pieces of legislation. It defines discrimination as where 'one person is treated less favourably than another is, has been or would be treated' and outlaws the following nine grounds of discrimination:

- Gender
- Marital Status
- Family Status
- Sexual Orientation
- Religious Belief
- Age
- Disability
- Race
- Membership of the Travelling Community

Discrimination is prohibited in the following areas:

- An employer shall not discriminate against an employee, prospective employee or agency worker in relation to access to employment, conditions of employment, training or experience for or in relation to employment, promotion or regrading or classification of posts.
- Discrimination is outlawed in collective agreements and with regard to equal pay for like work.
- Advertising in relation to employment is prohibited where it indicates (or may be reasonably understood to indicate) an intention to discriminate.
- An employment agency shall not discriminate against any person availing of their services or guidance.
- Instructors or providers of vocational training shall not discriminate in terms of any course offered or provided.
- Professional or trade organisations or vocational bodies shall not discriminate against any person in relation to membership or entry to that profession, vocation or occupation.

The Act reaffirms the principle that employers are responsible for the actions of their employees done in the course of their employment, regardless of whether the employer knew or approved of the actions. The Act also requires an employer to accommodate the needs of employees with disabilities, unless those needs would entail a cost, other than a nominal cost to the employer.

In terms of equality between men and women, the basic principle that men and women should receive equal pay for like work is underlined. An employee, under the Act, may bring a claim to the Equality Authority showing that differences in remuneration exist for comparable work being undertaken between themselves and another person of the opposite gender working for the same employer. In relation to the other grounds of discrimination, the Act provides that each contract of employment shall be deemed to include a non-discriminatory equality clause. This means that employees are entitled to the same rate of remuneration, despite differences in marital status, family status, sexual orientation, religious belief, age, disability, race and membership of the travelling community, provided they are engaged in like work for the same or associated employer.

Indirect discrimination is prohibited under the Act. This relates to a situation where provisions, which apply to both sexes, operate so as to prejudice unfairly one sex over the other. Sexual harassment in the workplace is similarly outlawed under the Act. Sexual harassment is defined as including acts of physical intimacy or requests for sexual favours of one employee from another employee of the opposite sex, as well as other conduct including spoken words, gestures or the production, display or circulation of written words, pictures or other material. In such situations, the employer will be held responsible for acts of sexual harassment carried out on employees by other employees, clients, customers or other business contacts, regardless of whether the acts take place inside or outside the work environment. Significantly, no remedy is provided under the Act for same-sex harassment.

The Act established the Equality Authority, which replaces the Employment Equality Agency. The functions of the Equality Authority are:

- to work towards the elimination of discrimination in relation to employment;
- to promote equality of opportunity in relation to matters covered under the Act;
- to provide information to the public and to review the working of certain specified Acts;
- to review the working of the Pensions Act 1990 as regards the principle of equal treatment.

Finally, the Act created the Office of the Director of Equality Investigations (OEDI) for the enforcement of the provisions laid down in the Act. In the event of a dispute, where one party is claiming to have been discriminated against by another and not receiving 'equal' remuneration in accordance with the Act, redress may be sought by referring a claim to the OEDI. If a dismissal results from discrimination outlawed under the Act, the appropriate forum for redress is stated to be the Labour Court. If the issue of discrimination centres on gender, the claim will be dealt with by the circuit court. In all three cases, appeal processes are specified under the Act.

TERMINATION OF EMPLOYMENT
Section 14 (1) of the Unfair Dismissals Act 1977, provides that within twenty-eight days of offering employment, an employer must give the employee a notice in writing setting out the procedure the employer will observe before and for the purpose of dismissing the employee. If an employee is dismissed, the employer must give a written statement of the reasons why, within two weeks of the date of dismissal.

It is wise to send all such statements by recorded delivery and where related previous correspondence exists – such as warning letters, dismissal letters – to include copies of these as well. Although all such earlier incidents or warnings should have been properly recorded and the employee given copies at the time that they occurred, it is advisable to include copies and refer to them again in the final written reasons for dismissal. An employee may take a case before the Employment Appeals Tribunal if written reasons are refused or if the reasons are perceived to be inadequate.

Notice of Termination

Both the employer and the employee are normally entitled to a minimum period of notice although either employer or employee may accept pay in lieu of notice. Under Section 4 (1) of the Minimum Notice and Terms of Employment Act 1973, an employee who has thirteen weeks continuous service is entitled to a statutory minimum notice. Section 4 (2) of the Act sets out the periods of minimum notice to which employees covered by the Act are entitled in figure 13.3.

Figure 13.3 Periods of minimum notice

Continuous Service of Employee *Minimum Notice*	
Less than 2 years	1 week
More than 2 years but less than 5	2 weeks
More than 5 years but less than 10	4 weeks
More than 10 years but less than 15	6 weeks
15 years or more	8 weeks

These are *minimum* periods: if a contract of employment gives entitlement to a longer period, the longer period will apply.

Under Section 6 the employer in turn is entitled to a period of notice of not less than one week from an employee who has been in continuous employment for thirteen weeks or more. This period does not increase in line with the length of service; however, the contract of employment may specify a period of notice that is required by the employer.

The Employment Appeals Tribunal has stated that the notice given by the employer must be sufficiently certain and precise, leaving no room for ambiguity or uncertainty. The precise expiry date (date of dismissal) must be clearly specified in writing and the period of notice given must be not less than the minimum statutory period or the formal contractual period of notice. Employees to whom the notice provisions apply are entitled to the same rights during the minimum notice period as they would enjoy but for the notice. Failure by an employer to give notice correctly can affect the effective date of dismissal and therefore the eligibility of an employee's claim of unfair dismissal to be heard by the Employment Appeals Tribunal.

If the employer fails to give the employee the proper period of notice, the employee may claim breach of contract through the courts (common law remedy) or, if he is covered by the Minimum Notice and Terms of Employment Act, through an action to the Employment Appeals Tribunal. Categories of workers not covered by these provisions include the Garda Siochana, defence forces, local authority employees and civil servants.

Unfair Dismissal

Under the Unfair Dismissals Act 1977, once an employee has been continuously employed for one year he/she has a right of action if he/she is unfairly dismissed. If an employee has been dismissed and perceives it as being unfair he or she can bring a case to the Employment Appeals Tribunal or a rights commissioner within six months of the date of dismissal. The Unfair Dismissals (Amendment) Act 1993, provides that, in exceptional circumstances, the time frame within which a case may be brought may be extended to within twelve months of the date of dismissal. The date of dismissal is taken to be the date on which notice of the termination of contract expires. When prior notice is not given, the date of dismissal is taken to be the date on which such notice would have expired if it had been given. (The Employment Appeals Tribunal and rights commissioners are discussed in chapter ten).

The following categories of employees are not eligible to submit a claim for unfair dismissal:

- employees who have less than one year's continuous service with the same employer (if it is shown that a dismissal resulted wholly or mainly from the employees membership, or proposed membership of a trade union, or from their activities on behalf of a trade union the requirement of one year's continuous service does not apply; a woman who claims she was dismissed because of pregnancy may bring her unfair dismissal claim even though she does not have a year's continuous service with her employer);
- those over the normal retiring age;
- close relatives of the employer who are members of his or her household and work in a private dwelling house;
- members of the Garda Siochana and defence forces;
- those employed by or under the state;
- those serving apprenticeships with FÁS;
- officers of local authorities, health boards and vocational educational committees.

Dismissal is automatically unfair where it is shown that it resulted wholly or mainly from any of the following causes:

- taking part in a strike or other industrial action;
- following a lockout;
- the employee's trade union membership or activities;
- religious or political opinion;
- involvement in legal proceedings against the employer;
- the age of the employee;
- the race or colour of the employee;
- the sexual orientation of the employee;
- the pregnancy of the employee;
- the employee's membership of the travelling community;
- unfair selection for redundancy.

In general, where a dismissal is contested, the burden of proving that the dismissal is fair rests firmly with the employer. However, in constructive dismissal cases, where the employee terminates the employment contract, because of the employer's conduct or because conditions in the organisation make it impossible to stay, the onus is first on the employee to prove that they were dismissed and subsequently on the employer to prove that the dismissal was fair.

The decision to dismiss must be taken carefully, as the penalties that may be incurred if a dismissal is ruled as unfair by the Employment Appeals Tribunal are severe. It is important, therefore, that one should know the conditions under which an employee may be fairly dismissed.

DISMISSAL FOR MISCONDUCT

The issue of reasonableness has great significance in the context of dismissal for misconduct. The Employment Appeals Tribunal will consider general industrial standards. There is no absolute definition of reasonableness since it depends on individual circumstances within the company. The EAT has emphasised that misconduct must be measured in the context of the employee's actions and not just the consequences or potential consequences of that behaviour to the employer. It has further decided that in misconduct cases, the employer must, before taking the decision to dismiss, consider whether there were mitigating circumstances, such as a record of good service, personal difficulties experienced by the employee or first instance.

In the case of minor misconduct – such as persistent lateness – an employer must show that all of the stages in the disciplinary procedure have been followed and, having exhausted these, have given written warning that further infringements would lead to dismissal. To prove that the employer had acted properly it is necessary to have kept a written record of all the procedures that had gone through in the case.

If the misconduct were more serious – such as fighting, breaking a works rule, or sleeping on duty – going through every stage of the procedure might be unnecessary. However the employer would need to observe the rules of natural justice.

- The employee has a right to be told the facts of the case against him/her.
- The employee has the right to a hearing (to tell his/her side of the story).
- The employee has the right to representation of his/her choice.
- The employee has the right to appeal to a higher level of his/her choice within the company.

Failure to comply with the rules of natural justice may render a dismissal unfair.
An employer should also:

- Enquire into the matter to find out what really happened. If fact-finding is going to take some time it may be necessary to suspend the employee on full pay.
- Interview the employee to get his/her side of the story, advising him/her of the right to be represented if appropriate.
- Decide on the basis of the information what action is reasonable in the circumstances. Did the employee know the rule that was broken? Was he/she aware of its significance? Would a clearly stated warning of dismissal for repetition be more reasonable than dismissal for a first time offence? How have similar cases been treated in the past, i.e. is the employer being consistent with previous 'custom and practice'?
- Make clear to the employee what action is to be taken and how he/she can appeal against the decision if the procedure allows this.

CAPABILITY, COMPETENCE OR QUALIFICATIONS

Section 6 (4) (a) of the Unfair Dismissals Act 1977, provides that a fair basis for dismissal relates to the capability, competence or qualifications of the employee for performing work of the kind which he/she was employed by the employer to do. While it may be fair to dismiss someone for incapability, if a complaint were made an employer would need to convince a Tribunal that they had a valid reason for dismissing the person, and that they had acted reasonably in treating that reason as a sufficient cause for dismissal.

Capability, as determined by the Employment Appeals Tribunal, usually relates to dismissals arising from illness, injury or similar inadequacy. The question of whether the employee was to blame for the illness or incapacity is irrelevant. In the case of capability the tribunal has introduced a number of exceptions:

1. Where an employee who is incapacitated due to injury or illness could be given lighter work that he would have been able to perform, the dismissal may be unfair.
2. Where an employee is absent it is up to the employer to try to find out why. It is not reasonable to assume, without further investigation, that the absence is due to illness that might justify dismissal.

INCAPABILITY BECAUSE OF ILL-HEALTH

Dismissals resulting from incapacity due to ill health may arise in cases of persistent short-term absenteeism or cases of long-term absence caused by prolonged illness or injury. In both instances, an employer needs to ask how reasonable it is to dismiss an employee who has been off work for an extended period of time. Reasonable action would again consist of being seen to follow fair procedures and securing the fullest possible information. Evidence of fair procedure might include the following:

- Visiting the employee (perhaps on more than one occasion) to find out how likely it is that they will be returning to work, and to make clear to them how long the company can wait.
- If the company cannot wait any longer, obtaining an independent medical report, which would be a useful element in making a decision.
- Considering whether alternative work could be made available.
- Advising the employee of the decision.

In the case of dismissal due to illness-related absence, the High Court has set out the following grounds placing an onus on employers to prove that the dismissal is fair by showing:

1. It was the employee's ill health that was the reason for the dismissal.
2. This was the substantial reason.
3. The employee received fair notice that the question of their dismissal for incapacity was being considered.
4. The employee was afforded an opportunity of being heard.

INCAPABILITY BECAUSE OF INCOMPETENCE

Competence issues arise when an employee is alleged to have demonstrated a poor work performance, for example failure to meet reasonable targets set by the employer. To act fairly in dismissing someone for this reason, an employer must detail evidence of the alleged incompetence, and must have discussed this with the employee. An employer would also need to establish that they did not contribute to the incompetence by failing to make requirements clear, or by not providing the necessary facilities to allow the job to be done competently.

A warning might be appropriate. If so, it should clearly state what is required of the employee within set time limits. In such instances, an employee must be given a reasonable time period within which to effect such improvement and a reasonable work situation within which to concentrate on their work defects. In the case of long-serving employees, it might be more reasonable to consider whether a less arduous job could be found.

As with misconduct, warnings are not necessary if an employer believes they serve no purpose, but the employer might have to convince a Tribunal of this. A case will obviously be much easier to make if an employee has been given warnings and a chance to improve with as much reasonable help from the employer as possible.

INCAPABILITY BECAUSE OF QUALIFICATIONS

The concept refers primarily to the absence of formal qualifications that are essential to the job, which is another fair reason for dismissal under certain circumstances. This category might include the case of an accountant, losing their professional qualifications, or the case of an employee who misled an employer into thinking they had certain qualifications or experience on joining, but in fact did not. It might also arise where the employee did not have the qualifications on joining, has agreed to take steps to obtain them, but who seems unable to obtain them despite repeated attempts and every assistance from the company.

Reasonable dismissal in this category would depend on how critical the qualification was to the job and the duties of the employee in question and how long the situation was likely to continue. As in other cases, an employer would need to consider whether an alternative job could be offered for which the person was qualified.

BREAKING ANOTHER STATUTE

It is fair for an employer to dismiss an employee who could not continue to work without breaking another law. The sales representative who loses his driving licence is a clear example. As usual, however, an employer would need to consider alternatives to dismissal. Could the employer offer alternative work? Could other arrangements be made for the period?

INDUSTRIAL ACTION

Section 5 (1) of the Unfair Dismissals Act 1977 provides that the dismissal of an employee by way of lockout is fair if the employee is offered reinstatement or re-engagement from the date of resumption of work. Section 5 (2) provides that the dismissal of an employee for taking part in a strike or other industrial action is unfair if any other employee or employees who took part in the strike were reinstated or re-engaged. Where an employer dismissed all the employees who took part, the onus is still on them to prove that they had fair grounds under one of the previous headings or on other substantial grounds. If they cannot do so the dismissal will be unfair.

OTHER SUBSTANTIAL GROUNDS

An employer may succeed even if a dismissal does not fall under any of the previous headings where they can claim that it qualifies on 'other substantial grounds'. This heading has not been used very often and furthermore there is little consistency in the decisions of the Employment Appeals Tribunal.

Redundancy

Section 6 (4) (c) of the Redundancy Payments Act 1991 provides that a dismissal resulting from a redundancy of an employee is not unfair. Redundancy is basically defined as dismissal caused by either the fact that the employer has ceased their business, or that they no longer requires the work carried out by the particular employee, or they are reducing the scope of their workforce. The onus is on the employer to prove the existence of redundancy. They cannot simply claim that a situation of redundancy exists, they must produce substantial evidence.

Even where there is a genuine redundancy not all dismissals will necessarily be fair. A number of qualifications have been introduced.

1. Where an employee was selected in contravention of a procedure that has been agreed between the employer and the employee or trade union or that was established by custom and practice and no special reasons are produced for departing from this procedure, then the dismissal will be unfair.
2. If the employer had an ulterior motive in selecting the particular employee, then the dismissal will be unfair even if there was a genuine redundancy.

An employer should not use arbitrary criteria in selecting employees for redundancy. The Employment Appeals Tribunal examines all aspects of an employee's conduct, including the observance of statutory obligations such as the Protection of Employment Act 1977 (this Act allows for consultation and information relating to mass redundancies). Not only must an employer use proper criteria, but they must also be applied in a fair manner.

Redundancy Payments
Under the Redundancy Payments Acts 1967–91, employees who have had at least two years continuous service and who work at least eight hours per week and have not reached retirement age, are entitled to a redundancy payment in the event of being made redundant. This payment is calculated as follows:

- a sum equivalent to the employee's normal weekly working remuneration; plus
- half of their normal weekly remuneration for each year of their continuous employment between their sixteenth birthday and their forty-first birthday (or up to the termination of the contract of employment); plus
- their full weekly remuneration for each year of continuous employment from their forty-first birthday until the dismissal i.e. up to the termination of the contract.

Employees are not entitled to a redundancy payment if they unreasonably refuse an offer of suitable alternative employment with their own employer, or with another company in the same group where continuity of employment can be maintained, provided the alternative employment does not involve a significant reduction in status or conditions.

Legal Regulation for Redundancy
Redundancy legislation is very complex, containing many detailed provisions and rules. As a general classification the Acts fall into two categories:

- Legislation dealing with collective redundancies; this lays down procedural regulations to be observed by employers, and bestows a number of rights on unions.
- Legislation on what constitutes redundancy, the right to a redundancy payment and the calculation of continuous service.

The Protection of Employment Act 1977 lays down procedural obligations in the case of collective redundancies. There are a number of specific provisions that a manager will need to be aware of:

1. The Act applies to a situation where in a period of thirty days a number of employees are dismissed for redundancy. The minimum number required varies, depending on the size of the total workforce.
2. The main obligation on employers is consultation and notification. If a company has a collective redundancy then the Minister for Enterprise, Trade and Employment must be notified at least thirty days before the final dismissal. The employer must also send a copy of this notice to the employees' representatives.
3. At least thirty days before the dismissal, the employer must enter into consultation with the employee's representatives with a view to reaching agreement on issues, such as the numbers to be made redundant, alternative courses of action and the implementation of the redundancies. The Act does not specify what happens in the event of an agreement not being reached.
4. Employers are also obliged to provide the employees with certain information relating to the redundancy. Examples include the reasons for the redundancy, the number of employees affected and the period during which it is to take place.
5. Employers are also obliged to keep adequate records of the situation.

In the event of a redundancy taking place, then the individual employees situation is governed by the Redundancy Payments Acts 1967–91. Under Section 7 of the 1967 Act as amended, redundancy is defined as ' . . . an employee who is dismissed shall be taken to be dismissed by reason of redundancy if the dismissal is attributable wholly or mainly to one of the following'.

- Where the employer has ceased or intends to cease to carry on business for the purpose of which the employee was employed.
- Where the requirements of the business do not require the particular type of work which the employee has to offer.
- Where the employer decides to carry on the business with fewer employees.
- Where the employer decides that the work which the employee does is to be done in a different manner.
- Where the employer decides that the work done by the particular employee should from now on be done by a person who is capable of doing other work for which the employee is not sufficiently qualified to do.

Once the employee fits one of the redundancy categories it is then necessary to examine whether they meet the additional requirements set out in the Acts. The main requirements are that the employee (i) must have a minimum of 104 weeks continuous employment, and (ii) be aged between sixteen and sixty-five. Other important provisions include the following:

1. The entitlement to a redundancy payment cannot be waived and any term in a contract of employment that purports to do so is invalid.
2. The employer must give notice in writing to the employee of the proposed dismissal and must send a copy to the Minister for Enterprise, Trade, and Employment thirty days in advance. The employer must also furnish the employee with a redundancy certificate.

3. The employer has an entitlement to offer the redundant employee suitable alternative employment if it exists. The job offered must be either on the same or similar terms. If the employee unreasonably refuses this alternative offer he may lose his entitlement to a redundancy payment.

- The Acts allow the employee time off to try out the alternative job to test its suitability. The employee has four weeks in order to test its suitability.
- Employees eligible for redundancy pay are entitled to reasonable time off work, with pay, to look for another job. An employer may in such circumstances seek evidence that the employee is actually using the time off in the intended manner. If an employer refuses to allow time off, the employee may bring the matter to the EAT.
- Furthermore, an employee who is under notice does not have to work this notice if it is agreed that he should receive any due payment in lieu.

However, where the employer terminates the contract, it is also important that they give notice correctly, as this could affect the effective date of dismissal and therefore the eligibility of an employee's claim of unfair dismissal to be heard by the Employment Appeals Tribunal. The effective date of dismissal should be made very clear (in writing) to the employee and any period of notice given must not be less than the minimum statutory period or the formal contractual period of notice.

This Worker Protection (Regular Part-time Employees) Act 1991, extends the benefit of the protective employment legislation to regular part-time employees i.e. those who are in continuous employment for at least thirteen weeks with the same employer and who normally work at least eight hours per week.

Section 14 (1) of the Unfair Dismissals Act 1977, provides that an employer must within twenty-eight days of offering employment, give the employee a notice in writing setting out the procedure which the employer will observe before and for the purpose of dismissing the employee. If an employee is dismissed, the employer must give them a written statement of the reasons why, within two weeks of the date of dismissal.

HEALTH AND SAFETY AT WORK[2]

Both common law and statute law lay down a number of provisions concerning health and safety in the workplace. A useful classification of the relevant statutes is as follows:

- those that deals exclusively with the safety and health of workers;
- those concerned with the regulation of hours of work;
- those not designed exclusively as worker protection measures, but nevertheless providing varying degrees of protection;
- those on the border line between issues of general environmental pollution and occupational health and safety.

Common Law

Outside all the legislation that exists on health and safety at work, an employer may incur liability at common law. The position here is that an employer is legally responsible for any injuries or diseases that occur on the job. Case law has clearly laid down that an employer must exercise reasonable care towards employees and must guard them against any likely injury or disease. If an employer fails to live up to this obligation, then liability for negligence will occur if an employee is injured. However, it is important to remember that liability will only arise when an employer's negligence actually caused an employee's injury or disease. Furthermore, the incident that occurs must be reasonably foreseeable. The reason for this is simple – the common law is not concerned with anticipating damages or setting standards of good behaviour in order to prevent accidents, it only comes into play after the event, and its main function is to compensate employees for any injuries they receive while at work.

As well as laying down a general principle of employers' liability for injuries, the courts have gone further and have specified different elements of the employers' duties. This is directly relevant and provides a useful framework within which to evaluate a company's safety effort. The four duties are worth considering in detail.

1. Safe Plant and Equipment

This duty covers machinery, raw materials, tools, etc. However, employers will not incur liability if they obtain supplies from a reputable company and had no reason to suspect that they were faulty.

Employers must also keep up to date with the potential dangers of new processes and machinery. They will have observed their duty of care if they keep up to date with information which already is known to exist: no liability will arise against a hazard that scientific knowledge is not yet aware of.

2. Competent Fellow Workers

Employers are expected to take reasonable steps to ensure that employees are able to do their jobs. This involves clarifying the personal qualities and skills required to do the particular job, ensuring that one has a systematic recruitment and selection procedure and providing the necessary training to do the job and special remedial training where necessary.

For an employee to succeed in an action under this heading he/she would have to show two things:

1. That the other worker was unsuitable for the job.
2. The employer had not been sufficiently careful in appointing or retraining the other worker.

If an employee undertakes quite unpredictable behaviour that causes injury to a fellow-employee, the employer will not be held responsible.

3. Provision of Safety Equipment and Effective Supervision

Employers are under an obligation to provide employees with the necessary protective equipment and clothing required to do the job without exposing them to risk or injury. Proper instructions should also be issued. The courts have also clearly stated that it is not enough for the employer to inform the employee that the equipment is available; they must take reasonable measures to see that the employee uses it.

4. Safe Premises and System of Work

Employers must take great care in the way work is laid out and organised. They must not expose employees to risks that could easily be avoided by more careful organisation. They are also expected to maintain their premises in a reasonable state.

The courts have held that this duty extends to a customer's premises. If an employee is injured while working on a customer's premises they may have a claim against the employer. The employer's responsibility will be less, however, than if it was on the employer's premises. Employers will be liable to their employees for injuries that arise out of defects in the customer's premises that would have been apparent, and that the employer should have taken reasonable precautions against.

Employers will not be liable as a general rule to employees on their way to and from work. However, if employers provide a company bus for transporting staff, they must have a competent driver and must ensure that the bus is properly maintained. Furthermore, if an employer allows their employees onto the premises outside of working hours then reasonable steps must be taken to ensure that the premises is safe. The law further indicates that employers are vicariously liable for any damage or injury caused by their employees, while in the course of their employment.

The Safety, Health and Welfare at Work Act 1989

The Safety, Health and Welfare at Work Act 1989, applies to all places of work and establishes regulations and codes of practice for dealing with specialist areas of safety, health and welfare at work. The Act established the National Authority for Occupational Safety and Health, which has a chairman and ten ordinary members (three nominated by employee organisations, three nominated by employer organisations, four representatives of Government departments, state agencies and other relevant bodies). The authority has a number of particular duties:

- Enforcement of the Act;
- The provision of advisory services;
- The promotion of a 'safety culture';
- Research into work practices.

In addition, the authority, with the assistance of specialist advisory committees, develops regulations and codes of practice for different work activities as the need arises.

DUTIES IMPOSED BY THE LEGISLATION – EMPLOYERS
1. To ensure the health, safety and welfare at work, of all employees (Section 6). The Act gives examples of some areas that must be considered:
   (a) Design, provision and maintenance of the place of work;
   (b) Safe means of access to and exit from the place of work;
   (c) The provision and maintenance of machinery without risk;
   (d) Safe systems of work;
   (e) The provision of information, instruction, training and supervision;
   (f) Where hazards exist that cannot be controlled or eliminated, the provision and maintenance of suitable protective equipment;
   (g) Adequate and current emergency plans;
   (h) Ensuring safety with regard to articles or substances in use;
   (i) The provision and maintenance of welfare facilities;
   (j) The use of specialist services to provide for health, safety and welfare of the workforce.
2. To ensure that those not in their employment who may be affected are not exposed to risks to their safety or health (Section 7).
3. To prepare a safety statement (Section 12). The safety statement must:
   - Specify the manner in which health, safety and welfare shall be secured;
   - Be based on an identification of hazards and an assessment of risks;

- Include arrangements made and resources provided;
- Specify the co-operation required from employees;
- Specify the names of the persons responsible.

The safety statement must be brought to the attention of all those who are affected by it.

4. To consult employees. Under this Act, employers must consult their employees so that they can make and maintain effective measures; they can co-operate in promoting and developing measures to ensure health and safety; that the effectiveness of their arrangements can be ascertained.

5. To take account of employees' views (Section 13). Not only must there be consultation, but employers must take account of representations made by the workforce.

Duties Imposed by the Legislation – Employees

Section 9 details the general duties of employees while at work.

1. They must take reasonable care for their own safety and that of any other person who may be affected.

2. They must co-operate to such an extent that all relevant statutory provisions are complied with.

3. They must use the equipment provided in a safe manner.

4. They must report any problems of which they become aware, or that might have an effect on safety, health or welfare.

In addition to imposing duties on various categories of participants, the Act confers quite specific rights on employees. They have the right to make representations to, and to consult their employers on, matters of safety, health and welfare in their place of work.

The Safety Representative

1. Must make representations to the employer;
2. Must investigate accidents and dangerous occurrences;
3. Must talk or write to inspectors;
4. Must receive advice and information from inspectors;
5. Must carry out inspections;
6. Must investigate potential hazards;
7. Must accompany an inspector on normal tours of inspection;
8. Must have paid time off to acquire required skills;
9. Must have paid time off to discharge functions;
10. Must not be placed at any personal disadvantage.

The Safety, Health and Welfare at Work Regulations

Since the inception of the Safety, Health and Welfare at Work Act 1989, a series of regulations has emerged to make explicit and operational the provisions implicit in the Act. While, to date, nineteen sets of regulations have been enacted covering areas such as construction, signage, carcinogens, biological agents, night-work and shift-work, the most prominent of these regulations have been the Safety, Health and Welfare at Work (General Applications) Regulations (S.I. No. 44 of 1993; S.I. No. 188 of 2001). They provide detailed information on safety management, particularly in relation to accident-reporting requirements, training, first aid, manual handling and personal protective equipment. (For additional information on Safety, Health & Welfare at Work Regulations consult the Health and Safety Authority [www.hsa.ie] or Garavan [1997].)

Also, the Safety, Health and Welfare at Work (Pregnant Employees) Regulations 2000 (S.I. No. 218 of 2000), which repeals the Safety, Health and Welfare at Work (Pregnant Employees) Regulations 1994 (S.I. No. 446 of 1994) obliges employers to carry out a risk assessment of the workplace to ensure the safety and health of employees during pregnancy and breastfeeding. Furthermore, it contains specific provisions regarding night-working and supplying employees (or their safety representative) with information on the results of the risk assessment and the measures to be taken concerning the employees' safety.

COLLECTIVE LEGISLATION

Collective labour law establishes the legal framework for employee/industrial relations, and is distinguished from individual labour law in that it is concerned with regulating the relationship between employers and collectivises of employees – normally trade unions (see chapter ten).

Industrial Relations

The Industrial Relations Act 1990 is the definitive piece of legislation governing relations between employers and employees and their representatives. The Act is the most comprehensive revision of the law governing trade unions, trade disputes and industrial relations generally in over eighty-four years, since the adoption of the Trade Disputes Act 1906. The provisions of the Act can be broadly divided between trade union law and industrial relations law.

Trade Union Law

Trade Disputes

The approach adopted in the area of trade disputes law was to repeal the Trade Disputes Acts of 1906 and 1982 and to reintroduce the main provisions of these Acts with amendments. The main features of the provision relating to trade disputes are as follows:

1. *Individual disputes:* The Act withdraws immunities from one-person disputes where agreed procedures have not been followed.
2. *Secondary action:* This is now restricted unless the union can show that the secondary employer directly sought to frustrate the aims of the dispute.
3. *Picketing:* Workers may now picket only their own employer at the employer's place of work.
4. *Immunities:* The Act places limitations on the blanket immunity which existed under Section 4 of the Trade Dispute Act 1906 in respect of tortuous acts (acts for which a civil action for damages could be brought). The immunity now exists only for acts 'committed in contemplation or in furtherance of a trade dispute'.
5. *Worker v. worker dispute:* These no longer fall within the definition of a trade dispute.
6. *Injunctions (an order issued by a court to a party to an action, to refrain from some act):* In trade dispute situations where a secret ballot has been held and one week's notice given, the granting of injunctions to employers, especially *ex-parte* injunctions is restricted.

Secret Ballots

From 18 July 1992 union rules must contain provisions for the holding of secret ballots before any form of industrial action can be taken. No injunction will be granted to an employer in the event of a secret ballot being held.

Trade Union Rationalisation

The Act makes a number of amendments to existing trade union law designed to encourage mergers and to discourage formation of new or breakaway unions. The Act essentially increases the minimum membership required for trade unions to secure a negotiating licence (to 1,000) and the sum of money required to be held on deposit with the High Court (varying according to the size of the union, but a minimum of £20,000 [€25,395]). The Act also amends the Trade Union Act 1975, by offering grants towards the expenses incurred in a two-year period prior to a merger attempt even if the attempt fails.

INDUSTRIAL RELATIONS LAW

The Industrial Relations Act 1990 provides for the establishment of the Labour Relations Commission and divides functions between it and the Labour Court. Previously, the Labour Court had two primary functions – a conciliatory and an investigative function along with a number of secondary functions, such as those of joint industrial councils, joint labour committees, rights commissioners. Under the Act all functions of the Labour Court with the exception of its investigative function has been taken over by the Labour Relations Commission (see chapter ten).

The Industrial Relations (Amendment) Act 2001 introduces additional provisions for promoting harmonious relations between employers and employees. It outlines a set of criteria allowing trade unions to petition the Labour Court to investigate a particular trade dispute. In such instances, the court may make a recommendation, giving its opinion on the matters under dispute. Where the matter is not resolved, the court may be asked by the trade union to make a determination. Such determinations are legally enforceable by court order.

Transfer of Undertakings

The Transfer of Undertakings Regulations (S.I. No. 306 of 1980 and S.I. No. 487 of 2000) provides employees with a series of rights on the transfer of a business. The regulations take effect in situations where there is a change in the identity of the employer and where the business transferred as a going concern continues or resumes with the same or similar activities under the new employer. Under such circumstances, the employment rights, seniority and continuity of service of employees is protected and employers are obliged to consult with their employees in the event of a proposed transfer. The regulations also outline a set of sanctions in the event of non-compliance by employers with the provisions contained therein.

For further information about employment law refer to the Act or consult the Department of Enterprise, Trade and Employment (www.entemp.ie), see also, Fennell and Lynch (1993) or Meenan (1999).

Note

1. This chapter provides an overview of Irish employment law, but is not a legal interpretation thereof. For detailed information readers should refer to the particular Act or consult with the Department of Enterprise, Trade and Employment (www.entemp.ie). Readers requiring a more detailed treatment on Irish employment law should refer to, for example, Fennell and Lynch (1993) or Meenan (1999).
2. Readers requiring more detailed information on Safety, Health & Welfare at Work Regulations should consult with the Health and Safety Authority (www.hsa.ie) or Garavan (1997).

Bibliography

Abramovitz, M., and David, P. (1996), 'Technological change and the rise of intangible assets: the U.S. economy's growth path in the twentieth century', *Employment and Growth in the Knowledge-based Economy*, Paris: OECD, 35–61.

Adams, J. (1965), 'Inequity in social exchange' in L. Berkowitz (ed.), *Advances in Experimental Social Psychology*, vol. 2, London: Academic Press.

Adkins, C., Russell, C., and Werbel, J. (1994), 'Judgements of fit in the selection process: the role of work value congruence', *Personnel Psychology*, 47 (3), 605–24.

Aldag, R., and Brief, A. (1979), *Task Design and Employee Motivation*, New York: Scott, Foreman and Company.

Alderfer, C. (1972), *Existence, Relatedness and Growth*, New York: The Free Press.

Alexander, L. (1985), 'Successfully implementing strategic decisions', *Long Range Planning*, vol. 18, no. 3, 91–7.

Allen, K. (2000), *The Celtic Tiger: The Myths of Social Partnership*, Manchester: Manchester University Press.

Allen, R. (2001), 'Aligning reward practices in support of total quality management', *Business Horizons*, May.

Anastasi, A. (1982), *Psychological Testing*, London: Macmillan.

Anderson, L., and Wilson, S. (1997), 'Critical incident technique' in D. Whetzel, and G. Wheaton (eds.), *Allied Measurement Methods in Industrial Psychology*, Palo Alto, CA: Davies-Black Publishing.

Anderson, N. (1992), 'Eight decades of employment interview research: a retrospective meta-review and prospective commentary', *The European Work and Organisational Psychologist*, 2, 1–32.

Anderson, N., and Shackleton, V. (1986), 'Recruitment and selection: a review of developments in the 1980s', *Personnel Review*, vol. 15, no. 4.

Anderson, N., and Shackleton, V. (1993), *Successful Selection Interviewing*, Oxford: Blackwell.

Appelbaum, S., and Shapiro, B. (1991), 'Pay for performance: implementation of individual and group plans', *Journal of Management Development*, vol. 10, no. 7.

Argyris, C. and Schön, D. (1978), *Organisational Learning: A Theory-in-Action Perspective*, Reading, MA: Addison Wesley.

Arment, L. (1990), 'Learning and training: a matter of style', *Industrial and Commercial Training*, vol. 22, no. 3, 16–21.

Armstrong, M. (1992), *Human Resource Management: Strategy and Action*, London: Kogan Page.

Armstrong, M., and Murlis, H. (1988), *Reward Management: a Handbook of Salary Administration*, London: Kogan Page.

Armstrong, M. (1987), 'Human resource management: a case of the emperor's new clothes', *Personnel Management*, vol. 19, no. 8, 30–5.

Armstrong, M. (1995), *A Handbook of Personnel Management Practice*, London: Kogan Page.

Armstrong, M. (1999), *A Handbook of Human Resource Management Practice* (7th ed.), London: Kogan Page.

Armstrong, M., and Baron, A. (1995), *The Job Evaluation Handbook*, London: Institute of Personnel and Development.

Armstrong, M., and Murlis, H. (1994), *Reward Management: A Handbook of Remuneration Strategy and Practice*, London: Kogan Page.

Armstrong, P. (1988), 'The Personnel profession in the age of management accountancy', *Personnel Review*, vol. 17, no. 1, 25–31.

Armstrong, P. (1994), 'Accountancy and HRM' in J. Storey (ed.), *Human Resource Management: A Critical Text*, London: Routledge.

Arnold, J., Robertson, I., and Cooper, C. (1995), *Work Psychology: Understanding Human Behaviour in the Workplace*, London: Pitman.

Ashton, D. (1986), 'Current issues in line/staff relationships', *Management Education and Development*, 10, 2, 105–18.

Atkinson, A. (1984), '*Flexible Manning: the Way Ahead*', London: Institute of Manpower Studies.

Atkinson, J. (1984), 'Manpower Strategies for Flexible Organisations', *Personnel Management*, August, 28–31.

Atkinson, J., and Meager, N. (1986), 'Is flexibility just a flash in the pan?', *Personnel Management*, September 1986, 26–9.

Attwood, M. (1989), *Personnel Management*, London: Macmillan.

Avery, R., Miller, H., Gould, R., and Burch, P. (1987), 'Interview validity for selecting sales clerks', *Personnel Psychology*, 40, 1–12.

Bacon, N., and Storey, J. (1993), 'Individualization of the employment relationship and the implications for trade unions', *Employee Relations*, vol. 15, no. 1, 5–17.

Bain, G. (1970), *The Growth Of White Collar Unionism*, Oxford: Clarendon Press.

Baird, L., Briscoe, J., Tuden, L., and Rosansky, L. (1994), 'World class executive development', *Human Resource Planning*, 17, 1–16.

Baldwin, T., Danielsen, C., and Wiggenhorn, W. (1997), 'The evolution of learning strategies in organizations: from employee development to business redefinition', *Academy of Management Executive*, 11, 4, 47–58.

Balkin, D., and Gomez–Mejia, L. (1987), *New Perspectives on Compensation*, New York: Prentice Hall.

Bandura, A. (1986), *Social Foundations of Thought and Action*, Englewood Cliffs, N.J.: Prentice Hall.

Barnett, R. (1999), 'Learning to work and working to learn' in D. Boud, and J. Garrick (eds.), *Understanding Learning at Work,* London: Routledge.

Barney, J. (1991): 'Firm resources and sustained competitive advantage', *Journal of Management*, 17: 99–120.

Barney, J. (1995), 'Looking inside for competitive advantage', *Academy of Management Executive*, 9, 49–81.

Barrow, M., and Loughlin, H. (1992), 'Towards a learning organisation: 1. the rationale', *Industrial and Commercial Training*, 24, 1, 3–7.

Bean, R. (1976), 'Industrial reactions' in E. Cohen, and G. Studdard (eds.), *The Bargaining Context*, London: Arrow.

Beardwell, I., and Holden, L. (1997), *Human Resource Management: a Contemporary Perspective*, London: Pitman.

Beardwell, I., and Holden, L. (2001), *Human Resource Management : a Contemporary Perspective* (3rd ed.), London: Pearson Publishing.

Beattie, R., and McDougall, M. (1998), 'Inside or outside HRM? Locating lateral learning in two voluntary sector organisations' in C. Mabey, D. Skinner, and T. Clark (eds.), *Experiencing Human Resource Management*, London: Sage, 218–35.

Beaumont, P. (1980), 'The success of white collar recognition claims', *Employee Relations*, vol. 2, no. 4.

Beaumont, P. (1985), 'New plant work practices', *Personnel Review*, vol. 14, no. 5, 15–19.

Beaumont, P. (1991), 'Trade unions and HRM', *Industrial Relations Journal*, vol. 22, no. 4, 300–08.

Beaumont, P. (1993), *Human Resource Management: Key Concepts and Skills*, London: Sage.

Beaumont, P. (1995a), *The Future of Employment Relations*, London: Sage.

Beaumont, P. (1995b), 'The European Union and developments in industrial relations' in P. Gunnigle, and W. Roche (eds.), *New Challenges to Irish Industrial Relations*, Dublin: Oak Tree Press.

Beaumont, P., and Townley, B. (1985), 'Greenfield sites, new plants and work practices' in V. Hammond (ed.), *Current Research in Management*, London: Frances Pinter.

Bechet, T., and Walker, J. (1995), 'Aligning staffing with business strategy', *Human Resource Planning*, 16, 2, 1–16.

Becker, G. (1964), *Human Capital*, New York: Columbia University Press.

Beer, M., Spector, B., Lawrence, P., Quinn–Mills, D., and Walton, R. (1984), *Managing Human Assets: The Groundbreaking Harvard Business School Program*, New York: The Free Press: Macmillan.

Beer, M., Spector, B., Lawrence, P., Mills, D., and Walton, R. (1985), *Human Resource Management: A General Manager's Perspective*, New York: The Free Press.

Bell, D. (1974), *Planning Corporate Manpower*, London: Longman.

Benchley, R. (2001), *The Value of Human Capital*, Chief Executive, February.

Benge, E. (1944), *Job Evaluation and Merit Rating*, Washington DC: US National Foreman's Institute.

Bennet, R. (1991), *Management*, London: Pitman.

Bennison, M. and Casson, J. (1984), *Manpower Planning*, Maidenhead: McGraw-Hill.

Berg, A. (1989), 'Part–time employment: a response to economic crisis' in S. Rosenberg (ed.), *The State of the Labour Market*, New York: Plenum.

Berggren, C. (1990), 'Det nya bilarbetet' ['The new automobile employment'], Ph.D. Dissertation, University of Lund, Sweden.

Berridge, J. (1992), 'Human resource management in Britain', *Employee Relations*, vol. 14, no. 5, 62–92.

Berry, J. (1990), 'Linking management development to business strategies', *Training and Development Journal*, vol. 44, no. 8, 20–2.

Bevan, S., and Thompson, M. (1992), 'How are companies interpreting performance management?', *Personnel Management*, November.

Biddle, D., and Evenden, R. (1989), *Human Aspects of Management*, London: Institute of Personnel Management.

Birchall, A. (1975), *Job Design: Planning and Implementation Guide for Managers*, London: Gower Press.

Black, J., and Boal, K. (1994), 'Strategic resources–traits, configurations and paths to sustainable competitive advantage', *Strategic Management Journal*, 15, 131–48.

Blackwell, J. (1990), 'The changing role of part–time work in Ireland and its implications', *Labour Market Review*, Issue 1, June.

Blennerhassett, E. (1983), *Work Motivation and Personnel Practices: a Study Of Civil Services Executive Staff*, Dublin: Institute of Public Administration.

Blennerhassett, E., and Gorman, P. (1986), *Absenteeism in the Public Service: Information Systems and Control Strategies*, Dublin: Institute of Public Administration.

Block, P. (1990), *The Empowered Manager*, San Francisco: Jossey Bass.

Bloom, M., and Milkovich, G. (1998), 'Relationships among risks, incentive pay and organizational performance', *Academy of Management Journal*, 41 (3).

Blyton, P., and Morris, J. (eds.), (1991), *A Flexible Future: Prospects for Employment and Organisation*, Berlin: De Gruyter.

Blyton, P., and Morris, J. (1992), 'HRM and the limits of flexibility' in P. Blyton, and P. Turnbull (eds.), *Reassessing Human Resource Management*, London: Sage.

Blyton, P., and Turnbull, P. (eds.), (1992), *Reassessing Human Resource Management*, London: Sage.

Blyton, P., and Turnbull, P. (1994), *The Dynamics of Employee Relations*, London: Macmillan.

Boerlijst, G., and Meijboom, G. (1989), 'Matching the individual and the organisation' in P. Herriot (ed.), *Assessment and Selection in Organisations: Methods and Practice for Recruitment and Appraisal*, Chichester: John Wiley.

Boisot, M. (1999), *Knowledge Assets: Securing Competitive Advantage in the Information Economy*, Oxford: University Press.

Boud, D. and J. Garrick (eds), *Understanding Learning at Work*, London: Routledge.

Bowey, A. (1975), '*Installing salary and wage systems*' in A. Bowey (ed.), Handbook of Salary and Wage Systems, London: Gower.

Bowey, A., and Thorpe, R. (1986), *Payment Systems and Productivity*, London: Macmillan.

Boxhall, P. (1992), 'Strategic human resource management: beginnings of a new theoretical sophistication', *Human Resource Management Journal*, 2, (3), 60–79.

Boyatzis, R. (1982), *The Competent Manager, A Model for Effective Performance*, New York: Wiley.

Boyd, A. (1972), *The Rise of Irish Trade Unions: 1729–1970*, Tralee: Anvil.

Boydell, T. (1983), *A Guide to Job Analysis*, London: BACIE.

Boyer, R. (ed.) (1988), *The Search for Labour Market Flexibility*, Oxford: Clarendon Press.

Bramham, J. (1989), *Human Resource Planning*, London: Institute of Personnel Management.

Brannick, T., and Doyle, L. (1994), 'Industrial conflict' in T. Murphy, and W. Roche (eds.), *Irish Industrial Relations in Practice*, Dublin: Oak Tree Press.

Brannick, T., Doyle, L., and Kelly, A. (1997), 'Industrial conflict' in T. Murphy, and W. Roche (eds.), *Irish Industrial Relations in Practice*, Dublin: Oak Tree Press.

Bratton, J., and Gold, J. (1999), *Human Resource Management: Theory and Practice*, Basingstoke: Macmillan Press.

Braverman, H. (1974), *Labour and Monopoly Capital: The Degradation of Work in the Twentieth Century*, London: Monthly Review Press.

Breen, R., Hannon, D., Rottman, D., and Whelan, C. (1990), *Understanding Contemporary Ireland: State, Class and Development in the Republic of Ireland*, Dublin: Gill and Macmillan.

Brewster, C. (1990), 'Flexible working and strategic HRM in Europe: research data', Brussels: MCE Industrial Relations Conference, November.

Brewster, C., Hegewisch, A., Lockhart, T., and Mayne, L. (1993), 'Flexible working patterns in Europe', *Issues in People Management*, no. 6, London: Institute of Personnel Management.

Brewster, C., and Hegewich, A. (1994), *Policy and Practice in European Human Resource Management: The Price Waterhouse Cranfield Survey*, London: Routledge.

Brooks, I. (1999), *Organisational Behaviour: Individuals, Groups and the Organisation*, London: Financial Times/Pitman Publishing.

Brown, J. (1994), 'The Juridification of the Employment Relationship', Aldershot: Aylesbury.

Brown, W. (1981), *The Changing Contours of British Industrial Relations*, Oxford: Blackwell.

Buchanan, D. (1979), *The Development of Job Design Theories and Techniques*, London: Saxon House.

Buchanan, D. (1994), 'Principles and practice of job design' in K. Sisson (ed.), *Personnel Management: A Comprehensive Guide to Theory and Practice in Britain*, Oxford: Blackwell.

Buchanan, D., and McCalman, J. (1989), *High Performance Work Systems: The Digital Experience*, London: Routledge.

Buckley, M., Ferris, G., Bernardin, H. and Harvey, M. (1998), 'The disconnect between the science and practice of management', *Business Horizons*, 41, 31–8.

Buckley, R., and Caple, J. (1992), *The Theory and Practice of Training*, London: Kogan Page.

Buller, P., and Napier, N. (1993), 'Strategy and human resource management: integration in FÁS growth versus other mid–sized firms', *British Journal of Management*, vol. 4, no. 2, 77–90.

Burack, E., Hochwarter, W., and Mathys, N. (1997), 'New management development paradigm', *Human Resource Planning*, vol. 20, 14–22.

Butler, P. (1985), 'Employer organisations: a study', unpublished BBS Final Year Project, Limerick: University of Limerick.

Byrne, T. (1988), 'IPM in Ireland 1937–87', *IPM News* vol. 3, no. 2.

Cairns, N., and Thompson, J. (1988), 'Manpower planning in Northern Ireland', *Irish Business and Administrative Research*, vol. 9, 38–45.

Calvert, G., Mobley, S., and Marshall, L. (1994), 'Grasping the learning organisation', *Training and Development*, June 1994.

Campion, M., Purcell, E., and Brown, B. (1988), 'Structured interviewing: raising the psychometric properties of the employment interview', *Personnel Psychology*, vol. 41, 25–42.

Cannon, F. (1995), 'Business driven management development', *Journal of European Industrial Training*, vol. 19, 26–31.

Cannon, T. (1999), 'Foreward' in J. Winterton, and R. Winterton (eds.), *Developing Managerial Competence*, London: Routledge.

Cappelli, P. (1995), 'Rethinking employment', *British Journal of Industrial Relations*, vol. 33, no. 4, 563–602.

Cappelli, P., and Crocker–Hefer, A. (1996), 'Distinctive human resources are a firm's core competencies', *Organizational Dynamics*, vol. 28, no. 2, 7–21.

Carey, A. (1967), 'The Hawthorne Studies: a radical criticism', *American Sociological Review*, June.

Cascio, W. (1986), *Managing Human Resources: Productivity, Quality of Work Life, Profits*, New York: McGraw-Hill.

Casey, B., Lakey, J., and White, M. (1992), *Payment Systems: A Look at Current Practice* (Research Series, no. 5), Department of Employment, London: Policy Studies Institute.

Central Bank of Ireland (2000), *Winter Bulletin*, Dublin: Central Bank of Ireland.

Chadwick, C., and Cappelli, P. (1999), 'Alternatives to generic strategy typologies in strategic human resource management' in P. Wright, L. Dyer, J. Boudreau, and G, Milkovich (eds.), *Research in Personnel and Human Resources Management*, supplement 4, 11–29, Greenwich, CT: JAI Press.

Chandler, A. (1962), *Strategy and Structure: Chapters in the History of the Industrial Enterprise*, Cambridge: MIT Press.

Cherns, A., and Davis, L. (1975), *The Quality of Working Life*, London: Macmillan.

Chubb, B. (ed.) (1992), *FIE: Federation of Irish Employers 1942–92*, Dublin: Gill and Macmillan.

Clarke, P. (1989), 'Payment by result schemes: a review of trends', *Industrial relations News*, no. 8, 23.

Clegg, H. (1979), *The Changing System of Industrial Relations in Great Britain*, Oxford: Blackwell.

Cole, G. (1988), *Personnel Management: Theory and Practice*, London: DP Publications.

Commission of Inquiry on Industrial Relations (1981), *Report of the Commission of Inquiry on Industrial Relations*, Dublin: The Stationery Office.

Commission on Industrial Relations, (1972), 'Employers Organisations and Industrial Relations', Study no. 1, London: HMSO.

Confederation of Irish Industry (1981), 'Jobs and the Workforce', Business Report no. 11.

Cowling, A. and Walters, M. (1990), Manpower planning – where are we today?, *Personnel Review*, 19, 3, 3–8.

Cox, B., and Hughes, J. (1989), 'Industrial relations in the public sector', *Industrial Relations in Ireland: Contemporary Issues and Developments*, Dublin: University College Dublin.

Cradden, T. (1992), 'Trade unionism and HRM: the incompatibles', *Irish Business and Administrative Research*, vol. 13, 37–48.

Cranet E./University of Limerick (1999), *Study of HR Practices in Ireland*, Limerick's Employment Relations Unit: University of Limerick.

Cropanzano, R. (2001), *Justice in the Workplace: From Theory to Practice*, New Jersey: Lawrence Erlbaum Associates.

Crouch, C. (1982), *Trade Unions: The Logic of Collective Action*, London: Fontana.

Culliton, J. (1992), *A Time for Change: Industrial Policy for the 1990s*, report of the Industrial Policy Review group, Dublin: Stationary Office.

Curson, C. (1986), *Flexible Patterns of Work*, London: IPM.

Dale, M. (1995), *Successful Recruitment and Selection: A Practical Guide for Managers*, London: Kogan Page.

Daniel, W., and Millward, N. (1983), *Workplace Industrial Relations in Britain: The DE/PSI/ESRC Study*, London: Heinemann.

Dastmalachian, A., Blyton, P. and Adamson, R. (1991), *The Climate of Workplace Relations*, London: Routledge.

Davis, L. (1966), 'The design of jobs', *Industrial Relations*, vol. 6, no. 1.

Deaton, D. (1985), 'Management Style and large scale survey evidence', *Industrial Relations Journal*, vol. 16, no. 2, 67–71.

De Cieri, H., and Dowling, P. (1999), 'Strategic human resource management in multinational enterprises: theoretical and empirical developments' in *Research in Personnel and Human Resources Management*, supplement 4, 304–26, Greenwich, CT: JAI Press.

DeGeus, A. (1997), *The Living Company: Growth, Learning and Longevity in Business*, London: Nicholas Brealey.

Delbridge, R., and Turnbull, P. (1992), 'Human resource maximization: the management of labour under just in time manufacturing systems' in P. Blyton, and P. Turnbull, (eds.), *Reassessing Human Resource Management*, London: Sage.

Delery, J., and Doti, H. (1996), 'Modes of theorising in strategic human resource management: tests of universalistic, contingency and configurational performance', *Academy of Management Journal*, vol. 39, 802–35.

Department of Enterprise and Employment, (1993), *Duties and Responsibilities of Employee Representatives and the Protection and Facilities to be afforded them by their employer*, Dublin: Department of Enterprise and Employment.

Dessler, G. (2001), *A Framework for Management*, New Jersey: Prentice Hall.

Dineen, D. (1987), *Employment Development in the Irish Economy Since 1979*, paper presented to the International Conference on 'The Changing Nature of Employment: New Forms and New Areas', Paris: BIPE.

Dineen, D. (1988), *Changing Employment Patterns in Ireland: Recent Trends and Future Prospects*, University of Limerick.

Dineen, D. (1992), 'Atypical work patterns in Ireland: short term adjustments or fundamental changes', *Administration*, vol. 40, no. 3, Autumn.

Dobson, P. (1989), 'Reference reports' in P. Herriot (ed.), *Assessment and Selection in Organisations*, New York: John Wiley.

Docherty, P., and Nyhan, B. (1997), *Human Competence and Business Development: Emerging Patterns in European Companies*, London: Springer-Verlag.

Doeringer, P., and Piore, M. (1971), *Internal Labour Markets and Manpower Analysis*, New York: Lexington Books.

Donnelly, E. (1987), 'The training model: a time for change?', *Industrial and Commercial Training*, May/June, 3–6.

Donovan, Lord (Chairman), (1968), Royal Commission on Trade Unions and Employers' Associations, 1965–68, Cmnd 3623, London: HMSO.

Downes, D. (1986), 'Manpower planning in Ireland: a survey of current practice in the mid-west region', unpublished final year project (BBS-Personnel), NIHE, Limerick.

Doyle, W., and Young, J. (2000), 'Management development: making the most of experience and reflection', *Canadian Manager*, Fall, 18–20.

Drejer, A. (2001), 'How can we define and understand competencies and their development?', *Technovation*, 21, 135–46.

Driver, M. (1982), 'Career concepts: a new approach to career research' in R. Katz (ed.), *Career Issues in Human Resource Management*, Englewood Cliffs: Prentice-Hall.

DuBrin, A. (1978), *Human Relations: A Job Oriented Approach*, Virginia: Reston Publishing Company.

Duffy, K. (1993), 'Training: why we lag behing our Euro partners', *Irish Independent*, Business and Recruitment Supplement, 18 Mar. 1993, 3.

Duggan, D., Hughes, G., Sexton, J. (1997), 'Occupational employment forecasts 2003', *FÁS/ESRI Manpower Forecasting Studies*, Report no. 6, November, Dublin: FÁS and The Economic and Social Research Institute.

Easterby-Smith, M. (1986), *Evaluation of Management, Training and Development*, Aldershot: Gower.

Economist, The (1988), 'A survey of the Republic of Ireland. poorest of the rich', *The Economist*, vol. 306, no. 7533, 1–26.

Economist, The (1997), 'Green is good – advantages of Ireland as a host for FDI', *The Economist*, vol. 343, no. 8017, 21–4.

Economist Intelligence Unit (EIU), (1999), 'Country Profile: Ireland', London: Economist Intelligence Unit.

Edwards, M., Ewen, A., and O'Neal, S. (1995), 'Using multisource assessment to pay people not jobs', *ACA Journal*, Summer, 4–17.

Eichel, E., and Bender, H. (1984), *Performance Related Pay: A Study of Current Techniques*, American Management Association.

Elger, T. (1991), 'Flexible futures? New technology and the contemporary transformation of work', *Work, Employment and Society*, vol. 1, no. 4.

Elliott, R. (1990), *Labour Economics – a comparative text*, Berkshire, UK: McGraw Hill.

Employment Appeals Tribunal (2000), *The Employment Appeals Tribunal Thirty-Second Annual Report 1999*, Dublin: The Employment Appeals Tribunal.

Equality Authority (2001), *The Equality Authority Annual Report 2000*, Dublin: The Equality Authority.

European Foundation for the Improvement of Living and Working Conditions (EFILWC) (1997), *New Forms of Work Organisation: Can Europe Realise its Potential?* Dublin: European Foundation for the Improvement of Living and Working Conditions.

European Foundation for the Improvement of Living and Working Conditions (EFILWC), (1999), *EPOC: Direct Employee Participation in the Public Services*, Dublin: European Foundation for the Improvement of Living and Working Conditions.

European Industrial Relations Review (1992), 'Lean production – more of the same or revolution', *European Industrial Relations Review*, no. 223, August.

Evenden, R., and Anderson, G. (1992), *Management Skills: Making the Most of People*, Wokingham: Addison Wesley.

Farnham, D. (1984), *Personnel in Context*, London: Institute of Personnel Management.

Farnham, D. and Pimlott, J. (1990), *Understanding Industrial Relations*, London: Cassell.

FÁS (2000), *Review of Labour Market Trends in 2000 and Outlook to 2001*, Labour Market Updates 4/2000 (www.fas.ie).

Feldman, D., and Doerpinghaus, H. (1992), 'Missing persons no longer: managing part–time workers in the 1990s', *Organizational Dynamics*, vol. 21, no. 1, 59–73.

Fennell, C., and Lynch, I. (1993), *Labour Law in Ireland*, Dublin: Gill and Macmillan.

Ferris, G., Hochwarter, W., Buckley, M., Harrell–Cook, G., and Frink, D. (1999), 'Human resources management: some new directions', *Journal of Management*, 25 (3), 385–427.

Field, L., and Ford, B. (1995), *Managing Learning Organisations*, Melbourne: Longman.

Fierro, F. (2001), 'Global human resource management: stock options in remuneration programmes', *Market Reporter*, 16 July.

Finn, G., and Morley, M. (2001), 'Expatriate selection: the case of an Irish MNC' in M. Linehan, M. Morley, and J. Walsh (eds.), *International HRM and the Expatriate Transfers: Irish Experiences*, Dublin: Blackhall Press.

Fisher, R., and Ury, W. (1986), *Getting to Yes*, London: Hutchinson.

Fitzgerald, T. (1971), 'Why motivation theory doesn't work', *Harvard Business Review*, July–August, 12–19.

Flamholtz, E. and Lacey, J. (1981), *Personnel Management: Human Capital Theory and Human Resource Accounting*, Los Angeles: Institute of Industrial Relations, UCLA.

Flanagan, J. (1954), 'The critical incident technique', *Psychological Bulletin*, 41, 236–358.

Flanders, A. (1968), *Trade Unions*, London: Hutchinson.

Fletcher, C., and Williams, R. (1985), *Performance Appraisal and Career Development*, London: Hutchinson.

Flood, P. (1989), 'Human resource management: promise, possibility and limitations', research paper, University of Limerick.

Flood, P. (1990), 'Atypical employment: core–periphery human resource strategies – the implications for corporate culture', *Industrial Relations News*, Nos. 9 and 10.

Flood, P., Gannon, M. and Paauwe, J. (1996), *Managing Without Traditional Methods: International Innovations in International Human Resource Management*, Wokingham: Addison Wesley.

Foley, A. (1990), 'Indigenous manufacturing' in A. Foley, and M. Mulreany (eds.), *The Single European Market and the Irish Economy*, Dublin: Institute of Public Administration.

Foley, K. and Gunnigle, P. (1994), 'The personnel/human resource function and employee relations' in P. Gunnigle, P. Flood, M. Morley, and T. Turner, *Continuity and Change in Irish Employee Relations*, Dublin: Oak Tree Press.

Foley, K., and Gunnigle, P. (1995), 'The personnel function: change or continuity' in T. Turner, and M. Morley, *Industrial Relations and the New Order*, Dublin: Oak Tree Press.

Foley, K., Gunnigle, P. and Morley, M. (1994), 'Financial rewards and company ownership: an examination of reward practices in the Republic of Ireland', *The International Executive*, vol. 36, no. 5, 575–99.

Fombrun, C. (1986), 'Environmental trends create new pressures on human resources' in S. Rynes and G. Milkovich (eds.), *Current Issues in Human Resource Management: Commentary and Readings*, Plasco (Texas): Business Publications.

Fombrun, C., Tichy, N., and Devanna, M. (1984), *Strategic Human Resource Management*, New York: John Wiley.

Foulkes, F. (1980), *Effective Personnel Policies: A Study of Larger Non–Union Enterprises*, Englewood Cliffs, NJ: Prentice Hall.

Fowler, A. (1988), 'New directions in performance pay', *Personnel Management*, November, 30–4.

Fowler, A. (1991), 'Performance related pay', *Personnel Management Plus*, June 1991.

Fowler, A. (1996), 'How To: pick a job evaluation system', *Personnel Management*, 8 February, 42–3.

Fox, A. (1966), 'Management ideology and labour relations', *British Journal of Industrial Relations*, vol. 4.

Fox, A. (1968), 'Industrial sociology and industrial relations', *Research Paper no. 3 to the Royal Commission on Trade Unions and Employers' Associations*, London: HMSO.

Fox, A. (1974), *Beyond Contract: Work, Power and Trust Relations*, London: Faber.

Fox, R. (1987), *Training of the Employed: Statistics for Ireland*, Dublin: AnCO, October.

Fox, R., and O'Reilly, A. (1979), *Corporate Manpower Planning in Ireland*, Dublin: AnCO.

Frawley, M. (2000) 'Year 2000 – Partnership Signed, Broken and Rescued?', *Industrial Relations News*, 48, 15–17.

Fulmer, R., Gibbs, P., and Goldsmith, M. (2000), 'Developing leaders: how winning companies keep on winning', *Sloan Management Review*, 42, 49–59.

Furnham, A. (1997), *The Psychology of Behaviour at Work: The Individual in the Organization*, London: Psychology Press.

Galbraith, J., and Nathanson, D. (1978), *Strategic Implementation: the Role of Structure and Process*, St Paul: West Publishing.

Galvin, P. (1988), *Managers for Ireland: The Case for Development of Irish Managers*, Dublin: Advisory Committee on Management Training, Department of Labour.

Garavan, T., Costine, P., and Heraty, N. (1995), *Training and Development in Ireland: Context, Policy and Practice*, Dublin: Oak Tree Press.

Garavan, T. (1991), 'Strategic human resource development', *Journal of European Industrial Training*, vol. 15, no. 1, 17–31.

Garavan, T. (1997), *The Irish Health and Safety Handbook*, Dublin: Oak Tree Press.

Garavan, T., Morley, M., and Flynn, M. (1997), '360 degree feedback: its role in employee development', *Journal of Management Development*, vol. 16, no. 2, 134–48.

Garavan, T., Morley, M., Gunnigle, P., and Collins, E. (2001), 'Human capital accumulation: the role of human resource development', *Journal of European Industrial Training*, 25, (2/3/4), 48–68.

Gatewood, R., and Fields, H. (1998), *Human Resource Selection*, Forth Worth, TX: Dryden Press.

Geary, J. (1994a), 'Task participation: employee's participation – enabled or constrained' in K. Sisson (ed.), *Personnel Management: A Comprehensive Guide to Theory and Practice in Britain*, Oxford: Blackwell.

Geary, J. (1994b), 'New Forms of Work Organisation: Implications for Employers, Trade Unions and Employees', working paper no. 9, Graduate School of Business, University College Dublin.

Geary, J. (1995a), 'Working at Teamwork: Lessons from Europe', working paper, Graduate School of Business, University College Dublin.

Geary, J. (1995b), 'World class manufacturing and the implications for industrial relations' in P. Gunnigle, and W. Roche (eds.), *New Challenges to Irish Industrial Relations*, Dublin: Oak Tree Press in association with the Labour Relations Commission.

Geary, J. (1998), 'New Work Structures and the Diffusion of Teamworking Arrangements in Ireland', paper presented at the Sixth Annual John Lovett Memorial Lecture, University of Limerick, 2 April.

Gee, J., Hull, G., and Lankshear, C. (1996), *The New Work Order: Behind the Language of the New Capitalism*, Sydney: Allen and Unwin.

George, J., and Jones, G. (1992), *Organizational Behaviour*, New Jersey: Prentice Hall.

Gill, D. (1977), *Appraising Performance: Present trends and the Next Decade*, London: IPM.

Gilliland, S. (1993), 'The perceived fairness of the selection system: an organisational perspective', *Academy of Management Review*, 18, 694–734.

Gladstone, A. (1984), 'Employers' associations in comparative perspective: functions and activities' in J. Windmuller, and A. Gladstone (eds.), *Employer's Associations and Industrial Relations: A Comparative Study*, Oxford: Clarendon.

Gleeson, J. (1998), 'A consensus approach to policy making: the case of the Republic of Ireland' in I. Finlay, S. Niven, and S. Young (eds.), *Changing Vocational Education and Training: an International Comparative Perspective*, London: Routledge.

Goffee, R., and Scase, R. (1986), 'Are the rewards worth the effort? Changing managerial values in the 1980s', *Personnel Review*, vol. 15, no. 4.

Goss, D. (1994), *Principles of Human Resource Management*, London, Routledge.

Government Publications Office, (1997), *White Paper on Human Resource Development*, (Pn. 3381), Dublin: Government Publications Office, May.

Government Social Survey (UK), (1968), *Workplace Industrial Relations*, (SS40Z), London: HMSO.

Grafton, D. (1988), 'Performance related pay: securing employee trust', *Industrial Relations News*, no. 44, 17 November, 11–12.

Graves, L., and Karren, R. (1996), 'The employee selection interview: a fresh look at an old problem', *Human Resource Management*, 35, 2, 163–80.

Gray, A. (ed.), (1997), *International Perspectives on the Irish Economy*, Dublin: Indecon Economic Consultants.

Green Paper on *Adult Education in an Era of Lifelong Learning* (1998), November, Dublin: Government Publications Office.

Green, F., Krahn, H., and Sung, J. (1993), 'Non–standard work in Canada and the United Kingdom', *International Journal of Human Resources*, vol. 14, no. 5, 70–86.

Griffin, R. (1987), 'Toward an integrated theory of task design', *Research in Organizational Behavior*, 9, 79–120.

Griffin, R., and McMahan, G. (1994), 'Motivation through job design' in J. Greenberg, (ed.), *Organizational Behaviour: The State of the Science*, Hillsdale: Lawrence Erlbaum Associates.

Grote, D. (1996), *The Complete Guide to Performance Appraisal*, New York: American Management Association.

Grundy, T. (1997), 'Human resource management: a strategic approach', *Long Range Planning*, 30 (4), 507–17.

Guest, D. (1983), 'Personnel management strategies, procedures and techniques' in D. Guest, and J. Kenny, *A Textbook of Techniques and Strategies in Personnel Management*, London: Institute of Personnel Management.

Guest, D. (1987), 'Human resource management and industrial relations', *Journal of Management Studies*, vol. 24, no. 5, 503–21.

Guest, D. (1989), 'Human resource management: its implications for industrial relations and trade unions' in J. Storey (ed.), *New Perspectives on Human Resource Management*, London: Routledge.

Guest, D. (1990), 'Human resource management and the American dream', *Journal of Management Studies*, vol. 27, no. 4, 377–97.

Guest, D. (1992), 'Right enough to be dangerously wrong: an analysis of the in search of excellence phenomenon' in G. Salaman (ed.), *Human Resource Strategies*, London: Sage/Open University Press.

Guest, D. (2001), 'Human resource management: when research confronts theory', *International Journal of Human Resource Management*, 12 (76), 1092–106.

Gunnigle, P. (1989), 'Management approaches to industrial relations in the small firm' in *Industrial Relations in Ireland: Contemporary Issues and Developments*, Dublin: University College Dublin.

Gunnigle, P. (1991), 'Determinants and nature of personnel policy choice: the context for human resource development', *Journal of European Industrial Training*, vol. 15, no. 3, 22–31.

Gunnigle, P. (1992a), 'Changing management approaches to employee relations in Ireland', *Employee Relations*, vol. 14, no. 5, 40–51.

Gunnigle, P. (1992b), 'Human resource management in Ireland' *Employee Relations*, vol. 14 no. 5, 5–22.

Gunnigle, P. (1993), 'Multinational companies and labour relations: a perspective on the experience of the Republic of Ireland'. Paper presented to OECD/Hungarian Ministry of Labour Seminar, 'Labour–Management Relations in Foreign Enterprises in Hungary', Budapest, June.

Gunnigle, P. (1995), 'Collectivism and the management of industrial relations in greenfield sites', *Human Resource Management Journal*, vol. 5, no. 3, 24–40.

Gunnigle, P., and Brady, T. (1984), 'The management of industrial relations in the small firm', *Employee Relations*, vol. 6, no. 5, 21–4.

Gunnigle, P., and Daly, A. (1992), 'Craft integration and flexible work practices: training implications', *Industrial and Commercial Training*, vol. 24, no. 10, 10–18.

Gunnigle, P., and Flood, P. (1990), *Personnel Management in Ireland: Practices, Trends and Developments*, Dublin: Gill and Macmillan.

Gunnigle, P., Flood, P., Morley, M. and Turner, T. (1994), *Continuity and Change in Irish Employee Relations* Dublin: Oak Tree Press.

Gunnigle, P., Foley, K., and Morley, M. (1994), 'A review of organisational reward practices' in P. Gunnigle, P. Flood, M. Morley, and T. Turner, *Continuity and Change in Irish Employee Relations*, Dublin: Oak Tree Press.

Gunnigle, P., Garavan, T., and Fitzgerald, G. (1992), *Employee Relations and Employment Law in Ireland*, Limerick: University of Limerick/Plassey Management and Technology Centre.

Gunnigle, P., and McGuire, D. (2001), 'Why Ireland? A qualitative review of the factors influencing the location of US multinationals in Ireland with particular reference to the impact of labour issues', *Economic and Social Review*, 32, 1.

Gunnigle, P., McMahon, G., and Fitzgerald, G. (1999), *Industrial Relations in Ireland: Theory and Practice – Revised Edition*, Dublin: Gill and Macmillan.

Gunnigle, P., and Moore, S. (1994), 'Linking business strategy and human resource management: issues and implications', *Personnel Review*, vol. 23, no. 1, 63–84.

Gunnigle, P., and Morley, M. (1993), 'Something old, something new: a perspective on industrial relations in the Republic of Ireland', *Review of Employment Topics*, vol. 1, no. 1, 114–43

Gunnigle, P., Morley, M., and Turner, T. (1994), 'Developments in industrial relations and HRM in the Republic of Ireland', *Irish Business and Administrative Research*, vol. 15, 76–92.

Gunnigle, P., Morley, M., and Foley, K. (1995), 'Human resource management in Ireland' in I. Brunstein (ed.), *Human Resource Management in Western Europe*, Berlin: De Gruyter.

Gunnigle, P., Morley, M., and Turner, T. (1997), 'Challenging collectivist traditions: Individualism and the management of industrial relations in greenfield sites', *Economic and Social Review*, vol. 28, no. 2, 105–34.

Gunnigle, P., Morley, M., Clifford, N., and Turner, T. (1997), *Human Resource Management in Irish Organisations: Practice in Perspective*, Dublin: Oak Tree Press.

Gunnigle, P., O'Sullivan, M., and Kinsella, M. (2001), 'Organised labour in the new economy: trade unions and public policy in the Republic of Ireland' in T. Turner, and D. D'Art (eds.), *Irish Employment Relations in the New Economy*, Dublin: Blackhall Press.

Gunnigle, P., and Roche, W. (eds.), (1995), *New Challenges to Irish Industrial Relations*, Dublin: Oak Tree Press/Labour Relations Commission.

Gunnigle, P., Turner, T., and D'Art, D. (1998), 'Counterpoising collectivism: performance-related pay and industrial relations in greenfield sites', *British Journal of Industrial Relations*, vol. 36, no. 4, 565–79.

Gunnigle, P., Turner, T., and Morley, M. (1998), 'Strategic integration and industrial relations: the impact of managerial styles', *Employee Relations*, vol. 20, no. 2, 115–31.

Hacker, C. (1997), 'The cost of poor hiring decisions . . . and how to avoid them', *HR Focus*, 74, 10, 13–16.

Hackman, J. (1977), 'Work design' in J. Hackman, and J. Suttle (eds.), *Improving Life at Work*, Santa Monica: Goodyear.

Hackman, J. (1987), 'The design of work teams' in J. Lorsch (ed.), *Handbook of Organizational Behavior*, New Jersey: Prentice Hall.

Hackman, J., and Oldham, G. (1980), *Work Redesign*, New York: Addison Wesley.

Hakim, K. (1991), 'Cross national comparative research on the European community: the EC Labour Force Surveys', *Work, Employment and Society*, vol. 5, no. 1, 101–17.

Hales, C. (1986), 'What do managers do? A critical review of the evidence', *Journal of Management Studies*, 23, 88–115.

Hall, D., and Foulkes, F. (1991), 'Senior executive development as a competitive advantage', *Advances in Applied Business Strategy*, 2, 183–203, JAI Press.

Hallier, J., and Butts, S. (1998), 'Employer's discovery of training: self–development, employability and the rhetoric of partnership', *Employee Relations*, 21, 1, 80–94.

Hamblin, A. (1974), *Evaluation and Control of Training*, Maidenhead: McGraw-Hill.

Hambrick, D.C. (1987), 'The top management team: key to strategic success', *California Management Review*, 30, 88–107.

Hannan, D. (1998), *Trading Qualifications for Jobs: Over-education and the Irish Youth Labour Market*, Dublin: Oak Tree Press.

Hannaway, C. (1987), 'New style collective agreements: an Irish approach', *Industrial Relations News*, no. 13, 16–22.

Hannaway, C. (1992), 'Why Irish eyes are smiling', *Personnel Management*, May, 38–41.

Hannigan, K. (1999), '*Survey of MNCs in Ireland: Results Of 2nd Annual Survey Of Competitiveness*', Dublin: Irish Management Institute.

Hannigan, K. (2000), 'Ireland's economic performance: a view from the MNCs', *Irish Business and Administrative Research*, vol. 21, no. 1, 69–83.

Hardiman, N. 1988, *Pay, Politics and Economic Performance in Ireland 1970–87*, Oxford: Clarendon Press.

Harrison, R. (1997), *Employee Development*, London: IPD.

Hart, T. (1993), 'Human resource management: time to exorcize the militant tendency', *Employee Relations*, 15 (3), 29–36.

Hawkins, K. (1979), *A Handbook of Industrial Relations Practice*, London: Kogan Page.

Hay Associates, (1975), *Survey of Human Resource Practices*, London: Hay Associates.

Heery, E. (1992),'Divided we fall? Trade unions and performance related pay'. Paper presented to London School of Economics/Trade Union Congress Seminar: London School of Economics, 19 March.

Hegewisch, A., and Bruegel, I. (1992), 'Flexibilisation and part–time work in Europe', paper at BSA 92 Conference, Canterbury, April.

Hendry, C. (1995), *Human Resource Management: A Strategic Approach to Employment*, Oxford: Butterworth Heinemann.

Hequet, M. (1995), 'Not paid enough? You're not alone', *Training*, vol. 32, no. 11, 44–55.

Heraty, N. (1992), 'Training and Development: a Study of Practices in Irish Based Companies', MBS Thesis, University of Limerick.

Heraty, N., and Garavan, T. (2001), *Training and Development in Ireland 2001*, Dublin: CIPD.

Heraty, N., and Morley, M. (1994), 'Human resource development in Ireland: position, practices and power', *Administration*, 42, 3, 299–319.

Heraty, N., and Morley, M. (1995), 'A review of issues in conducting organisational level research with reference to the learning organisation', *International Journal of the Learning Organization*, 2 (4), 27–36.

Heraty, N., and Morley, M. (1998), 'In search of good fit: policy and practice in recruitment and selection in Ireland', *Journal of Management Development*, 17 (9), 662–86.

Heraty, N., and Morley, M. (1998), 'Recruitment and selection practices' in W. Roche, K. Monks, and J. Walsh (eds.), *Human Resource Strategies: Policy and Practice in Ireland*, 109–47.

Heraty, N., and Morley, M. (1998a), 'Training and development in the Irish context: responding to the competitiveness agenda', *Journal of European Industrial Training*, vol. 22, Nos. 4 and 5, 190–204.

Heraty, N., and Morley, M. (2002), 'Management development in Ireland: the new organisational wealth?', *Journal of Management Development*.

Heraty, N., Morley, M., and McCarthy, A. (2000), 'Vocational education and training in the Republic of Ireland: institutional reform and policy developments since the 1960s', *Journal of Vocational Education and Training*, 52, 2, 177–98.

Heraty, N., Morley, M. and Turner, T. (1994), 'Trends and developments in the organisation of the employment relationship' in P. Gunnigle, P. Flood, M. Morley, and T. Turner (eds.), *Continuity and Change in Irish Employee Relations*, Dublin: Oak Tree Press, 82–102.

Herriot, P. (1989), *Recruitment in the 90s*, London: Institute of Personnel Management.

Herzberg, F. (1968), 'One more time: how do you motivate employees', *Harvard Business Review*, January–February, 115–25.

Higgins, C. (1992), 'Executive search – an essential requirement for the 1990s', *Industrial Relations News*, 38, 8 October.

Hill, J., and Trist, E. (1955), 'Changes in accidents and other absences with length of service', *Human Relations*, 8 May.

Hillery, B. (1989), 'An overview of the Irish industrial relations system' in University College Dublin, *Industrial Relations in Ireland: Contemporary Issues and Developments*, Dublin: University College Dublin.

Hillery, B. (1994), 'The institutions of industrial relations' in T. Murphy, and W. Roche, (eds.), *Irish Industrial Relations in Practice*, Dublin: Oak Tree Press.

Hoevemeyer, V. (1989), 'Performance based compensation: miracle or waste', *Personnel Journal*, July.

Hofer, C., and Schendel, D. (1978), *Strategy Formulation: Analytical Concepts*, St. Paul, Minneapolis: West Publishing.

Horwitz, F. (1999), 'The emergence of strategic training and development: the current state of play', *Journal of European Industrial Training*, 23 (4/5), 1–10.

Hourihan, F. (1996), 'The Labour Court – fifty years on', *Industrial Relations News*, 12, 21, March.

Hourihan, F. (1997), 'The European Union and Industrial Relations' in T. Murphy, and W. Roche (eds.), *Irish Industrial Relations in Practice: Revised and Expanded Edition*, Dublin: Oak Tree Press.

Hucznyski, A., and Buchanan, D. (1991), *Organizational Behaviour: an Introductory Text*, Hemel Hempstead: Prentice Hall.

Hunt, N. (1992), *How to Conduct Staff Appraisals*, Plymouth: How To Books.

Hunter, J. and Hunter, R. (1984), 'Validity and utility of alternative predictors of job performance', *Psychological Bulletin*, 96, 72–98

Hunter, L. and McInnes, J. (1992), 'Employers and labour flexibility: the evidence from case studies', *Employment Gazette*, June, 307–15.

Huselid, M. (1995), 'The impact of human resource management practices on turnover, productivity, and corporate financial performance', *Academy of Management Journal*, vol. 38, no. 3, 635–72.

Huseman, R., Hatfield, J., and Miles, E. (1987), 'A new perspective on equity theory: the equity sensitivity construct', *Academy of Management Review*, vol. 12, 222–34.

IBEC (1998), *Survey of Reward/Payment Schemes*, Dublin: IBEC.

IBN (Internet Business Network) (1999), *Electronic Recruiting Index: The Industry Matures*, Road Mill Valley, CA: www.interbiznet.com.

Iles, P. (1999), *Managing Staff Selection and Assessment*, Buckingham: Open University Press.

Iles, P., and Mabey, M. (1993), *Strategic Human Resource Management*, London: Blackwell.

International Labour Organisation, (1975), *Collective Bargaining in Industrialised Market Economies*, Geneva: International Labour Organisation.

International Labour Organisation, World Labour Report (1997–98), *Industrial Relations, Democracy and Social Stability*, Geneva: International Labour Organisation.

Irish Business and Employers Confederation, (1993), *IBEC: An Introduction*, Dublin: Irish Business and Employers Confederation.

Irish Business and Employers Confederation (various), *IBEC Annual Reviews*, Dublin: Irish Business and Employers Confederation.

Irish Congress of Trade Unions (1993), *New Forms of Work Organisation: Options for Unions*, Dublin: Irish Congress of Trade Unions.

Irish Congress of Trade Unions (1995), *Managing Change*, Dublin: Irish Congress of Trade Unions.

Irish Industrial Relations Review (1993), *Trade Union Organisation in the Republic*, vol. 2, no. 7, July.

Jackson, M. (1982), *Industrial Relations: A Textbook*, London: Kogan Page.

Janson, R. (1979), 'Work redesign: a results oriented strategy that works', *S.A.M. Advanced Management Journal*, 44 (1), 21–4.

Kakabadse, A. (1990), 'Top people, top teams', paper presented to the Annual Conference of the Irish Institute of Training and Development, Limerick.

Kamoche, K. (2000), 'Developing managers: the functional, the symbolic, the sacred and the profane', *Organization Studies*, 21, 4, 747–74.

Keenoy, T. (1990), 'HRM: A case of the wolf in sheep's clothing?' *Personnel Review* vol. 19, no. 2, 3–9.

Kelly, A. (1975), 'Changes in the occupational structure and industrial relations in Ireland', *Management*, no. 2.

Kelly, A. (1989), 'The worker director in Irish industrial relations', *Industrial Relations in Ireland: Contemporary Issues and Developments*, Dublin: University College Dublin.

Kelly, A., and Brannick, T. (1983), 'The pattern of strike activity in Ireland, 1960–79: some preliminary observations', *Irish Business and Administrative Research*, vol. 5, no. 1, 65–77.

Kelly, A., and Brannick, T. (1985), 'The strike-proneness of public sector organisations', *Economic and Social Review*, vol. 16, no. 4, 251–71.

Kelly, A., and Brannick, T. (1986), 'The changing contours of Irish strike patterns: 1960–84', *Irish Business and Administrative Research* vol. 8, no. 1, 77–88.

Kelly, A., and Brannick, T. (1988a), 'Explaining the strike proneness of British companies in Ireland', *British Journal of Industrial Relations*, vol. 26, no. 1, 37–57.

Kelly, A., and Brannick, T. (1988b), 'The management of human resources: new trends and the challenge to trade unions', *Arena: Journal of Irish Institute of Training and Development*, August, 11–15.

Kelly, A., and Brannick, T. (1988c), 'Strike trends in the Irish private sector', *Irish Business and Administrative Research*, vol. 9, 87–98.

Kelly, A., and Brannick, T. (1989), 'Strikes in Ireland: measurement, indices and trends', *Industrial Relations in Ireland: Contemporary Issues and Developments*, Dublin: University College Dublin.

Kelly, A., and Brannick, T. (1991), 'The impact of new human resource management policies on US MNC strike patterns', Department of Business Administration, University College Dublin (unpublished).

Kelly, A., and Monks, K. (1997), 'Performance related pay: what makes a successful scheme?', *Research Paper Series*, Dublin City University Business School.

Kelly, J. (1980), 'The costs of job redesign: a preliminary analysis', *Industrial Relations Journal*, vol. 11, no. 3.

Kerr, A. (1997), 'Collective labour law' in T. Murphy, and W. Roche (eds.), *Irish Industrial Relations in Practice*, Dublin: Oak Tree Press.

Kerr, A., and Whyte, G. (1985), *Irish Trade Union Law*, Abington: Professional Books.

Kessler, I., and Purcell, J. (1992), 'Performance related pay: objectives and application', *Human Resource Management Journal*, vol. 3, no. 2.

Keynes, J. (1936), *The General Theory of Employment, Interest and Money*, London: Macmillan

Kilibarda, P., and Fonda, N. (1997), 'Random selection', *People Management*, December, 36–9.

Kirkpatick, D. (1959), 'Techniques for evaluating programmes', *Journal of the American Society for Training Directors*, 13.

Klein, J. (1989), 'The human cost of manufacturing reform' *Harvard Business Review*, March–April.

Kochan, T., Katz, H., and McKersie, R. (1986), '*The Transformation of American Industrial Relations*', New York: Basic Books.

Kochan, T., and Osterman, P. (1994), *The Mutual Gains Enterprise*, Cambridge, MA: Harvard Business School Press.

Kohn, A. (1993), 'Why incentive plans cannot work', *Harvard Business Review*, September–October, 54–63.

Kolb, D.A. (1984) *Experiential Learning – Experience as a Source of Learning and Development*, New Jersey; Prentice Hall.

Kopelman, R. (1985), 'Job redesign and productivity: a review of the evidence', *National Productivity Review*, Summer, 237–55.

Labour Court, (various) *Labour Court Annual Reports*, Dublin: Labour Court (various).

Labour Market Study: Ireland (1997), *Series No. 1*, Brussels: European Commission.

Labour Relations Commission (2001), *Annual Report 2000*, Dublin: Labour Relations Commission.

Laffan, B. (1984), 'The youth employment scheme in Ireland' University of Strathclyde: Strathclyde Papers.

Lane, C. (1988), 'Industrial change in Europe: the pursuit of flexible specialisation in Britain and West Germany', *Work, Employment and Society*, vol. 12, no. 2, 141–68.

Latham, G., and Crandall, S. (1991), 'Organisational and social influences affecting training effectiveness' in J. Morrison (ed.), *Training for Performance*, Chichester: Wiley.

Lawler, E., Mohrman, S. and Ledford, G. (1995), *Creating High Performance Organizations: Practices and Results in Employee Involvement and Total Quality Management in Fortune 1000 Companies*, San Francisco: Jossey-Bass.

Lawler, E. (1977), 'Reward systems' in J. Hackman, and J. Suttle (eds.), *Improving Life at Work: Behavioural Science Approaches to Organisational Change*, New York: Goodyear.

Lawler, E. (1978), 'The new plant revolution', *Organisational Dynamics*, Winter, 3–12.

Lawler, E. (1982), 'Increasing worker involvement to enhance organisational effectiveness' in P. Goodman, (ed.), *Change in Organisations*, San Francisco: Jossey Bass.

Lawler, E. (1986), *High Involvement Management*, San Francisco: Jossey Bass.

Lawler, E. (2000), *Rewarding Excellence*, San Francisco: Jossey Bass.

Leadbeater, C. (1999), 'The Knowledge Driven Economy', paper at Association for Management Education and Development Conference, August, Cranfield.

Leddin, T., and Walsh, B. (1994), *The Macro Economy of Ireland*, Dublin: Gill and Macmillan.

Lees, S. (1992), 'Ten faces of management development', *Management Education and Development*, 23, 89–105.

Legge, K. (1989), 'Human resource management: a critical analysis' in J. Storey (ed.), *New Perspectives on Human Resource Management*, London: Routledge.

Legge, K. (2000), 'Personnel management in the lean organisation' in S. Bach, and K. Sisson (eds.), *Personnel Management: a Comprehensive Guide to Theory and Practice*, Oxford: Blackwell, 43–69.

Lehmbruch, G., Schmitter, F., and Philie, C. (1982), *Patterns of Corporatist Policy Making*, London: Sage.

Lenz, R. (1980), 'Strategic capability: a concept and framework for analysis', *Academy of Management Review*, 5, 225–34.

Lepak, D. and Snell, S. (1999), The Human Resource Architecture: Towards a Theory of Human Capital Allocation and Development, *Academy of Management Review*, 24, 1, 31–48.

Lewis, C. (1984), 'What's new in selection?', *Personnel Management*, January.

Liitt, G. (1981), 'Management development as the key to organisation renewal', *Journal of Management Development*, 1, 34–40.

Litwin, G., and Stringer, R. (1968), *Motivation and Organizational Climate*, Boston: Harvard University Press.

Locker, A., and Teel, K. (1977), 'Survey of human resource practices', *Personnel Practices Journal*, March.

Lockett, J. (1992), *Effective Performance Management: a Strategic Guide to Getting the Best from People*, London: Kogan Page.

Long, P. (1986), *Performance Appraisal Revisited*, London: IPM.

Long, P. (1988), 'A Review of Approved Profits Sharing (Trust) Schemes in Ireland and the UK', dissertation, Dublin Institute of Technology.

Longenecker, C., and Ludwig, D. (1990), 'Ethical dilemmas in performance appraisal revisited', *Journal of Business Ethics*, 9, 961–69.

Lowery, C., Petty, M., and Thompson, J. (1996), 'Assessing the merit of merit pay: employee reactions to performance based pay', *Human Resource Planning*, vol. 19, no. 1.

Lundy, O., and Cowling, A. (1996), *Strategic Human Resource Management*, London: Routledge.

Luoma, M. (2000), 'Investigating the link between strategy and HRD', *Personnel Review*, 29 (6), 769–90.

Lupton, T. (1976), 'Best fit in the design of organisations' in E. Miller (ed.), *Task and Organisation*, New York: John Wiley.

Mabey, C., and Salaman, G. (1995), *Strategic Human Resource Management*, Oxford: Blackwell.

MacDuffie, J, (1995), 'Human resource bundles and manufacturing performance: organisational logic and flexible production systems in the world auto industry', *Industrial and Labor Relations Review*, vol. 48, no. 2, 197–221.

Mackay, L., and Torrington, D. (1986), *The Changing Nature of the Personnel Management*, London: Institute of Personnel Management.

Macon, T., and Dipboye, R. (1988), 'The effects of interviewers initial impressions on information gathering', *Organisational Behaviour and Human Decision Processes*, 42, 364–87.

Magee, C. (1991), 'Atypical work forms and organisational flexibility'. Paper presented to the Institute of Public Administration Personnel Management Conference, Dublin, 6 March.

Makin, P., and Robertson, I. (1986), 'Selecting the best selection technique', *Personnel Management*, November.

Marchington, M. (1982), *Managing Industrial Relations*, London: McGraw–Hill.

Marchington, M. (1990), 'Analysing the links between product markets and the management of employee relations', *Journal of Management Studies*, vol. 27, no. 2, 111–32.

Marchington, M., and Parker, P. (1990), *Changing Patterns of Employee Relations*, Hemel Hempstead: Harvester Wheatsheaf.

Marginson, P. (1991),'Continuity and change in the employment structure of large firms' in A. Pollart (ed.), *Farewell to Flexibility*, Oxford: Blackwell.

Marsden, D. (1986), *The End of Economic Man? Custom and Competition in Labour Markets*, New York: St. Martin's Press.

Marsh, A. (1973), *Managers and Shop Stewards*, London: Institute of Personnel Management.

Marshall, A. (1928), *Principles of Economics* (8th ed.), London: Macmillan.

Martin, J. (2001), *Organizational Behaviour*, London: Thomson Learning.

Maslow, A. (1943), 'A Theory of human motivation', *Psychological Review*, vol. 50, no. 4.

Mathis, R. and Jackson, J. (1994), *Human Resource Management* (7th ed.), St Paul, Minneapolis: West Publishing.

Matthews, J. and Candy P. (1999), 'New dimensions in the dynamics of learning and knowledge' in D. Boud, and J. Garrick (eds.), *Understanding Learning at Work*, London: Routledge.

Mayo, A. (1991), *Managing Careers: Strategies for Organisations*, Wimbledon: IPM.

Mayrhofer, W., Brewster, C. and Morley, M. (2000), 'The concept of strategic European human resource management' in C. Brewster, W. Mayrhofer, and M. Morley (eds.), *New Challenges for European Human Resource Management*, London: Macmillan, 3–31.

McBeath, G., and Rands, N. (1989), *Salary Administration*, (4th ed.), London: Gower.

McCarthy, A., and Pearson, J. (2000), *Performance Feedback is Coming Full Circle*, CIPD News, vol. 1, no. 2, 12–14.

McCarthy, A., and Pearson, J. (2001), '360° feedback in the global HRM arena and the expatriate management process' in M. Linehan, M. Morley, and J. Walsh (eds.), *International Human Resource Management and Expatriate Transfers: Irish Experiences*, Dublin: Blackhall Press.

McCarthy, C. (1977), 'A review of the objectives of the national pay agreements 1970–77', *Administration*, vol. 25, no. 1.

McCarthy, W., O'Brien, J. and Dowd, V. (1975), *Wage Inflation and Wage Leadership*, Dublin: Economic and Social Research Institute.

McClelland, D. (1961), *The Achieving Society*, New York: Van Nostrand.

McClelland, D. and Boyatzis, R. (1982), 'Leadership motive pattern and long term success in management', *Journal of Applied Psychology*, vol. 67, no. 2.

McEwan, N., Carmichael. C., Short, D. and Steel, A. (1988), 'Managing organisational change: a strategic approach', *Long Range Planning*, 21, 6, 71–8.

McGinley, M. (1989a), 'Pay increases in the 1980s: the issue of control', *Industrial Relations News*, no. 30, August.

McGinley, M. (1989b), 'Pay increases between 1981 and 1987', *Personnel and Industrial Relations Directory*, Dublin: Institute of Public Administration.

McGovern, P. (1988), 'Increasing opposition to unionisation in the 1980s', *Industrial Relations News*, no. 45, 24, 15–18 November.

McGovern, P. (1989a), 'Union recognition and union avoidance in the 1980s', *Industrial Relations in Ireland: Contemporary Issues and Developments*, Dublin: University College Dublin.

McGovern, P. (1989b), 'Trade union recognition – five case studies', *Industrial Relations News*, 9 February, no. 6, 12–16.

McGrath, P., and Geaney, C. (1998), 'Managing organisational change' in W. Roche, K. Monks, and J. Walsh (eds.), *Human Resource Strategies: Policy and Practice in Ireland*, Dublin: Oak Tree Press, 311–48.

McGregor, A., and Sproull, A. (1992), 'Employers and the flexible workforce', *Employment Gazette*, May, 225–34.

McGregor, D. (1960), *The Human Side of Enterprise*, New York: McGraw-Hill.

McLagan, P. (1989), 'Models for HRD practice', *Training and Development Journal*, September, 49–59.

McMahon, G. (1988), 'Personnel selection in Ireland: scientific prediction or crystal ball gazing', *IPM News*, vol. 3, no. 3, 20–3.

McMahon, G. (2001), 'Special Feature on Web Recruitment', *Irish Times*, May.

McMahon, G. (1989), 'The joint labour committee system', *Industrial Relations in Ireland: Contemporary Issues and Developments*, Dublin: Department of Industrial Relations, University College Dublin.

McMahon, G., and Gunnigle, P. (1994), *Performance Appraisal: How to Get it Right*, Dublin: Productive Personnel Ltd. in association with IPM (Ireland).

McMahon, G., Neary, C., and O'Connor, K. (1988), 'Multinationals in Ireland three decades on', *Industrial Relations News*, no. 6, 11 February.

McMahon, J. (1994), 'Employee relations in small firms' in P. Gunnigle, P. Flood, M. Morley, and T. Turner, *Continuity and Change in Irish Employee Relations*, Dublin: Oak Tree Press.

McNamara, G., Williams, K., and West, D. (1988), *Understanding Trade Unions: Yesterday and Today*, Dublin: O'Brien Educational Press.

Meenan, F. (1999), *Working within the Law*, Dublin: Oak Tree Press.

Menagh, M. (1999), 'IT costs per hire: finding net (and other) savings', *Computerworld*, 44, 18 January.

Merrick, N. (1997), 'Broadbanding not a corporate quick fix', *People Management*, 16, 20 February.

Meulders, P., and Tytgat, B. (1989), 'The emergence of atypical employment in the European community' in G. Rodgers, and J. Rodgers (eds.), *Precarious Jobs in Labour Market Regulation: The Growth of Atypical Employment in Western Europe*, Geneva: International Labour Office.

Meyer, H. (1975), 'The pay for performance dilemma', *Organisational Dynamics*, vol. 3, no. 1.

Miles, R., and Snow, C. (1978), *Organizational Strategy, Structure and Process*, New York: McGraw-Hill.

Miles, R., and Snow, C. (1984), 'Designing strategic human resources systems', *Organisational Dynamics*, Spring, 36–52.

Miller, D., and Lee, J. (2001), 'The people make the process: commitment to employees, decision making and performance', *Journal of Management*, March.

Mintzberg, H. (1978), 'Patterns in strategy formulation', *Management Science*, May, vol. 24, 934–48.

Mintzberg, H. (1988), 'Opening up the definition of strategy' in J. Quinn, H. Mintzberg, and R. Rames (eds.), *The Strategy Process: Concepts, Contexts and Cases*, New Jersey: Prentice Hall.

Mintzberg, M. (1973), *The Nature of Managerial Work*, New York: Harper and Row.

Molander, C. (1986), *Management Development*, Bromley: Chartwell-Bratt.

Mondy, R., and Noe, R. (1984), *Personnel: The Management of Human Resources*, New York: Allyn and Bacon.

Monks, K. (1992), 'Personnel management practices: uniformity or diversity? Evidence from some Irish organisations', *Irish Business and Administrative Research*, vol. 13.

Monks, K. (2001), 'The role of the corporate human resource function in Irish international firms' in M. Linehan, M. Morley, and J. Walsh (eds.), *International Human Resource Management and Expatriate Transfers: Irish Experiences*, Dublin: Blackhall Press.

Mooney, M. (1988), 'From Industrial Relations to Employee Relations in Ireland', Ph.D. Thesis, Trinity College, Dublin.

Mooney, P. (1980), *An Inquiry into Wage payment Systems in Ireland*, Dublin: Economic and Social Research Institute/EFILWC.

Moorhead, G., and Griffin, R. (1989), *Organizational Behaviour*, New York: Houghton Mifflin Company.

Morley, M. (1994), 'A team approach to job design', *Irish Business and Administrative Research*, 15 (1), 20–34.

Morley, M., and Garavan, T. (1993), 'The new organisation – it's implications for training and development'. Paper presented to the Irish Institute of Training and Development, National Conference, Galway, April.

Morley, M., Garavan, T., Gunnigle, P., and Collins, E. (2001), 'Human capital accumulation: the role of human resource development', *Journal of European Industrial Training*, vol. 25, Nos. 2–4, 48–68.

Morley, M., and Gunnigle, P. (1993), 'Trends in flexible working patterns in Ireland' in P. Gunnigle, P. Flood, M. Morley, and T. Turner (eds.), *Continuity and Change in Irish Employee Relations*, University of Limerick.

Morley, M., Gunnigle, P. and Heraty, N. (1994) 'The Flexibilisation of Working Practices in Ireland', Administration, vol. 41, no. 1.

Morley, M., Gunnigle, P., and Heraty, N. (1999), 'Constructing the reward package: the extent and composition of change in wage and non wage increases in Ireland', *International Journal of Employment Studies*, vol. 7, no. 2, 121–50.

Morley, M., Gunnigle, P., Heraty, N., and Garavan, T. (2001), 'Human resource development: sectoral and intervention level evidence of human capital accumulation', *Journal of European Industrial Training*, 25 (2/3/4), 48–229.

Morley, M., and McCarthy, A. (1999), 'The management of rewards' in P. Gunnigle (ed.), *The Irish Employee Recruitment Handbook: Finding and Keeping a High Quality Workforce*, Dublin: Oak Tree Press.

Morley, M., Moore, S., Heraty, N., and Gunnigle, P. (1998), *Principles of Organisational Behaviour: An Irish Text*, Dublin: Gill and Macmillan.

Morrissey, T. (1989), 'Employee participation at sub–board level', *Industrial Relations in Ireland: Contemporary Issues and Developments*. Department of Industrial Relations, University College Dublin.

Moss Kanter, R. (1983), *The Change Masters*, London: Unwin.

Mowday, R. (1987), 'Equity theory predictions of behaviour in organisations' in R. Steers, and L. Porter, *Motivation and Work Behaviour*, New York: McGraw-Hill.

Mowday, R., Porter, L., and Steers, R. (1982), *Employee-Organization Linkages: The Psychology of Commitment, Absenteeism and Turnover*, New York: Academic Press.

Muchinski, P. (1986), 'Personnel selection methods' in C. Cooper, and I. Robertson (eds.), *International Review of Industrial and Organisational Psychology*, New York: John Wiley.

Mumford, A. (1986), 'Learning to learn for managers', *Journal of European Industrial Training*, 10, 2, 1–22.

Munns, V. (1968), 'The functions and organisation of employers' associations in selected industries', Employers' Associations (Royal Commission on Trade Unions and *Employers' Associations* Research Paper no. 7), London: HMSO.

Munro-Fraser, J. (1954), *A Handbook of Employee Interviewing*, London: McDonald and Evans.

Murphy, T., and Roche, W. (eds.) (1997), *Irish Industrial Relations in Practice: Revised and Expanded Edition*, Dublin: Oak Tree Press.

Murray, B., and Gerhart, B. (1998), 'An empirical analysis of a skill–based pay program and plant performance outcomes', *Academy of Management Journal*, vol. 41, no. 1.

Murray, S. (1984), *Employee Relations in Irish Private Sector Manufacturing Industry*, Dublin: Industrial Development Agency (IDA).

Nevin, E. (1963), *Wages in Ireland*, Dublin: Economic and Social Research Institute.

Newell, S. (1995), *The Healthy Organization: Fairness, Ethics and Effective Management*, London: Routledge.

Newell, S. (2000), 'Selection and assessment in the "knowledge" era' (editorial), *International Journal of Selection and Assessment*, 8, 1, 1–6.

Nicholson, N., and Arnold, J. (1989), 'Graduate early experience in a multinational corporation', *Personnel review*, 18, 4, 3–14.

Nicholson, N., and West, N. (1988), *Managerial Job Changes: Men and Women in Transition*, Cambridge: Cambridge University Press.

Nierenberg, G. (1968), *The Art of Negotiating*, New York: Cornerstone.

Niven, M. (1967), *Personnel Management 1913–63*, London: Institute of Personnel Management.

Nollen, S., and Gannon, M. (1996), 'Managing without a complete full–time workforce' in P. Flood, M. Gannon, and J. Paauwe (eds.), *Managing Without Traditional Methods: International Innovation in Human Resource Management*, Wokingham: Addison Wesley.

Nonaka, I. (1991), 'The knowledge creating company', *Harvard Business Review*, vol. 69, 96–104.

Nonaka, I., and Takeuchi, H. (1995), *The Knowledge–Creating Company: How Japanese Companies Create the Dynamics of Innovation*, Oxford: Oxford University Press.

Nooteboom, B. (1999), 'Innovation, learning and industrial organisation', *Cambridge Journal of Economics*, 23, 127–50.

Nowack, K. (1993), '360 degree feedback: the whole story', *Training and Development*, 47 (1), 69–73.

O'Brien, G. (1998), 'Business strategy and human resource management' in W. Roche, K. Monks, and J. Walsh, *Human Resource Strategies: Policy and Practice in Ireland*, Dublin: Oak Tree Press.

O'Brien, J. (1981), *A Study Of National Wage Agreements in Ireland*, (paper no. 104), Dublin: Economic and Social Research Institute.

O'Brien, J. (1989), 'Pay determination in Ireland', *Industrial Relations in Ireland: Contemporary Issues and Developments*, Dublin: University College.

O'Connell, P. and Lyons, M. (1995), Enterprise Related Training and State Policy in Ireland: The Training Support Scheme, Economic and Social Research Institute

O'Connor, E. (1995), 'World class manufacturing in a semi–state environment' in P. Gunnigle, and W. Roche (eds.), *New Challenges to Irish Industrial Relations*, Dublin: Oak Tree Press in association with the Labour Relations Commission.

O'Connor, K. (1982), 'The impact of the Unfair Dismissals Act, 1977 on personnel management and industrial relations', *Irish Business and Administrative Research*, vol. 5, no. 2.

OECD (1996), *Education at a Glance*, Paris: OECD.

OECD (1997), *Economic Surveys: Ireland*, Paris: OECD.

OECD (1999), *Economic Survey: Ireland*, Paris: OECD.

Oechslin, J. (1985), 'Employers' organisations' in R. Blanpain (ed.), *Labour Law and Industrial Relations*, Deventer: Kluwer.

O'Hara, B. (1981), *The Evolution of Irish Industrial Relations: Law and Practice*, Dublin: Folens.

Olian, J., Durham, C., Kristoff, A., Brown, K., Pierce, R., and Kunder, L. (1998), 'Designing management training and development for competitive advantage: lessons from the best', *Human Resource Planning*, 21, 20–30.

O'Mahony, D. (1958), *Industrial Relations in Ireland*, Dublin: Economic and Social Research Institute.

O'Malley, E. (1983), 'Late Industrialisation under Outward Looking Policies: the Experience and Prospects of the Republic of Ireland', Ph.D. Thesis, University of Sussex.

O'Neill, G., and Lander, D. (1994), 'Linking employee skills to pay: a framework for skill–based pay plans', *ACA Journal*, Winter, 14–27.

Ost, E. (1990), 'Team based pay: new wave incentives', *Sloan Management Review*, Spring.

O'Sullivan, C. (1996), 'Time ripe for the Irish annual hours contract?', *IR Data Bank*, vol. 14, February, 21–3.

Ouchi, W. (1981), *Theory Z: How American Business Can Meet the Japanese Challenge*, Reading, MA: Addison–Wesley.

Pearse, J. (1987), 'Why merit pay doesn't work: implications for organisations theory' in D. Balkin, and L. Gomez–Mejia (eds.), *New Perspectives on Compensation*, New York: Prentice Hall.

Pedler, M., Boydell, T., and Burgoyne, J. (1989), 'Towards the learning company', *Education and Development*, vol. 20, part 1.

Perry, B. (1984), *Enfield: A High Performance System*, Bedford, Massachusetts: Digital Equipment Corporation, Educational Services Development and Publishing.

Personnel Standards Lead Body (1993), *A Perspective on Personnel*, London: Personnel Standards Lead Body.

Peters, T., and Waterman, R. (1982), *In Search of Excellence*, New York: Harper and Row.

Pettigrew, P., Hendry, C., and Sparrow, P. (1988), *Linking Strategic Change, Competitive Performance and Human Resource Management: Results of a UK based Empirical Study*, University of Warwick.

Pettinger, R. (1994), *Introduction to Management*, London: Macmillan.

Phelps-Brown, H. (1986), *The Origins of Trade Union Power*, Oxford: Oxford University Press.

Philpott, L., and Sheppard, L. (1993), *Managing for Improved Performance*, London: Kogan Page.

Plumbley, P. (1985), *Recruitment and Selection*, London: Institute of Personnel Management.

Pollert, A. (1988), 'The flexible firm: fact of fixation?' *Work, Employment and Society*, vol. 2, 3, 281–316.

Pollert, A. (ed.) (1991), *Farewell to Flexibility*, Oxford: Blackwell.

Pollock, H., and O'Dwyer, L. (1985), *We Can Work It Out: Relationships in the Workplace*, Dublin: O'Brien Educational Press.

Poole, M. (1986), 'Managerial strategies and styles in industrial relations: a comparative analysis', *Journal of General Management*, vol. 12, no. 1, 40–53.

Porter, M. (1980), *Competitive Strategy: Techniques for Analysing Industries and Competitors*, New York: The Free Press.

Porter, M. (1985), *Competitive Advantage: Creating and Sustaining Superior Performance*, New York: The Free Press.

Porter, M. (1987), 'From competitive advantage to corporate strategy', *Harvard Business Review*, May–June, 43–59.

Porter, M. (1990), *The Competitive Advantage of Nations*, New York: The Free Press.

Porter, M. (2000), in *Global Competitiveness Report 2000*, World Economic Forum, Geneva: Switzerland.

Prahalad, C., and Hamel, G. (1990), 'The core competence of the corporation', *Harvard Business Review*, 68, 79–91.

Prahalad, C., and Hamel, G. (1994), 'Strategy as a field of study: why search for a new paradigm?', *Strategic Management Journal*, 15, 5–16.

Probst, G., and Buchel, B. (1997), *Organisational Learning: The Competitive Advantage of the Future*, London: Prentice Hall.

Pulakos, E. (1997), 'Ratings of job performance' in D. Whetzel, and G. Wheaton (eds.), *Applied Measurement Methods in Industrial Psychology*, Palo Alto CA: Davies-Black Publishing.

Purcell, J. (1987), 'Mapping management styles in employee relations', *Journal of Management Studies*, vol. 24, no. 5, 533–48.

Purcell, J. (1989), 'The impact of corporate strategy on human resource management' in J. Storey (ed.), *New Perspectives on Human Resource Management*, London: Routledge.

Purcell, J., and Gray, A. (1986), 'Corporate personnel departments and the management of industrial relations: two case studies in ambiguity', *Journal of Management Studies*, vol. 23, no. 2, 205–23.

Purcell, J., and Sisson, K. (1983), 'Strategies and practice in the management of industrial relations' in G. Bain (ed.), *Industrial Relations in Britain*, Oxford: Blackwell.

Quinn Mills, D. (1991), *Rebirth of the Corporation*, New York: John Wiles and Sons.

Raghuram, S. and Arvey, R. (1996), 'Business strategy links with staffing and training practices', *Human Resource Planning*, 17, 3, 55–73.

Randell, G. (1994), *Performance Appraisal in Personnel management: A Comprehensive Guide to Theory and Practice in Britain*, Oxford: Blackwell.

Redman, T., and Mathews, B. (1995), 'Trends in recruitment: a ten year retrospective view', *International Journal of Career Management*, 7, 2, 10–16.

Regalia, I. (1995), *Humanize Work and Increase Productivity*, Dublin: European Foundation for the Improvement of Living and Working Conditions.

Reid, M., Barrington, M., and Kenney, J. (1992), *Training Interventions: Managing Employee Development*, London: Institute of Personnel Management.

Reilly, P. (1996), *Human Resource Planning: An Introduction, Institute for Employment Studies Report 312*, Brighton: IES.

Reilly, R., and Chao, G. (1982), 'Validity and fairness of some alternative selection procedures', *Personnel Psychology*, 35.

Reilly, R., and Warech, M. (1993), 'The validity and fairness of alternatives to cognitive tests' in L. Wing (ed.), *Employment Testing and Public Policy*, Boston: Kluwer.

Report of the Commission of Inquiry on Industrial Relations (1981), Dublin: Stationery Office.

Revans, R. (1982), *Action Learning: the Skills of Diagnosis, Management decision*, 21, 2, 46–52.

Reynaud, J.P. (1978), *Problems and Prospects for Collective Bargaining in the EEC Member States* (document no. V/394/78–EN), Brussels: Commission of the European Community.

Ricardo, R., and Pricone, D. (1996), 'Is skill based pay for you?', *SAM Advanced Management Journal*, 61, (4), 16–22.

Ridgely, P. (1988), 'How relevant is the FUE?', *Irish Business*, February.

Robbins, S. (2001), *Organizational Behaviour*, New Jersey: Prentice Hall.

Roberts, K., and Glick, W. (1981), 'The job characteristics approach to task design: a critical review', *Journal of Allied Psychology*, vol. 66, no. 2, 193–217.

Robertson, I., and Makin, P. (1986), 'Management selection in Britain: a survey and critique', *Journal of Occupational Psychology*, 59.

Roche, W. (1988), 'Ireland: trade unions in Ireland in the 1980s', *European Industrial Relations Review*, no. 176.

Roche, W. (1989), 'State strategies and the politics of industrial relations in Ireland since 1945', *Industrial Relations in Ireland: Contemporary Issues and Developments*, Dublin: University College Dublin.

Roche, W. (1990), 'Industrial Relations Research in Ireland and the Trade Union Interest'. Paper presented to the ICTU Conference, Joint Research between Trade Unions, Universities, Third Level Colleges and Research Institutes, Dublin.

Roche, W. (1992), 'Modelling trade union growth and decline in the Republic of Ireland', *Irish Journal of Business and Administrative Research*, vol. 14, no. 1, 87–103.

Roche, W. (1995), 'The New Competitive Order and Employee Relations in Ireland: Challenges and Prospects'. Paper presented to the Irish Business and Employers Confederation Conference, 'Human Resources in the Global Market', Dublin, November.

Roche, W. (1997a), 'The trend of unionisation' in T. Murphy, and W. Roche (eds.), *Irish Industrial Relations in Practice: Revised and Expanded Edition*, Dublin: Oak Tree Press.

Roche, W. (1997b), 'Pay determination, the state and the politics of industrial relations' in T. Murphy, and W. Roche (eds.), *Irish Industrial Relations in Practice: Revised and Expanded Edition*, Dublin: Oak Tree Press.

Roche, W., and Ashmore, J. (2000), 'Irish unions in the 1990s: testing the limits of social partnership' in G. Griffin (ed.), *Changing Patterns of Trade Unionism: Comparisons Between English–speaking Countries*, London: Mansell.

Roche, W., and Geary, J. (1994), 'The Attenuation of Host–Country Effects? Multinationals, Industrial Relations and Collective Bargaining in Ireland'. Working paper, Business Research Programme, Smurfit Graduate School of Business, University College Dublin.

Roche, W., and Gunnigle, P. (1997), 'Competition and the new industrial relations agenda' in T. Murphy, and W. Roche (eds.), *Irish Industrial Relations in Practice: Revised and Expanded Edition*, Dublin: Oak Tree Press.

Roche, W., and Larragy, J. (1989), 'The trend of unionisation in the Irish Republic', *Industrial Relations in Ireland: Contemporary Issues and Developments*, Dublin: University College Dublin.

Roche, W., and Tansey, P. (1992), *Industrial Training in Ireland: Report Submitted to Industrial Policy Review Group*, Dublin: Department of Industry and Trade.

Roche, W., and Turner, T. (1994), 'Testing alternative models of human resource policy effects on trade union recognition in the Republic of Ireland', *International Journal of Human Resource Management*, vol. 5, no. 3, 721–53.

Rodger, A. (1952), *The Seven Point Plan*, London: National Institute of Industrial Psychology.

Roethlisberger, F., and Dickson, W. (1939), *Management and the Worker*, Cambridge, MA: Harvard University Press.

Rollinson, D. (1993), *Understanding Employee Relations: A Behavioural Approach*, Wokingham: Addison Wesley.

Ross, J. (1981), 'A definition of HRM', *Personnel Journal*, 60, 10, 781–83.

Roth, S. (1993), 'Lean production in German motor manufacturing', *European Participation Monitor*, no. 5. 35–9.

Russo, G., Rietveld, P., Nijkamp, P., and Gorter, C. (1995), 'Issues in recruitment strategies: an economic perspective', *The International Journal of Career Management*, 7, 3, 3–13.

Salaman, G. (1992), *Human Resource Strategies*, London: Sage/Open University Press.

Salamon, M. (1998), *Industrial relations: Theory and practice*, Hemel Hempstead: Prentice Hall.

Sandico, C., and Kleiner, B. (1999), 'How to hire employees effectively', *Management Research News*, 22, 12, 33–7.

Sanfilipo, F., and Weigman, G. (1991), 'A compensation strategy for the 1990s', *Human Resource Professional*, vol. 4, no. 1, Fall.

Sappey, R., and Sappey, J. (1999), 'Different skills and knowledge for different times: training in an Australian retail bank', *Employee Relations*, 21, 6, 577–89.

Sargent, A. (1990), *Turning People On: The Motivation Challenge*, London: Institute of Personnel Management.

Saul, R. (1997), *The Unconscious Civilisation*, Melbourne: Penguin.

Scarbrough, H., Swan, J., and Preston, J. (1999), *Knowledge Management: A Literature Review*, Wimbledon: Chartered Institute of Personnel and Development.

Schermerhorn, J., Hunt, J., and Osborn, R. (1985), *Managing Organizational Behavior*, New York: John Wiley.

Schneider, B., and Schmitt, N. (1986), *Staffing Organisations*, Illinois: Waveland.

Schuler, R. (1987), 'Personnel and human resource management choices and organizational strategy', *Human Resource Planning*, vol. 10, no. 1, 1–17.

Schuler, R. (1989), 'Strategic human resource management', *Human Relations*, vol. 42, no. 2, 157–84.

Schuler, R. (1992), 'Strategic human resource management: linking the people with the strategic needs of the business', *Organisational Dynamics*, vol. 21, no. 1, 18–31.

Schuler, R. (1995), *Managing Human Resources* (5th ed.), St Paul, Minneapolis: West Publishing.

Schuler, R., Dowling, P., and De Cieri, H. (1993), 'An integrative framework of strategic international human resource management', *International Journal of Human Resource Management*, 4 (4), 717–64.

Schuler, R., Galante, S., and Jackson, S. (1987), 'Matching effective HR practices with competitive strategy', *Personnel*, September, 18–27.

Schuler, R., and Jackson, S. (1987a), 'Linking competitive strategies with human resource management practices' *Academy of Management Executive*, vol. 1, no. 3, August, 209–13.

Schuler, R., and Jackson, S. (1987b), 'Organizational strategy and organizational level as determinants of human resource management practices', *Human Resource Planning*, vol. 10, no. 3, 125–41.

Schuler, R., and Jackson, S. (1996), *Human Resource Management: Positioning for the 21st Century*, St. Paul, Minneapolis: West Publishing.

Schuler, R., and Jackson, S. (1999), *Strategic Human Resource Management*, Malden: Blackwell Publishers.

Scott-Lennon, F. (1995), *The Appraisals Pocketbook*, Alresford: Management Pocketbooks Limited.

Senge, P. (1990), *The Fifth Discipline*, New York: Doubleday.

Sexton, J., Canny, A., Hughes, G. (1996), *Changing Profiles in Occupations and Educational Attainment, FÁS/ESRI Manpower Forecasting Studies*, Report no. 5, November, Dublin: FÁS and The Economic and Social Research Institute.

Sexton, J., Hughes, G., McCormick, B., and Finn, C. (2001), *Estimating Labour Force Flows, Job Openings and Human Resource Requirements 1990–2005*, Dublin: FÁS/ESRI Manpower Forecasting Studies.

Sheehan, B. (1997), 'Broadbanding pay system encourages sideways movement', *Industrial Relations News*, no. 6, 6 February, 17.

Shivanath, G. (1987), 'Personnel practitioners 1986: their role and status in Irish industry', MBS Thesis, NIHE Limerick.

Sisson, K. (1983), 'Employers organisations' in G. Bain (ed.), *Industrial Relations in Britain*, Oxford: Blackwell.

Sisson, K. (1989), *Personnel Management in Britain*, Oxford: Blackwell.

Sisson, K. (1994), 'Workplace Europe. Direct Participation in Organisational Change: Introducing the EPOC Project'. Paper presented to the International Industrial Relations Association Fourth European Regional Congress, 'Transformation of European Industrial Relations: Consequences of Integration and Disintegration', Helsinki.

Sisson, K. (1997), 'Towards New Forms of Work Organisation – Can Europe Realise its Potential?' An interim report of the results of the EPOC questionnaire survey of direct employee participation in Europe. Luxembourg: European Foundation/Office for the Official Publication of the European Communities.

Sisson, K. and Timperley, S. (1994), 'From Manpower Planning to Strategic Human Resource Management', in K. Sisson (ed.), *Personnel Management: A Comprehensive Guide to Theory and Practice in Britain*, Oxford: Blackwell.

Skinner, B. (1938), *The Behaviour of Organisation*, New York: Appleton-Century-Crosts.

Skrovan, D. (1983), *Quality of Work Life*, Reading, MA: Addison Wesley.

Smith, A. (1970), *The Wealth of Nations*, London: Pelican.

Smith, I. (1992), 'Reward management and HRM' in P. Blyton, and P. Turnbull (eds.), *Reassessing Human Resource Management*, London: Sage.

Smith, M., and Robertson I. (1986), *The Theory and Practice of Systematic Staff Selection*, London: Macmillan.

Smith, M., Gregg, M., and Andrews, D. (1989), *Selection and Assessment – A New Appraisal*, London: Pitman.

Smith, M., and Robertson, I. (1993), *The Theory and Practice of Systematic Staff Selection*, London: Macmillan.

Smith, P., and Kendall, L. (1963), 'Retranslation of expectations: an approach to the construction of unambiguous anchors for rating scales', *Journal of Allied Psychology*, 47, 149–55.

Snell, S., Youndt, M. & Wright, P. (1996), 'Establishing a Framework for Research in Strategic Human Resource Management: Merging Resource Theory and Organizational Learning', in G. Ferris (ed.), *Research in Personnel and Human Resources Management*, Greenwich, CT: JAI Press.

Snyder, W. (1996), 'Organizational Learning and Performance: An Exploration of the Linkages Between Organizational Learning, Knowledge and Performance', doctoral thesis, University of Southern California.

Solomon, N. (1999), 'Culture and Difference in Workplace Learning', in Boud, D. and J. Garrick (eds), *Understanding Learning at Work*, London: Routledge.

Sparrow, P. (1996), 'Too good to be true'?, *People Management*, 5 December, 22–7.

Sparrow, P., and Bognanno, M. (1993), 'Competency requirements forecasting: issues for international selection and assessment', *International Journal of Selection and Assessment*, vol. 1, no. 1, 50–8.

Sparrow, P., and Hiltrop, J. (1994), *European Human Resource Management in Transition*, London: Prentice Hall.

Stata, R. (1989), 'Organisational learning: the key to management innovation', *Sloan Management Review*, vol. 30, no. 3, Spring 1989.

Steers, R., and Mowday, R. (1987), 'Employee turnover in organisations' in R. Steers, and L. Porter. (eds.), *Motivation and Work Behaviour*, New York: McGraw-Hill.

Steers, R., and Porter, L. (1987), *Motivation and Work Behaviour*, New York: McGraw-Hill.

Steers, R., and Rhodes, S. (1978), 'Major influences on employee attendance: a process model', *Journal of Applied Psychology*, 63, 391–407.

Stewart, A. (1991), 'Performance appraisal' in J. Prior (ed.), *Handbook of Training and Development* (2nd ed.), Aldershot: Gower.

Stewart, R. (1979), *Contrast in Management: a Study of Different Types of Managers' Jobs, their Demands and Choices*, Maidenhead: McGraw-Hill.

Storey, J. (ed.), (1989a), *New Perspectives on Human Resource Management*, London: Routledge.

Storey, J. (1989b), 'Management development: a literature review and implications for future research part 1', *Personnel Review*, 18, 2–15.

Storey, J. (1992), *Developments in the Management of Human Resources*, Oxford: Blackwell.

Storey, J. (1995), *Human Resource Management: a Critical Text*, London: Routledge.

Strauss, G., and Sayle, L. (1972), *Personnel: The Human Problems of Management*, London: Prentice Hall.

Sugarman, L. (1986), *Life Span Development*, London: Methuen.

Suttle, S. (1988), 'Labour market flexibility', *Industrial Relations News*, vol. 38, no. 6, 13–16.

Sveiby, K. (1997), *The New Organizational Wealth: Managing and Measuring Knowledge Based Assets*, San Francisco: Berrett–Koehler.

Sweeney, P. (1998), *The Celtic Tiger: Ireland's Economic Miracle Explained*, Dublin: Oak Tree Press.

Tansey, P. (1998), *Ireland at Work: Economic Growth and the Labour Market 1987–97*, Dublin: Oak Tree Press.

Taylor, F. (1911), *The Principles of Scientific Management*, New York: Harper and Row.

Taylor, F. (1947), *Scientific Management*, New York: Harper and Row.

Taylor, S. (1998), *Employee Resourcing*, London: IPD.

Teague, P. (1995), 'Pay determination in the Republic of Ireland: towards social corporatism?', *British Journal of Industrial Relations*, vol. 333, no. 2, 253–73.

Terpstra, D. (1996), 'The search for effective methods (employee recruitment and selection)', *HR Focus*, 17, 5, 16–18.

Terpstra, D., Mohamed, A., and Kethley, R. (1999), 'An analysis of federal court cases involving nine selection devices', *International Journal of Selection and Assessment*, 7, 1, 26–34.

Thelen, H., and Withall, J. (1979), 'Three frames of reference: the description of climate', *Human Relations*, vol. 2, no. 2, 159–76.

Thomas, S., and Ray, K. (2000), 'Recruiting on the web: hi-tech hiring', *Business Horizons*, 43, 3, 43–61.

Thomason, G. (1984), *A Textbook of Industrial Relations Management*, London: Institute of Personnel Management.

Thompson, A., Mabey, C., Storey, J., Gray, C., and Iles, P. (2001), *Changing Patterns of Management Development*, Oxford: Blackwell.

Thompson, P. (1983), *The Nature of Work – an Introduction to Debates on the Labour Process*, London: Macmillan.

Thurley, K., and Wood, S. (1983), *Industrial Relations and Management Strategy*, Cambridge: Cambridge University Press.

Tiernan, S., Morley, M., and Foley, E. (1996), *Modern Management: Theory and Practice for Irish Students*, Dublin: Gill and Macmillan.

Tomlinson, J. (1993), 'Human resources: partners in change', *Human Resource Management*, 32, (4), 545–554.

Tregaskis, O., Heraty, N., and Morley, M. (2001), 'HRD in multinationals: the global/local mix', *Human Resource Management Journal*, 11, (2), 34–56.

Turner, H. (1962), *Trade Union Growth, Structure and Policy*, London: Allen and Unwin.

Turner, T. (1988), 'Wage bargaining in Ireland: future strategies', *Industrial Relations News*, no. 27, July.

Turner, T. (1994), 'Unionisation and human resource management in Irish companies', *Industrial Relations Journal*, 25, 1, 39–51.

Turner, T., and Morley, M. (1995), *Industrial Relations and the New Order*, Dublin: Oak Tree Press.

Tyler, K. (1998), 'Compensation strategies can foster lateral moves and growing in place', *HR Magazine*, vol. 43, no. 5, 64–71.

Tyson, S. (1985), 'Is this the very model of the modern personnel manager', *Personnel Management*, May.

Tyson, S. (1987), 'The management of the personnel function', *Journal of Management Studies*, vol. 24, no. 5, 523–32.

Tyson, S. (1992), 'Business and human resource strategy', *Irish Business and Administrative Research*, vol. 13, no. 1, 1–5.

Tyson, S., and Fell, A. (1986), *Evaluating the personnel function*, London: Hutchinson.

Tyson, S., Witcher, M., and Doherty, N. (1994), *Different Routes to Excellence*, Cranfield, UK: Cranfield University School of Management, Human Resource Research Centre.

Ulrich, D., and Lake, D. (1991), 'Organizational capability: creating competitive advantage', *Academy of Management Executive*, 5, 77–91.

Umstot, D. (1988), *Understanding Organisational Behaviour* (2nd ed.), St. Paul, Minneapolis: West Publishing.

Vaill, P. (1982), *The Purposing of High Performing Systems, Organizational Dynamics*, Autumn, 23–39.

Vogeley, E., and Schaeffer, L. (1995), 'Link employee pay to competencies and objectives', *HR Magazine*, vol. 40, no. 10.

Von Prondzynski, F. (1985), 'The death of the pay round', *Industrial Relations News*, no. 43, November.

Von Prondzynski, F., and McCarthy, C. (1984), *Employment Law in Ireland*, London: Sweet and Maxwell.

Von Prondzynski, F., and Richards, W. (1994), *European Employment and Industrial Relations Glossary: Ireland*, London: Sweet and Maxwell and Luxemburg: Office for Official Publications of the European Communities.

Vroom, V. (1964), *Work and Motivation*, New York: John Wiley.

Wagner, R. (1949), 'The employment interview: a critical summary', *Personnel Psychology*, 2, 17–46.

Waldman, D., Atwater, L., and Antonioni, D. (1998), 'Has 360 degree feedback gone amok?', *Academy of Management Executive*, vol. 12, no. 2, 86–94.

Walker, C., and Guest, R. (1952), *The Man on the Assembly Line*, Boston: Harvard University Press.

Walker, J. (1980), *Human Resource Planning*, New York: McGraw-Hill.

Wall, T. (1982), 'Perspectives on job redesign' in J. Kelly and C. Clegg (eds.), *Autonomy and Control at the Workplace: Context for Job Redesign*, London: Croom Helm.

Wallace, J. (1988a), 'Unofficial strikes in Ireland', *Industrial Relations News*, no. 8, 15 February.

Wallace, J. (1988b), 'Workplace aspects of unofficial strikes', *Industrial Relations News*, no. 9, 3 March.

Wallace, J. (1989), 'Procedure agreements and their place in workplace industrial relations', *Industrial Relations in Ireland: Contemporary Issues and Developments,* Dublin: Department of Industrial Relations, University College Dublin.

Wallace, J. (1991), 'The Industrial Relations Act 1990 and other developments in labour law', paper presented to the Mid-West Chapter of the Institute of Personnel Management, University of Limerick.

Wallace, J. and O'Shea, F. (1987), *A Study of Unofficial Strikes in Ireland,* Dublin: Stationery Office.

Walsh, J. (1998), 'Managing human resource development' in W. Roche, K. Monks and J. Walsh (eds.), *Human Resource Strategies: Policy and Practice in Ireland,* Dublin: Oak Tree Press.

Walton, J. (1999), *Strategic Human Resource Development,* London: Prentice Hall.

Walton, R. (1973), 'Quality of working life: what is it?', *Sloan Management Review,* vol. 15, Fall, 11–21.

Walton, R. (1985), 'From control to commitment in the workplace', *Harvard Business Review,* March–April, 77–84.

Walton, R. and Lawrence, P. (1985), *Human Resource Management – Trends and Challenges,* Harvard, MA: HBS Press.

Walton, R. and McKersie, R. (1965), A *Behavioural Theory of Labor Negotiations,* New York: McGraw-Hill.

Ward, P. (1995), 'A 360 degree turn for the better', *People Management,* February, 20–2.

Wareing, R., and Stocjdale, J. (1987), 'Decision making in the promotion interview: an empirical study', *Personnel Review,* 16, 4.

Way, S., and Johnson, D. (2001), 'The Evaluative Process Model: a Multiple Stakeholder Framework for Strategic Human Resource Management Research'. Paper read to the Washington meeting of the Academy of Management, August.

Webb, S., and Webb, B. (1920), *The History of Trade Unionism,* Harlow: Longman.

Webster, B. (1990), 'Behind the mechanics of HRD', *Personnel Management,* 22, 3, 44–7.

Webster, E. (1964), *Decision Making in the Employment Interview,* Quebec: Eagle Publishing.

West, P. (1994), 'The learning organisation: losing the luggage in transit?', *Journal of European Industrial Training,* vol. 18, no. 11.

Westwood, R. (1992), *Organizational Behaviour,* London: Longman.

Wexley, K., and Latham, G. (1991), *Developing and Training Human Resources in Organisations,* New York: HarperCollins.

Whelan, C. (1982), 'Worker Priorities, Trust in Management and Prospects for Worker Participation' (paper 111), Dublin: Economic and Social Research Institute.

White Paper on Education (1995), *Charting our Education Future,* Pn. 2009, Dublin: Government Publications Office, April.

White Paper on Manpower Policy (1986), Pn. 4306, Dublin: Government Publications Office, September.

Whittington, R. (1993), *What is Strategy and Does it Matter?,* London: Routledge.

Wickham, J. (1993), *New Forms of Work in Ireland: an Analysis of the 'New Forms of Work and Activity' Data Set,* (Working Paper no. WP/93/31/EN), Dublin: European Foundation for the Improvement of Living and Working Conditions.

Wiesner, W., and Cronshaw, S. (1988), 'A meta–analytic investigation of the impact of interview format and degree of structure on the validity of the employment interview', *Journal of Occupational Psychology,* 61, 275–90

Williams, M., and Dreher, G. (1992), 'Compensation system attributes and applicant pool characteristics', *Academy of Management Journal,* vol. 35, no. 3, 571–96.

Williamson, O. (1975), *Markets and Hierarchies,* New York: The Free Press.

Williamson, O. (1978), *Markets and Hierarchies: Analysis and Anti–trust Implications,* Glencoe: Free Press.

Windmuller, J. (1984), 'Employers' associations in comparative perspective; organisation, structure and administration' in J. Windmuller, and A. Gladstone (eds.), *Employers' Associations and Industrial Relations,* Oxford: Clarendon.

Womack, J., Jones, D., and Roos, D. (1990), *The Machine that Changed the World,* New York: Rawson Associates

Wright, V., and Brading, L. (1992), 'A balanced performance', *Total Quality Magazine,* October.

Zeleny, M. (1990), 'Knowledge as capital/capital as knowledge', *Human Systems Management,* 9, 129–30.

Index